in
france

Hangingout™

in

france

First Edition

A Balliett & Fitzgerald Book

Hungry Minds, Inc.

Balliett & Fitzgerald, Inc.
Project Editor: Kristen Couse
Production Managers: Maria Fernandez, Mike Walters
Production Editor: Paul Paddock
Map Artist: Darshan Bhagat
Line Editors: Jo Ann Baldinger, Alix McNamara
Copy Editors: Carolyn Kuebler, Erin Furguson
Proofreaders: Shoshanna Wingate, Rick Willett, Joshua Mehigan
Associate Editors: Simon Sullivan, Lauren Podis, Nathaniel Knaebel,
Chris Varmus
Editorial Intern: Joanna Cupano

Published by
Hungry Minds, Inc.
909 Third Avenue
New York, NY 10022

ISBN: 0-7645-6244-4
ISSN: 1531-1554

Book design: Sue Canavan and Mike Walters

Special Sales: For general information on Hungry Minds' products and services please contact our Customer Care Department within the U.S. at 800-762-2974, outside the U.S. at 317-572-3993 or fax 317-572-4002.

For sales inquires and reseller information, including discounts, premium and bulk quantity sales, and foreign-language translations, please contact our Customer Care Department at 1-800-434-3422 or fax 317-572-4002.

Manufactured in the United States of America

5   4   3   2   1

CONTENTS

france

backmatter

france

maps

a disclaimer

Please note that prices fluctuate in the coarse of time, and travel information changes under the impact of the many factors that influence the travel industry. We therefore suggest that you write or call ahead for confirmation when making your travel plans. Every effort has been made to ensure the accuracy of information throughout this book and the contents of this publication are believed correct at the time of printing. nevertheless, the publishers cannot accept responsibility for errors or omissions or for changes in details given in the guide or for the consequences of any reliance on the information are based upon the author's own experience on another occasion. Readers are invited to write the publisher with ideas, comments, and suggestions for future editions.

Your safety is important to us, however, so we encourage you to stay alert and be aware of your surroundings. Keep a close eye on cameras, purse, and wallets, all favorite targets of thieves and pickpockets.

an invitation to the reader

In researching this book, we discovered many wonderful places—hotels, restaurants, shops, and more. We're sure you'll find others. Please tell us about them, so we can share the information with your fellow travelers in upcoming editions. If you were disappointed with a recommendation, we'd love to know that, too.

Please write to:
Hanging Out in France
Hungry Minds, Inc.
909 Third Avenue
New York, NY 10022

foreword

most of us have had the experience of going to a new school or moving to a new neighborhood and not knowing a soul there, not knowing the laws of the land, feeling lost and uncool. But if you're lucky, someone comes along who invites you in and shows you where the action is. The same can be said for travel—unless you're committed to seeing Europe through the moving tinted window of a tour bus, pretty soon you're going to want to get past the initial strangeness and get with it. And to really be able to do that, you need someone or something to help you along, so that what could have been just another cute postcard turns into a new chapter in your life.

Going to Europe is infinitely more complicated—and ultimately more rewarding—than just going on a road trip. Without some help, you may repeatedly find yourself surrounded by a numbed-out tour group, scratching your head and wondering what all the fuss is about. We sent out our teams of writers with just that in mind. Go to where the action is, we instructed them, and tell us how to find it.

Of course we tell you how to see all the cultural and historical goodies you've read about in art history class and heard about from your folks, but we also tell you where to find the party, shake your butt, and make friends with the locals. We've tried to find the hottest scenes in Europe—where traditions are being reinvented daily—and make these guides into the equivalent of a hip friend to show you the ropes.

So, welcome to the new Europe, on the verge of mighty unification. The European Union (EU)—and the euro's arrival as a common currency—is already making many happy, others nervous, and setting the entire continent abuzz with a different kind of energy. As the grand tour of Europe meets the Info Age, the old ways are having to adjust to a faster tempo.

But even as the globe is shrinking to the size of a dot com, Europe remains a vast vast place with enough history and art and monuments to fill endless guides—so we had to make a choice. We wanted the *Hanging Out Guides* to live up to their title, so we decided to specialize and not only show you the best spots to eat, shop, sightsee, party, and crash, but also give you a real feeling for each place, and unique but do-able ways to get to know it better. So we don't cover *every single* town, village, and mountaintop—instead, we picked what we felt were the best and serve them up with plenty of detail. We felt it was crucial to have the room to go deeper, and to tip you off as to how to do the same, so that after you see the sights, you'll almost certainly end up in a place where you'll get to know the secret to the best travel—the locals.

Aside from the basics—neighborhoods, eats, crashing, stuff (shopping), culture zoo (sightseeing stuff), and need to know (the essentials)—we cover the bar scene, the live music scene, the club scene, the gay scene, the visual arts scene, and the performing arts scene, always giving you the scoop on where to chill out and where to get wild. We take you on some beautiful walks and show you great places to hang (sometimes for no money). Things to Talk to a Local About actually gives you some fun conversation openers. Fashion tells you what people are wearing. Wired lists websites for each city—some general, some cool, some out-of-the-way—so you can start checking things out immediately. It also takes you to the best cybercafes in each place. Rules of the Game lays out local liquor and substance laws and also gives you the vibe on the street. Five-0 does a quick sketch of cops in each city. Boy meets Girl dares to speculate on that most mysterious of travel adventures. And Festivals & Events lists just that. We also take you out to all the best outdoor spots, where you can hike, bike, swim, jump, ski, snorkel or surf till you've had enough.

Our adventurous team of writers (average age, 24) and editors let you in on the ongoing party. We want to make sure that your time abroad is punctuated by moments when you've sunk deep enough into the mix (or danced long enough to it), so that you suddenly get it, you have that flash of knowing what it's like to actually *be* somewhere else, to live there—to hang out in Europe.

INTRODUCTION

you're sitting in an outdoor cafe on a tree-lined boulevard or a shady plaza, getting wired on a bowl-sized mug of joe and eavesdropping on the styling crew at the table next to yours. Or you're kicking back on the banks of a river with the new pals you've just hooked up with at the local hostel, enjoying a feast of baguettes 'n' cheese along with some vino you'd have to break the bank for back in the states. Or you're getting some tips from the pros through some visual osmosis— Van Gogh, Picasso, or Monet, anyone?—in a museum. Where are you? In France, *bien sur.*

Chances are you're probably here because you've been dying to come here for years. No matter how many times your well-meaning parents, or uncle, or roommate, or neighbor have regaled you with the story about those awful waiters at that crummy, overpriced dive in Paris, you still wanted to go. You've heard about Uncle Harry's stolen luggage and your friend Joann's fruitless attempts to order something off the menu, but it's done nothing to dampen your enthusiasm. You suspect that there's more to France than the Eiffel Tower and stuck-up waiters—and you're right.

But where to start first? For a country that's barely the size of Texas, there's an awful lot going on. One day you're playing the slots in Monte Carlo, the next you're learning how to hang-glide off the top of a mountain, and the day after that you're on the back of a bus headed to some vineyard, learning more than you ever imagined you could from the wine geek sitting next to you.

the regions of france

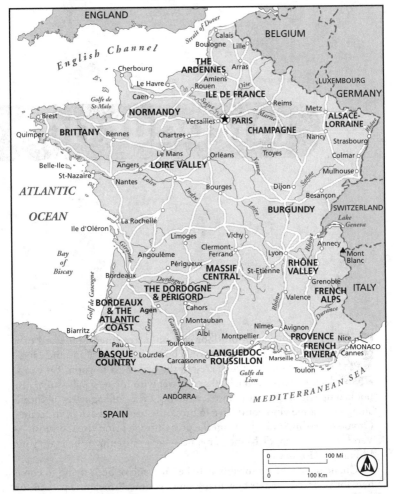

Even when you think you've done your homework and know everything about the place you're headed, you can expect a surprise or two: There are 17 distinct regions in France, and each one of them is different—from the tough, wind-battered towns of Normandy in the north; to the gamble-hard, party-hard beaches and casinos of the glitzy, sun-drenched Riviera in the south. Plus there's so much more in between. You'll get your fill of picture-perfect lavender fields in Provence; in the Loire Valley, you'll find the big ol' chateaux you may (or may not) have been dying to see. You could lose yourself for weeks alone in Paris, or spend those weeks tooling around Burgundy, Bordeaux, or the Rhône Valley for a leisurely wine lesson.

Thanks to its history and its neighbors, France is also home to a few regions that promise a flavor that's surprisingly un-French. When you've had one baguette too many, they can be the perfect remedy to a momentary overdose of, well, Frenchness. In Alsace-Lorraine, there's sausages and *choucroute* (sauerkraut) and so many German day-trippers that you may momentarily think you crossed the border without realizing it. In Brittany, you'll find weird old megaliths perched amidst a sea of greener-than-Ireland green, plus friendly kids hanging out in hemp sweaters, buckets of oysters, a lilting Breton dialect, and rain. And in Basque Country, you'll feel the warmth of Spain radiating across the tall mountains.

Where you go in France will depend on what your scene is, how much time you have, and how far you're trying to stretch your dime. Culture vultures, city slickers, and club kids will feel right at home hanging out in the record stores, cafes, museums, and plazas of Paris, Lyon, Strasbourg, and Marseilles, all with their share of hoppin' pubs, bars, and clubs (pack black); bookworms, art addicts, and history buffs may prefer the medieval charms and artsy bent of towns like Aix-en-Provence and Avignon. As far as nightlife goes, while it's true you'll suffer your share of French club house, Bossanova, down tempo trip hop, drum and bass, rap, and reggae also heat up the local scene. College towns (and cities) like Nancy, Rennes, and Montpellier tend to be pretty happening, too—although make sure you time your visit while school is still in session, otherwise the ville could turn into Deadsville.

Maybe you'd rather be far from the madding crowds, which is fine too. You can bike, or hike, or rollerblade, or ski, or snowboard, or hang-glide your way across France, if you choose. You'll find your fill of off-the-beaten track country roads and trails, and they're usually pretty easy to get to. The French are mad for biking, and you'll likely find a rental shop wherever you go. As far as the great outdoors goes, while it ain't the Wild West, France does have its share of cool spots. We recommend the Alps, home to really amazing tall mountains, fondue, and really cold lakes; the Massif Central, a weird landscape of extinct volcanoes, wide valleys, forests, and little towns made out of lava; and Languedoc-Roussillon, where you can rent a *gîtes* (it's like a very basic mountain lodge) for a day or a week of mountaineering in the Pyrénées. Or you may want to rent a bike and head into Loire River country, where tons of trails and excellent scenery make for an easy ride.

Wherever you go in France, you're bound to find yourself embarked on a parallel culinary adventure. After all, this is the country that put the crème in brulee, the p in paté, and the quiche in Lorraine, so why not enjoy it while you're here? While you'll find your standard French staples everywhere (like baguettes, and coffee), many foods tend to taste even better in the region they come from, and you'll be smart to sample the local specialty: Roquefort cheese in the Massif Central, bouillabaisse and ratatouille in Provence, fresh paté in Alsace-Lorraine—the list goes on and on. The same goes for wine: You'll find this season's Beaujolais nouveau in Lyon, Bordeaux (and dozens of other wines) in Bordeaux, and champagne in (where else) Champagne. In fact, sometimes your travels may feel a little like a walking wine lesson—but who's complaining?

Of course, France isn't just all about food; it's art, and architecture, and history, too. Wherever you go an amazing cathedral is sure to await you, not to mention twisty-turny cobblestone streets, medieval buildings, wide boulevards, gold-gilded public squares, fountains, and neighborhoods laced with tiny canals. Finally you'll get a chance to make all those dull French history lessons come alive: You can follow in the footsteps of Van Gogh and hop a train to Arles, where the poor guy eventually sliced off his ear, plus painted some pretty good stuff. Or pay homage to Joan of Arc in Rouen, where she was burned at the stake. Or count the lily pads in Monet's old garden in Giverny.

Just as you'll want to schedule your time wisely, you'll also want to be picky about when you come. When it comes to visiting France, timing is everything. A visit to Louis XIV's chateaux in July is about as pleasant as riding the subway during rush hour; go in October or May, on the other hand, and you'll at least have a little more elbow room while you're checking yourself out in the trippy Galerie des Glaces (Hall of Mirrors). Do as the locals do and avoid Paris (and the rest of France, for that matter) in July and August; if you time your visit for the spring (April through June) or the fall (September through November), you'll miss the crunch of the tourist season. Most people avoid the country between November and February, but if dreary, drizzly skies don't dampen your spirits but only send 'em soaring, you'll probably be able to score cheap airfare.

Finally, you can leave your preconceptions about rude Frenchies at home: You'll find you won't need them in most parts of France. People here aren't as snooty as your Aunt Martha remembers them, and lots of them are just waiting to practice their already perfect English on you. That's not to say that all of France is 'tude-free (hello, what country is?), but it's also not as frosty as you might imagine. And while kids in the big cities tend to be on the snooty side, usually that's nothing a big ice-breaking smile can't fix. Our book will help you find the *branché,* or in, spots, but we can't do all the work for you: Hanging out with the locals will just add to the experience, plus double your list of cool places to tell your friends about when you get home. So pack some black and some comfortable shoes, and get ready to have a *bon voyage.*

The best of france

party spots

Rue Saint Michel [Rennes]: If only to share a bottle of cheap wine with the sidewalk hippies, you'll do yourself a favor by checking out this infamous Rennes street. Bars compete side by side for your money and affection, so it's a given that nearly any dive will offer up a story to tell the grandkids or, at the very least, a pint to remember.

L'Oxford [La Rochelle]: Airbrushed palm trees! Tight-lipped bouncers in denim! Britney Spears! No, it isn't an N'Sync concert... but the "hip to be square" crowd at this charmingly cheesy discotheque might make you wanna smile like a preteen in love regardless of age, status, or musical tastes.

The Loco Mosquito [Grenoble]: Their happy-hour takes place every night of the week from 7 to 8:30, and offers 5F pastis and 8F beers, a raucous student crowd, friendly waiters, and music that goes from punk to ska to reggae to disco.

The Festival of Avignon (and the simultaneous Festival Off) [Avignon]: It's one of the crazier festivals, with a huge ongoing party on the streets, as well as theater shows, dancing, art displays, lectures, etc.

Place de la Victoire [Bordeaux]: On and around this square is one of the best concentrated areas for hanging out, bar hopping, and meeting up with young French people. There's lots of choices for every taste, smooth jazz, hot salsa, or beating electronic music.

Batofar [Paris]: This old boat parked permanently along the Seine boasts the dopest sound system in Paris. If you don't rock the boat, it will rock you. Drinks are cheap. The crowd is surprisingly unpretentious and laid-back (especially by Parisian standards). And the music is either eclectic, if you're conservative, or just cutting edge, if you're in the know (or *branché*, as they say).

Place de Zurich [Strasbourg]: Outside of Paris, Strasbourg has one of the best nightlifes in France. Though the neighborhood around this infamous *place* has a low-key Williamsburg, Brooklyn, feel about its student-populated streets, there is no mistaking the larger Germanic influence on the town. But when the sun goes down, there is something for just about everyone, from rhyming French urban griots to salsa to thundering drum and bass.

CULTURE

Musée des Beaux-Arts [Quimper]: Yes, nearly every town in France has its own fine arts museum, and Paris might seem to corner the market of impressive and expensive pieces of artwork, and Quimper might be a little out of the way—but nonetheless its collection kicks proverbial arse. An intense collection of works by Gaugin and his followers is the backbone of the museum, which is bolstered by tasteful smaller collections spanning centuries from the Italian Renaissance to the Modern Era.

Provence: This entire region is one of the best places to go to see art and the landscape that has inspired art throughout French history. If you enjoyed the Musée D'Orsay in Paris, with its impressive Impressionist exhibit, you can't miss Provence—particularly Van Gogh's Arles and Cézanne's Aix-en-Provence.

Toulouse: A lot of the architecture in France reminds you of bits and pieces of Paris, but Toulouse, La Ville Rose, is unique. The elaborate old mansions—**Hôtel d'Assézat, Hôtel Dieu Saint Jacques, Hôtel de Police, Hôtel Vieux Raisins** and more—that spread out through the streets help paint the town's rose colored picture.

Centre National d'Art et de Culture Georges Pompidou [Paris]: After wandering the slick galleries and clicking your way through the multimedia computer projects, hang out at the free arts library here, where the trendy arts students browse with furrowed brows through texts analyzing Europe's foremost artists and arts theorists.

Château de Versailles [Versaillé]: Lose yourself amongst the flowers, fountains, reclining nymphs and grinning Greek gods in the gardens. Though the Château itself can be like midtown Manhattan during rush hours, the gardens offer the weary traveler solitude, and are best explored in the long summer twilight when the sunset sends light cascading through the foliage.

outdoors

Mont Frugy [Quimper]: An enlightening experience to say the least, attaining the summit of Mont Frugy is a nearly religious experience. Sure, it isn't that difficult to get there, but the payoff is in the scenery. Go on a day the weatherman predicts a rainstorm, and you'll feel like the sky is laying right on top of your head.

Chamonix: Hands down, *the* best place for anything involving mountains—skiing, hiking, mountain-climbing, etc. It's a place that's hard to describe without using cheesy words like "breathtaking" and "jaw-dropping" in every sentence.

Lac d'Annecy [Annecy]: The best trail for walking, biking, and rollerblading is around Lake Annecy at twilight.

Anglet: Surfing the ocean blue has never been so energizing. There's something in the salty air that makes you feel one with nature—the ocean mist on your skin penetrates to your soul.

Biking in Bordeaux: Taking a spin on two wheels is the best way to traverse the city although it can be a challenge pedaling through the cars and holding your map up at the same time. Getting on one of the trails out of town is also a good way to gallivant about the countryside.

Route du Champagne [Champagne Region]: Even if biking drunk isn't your thing, you have to hit up at least a portion of this seventy-five kilometers trek from Épernay to Reims. The national forest lined route has dizzying fields of grape trestles, and enough inclines to keep you sober and enough declines to keep you buzzing, while the frequent *dégustations* at small champagne houses along the way keep the wheels well oiled.

Centre de Vol à Voile [Chartres]: Gliding in an engineless aircraft in quiet skies above the gorgeous cathedral of Chartres in Île de France will give you a new perspective on the world, or maybe just make your life flash before your eyes. But you'll be in good hands here, as this operation has a team of some of the best engineless aircraft pilots in France.

weird and bizarre

Musée des Automatons [La Rochelle]: Forget Little Shop of Horrors—for a truly strange experience, try this little museum on for size. Like the penny arcades of Northern Californian boardwalks, the pint-sized mechanical figures of the museum dance, smile scarily, or just sit there for your viewing enjoyment.

The Musée Crozatier [Puy en Velay]: It's one of the campiest museums that we found in France, with a strange conglomeration of contemporary art, old lace, stuffed animals, information on volcanoes, and crumbling Roman artifacts. A real small-town museum.

Antigone [Montpellier]: A walk through the new neoclassic architectural baby of Montpellier's governor is like walking through a brave new world. The sparse long sidewalk's design is called *la perspective* and can also be seen in Paris looking from L'Arc de Triomphe to L'Arc de la Défense. Antigone's leads you to the river which they've so neatly cemented into a fountain.

Moët et Chandon [Epernay]: The enormous, eerily half-lit caves of this venerable Champagne house are dreamlike. Rows and rows of champagne bottles older than your grandparents will give you new appreciation for the bubbly that filled Biggie Smalls' champagne flute during his short Dom Perignon–sipping life. Admiring the minuscule size of the bubbles (a sign of high quality and careful fermentation), you may never want to emerge from caves into the light of day.

Vole Hole [Boulogne-sur-Mer]: The tiniest wine bar in all of France, this English-expatriot-run spot has the biggest heart. Whether sitting at the bar alone or nestled in the corner with a loved one, you'll never feel alone or out of place at this friendly establishment that has an extensive wine list and delicious beer on tap.

paris and
île de france

paris and île de france

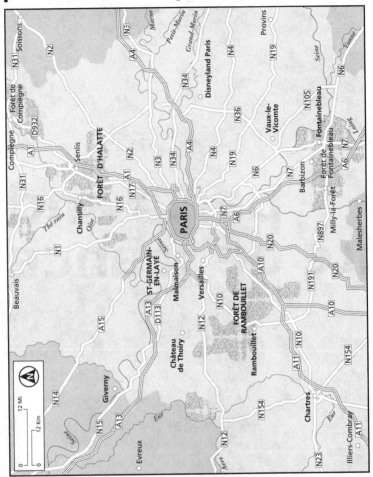

f Paris is the first place you see in Europe, it's definitely going to blow your mind. Once you get over the initial jolt of just how damn *beautiful* it is, you start enjoying all its little quirks, delighting in Europe's most proper populace spending its time elegantly dodging the ubiquitous dog poop, and trying not to get run over by maniac drivers. Paris has more class—not to mention history, exquisite food, breathtaking museums, chi-chi boutiques, idyllic cafes, expansive *avenues,* and beautiful people—in one little *rue* than most cities have in their entire square mileage. You could fill a couple of weeks of your time here, easy—hell, you could probably spend two weeks in the Louvre alone. But don't let yourself get stuck in the city for the whole of your trip—the Île-de-France isn't only about Paris.

Since the end of the 18th century, the surrounding countryside has attracted painters from Corot to Monet, and now it soaks up the runoff of millions of tourists who visit Paris each year. Enclosed in the circle of four great rivers—the Aube, the Oise, the Marne, and the Seine—the Île-de-France is made of many small towns and lush countryside. The Île is also filled with forests—the **Fontainebleau,** Chantilly, Compiègne, and more—châteaux, and cathedrals. All of them are an easy day trip away from Paris, and a great way to shed your club gear and *branche-*conscious mindset for a while and enjoy something more soothing. So go ahead and join the hoards of tourists (and yes, we do mean hoards) flocking to Louis XIV's fabulous chateaux in **Versailles,** get religious with the pilgrims at the Cathédrale Nôtre Dame in **Chartres,** or pack some bread crumbs and plan a hike to one of the Hansel 'n' Gretel forests outside of town. Just don't expect to find a star-studded nightlife on your excursions: The region's towns act as the dark cosmos over which Paris's heavenly bodies shine, burning brighter than ever.

getting around the region

Served by both the **RER** and **SNCF** rail lines, the Île-de-France is quite tourist friendly (perhaps even too friendly). The region's sites are best

m-i-c k-e-y s-o-u-r-i-s

Had your fill of baguettes and need to gorge on funnel cakes? Got some pint-sized acquaintances back home counting on your souvenir largesse? Does a trip on Dumbo the Flying Elephant sound more fun than another ride on the TGV? If you answered "yes" to any of these questions, then you might want to consider spending a day at **Disneyland Paris** (*Tel 01/60-30-60-53; www.disneylandparis.com; One-day admission 160F Jan-Mar, 200F April-Sept and 3rd week of Dec-1st week of Jan;* **Note: these hours are highly subject to change!:** *10am-8pm Mon-Fri, 9am-8pm Sat, Sun Sept 4-Oct 20; 9am-8pm daily Oct 21-Nov 5; 10am-8pm from Mon-Fri, 9am-8pm Sat, Sun Nov-Dec 22; 9am-8pm daily Dec 23-Jan 1 (except Dec 31: 9am-1am); 10am-8pm Mon-Fri, 9am-8pm Sat, Sun Jan 2-March 16th; 10am-8pm Mon-Fri 9am-11pm Sat, Sun Mar 17-March 31)* Built at cost of nearly $5 billion, the park is located about 19 miles east of Paris and is easily reached by taking the Metro/RER A4 line to Marne-la-Vallee-Chessy (expect a 35-40 minute journey). In addition to fried dough, park highlights include Euro versions (which are pretty much exactly the same as the U.S. versions) of the Space Mountain and Mad Hatter's Tea Cups rides, and Main Street U.S.A. (in case you're feeling homesick...for turn-of-the-century America, that is). Adventureland is pretty rockin', boasting a ride modeled on Indiana Jones and the Temple of Doom, or Frontierland with the Big Thunder Mountain rollercoaster—a pretty accurate rendition of a runaway mining car. Discoveryland offers the opportunity to take a ride in a replica of the Nautilus from *20,000 Under the Sea* or watch a 3-D film featuring Michael Jackson, among other "educational" treats. Up for a rootin', tootin' good time? You're in luck, partner (though you'll be out 325F)—among the many shows and parades to choose from is Buffalo Bill's Wild West Show, an extravaganza including horses, bison, and real six-shooters.

seen on day or overnight trips from Paris. For train departure times and real-time traffic reports around Paris and the Île-de-France, check the site **www.citefutee.com,** from which you can plot routes by both road and rail. For places farther away, like Chartres and Giverny, **www.bison-fute. equipement.gouv.fr** can plot road routes.

TraVEL TIMES

*TGV (Fast Train—more expensive) **By car	Versailles	Chartres	Paris
Paris	:20**	1:00	-
Versailles	-	:45**	:20**
Chartres	:45**	-	1:00

▶▶ROUTES

There are lots ways to get to **Versailles** from **Paris.** The easiest and most cost-effective is to take the **RER C** to Versailles' Gare Rive Gauche. Located along the same SNCF rail line, Versailles and **Chartres** together make a nice two-day getaway. Trains depart from Paris Montparnasse, stop at Versailles Chantiers, and then in Chartres.

paris

"L'art c'est la decouverte de l'autre."—Ben Vautier

"Paris speaks to me through pictures, myths of romance."
—Kevin Barker, singer-songwriter, Currituck County

The first things you may notice about Paris, probably the most visited city on earth, is that the pigeons, like the people, are well-fed and -plumed and that the female mannequins in the shop windows have nipples. Myths of romance hang around Paris like stale smog in Los Angeles, obscuring the dynamic reality of modern Parisian life. The couples lip-locked on park benches and the cult of femininity that Parisian women obsessively cultivate with their cooler-than-thou coiffed stares and their ever-put-together outfits only enliven the myths every person in the world seems to entertain about Paris. French advertisements use the female body sans clothing to sell everything from toothpaste to cars. It doesn't take long to realize from the way they stare at and approach women that French men are some of the last bastions of male chauvinism on the planet. In other words, they're suckers for women. Take a stroll through the sleaze of **rue St.-Denis,** and the beauty sheltered in the gorgeous architecture of the ritzy Right Bank will devolve into sticky peep shows and hardened prostitutes.

The mythology and even the history of Paris are steeped in its literary and artistic past, from the romantic visions of Victor Hugo and the darkness of Émile Zola, to the crazed ravings of Louis Aragon, the depressive ponderings of Sartre, and the intensely intelligent observations of Simone de Beauvoir. In modern times the cinematic has replaced the literary, and the great Jean-Pierre Melville, Jean-Luc Godard, François Truffaut, even foreigners such as Luis Beñuel, Bernardo Bertolucci, and Woody Allen have used the city as the backdrop for their kaleidoscopic hallucinations.

Today, not only is the profile of the city transforming with the influx of immigrant populations from Africa, the Arab world, Asia, and Eastern Europe—creating both excitement and political tension—but the European Union (EU), the Chunnel, and the juggernaut of globilization has made Parisians generally more open and friendly than they've ever been. People think of the City of Light as a place for lovers, and in fact, getting to know Paris can be as intoxicating as a good love affair. Sometimes, strolling down a broad boulevard under the chestnut trees and blue sky, sun glinting off the cafe tabletops, you could swear that Paris is embracing you. But then you find yourself backed against the window of a drafty, overpriced brasserie, coldly ignored, waiting to be charged tourist rates for a cheese sandwich, and you suspect Paris might've been stringing you along the whole time. And you think, was I ever in? Was I even close?

In fact being *in,* or *branché* (literally, "plugged in"), is what Paris is all about. A joint can be dead and dull, but still keep its rep if the right people are there, if it's *branché.* Most young Parisians will affect total ignorance about what spot is or is not *branché,* but in fact they're in constant anxiety over not being *branché.* Those who are, in fact, in, won't even use the word; they may say that a scene is trendy or say nothing about it at all.

So, if you want to be in with the in crowd, it's essential—more so than in any other place in Europe—that you meet and interact with real, live, groovy French people. There's no way in without them, unless you're wildly rich, beautiful, or powerful (in which case, who needs you?). We've scoped out the best spots for this eventuality, and then all it'll take from you is a little initiative. Parisians can seem forbidding at first, but they're not the snobs of lore. The young especially are more apt to attempt communicating in English, either to go on about the latest Q-Tip album or to inform you that they're vehemently opposed (they *oppose* things *vehemently* here) to an Americanized McParis. Either way, once you crack 'em, your new friends will surprise you with their generosity and hospitality. And when you catch that look of unease on their faces ("Is this cool enough, should we be somewhere else...?") you can smile to yourself that you know you're exactly where you want to be.

The best way to find out about underground club happenings is, as ever, the old-fashioned flyer, placed in the entry ways of record shops like **Marché Noir** [see *stuff,* below]. Sometimes you'll even luck out and score free entry passes if you're savvy enough to pick up the right flyer. With so much happening all at once, and new venues gaining reps with the seasons, you've got to have good resources. The best all-around listings are in *l'Officiel des Spectacles,* a weekly that comes out every Wednesday and can be had at any newsstand for 2f. It's better, cheaper, and more exhaustive than its competitor *Pariscope,* though *Pariscope* includes *TimeOut's* weekly listings. If you read French, even just enough to get by, the funky monthly mag *Nova* (10f) has a "hot guide" with day-by-day cool picks. *TimeOut* recently started putting out free English-language quarterlies, with a sparer list of events, special features, and decently cool venues, with a map. The free English monthly **FUSAC** hasn't got much of anything except listings for apartment shares and short-term digs [see *crashing*, below]; same goes for its geeky competition, *Paris Voice*. Both can be found just about everywhere—try in front of Shakespeare & Co. [see *stuff*, below]. Oh, and remember, most businesses close for an hour or more at 1pm, so the staff can enjoy a proper *déjeuner*. Now there's civilization for you.

neighborhoods

The Paris *arrondissement* system can appear at first to make as much sense as the scoring system on a dartboard (the 17th is next to the 8th is next to the 1st. Right.), but you'll get used to it. We've indicated the *arrondissement* for each venue listed after the address, below. The Seine river runs east-west through the middle of the city. The *arrondissements* begin with the 1st on the **Right Bank** (north) of the Seine, smack-dab in the center of town, then swing up and out, uncoiling clockwise. The city is bounded by the périphérique, a beltway that runs up against the far ends of the double-digit *arrondissements*. In general, it's best to disregard the linear order of the *arrondissements* and to think, instead, in terms of the neighborhoods associated with the number: The **1st** is the **Louvre** [see *culture zoo* below], the **4th** is the **Marais**, the **5th** the **Latin Quarter**, the **6th St. Germain,** etc.

Most of postcard Paris—the Louvre, the majestic quays along the Seine, the **Champs Elysées,** and the **Arc de Triomphe**—is in or around the **1st** and **8th** *arrondissements*. Needless to say, this is also tourist Paris, more and more a spiritual extension of Disneyland Paris, and not where you'll want to be spending most of your time. The great big megaclubs like **Le Queen** [see *club scene*, below] are still to be found around here, but the funkier neighborhoods pop up all over the city without warning.

The **place de la Concorde**—the broad, beautiful plaza of obelisks and *belle époque* lamps on the western edge of the **Tuileries** gardens on the **Right Bank**—is the center of the city, the border between the 8th and 1st *arrondissements*. It is the midway point of the **Voie Triumphale**, the trail which aligns the **Arc de Triomphe**, the Champs Elysées, and the **Palais du Louvre.** Across the Seine from the place de la Concorde on the **Left Bank,** is the ritzy, meticulous **7th** *arrondissement*, full of ministries and high-price antique shops. The massive railway-station-looking building you'll see is the **Musée d'Orsay** [see *culture zoo*, below]. Away and to the east you'll see the **Eiffel Tower** [see *culture zoo*, below] standing astride the **Champs de Mars,** on the edge of the 7th. Push on as far as the **boulevard Saint-Germain** and follow it east and you'll pass first through the **Saint-Germain** district in the **6th** *arrondissement,* full of great little boutiques and cafes, and then the **Quartier Latin,** the student

paris

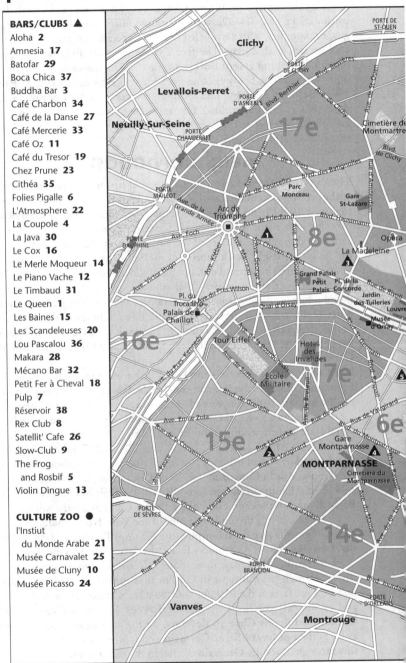

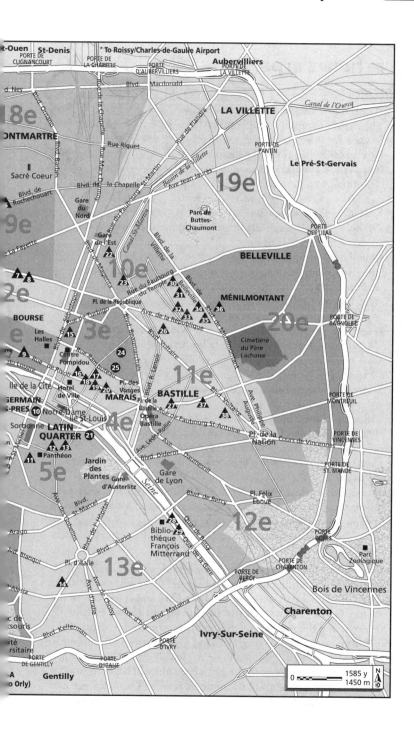

12 hours in paris

1. Walk down the Voie Triumphale from the Arc de Triomphe to the **Louvre** [see *culture zoo*, below], through the Place de la Concorde and Tuileries garden.
2. Go to the Louvre after 3pm and visit the paintings section of the Richilieu wing, see Delacroix's *Liberty Leading the People* and other faves [see *culture zoo*, below].
3. Wander the two small islands in the Seine: the Île de la Cité, which was the whole of Paris c. 50 A.D., and the Île Saint-Louis.
4. Wander up into the Latin Quarter from the rue des Écoles and the little medieval streets on this side of the **Panthéon** [see *culture zoo*, below] at night, when the vampires come out.
5. Nearby, visit the **Musée de Cluny** [see *culture zoo*, below] and see the allegorical five tapestries of *The Lady and the Unicorn*.
6. Have a pot of tea and some scones at **Mariage Frères** in the Marais at 4pm, and watch the ladies who lunch pour in [see *only here*, below].
7. Wander and explore the Marais and walk elegantly around the Place des Vosges at sunset, when the galleries cast long shadows over the court.
8. After 11pm, live it up along the rue Oberkampf, at **Café Charbon, Mécano Bar,** and **Cithéa** [see *bar scene*, below for all].
9. If it's a moody day, stroll along the banks of the Canal Saint-Martin beginning at the François le Maître Square *(Métro to République)* and soak up the atmosphere.
10. Have dinner, or at least dessert, at **Bofinger** [see *eats*, below] the extraordinary, bustling brasserie, at midnight, when the best people are only just sitting down to sup.

quarter, a vestige of medieval Paris, with the greatest density of tiny movie houses, cafes, and attitude in Western Europe. Cut back to the Right Bank here and you'll pass over the **Île de la Cité** and stand before the bright white facade of **Notre Dame** [see *culture zoo,* below] cathedral.

Due east along the **rue Saint-Antoine** brings you to the **Marais** ("the swamp"), a hip and gorgeous neighborhood of tight streets, 16th-century mansions, and artsy bars. This used to be the Jewish quarter, but now it is equally, if not more, the heart of the gay scene, and you begin to wonder what the trim, chic gay men and the nervous, bearded Orthodox make of each other as they brush past. The Marais offers the rare combination of a great place to poke around during the day—for instance, at the **Musée Carnavalet** or the **Musée Picasso** [see *culture zoo*, below, for both] or at the tea room **Mariage Frères** [see *only here*, below]—and a thumping night scene, at for instance **Petit Fer à Cheval** or **Café du Trésor** [see *bar scene*, below, for both]. Push on east along the shop-lined, aptly named, **rue de Francs Bourgeois** and you'll come to the splendid **Place des Vosges**, an enclosed plaza of perfect harmony, then brace yourself for the bustle of the **Place de la Bastille**, at the mouth of the cool **11th**, just beyond.

Bastille was the heart of the Paris nightscene in the '80s and still has a mighty draw, but the glitzy crush everywhere along the **rue du Faubourg Saint-Antoine**, the **rue Charonne**, and, most of all, the bombastically over-hyped **rue de Lappe** has the hashed-over and has-been feel of a glam band of the same era that's "still rockin." Look out for vomiting Dutch tourists. Half a mile to the north of Bastille, along the **boulevard Richard Lenoir**, you come to **Ménilmontant** and the **rue Oberkampf**. For the past few years, this nondescript little street—nothing at all to see in daylight—has reigned as uncontested king of the bar scene. It, too, shows signs of wear and creeping Disneyland Paris, but **Café Charbon** and the **Mécano Bar** [see *bar scene*, below, for both] are still the place to be seen for those of us who crave it.

East, along the rue Oberkampf and along the **boulevard de Belleville** brings you to the dizzying and increasingly coolifying immigrant swirl of

nique les flics

Since the 1970s, when they were imported to work in the mines and heavy industry, North Africans have occupied a special place in French society. North African couscous and the *tangines* of delicious stewed meats seasoned with vegetables and raisins have become accepted standards of the Parisian diet, but the same acceptance cannot exactly be said of the North Africans themselves. They are French without being French, and have the brunt of the French paranoia about national and cultural identity. Films like *La Haine* only capture part of the picture. Walk certain streets of Paris, like the quays bordering the Seine and the area surrounding Pont Neuf, and you're bound to have a North African kid try to sell you some hash, but don't be suckered. High unemployment has pushed a lot of North African teenagers towards selling drugs (or pretending they have drugs to sell) and created a lot of resentment from many native-born French against all North Africans, even those who actually do hold honest, paying positions.

paris

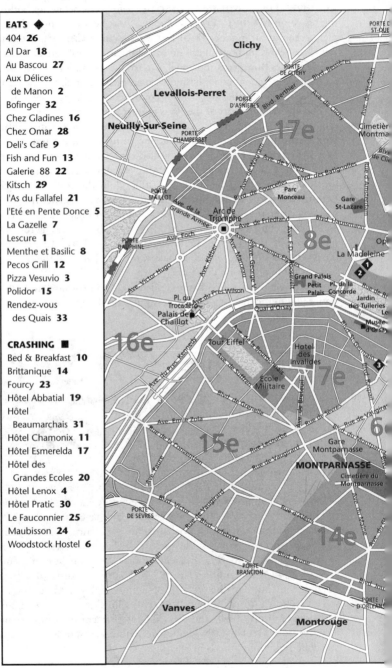

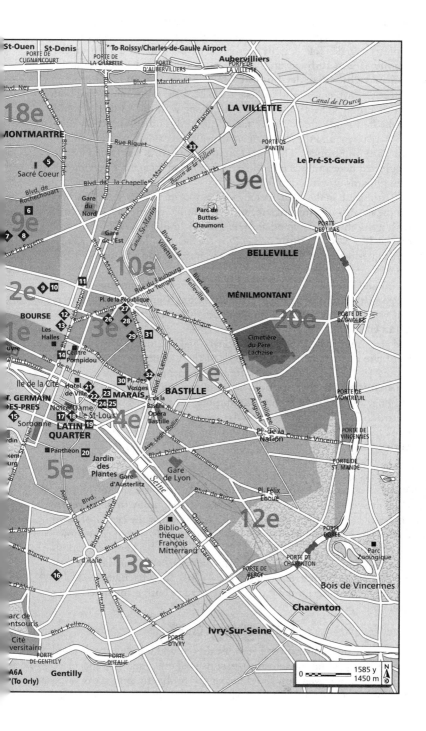

Belleville (now in the 20th), where West Africans, Maghrebins (North African Arabs), Sephardic Jews, Chinese, Vietnamese, and white Parisian hep cats mingle. Take a right on the rue de Belleville and a left on the **avenue Simon Bolivar,** and you'll find yourself in the **19th** and the uncharacteristic **Parc des Buttes Chaumont,** perhaps Paris' most beautiful park, with craggy cliffs, Greek temple follies, the Sublime, and that sort of a thing. The 19th and the 20th, along with the 13th, way south on the Left Bank, are havens of radicalism in this otherwise solidly conservative town, and the electorate here loyally keeps the French Communist Party in business. The Paris Commune of 1871 was fueled by the disaffected here and was put down here in bloody slaughter, costing the communards upwards of 3,000 lives.

To the west, in the **18th,** past the lowlands of the largely Arabic **Barbès,** are the heights of **Montmartre,** still a charming, quiet place to get lost, with a number of its wooden *moulins* (windmills) still standing, and crowned by **Sacré-Coeur** [see *culture zoo,* below], the painfully gaudy, meringue-like church perched atop the mount, and glimpsable from almost anywhere in Paris.

Far and away to the south, in the 13th, is the hilly, charming, no-frills haven of the communard spirit, the **Butte aux Cailles,** where students and workers unite. The proletarian spirit survives in simple bistros like **Chez Gladines** [see *eats,* below], where folks are likely to curse the state and sing hundred-year-old revolutionary ballads; many of the bars, in fact, take their name from the words of the Commune's anthem, "Le Temps des Cérises." West of that, through residential no-man's lands, lies **Montparnasse,** the sometime haunt of the Lost Generation and now of aging, lost American expats. **La Coupole,** the preferred brasserie of the Gertrude Stein set, and its new salsa-pumping lower level are worth a look, however [see *club scene,* below]. The west of Paris—the **17th** and **16th** *arrondissements* on the Right Bank, and the **15th** on the Left—you can skip with minimal loss.

Paris is served by the best public transport system in the world, the Métro. Clean, fast, convenient, it's a city planner's dream. You're never more than five minutes from a **Métro** stop or 30 minutes from the center of town. The suburban **RER** lines also run through the center of town and can be quicker. The only hitch is that the whole system closes down sometime around 12:30 or 1am. (The time of the last train is listed on the destination sign when you enter). After that, you're at the mercy of Paris' pricey and underrepresented taxis. On a Saturday night, available taxis don't reappear until 3am, so be prepared to burn some shoe-leather after dancing or wait.

hanging out

In autumn and winter, Paris gets gray, dreary, and a little on edge, and people busily withdraw into their newspapers, cafes, and hot chocolats. In summer, however, you should have no trouble finding spots to do nothing in and locals to not do it with. Nearly every cafe puts out tables,

fIVe ThIngs To TaLk To a LocaL about

1. **Paris:** Parisians are more than half in love with their city, and each has a stomping-ground all his or her own. Ask them about it. It's a great way to learn more about the place and its history, and listening to them go on and on is kind of endearing.

2. **Globalization:** If they're young, they're probably against the imminent decline of things French and the rise of all things American, like multinationals and fast food. Their unlikely hero is José Bove, the shepherd from the south who bulldozed a McDonald's in 1999.

3. **What a racist, terrible country France is:** The prejudice against Maghrebin (North African Arab) immigrants is often very severe, and the plight of the sans-papiers (illegals) is the cause célébre of the young left.

4. **What a racist, terrible country the U.S. is:** If possible, the French are even more obsessed with race in America than the Americans. Nod your head, agree, rail freely against the States. This will bring the conversation around to...

5. **American movies:** The French don't only love Clint Eastwood, they love Westerns you've never heard of, Marilyn as a serious comedienne, and Hitchcock, and probably know far, far more than you about, say, Ernst Lubitsch. And skip the whole Jerry Lewis thing....Just let it go.

and most every plaza or park is full of the most jaw-dropping slackers you've seen. The primest spot to spark up a conversation is either the **Place de la Sorbonne**—on the Place itself or in one of its many cigarette smoke-clogged cafes—or immediately inside the **Sorbonne** *(Sorbonne III and IV; Métro to Cluny-La Sorbonne),* in the courtyard. The gorgeous **Place des Vosges** *(Métro to Bastille or Saint-Paul),* until recently a solemn, residential cloister, is where the cool and beautiful from the Marais now come to warm themselves and spread the wealth.

With so much of the population here in cafes so much of the time, the question arises: Don't these people work? The answer to which is: sort of. With three-course lunches, 12 percent unemployment, and a freshly-minted law enforcing a 39-hour-max work week, Parisians have a lot of time to dawdle. There are also indications that some of the more picturesque cafe-dwellers are in fact paid employees of the French Tourist Bureau, strategically placed to promote the city's romantic image (no, they're not hiring). So if you're going to get in with the locals, join them at the cafes and *salons de thé* where they linger and try to look serious doing very little.

Right off the rue de Rivoli, with a view of the Seine and the dome of the Institut de France, **Le Fumoir** *(6 rue de l'Amiral-de-Coligny, 1st; Tel 01/42-92-00-24; Métro to Louvre or Louvre-Rivoli; 11am-2am daily; AE, MC, V)* is how you imagined Paris would be. With the yellow blinds shutting out any daylight, this long, ersatz-'30s speakeasy is peopled with just about everyone who's anyone: cigar-chomping suited men in leather smoking chairs; tall, gesticulating stubble-cheeked artists; and the occasional dumbfounded onlooker. The rear room holds a reading library and the all-day-long-ers, chowing on the decent-but-pricey food.

Just the opposite effect is had at **Le Reflet** *(6 rue Champollion, 5th; Tel 01/43-29-97-27; Métro to Cluny-La Sorbonne; 10am-2am daily; MC, V)* in the Latin Quarter, a cramped little room opposite an art-house theater of the same name. It's still one of the best places in Paris to work on your novel, have an espresso, maybe a little tempeh salad, flirt with the waitstaff, and meet the coolest and most low-key of the university student set.

Right on its heels is the **Café de la Mairie** *(8 place Saint-Sulpice, 6th; Tel 01/43-26-67-82; Métro to Saint-Sulpice or Odéon; 7am-2am Mon-Sat, daily in June; No credit cards)*. Don't let the mustard-yellow ceiling or the early-'60s naugahyde banquettes and fluorescent lighting throw you—this is one of the local egghead faves. The glass-enclosed terrace has the best seats for spying on the place de Saint-Sulpice, and the second level is that holy grail (for some) of Paris cafes—it has a great nonsmoking section.

The tea room at **La Mosquée de Paris** *(39 rue Géoffroy-Saint-Hillaire, 5th; Tel 01/43-31-38-20; Métro to Censier-Daubenton; 9am-midnight daily; MC, V)*, the big exotic draw for the student set, is *hypercool* (pronounced ee-pehr-kul). The waitstaff gets a little *ee-pehr* here, and snappy, too, and you can't blame them—amazing numbers of funky students crush into the low copper tables, downing delicious spiced-almond tea and baklava under low-hung brass lamps. By the Jardin des Plantes on the far eastern end of the Latin Quarter.

A nice pit stop after a little excursion to the Pompidou, or shopping in Les Halles and the alternately chic and sleazy side streets surrounding the shopping center, is the ornately carved wood bar of **JIP's Cafe** *(41 rue St.-Denis; Tel 01/42-21-33-93; Métro to Chatelet; 11am-2am daily; MC, V)* for a taste of Kingston beer, sweetened by a bit of rich rum, or an *exotique* Caribbean cocktail. The atmosphere of the place is laid-back, attentively serviced by cutely braided help, soothed by a bit of ragga, reggae, and roots R&B, and covered by a ceiling decorated with African wood carvings.

The narrow, moody Canal Saint-Martin, with its stunted trees, tall green locks, high pedestrian bridges, and quiet, is becoming a refuge for cool Parisians fed up with cool-hunting. Before elbowing your way into

L'Atmosphère [see *live music scene,* below] stop at **Chez Prune** *(74 quai de Valmay, 10th; Tel 01/42-41-30-47; Métro to République; 7:30am-2am Mon-Sat, 10am-2am Sun; No credit cards),* a funky corner cafe/bar with reggae in the air, and check out the beautiful, happy inhabitants in their still-unspoiled environment.

The upper reaches of Canal Saint-Martin widen into the Basin de la Villette in the 19th, where a converted boathouse right on the wide cobblestone quay is now a small, ultra-modern multiplex movie theater. Stop into the restaurant inside, the **Rendez-vous des Quais** *(10 quai de la Seine, 19th; Tel 01/40-37-02-81; Métro to Stalingrad; 11:30am-1am daily in winter, 10:30am-2am daily in summer; AE, MC, V)* with its awkward, sloping cement roof, low lights, and cozy atmosphere, and savor a frothy Cafe crème while you enjoy the view (skip the food, though).

Though it's a little nasty, what with the fumes from the highway and that foaming brown city river water, the **banks of the Seine** are always elbow-to-elbow with locals sporting their little Speedos in the warmer months. A less Coney Island feel is found along the shady banks of the up-and-coming Saint-Martin Canal in the 10th and 19th *arrondissements.* Pickup ultimate frisbee games happen on the grass of the **Bois de Vincennes** (Métro to Château-Vincennes), just on the eastern edge of town.

bar scene

The bar scene is the site of Paris nightlife; it is here that Parisians feel most at home, mugging under the dim lights, dangling Gauloises and Marlboros from their puckered lips, and frightening their little dogs. Though Paris has plenty of club kids and music lovers, as everywhere, the bar allows the Parisians to show off what they've got going on, and hide away what they don't (like rhythm) [see *club scene,* below]. Dress code varies, but is generally more formal than in the States, and (big surprise) you can't go wrong with black; the bucket-jeans with dragging, shredded cuffs and sneaks (except if they're a bright pair of New Balance) probably won't wash.

Still hip after all these years, rue Oberkampf, the main drag of Ménilmontant, is lined with bar after bar, stretching toward Belleville. Mondays and Tuesdays are slow here, but after that it can feel like every youth in Paris is trying to squeeze their way into this narrow little lane. The biggest and baddest of the lot are Café Charbon and Mécano Bar, only a few buildings apart from each other and both jammed full of the coolest and drop-deadest of the 18-to-25 set.

Café Charbon *(109 rue Oberkampf, 11th; Tel 01/43-57-55-13; Métro to Parmentier or Ménilmontant; 9am-2am daily; MC, V)* is a beautiful space, a belle époque dance hall with a long wide bar, gas lamps, tall mirrors, and 20-foot ceilings. The DJ spinning house and jungle gives a nice counterpoint, making this the perfect spot to linger and neck with a coquette or French loverboy before a wide audience at 3am.

Mécano Bar *(99 rue Oberkampf, 11th; Tel 01/40-21-35-28; Métro to Parmentier or Ménilmontant; 9am-2pm Mon-Sat, 10am-2am Sun; AE,*

garçon meets fille

Are the French the seducers and seductresses they're fabled to be? They've got something, there's no denying it. Maybe it's that Paris is in some haunting way a lonelier place than you might have imagined, or maybe it's that the fear (of sex crime or insult) we know as PC has never crossed the Atlantic—but arts long-lost in the States such as innuendo, drawn-out flirtation, shameless meaningful looks between strangers, sexy PDA, and the asking-for and giving-out of phone numbers without a lot of to-do, are still alive here and charge almost every exchange with a little *frisson.* The two little kisses upon greeting and parting are not always totally innocent; nor are those lingering looks on the Métro: I heard tell of a friend of a friend, not bad-looking, who sat beside a not bad-looking total stranger, and after a 15-minute wordless ride, the two rose in unison and walked silently back to her place. Or maybe people just tell these stories to make everyone else miserable. Note: a *préservatif* is a condom, not some additive.

MC, V) despite the name, is far from a "tool shed" (though with the bus engines and monkey wrenches hanging from the ceiling, it does over-reach for the "theme bar" thing), and its more friendly layout leads to more mixing between the tables and spontaneous dancing—for more of this lip-biting, fist-pumping, endearing French phenomenon, hop across the street to **Cithéa** [see *club scene,* below]. Mécano hasn't quite got the same erotic patina as Charbon [see above], and attracts a slightly younger crowd, but is just as wildly popular.

A slightly older, more meditative crowd can be found across the street at **Café Mercerie** *(98 rue Oberkampf, 11th; Tel 01/43-38-81-30; Métro to Parmentier or Ménilmontant; 5pm-2am Mon-Fri, 3pm-2am Sat, Sun; MC, V)* with its oversized sewing machines, stripped walls, and back lounge.

Also located on the plain-jane-by-day, party-girl-by-night rue Oberkampf, the **Underworld Cafe** *(25 rue Oberkampf; Tel 01/48-06-35-36; Métro to Oberkampf; 6-2pm daily; underworld@libertysurf.fr; Cover varies, free-30F; AE, MC, V)* is a good place to mellow out or get hot around the collar, but only if the moment is right. With tables, chairs and couches, three large-screen TVs, and wall projections broadcasting a range of visual stimuli, there is plenty to keep you occupied, if the beautiful girl working behind the counter or gay boys sitting alone at the bar don't. Evenings feature a mellow mix of musical styles—from pop, house, and garage to drum 'n' bass and hard techno during the week, to higher-quality DJs and events on the weekends. During the hottest all-round get-downs, the tables and chairs part to create a dance floor.

Further up along Oberkampf, just after it crosses the roundabout boulevard de Belleville and down a sneaky side street to the right, is the rue de Panoyaux, the chillest corner of Ménilmontant. Here you'll find the solid, spacious, and far calmer **Lou Pascalou** *(14 rue des Panoyaux, 20th; Tel 01/46-36-78-10; Métro to Ménilmontant; 9am-2am daily; MC, V)*, a local fave and the place to come if you're actually interested in preserving your vocal cords, and not just pretending to comprehend Jean-Claude's responses to your questions.

With the all the disorienting scene-y-ness of Oberkampf, it can be shocking to realize you're a hop, skip, and stagger away from Belleville and its distinctly un-French buzz. Except for the occasional nose-ringed student here to check out "the other," Belleville (beginning, really, on the next street parallel to Oberkampf, the rue Timbaud) is a great place to wander aimlessly, but can be a bit forbidding. Though not the mecca of integration many tout it to be, Belleville does boast more genuine mingling than elsewhere in Paris.

Try the **Le Timbaud** *(99 rue Jean-Pierre Timbaud, 11th; Tel 01/49-23-08-96; Métro to Couronnes; 7:30am-1am daily, 6pm-6am month of Ramadan; No credit cards)* for just such a place, absolutely blasting West African tunes to its far-from-exclusively Arabic clientele, featuring live jazz, African, or Algerian Raï after Ramadan, and appropriately skeptical about (but nonetheless welcoming to) you.

Deep in the 13th, among the workers of the world, the Butte aux Cailles is coming into its own, and it is where you'll find the cheapest beers and the least English. After a meal at **Chez Gladines** [see *eats*, below], run around the corner to **Le Merle Moqueur** *(11 rue de la Butte-aux-Cailles, 13th; Tel 01/45-65-12-43; Métro to Corvisart or Place de l'Italie; 5pm-2am daily; AE, DC, MC, V)*, where the bamboo plants choke on smoke and the French pop is played unabashedly; your new friends will tell you when to show up at the anti-Chirac rally.

Students who can't bother to shave and put on a tie still go out in the Latin quarter, and the student dive is **Le Piano Vache** *(8 rue Laplace, 5th; Tel 01/46-33-75-03; Métro to Maubert-Mutualité; Noon-2am Mon-Fri,*

rules of the game

There is no enforced drinking age in France, but neither are there great drunks; people consume moderately and get drunk with great composure. It's only tourists you'll hear shouting yahoo while under the influence. As for narcotics, we would definitely not recommend you head out to the rough streets of the *banlieue,* the outskirts, the only areas in Paris where they're hawked in the street. In most public parks, like the Champ de Mars, you'll find kids sneaking a toke, though busts are extremely rare.

9pm-2am Sat, Sun; MC, V), on a medieval street on the northern slope of the Panthéon. Dingy and wonderful, its walls are all plastered and charred. A DJ spins Wednesday through the weekend, but Friday—*American Rock* night—somehow feels the most French.

British-style bars and pubs are relatively foreign to Paris's bar, brasserie, and cafe culture. Indeed, across France, Irish and British pubs tend to be more expensive and style-conscious than your average dive bar, but in Paris, kids who want to drink seriously will look to foreign-run bars or bars catering to foreigners.

Tucked off of rue Sentier in the 2nd Arrondissemont, south of boulevard Poissonnière, and situated (surprisingly enough) next to a police station, **Café le Port d'Amsterdam** *(20 rue du Croissant; Tel 01/40-39-02-63; Métro to Sentier; 5pm-2am; Happy hour 5-7pm)* is a dive bar run by a cabal of Dutch chauvinists, reputed to entice female patrons into dancing on the scarred wood tables. Music varies from Brit-pop to commercial Euro-dance, and at night the bar becomes a dark smoky den of sin, fueled by cheap Grolsch and testosterone.

Also located in the 2nd Arrondissement, on the laughably sleazy rue St.-Denis, **The Frog & Rosbif** *(116 rue St.-Denis; Tel 01/42-36-34-73; Métro to Entienne Marcel; Noon-2am)* is the spot to gab with ex-pat Brits and butt heads with European football fans over pints and pitchers of lager and groovy microbrews. With heavy wood furniture, floors, and bar, this place has the well-trodden look and relaxed feel of an English pub, and crazy patrons to match. Remember as you settle into a booze-laden haze that they offer student discounts on their brew. Look for the live broadcasts of European football and English rugby, and watch out for that English nutter doing card and coin magic tricks. A note for the crime-weary urbanite in all of us: He's not trying to take your money, he just wants to make you smile.

And if you're feeling homesick, run around to the **Violon Dingue** *(46 rue de la Montagne Sainte-Geneviève, 5th; No phone; Métro to Maubert-Mutualité; Regular bar 6pm-1:30am Sun-Thur, 8pm-3:30am Sat, Sun, lower level 4:30pm-3:30am Fri, Sat; V, MC),* designed and run by a Minnesota local and ex-Navy man, where you can watch NFL whenever in season, and get blitzed beneath old tin Coors signs and sports pennants to the sweet sounds of James Brown on the juke.

On the western edge of the Latin Quarter, on a main street, **Café Oz** *(184 rue St.-Jacques, 5th; Tel 01/43-54-30-48; RER to Luxembourg, Métro to Cluny-La Sorbonne; 4pm-2am daily; MC, V)* is where to get your Australian fix (if the quotient was too low at the hostel). Travel yarns, sleepy 1am chess games, and Fosters is what you'll 'ave 'ere, mate.

The Marais can have a sultry, New Orleans feel at night, and a number of slick venues and American-style bars have opened up alongside the gay old-timers. The truly petit **Petit Fer à Cheval** *(30 rue Vieille-du-Temple, 4th; Tel 01/42-72-47-47; Métro to St.-Paul; 9am-2am daily; MC, V),* with its tin ceiling, zinc bar, and old Paris charm, is one of the best bars in the area, if you can squeeze in. Were the talented Tom Ripley to seduce you, kill you, and steal your identity, he'd start the process here.

Just around the corner in a wide, cobbled cul de sac is the very young and very cool **Café du Trésor** *(5 rue du Trésor, 4th; Tel 01/43-26-62-93; Métro to St.-Paul; 2:30pm-2am daily; MC, V)* with a stocking-capped DJ spinning the latest house grooves in his little booth, and sultry kids on every divan.

You find an entirely different set at **Buddha Bar** *(8 rue Boissy d'Anglas, 8th; Tel 01/53-05-90-00; Métro to Concorde; 6pm-2am daily; AE, V, MC)* the transcendent shrine of the BCBGers *(bon chic bons gens)*, that unique creation of modern French society: yuppies with ascots. Though not as exclusive, of course, as the *clubs privés* many of this crowd belong to, Buddha Bar is where the Donald might decline shaking hands with Lenny Kravitz or his entourage. Dominated by a huge Golden Buddha, and filled with strains of sitars, double violins, and other signals that you're firmly in France, this massive split-level, grotto-like, and hugely pricey restaurant/bar in the 8th still has to be visited at least once.

And then, of course, there's the Bastille scene, where you'll wind up despite yourself and where a good time can still be had with selective vision. The spawn of the European Union still congregate here and subject themselves to the unjustifiably snooty whims of the door along the rue du Faubourg Saint-Antione at La Fabrique, SanZSanS, Barrio Latino, and the whole sleazy stretch of the rue de Lappe.

A chill spot to grab a cheap espresso or midday pint of beer in the Bastille area is the colorful **Café des Anges** *(66 rue de la Roquette; Tel 01/47-00-00-03; Métro to Bastille; 8am-midnight daily; MC, V).*

If you must, you might as well at **Boca Chica** *(58 rue de Charonne, 11th; Tel 01/43-57-93-13; Métro to Ledru-Rollin; 11am-2am daily; AE, MC, V)* where the "Latino" pretensions of the Bastille scene are brought to fever pitch, and the vivacity, genuine fun-lovingness, and tasty tapas make you feel hotta' than they do in Granada. Low tables, painfully loud Cesaria Evora remixes, and burnt umber are the call of the hour.

LIVE MUSIC SCENE

Paris was patron to jazz's cutting edge in the '40s and '50s, but since then we haven't consistently been able to depend on their taste, to say the least. Sometimes they treat a fledgling comer seriously—take Charlie Parker—and elevate him to his rightful place, and sometimes they elect others—say Serge Gainsbourg or Céline Dion (for which we've got to accept partial responsibility)—and treat them with the same seriousness. The current Parisian enthusiasm is world music, that catch-all phrase that can mean anything—it can lump together respectable ska, Algerian Raï, Gypsy fiddlers, and klezmer acts, with, say, a Frenchman in red suspenders singing in Arabic to the accompaniment of a gypsy violin, a Jewish clarinet, and a tabla. It's hit-or-miss.

▶▶JAZZ
L'Atmosphère *(49 rue Lucien Sampaix, 10th; Tel 01/40-38-09-21; Métro to Gare de l'Est; Bar 11am-2am Tue-Fri, 5pm-2am Sat, Sun, sets begin 8pm Tue-Sat, 5pm Sun; No cover; No credit cards),* a tiny

la di da dj

Rap has busted through the charts in France, but it pretty much remains the music of the *cité,* the generally black, Arab, and Jewish dominated, housing project-like suburbs surrounding Paris. Paris and Marseille, much like the East and West coasts of the United States, compete in verbal sparring contests. In the headlines of French newspapers and in the minds of many elders and young people, rap gets a bad rap and is still associated with questionable indictments of police racism, violence, and the gangster-like lifestyles prevalent in its lyrics. While the charts play host to a number of artists, often mimicking the styles of American rap, French rap has come a long way since the late eighties and the days of **MC Solaar,** one of the few French rappers to break through to the American scene. Nowadays, **NTM** is arguably one of the best and most distinguished groups on the French scene for its uncompromisingly sharp rhymes and tight beats, and the influence of American independent hip-hop is evident in the raw energy of such groups as **Supa Sian Crew.**

The obvious difference between American and French rap is the influence of ragga and dancehall (the difference between ragga and dancehall being largely one of semantics). The white dreads now sported by both girls and boys in cities like Rouen and Lille are less a statement of roots culture or Rastafarianism than a fashion statement, but they hint at larger influence in French popular culture. Afro-beat, reggae, dancehall, and ragga are wildly popular in France, as the popularity of Nigerian-born **Femi Kuti,** the son of eighties Afro-beat superstar Fela Kuti, and **Les Nubiennes,** the West African rooted R&B pop group, attest.

Ragga and dancehall have very heavily influenced rap in France and even in the most commercial of French rap, you'll hear dancehall-style back-up vocals. Songs usually feature a break down, where an MC will kick a few rhymes in a dancehall-stylee flow. The inevitable result of such influence is a blurring of the genres. At the **Slow-Club,** [see *club scene,* above] you'll hear rap vocals thrown over dancehall bass lines, and dancehall vocals laid down over rap beats, often with R&B back-up vocals to boot. Groups like **Raggasonic** are some of the most popular innovators of such musical miscegenation.

Essential Listening:
Supa Sian Crew, *KLR* (Virgin)
NTM, *Paris sous les Bombs* (Sony)
Premiere Classe compilation (Virgin)
Le Flow 1 & 2 compilations (Virgin & Ultra)

bistro/cafe/bar on the Canal Saint-Martin, is one of the best jazz venues out there, with the energetic blowing out of home-grown talent, and sometimes inspiring, fanciful solos, though the influence of Ornette Coleman is a little overwhelming. Linger over a glass of wine before the first set starts around 8pm—the weekend crush can be impossible—stay for the first set, and then retire to **Chez Prune** [see *hanging out*, above].

While the atmosphere at l'Atmosphere can run to the ponderous, **Cithéa** [see *club scene*, below]—whether a funk, reggae, world, or jazz show is on—makes sure its groove is front and center. With groovy bass lines and the occasional barri sax, Cithéa can make you never want to go home again—and with the DJ spinning funk faves after the set, you won't have to, till dawn.

Should you require a chiller ambiance with the possibility of release into the Oberkampf mayhem, check out the **Satellit' Cafe** *(44 rue de la Folie Méricourt, 11th; Tel 01/47-00-48-87; Métro to Oberkampf; 8pm-3am Tue-Thur, 10pm-6am Fri, Sat, shows at 9:30pm Tue-Thur; www. satellit-cafe.com; No credit cards)* where acoustic world acts range from downright slamming to self-serious crud. The space itself, with black walls and a glow-in-the-dark solar system painting, feels like an 11-year-old's dream of an ideal club. When the friendly staff switches on the turntable on the long weekends, it can be a swinging floor, too.

The péniches (canal barges) **Batofar** [see *club scene*, below] and **Makara** *(quai de la Gare, 13th; Tel 01/44-24-09-00; Métro to quai de la Gare; 7pm-2am Tue-Sun, shows 9pm Tue-Sun; 30-50f cover; MC, V)* are rarely—at least not yet—packed, and can host everything from flamenco to funk. The multi-act shows are long, and loud.

A favorite of the *Nova*-reading set, the beguilingly eclectic **Café de la Danse** *(5 Passage Louis-Philippe, 11th; Tel 01/47-00-57-59; Métro to Bastille; Shows 8:30pm most nights; 80-120f cover; No credit cards)* is impossible to characterize, booking fast-and-furious rock acts like the Cramps as much as it pushes its Arabic character. The mood of this dank, stony place can shift from Château Dracul to Soho London between gigs. The high quality of the acts is worth the price, as are the funky young things who shell it out nightly.

Nearby, the tight but hip **Réservoir** *(16 rue de la Forge Royale, 11th; Tel 01/43-56-39-60; Métro to Faidherbe-Chaligny; Bar 8pm-2am daily, shows at 11:30pm Tue-Sat; No cover; AE, MC, V)*, is a slicker affair, hooked deeply into the music biz and its double-breasted, pinky-ringed sleaze factor. It's still one of the better places to hear hot labels trying out the newly-signed on a beautiful, made-up clientele on Thurdays, and its one of the Paris layover blips on the migratory path of freshly-hot musicians.

If you're looking something eclectic, take a seat on **Le Divan du Monde** (Couch of the World) *(75 rue des Martyrs; Tel 01/44-92-77-66; Métro to Pigalle; Concerts start at 7:30pm Mon-Sat, 4pm Sun; Cover varies, free-120F, 20-40F drinks; No credit cards)*. Housed in a two-tiered former cabaret club in the popping Pigalle area, this casually sized concert space hosts everything from intense drum'n'bass, ragga, and raï events to world beat, Brit-pop, rock, and the odd hip-hop concert, and the crowd is as diverse as the music. You don't want to dally, because concerts start on time and end promptly.

club scene

The Paris club—or *boîte*—is kind of an unnatural graft onto Paris's nightlife, and this can make some of its excesses—the scoping, the over-the-top grinding, and the leaping up and down on the cushions—a little embarrassing to witness. The best dancers here are generally not nationals, but Americans, Spaniards, and the boogying huddled masses from every-where else who flock here. Unless you are gorgeous, famous, or know someone (and, hey, don't sell yourself short), it can be hard to get into the big, *branché* (literally "plugged in") clubs along the Champs Elysées or elsewhere. There is no list you can lie and say you were left off of, and smooth-talking the bouncers is definitely harder in French. Most *branché* nighthawks get private invitations to parties in the mail in lieu of being put down on a list. If you're dying to get into one of these joints, make friends with one of the elect or get your mitts on one of those invites by whatever means necessary—the velvet rope parts the minute they check it out.

The king of these *boîtes branchées* is **Les Bains** (*7 rue du Bourg-l'Abbé, 3rd; Tel 01/48-87-01-80; Métro to Réaumur Sébastopol; 11:30pm-5am daily, restaurant 8:30pm-1am; 100F cover, drinks 70F; AE, MC, V*), with an upstairs restaurant that doubles as a roped-off VIP room (read: models and those who can bed 'em, like celebs). The fiftysomething prowlers stand around looking worried as those only slightly less beautiful than their sisters upstairs (or else still unsigned) cavort before their eyes. A former bathhouse, the intermittent open pools function largely as ash-trays these days. Wednesday's *Glam Parade*—when the glam beats are laid down—is the night to come, otherwise it's generally house.

If Les Bains is King, God save **Le Queen** (*102 ave. des Champs Elysées, 8th; Tel 01/53-89-08-90; Métro to Charles de Gaulle-Étoile, George V, Franklin Roosevelt; Daily 11:30-dawn; Cover 100f Fri, Sat, 50f Mon, free Tue-Thur; Exclusively gay Thur, Sat, Sun; V, MC, AE*), where the most outrageous element of the Paris gay scene taught its straight brothers and sisters how to get down. Still ostensibly a queer club (meaning women might be scrutinized at the door longer than they're used to), this is where the big wet kiss Paris has decided to bestow on its queer demimonde is sloppiest. Huge, with go-go dancers, six-foot transsexuals, and ear-shat-tering techno mixes, there is no better dance floor in Paris. For full-out delicious drag, Monday is the night to see Paris Burning. The *Respect Is Burning* party on Wednesday nights is the club's only truly mixed night, and the place kicks to the tunes of big-name house DJs like Dimitri From Paris and the occasional American import like Armand Van Helden. For much of 1999-2000, the party toured the globe as if bent on world dom-ination. Now the party is back in town at its rightful home in the metal and slick, black industrial interior of Le Queen.

The first Thursday of the month **Pulp** *(25 blvd. Poissonière; Tel 01/40-26-01-93; Métro to Grands Blvds; Midnight-dawn Wed-Sat; 50F Fri & Sat; AE, MC, V)* [see *gay and lesbian scene,* below] tolerates unaccompanied men for a fun, mixed gay and straight party (but guys, don't expect any generosity from the less-than-*gentille* girls working the bar). While music varies from house to Latin and lacks the superstar quality of Le Queen, the vibe of this intimate place is decidedly positive.

Up in Pigalle, the seedy, Times Square-like area south of Montmarte, **Folies Pigalle** *(11 place Pigalle, 9th; Tel 01/48-78-25-56; Métro to Pigalle; Midnight-dawn daily, till noon weekends; Cover 100f; MC, V),* once a strip joint, has managed to spin tassles into gold (or at least lamé). Not nearly as plugged-in as Les Bains or Le Queen, a younger crowd comes here to enjoy itself on the runway and in the pit (rather than to hang on the pavement outside, call friends on their cell phones and *talk* about enjoying themselves.) The weekends are solidly techno, while Sundays from 5:30 to 11pm see the *United Colours of Gays* tea dance, a pseudo-belly dancing event the young things just can't seem to resist in this town.

The only option for straight-ahead dancing along the Oberkampf strip is **Cithéa** *(112-114 rue Oberkampf, 11th; Tel 01/40-21-70-95; Métro to Parmentier; 10pm-5am daily, shows 11pm Wed-Sat; Admission free Mon, Tue, Sun, 30f including a drink Wed, Thur, 60F Fri, Sat; MC, V),* a small space with a '50s-marquee exterior that does triple service as a bar, a live venue [see *live music scene,* above], and a club. Cithéa feels a bit like the disco at the University Student Union, but on a good night. Here you will come to understand why Oberkampf doesn't have more dance spots, however: No matter how deep a groove is playing, the would-be Jean-Paul Belmondos from **Café Charbon** across the street [see *bar scene,* above] work the same wiggle, and that same, "oh god I need a toilet" demi-crouch, tune after tune. If you have the teensiest bit of soul in your moves, you will be scoped and asked to give lessons. Great selection of acid jazz and Stevie and (he who was) Prince.

Evolving from the hair-metal nights and rock free-for-alls of the late eighties and early nighties, **Gibus** (*18 rue du Faubourg-du-Temple; Tel 01/47-00-78-88; 9pm-dawn Tue, midnight-dawn Wed-Sun; Cover 50F-100F, depending on the night*) has had a varied clientele to match its ever-changing cast of promoters. Currently under the eyes of "Bitchy Jose," the clientele is mostly gay, except for the annoying, cloying (alternately either empty or packed) VIP section. The VIP section, basically the only place to sit except for a single table tucked behind the DJ booth, features sleazy looking guys with greasy hair holding court with their preening model girlfriends. Except for the headlining U.K. or U.S. DJ on the weekends, you will probably want to avoid this bastion of sweaty, hedonistic, over-the-top exploits, unless you want to grope or be groped.

A recent, slightly unholy renovation has added a Latin cafe downstairs at **La Coupole** (*102 blvd. de Montparnasse, 14th; Tel 01/43-20-14-20; Métro to Vavin; 7:30pm-2am daily, dancing 11:30pm-4am Tue-Thur; 100f cover includes drink; AE, V, MC*), the famous Montparnasse brasserie where Hemingway and all those cats never once heard, let alone boogied to, Gypsy Kings house remixes. Yet the spacious, tiled lower level is now an all-out salsa fiesta on the weekdays. It may be worth heading all the way down to Montparnasse to see the famous dining room, which, though slightly disfigured by the renovation, still retains the famous murals commissioned in exchange for free drinks from artist-regulars.

Should you grow weary of the Parisian craze for the traditional, with all its meandering "world" rhythms that are easier to talk about than dance to, **Rex Club** (*5 blvd. Poissonnière, 2nd; Tel 01/42-36-83-98; Métro to Bonne-Nouvelle; 11pm-dawn Wed, Thur, Fri, 11:30pm-dawn Sat; Cover 60f Wed, 70f Thur, Fri, 80f Sat; AE, MC, V*) will rev you up with techno and house, pumped out with no apologies, on a bass system so seismic you'll be asking, "What is that—do you hear that?" the whole next day. This is the house that Laurent Garnier—to many, the father of techno—built, and DJ Charles Schillings keeps the tradition hard and heavy on Friday night's *Automatik;* Garnier himself spins when the spirit in the machine moves him. Housed in a wing of the *Metropolis*-esque, Art Deco Rex moviehouse, the Rex may not be as hot as it was in the '90s, but it's true to its roots.

And if you've brought your four-inch, electric red patent-leather dancing shoes, you can salsa into one of Edith Piaf's haunts, **La Java** (*105 rue du Faubourg-du-Temple, 10th; Tel 01/42-02-20-52; Métro to Belleville; 11pm-6am Thur-Sat; Cover 60-80f Thur, 100f Fri, Sat; AE, MC, V*) unquestionably the best thing about Paris's Latin craze. Salsa, meringue, and tango dancers who actually know what the hell they're doing pack it into this classic old dance hall, with a great wide lacquered dance floor and period tables, lamps, and bandstand, for a sweat-drenched cha-cha-cha on the weekends. A live Latin horn band is followed by a DJ.

And a good idea whose time may have finally come are the péniches—small party boats—many of which have theater, live shows, and clubbing after the curtain. The vast majority are moored—and stay that way—in the distant, eastern 13th *arrondissement (Métro to quai de la Gare or Bibliotèque),* on the quay just down from the new massive Bibliotèque Nationale on the allée Arthur Rimbaud.

Batofar *(facing 11 quai Francois-Mauriac; Tel 01/56-29-10-00; Métro to Bibliothèque; 8pm-2am Tue-Sun; Free-60F, 15-60F drinks; MC, V),* the hippest, most avant-garde bar, club, and concert space in all of Paris, hosts a consistently interesting mix of concerts and DJ gigs featuring live local, British, European, and American dub, trip-hop, hip-hop, ragga, minimal house, techno, Brit-pop, rock, post rock, and the odd big-name heavy hitter like DJ Krush. In the smallish hull of the boat, the sound system, unencumbered by sound-wave-bending concrete pilings and bedrock, shakes the entire boat with viciously deep bass sans ugly reverb and distortion. (To test the bass, place a cigarette wrapper on the ground and watch it dance along the vibrating dance floor.) The most interesting projects are often the monthly experimental shows, throwing together live DJs and live musicians. For a complete listing of concerts, check record stores and hip shops around town for Batofar's flyers. You'll want to arrive promptly because it closes early by Parisian standards (2am) and because drinks at the well-stocked bar are cheap. Because of the club's relative isolation from the city center, ask the guys at the door to call you a taxi when you're ready to leave—taxis can be hard to come by late at night in the 13th Arrondissement.

Kids will tell you, with forlorn faces, that Paris has no hip-hop clubs. But they're wrong. Paris *had* no hip-hop clubs, until the appearance of the **Slow-Club** *(130 rue de Rivoli; Tel 01/42-33-84-30; Métro to Chatelet; 11:30pm-4:30am Mon & Wed; 80F men, Mon free for women, Wed 50F for women; Until 12:30 admission includes a free drink; MC, V),* located elegantly enough across from the *Grand Magasin,* La Samaritaine. Almost as rare as clubs in Paris with generally all-black clientele are white kids at the Slow-Club, which is not to say that they're not welcome. Quite the opposite. If you're down with the hip-hop, R&B, dancehall, and interesting percussive combinations of the three, you'll be down and you'll get down at the Slow-Club, no matter what the color of your skin. Don't be intimidated by color line, the monster-sized bouncers, or the intimate frisk. While drinks are expensive at 50F a bottle, cigarette packets sit open on the coffee tables and joints move secretively around the club. Wednesdays, the club fills out with the silhouetted curves of beautiful girls singing along to their favorite R&B songs in the dim club smoke.

arts scene

▶▶VISUAL ARTS

Almost all of Paris is a giant gallery, with windows full of photographs, canvasses, sculptures, antiques, and curiosities. In the Marais, Saint-Germain-des-Prés, along the rue de Rivoli in the 1st, the backstreets of

festivals and events

Banlieue Blues *(Mar/Apr; Seine St.-Denis; 01/49-22-10-10; Free-150f):* Big funk-fest in the suburbs, known to attract nobodies and somebodies with soul.

Festival du Film de Paris *(Early Apr; Cinéma Gaumont Marignan, 27 ave. des Champs Elysées, 8th; Tel 01/42-65-12-37; Métro to Franklin Roosevelt; 35f per day, 150f per wk):* Directors, actors, and writers from all over the world come to show their films, speak about them and themselves, and look for a distributor.

Fête du Travail *(May 1):* May Day is taken very seriously, with a big parade of the proletariat and trade unions, colorfully losing their chains together.

Fête de la Musique *(June 21; Tel 01/40-03-94-70):* Every street of the city is packed with buskers playing every conceivable genre of music, while big names (James Brown and Sting have come in the past) take to the plazas for free outdoor shows.

Gay Pride March *(End of June):* Bigger by the year, if not yet on par with New York's. Expect floats, queens, and general gaiety. Info at **Centre Gai et Lesbien** [see *gay scene*, below].

Course des Garçons et Serveuses de Cafe: *(Late June; At the Hôtel de Ville; Tel 01/42-96-60-75; Métro to Hôtel-de-Ville):* One of the more ridiculous contests, with cafe waiters and waitresses in full regalia racing viciously against each other, platter in hand. No tipping.

Jazz à la Villette *(Early July; 211 ave. Jean Jaurès, 19th; Tel 08/03-07-50-75; Métro to Porte de Pantin; Free-160f):* Just as venerable as the other two music fests, this is held in the Epcot Center-ish Parc de la Villette, on the Canal St.-Martin. From big names to no names.

Bastille Day *(July 14th):* The city explodes with celebrations, especially around the Place de la Bastille, and on the Champ de Mars, watching the fireworks at Trocadéro, across the water. The greatest and strangest aspect of the French independence day celebrations are the fireman's *(pompiers)* balls, held in the courtyards and streets adjacent to their firehouses.

the 7th, and across the Bastille, Paris serves up images of itself, its pretensions, its history, and its slightly dirty conscience everywhere.

To find the most cutting-edge of the lot, go to the northern reaches of the Marais and its extension into Beaubourg, in the 3rd arrondissement. There must be at least 100 galleries in this otherwise quiet area, and more opening all the time, so it's a place to get lost in.

One of the best of the area is surely the **Galerie Aréa** *(10 rue de Picardie, 3rd; Tel 01/42-72-68-66; Métro to Temple; 2-7pm Wed-Sat, 3-*

Quartier d'Eté (*Mid-July through mid-Aug; All over Paris; Tel 01/44-94-98-00*): The largely emptied city is given shows of classical and world music, circuses, and spectacles, mostly out-of-doors and free.

Le Cinéma en Plein Air (*Mid-July through mid-Aug; Parc de la Villette, 19th; Tel 01/40-03-76-92; Métro to Porte de Pantin*) Free outdoor festival of classic cinema, projected onto a large screen.

La Tour de France (*End of July; Finish line on the Champs Elysées; Tel 01/41-33-15-00*): Watch 'em roll in past the **Arc de Triomphe.**

Artists' Open Studios (*Oct*): **Artistes à la Bastille** (*Tel 01/53-36-06-730*), **Ménilmontant** (*Tel 01/40-03-01-61*), **13th** (*Tel 01/45-86-17-67*). Working studios are open for your inspection; a good time to see the work of the collectives and squats of Belleville, like **La Forge** (*32 rue de Ramponneau*), or the **Collective de Grange** (*10th; 31 rue de la Grange-aux-Belles*), and in the Barbès area of the 18th [see *arts scene*, above].

Festival FNAC-Inrockuptibles (*Early Nov*): Sponsored by *Inrockuptibles*, the French *Rolling Stone*, a big indie-music event of the year, where American alternative musicians are sold to the French market.

Armistice Day (*November 11*): Solemn commemoration of the end of WWI, which cost so many French lives.

Salon des Grands Vins (*Mid-Dec; Paris-Expo, Porte de Versailles, 15th; Métro to Porte de Versailles; 50f*): Wine expo. Great way to refine your palette and get smashed at the same time. 50 francs buys you a glass, and from there it's just you and 1,000 vintners of France, including some of the very best; if you like, you can buy for 30 to 40 percent under retail. Spitting is classier than swallowing.

Africolor (*Late Dec; Théâtre Gérard Philippe, 59 blvd. Jules Guesde, 93200 St.-Denis; Tel 01/48-13-70-00; Métro to St.-Denis Basilique; 50f*): An African festival celebrating the cultures of the largest minority in France, held in the suburb of St.-Denis.

7pm Sun) devoted exclusively to French contemporary painting. Housed in a small, two-story converted office, the Galerie shows its stuff by flouting the conceptual aesthetic conventions of many of its neighbors.

Yvon Lambert (*108 rue Vieille-du-Temple, 3rd; Tel 01/42-71-09-33; Métro to Filles du Calvaire; Open 10am-1pm/2:30-7pm Tue-Fri, 10am-7pm Sat*) shows all the heavy hitters, like Anselm Kiefer, Nan Goldin, and Julien Schnabel, as well as video and photo shows. In its massive, well-lit warehouse space on a main thoroughfare of the Marais, Yvon Lambert is where you show once you've "arrived."

Everyone has a different opinion on the bizarre architecture of the **Centre National d'Art et de Culture Georges Pompidou** *(1 rue Beaubourg; Tel 01/44-78-12-33; Métro to Chatelet/Les Halles or Hôtel de Ville; 11am-10pm Wed-Mon, until 9pm for exhibitions; Closed May 1; Prices vary depending on exhibitions, 30-50F, 20-40F students, under 18 free)*, designed by Richard Rogers and Renzo Piano in the 1970s. Certainly the air-conditioner-turned-inside-out building containing the Centre d'Art Moderne—which after the **Louvre** should be the second stop of any art lover in Paris—has not aged as well as it was intended. The glass, steel, and brightly colored plastic exterior is grayed and dirty, and the slightly seedy Place Georges Pompidou is home to throngs of pigeons, hippie bongo players, and cheesy portrait painters. But do not be put off: The center is easily navigable and always changing, displaying everything from sleek '60s Modern Braun products to Giacometti's statuary to the models of the designs of Achille Castiglioni and films of Luis Buñuel, as well as a host of temporary exhibitions. No two visits are ever quite the same.

Recently opened, **l'Espace Nouveaux Media** *(4th floor; 1-9pm)* allows the normally passive museum-goer to navigate through the multimedia computer projects of such artists as Claes Oldenburg and Chris Marker (best known for his film *La Jetée*, on which the obnoxious Terry Gilliam–Bruce Willis project *12 Monkeys* was based). Give yourself several hours to meander the three floors of the museum, serviced by the elevators and escalators attached to the exterior of the building.

A firmly unofficial place to witness the Birth of Art is in the many collectives and squats that are generally ignored by officials. One is the converted smithy **La Forge,** in Belleville *(32 rue de Ramponneau);* another is the **Collective de Grange** in the 10th *arrondissement (31 rue de la Grange-aux-Belles).* During the *portes ouvertes* (open studios) [see *festivals & events,* above] you can get a peak inside, or try knocking anytime; providing you don't look like a narc, they'll probably let you in.

▶▶PERFORMING ARTS

The second best thing (and let's face it, sometimes the best thing) to do in a darkened room in Paris is to watch a movie. Film in Paris is venerated as nowhere else on Earth, except, sadly, as it was in the New York City of the '60s and '70s. There are megaplexes here like the Cineplex Odeon, but the number of small revival houses, art film theaters, foreign cinema theaters, festivals [see *festivals & events,* above] both official and informal, and spontaneous screenings of classics and cult classics, makes first-run films beside the point. Most foreign-language films are screened here in *version originale* (VO); that is, with the original dialogue and French subtitles. There are continual festivals of Hitchcock, Kubrick, Cassavetes, and other adored Anglo/American directors. The greatest variety and number of theaters are in the Latin Quarter (5th) and the St.-Michel area (6th).

A veritable compendium of listings for 'round-the-clock screenings can be found in *l'Officiel des Spectacles,* but you should devote a good hour to pinpointing what you want to see. Beside the title of the film (in French, even if the movie's not) are the day (*lun* = Mon, *mar* = Tue, *mer* = Wed, *jeu* = Thur, *ven* = Fri, *sam* = Sat, *dim* = Sun, *tlj* = daily) and the hour of the screening (in military time). Some of the best theaters are found on the Rue des Écoles, like the **Action Ecoles** *(23 rue des Écoles; Tel 01/43-29-79-89; Métro to Maubert-Mutualité; 40f admission, 30f students; No credit cards)*, the **Champo** *(51 rue des Écoles; Tel 01/43-54-51-60; Métro to Odéon or St.-Michel; 45f admission, 35f students; No credit cards)*, and the **Grand Action** *(5 rue des Écoles; Tel 01/43-29-44-40; Métro to Cardinal Lemoine or Jussieu; 42f admission, 32f students; No credit cards)*. The Mk2 chain, including **Rendez-vous des Quais** [see *hanging out,* above] shows arty French and foreign new releases.

Theater in Paris is thriving, owing to a devoted following, heavy government subsidies, and a French penchant for putting on a good show and being looked at. While the Comédie Française is still the height of culture and poise, performing the experimental and the classic (Shakespeare, Molière, Ibsen); the more informal dirt-on-the-floor, in-your-face pits may be more authentically French. Rather than the rise of a curtain, many of the grass-roots theater troupes signal the show's beginning as they did in the Middle Ages, with the dramaturge's repeated pounding of a pole solemnly on the ground.

For this elemental, timeless soul of French theater, head out to the avant-garde **Théâtre du Soleil** at the **Cartoucherie de Vincennes** *(Route du Champ de Manoeuvre, Bois de Vincennes, 12th; Tel 01/43-74-24-08; Métro to Chateau de Vincennes, from there shuttle bus or Bus 112; Reserve seats daily from 1-6pm, shows 7:30pm Wed-Sat, 1pm Sun; Tickets 150f; No credit cards)* where the legendary, radical Ariane Mnouchkine and her cast stage political and provocative interpretations of plays, from the contemporary to the Greek, that can border on events. Mnouchkine was known for staging productions in working-class neighborhoods before she opened in this location in 1970. The theater, just out of town on its far-eastern fringe, is in a massive overgrown industrial space—a converted military cartridge factory—a post-post-apocalyptic landscape à la *Logan's Run.* The Cartoucherie houses several companies and a number of performance spaces—with work almost always in French—and the cast even cook you dinner (reserve at the above number). Check any of the major listings mags for showtimes and ticket info.

gay scene

Increasingly, Gay Paree is openly just that, and straight Paris's fascination of the moment is watching while Paris flames. But the straight world's interest in venues like **Le Queen** [see *club scene,* above] and its mass intrusion into the Marais can feel a little obnoxious, so you may want to seek refuge at one of the many gay spots that still pride themselves on being somewhat exclusive. Gay-bashing or outright bigotry are almost unheard-of in this sophisticated city, and if there is still prejudice here, you may sense it in the over-use of the word *pédé*—"fag"—by heteros to describe a venue or style. But then again, this insensitivity may be nothing more than a nasty reflex of the straight French boys who are often mistaken for the other team, thus the refrain: "Is he gay? Maybe he's just French...."

The **Centre Gai et Lesbien** *(3 rue Keller, 11th; Tel 01/43-57-21-47; Métro to Ledru-Rollin; 2-8pm Mon-Sat, 2-7pm Sun)* is a popular meeting ground, information center, and activist HQ with a cafe where you're free to peruse the plentiful materials and fliers stashed around. Many of the main parks and public spaces become prime cruising grounds after dark. Note especially the quays of the Seine, the Parc des Buttes Chaumont, and the Tuileries gardens. The endless paths of the Bois de Boulogne are daytime cruising spots, but at night, the park is turned over to extremely gorgeous and extremely butch (no joke: blade-wielding) Brazilian transvestite prostitutes, who've driven straight trick-seekers out of the Bois almost entirely.

Even with the intrusion of straight Paris, the Marais retains that West Village or French Quarter sensuousness that characterizes the best gay neighborhoods. The main stretch, up the rue Vielle du Temple, is half-straight, half-gay, and may be yielding to the former. But the area further west, closer to the Métro stop Hôtel de Ville, is still dominantly queer and dotted with dark-tinted windows, mysterious goings-on, and campy cabarets.

Bite your tongue and enter **Le Cox** *(15 rue des Archives, 4th; Tel 01/42-72-08-00; Métro to Hôtel de Ville; 1pm-2am daily; No credit cards)*, one of the more popular additions to the check-out and pickup scene, a roomy cafe/bar where you can, ahem, log on in the rear (with a name like that, everything seems like a double-entendre).

Amnesia *(42 rue Vielle du Temple, 4th; Tel 01/42-72-16-94; Métro to Hôtel de Ville; 10:30am-2am daily; MC, V)* catering equally to the gay and dyke crowds, as well as to the requisite straight hangers-on, is a local favorite, split-level, with sofas and a less severely body-conscious vibe.

Les Scandeleuses *(8 rue des Ecouffes, 4th; Tel 01/48-87-39-26; Métro to Hôtel de Ville or St.-Paul; 6pm-2am daily; MC, V)* on a small street with a yeshiva and several Jewish markets, is a laid-back, artsy dyke bar with the post-industrial installation look, and the cropped-hair, lip-stickless girls to match.

At night, **Le Queen** [see *club scene*, above] is still the address for lumberjacks who put on women's clothing and hang around in bars; if any boy has packed a fabulous rhinestone gown especially for Paris, here is where she can make her grand entrance.

Pulp *(25 blvd. Poissonnière, 2nd; Tel 01/40-26-01-93; Métro to Grands Boulevards; Midnight-dawn Wed-Sat; 50f cover weekends; AE, MC, V)* the dyke club of Paris, is poised to become the next **Le Queen,** so brace yourself, girls. More intimate than the former, with more emphasis on Latin, and less robotic dance tracks.

cULTURE ZOO

You can't come to Paris and skip the museums; visiting the Louvre at least is a duty akin to getting blitzed on Saint Paddy's, or cursing at taxi drivers

"Old Paris is no more. The shape of a city changes more swiftly, alas! than a man's heart." That's what Baudelaire, the preeminent *flâneur* (stroller) of all time, wrote of his town in 1857. The verb *flâner* means a kind of foot-dragging, ponderous stroll, a trance that Paris induces in the curious and restless. But following Baudelaire's lead, we can hardly send you strolling down the lacquered-up and packaged central boulevards of Paris, picturesque as they may be; the trick is to see the city as it changes. And nowhere is it changing more swiftly, in as many different directions and under as many different influences, than in the volatile, varied, and exuberant northeast corner of the city.

Start at the tourist hub of **place de La République,** where the 3rd, 11th, and 10th **arrondissements** collide, and take **rue du Faubourg du Temple,** heading east. You are still solidly in white Paris when you come to the **Square François Lemaître.** This placid retreat from République is where the Canal St.-Martin goes underground, to reemerge at Bastille. Stroll up the canal a ways, cross over the bridge, and come back up rue du Faubourg du Temple. As you continue on, you'll notice that the number of Chinese takeout places multiplies, complemented by *halal* butcher shops and, increasingly, little stores selling low-rate international phone cards for the lonesome and the far from home. When you come to the **rue Bichat,** on your left, you may want to take a quick jaunt up it to the **Hôpital Saint-Louis,** built in 1607, a massive and austere structure still penned-in by surrounding buildings, as **Nôtre Dame** used to be. Return on up the rue du Faubourg du Temple as it starts to climb. When it crosses the **boulevard de Belleville,** you've arrived in, yes, Belleville, now the 20th *arrondissement.* To your right is the hugely popular local Chinese restaurant **Président,** with its guardian lions and glitzy red-and-gold decor. Try to grab a seat if you're hungry; otherwise, hang a right along the boulevard de Belleville and you'll find yourself, after a few steps, deep in the Islamic neighborhood. On Tuesday and Friday mornings, this wide boulevard becomes an African market, with purchased goods carefully balanced on the buyers' heads. On your right there are many inviting pastry shops, where the goods are sold no-nonsense style in their baking trays, amid bare walls and blazing white light. Should you need to book a flight to Mecca, you'll pass several agencies that specialize in it. When you get to the **rue Timbaud,** you can turn and head down to **Le Timbaud** [see *bar scene,* above] should you so desire, or continue to **rue Oberkampf,** just beyond. If you continue on the boulevard de Belleville, it will take you to **Cimetière de Père Lachaise** [see *culture zoo,* below], where you can conclude your meditation on tradition and change.

in New York. But as if recognizing that the clogged, stodgy museums of old and their overwhelming collections had made this duty into somewhat of a chore, Paris has revamped the old venerables over the past decade or so, and learned the importance of not just throwing everything it's got—which is, pretty much, everything—at you at once.

Musée du Louvre *(99 rue de Rivoli, 1st; Tel 01/40-20-50-50; Métro to Palais-Royal or Louvre-Rivoli, 9am-6pm Mon, Thur-Sun, till 9:45pm Wed, closed Tue; 45f admission, 26f after 3pm):* Divided into three wings—Richelieu, Sully, and Denon—a tenth of each of which will take you several hours. To avoid the it's-too-much-the-world-is-closing-in-on-me freakout, it's best to decide beforehand what you're going to see. Aside from the famous smilin' lady that you'll have to push through a million people to see, some ignored prizes are a Van Eyck *Madonna and Child* in the last room of Northern Painting (in Richelieu), and a Hellenistic crouching Venus in Greek Antiquities (in Denon). Go after 3pm for the cut-rate ticket and you'll still have plenty of time.

Musée d'Orsay *(1 rue de Bellechasse, 7th; Tel 01/40-49-48-14; Métro to Solférino; 10am-6pm Tue, Wed, Fri, till 9:45pm Thur, 9am-6pm Sun, closed Mon; 40f admission, 30f if 18-25, free Sun if under 18):* Same deal as in the Louvre: plenty to see, many to dodge. The Impressionists and the post-Impressionists are all on the top level, and so are the mobs with their audio-phones. Off the main concourse on the ground floor, and especially off the sculpture deck on the mezzanine, are many smaller galleries of greats—like Daumier and Courbet—and wackos the curators didn't know what to do with. Don't miss the Art Nouveau wooden chamber in the rear.

The Eiffel Tower *(Champ de Mars, 7th; Tel 01/44-11-23-45, Tel 01/44-11-23-23, Métro to Bir-Hakeim; 9am-11pm Sept-Jun 12, till midnight June 13-Aug; Admission charged by level, 20f Level 1 or 59f to go the top; www.paris.org/monuments/eiffel; AE, MC, V):* Decidedly the most famous structure on earth, though the jury's still out on whether this massive erection is in good taste or not. More a showpiece of materials and engineering than a functional building—it was built to be torn down 10 years after construction—the Tower foretold the rise of steel-frame construction in the 20th century. The Jules Verne retro-restaurant on the second level is worth a gander but not for a bite. The views from the observation deck can't be beat. No tossing of monogrammed berets permitted, Rusty.

Musée Carnavalet *(23 rue de Sévigné, 3rd; Tel 01/42-72-21-13; Métro to St.-Paul; 10am-5:40pm Tue-Sun, closed Mon; 27f admission, 14.50f students and ages 18-25; AE, MC, V):* Housed in a creaky and beautiful old mansion in the center of the Marais, this is one of the best places to orient yourself to the feel of French history. Paintings and artifacts tell the story of the periodic demolition and reconstruction of the city over the past 500 years.

Musée des Arts d'Afrique et d'Océanie *(293 ave. Daumesnil, 12th; Tel 01/44-74-84-80; Métro to Porte Dorée; 10am-5:20pm Mon-Sun, closed Tue; 30f admission, 20f ages 18-25, free Sun if under 18):* It may not

only here

You've walked along the banks of the Seine, you've marveled at the endless vista of hazy roofs and shimmering domes from the **Eiffel Tower,** beheld the grandeur of the **Louvre,** and then you think...naked girls in high heels and garters. That's right, you haven't done Paris unless you've been to the one and only **Crazy Horse Saloon** *(12 ave. George V, 8th; Métro to Alma-Marceau or George V; Tel 01/47-23-32-32; Two shows nightly, 8:30pm, 11pm, three shows Sat; 560f orchestra, 450f mezzanine, 290f bar; www.crazy-horse.fr; No credit cards)* the tackiest (sexiest?) "erotic revue" this side of Vegas, now 45 years old. Go to the show as an expression of irony or put on an ironic expression to cover up for going to the show.

If the Crazy Horse is the French version of the Rockettes, **Mariage Frères** *(30 rue du Bourg-Tibourg, le Marais, 4th; Métro to St.-Paul; Tel 01/42-72-28-11; 10:30am-7:30pm daily; 37-59f pot of tea; MC, V)* is their interpretation of teatime. With well over 200 different kinds of tea, each to be served at the correct hour, at its own precise temperature, it's kind of like a grandma-sensualism behind the potted palms. The warmed scones are scrumptious, and the tea-based *gelées* better than you dreamed they could be. Also the place to buy that classy souvenir the folks are expecting.

For the historical rubber-necker in you, head over to the **Place de l'Alma** *(Métro to Alma-Marceau),* where, in the traffic tunnel beneath a replica of Lady Liberty's torch, Lady Di was hounded to her death by paparazzi (graffiti on the gilded flame will tell you where exactly). Officials have allowed this symbol of liberty to become a *de facto* shrine to her Ladyship, and it is now plastered-over with hundreds of awfully begrieved notes in every language.

be the most PC of museums in terms of how they got the stuff, okay, but this storehouse of colonialist treasures is probably one of the coolest. Stored in this unfrequented corner of the city, Vanuatan slit-gongs, West African masks, and live crocs a-snappin' in the basement (just like in your nightmares) will wow you, albeit with a guilty conscience.

Musée de Cluny *(6 place Paul-Painlevé, 5th; Tel 01/53-73-78-00; Métro to Cluny-La Sorbonne; 9:15am-5:45pm Mon, Wed-Sun, closed Tue; 28f admission, 18f if 18-25, free Sun if under 18; No credit cards):* An old cloister, itself occupying the ruins of a Roman bath, has in turn been converted into a place of cool serenity. Don't miss the radiant five tapestries of *The Lady and the Unicorn,* an allegory of the five senses. Between the oh-so-delicate fondling fingers of the lady, and the collar around the neck of her pet chimp, the tapestry depicting touch gives a whole new meaning to the question, "Would you like to touch my monkey?"

Musée Picasso *(Hôtel Salé, 5 rue de Thorigny, 3rd; Tel 01/42-71-25-21; Métro to Chemin-Verte; 9:30am-5:30pm daily except Tue; 30f admission, 20f if 18-25, free Sun if under 18):* The master's progress from hard-toiling figurative nobody (until he was exactly 15) to experimental superstar is housed here at one of the best art museums in town.

l'Institut du Monde Arabe *(1 rue des Fossés-Saint-Bernard, 5th; Tel 01/40-51-39-53; Métro to Jussieu; 10am-6pm, closed Mon, closed May 1; 25f admission, 20f students, 18-25, or over 60, free under 18, additional 5f for exhibitions):* The modern structure of this museum is an uncontested success: a wedge-shaped, ultramodern metal and glass library-cum-gallery-cum-*salon de thé*-cum-cutural emblem. The whole southern facade is a reinterpretation of a traditional Arabic lattice-work screen, with light-responsive diaphragms that let through just the right amount of dappled light. There's also a museum shop and bookstore (AE, MC, V).

Cimetière du Père Lachaise *(Blvd. de Ménilmontant, 20th; Métro to Père Lachaise; 8am-6pm Mon-Fri, 8:30am-6pm Sat 9am-6pm Sun; Free admission, free map at newsstand):* The ultimate shrine to the dead white male—Balzac; the dead white gay male—Proust; the dead white female—George Sand; the dead white gay female—Gertrude Stein, side-by-side with Alice B. Toklas; and, of course, the dead white lizard, Jim Morrison.

Nôtre Dame Cathedral *(Place du Parvis Notre Dame, 4th; Tel 01/42-34-56-10; Métro to Cité; Cathedral 8am-6:45pm daily, towers 10am-4:30pm daily; Free admission to cathedral, 35f admission to towers, 25f ages 12-25; No credit cards):* The scaffolding has just come off the facade after an elaborate "photonic disencrustation." The verdict? The old dame's white and shiny, just like in her youth, but she looks a little shorter and more commonplace after the bleach job. Still maybe the most impressive *Last Judgment* ever sculpted.

The following two monuments need to be mentioned if only for their distinctly Parisian self-importance:

Sacré-Coeur *(Place St-Pierre, 18th; Tel 01/53-41-89-00; Métro to Abbesses, then take elevator to surface and take the funicular; Bascilica 6:45am-11pm daily, Dome and Crypt 9:15am-7pm daily Apr-Sept, 9:15am-6pm daily Oct-Mar; Basilica free, Dome and Crypt 15F adult, 8F under 24):* A monstrosity. "Wedding cake architecture," the common epithet, doesn't go far enough; you can do better. Gaudy and inescapable when it was built, it now spoils much of beautiful Montmartre with its spillover, a massive funicular for those too feeble to scale the "mount," and the vendors it breeds, selling painting after painting of it, infecting bedrooms in Idaho or Manhattan with its likeness; plus it squanders prime real estate.

Panthéon *(Place de Panthéon, 5th; Tel 01/43-54-34-51; Métro Cardinal-Lemoine or Maubert-Mutualité; 9:30am-6:30pm daily Apr-Sept, 10am-6:15pm daily Oct-Mar; 32F adult, 21F ages 12-25):* A failure of a

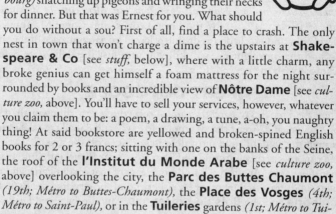

down and out

Hemingway, when he was here, strolled through the **Jardin de Luxembourg** *(6th; RER to Luxembourg)* snatching up pigeons and wringing their necks for dinner. But that was Ernest for you. What should you do without a sou? First of all, find a place to crash. The only nest in town that won't charge a dime is the upstairs at **Shakespeare & Co** [see *stuff,* below], where with a little charm, any broke genius can get himself a foam mattress for the night surrounded by books and an incredible view of **Nôtre Dame** [see *culture zoo,* above]. You'll have to sell your services, however, whatever you claim them to be: a poem, a drawing, a tune, a-oh, you naughty thing! At said bookstore are yellowed and broken-spined English books for 2 or 3 francs; sitting with one on the banks of the Seine, the roof of the **l'Institut du Monde Arabe** [see *culture zoo,* above] overlooking the city, the **Parc des Buttes Chaumont** *(19th; Métro to Buttes-Chaumont),* the **Place des Vosges** *(4th; Métro to Saint-Paul),* or in the **Tuileries** gardens *(1st; Métro to Tuileries),* you may feel that Paris is best viewed from an empty pocket.

All the churches in town are free: **Saint-Eustache** *(1st; Métro to Les Halles)* at Les Halles still stands in its unrenovated glory, and the three-tiered **Art Nouveau** gallery of the synagogue on the rue Pavée in the Marais *(Métro to St.-Paul),* designed by Hector Guimard himself, is definitely worth a look (but be sure to cover your head!). Many of the larger museums are free the first Sunday of the month. Any and every *cafe* will let you linger over a cafe, which at most will cost you 18f, and the sips of ambiance are absolutely free.

building named for one of the most beautiful in the world (in Rome), renowned for who's under the floor (Voltaire, Zola, Hugo, among others) and for the mathematician Foucault hanging a pendulum from its dome; a jumble of imbalanced classical elements built of flinty stone and possessed of a vast, echoing, and cheerless interior. The "gods" enshrined here are the French *grands hommes,* so you can add hubris to its list of sins, too.

modification

Hey, why not stick metal in your face and inject ink under your skin in the city that coined the term "primitivism"? From Ménilmontant to the Marais, kids are dying to be dyed like Queequeg. C'mon, everyone's doing it....

Near the hip, clubsy boutiques of the rue des Abbesses in Montmartre, **Studio Titane** *(44, rue des Abbesses, 18th; Tel 01/53-41-01-34 Métro*

Abbesses; Open irregular hours, from 50f; AE, MC, V) is one of the newest additions, and one of the best in the area. Specializing in Polynesian patterns and delicately rendered images, Titane keeps a small, sterile, friendly shop. Plus, they'll give you a cafe while you bleed.

And if before going out you wouldn't feel presentable with out extensions, or a fresh, clotted wash of henna in your hair, stop into **Tomasso Coiffeur** *(127, bis rue de la Roquette, 11th; Tel 01/43-79-20-01; Métro Voltaire; 10:30am-7pm Mon-Sat; 2pm-7pm Sun; Men's cuts, 115f; women's from 195f; AF, MC, V)*, by the Place Leon Blum, where M. Tomasso offers funky and exotic do's at doable prices. The narcotic pace of the stylists, and the dim lighting, will lull you into just the right state before kicking it with the new coiffure.

great outdoors

When the French say *parc,* they mean something very different than we do. They mean, "Aren't the sycamores lovely?" and "Shall we take a turn through the garden?" and most definitely, "Keep off the grass." "Let's go for a run, toss a frisbee around and blast *Regatta de Blanc*" is definitely not what they mean. At all. You'll find no release of that sort in Paris, and the huge woods traversed by paths on either end of the city, like the **Bois de Boulogne** and the **Bois de Vincennes,** can also be a real let-down because of their dull terrain and flat, featureless paths.

A more Anglo-American-style park is the **Buttes Chaumont** [see *neighborhoods,* above], once a quarry, where the craggy cliffs and steep ascents can give you a good workout.

If you're a jogger, there's nothing like the quays along the Seine; you may have to stop occasionally for tourists or traffic, but it's worth it. Otherwise, the cobblestone banks of the Canal St.-Martin and Basin de la Villette are uninterrupted and traffic-free.

The lunatic driving and cobblestones of Paris discourage biking for those of sound mind; if you're certifiable, go get yourself a cycle at **Paris à vélo, c'est sympa!** *(37 blvd. Bourbon, 4th; Tel 01/48-87-60-01; Métro to Bastille).*

A "safer," or at least chaperoned, option is joining the shrieking mass-rollerblading horde (the record to date is 28,000 people!) with police escort, leaving from 40 place de l'Italie *(Métro to place de l'Italie)* every Friday at 10pm and returning to the same spot three hours later. Check with **Pari Roller** *(62 rue Dulong, 17th; Tel 01/43-36-89-81; www.pari-roller.com).* They rent skates, too.

It's not inconceivable that you might want to bike out of the city, and not unrealistic, either; after the *banlieue,* the suburbs of Paris, the metropolis stops abruptly, particularly to the south. A good day trip could be had by taking your bike on the train to **Chartres** [see **everywhere else,** below], getting off wherever you decide the sprawl has sufficiently thinned, and pedaling the rest of the way. A good leaping-off point might be at Villiers, roughly the halfway point and positively rustic. The cathedral itself is, of course, extraordinary, with its famous lopsided spires, brass labyrinth, and stained glass dating to the 13th century. If you get fagged-out on the way back, hop back on the train wherever you like.

STUff

Some have called Paris the largest mall in the world, and it's true that there are more opportunities to part with cash here than almost anywhere. You can buy the very latest fashions—at the very highest prices—along the boulevard Saint-Germain (6th), or any of the designer outlets on its endless side streets, or that diamond-studded, lizard-skin pocketbook you've been hankerin' for, along with the platinum clip, at Place Vendôme. But Paris also has incredible bargains, especially considering the strength of the dollar over the past few years.

So after you've drooled outside the shops in Saint-Germain or in the 1st, it's actually very worth your while to visit the two mega-department stores **Printemps** (*64 blvd. Haussman, 9th; Tel 01/42-82-50-00; Métro to Havre-Caumartin; 9:35am-7pm daily except Sun, till 10pm Thur; AE, MC, V*) and **Galeries Lafayette** (*40 blvd. Haussmann, 9th; Tel 01/42-82-30-25; Métro to Chausée d'Antin; 9:30am-7pm daily except Sun, till 9pm Thur; AE, MC, V*), its more veteran and expensive cousin, and pick up name brands and knockoffs at significantly less than you could find them for in the States.

The shrine of stuff is the all-in-one **FNAC** (*Forum des Halles, 1st; Tel 01/40-41-40-00; Métro to Les Halles; 10am-midnight, Mon-Sat; AE, MC, V*), where your one-stop shopping could snag you every CD you've ever wanted, a book from every major literature in the original language, a new stereo, and a comic book.

▸▸BIZARRE BAZAAR

For the young and impressionable traveler, the shopping experience is found at the puces on the outskirts of town. The *puces*—"fleas"—is where the flea market got its name. At the **Puces de Clignancourt,** the largest of the lot, there's an endless labyrinth of permanent stalls—here's where you can buy that roccoco walnut four-poster bed—and bin after bin of the best and cheapest junk in France; where you can get, say, every incarnation of the Michelin man since 1970 at 10f for the bunch.

Outside the **Puces de Clignancourt,** vendors hawk pot bowls, army-navy surplus, and knockoff jeans, but also almost unbelievable vintage finds: Leather jackets that would run into the high hundreds in a Soho boutique can be gotten here for 200f.

To get to the puces, take Métro 4 to Porte de Clignancourt and follow the traffic signs toward the puces. This will take you under the périférique highway and into a knot of people on the other side along the avenue de la Porte de Clignancourt. Keep elbowing your way through and, on your left, a small lane will appear, and you found 'em. The puces are open 7am till 6pm everyday except Sunday. Get there early.

▸▸HOT COUTURE

The fashion world of Paris is likewise everywhere you turn, but if you weren't invited to the latest catwalk show of Givenchy, Chanel, or Yves Saint-Laurent, or can't afford the very heights of haute couture, several

The forests of île-de-france

▶▶ THE FÔRET DE COMPIEGNE

One of the most magnificent forests of Île de France, *Fôret de Compiegne*, a 200-square-kilometer district, surrounds the town of **Compiàgne**, 50 miles north of Paris. Most of the trails here were originally laid out by François 1er, Louis XIV, and Louis XV as a means of facilitating their hunting parties. Outdoorspeople and novices alike hike or bike through this forest since most of it is relatively flat, with only two steep trails. Watch your footing—some of the unpaved trails are a bit sloshy when it rains. On a summer day, head for one of the oak or beech groves with a picnic basket; there are countless idyllic spots where you can pretend you're a princess out on the palacial estate....

Trains make the 50-minute trip to Compiègne from Paris's Gare du Nord several times a day. Compiègne's train station is a 10-minute walk from the center of town, across the **River Oise.** At the local **tourist office** (*Place Hotel-de Ville; Tel 03/44-40-01-00*), you can purchase detailed maps of the *Fôret de Compiègne*, which show all hiking and biking trails, monuments, geological oddities, bodies of water, and the general topography.

If you're not up for a big hike, take Bus 5 from the railway station to the edge of the Oise—ask your driver to let you out at *"le bord de l'Oise"*. From there you can meander down a riverside promenade that, although not technically within the forest, will convey much of what the topography of the forest, is all about. If you really want to delve into the hiking goodness, take STEPA bus 25—it's marked "Compiègne-Soissons"—from the train station to the Rotonda, where the German Armistice was signed. From here, paths radiate off into other parts of the forest.

And if you'd rather pedal, rent a bike from **Picardie Fôrets Vertes,** (*4 rue de la Gare; Tel 06/07-54-99-26; 100F to 180F per day*). From behind the Hôtel de Ville, bikers can take **avenue Royal du Baron de Soultrait** southwest for about a mile, to the edge of the forest. From there, using the map you grabbed at the tourist office, you can attack the forest however you please.

areas will satisfy your craving for Parisian cool and sartorial savvy. The Marais, once again, has some of the best, if pricey and a bit on the conservative side, for anyone feeling desperately underdressed. Try the prophetically named rue des Francs Bourgeois for the sharpest duds. But for experimentation, the otherwise touristy lower slopes of Montmartre are the province of a number of ultracool, club/street boutiques, very often with the seamstress/designer doing triple duty as saleswoman.

▶▶THE FORÊT DE CHANTILLY

The *petit* Fôret de Chantilly, covering some 65 square miles around the town of Chantilly, lies 26 miles north of Paris. Trains leave frequently throughout the day from Paris' Gare du Nord, arriving in Chantilly in only 30 minutes.

About a century ago, the private estate (about 15,500 acres) of the Duc d'Aumale was given (willed) to the *Institut de France,* which preserves and maintains it today, defining it as a "Private Forest." The primary motivation for the eco-folks maintaining this park involves protecting both the colonies of deer that have been the hallmark of the park since the French kings used it as their hunting grounds during the Renaissance, and the thousands of trees (especially oak, linden, elm, and various species of pine) that cover the grounds. Maintaining a good deer/sapling balance is a constant ecological battle—more than 100,000 saplings are planted every year to replace those chomped by the deer population.

Since Chantilly is "horse country," the forest is full of riding trails—as well as hiking trails—many dating from the Middle Ages. The most scenic route appears on maps as GR11. This trail links the château at Chantilly with the little town of Senlis, which is most well known for its Cathédrale Nôtre-Dame, begun in 1153. The forest is known for a series of scenic ponds and lakes. The largest of these are *les Étangs de Comelle,* the first of which were formed in the 1200s by monks who dammed local streams and rivers for irrigation of their crops. Today, they're a permanent part of the landscape. One of the most gorgeous trails in the forest is the one that winds around these bodies of water, about a 90- to 120-minute trek.

The **Chantilly tourist office** *(60 ave. Maréchal-Joffre; Tel. 03/44-57-08-58)* sells maps of the forest for 58F, showing all topographical, hiking, and biking features. Bike rentals are arranged through **Orry Evasion** *(5 rue Neuve, Orry la Ville (a suburb of Chantilly); 90F per day).*

Futurewear Lab *(2 rue Piémontési, 18th; Tel 01/42-23-66-08; Métro to Abesses; 11am-8pm Mon-Sat, 2pm-8pm Sun; AE, MC, V)* is where ex-costume designer Tatiana Lebedev fuses industrial materials with streetwise clothes.

Bonnie Cox *(38 rue des Abbesses, 18th; Tel 01/42-54-95-68; Métro to Abbesses; 11am-8pm daily; AE, MC, V)* runs the gamut from club gear to East Village chic, at slightly steeper prices.

And incredible designer women's clothes worn only once or twice in shows are a steal at **Passé Devant** *(62 rue d'Orsel, 18th; Tel 01/42-54-*

fashion

Paris may not be the city of women in extravagant silk gowns, corsets, and bonnets that it once was, but there is still a latent elegance to the way people are turned out; clothes here make the man, woman, or androgyne more than almost anywhere else, and they make the man much more than most men are used to. While the American uniform of frayed baseball caps, jeans, and anoraks is forgiven as endemic, ratty T-shirts and jeans will not be. Even if you want to do the arm-the-battlements, revolutionary thing, you'd better have the right flight jacket, clean desert boots, and well-worn but not overworn jeans. The way to dress for dinner or a party is in pressed clothes and matching tones. A sports jacket is never frowned at. Dress tends toward the conservative, and real experimental outrageousness is rare, Jean-Paul Gaultier notwithstanding; but while your over-the-topness may get stares, Paris depends on people like you to set their trends.

75-15; Métro to Abbesses; 10:30am-7pm Tue-Sat, 1pm-7pm Sun, Mon; MC, V).

The Parisian portal into the street-cum-club fashion of New York's East Village is the perfectly named **Le Shop** (3 rue d'Argout; Tel 01/40-28-95-94; Métro to Entienne Marcel; 11am-7pm Tue-Sat, 1-7pm Mon; www.leshop.voice.fr; MC, V). A sort of department store of hip, the store is composed of 24 separate clothing vendors, each with their own phone, crammed into a medium-sized two-level space, and serviced by their own sales people. Here you'll find hundreds of different styles of denim and polyester **Carhartt** work clothing for that Beastie Boys-circa-1989 look, **Aem'kei,** a sophisticated NYC-German rework of that skater-hip-hop look, and the environmentally conscious and free-Tibet-oriented **Komodo,** for baggy clothing that actually fits well, thanks to carefully placed pleats, cool fabric choice, and hip patterns. Shoes, handbags, and all kinds of accessories are carried here for the downtown hipsters on holiday. Downstairs, there's a coffee shop and a piercing and tattoo parlor.

But the real hip-cat b-boy or b-girl wannabe will not want to go without their own custom-made necklace or jewelry, with their name emblazoned in graffiti-like scrawl in brass, silver, or gold knuckles. Think of Run DMC in 1984, all the Big Daddy Kanes of yesteryear, or LL Cool J yesterday. Because no one should ever have to ask you your name, contact **Anjuna Bijoux** (Tel 01/48-39-38-39, Mobile 06-15-74-71-85, Fax

01/48-34-78-42) and arrange the production of your own "look." Be sure to negotiate the price down.

▶▶BOUND

This is the town of the revered writer. Shrines are built to Zola, Hugo, and Balzac, and even formerly fringe authors like Rimbaud and Baudelaire are now solidly ensconced in street names and public statues. It is also where most American authors of note came at least once, including Poe, Faulkner, and Dos Passos. Most girls and boys you see here will be reading finer literature and philosophers like Lévi-Strauss or Bergson. Yikes! What to do if you're not up to cultural speed? There are several excellent English-language bookstores, with as wide selection as you'd find at the best back home, where you can find that last novel of the *comédie humaine* you've always meant to read in English, or even English books by that Paul Auster guy everyone's talking about.

Shakespeare & Co. *(37 rue de la Bûcherie, 5th; Tel 01/43-26-96-50; Métro to Maubert-Mutualité, St.-Michel; Noon-midnight daily; No credit cards)* is the heir to the famous bookstore/colony that self-published Joyce's *Ulysses* when all else failed. A swell collection of used and new books, plus free bunks [see *down and out,* above] in the attic!

The stock at **Village Voice** *(6 rue Princesse, 6th; Tel 01/46-33-36-47; 2pm-8pm Mon, 10am-8pm Tue-Sat, 2-7pm Sun; MC, V, AE)* is more academic than the rest with a helpful, bilingual staff that'll help you navigate the egghead terrain.

The English bookstore **WH Smith** *(248 rue de Rivoli, 1st; Tel 01/44-77-88-99; Métro to Concorde; 9:30am-7pm Mon-Sat, 1-7pm Sun; MC, V, AE)* also sells American and British magazines and newspapers.

▶▶TUNES

You can get any CD you want for the best prices at the **FNAC** [see above] but if it's vinyl you crave, the major supplier for the DJ world in Paris is **Techno Import** *(16-18 rue des Taillandiers, 11th; Tel 01/48-05-71-56; Métro to Bastille; 11am-midnight daily, but irregular; MC, V),* world-renowned for its huge collection and variety of vinyl and rarities. Another resource for vinyl is the discussion boards on ***www.france-techno.com*** or on ***www.planet-tekno.com.***

Rue d'Argout is lined with hip stores from **Le Shop** to **Marché Noir** *(52 rue d'Argout; Tel 01/42-21-02-72; Métro to Entienne Marcel; noon-8pm; MC, V),* the Parisian translation of London's Black Market record store and the place to pick-up vinyl from deep to disco house to drum 'n' bass and rare groove. As at all record stores in Paris and indeed France, prices are decidedly high, so you'll want to confine yourself to strictly Parisian vinyl, which of course is reasonably cheap, even though their selection of American imports is quite cool.

Ragga and hip-hop find their home in Paris at **Sound Record** *(5 rue des Prêcheurs; Tel 01/40-13-09-45, Fax 01/45-23-03-88; Métro to Les Halles; 11am-7:30pm Mon-Sat; www.sound-record.fr; MC, V),* located between Rue St.-Denis and Les Halles. This nook-like store's got a decent selection of American and import releases, though the selection of French rap is limited to current releases. The staff will happily guide you through their inventory, but unfortunately will not let you listen to full-length LPs.

eats

That the French eat so well and stay so thin and healthy is the constant gripe of the non-French. Hate the French all you want, they know something about how to eat. Take a lesson from them: Put aside, if you can, your quest for skim milk, your fear of cream sauce and butter, or any other "healthy habits" you might have, and *eat*—meaning several courses, with wine and coffee. You may even feel trim and well in the end (or bloated yet happy, which is fine, too).

Depending on the place, it's usually wise to go for one "menu" (*prix fixe* or "fixed-price" meal) for dinner. You usually have the option of a three-course menu with *entrée* (appetizer), *plat* (entree), and dessert, with

garçon means "boy"

The cafe waiter—these days known as *monsieur*, not *garçon*—is one of the obnoxious fixtures of Paris life. Yes, he may mock you if you don't understand French. Yes, he will present your coffee with an exaggerated flourish that comes off as somehow even more insulting than just plopping it down. No, he will never come back with your change. Jean-Paul Sartre, the now largely ignored father of Existentialism, wrote many of his works in cafes [see *Cafe de la Mairie* in *hanging out*] and evidently got just as pissed off as us. In *Being and Nothingness* he used the waiter as an example of someone who vanishes so completely into his role as "waiter" that he ceases to be a person. You may think you can lube him up like we do the DMV guy back home: a wink and a smile that says, "Yeah, I feel for you, crappy job." But he's not acting like that 'cause he hates his job; *au contraire,* it's 'cause he takes his job just a wee bit too seriously. This stickler mentality is what many a French lefty will unflinchingly call *petit bourgeois:* the train conductor will absolutely demand proof of age if you buy the youth-rate ticket, and the baker will give you a baker's singsong "Bon-jour" every time. Javert, the mean old inspector in *Les Misérables,* was doing the same thing when he hunted poor Jean Valjean to his death for a stolen loaf of bread. Visit the Daumier room at the **Musée D'Orsay** [see *culture zoo*, above], and see if those pinched little bureaucrats don't seem to be overplaying the part. Still true, still annoying as hell.

wine and coffee included; or a cheaper two-course menu with choice of appetizer and entree or entree and dessert, plus wine and coffee. Tax and tip are always included, so the price you see is the price you pay. And if you just ask for water, the waitstaff will think you want mineral water—perfectly potable free tap water is brought when you order *une carafe d'eau.*

Besides the indigenous cuisine—that is, regional French and old, established, immigrant cuisine—which we've focused on here, there are of course great Chinese and Thai restaurants (particularly in the China-town in the 13th *arrondissement),* Turkish shwarma stands, and whatever other cuisine you could imagine here. If you're dying for a quick bite, the Rue des Rossiers in the Marais is dotted with falafel stands side by side, each as good as the next. The same is true for the crêpe stands everywhere, with uniform prices and quality, even outside the **Louvre.**

▶▶CHEAP

You may have to line up for **Polidor** *(41 rue Monsieur-le-Prince, 6th; Métro to Odéon; Tel 01/43-26-95-34; Noon-2:30pm/7pm-12:30am Mon-Sat, till 11pm Sun; 60-80f per entree; No credit cards)* a popular, charming, century-old bouillon or brothhouse (worker's dining hall) in the Latin Quarter. Once you're seated here, choose what you want and snap out your order quick-like, and don't ask what's in what and can you get a sub-stitution, or you'll get an earful from the *bouillon*-Nazi waitresses. Excel-lent down-home cooking, like tender veal in crème fraîche, or breast of duck, served in a brusk but warm-hearted atmosphere to chatty grad-student types.

In the heart of the Butte aux Cailles, is the teeny, rugged bistro **Chez Gladines** *(30 rue de Cinq Diamants, 13th; Métro to Corvisart or Place de l'Italie; Tel 01/45-80-70-10; Noon-3pm/7pm-midnight daily, closed Aug; 50-90f per entree; No credit cards).* Peanut shells cover the floor, and big clay bowls full of country salads and southwestern and Basque dishes like *canard à la basquaise* (duck Basque-style) are tossed to you over the heads of that happy couple sharing the bench with you. Have a beer, put your elbows on the oilcloth, and chow down.

The minibistro **Lescure** *(7 rue de Mondovi; 1st; Métro to Concorde; Tel 01/42-60-18-91; Noon-2:15pm/7-10:15pm Mon-Fri; Closed 2 weeks in Aug; 40-80f per entree, 100f s4 course prix fixe; MC, V)* is a major find because reasonably priced restaurants near Place de la Concorde are rare. The tables on the sidewalk are tiny and there isn't much room inside, but what this place does have is rustic charm to burn. The kitchen's wide-open, and the aroma of drying bay leaves, salami, and garlic hanging from the ceiling lends the room a homey vibe. House specialties include *confit de canard* (duckling) and salmon in green sauce. A favorite dessert is one of the chef's fruit tarts.

The line of hungry Parisians extending out the door of **Aux Délices de Manon** *(400 rue St.-Honoré; Tel 01/42-60-83-03, Fax 01/49-27-02-51; Métro to Concorde or Madeleine; 7am-10pm daily; MC, V),* waiting to get a sandwich for take-out, speaks volumes about this small restaurant/boulangerie just a block from the Champs-Elysées. On a pretty day, pick up a sandwich *à emporter* (for take-out) and walk with it towards the Tuileries to dine on a park bench among the splendor of the gardens.

Paris may go coo-coo for couscous, but some of the best falafel outside of Jerusalem can be found along rue des Rosiers in the Marais. While the bustling street is lined with falafel joints, the best is **L'As du Fallafel** *(34 rue des Rosiers; Tel 01/48-87-63-60; Métro to St.-Paul; Noon-midnight Mon-Thur & Sun, noon-5pm Fri, 8pm-midnight Sat; MC, V),* whose cheaply priced sandwiches are seasoned with Middle Eastern spices, dripping with tahini, and stuffed with delectable beets, lettuce, tomatoes, and other veggie goodies. The interior of the place gets super-crowded around lunch and dinner, so you may have to wait, but pay no mind and make yourself completely known to the stylish looking family that runs the place to get the next possible seat.

The best slice of pizza for your *franc* in Paris is made in the stone ovens of **Pizza Vesuvio** *(1 rue Gozlin; Tel 01/43-54-94-78; Métro to Saint-Germain-de-Prés; 11am-midnight; 17F slice; MC, V),* which is tucked off Boulevard St.-Germain across from the St.-Germain church. They also have two other locations around the city, both with the same hours: *(25 rue Quentin-Baucard; Tel 01/47-23-60-26, Fax 01/47-23-63-24)* and *(144 ave. Champs-Elysées; Tel 01/43-59-68-69).* Order your slice at the counter for take out. Slices are delicately thin-crusted and delectably seasoned with a small amount of sauce, and the guy who molds the dough and works the oven is really Italian.

Proletarians sit alongside the smart set in the colorful Asian, Ikea-meets-cafeteria styled **Fish and Fun** *(55 blvd. de Sébastopol; Tel 01/42-21-10-10; Métro to Entienne Marcel; noon-4:30pm/6:30-midnight; No credit cards).* The centerpiece of this order-at-counter restaurant is the super-healthy and super-cheap flash-fried fish with sides of cold pasta, tabouli, mashed potatoes, and rice served in bamboo bowls. You can eat a complete reasonable meal for around 50F, and there's never any need to ask for water as carafes adorn every table.

A safe spot to grab a late-night snack is **Deli's Cafe** *(5 blvd. Poisson-nière; Tel 01/42-24-24-04; Métro to Bonne Nouvelle; Hours vary; No credit cards),* which serves tasty standard baguette and *crudité* sandwiches and *crêpes* along with sodas, beer, and liquor from behind a sleek, curved-glass display jutting out of the cafe onto the sidewalk. Conveniently located next to the Rex Club [see *clubs,* above], Deli's evening hours vary with the crowds that spill in from the shows next door.

A slightly more suspect choice is the late-night window of the **Pecos Grill** *(112 rue St.-Denis; Tel 01/42-21-47-66; Métro to Entienne-Marcel; evening hours vary; No credit cards),* which serves the perfect Parisian drunk fare of kebabs and *steak-frites* steps from the sketchy Les Halles. The hours generally depend on whether they have any meat left on the skewer or whether you can cajole the North African guy behind the counter to serve you one of their large steak sandwiches with lettuce and tomato topped with *pommes frites.* Order anything sounding remotely

American Western from the menu at any other time besides late at night, and you put yourself in risk of fiery bowel movements—and remember, the scratchy French toilet paper isn't kind on the nether regions.

The name of **Kitch** *(10 rue Oberkampf; Tel 01/40-21-94-14; Métro to Filles de Calvaire; 10am-midnight; MC, V)* adequately describes both the fun atmosphere and the junk aesthetic interior of this hip bar-restaurant. Unwind with a snack and drink and listen to the mellow world beat music before retiring for an afternoon siesta after a day of rigorous sightseeing. The menu is slim, but the drink list is long and includes bottles of Red Stripe for those lonesome for Jamaica's white sands. Try the tasty bagel sandwiches for an interesting commentary on the globalization of American culture.

▶▶DO-ABLE

Just north of the Marais, charming **Chez Omar** *(47 rue de la Bretaigne, 3rd; Métro to Arts et Métiers; Tel 01/42-72-36-26; Noon-2:45pm/7pm-midnight Mon-Sat, 7pm-midnight Sun; 60-100f per entree; No credit cards)* offers simple, reasonable couscous dishes for anything but a simple crowd. By 9pm every table of this unassuming, ragged old brasserie is packed with glitterati and artists from the nearby galleries. Show up early around 7pm, stuff yourself on chicken or lamb couscous and flaky *merguez* sausage and drink your fill of the perfumed Algerian wine, then get kicked out by Omar himself when the crush starts.

If you've wandered the streets of Montmartre, but'll be damned if you'll eat with the hordes around **Sacré-Coeur,** you're in luck: Wander all the way around the eastern, sheer slope of the mount along the rue Ronsard, past the little pagan grottoes cut into the rock, and you'll arrive at **l'Eté en Pente Douce** *(23 rue Muller, 18th; Tel 01/42-64-02-67; Métro to Château-Rouge; Noon-midnight daily; 60-80f per entree; MC, V).* Here you can lunch on light, simple salads or smoked fish, or one of the fresh mushroom specialties of the proprietor, and linger for hours over a good pot of tea on a sunny, crowded terrace at the foot of the mount. Little-known to tourists but a favorite of the locals, down here you get all the charm of Montmartre without a glimmer of a single gaudy spire of the cathedral.

Al Dar *(8 rue Frédéric Sauton, 5th; Tel 01/43-25-17-15; Métro to Maubert-Mutualité; Noon-midnight daily; 85-92f per entree; AE, DC, MC, V)* works hard to popularize Lebanon's savory cuisine. In a room lined with photographs of Lebanese architecture and scenery, you can relish their refreshing *taboulé,* and their creamier-than-thou *baba ganush* and *hummus.* Follow any of these with excellent roasted chicken; minced lamb prepared with mint, cumin, and Mediterranean herbs; and any of several kinds of *tagines* (clay pot stews) and couscous. Reservations recommended.

Tunisian and West African restaurants line the Belleville and rue du Faubourg du Montmartre. Tunisian starters include *brik,* a puffed pastry with egg, cheese, and different meat fillings, and a tomato and roasted red pepper salad massaged in olive oil. Perfumed couscous and delicately spiced *tangines,* like lamb with tomato and onions, are the specialties of **La Gazelle** *(33 rue Lamartine; Tel 01/48-78-25-69; Métro to Cadet; 11am-2pm/5-11pm daily; MC, V),* a popular Tunisian restaurant nestled above the Grands Boulevards in the 9th Arrondissement.

Just south of the Montmartre area, chef Stephane Michot serves fresh, contemporary Provençal cuisine at **Menthe et Basilic** *(6 rue Lamartine; Tel 01/48-78-12-20, Fax 01/48-78-12-21; Métro to Cadet; 11am-2pm/6-11pm daily; MC, V).* While the dining is decidedly button-down collar, the service is quite kind. The menu is light, delicious, and reasonably priced, and varies seasonally. Specialties include honey and cinnamon pork chops, exquisite fresh grilled salmon, and fresh strawberry "soup", which includes blended currants, raspberries, and strawberries with crushed fresh basil, topped with a single mint leaf.

For more eclectic dining, **Galerie 88** *(88 quai de l'Hôtel de Ville; Tel 01/42-72-17-58; Métro to Hôtel de Ville; Noon-2am daily; No credit cards)* offers a version of vegetarian cuisine that includes fish and resembles a meatless Mediterranean-North African fusion cuisine. The Anisette 88 comes with guacamole, assorted different salads, and tabouli. Come early lest you have to wait for a seat, as the cozy yellow and red interior fills early with young Parisian trendies and unpretentiously hip cats.

▶▶**SPLURGE**

If you've grabbed a cheese sandwich at something that said brasserie on the front window, you've been duped. Just off the Place de la Bastille, **Bofinger** *(5-7 rue de la Bastille, 11th; Tel 01/42-72-87-82; Métro to Bastille; Noon-3pm/6:30pm-1am Mon-Fri, noon-1am Sat, Sun; 80-150f per entree, 119f weekday lunch menu, 179f dinner menu all week; AE, MC, V)* is the real deal, with rich dark wood paneling, brass banisters, and serious, attentive waiters in black ties standing by with hands clasped. Built in 1864, this was the first *brasserie* here, and remains one of the most magnificent examples of these Alsatian-style "brewery" restaurants that gained popularity after the Franco-Prussian war. Come for a late-night dinner, around 11, and linger either in the bright, busy main dining room under a high stained-glass dome, or on the *1er étage* (second floor) in quiet rooms with magnificent inlaid wood tableaux. For the quality, the 179f menu is a bargain. Try the *jarret de porc* (ham hocks), served with a heaping plate of buttery *choucroûte* (sauerkraut), and the *île flottant* (floating island) for dessert. Reservations are necessary on the weekends.

The literal pinnacle of hip in Paris is perhaps **Chez Georges** *(6th Floor, Centre Georges Pompidou, entrance place Georges Pompidou; Tel 01/44-78-12-33; Métro to Les Halles/Chatelet; Hours vary; AE, MC, V, DC).* It's the perfect place to sip an *après musée* apéritif in the sumptuous quietude of the skyline of Paris. The architecture of the restaurant is decidedly Modern, but unlike the rest of the museum, it eschews right angles in favor of organic shapes and forms. Ignore the expensive, uninteresting, and poorly prepared food and check out the quietly cursing, rakishly dressed, three-button-suit clad wait staff. Weekend evenings DJs play to the who's who of hip Paris.

On a desolate side street full of tailors and Chinese takeout spots in the 3rd, south of République, hides the extraordinary **404** *(69 rue de Gravelliers, 3rd; Métro to Arts et Métiers; Tel 01/42-74-57-81; Noon-2:30pm/8pm-midnight Mon-Fri, noon-4pm/8pm-midnight Sat, Sun, closed 2 weeks in Aug; 80-120f per entree; AE, MC, V),* where the Arabic inscriptions in the high stone wall, the floor cushions, low tables, weepy Arab ballads, and an open stove transport you to a very comfy, if pricey, corner of the Sahara. The unusual spicy *tagines,* cooked with olives or dried fruits, are a little much at 110f, but you've got to see the dare-me-not-to-scald-you-long-distance-tea pour-off at the end of the meal. Brunch is served noon to four Saturday and Sunday.

Not far from 404 in the 3rd is another gem, if not so glittery. **Au Bascou** *(38 rue Réaumur, 3rd; Métro to Arts et Métiers; Tel 01/42-72-69-25; Noon-2pm/8-10:30pm Mon-Fri, 8pm-10:30pm Sat, closed Sun, Aug 24, Dec 2-Jan; 90-130f per entree; AE, MC, V)* offers the salty, earthy, and rich cuisine of those independent-minded Basques in a quiet bistro setting that doesn't prepare you for the excellent food and service. Robust proprietor Jean-Guy Loustau personally oversees the presentation of dishes such as *chipiron* (baby squid and rice over crisp grilled spinach) or *axoa de veau* (a slow-cooked lamb stew). Eccentricities are revealed quietly— M. Loustau's handlebar moustache gives the first hint, then his transplanted velvet movie seats, then the free Basque liqueurs he keeps pushing on you....

crashing

Wonderful thing about Paris: Even though you know there are people— rich people—staying at the Crillon and the Plaza Athénée, with the billowing drapes, the French doors, and the silver coffee set beside the bed in the mornings, there are mid-range and budget options of such charm and taste you never need eat your heart out with envy. However, if you haven't booked months in advance for a Paris visit between June and mid-August or around Christmas, finding a place to stay can be like trying to lose your virginity in the back of your parents' Toyota Camry: Very difficult, and in the end, kind of unsatisfying. So book well in advance.

Rates may vary with the seasons, too. If you're planning on lingering, the *FUSAC* free magazine (in English) has ads for shares, apartment exchanges, and short-term sublets, many of which, in the suburbs or less-fashionable areas of Paris, might be worth your time.

▶▶CHEAP

The colorful, clean, well-kept interior of the centrally located **Woodstock Hostel** *(48 rue Rodier; Tel 01/48-78-87-76, Fax 01/48-78-01-63; Métro to Anvers or Poissonière; www.woodstock.fr; Bed in double 97F winter, 107F summer, bed in a 4-person room 87F winter, 97F summer, breakfast included; MC, V)* radiates that relaxed hippie vibe to receptive backpackers from around the world. Located just blocks from Gare du Nord, the hostel is the better part of the CHEAP syndicate of six hostels in Paris. The bushes adorning the exterior at first glance might be mistaken

wired

Web-wise, Paris isn't quite up to speed. The official tourist site, ***www.paris.org,*** is functional if you want to check exhibition times or dates, but it's far simpler to buy one of the weeklies [see intro] than to go online. But when Paris catches up, it naturally does it with a lot of style. A number of portals will be opening soon which will, at the same time, function as ISP's (Internet Service Providers) free of charge—a great idea. In French, Nova has an online shadow, ***www.novaplanet.com*** with listings, bizarre links, a Nova radio station, and picks distinct to its online incarnation. As webspeak is largely English anyway, you should have little difficulty navigating the site.

A similarly attitude-laden site is ***www.thinkparis.com,*** a would-be city ***search.com*** without quite the scope, but with chatty reviews and an emphasis on the English-speaking twentysomethings of Paris. *TimeOut's* website ***www.timeout.com/fr*** is a little clunky and has no sections distinct from its guide, but it's worth visiting if you can't get your hand on one of its free supplements. For rave and techno party news, visit the all-French but rather simple ***www.france-techno.fr*** where you can find out where the local quasi-legal raves are being thrown and enter your e-mail on its mailing list. And in case you haven't run into enough drunken Anglos, ***www.net-europa.com/gap*** gives an extremely Anglo-slanted portrait of "Paris' best pubs."

The Cybercafe is another idea the French won't accept until they make it their own, and here are three distinct riffs:

Cyber Cafe Latino *(13 rue l'École Polytechnique, 5th; Tel 01/40-51-86-94; Métro to Maubert Mutualité; 11:30am-2am Mon-Sat, 7pm-9pm Sun; 40f/hour; MC, V, AE),* except for the insistence on Latino-chic, is about how they do things back in the States, with

for their smokable cousins, all too familiar to actual attendees of the first Woodstock, but don't worry, the management is decidedly clean-cut and extraordinarily helpful in the event that the hostel is full, which often occurs as they don't take reservations during the summer. So show up early and try to badger your way into a room. Internet access available.

If Woodstock is full, a good bet is the less centrally located, blander **Aloha** *(1 rue Buromée; Tel 01/42-73-03-03, Fax 01/42-73-14-14; Métro to Volontaire; www.aloha.fr; Bed in double 107F winter, 127F summer, bed in 4-person 97F winter, 107F summer, breakfast included; MC, V),* which has a similar room setup and international clientele and staff.

The cheapest choice for backpackers who don't mind slightly cramped conditions and dormitory-style triple-bunk sleeping is the no-frills, floral wallpapered **Bed & Breakfast** *(42 rue Poissonière; Tel 01/40-26-83-08;*

fruit smoothies and tapas: Six Macs on simple work desks, in a spacious room, with the salsa just turned up high enough so that you can't hear the guy beside you mutter for the 80th time that he doesn't understand how to log off. The Venezuelan staff speaks neither French nor English.

You may think you're in an '80s arcade revival at very small, very spare **Clickside** (*14 rue Domat, 5th; Tel 01/56-81-03-00; Métro to Maubert Mutualité or Cluny-La Sorbonne; 10am–midnight Mon-Sat, 1pm-11pm Sun; 11 PC terminals, 45f/hour; www.clickside.com; MC, V, AE*), where the future French Steve Jobses squander their intellect on the lastest video games, sampled here for a small fee (at an elaborate pricing system—prorated, as opposed to the Latino). This is no-nonsense gameplaying; the cafe part seems almost like an afterthought.

And the big geniuses behind the **Webbar** (*32 rue de Picardie, 3rd; Tel 01/42-72-62-50; Métro to Filles du Calvaire; 11:30-2am, daily; 12 PCs, 40f/hour; www.webbar.fr; MC, V, AE*) want you to understand that their complex is not a cybercafe, it's a, well, you can figure it out. Certainly more business/suit oriented, the two-level, bar/cafe/gallery also addresses the scourge of French computer illiteracy with private lessons, in a tactfully private room. The requisite salsa, jungle, and world beats laid down by, of course, DJ Replicant.

A note to the notebook carrier: though French phone plugs may appear compatible with American ones, they're not: the order of the wires you see in the clear plastic head is reversed. There's nothing for it but an adapter, best bought at home, but findable at the **FNAC** [see *stuff*, above].

Métro to Bonne Nouvelle; 100F bed, breakfast included; No credit cards) run by Michel, a fluent English speaker and former resident of Queens, New York, and John, his Californian help. As with most hostels, Bed & Breakfast is reasonably safe and a good place to meet and commune with fellow trekkers. It is centrally located next to the Rex Club and a 20-minute walk from Les Halles. Like the other hostels in town, it doesn't take reservations, so show up early to snag a bed. Internet access available.

Between Nôtre Dame and the rue Saint-Antoine, are some of the most luxuriant, pristine hostels you'll visit, run by the **Maison Internationale de la Jeunesse et des Etudiants** (*Tel 01/42-74-23-45; www.mije.com*) in three spic-and-span renovated 17th-century buildings with three addresses: **Le Fauconnier** (*11 rue du Fauconnier, 4th; Métro to St.-Paul*), **Fourcy** (*6 rue de Fourcy, 4th; Métro to St.-Paul*), and **Maubuisson** (*12 rue* *des Barres; Métro to Hôtel-de-Ville).* Rates are the same for all three *(140f/person dorm, 150f/person triple room, 170f/person double room, 220f/person private room, plus 12f membership fee, breakfast included; No credit cards),* and all three have the right mix of teenage tour groups, spooky loners, and attractive traveling duos, along with the indispensable attentive and efficient cleaning staff. It can be a trick to find the Fourcy address, housed in a converted convent: The huge, unmarked double doors on the Rue de Fourcy have a smaller, almost hidden door that opens up into an immense courtyard. Great vaulted breakfast room in the basement, too.

Probably the best deal in the Latin Quarter is the **Hôtel Esmerelda** *(4 rue St.-Julien le Pauvre, 5th; Tel 01/43-54-19-20; Métro to St.-Michel; 160-420f single, 450-490f double, 550f triple, 600f quad, breakfast 40f; No credit cards),* which, despite its name and the view of **Nôtre Dame,** is the place most reminiscent of Balzac's *Maison Vauquer* that we visited, with the sickly-sweet decrepitude, the velvet, the ubiquitous plants, the cat, and the ancient, warped floors. The rooms are smaller and more rickety than at Grandes coles [see below], but they've got facilities, too, and less of the industrially sanitized feel.

Around the Place des Vosges in the Marais, where you'd expect rates to soar, there are a number of elegant hotels that seem miniaturized; small beds, small elevator, and shrunken rates. One such is the **Hôtel Pratic** *(9 rue d'Ormesson, 4th; Tel 01/48-87-80-47; Métro to St.-Paul or Bastille; 230f single w/toilet, 280f double w/toilet, 380f double w/shower, 420 double w/toilet and shower, breakfast 20f; MC, V),* a fairly dull and spare place, exceptional only for the vague sense that you've just eaten a little Gulliver pill. With a prime location on the peaceful Place du Marché Sainte-Cathérine, just a walk away from the heart of the Marais.

▶▶DO-ABLE

For an ultramodern, ultrahip option, the **Hôtel Beaumarchais** *(3 rue Oberkampf, 11th; Tel 01/53-36-86-86; Métro to Filles de Calvaire; 350-400f single, 450-500f double, 700f suite, breakfast 30f; AE, MC, V)* has just opened for those who simply cannot get enough Oberkampf [see *bar scene,* above] in their life. Clearly designed to be party central, it was on its way when we visited, with the sleek New York ultramodern hotel look in primary colors, albeit a little stage-set-y. Toilets and showers in every room and brand-new fixtures after a recent renovation.

A favorite hotel for the study-abroad crowd in the Latin Quarter is the **Hôtel des Grandes Écoles** *(75 rue du Cardinal Lemoine, 5th; Tel 01/43-26-79-23; Métro to Cardinal Lemoine; 530-690f single or double, 670-790f triple, 890f quad, extra cot 100f, breakfast 45f; MC, V),* shutting out the noise of the city with many large rooms with exposed rafters and other little country touches, opening onto a large cobblestone courtyard where breakfast can be taken in the summer. When fellow guests start asking if maybe you know their son, he's studying French at the Sorbonne and he's just about your age, this becomes the perfect spot to perfect your incomprehension of English. All rooms have shower, toilet, and phone.

Though the 1st arrondissement has better hotels, the **Britannique**

(20 ave. Victoria, 1st; Tel 01/42-33-74-59, Fax 01/42-33-82-65; Métro to Châtelet; 680-950f double; AE, DC, MC, V) is a good deal. The rooms may be small, but they're clean, comfy, and have the basics. Located in the heart of Paris, near **Les Halles,** the **Centre Pompidou,** and **Nôtre-Dame,** the Britannique was completely renovated in 1998. Bedrooms are cozy and conservatively decorated with traditional furniture. Bathrooms are small but well organized with enough shelf space for your beauty creams and a hair dryer. Minibar and TV make it positively luxurious.

The standard three-star **Hôtel Chamonix** *(8 rue d'Hauteville; Tel 01/47-70-19-49, Fax 01/45-23-14-81; Métro to Strasbourg-St.-Denis; 640F single, 740F double, 860F triple)* is fully air-conditioned, recently remodeled, and centrally located between Strasbourg-St.-Denis and the place de la République. While rooms tend towards the nondescript, they are soundproofed and quite comfortable, with cable television and fully outfitted bathrooms. You'll get a 15 percent discount when you mention this guide.

▶▶SPLURGE

In 1996, a radical restoration of **Hôtel Abbatial St-Germain** *(46 blvd. St.Germain, 6th; Tel 01/46-34-02-12, Fax 01/43-25-47-73; Métro to Maubert-Mutualité; 680-820f double; abbatial@hotellerie.net; AE, DC, MC, V)* brought the six stories of this 17th-century building up to modern, smallish, but very comfortable standards. Rooms are very much French boudoir in style, with faux-Louis XVI and many lovely decorative touches. All rooms are double-glazed to keep out the busy and noisy surrounding neighborhood, and many rooms on the fifth—some with small balconies— and sixth floors enjoy views over the **Notre-Dame.** Plus AC, TV, and a minibar!

Swank and style predominate at the leather, wood, marble and leafty-ferned lobby of **Hôtel Lenox** *(9 rue de l'Université; Tel 01/42-96-10-95, Fax 01/42-61-52-63; 700-1150F single or double, 50F breakfast; AE, DC, MC, V),* whose bar Hemingway was said to have hung out at. Today, for better or worse, you'll find pinch-nosed arty types at the Art Deco-ish bar. Rooms stylishly hark back to *les années folles* (the rough equivalent of the Roaring Twenties), with their hand-painted furniture and sleek bathrooms.

nEEd TO KnOW

Currency Best way to change money is to use **ATMs,** which give the best rates. Both airports also have 24-hour *bureaux de change.* At the Gare du Nord, where the RER B train arrives from Charles de Gaulle Airport, there is a **Thomas Cook** *(Tel 01/42-80-11-50; 6:15am-11:25pm daily).*

Public Transportation A 48f *carnet* buys you ten **Métro** rides; if you're sticking around, a monthly, which can be used as often as you like (in Zone 1, the urban center) is 279f. The **trains** to the suburbs, the **RER** lines, also run through the center of town and can be quicker; tickets must be bought separately, and prices vary. Keep your yellow RER ticket—you'll need it to get out from the tracks. Two can—and often do—slip through the turnstiles on one ticket, but checks happen, so be careful [see *five-o*, above]. First and last train *(5-6am/12:30-1am)* are listed on the platform signs. **Taxis** are your only option then, and on Saturday nights there aren't enough.

Health/Emergency Police: *17;* Fire: *18;* Ambulance: *15.* The 24-hour **American Hospital** is just out of town in Neuilly *(63 blvd. Victor-Hugo; Bus 82; Tel 01/46-41-25-41, direct emergency line Tel 01/47-47-70-15).*

Pharmacies Pharma Presto *(Tel 01/42-42-42-50)* is a 24-hour pharmacy that delivers for a fee of 150f 8am-6pm, 250f after. Otherwise, try the **Pharmacie des Champs** *(84 ave. de Champs Elysées, 8th; Tel 01/45-62-02-41; Métro to Georges V).*

Bike/Moped/Whatever Rental Atelier de la Compagnie *(57 blvd. de Grenelle, 15th; Tel 01/45-79-77-24; Métro to Dupleix; 10am-7pm Mon-Fri, till 6pm Sat; MC, V, AE)* rents scooters for 250f/day, 950f/week, motorcycles from 340f/day, 1,500f/week, requires 14,000f refundable deposit, w/valid driver's license.

American Express *(38 ave. de Wagram, 8th; Tel 01/42-27-58-80; Métro to Ternes; 9am-5pm Mon-Fri)*

Telephone Country code: *33;* city code: *01;* information: *12;* international operator (USA): *00/33-12-11.* Phone cards, ***télécartes,*** can be bought at most tobacco shops, magazine stands, and at any post office, in 50f or 120f denominations. **AT&T:** *Tel 08-00-99-00-11;* **MCI:** *Tel 08-00-99-00-19;* **Sprint:** *Tel 08-00-99-00-87.*

Airports Charles de Gaulle (Roissy) *Tel 01/48-62-22-80;* **Orly** *Tel 01/49-75-15-15;* 20 miles north of town. International flights arrive at Aérogare 1 at Charles de Gaulle; bus it to Aérogare 2, from there, catch the RER B train into town *(4-5 departures an hour 5:20am-midnight; 48f).* **Air France** buses *(4-5 departures an hour 6am-11pm daily; 60f)* leave from both Aérogares and stop at more locations. **Roissybus** *(4-5 departures an hour 5:20am-midnight; 45f)* drops you near Place de l'Opéra. **Taxis** *(around 200f w/no traffic, 300f during the day)* are the only choice in off-hours.

From Orly, catch the **Orlyval** shuttle train *(6am-10pm Mon-Fri; 7am-11pm Sat, Sun)* to RER B station **Antony** *(57f together),* and from there into Paris. Or shuttle bus to RER C station **Pont de Rungis,** then Orlyrail train to central Paris *(Every 12 minutes 5:45am-11pm daily; 30f).* Taxi same cost and time as from De Gaulle.

Trains General info for all trains: *Tel 08-36-35-35-35.* The six stations: **Gare d'Austerlitz, Gare Saint-Lazare, Gare Montparnasse, Gare d'Est, Gare d'Ouest,** and **Gare du Nord** are all major Métro hubs.

Bus Lines Out of the City Most buses arrive at **Gare Routière Internationale de Paris** *(28 ave. de Général de Gaulle Tel 01/49-72-51-51; Métro to Galliéni)* in the suburb of Bagnolet. From the bus station take the Métro line 3 from Galliéni into town.

everywhere else

versailles

Certainly no first-time visit to Paris would be complete without visiting "Sun King" Louis XIV's posh **château** at Versailles. The seat of power between 1682 and 1789, and later the digs of Louis XVI and Marie-Antoinette before they were dragged off to Paris and beheaded, this imposing palace can be a major trip, especially if you endured a few too many lessons on ol' Louis in your high school history class. In fact, it's a great place to bring those history lessons alive.

Sadly, a lot of *other* folks have the same thing in mind: During the high tourist season in summer, the halls of the château are like the sidewalks in midtown Manhattan at rush hour. Expect to find yourself standing in lines and wading your way through crowds just to get to the *Grands Appartements*. Despite the signs reminding tourists that "only the bearers of the official badge are allowed to make commentary," you'll hear many an American Ivy League prepster enjoying the sound of his own voice as he brings his sandal-footed companions up to speed on the chateaux' history. Besides rich kids on their postgrad junket to Europe, there are also herds of obnoxious, squabbling French kids being chaperoned through the halls by their overwhelmed instructors. Your best bet for a successful visit is to come very, very early in the morning or late in the afternoon.

Versailles tourists spend freely and everyone seems to benefit, from the legions of street salesmen clad in umbrella hats and armored in postcards and the self-interested unofficial tour guides, to the pickpockets who've recently made an arrival here. But the château itself is actually quite under-funded. Time has tarnished it somewhat: The once regal Place d'Armes in the front is now a parking lot for tour buses, and a freak wind-storm recently damaged the gardens. But the place is still truly awesome, and you may even find some peace and quiet in the acres of landscaped gardens outside.

versailles

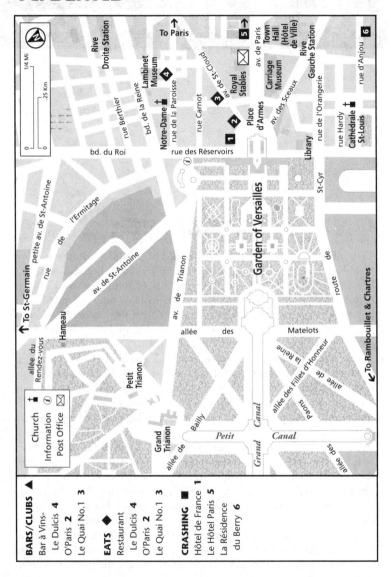

BARS/CLUBS ▲
Bar à Vins-
Le Dulcis **4**
O'Paris **2**
Le Quai No.1 **3**

EATS ◆
Restaurant
Le Dulcis **4**
O'Paris **2**
Le Quai No.1 **3**

CRASHING ■
Hôtel de France **1**
Le Hôtel Paris **5**
La Résidence
du Berry **6**

Versailles the city flows out from the châteaux in a series of leafy, cobblestone streets. It's worth a quick visit, if only to cool off at a local bar or cafe before heading back to gay Par-ee. Or, if you're a big-time Louis XIV fan, time your visit to coincide with one of **Les Fêtes du Nuit de Versailles,** [see *festivals,* below] when the old royal court comes back to life with the help of some French actors in costumes.

hanging out-neighborhoods

There's more to Versailles than just the actual Château, its parks and gardens. The town contains two distinctive 18th century neighborhoods that were inaugurated (though not completed) during the reign of Louis XIV. **Quartier St-Louis,** begun around 1730, is a ten-minute walk south of the château; **Quartier Notre Dame,** begun around 1680 but mostly rebuilt around 1730, is a ten-minute walk north of it. Either gives an interesting overview of the vast support mechanism needed to provide for the French kings. Of the two, the one that's less altered by later generations is the Quartier St-Louis. To reach it from the main (east) facade of the Château (the entrance that faces the town, not the one facing the gardens), turn your back to the Château, and walk down **Avenue de Sceaux,** the large boulevard that funnels off diagonally to the right (i.e. to the southeast). Walk along it for about four minutes till you reach the **rue Satory,** where you'll turn right (south). Rue Satory changes its name within three blocks to the **rue du Maréchal Joffre.** Within two blocks, turn right onto the **rue d'Anjou,** site of low-slung, stucco-covered buildings which, during the heyday of the *ancien régime,* were the subject of rapidly inflating real estate prices (yes, it's been happening for centuries...). You'll get a general sense of the 18th century sprawl of the Versailles community by walking along these streets. The neighborhood's most interesting feature is the **Potager du Roy,** site of the kitchen gardens that kept the king and his court in fresh salads and vegetables throughout the long Île de France winters.

culture zoo

Château de Versailles *(Tel 01/30-84-74-00; 9am-6:30pm Tue-Sun May-Sept; 9am-5:30pm Tue-Sun Oct-Apr, last entrance half an hour before closing; Grands Appartements, Galerie des Glaces: 45F, 35F students and young adults aged 18-25 after 3:30pm, free for seniors 65 and older; Chamber du Roi, Galerie des Glaces, Appartements Dauphin Daupine, 70F):*There are four entrances to the Château on the place d'Armes. Unless you are an absolute monarchist, you'll probably be content to wander through the Grands Appartements alone or with the aid of a self-guided audio tour, and afterwards stroll through the gardens. This is the easiest and most efficient way to see Versailles. Head straight to entrance A, pick your brochure and map, avoid the queues for the King's Chambers, and if you so desire, flatter your penchant for minute, often meaningless detail by spending an extra 30F on the audio tour. If you want the full effect of the royal pomp and splendor, queue up at entrance C for the

Seven to ten times a summer, the Château plays host to **Les Fêtes de Nuit de Versailles (Rêve du Roi)** *(10:30pm Apr-Oct; 9:30 Jul-Aug; Tickets 250-70F)* in which you see French actors bandy about in period costume portraying Louis XIV and his royal court. The 90-minute show successfully captures the glorious insanity of court life. Spectators gaze from bleachers along the Boulevard de la Reine, adjacent to the Bassin de Neptune, which open 90 minutes prior to show time. Inquire on show times at the Château's website, ***www.chateauversailles.fr***, and at the **Office de Tourisme** [see *need to know*, above]. Tickets can be bought in advance at the **Office de Tourisme** or any **FNAC** *(Tel 01/49-87-50-50)* in Paris, or at the door an hour before show time.

It remains to be seen how the Sunday and Saturday **Grandes Eaux Musicales** *(Gardens de Château de Versailles; 11am-noon/3:30-5:30pm Sun April-mid-Oct; same hours Sat Jul-Aug; 25F)*, in which the gardens' numerous fountains gloriously spray forth water to the strains of piped-in classical music, will be affected by the wrenching storm that took so heavy a toll on the gardens' tree life. In any case, these romantic weekend spectacles are a pleasant way to experience the gardens, given good weather.

King's Chambers. If you want a guided tour, head to entrance D. (Time Note: It takes an hour to go through the Grands Appartements and a minimum of three hours (or more if you have the time) to tour the château. You can easily spend another 3 hours touring the Trianons and strolling through the gardens. Our recommendation? Make Versailles a day-long event.)

You can almost sense the massive arrogance of court life that helped bring about the Revolution as you wander the Grands Appartements. Each room is individually decorated, richly brocaded in velvet, marble-accented, and touched up with fleur-de-lis flourish and gold-leaf luxury, and has a ceiling painted in 17th-century allegory. The most impressive ceiling painting is in the Hercules Salon, out-dazzling all the others and created in 1712, its ceiling painted between 1734 and 1736 by François Lemoine. When he'd finished, he surveyed his splendid achievement and committed suicide. Other apartments are dedicated to Venus, Diana, Mars, Mercury, and Apollo. The outlandish Salon d'Apollon or Apollo is of special interest, as it was once the throne room and honors the Sun God, the mythical hero who was the symbol of Louis XIV. The rooms are only partially furnished with period (but not original) furniture. At the end of the Grands Appartements, you find the impressive Hall of Mirrors.

In the 236-foot-long room, the European and American leaders forced the signing of the Treaty of Versailles that ended World War I.

Gardens de Château de Versailles *(Tel 01/30-83-78-88; 7am-9:30pm daily May-Sept; 8am-5:30pm Oct-Apr, closed in inclement weather; Free except Grandes Eaux* (fountain displays) *-28F)*: More than 10,000 of the gardens' trees were uprooted by an unprecedented storm in December 1999. At this point, it is questionable whether they can ever be restored to a semblance of their former selves, but nonetheless the gardens still are one of the most impressive components of the Château—during the summer months they get just as crowded as the Château, with the same long lines. The 250 acres, planned by André Le Nôtre, feature geometrically arrayed flower beds, numerous little grottos accented with Neoclassical statuary, and beautiful fountains featuring nymphs in elegant states of repose and muscled Greek gods with furrowed brows. The particularly impressive fountains are the Bassin de Neptune and the Bassin d'Appollo, both located on your right as you emerge from the Château. The Bassin de Neptune depicts the Greek sea god among innocent cherubs and vicious-looking sea dragons. In the Bassin d'Appollo, the Greek god of the sun is shown bringing light to the world astride his horse-drawn chariot as he emerges from the depths of the sea flanked by sea monsters.

These two beautiful fountains greet you as you approach the gardens, but the beauty of the romantic gardens is the escape they provide from the herds of grazing tourists. Wander for a while along the prim and trim walkways, lose yourself in the splendor of the statuary, and if you're lucky, you'll find yourself alone for the first time since you set foot in Versailles.

Grand et Petit Trianon *(Noon-5:30pm Nov-Mar; Noon-6:30pm Apr-Oct; Grand: 25F, 15F young adults 18-25 and after 3:30pm; Petit: 15F, 10F young adults and after 3:30pm; Grand et Petit 30F, 20F young adults, free for those under 17)*: A long walk across the gardens will lead you to these small châteaux, once the guest houses for visitors to the royal Château. They are not particularly impressive and lack the splendor and period furnishings of the main château.

bars and eats

After soaking up as much of the overblown royal display of the Château as you can possibly endure, you will probably be ready for a pint. A quick retreat from the tourist circus is the **O'Paris Pub** *(15 rue Colbert; Tel 01/39-50-36-12; 11am-midnight, happy hour 4-8pm; V)*, just off place d'Armes. Sit at the bar and dig the Brit-pop music playing on the pub's stereo or retreat further into its murky, dark, varnished-wood interior with a pint of the dark stuff, and even the most nervous temperament will loosen in the relaxed atmosphere. Stay a while and the place will probably begin to crowd with Versailles' young hip anglophiles.

If you're looking for something ever-so-slightly more sophisticated but no less relaxed, work your way over to the **Bar à Vins-Restaurant Le Ducis** *(13 rue Ducis; Tel 01/39-49-96-51; 11am-midnight V)* on the quiet place du Marché Notre-Dame. Study the long wine list, order a glass or a bottle, and let your toe start to tap to the classic Serge Gainsbourg and Rolling Stones playing on the stereo. Or order a meal off the short, but classic, chalkboard menu. The food is light, delicious, carefully prepared, and reasonably priced. On summer days, the patio furniture spills onto the quiet adjacent side street, making it a nice place to take in the long, temperate evenings. Few foreigners frequent the bar so rest easy among Versailles' twenty- and thirtysomething smart set.

For classy "date" dining, try the seafood of **Le Quai No. 1** *(1 ave. St.-Cloud; Tel 01/39-50-42-26; Noon-2:30pm, 7:30-11pm; Reservations required; Fixed price lunch menu 110-185f, main course 85F; MC, V)*. The interior of the restaurant is "tastefully" decorated with lithographs and wood paneling, though during the summers you'll want to bask on the outdoor terrace. While the food isn't astounding, the general care put into the preparation and presentation is quite high, and seafood probably doesn't get much better so far from the sea. The chef's specialties are seafood sauerkraut, *fruit de mer* paella, bouillabaisse, and home-cooked salmon, but you may notice a fair number of surf-and-turf platters with sizzling steaks saddled next to grilled lobsters flying by, carried with panache by the professionally polite waitstaff.

crashing

A short walk east of the Château, the recently remodeled two-star **Le Hôtel Paris** *(14 ave. de Paris; Tel 01/39-50-56-00, Fax 01/39-50-21-83; www.paris-hotel.fr; 210F single, 360F double)* is your best bet to stay in Versailles without busting your budget. It has an accommodating, helpful front desk and provides nondescript but neat and cozy rooms, all with sinks, televisions, and either showers or baths. The beds are mostly doubles and twins and quite comfortable. Mention that you are using this guide and you will receive a 10-percent discount. You can make reservations over the Internet.

Located in the quaint St.-Louis neighborhood southeast of the Château, the three-starred **Hôtel La Résidence du Berry** *(14 rue d'Anjou; Tel 01/39-49-07-07, Fax 01/39-50-59-40; 520F single, 550-650F double, 55F breakfast; AE, MC, V)* is probably the most intimately charming hotel in Versailles, with its exposed wood-beam ceiling, flowery courtyard garden, and individualized rooms with private baths. Each room is discreet and calmly decorated with carefully chosen colors and warm prints. Beds are predictably soft, and the bathrooms have plush towels.

For almost opulent accommodations, try the recently remodeled and renovated **Hôtel de France** *(5 rue Colbert; Tel 01/30-83-92-23, Fax 01/30-83-92-24; www.hotelfrance-versailles.com; 780-820F single, 820F double, 60f breakfast; MC, V)*. Housed in the former offices of Napoleon, the hotel has a rather curious layout, with only 23 rooms spread over several long corridors. Each room was painted and decorated along the hotel's fleur-de-lis theme by the same craftsmen who did the famous George V hotel in Paris. Beds are comfortable and inviting, and bathrooms (private of course) are quite beautiful. You can probably skip eating there though, as the food service is contracted out through the Maitre de Kanter chain.

need to know

Currency The best place to change money in Versailles is the central **post office's** automatic teller machine which is open 24 hours a day.

Tourist Information There are three branches of the **Office de Tourisme** in Versailles. The **central branch** *(7 rue des Reservoirs; Tel 01/39-24-88-88, Fax 01/39-24-88-89; 9am-6pm, closed Sun; www. chateauversailles.fr)* is just north of the Château. **Another branch** *(Les Manèges; Tel 01/39-53-31-63; 9am-6pm, closed Mon)* is just opposite the Rive Gauche train station. The third is open May through September in a temporary booth near the gates of the Château and is usually mobbed with tourists. The first two branches offer a wealth of information and will arrange hotel accommodations.

Public Transportation The only time you'll want to use the public transportation system in Versailles is coming and going from either the **Gare Chantiers** or **Gare Rive Droite,** both only 15 minutes by foot from the Château. The **bus system** in Versailles is run by **Phébus** *(12 ave. du Général de Gaulle; Tel 01/39-20-16-20, Fax 01/39-49-99-96; www.phebus.tm.fr)* and it runs often. One-way tickets cost 8F. Line B connects Gare Chantiers to the Office de Tourisme, just opposite the Rive Gauche train station in a shopping center along avenue Paris and avenue Royale. Line H connects Gare Rive Doite to the Avenue de Paris.

Health and Emergency Police *17;* **Fire:** *18;* **Medical Emergency Response** (SAMU): *15.* The central hospital of Versailles is the **Hôpital Richaud** *(1 rue Richaud; Tel 01/39-63-91-33; Bus I to Hôpital Richaud).*

Pharmacy Pharmacie Boussiron Marie-Christine *(10 rue Georges Clémenceau; Tel 01/39-50-12-89, Fax 01/39-50-18-60; 8:30am-8pm Mon-Sat)* has a wide array of over-the counter medicines.

Trains The easiest and cheapest way to get to Versailles from Paris is to take the yellow RER Line C that runs along the left bank of the Seine to Gare Austerlitz, St.-Michel, Musée d'Orsay, and so on, and deposits you at the **Gare Rive-Gauche** *(rue du Gén. de Gaulle; Buses A, D, F, H, K, L, P to Gare Rive Gauche a 5-minute walk from the Château).* Trains also run from Gare St.-Lazare to **Versailles Rive-Droite** *(rue du M. Foch; Buses A, D, G, H, H Express, I, S, T to Gare Rive Droite, 5-minute walk from the Château),* which is about a 10-minute walk from the Château. If you must take a bus from here, grab one marked "Château" or "Hôtel de Ville". Trains run from Paris Montparnasse and other destinations in the Île-de-France, such as Chartres, to **Versailles Chantiers** *(rue des États-Généneraux; Buses B, G, H Express, K, L, P, R, T, X to Gare des Chantiers).* You can plot your trip and train departure times most easily using the website, ***www.citefutee.com.***

Bus You can take the **bus** to Versailles from Paris by riding the *Métro* to the Pont-de-Sèvres stop, then transferring to **Bus 171,** which lets you off five minutes from the Château. Depending on the traffic, the trip takes about 20 to 45 minutes and costs three *Métro* tickets. Before embarking, you will probably want to check the traffic reports using the ***www.citefutee.com*** website.

Laundry Located off of rue Georges Clemenceau, the **Laverie Lavo-matique** *(10 rue de Phillipe Dangeau; Tel 01/39-49-04-61; 7am-9:30pm)* has self-serve, coin-operated machines in which you can wash 14 kilograms (about 31 pounds) of clothing for 30F.

Postal There is a **Post Office** *(3 ave. de Paris; Tel 01/39-67-63-00, Fax 01/30-21-82-37; 8am-7pm Mon-Fri, 8am-noon Sat)* just across from the branch of the Office de Tourisme in the shopping center, Les Manèges, which handles all the typical postal operations, including faxes, and offers internet access with a shiny-new blue iMac. See ***www.cyberposte.com*** for more information about the French cyber-postal program.

fontainebleau

Surrounded by the aptly named the Forêt de Fontainebleau, the Château of Fontainebleau is an impressive castle—you might think of it as a small-scale Versailles, if you're familiar with the other French royal getaways. Fontainebleau is just 37 miles south of Paris, and the castle was favored by Renaissance kings, who loved to escape the grime and crime of Paris to hunt in the Forêt de Fontainebleau. Post-Renaissance, the castle was re-decorated by Emperor Napoléon, who called the castle "the house of the centuries." You may remember, from a European History class, the image of Napoleon descending Fontainebleau's horseshoe-shaped exterior stairway as he departed for Elba, the island where he lived the end of his life in exile. The palace now houses a museum dedicated to the life of Napoleon, and the interior still contains his lavish decorations. You can visit either selected rooms or the whole dang thing. Don't go to Fontainebleau without visiting at least the Napoleonic rooms, which are filled with his famous monograms and designs. The *grands appartements* are definitely worth a visit too, especially if you're interested in French royal history. If you're interested in other walks you can take in both the town Fontainebleau or its surrounding forest, visit the Office du Tourisme [see *need to know*, below].

Visiting Fontainebleau is a good half-day trip from Paris: It's a nice place to take a little break from the city, and the surrounding forest is a great place for a relaxing walk or a picnic.

need to know

Contact Info *Tel 01/60-71-50-70* or *01/64-22-27-40.*

Hours/Days Open The Chateau is open 9:30am-12:30pm and 2-5pm Wed-Mon Sept-June, and 9:30am-6pm Wed-Mon July-Aug.

Tourist Info The Office de Tourisme *(4 rue Royale; Tel 01/60-74-99-99;)* and their website can give you hotel information as well as a local event guide (it's all in French, alas).

Directions/Transportation Trains to Fontainebleau depart from the **Gare de Lyon** in Paris. The trip takes between 45 and 60 minutes each way, and costs 94F round-trip. When you get to the Fontainebleau train station, **Fontainebleau Avon,** you'll still be about 3 miles from the chateau. You can get to the chateau by taking a local bus—you can take bus A or B, each of which are labeled simply "Chateau". The bus makes the round trip journey between the train station and the castle every 15 minutes Monday through Saturday, and every 30 minutes every Sunday. It costs 10 F each way.

Cost Access to the *grands appartements* is 35F for adults and 23F for students age 18 to 25. Access to the *petits appartements* and the Napoleonic Rooms is 16F for adults and 12F for students age 18 to 25. It is all free for those under age 18. Ah, youth....

Eats Buying a picnic in Paris to bring on your journey is the best bet.

Crashing You're best off staying in Paris and just making Fontainebleau a day trip—hotels in Fontainebleau tend to be fancy and pricey. However, if you're stuck here for the night, try the one-star **Hôtel Terminus** *(93 avenue Franklin-Roosevelt, Tel 01/64-22-38-25),* which is in Avon, near the train station. Alternatively, if you're ready to splurge on a quaint old forest-cottage style hotel, pull in to the charming **Hôtel Legris et Parc** *(36 rue Paul Seramy, 77300 Fontainebleau, Tel 01/64-22-24-24, 300F singles, 350F-570F doubles).*

chartres

While Versailles and Fontainbleau attract tourists to their flamboyant châteaux, Chartres is a truly sleepy small town of 42,000 inhabitants, 60 miles southwest of Paris. The main draw here is the Gothic **Cathédrale Nôtre Dame** [see *culture zoo,* below]. It is huge, towering over the town, and also very old, dating back to 1260, when it was completed. It also has 600 square feet of rose-colored glass, creating a calm, unearthly glow inside.

The church has drawn religious pilgrims from far and wide since the Middle Ages, who come to ogle at the stark spires and the various religious relics inside. One especially important one is the famous *Voile de la Vierge,* or sacred tunic of the Virgin Mary. The robe's history is even longer than the church: Constantine Porphyrogenitus and Irene presented it to Charlemagne in the fourth century, and Charles the Bald delivered it to Chartres around 876.

Besides the cathedral, there is not a whole lot happening here. The local bars are good for a mellow drink at night, but not much else. For a real energy buzz, you might consider arranging a ride in an ultra-light aircraft [see *outdoors,* below] over the town: It's sure to get your heart a-racing, even if the spires of the Cathedral don't.

neighborhoods and hanging out

Most visitors view the cathedral's stained glass, have lunch, then move on, but you can spend an hour or two wandering the medieval streets of **Vieux Chartres.** These ancient streets tumble down from the cathedral, leading east to the **River Eure.**

Our favorite stroll is along **rue du Point-St-Hilaire,** from which you can see a panorama of the rooftops beneath the cathedral. St-Hilaire begins immediately east of the Gothic church of St. Pierre, which stands on **rue St-Pierre,** a 10-minute walk south of the cathedral. Two other streets ideal for neighborhood strolls are **rue des Écuyers** and **rue du Cygne,** both of which lie a 3-minute walk south of the cathedral.

The most evocative neighborhood is the *St-André quartier,* a district east of the cathedral and the banks of the river. This was the old merchants' district, housing everybody from cobblers to tanners. Most of these old houses have been restored, many dating from the 18th century. Check out the embossed doorways topped with bull's-eye glass.

bar scene

Don't expect to find much nightlife in Chartres, except perhaps a mellow drink at **La Bodega** *(20 place des Halles; Tel 02/37-36-05-05; Noon-midnight, closed Mon; MC, V)* in a lively Cuban-inspired interior. It offers a wide selection of beers and spirits, but you'll notice the coolest customers sipping their potent rum and lime cocktails. If you're in town over the weekend, be sure to check in and see if there's any live music scheduled here.

culture zoo

Cathédrale Notre Dame de Chartres *(16 Cloître Nôtre-Dame; 7:30am-7:15pm Mon-Sat, 8:30am-7:15pm Sun, holidays):* The only requirements for gaining entry into the Cathédrale's hallowed walls are silence and dignity. Consecrated in 1260 on the site of a Romanesque church that had been destroyed by fire in 1194, it was the first building to use the structural innovation of flying buttresses to displace the weight of the stone walls and permit light to shine through an astonishing 3,000 square yards of stained-glass. The quality of the light blazing through the three rose windows is quite amazing. Masses are held Monday through Saturday at 11:45am and 6pm, and on Tuesdays and Fridays at 9am and 6pm. A Dominican mass is held Saturdays at 6pm, and Sundays at 9:30, 11am, and 6pm.

The sharp wit and laborious scholarship of **Malcolm Miller** *(Tel 02/37-28-15-58, Fax 02/37-28-33-03),* an English expatriate who has devoted his life to studying the Cathédrale and has given tours of the structure for 42 years, is a must for anyone seeking to understand the colossal beauty of the stone and glass structure. The 75-minute tours cost 20F for students, and start at noon and 2:45pm daily.

outdoors

If the Cathédrale doesn't leave you breathless, surely a 20- to 30-minute trip gliding above the countryside surrounding Chartres in an ultra-light aircraft of the **Centre de Vol à Voile** *(Aérodrome de Chartres, Route d'Albis; Tel 02/37-34-14-27, Fax 02/37-30-01-87; Bus 3 to Chartrexpo, then 10 minutes on foot; www.cvv-chartres.claranet.fr; 200-400F introductory flight depending on the type of plane)* will do the trick. But you will feel safe guided by the expert hands of your instructor: Members of the club, founded in 1951, hold the world championship in engineless gliding and are consistent national champions in French gliding competitions. The views of the Cathédrale, the geometrically carved countryside, and even the nuclear power plant of a neighboring town are amazing from the sky. Air conditions within the Eure-Loir region make for excellent, occasionally optimal gliding. Even if your life doesn't flash before your eyes, you may find God in the sky above Chartres. Unfortunately, getting to the aeroclub is bit difficult, so you may want to break down and pay for a taxi.

eats

Located in the long shadow of the majestic cathedral, **Café-Restaurant Serpente** *(2 Cloître Nôtre-Dame; Tel 02/37-21-68-81; 11am-10pm daily; MC, V)*, with its classy, well-stocked, dark-wood-varnished bar, delicious menu, and hopping table service is the place to have a quick drink (to steel your nerves before a trip into the Cathédrale or the atmosphere above it) or a deliciously bloody rare steak to fill your stomach. Unfortunately things can get a bit pricey if you order à la carte, so you'll probably want to pick and choose from the daily specials chalk menu and wine list. Dinner for two can easily run up to 300F, but is worth it if you want food that's going to stick with you.

Around the corner from the Cathédrale, **Crep'Salade** *(7 rue Serpente; Tel 02/37-21-53-12; 11am-2pm/6-10pm daily Apr-Aug; MC, V)* serves delicious, reasonably priced crêpes and salads, often best in combination. Vegetarians will appreciate the variety of meatless crêpes on the menu. The "vegetarian" crêpe comes with mustard vinaigrette, garnished with a mixed salad. During the summer, the sunny sky-lit courtyard is the place to grab a glass of cider and enjoy some delicately spiced crêpes.

crashing

Located toward the end of the old town across the river from the Cathédrale, the **Auberge de la Jeunesse** *(23 ave. Neigre; Tel 02/37-34-27-64, Fax 02/37-35-75-85; Bus 3 to Rouliers; Reception open noon-10pm; closed mid Dec-mid Jan; 70F a bed, sheets 17F; MC, V)* is housed in a predictably unattractive, well-worn building. The 11:30pm curfew is annoying not because it gets you out of the bars early, but because it keeps you locked in your two- to eight-person room for so long.

The best place to stay in Chartres on a tight budget is the **Maison Saint-Yves** *(1 rue Saint-Eman; Tel 02/37-88-37-40, Fax 02/37-88-37-*

49; 135F single, 180F double, 20F sheets, 20F towels, 30F breakfast, 70F lunch or dinner; MC, V), which is tucked behind the Cathédrale on a narrow street and run by the Chartres Diocese. From their super-new, clean, and reasonably comfortable rooms, all with private baths, you are afforded sweeping views of the Cathédrale and the surrounding countryside. You can also have a hearty meal at a very reasonable price while you're here. One should definitely make reservations, because the rooms tend to go very fast. Also, be aware that they give priority to pilgrims on religious visits to Chartres or people with an interest in local history and architecture, so it might be best to change out of that beer-soaked T-shirt you've been wearing for the past week and show some manners when trying to snag a room.

Opposite the Art Deco post office, **Hotel de la Poste** *(3 rue du Général-Koenig; Tel 02/37-21-04-27, Fax 02/37-36-42-17; hotelposte. chartres@wanadoo.fr; 290F single with shower, 320F with bath, 320F double with shower, 350F with bath; AE, DC, MC, V)* is conveniently located 15 minutes from the station and 10 minutes from the cathedral. Rooms are sound-proofed and carpeted, and have comfortable beds, in this reasonable two-star hotel. The decent restaurant serves well-prepared French standards and a large buffet-style breakfast.

need-to-know

Currency You can change money at the **Bureau de Change** *(Parvis de la Cathédrale; Tel 02/37-36-42-33; 9am-6pm Mon-Sat, 10am-noon/2-5pm Sun Mar-Oct; Closed Nov-Feb),* but don't expect exciting rates of exchange. Your best bet is probably the 24-hour automatic teller machine at the **Société Générale** *(15 rue Sainte-Même; Tel 02/37-23-57-00),* which is just southwest of the Cathédrale on the last cross street before you approach the Parvis de la Cathédrale.

Tourist Information The **Office de Tourisme** *(Place de la Cathédrale; Tel 02/37-18-26-26, Fax 02/37-21-51-91; 9am-7pm Mon-Sat, 9:30am-5:30pm Sun, holidays Apr-Sept; 10am-6pm Mon-Sat, 10am-1pm/2:30-4:30pm Oct-Mar; closed Jan 1, Nov 11, Dec 25)* dispenses information on Chartres and the Loire valley and makes hotel bookings.

Public Transportation You can obtain maps and information on Chartres' bus system, **Filibus** *(Place des Épars; Tel 02/37-36-26-98)* from a kiosk on the central place des Épars or at the Office de Tourisme. All buses stop at the Gare and run from the city center to the suburbs in all directions. Tickets are 6F. **Taxis:** Tel 02/37-36-00-00.

Health and Emergency Police: *17* or *Tel 02/37-24-75-39;* **Fire:** *18;* **Medical Emergency Response (SAMU):** *15.* **Non-emergency medical attention after-hours** (after 8pm Mon-Fri, after 6pm Sat, Sun): *Tel 02/37-36-20-20.* Other medical needs, go to **Hôpital de Chartres-Le Coudray** *(rue Claude, Le Coudray; Tel 02/37-30-30-30; Bus 8 to Hôpital).*

Pharmacy **Pharmacie des Épars** *(3 place des Épars; Tel 02/37-21-08-47, Fax 02/37-21-49-77)* should fulfill all your medicinal needs.

Trains Trains run hourly to and from Paris Montparnasse to Chartres' **train station** *(Place Pierre Sémard; Tel 02/37-84-61-65)*, which is within five minutes of the Cathédrale. The trip costs about 71F and lasts 70 minutes.

Laundry Down Boulevard Charles from place des Épars, you'll find the **Laverie Libre Service** *(Place Pasteur; Tel 02/37-34-42-33-13; 10am-7pm daily)*.

Postal The **central post office** *(1 blvd. Maurice Violette; Tel 02/37-27-40-70; 8am-7pm Mon-Fri, 8am-noon Sat)* is a distinctive yellow brick building with Art Deco mosaics. You can check your e-mail, send faxes, make long distance phone calls, and perform other postal operations here.

the north

the north

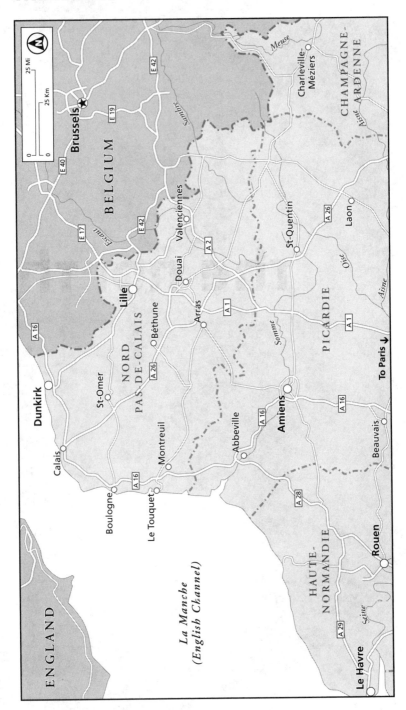

The north of France, the area stretching from the lush Picardy country-side of **Amiens** to the windblown Opal Coast off **Boulogne-sur-Mer,** is one of the country's least visited. As you travel north from town to countryside, the scenery becomes one part the 1959 David Ladd film *Dog of Flanders* and one part the Zola novel *Germinal*—and as fans of these works will tell you, neither has a happy ending. But if you're looking for a relatively authentic, untouristy adventure, you can safely head north. The cities and towns here also make for cozy stops on trips to larger destinations, like Amsterdam, Brussels, or London.

During your stay you'll be introduced to exotic Flemish cuisine, stick-to-the-ribs fixings that are testament to the cold, windswept, and craggy coast of the north. These include *Potjevleisch,* a potted meat product that's a far cry from its American cousin, Spam, *Anguilles au vert,* eels fried with spinach and white wine, and *Andouillettes,* a small offal-stuffed sausage normally served with mashed potatoes. Why more tourists have not been lured to the region by its food says more about the bad name sausage has gotten across the globe (think Jimmy Dean, pigs-in-a-blanket, Vienna sausage in a can...) than it does about the culinary merits of the region.

Lille, a historic regional capital, has a large, dynamic student popula-tion that keeps the city's nightlife changing constantly, while memories of its 17th-century Flemish glory are as close as Brussels, just across the Bel-gian border. For a large town with a student population of around 150,000, the people are remarkably friendly, though the gray northern skies can sometimes put a damper on things. **Boulogne-sur-Mer,** sand-wiched between Le Touquet-Paris Plage and Calais, is neither as seedy as Calais nor as ritzy as Le Touquet. Its cobblestone streets and medieval ramparts have a distinct charm of their own, while the fishing docks, a major hub for France's fishing industry, offer a sobering glimpse into a troubled industry. You can also visit Nausicaä, the town's UNESCO-crowned marine environment museum. A little over 90 minutes from both Paris and Lille, **Amiens'** quiet, lazy small-town feel and gorgeous Gothic cathedral, built during the 13th and 16th centuries, offer a relaxing diversion from Paris. The gentle, rolling countryside surrounding this capital of the Picardy region is flaxen with golden fields of grains in the summer and autumn and speckled with large commercial farms.

Compared to the hot tempers and quick smiles of the south of France, the coolness or suspiciousness of strangers in the north can often be mistaken for a lack of kindness. But if you sit long enough at a bar, someone is bound to start talking to you, and once the ice is broken, you'll find the northerners as friendly as anyone you're likely to meet in France. Since tourists are rare here, you'll definitely attract attention, and if you speak French, you're likely to find yourself engaged in a long conversation. You'll find some native English-speaking folk, too: In Boulogne-sur-Mer, the tidal flow of English day-trippers has deposited quite a number of expatriates who came for a day and stayed for a lifetime. Overcrowding, high cost of living, and pollution in the British isles has only seen the number of English living in France grow.

Fierce tumult not only describes the waters of the North Sea, but also the history of the Pas-de-Calais du Nord region. The coastal towns were the front lines of defense against attack from across the English Channel. Further north, Protestants and Catholics clashed with the conviction that only religion can stir. In an effort to stave off the threat of Protestantism rising in the Dutch Republic (c. 1568), the Catholic church spent a considerable largesse on art to reassure its questioning diocese, sending artists to Italy for training and commissioning countless masterpieces. The indelible influence of Rubens, Van Dyck, and Rembrandt is unmistak-

TraveL TIMES

* TGV (Fast Train—more expensive
**By car

	Amiens	Calais	Boulogne-sur-mer	Le Touquet	Paris	Lille
Lille	:40	1:10**	1:30**	1:50**	1:05*	-
Amiens	-	1:15**	1:20**	1:10**	1:20	:40
Calais	1:45**	-	:25**	:45**	1:30* 3:00	1:10**
Boulogne-sur-mer	1:20**	:25**	-	:20**	2:40**	1:30**
Le Touquet	1:20**	:45**	:20**	-	2:25**	1:50**

able, even as far south as Lille, and a sizable collection of Flemish art is on display in Lille's **Musée des Beaux-Arts.**

getting around the region

The best way to get around this region is by rail. Lille and Calais are serviced by high-speed TGV trains, though you will probably want to avoid Calais, because there's nothing to see there. Local buses connect Boulogne and Calais and are cheaper but less comfortable than the train.

▶▶ROUTES

Lille is a good base for trips to London and Brussels. Trains leave from the city's brand-new international train station, a long couple of blocks from the local Lille Flanders train station.

If you're short on time, you could make Lille a day or weekend trip from Paris, as commuter TGV trains zip back and forth on the hour-long run both bright and early, and late at night.

Amiens, an easy day trip from Paris, is a quiet getaway from the capital's hustle and bustle. From the Gare du Nord, it takes about 70 minutes to reach Amiens.

If given a week to tour the north from Paris, a good plan would be to head to Amiens first and enjoy one of the most glorious Gothic cathedrals in France for a day. From Amiens, head to Boulogne, which makes a good base of operations to visit Le Touquet for a day. In Le Touquet, sun yourself on the beach and have a bowl of fish soup at **Perard's**. Then head to Lille for the weekend to enjoy the nightlife.

LILLE

Lille's student population of over 150,000 makes it startlingly hip for a town that is almost completely, remarkably tourist free. Kids here regularly make the 35-minute commute across the border to Brussels, or hop the Eurostar train for the two-hour trip to London if they can afford it. Maybe it's because of those weekend overnighters that the youth culture here is very much in tune with the latest European trends. Be forewarned though: the town kind of hibernates in the summer, when most students disappear.

The economic hardship that has hit the entire du-Nord-Pas-de-Calais region has undermined Lille's status as one of the richest cities in France. But that slump has also had its pluses: Thanks to the steep drop in neighborhood rents, the oldest part of the city has become the hippest, with bohemian bars, cool cafes, and lots of record stores catering to the local youth scene. This is by far the best part of town to hang, since outside the old city Lille is mostly suburban and industrial sprawl. You can also check out the ramparts of the old **Citadelle,** [see *culture zoo*, below] or spend a few hours (or days) in the massive **Palais des Beaux-Arts de Lille** [see *culture zoo*, below], which has the largest collection of art in France outside of Paris.

For years French and European hipsters banished what Americans considered acceptable urban street culture and clothing to the dark, dungeon-like shadows of clubland. With the explosion of electronic music across Europe in the last decade, however, the culture of dreadlocks, baggy clothing, and brightly colored sneakers is moving into the mainstream, becoming easily the most international youth subculture around.

In Lille, the growth of club culture is evidenced more by the number of cool record stores than by actual clubs. But the savvy young traveler will also find hints of other quiet underground subcultures here. In addition to your usual drink-too-much, study-too-little skater crew, there's a cool indie rock scene, an underground arts clique, and a roots-reggae subculture.

Pick up a copy of *Sortir*, a weekly guide to goings-on around town, which you can find just about everywhere, from the tourist office to record shops. Even if you don't read French, you'll probably be able to decipher enough of the short blurbs on concerts to figure out if a given art show or concert falls within your interests. If you do read French, several good online guides can offer you, if not the most up-to-date happenings, a good knowledge of the different bars and venues around town. Of these guides, *www.lechti.com* is the best.

neighborhoods

The two neighborhoods where you'll want to spend the most time are easily reached on foot from the train station. The **city center,** which is marked by a number of pedestrian streets, is home to the fascinating **Palais des Beaux-Arts de Lille** [see *culture zoo,* below], the **Lille Flanders train station** [see *need to know,* below], the **Office de Tourisme** [see *need to know,* below], and **Auberge de Jeunesse** [see *crashing,* below]. On the whole it can feel a bit commercial, with its FNAC, McDonald's, and Au Bureau (a chain of English-style pubs across France). To get from the train station to the heart of the city center, just walk up rue Faidherbe.

Just north of the center and east of the **Citadelle** fortress [see *hanging out,* below], is the *vieille ville,* Lille's coolest neighborhood, with a wealth of fresh bars, little cafes, independent record stores, and small hip shops. To get from the Office de Tourisme to the *vieille ville,* turn left onto la rue Rihour and walk north until you reach the very large, very busy **place de Général-de-Gaulle.** Here, turn left onto **rue Esquermoise.** Eventually you will come to a fork in the road, at which point rue Esquermoise branches into **rue de la Barre** and **rue Royale.** Turn right onto rue Royale to get to the *vieille ville's* hip bars, or turn left onto rue de la Barre to get to the Jardin Vauban and the Citadelle. The walk should take about 15 minutes.

hanging out

Adolescent skaters do their best to tear things up at **place de la République,** and the arty kids smoke joints and watch them after trips to the Palais des Beaux-Arts. The cement square doesn't appeal to all tastes, so other teenage Lillois flirt, people-watch, and sunbathe in the **Parc Henri Matisse,** off avenue le Corbusier in front of Gare Lille Europe with the appropriate musical aides, such as boom-boxes and guitars. The park is not the most aesthetically pleasing, having been recently replanted and redesigned, but Lille's teens aren't there for the scenery, but to see and be seen.

LILLE

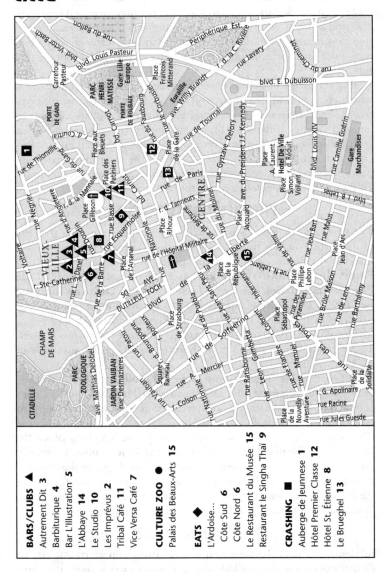

BARS/CLUBS ▲
Autrement Dit **3**
Barbiturique **4**
Bar L'Illustration **5**
L'Abbaye **14**
Le Studio **10**
Les Imprévus **2**
Tribal Café **11**
Vice Versa Café **7**

CULTURE ZOO ●
Palais des Beaux-Arts **15**

EATS ◆
L'Ardoise...
Côte Sud **6**
Côte Nord **6**
Le Restaurant du Musée **15**
Restaurant le Singha Thaï **9**

CRASHING ■
Auberge de Jeunnese **1**
Hôtel Premier Classe **12**
Hôtel St. Étienne **8**
Le Brueghel **13**

If the city's public spaces aren't green enough for you, head northwest of the rue Royale to the parks of the **Citadelle** [see *culture zoo,* below], including the **Bois de Boulogne** with its large pond and its exotic flowering **Jardin Vauban**—a great place to lounge or enjoy a picnic. The area enclosed within Citadelle walls is still used by the military, and tours can only be arranged through the Office de Tourisme [see *need to know,* below], but you can stroll around the rampart walls and admire the city.

In the city center, the pedestrian-only rue Bethune, which begins at place de la République, and the rue Neuve, make for fine strolling. The **Grand'Place,** the casual name for the collection of squares surrounding the flamboyantly Flemish **Baroque Vieille Bourse** (Old Stock Exchange) [see *culture zoo,* below] and the Opera, is where teens and kids, young and old, sit by the fountain to chat, flirt, and snack. (Though you probably won't spend more than 10 minutes here before you start to feel the grease in the air from the nearby McDonald's.) The Vieille Bourse is across the square from the Office de Tourisme, and directly in front of a fountain.

To hang with the local college crew, your best bet is to hit the bars, since that's where you're most likely to find them.

bar, cafe, and club scene

Bars cluster along rue Royale, a main thoroughfare of the *vieille ville.* The vibe at bars and clubs in Lille is decidedly intimate. Sit long enough at the

wired

The Central post office does not yet have an iMac for e-mail, though one may be installed by the time you read this. The best place to check your e-mail is **Le Smiley** *(2 rue Royale; Tel 03/20-21-12-19; 7am-midnight Tue-Thur, 7-2am Fri, 9-2am Sat, 4pm-midnight Sun, Mon; Cocktails 20F, beer 13F).* The more time you spend online, the cheaper it is. For 15 minutes, its 15F, an hour is 40F, and so on, which is fine because you might wind up staying longer than you expected, as the place has a comfortable atmosphere, cheap drinks, and friendly service.

There are a several good Internet sites about Lille. All of them are private, so they lack key information about post offices and other useful public information, and the information is not necessarily targeted to tourists but rather to people who actually live in Lille. Any gaps in information about Lille you can probably fill from the French national online yellow pages in English, ***http://wfa.pagesjaunes.fr/pj.cgi?lang=en,*** by specifying the Lille locality.

www.cityvox.com/home has a decent site about Lille that is suitably multilingual and updated reasonably regularly but lacks certain key tourist-type information. If you read French, ***http://lille.webcity.fr*** is also useful, with lots of articles, venue write-ups, and current happenings. For nightlife, study the reviews and venue listings on ***www.lechti.com.*** For each venue, it provides hours, phone numbers, and addresses. Overall, the site is nicely put together, easily searchable, and on-the-mark.

bar and someone is going to start talking to you. But at the same time, kids in Lille are practiced in that aloof art of maintaining a "cool" attitude. They tend to be more style-conscious than kids in other parts of provincial France, and thus maintain an aloof air that stylish sophistication demands.

Egon Schiele could have hung out at the **L'Illustration** *(18 rue Royale; Tel 03/20-12-00-90; 12:30pm-2am Mon-Fri, 3pm-2am Sat, 6pm-2am Sun; Cocktail 35F, beer 14F; MC, V)*. The twisted work of local artists competes with shriveled dried vines for wall space and the *garçon* and *serveuse* behind the bar are works of art themselves. Mixed groups of gay and straight kids recline in elegant states of repose, play chess, or flirt animatedly, while atmospheric down-tempo, dark trip-hop, and the occasional pop tune make the place feel warm and friendly no matter what the weather. Brunch is served at 10:30am Sundays.

While you could accuse the hiply elegant kids at L'Illustration of affectation, **Autrement Dit** *(rue Royale; Tel 03/20-51-02-22; 11am-2am Mon-Fri, 2pm-2am Sat, 4pm-2am Sun; Cocktails 40F, beer 14F)* is a bar that makes no fronts. Music from across the Channel, in the form of trip-hop and drum 'n' bass, is what comes first here. If you need something more than a deep rolling bass line, you might want to practice your pick-up lines on the cute *serveuse* or *garçon*. Occasionally the place hosts concerts, so inquire at the bar or peruse the weekly guide, *Sortir*, for details.

The tiny rue de la Clef, hidden behind the Opéra, is another interesting street for its record shops as well as its bars and clubs. Skaters, hip-hop-heads, and assorted disreputables frequent one bar in particular, the **Tribal Café** *(46 rue de la Clef; Tel 03/20-31-71-60 10:30am-midnight Mon-Thur, 10:30am-1am Fri, 10:30am-2am Sat, 2pm-10pm Sun; Beer 13F)* which, despite the dark drum 'n' bass and aggressive hip-hop, manages to be quite mellow, friendly, and easygoing. During the day, skaters rest their wearied feet in its booths, and underachieving school kids struggle with their homework assignments at the tables. This small cafe hosts a number of events, from concerts and DJ gigs to video installations and art shows.

All manner of beats are broadcast over the dance floor from the elevated DJ booth at **Le Studio** *(20-22 rue de la Clef; Tel 03/20-63-22-33; 10pm-4am Wed-Sat; Cocktails 40F, beer 25F)* every weekend. The crowd is young, hip, and dressed to leave earth, though not to be confused with the mannequins and androids that decorate the futuristic blue and silver interior.

In the center of town, a stone's throw from the **Palais des Beaux-Arts de Lille** [see *culture zoo*, below] on the place de la République, **L'Abbaye** *(119 blvd. de la Liberté; Tel 03/20 57-11-62; 8am-2am daily)*, a medieval-themed Art Nouveau-style bar/cafe, offers all your favorite European beers, and more than a few you probably haven't had the pleasure of trying. Varnished wood, bright fun colors, painted cloth ceiling hangings, tapestry-like cushions, and flora make the atmosphere light and easygoing. Though the .75-liter Jenlain is reasonably priced, and it's not uncommon to see the French drinking in the morning, ordering one at midday will draw smirks from the wait staff. Special bonus How-to-Look-Like-a-Regular tip: Don't bother looking for the switch for the light in the john—it turns on when you lock the door.

gay scene

Lille is a largely gay-friendly city and has a number of hip gay bars that also happen to be straight-friendly. The two-level **Les Imprévus** *(21 rue Royale; Tel 03/28-36-26-26; 3pm-2am Mon-Sat, 4:30pm-2am Sun; Cocktails 25-30F, beer 12F)* has regular techno and house nights with an attractive mixed gay and lesbian crowd hanging out both upstairs and downstairs. The downstairs features a large well-stocked bar; upstairs you'll find tables and chairs at which to sit and make mischief. DJs play regularly on weekends.

While other bars are content to serve their dull and drab mixed drinks, **Vice Versa Café** *(3 rue de la Barre; Tel 03/20-54-93-46; 11am-2am Mon-Fri, 2pm-2am Sat; Cocktails 35F, beer 13F)* has a superior collection of extraordinarily inventive cocktails to titillate and stimulate conversation. It's always fun when a flaming B-52 shooter singes an eyelash or better yet ignites the the hairsprayed 'do of the patron sitting next to you. The interior is nothing to write home about, but the bar is comfortable, friendly, and warm, and if you've got non-queer friends along, they're also welcome in this bar.

Only at a bar so aptly named **Barbiturique** *(4 rue Doudin; Tel 03/20-31-28-10; 11am-2am Thur-Sun; Cocktails 15F, beer 16F)* could the beer be more expensive than the cocktails. The interior of this hip new second-floor bar, lavishly decorated in shades of pink with faux-fur accents, might make you think someone slipped you a barbiturate, but fortunately the laid-back but animated clientele are more likely to be popping Valium.

culture zoo

Lille has a number of attractions to appeal to all sorts of tastes. In the 17th century, the city reached the peak of its power under the rule of the Dukes of Burgundy. It was during this time that the regal Vieille Bourse (Old Stock Exchange), and the star-shaped Citadelle fortress, which presides over the northern end of the Lille's vieille ville, were built. There is also the newer Palais des Beaux-Arts de Lille, Lille's Museum of Fine Arts, for rainy days.

Vieille Bourse *(Grand'Place):* Under the orders of Philippe IV, king of Spain, the architect Julien Destrée constructed the building in 1653. The attraction here is definitely the exterior: The red brick façade, garnished with sculptural flourishes, is a powerful testament to the power of the Flemish merchant class, while the interior, with its plaques dedicated to France's innumerable cadre of famous dead white men, is pretty forgettable. It's not really even worth going inside unless you want to buy some flowers or used books from the market that is held here [see *stuff,* below].

Citadelle *(Bus 14 or M. Porte de Douai; Gardens Free, Tours 35F Sun Apr-Oct):* Unless you're a military buff, you'll probably be content to take in the city from the ramparts, which are always open to the public [see *hanging out,* above]. In nice weather, you'll want to take some time to explore the beautiful parks that surround the ramparts. The Citadelle, built by Vauban, can be toured only on weekends from the late spring through early fall through arrangements made with the Office de Tourisme [see *need to know,* below]. You'll learn about the layout and construction of the fortress, and get to see the arsenal and the Governor's mansion.

Palais des Beaux-Arts de Lille *(18 rue Valmy or place de la République; Tel 03/20-06-78-00; 2-6pm Mon, 10am-6pm Wed, Thur, Sat, Sun, 10am-7pm Fri; 30F):* The three floors of the Palais house the largest collection of art in France outside of Paris. On the second floor, works by Dutch and Flemish masters as well as works by Delacroix, Goya, Raphael, and Courbet make the visit worth your while. Sculpture, a gift shop, and the bag check round out the first floor. The dimly lit basement has a bunch of local Medieval sculptures and bas-reliefs, which sit in the dim gray shadows like treasures waiting to be discovered. The sub-basement level has temporary exhibits, some worth your time and some not, which can only be accessed if you specifically pay for them at the front desk.

STUFF

For the intrepid shopper, Lille has a bit of everything. Rue Esquermoise and the other streets just north of the center's pedestrian walkways host a number of high-fashion women's clothing stores, hocking everything from Hermes handbags to six-inch stillettos. Some of the hippest shopping in Lille is on the rue de la Clef.

▶▶BAZAAR

Right on the Grand'Place, the inner courtyard of the Vieille Bourse, ringed by flamboyant arches and collumns, hosts a small open-air market from Tuesday to Sunday. When the weather permits, you can browse for flowers or used books.

▶▶TUNES

Three good record stores are clustered along the rue de la Clef. While records and CDs are not always the cheapest in Lille, you should stop in even if you don't intend to make a purchase: By talking with the owners, you'll find out about underground happenings around town that you won't find in *Sortir* or any other sources.

At **Stamina Records** *(17 rue de la Clef; Tel 03/20-31-88-50; 11:30am-7:30pm Tue-Sat; MC, V)* you can listen to and then buy a smooth selection of vinyl dancehall, reggae, dub, soul, groove, hip-hop, and drum 'n' bass. They have two turntables at the customers' disposal. The owner is also a DJ, and the front of the store is flyer-laden for those looking to get in on the underground goings-on.

Farther up the street, the butterfly-collared, flowery-shirted owners of **Key Records** *(54 rue de la Clef; Tel 03/20-51-37-79; 11am-5pm Mon-*

Sat; MC, V) are anxious to help you sort through bins of vinyl and CDs. Riding the waves of the retro trend, they've got a wide selection of both American and European *indé* (indie) rock, soul, funk, and pop music. Unfortunately, they do not have a turntable or a disk player to preview selections.

At the end of rue de la Clef, techno and house music find their home at **USA Import Music** *(14 place des Patiniers; Tel 03/28-36-28-88; www.usaimport.com; MC, V)*. While the name may suggest otherwise, it has a good selection of the most popular and current Parisian and French house, as well as lots of hard-banging techno. To listen to the records, you must provide a photo ID, and they'll give you a needle to put on the turntable.

If you're looking for a piece of vinyl that's rare or hard to find, try **Music Line** *(34 rue Royale; Tel 03/20-51-96-92; 10am-10pm Tue-Sat; MC, V)*, a block or two north of L'Illustration [see *bars, cafe, and club scene* above] in *Vieux Lille*. It's famed for its sometimes obscure stock and depth of selection of techno, house, and electro. You can listen as long as you like, and if you have a problem finding something just ask the staff. Just around the corner from the record shops on rue de la Clef, the **Hermès store** *(8 rue Grande Chaussée; Tel 03/20-51-44-51)* does the brand's briskest business outside of Paris. Established in 1837, Hermès is world reknowned for its leather goods and scarfs. Under the watchful eye of Jean-Louis Dumas, the fifth generation of the Hermès *famille,* the company recently introduced a ready-to-wear line, which you can check out at the rather opulent store.

EATS

Eating in Lille is an exercise in eclecticism, offering just about everything to please the discriminating gourmande, from the distinctively local Flemish cuisine to succulent Thai food.

Le Singha Thaï *(66 rue Esquermoise; Tel 03/20-34-38-86; 11am-2pm/6-10pm Tue-Sun; 204F for three-course meal)* should be a must for any visitor to Lille enamored of Thai cuisine. Before you can say "word," their tasty palate-cleansing *hors d'oeuvres,* in the form of fried toast with a gingered chicken fat, are placed on your table. This delicate concoction contains flavors that will be brought to full bloom over the course of your meal. The soup *Tom Yom Kung* includes shrimp, ginger, lemongrass, pineapple, and tomato, and also subtly suggests flavors that will show up in more robust dishes such as the duck in basil sauce. Order a dessert and you won't be disappointed.

Surprisingly enough, **Le Restaurant du Musée** *(Musée des Beaux-Arts, 18 rue Valmy; Tel 03/20-13-92-40; noon-2:30pm daily; Menus from 79F; MC, V, AE)*, housed in an ultra-modern glass and steel edifice facing the Musée des Beaux-Arts, serves fine, tasty Flemish cuisine with reasonable prix-fixe menus. Served cold, *potjevleisch* is a terrine of three meats: veal, pork, and rabbit; or chicken, duck, and rabbit, cooked with onions, garlic, white wine, lemon and tomatoes. On cold winter days, try the hot beef stew, *carbonade à la flamande,* painstakingly cooked in beer and onions, and slightly sweetened with a little brown sugar. The clientele consists of well-dressed collection of arty business types and tourists, and the service is swift. A lunch here is the perfect cap to a morning spent at the Musée.

For Flemish classics or southern French-Mediterranean fusion food, try the **L'Ardoise...Côte Nord** *(4 rue des Bouchers; Tel 03/20-63-95-51; 11am-2pm/5pm-midnight; Average entrée 45F; MC, V),* in the *vieille ville,* or its sister restaurant, **L'Ardoise. . .Côte Sud** *(22 rue de la Barre; Tel 03/20-51-23-45; Similar hours and prices; MC, V),* a few blocks south of the *vieille ville.* Though suffering from occasionally flighty service, these two family-run restaurants offer innovative seasonal menus that delight the palate. The Côte Sud's gazpacho garnished with watermelon and orange is smart, light, and fanciful.

crashing

Unfortunately Lille's hotel situation is not kind to the young, budgeted traveler. There are a wealth of hotels around the Gare Lille Flanders, but they tend to be seedy, sleazy, dirty, or an unhealthy combination of the three. Hotels also fill up in the town center, and rooms even in the unsightly hotels can be hard to come by, so your best bet is to reserve ahead.

While the building that holds the **Auberge de la Jeunesse de Lille** *(12 rue Malapart; Tel 03/20-57-08-94, Fax 03/20-63-98-93; 72F bed, 17F sheets; MC, V)* seems as if it was once an institution of some kind, its rooms (singles, doubles, and 6-person dorms) are comfortably clean (if not sterile), and the staff is helpful and courteous. The harsh 1am curfew, however, makes it a rather unfestive choice of accommodations. The free breakfast consists of stale bread, jam, and some cheese, and is served at the almost ungodly hour of 7am. Because most of the bars close at 2am, leaving early definitely throws a wet blanket on being able to really cut loose.

A decent budget solution is to stay at the **Hôtel Premier Classe** *(19 place des Reignaux; Tel 03/28-36-51-10, Fax 03/28-36-51-11; Single 155F),* tucked around the corner from the train station on an unseemly block. Say what you like about the sex shops across the street, but the hotel, though it embodies all the charm of a McDonald's, is very clean and new, with a kind, helpful staff. Every single room has a shower, toilet, and television.

The same, unfortunately, cannot be said of the **Hôtel St. Étienne** *(13 rue du Curé St. Étienne; Tel 03/20-51-82-51; 160F room with wash-basin, 210F with shower, 245F with toilet),* but what the hotel lacks in terms of cost-to-amenity ratio, it perhaps makes up for in its awesome location, less than a block from the cool nightlife of the *vieille ville's* rue Royale. The hotel has a slightly unkempt, dive-like feeling, and the beds are thinly mattressed, but the rooms are clean. And if you're feeling stressed about finding a place to stay at the last minute, chances are they have a room.

Another hotel that benefits from its central location is **Le Brueghel** (*5 parvis Saint-Maurice; Tel 03/20-06-06-69, Fax 03/20-63-25-27; 235F single with sink, 480F double with bath; MC, V, AE*). The rooms were renovated in 1996, with well-made coordinated furniture, but have a geriatric feeling that's reinforced by the fussy décor and the large elderly clientele. On the upside, the kind folks at the front desk are willing to go out of their way to make sure your stay is pleasant.

need to know

Currency Exchange You can exchange travelers checks at the **Office de Tourisme** or the **Post Office** and, before you do, you might want to make a little comparative survey of the two. The best way to obtain local currency is through one of the many **ATMs** that are open 24 hours a day on the street. There is one such machine at the train station.

Tourist Information The **Office de Tourisme** (*place Rihour; Tel 03/20-21-94-21; 9:30am-6:30pm Mon-Sat; 10am-noon/2pm-5pm Sun*) is five minutes west of the Gare Lille Flanders, just off the central pedestrian walkway, rue Neuve. There you can collect maps and brocheres, and book hotel rooms or guided tours of various sites around town.

Public Transportation Unless you decide to head out to the suburbs, you won't need the two-line subway system. You'll spend most of your time traveling by foot around Lille's tangled streets, so getting a map from the Office de Tourisme is essential.

Health and Emergency Police emergency: *17;* non-urgent police: *03/20-62-47-47;* ambulance: *15,* or go to **Centre Hospitalier Saint-Vincent** (*51 blvd. de Belfort; Tel 03/20-87-48-48; Metro Porte de Doual*).

Pharmacy Try the **Pharmacie de France** (*1 rue Faidherbe; Tel 03/20-63-11-11*), in the center of town.

Trains Lille has two train stations within seven minutes of each other. **Lille Flanders** (*place de la Gare; Tel 03/20-44-59-62*) handles all local and regional trains, such as the train to Amiens. **Lille Europe** (*Tel 03/20-55-57-16*) down the long elevated avenue le Corbusier, handles trains to Paris and the rest of Europe. The TGV departs for the one-hour trip to Paris at a cost of 203F, the four-hour trip to Amsterdam at 250F, and the 75-minute trip to Brussels at 113F. Trains to Calais depart from both Lille Flanders and Lille Europe.

Laundry There's a very central laundromat in the center of the student district: **Lavotec** (*137 rue Solférino; Tel 03/20-70-14-45*).

Bike Rentals Localille (*Place Rihour, Tel 03/20-85-25-66; or esplanade de Champs de Mars, Tel (cell phone) 06/88-65-10-55; 10am-7pm daily; 15F/hour, 30F/half-day, 45F/full day, 90F/weekend*), a well-inventoried bike rental chain, offers two branches in Lille.

Postal The **central post office** (*8 place de la République; Tel 03/20-12-81-00; 8am-7pm Mon-Fri, 10am-noon/Sat*) handles all the usual post operations.

Internet See *wired,* above.

everywhere else

amiens

This town of 50,000 was once a powerful medieval textile center; now it's a quiet town with quaint canals and leafy-green avenues. Come admire the largest Gothic cathedral in France, the **Cathédrale Nôtre Dame** [see *culture zoo*, below], wander through the 300 hectares of beautiful lush gardens and 55 kilometers of canals in the **Hortillonages** [see *hanging out*, below], and nose around the lively Saint Leu *quartier*, sandwiched between the Hortillonages and across the river from the cathedral. Save your dancing shoes for other parts of the country: Amiens' proximity by train to both Lille and Paris (some 105 minutes and 90 minutes, respectively) means that if kids want to really throw down and have a wild time, they hop a train out of town. However, since Amiens is a college town, it's not completely dead, either, and you'll find some interesting bars and clubs to check out while you're here.

Amiens is as solidly white-bread middle class as just about any medium-size French town, and its youth are as sophisticated as their comfortable upbringing requires. As the capital of the Picardie *departement*, Amiens has several small schools and universities, the most prominent of which is the Université de Picardie Jules Verne, a relatively young (30 or so years old) science and technology research university. The college kids tend to hang out in the Saint Leu *quartier*, where equally sophisticated high school kids studying to pass their BACs attempt (successfully) to blend in.

A good landmark in Amiens is its huge cathedral, right on the place Nôtre Dame. A couple blocks to the west of the cathedral is the place Gambetta, which marks the center of town; to the north of the cathedral are the canals, the Saint Leu *quartier*, and the **Parc Saint Pierre** [see *hanging out*, below]. The train station is south of the cathedral and is about a 10-minute walk from place Gambetta, where you'll also find the tourist office.

hanging out

The Saint Leu area with its pedestrian walkways is the primary place where kids hang out in Amiens. The best place to meet students is the gaslit cobbled square, **place du Don,** directly below the cathedral, and the **rue Belu,** both in the Saint Leu quartier. In winter, you can retreat inside the clubs, but in summer, the best place to be is sitting and sipping on place du Don. When you tire of that, stroll through the quartier itself. With its network of canals and antique cottages it evokes a true Flanders setting. The large student population keeps most of the clubs and bars in the neighborhood jumping until late. You'll see couples sneaking off into the gardens adjacent to the cathedral to make out. But if gardens and romance are to be the subtext of your visit to Amiens, you'll want to head straight to the 22 hectares of **Parc Saint Pierre** between boulevard Alsace-Lorraine and Boulevard Beauvillé and just north of the train station. It's the ideal starting point for a romantic visit to the nearby **Hortillonages,** a series of gardens that run along the winding canals that separate them from the city. Originally marshlands that were drained by the Romans in order to build an intricate system of canals, these gardens gradually grew and expanded over the centuries, helped along by the efforts of local residents. Today they take up 300 hectares (about the size of a neighborhood park) and are the source of the produce you'll find at the Thursday and Saturday market in Saint Leu. Sit by the idyllic pond under ivy-covered trees, watch kids do their thing in the playground, or just enjoy the day and the view of the cathedral. The most picturesque views of the cathedral, however, are not from the park, but from the boats of the **Society for the Protection of the Hortillonages** *(54 blvd. Beauvillé; Tel 03/22-92-12-18; 30F boat tour, Jan 4-Oct 10).* The tours vary in length and can be a bit much if you want to keep things low key, but can be just what the captain ordered if you want to rest your legs and woo your way to smooth sailing. Check ahead with the Office de Tourisme [see *need to know,* below] to make sure the tours are indeed running. From the Parc Saint Pierre, stroll southeast and cross the avenue d'Alsace Lorraine to the entrance and boat dock. Lose yourself in the quiet as the boatman glides you through a portion of the canals, past verdant gardens, with their flowering trees, quacking ducklings, and marsh grasses. If boats aren't your thing, walk through the Hortillonages on the tow path, Chemin de Harlage, which runs along the River Somme.

bar and live music scene

Sip a rum and lime cocktail and gaze at the carved wood masks and statuettes at the colorfully decorated **Café Bissap** *(50 rue St. Leu; Tel 03/22-92-36-41; 11am-3am; Happy-hour 6-8pm),* and you'll feel closer to Africa than to Amiens. Ragga, dancehall, reggae, music from the French Antilles, and even hip-hop thump from the sound system. On Wednesdays you can hear live African and Antillian music and drumming; Thursdays are for reggae, dub and dance hall, or Antillian *soirées;* Fridays and Saturdays

amiens

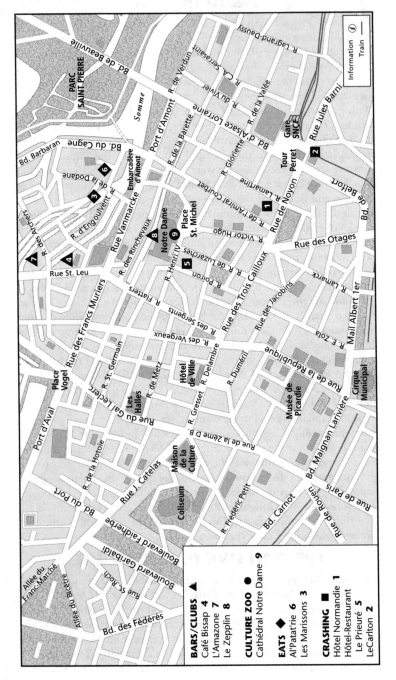

BARS/CLUBS ▲
Café Bissap **4**
L'Amazone **7**
Le Zepplin **8**

CULTURE ZOO ●
Cathédral Notre Dame **9**

EATS ◆
Al'Patat'rie **6**
Les Marissons **3**

CRASHING ■
Hôtel Normandie **1**
Hôtel-Restaurant
Le Prieuré **5**
LeCarlton **2**

Information ⓘ
Train —

feature various events. The searingly beautiful servers and the hip clientele just might make you feel more beautiful and hip yourself. Located just four blocks west of Parc Saint Pierre.

Just a few blocks north of Café Bissap, ferns, potted plants, and exposed teak and bamboo make **L'Amazone** *(14 rue des Archers; Tel 03/22-91-98-00; 9pm-2am weekdays; 9pm-4am weekends; Cover varies)* a true *bar d'ambiance discothèque.* Don't come dressed down, however—sneakers will earn you a distinct *"Non"* at the door. You'll have to have a pair of dress shoes, a bit of salsa in your blood, and samba in your slacks, though kids at L'Amazone tend to strike surprisingly sophisticated too-cool-for-dancing poses for Amiens' overall small-town feel—until the cocktails take control of the dance floor.

Prepsters and rockers will probably want to ignite their nights at **Le Zepplin** *(2 rue Blondes; Tel 03/22-92-38-16; Noon-3am),* which blasts the rock odes of the seventies and bustles with Amiens' young set. There are televisions over the bar for the attention-deficient, and the servers are reputed on occasion to parade around in kilts (in the traditional style: with no underwear). Next to the bar, there are also the ubiquitous (in France, anyway) pay-as-you-play electronic darts games abhorred by all true dart players. Easy to find, right next to (north of) the Cathédrale Nôtre Dame.

CULTURE ZOO

Amiens is kind of a cultural one-trick pony, but what a trick it is.

Cathédrale Nôtre Dame *(Place Nôtre Dame; Tel 03/22-80-03-41; 8:30am-6:45pm Easter-Halloween; 8:30-noon/3-6pm All Saints Day-Easter; Closed Oct and May 18; Admission free):* Constructed from 1220 to 1533, this is the tallest Gothic cathedral in France at an astounding 112.70 meters. Miraculously, the cathedral escaped both

20,000 LEAGUES under the ground

Attention all sci-fi aficionados: One of the forefathers of the genre, the great Jules Verne, made his home in Amiens. Yes, the man who brought you *20,000 Leagues Under the Sea* and *Journey to the Center of the Earth* lived and died here, and you can pay your respects at the **Cimetière de la Madeleine** *(on rue St. Maurice, a half-mile northwest of the town center; 9am-7pm daily).* Even in repose he gets his sci-fi dues; the monument on Jules's gravesite shows him coming back from the dead!

World Wars unscathed. As you approach it, you're dwarfed by its massive imposing structure and blinded by its bright, sandy color. The blinding is new—the front façade was meticulously cleaned in 1996 (to the chagrin of many), and the rest of the cathedral is due for a cleaning. The three front portals and swirling circular rose window merit a close examination. The 126 columns that support the interior are so amazingly slender that they make the space feel twice as large as it actually is. Check out the intricately carved stalls and choir screen. Whether you're religious or just admire the rich ceremony of the Catholic Church, you'll want to experience mass in the cathedral. Dominican masses are held in the mornings at 6, 9, 10:15, and 11:30, and Sacré Cœur services are at 10am Monday, Tuesday, Friday, and Saturday. You can also take a tour of the cathedral's towers. They are open from 10:30 to 11:30am and 2 to 6pm April through September; closed Tuesday and Sunday mornings and January 1, May 1, and September 25. If you have the lungs, it's worth it to climb the almost endlessly steep stairs to the top of the towers, because an amazing panoramic view awaits you at the top.

eats

The short rue Bélu is lined with restaurants that make for nice canal-side dining during the summer. They all have a similar menu of French classics, and their equally similar level of quality makes it hard to distinguish between them.

One standout, however, especially for vegetarians, is **Al'Patat'rie** (*25 quai Bélu; Tel 03/22-80-90-20; 11am-2pm/5-11pm Tue-Sat; Closed three weeks from Jan-Feb; MC, V*), which specializes in serving the potato in just about every way possible. The meals can seem a bit carelessly put-together, but they're affordable, tasty, and always filling.

Celebrating fresh ingredients and Picardy specialties, **Les Marissons** (*68 rue des Marissons; Tel 03/22-92-96-66; Noon-2pm Mon-Fri, 7-10pm Mon-Sat; Menus 110F; www.les-marissons. fr, MC, V, DC, AE*) is the kind of place you might want to take your parents. It offers truly elegant dining in a half-timbered 15th-century building situated right on the water, with a beautifully kept terrace and garden. Try the saffron crayfish with mixed vegetables and see if you can replicate chef Antoine Benoit's brilliance at home with the recipe available on the website. After an afternoon enchanted by the wildlife of the Hortillonages, the *pâté* of local duckling might break your heart, if just because it's so good.

crashing

For your two-star budget home base, **Hôtel Normandie** (*1 rue Lamartine; Tel 03/22-91-74-99, Fax 03/22-92-06-56; 155F minimum single, 255F maximum double*) offers comfortably bland rooms with televisions and clean functional fixtures. All rooms have showers, two come with full baths. Be prepared for thin walls—you may get to listen to what your neighbor is watching on television. Its location, five minutes from the station, the cathedral, and the Tourist Office, make it perfect if you made the mistake of overpacking.

Hôtel-Restaurant Le Prieuré *(17 rue Porion; Tel 03/22-92-27-67, Fax 03/22-92-46-16; 250F-400F)* is conveniently located directly adjacent to the cathedral. It also has a restaurant reputed for regional home-style cuisine.

If you feel like seeing how the other half travel, try the three-star **Carlton** *(42 rue de Noyon; Tel 03/22-97-72-22, Fax 03/22-97-72-00; Reception open 11am-11pm; 400F minimum single, 610F maximum double; AE, DC, V)*, where you can rub elbows with business-people and seniors. Ignore the looks your youthful face gets, and just enjoy the amenities of the primo cable network Canal+, newish bedding, somewhat generically muralled rooms, and beautiful bathrooms. They also have a restaurant that serves tasty but expensive food.

need to know

Currency Exchange Currency can be exchanged at **BNP,** *(Place Darnétal).*

Tourist Information The people in the **Office de Tourisme** *(6 rue Dusevel; Tel 03/22-71-60-50, Fax 03/22-71-60-51; 9:30am-6pm Mon-Sat, till 7pm summers, 10am-noon/2-5pm Sun, www.amiens.com)* make hotel reservations, dispense very complete information, and will go out of their way to make your stay a comfortable one.

Public Transportation City buses servicing the city of Amiens and the hamlets in the surrounding *département* are based in **La Gare Routière** *(rue de la Vallée, behind the Gare SNCF; Tel 03/22-92-27-03).* For bus information, call **SEMTA** *(Tel 03/22-71-40-00).* Bus tickets to anywhere in Amiens cost 6.50F, and are purchased directly from the driver.

Trains and Buses Amiens' seedy-looking but reasonably central **train station** *(Place Alphonse-Fiquet; 08/36-35-35-35)* is 75 minutes by train from Paris (116F), and 105 minutes from Calais and Lille Flanders (116F and 96F, respectively). Adjacent to the train station is an ugly strip mall from which **Couriers Automobiles Picards** *(Tel 03/22-91-46-82)* runs buses to Arras daily for 48F.

Boat Rentals Rent rowboats and small putt-putt motorboats from **l'Auberge de la Mère Boule,** *(Chemin de Halage, Tel 03/22-91-31-66).* Within a 15-minute walk northwest of the cathedral, it operates from a base directly beside the River Somme.

Bike Rental Société Buscyclette, *(Gare SNCF, Tel 03/22-72-95-95).*

Laundromat Net Exprès *(10 rue André, Tel 03/22-72-33-33).*

Postal The **post office** *(35 place Alphonse-Fiquet; Tel 03/22-71-56-99; 8am-7pm Mon-Fri, 10am-noon/2-5pm Sun)* runs all the usual postal operations, including the *Cyberposte* at the train station.

calais

The port town of Calais, situated 40km up the Côte d'Opale from Boulogne, is shrouded in gray and smog most of the year. It's most notable for the smothering masses of English day-trippers who visit from a mere 38km away via ferry and the Channel Tunnel (more affectionately known as the Chunnel) for the same treats they enjoy at home, but for less: booze and French *frites* (which they recognize as the latter half of fish 'n' chips). Calais' prevailing British-ness—it's been called "the most English town" in France—has a historical basis: in 1346, King Edward III seized the port town in the Battle of Crécy, and it became an English beachhead in the Hundred Years War. British troops remained in power until 1558 when the Duke of Guise managed to retake England's last colonial possession in France.

You won't want to spend more than a couple of hours here, as Calais is short on charm and there's really little to do—you come to Calais for transportation purposes, not to view ancient relics. But if you're only here for a few hours, you *can* make the most of it. If the weather's fair, head for the beach: Follow **rue Royale** toward the sea until you reach **rue de Mar.** At the end of that road, walk west along the coast away from the harbor until you come to the sands of Calais. It's fascinating just to sit here on the beach, watching the big ships go by. Back in the town center you'll find canals splitting the old part of town, *Calais-Nord,* from the newer part of town, *Calais-Sud.* Calais-Nord is centered on the **place d'Armes** and **rue Royale.**

Calais was virtually leveled by the bombings of WWII. After the war, reconstruction was haphazard, leading to dull architecture and petrochemical plants tainting the skyline. The only building in *Calais-Nord* to survive the bombings is the 13th-century **Tour du Guet,** still a landmark. The tower's belfry—completed a bit after the original structure, in 1926—rises 60 meters into the Calais cityscape. In *Calais-Sud,* the only building to survive the bombings is the **Hôtel de Ville,** the town hall at the juncture of rue Royale and boulevard Jacquard. If Calais has a "must see," it is Auguste Rodin's fabled bronze statue, *The Burgers of Calais,* standing in front of the Hôtel de Ville. Rodin cast this statue in 1895, honoring these brave but starving men who surrendered the keys of the city to the forces of Edward III. To save their city, they offered to give up their lives, but the English spared them.

The town's most worthwhile attraction is the **Musée de la Guerre (war museum)** *(Opposite the Hôtel de Ville in Parc Saint Pierre, Tel 03/21-34-21-57 10am-6pm daily Apr-Sept, 11am-5pm Wed-Mon Oct, Nov, Feb, Mar; Admission 25F adults, 20F students and children).* This former bunker served as the Nazi naval headquarters for the English Channel; today it contains exhibitions tracing the tragic events enveloping Calais in WWII. The collection includes WWII newspapers, models of battlegrounds, and bits and pieces of aircraft (both Nazi and Allied) shot down near Calais.

Another museum of note is the **Musée des Beaux-Arts et de la Dentelle** *(Rue Richelieu; Tel 03/21-46-48-40 10am-noon/2-5:30pm Mon, Wed, Fri, till 6:30pm Sat; 2-6:30pm Sun; Admission 10F; Free on Wed)*, which contains the city's pride, a collection of 19th and 20th century art, including some other sculptures (minor) by Rodin. Most of the art is by painters from Flanders, but there is Modern art as well, with works ranging from Dubuffet to Picasso. The museum lies in the center of Calais-Nord, sandwiched between place d'Armes and Parc Richelieu close to Église Notre-Dame.

If you're stranded in Calais for a day or a night, **Le Channel** *(3 blvd. de la Résistance; Tel 03/21-34-42-30; 12pm-2:30pm/7pm-10:30pm Tue-Sat, 12pm-2:30pm Sun; www.solemeumiere.com; Prix-fixe menus 89f-160f; MC, V)*, sandwiched between two reasonably decent restaurants facing Calais' port basin, serves a mean *foie gras*, as well as the delicious *fruits de mer* standards of the Pas-de-Calais region under the watchful eye of the Crespo family. If you must rest your wearied bones in Calais, the quaint, friendly family-run **Hôtel Pacific** *(40 rue du Duc de Guise; Tel 03/21-34-50-24, Fax 03/21-97-58-02; www.cofrase.com/hotel/pacific/index.htm; single 160, family double 330f; MC, V, AE)* has cozy (if-not-Manhattan-apartment-cramped) rooms for wallets that are on Kate Moss model diets. There's a bar on the premises and rooms have televisions that pick up English channels so you can get your fill of *Eastenders*.

need to know

Currency Exchange The English bank **Barclay's** *(129 blvd. LaFayette; Tel 03/21-96-63-95; Fax 03/21-34-80-58)* has a branch in Calais.

Tourist Information Located to the left of the train station, right past a park, the **Office de Tourisme** *(12 blvd. Cleménceau; Tel 03/21-96-62-40, Fax 03/21-96-01-92; 9am-7:30pm Mon-Sat, 10am-1pm/4:30-7:30pm Sun Jul, Aug; 9am-7pm Mon-Sat, 10am-1pm Sun Sep-Jun)* has everything you'll need for a brief visit to Calais. They'll even help you make a hotel reservation if you roll into town without one.

Trains Calais has two train stations: **Calais-Ville** *(blvd. Jacquard; Bus 7 from the docks; Tel 08/36-35-35-35)*, which is next to the Hôtel de Ville, and **Calais-Frethun** *(Tel 08/36-35-35-35)*, near the opening of the Chunnel. Calais-Ville handles all the local and regional train traffic; Calais-Frethun handles the **Eurostar** and high-speed TGV traffic. A TGV trip from London to Calais costs approximately 470F. The half-hour trip from Calais to Lille aboard the TGV costs 107F, and the 90-minute trip to Paris from Calais aboard the TGV costs approximately 274F.

Boat The best way to travel to the Queen's country is still the old-fashioned way, by ferry or by hovercraft. Though you might be tempted by the Freudian ride through the long dark Chunnel to reach the U.K., the ferry ride in the salty Channel air is much more pleasant, if only because you get to gaze at the sterling cliffs of Dover. **Sealink** *(Car-Ferry Terminal; Tel 03/21-46-80-00)* costs approximately 190F for the 90-minute trip, with bicycles free. **P&O Ferries** *(Car-Ferry*

Terminal; Tel 03/21-46-04-40) costs 200F for the similarly long trip, again with bicycles free. Tickets are usually good for return within a five-day period. **Hoverspeed** *(Hoverport; Tel 03/21-46-14-14)* costs 200F and gets to Dover in half the time of the ferry. Catch a free shuttle to both the Hoverport and the Ferry Terminal from the *gare.*

boulogne-sur-mer

As you travel north, the flat fields of Picardy dissolve into less-populated green hills, hollowed with gray quarries, speckled with the odd house or medieval château, ruffled with scattered trees, and edged by exposed rocks. Like most towns on France's Côte d'Opale, Boulogne-Sur-Mer was fortified with heavy stone ramparts in the 12th century to defend France against English invasion. A promenade on the remains of the ramparts offers beautiful views of the sun melting like butter over the town and the distant water. To get the most of those views, stay at **Folie Roger** [see *crashing,* below], the only bed and breakfast that's actually located on the ramparts, where you can watch such scenes from bed, then get up and pour yourself some tea, spread some preserves on your toast, and start your day off right with a proper continental breakfast.

Unlike the ritzy modern resort of Le Touquet, Boulogne-Sur-Mer used to be an important Roman outpost and continues to be a major hub for the French fishing industry. The port sits at the northwestern end of town; the Liane River runs south through town from there. The nightlife here is pretty much one bar, but what a bar—the tiny **Vole Hole** may make you want to delay your ferry for a few days. You can find enough things to do to occupy a day or two (or an hour or two while you wait for your ferry), including learning about all things fishy at the watery aquarium/museum **Nausicaä,** and wandering around quirky **Château Musée,** with its hodgepodge collection of dumpster-divin' finds [see *culture zoo,* below, for both].

hanging out

You'll want to spend most of your daytime hours within the rampart walls of the *vieille ville,* which sits on the east bank of the **Liane,** at the east end of **Grand Rue.** The newer part of the city has a slightly shabby, paint-peeling-at-the-edges quality that's only exacerbated when the weather turns gray and unfriendly. Unfortunately, during the height of the tourist season, the charming ivy-lined streets of the old town overflow with plump, middle-aged English day-trippers and their sullen offspring. (Sometimes it's nice to go where Americans are not consistently the loudest, most obnoxious tourists.) If you need a stinging sip of reality, perhaps after a rosy trip to **Nausicaä,** the aquarium/museum [see *culture zoo,* below], take a stroll just across the river to the work-a-day harbor, where you can trip out on the mammoth ship-loading equipment, huge warehouses, puddles of oil, and, the pervasive smell of dead fish.

Most French universities are decentralized and scattered throughout many neighborhoods of a city, but the one in Boulogne is especially fragmented. It's made up of about ten loosely defined academic "pods" scattered on both sides of the river. The most visible academic nugget is within the *Palais Imperial* (built by Napoleon), on the place Godefroy-de-Bouillon, in the *vieille ville,* but even it can't really be defined as a "campus." The place to meet students is in the area between the Haute Ville and the river, called **La Basse Ville.** The central hub there is **place Dalton,** at the union of the Grand'Rue and **la rue Thiers,** where there is a cluster of restaurants, cafes, bars where the student population kills time between classes.

bar scene

Nights in Boulogne are quiet and serene, so save your energy for livelier towns. There is one essential stop here: the tiny **Vole Hole** *(52 rue de Lille; Tel 03/21-92-15-15; 11:30am-1am Tue-Thur, till 2am Fri-Sun; MC, V),* the patron saint of which is bartender Pamela Cook. Afternoons, she bestows the nectar-like Angellus beer upon customers like a high priestess granting life to the sick. Evenings, the ever-so-sexy Richard serves wine and wit to an audience of admirers of both sexes. It's almost impossible to come here and not strike up a conversation with the person sitting next to you, both because the regulars and help are so friendly and because the bar is so damned small and intimate.

culture zoo

The cultural sites in Boulogne are limited but worth your time.

Nausicaä *(Blvd. Ste-Beuve; Tel 03/21-30-99-99; 9:30am-6:30pm Sept-June, 9:30am-8:00pm July, Aug; 68F adults, 62F students):* Part museum, part aquarium, part Cousteau-style documentary ode to the sea, this center for all things oceanic has been declared a UNESCO Center of Excellence for Marine Environmental Education. Its intricately shaped, 600-cubic-meter aquariums and interactive video projects really do put one in awe of the sea—an awe which, of course, lasts as long as it takes to read what the catch of the day is at the museum restaurant. There's a small room dedicated to the debates over the different types of fishing and the problems caused by over-fishing.

Château Musée *(Rue Bernet; Tel 03/21-80-00-80; 10am-5pm Wed-Mon Apr-Oct; 11am-4pm Wed-Mon Nov-May; 20F]):* The château contains a yard-sale–like collection of things that history has tossed aside—Egyptian antiquities, Greek vases, exotic Alaskan fishing gear, and medieval odds and ends—the crowning jewel of which is the largest hat ever to grace the greasy scalp of the short-in-height-but-tall-in-stature, champagne-swilling emperor, Napoleon. This is the museum for anyone who has ever practiced the fine art of dumpster diving.

boulogne-sur-mer

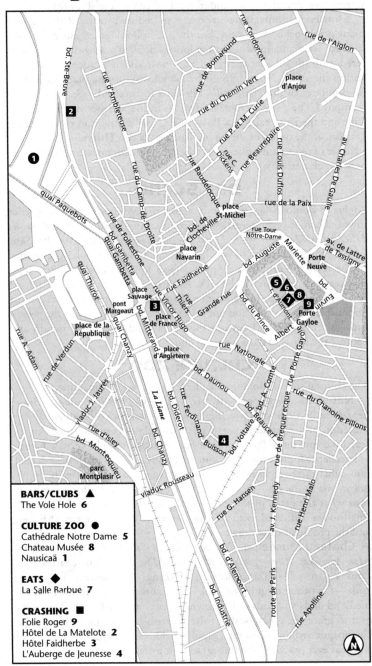

BARS/CLUBS ▲
The Vole Hole **6**

CULTURE ZOO ●
Cathédrale Notre Dame **5**
Chateau Musée **8**
Nausicaä **1**

EATS ◆
La Salle Barbue **7**

CRASHING ■
Folie Roger **9**
Hôtel de La Matelote **2**
Hôtel Faidherbe **3**
L'Auberge de Jeunesse **4**

Cathédrale Nôtre Dame *(Parvis Nôtre Dame; 9am-5pm Tue-Sun):* The distinctive elongated dome of this Neo-classical cathedral can be seen far out into the English Channel from aboard ships. The original church was built over the remains of a 3rd-century Roman temple which can be seen in the crypt today. The *basilique* was destroyed during the French Revolution but rebuilt from 1827 to 1866. It is an architectural bastard, borrowing something from Saint Peter's in Rome, something from Saint Paul's in London, etc. Its interior isn't spectacular, except for the tapered dome behind the choir, but it does contain a curious white statue of the Madonna and Child on a boat-chariot that was transported on its own wheels to Boulogne from Lourdes in the 1940s as part of a religious pilgrimage that took six year to complete. (Obviously there were a lot of stopovers on the way.) The collection of Roman ruins and assorted religious treasures kept in the crypt keeps growing as more artifacts are discovered beneath the building. It's worth a bit of your time to nose around.

Eats

In the old town, rue de Lille is home to a number of popular restaurants, all specializing in *moules et frites* (mussels and fries). **La Belle Barbue** *(22 rue de Lille; Tel 03/21-10-47-46; 10am-2pm/5-10pm Mon-Sat; Set menus 55-60F)* is not the most glamorous of the bunch, but the service is brisk, the fries crisp, and the mussels fresh. You can taste the sea in every one. Snag a table on the sidewalk at any of these spots, where you can people-watch.

Thanks to an oft-returning English clientele, **Cyrano** *(9 rue Coquelin; Tel 03/21-31-66-57; Noon-9pm daily, till 10pm Jun-Aug; Main courses 45-55F, set menus 51 and 88F; MC, V)* has decorated itself in a style that the owners identify as British. That means hunting scenes in wooden frames, lots of exposed wood, and a sense of conservative dignity. Menu items—especially the set-price menus—are among the most reasonably priced of any restaurant near the port. They include the north coast classics frogs' legs, duck thighs, faux filet in pepper sauce, and steamed mussels with French fries.

Set adjacent to the port, within a building that, as we want to press, was about to be expanded for the creation of 12 simple bedrooms, **Restaurant Hamiot** *(1 rue Faidherbe; Tel 03/21-31-44-20; Noon-midnight daily; Main courses 45-80F, set-price meals 87-169F; MC, V)* serves flavor-filled food that's well-known to many cost-conscious diners. Within a mostly Bordeaux and forest-green décor that the owners say was influenced by the tastes of Napoleon, it stocks lots of shellfish and seafood. The *plat du jour* is usually very generous in its portions—in many cases a meal unto itself.

crashing

The lively **Auberge de Jeunesse** *(Place Rouget-de-Lisle; Tel 03/21-80-14-50; 80F a bed, including sheets)* is located just across the street from the Gare Boulogne Ville, about 1km from the town center, and is staffed by kind, gentle folk. Though you may find yourself rooming with seniors, it doesn't get any cheaper than this in Boulogne. Rooms range from singles and doubles to 3-4-person suites. On weekends the place gets crowded with young people, so reserve ahead (HI card required).

The place to stay in Boulogne is the bed and breakfast, **Folie Roger** *(50m east of Porte Gayole on the ramparts of the vieille ville; Tel 03/21-80-97-66; 250F single, 295F double; No credit cards)*, housed in a pre-Revolutionary building on the ramparts of the *vieille ville*. Rooms are charmingly decorated with neat, new furniture, and the views of the town—punctuated by the 19th-century clock tower, which you can see from the higher rooms—can't be beat. The continental breakfast, included in the price of the room and served by Roger himself, hits the spot.

A slew of one- and two-star hotels is spread out in front of the Gare Maritime. The best bearer of the two-star standard is **Hôtel Faidherbe** *(12 rue Faidherbe; Tel 03/21-87-60-93, Fax 03/21-87-01-14; 230F single with shower, 320F doubles with bath and toilet)*. The lobby and downstairs breakfast room are strikingly strange, with red wallpaper, heavy red leather, and gold-colored highlights. *"Ouaaai!"* (yeaaah!) the caged bird in the lobby will squawk at you, but don't let the lobby or padded doors make you hesitate. Though the rooms are studiously bland, they have private baths, comfortable mattresses, televisions, and phones.

need to know

Currency Exchange Money is most easily changed at the **Société Général,** *(6 rue Victor Hugo; Tel 03/21-87-75-00)* or the **Banque Populaire** *(87 rue Thiers; Tel 08/20-00-09-20)*.

Tourist Information The tiny **Office de Tourisme** *(24 quai Gambetta; Tel 03/21-10-88-10, Fax 03/21-10-88-11; 8:45am-12:30pm/1:30-6:15pm Mon-Sat, 10am-12:30pm/2-5pm Sun)*, on the east bank of the Liane right near the port, has a startling multiplicity of brochures to suit just about every interest.

Health & Emergency Boulogne's biggest hospital is **Hôpital de Chenne** *(Rue Jacques Monad; Tel 03/21-99-33-33)*, 2km east of the town center.

Pharmacies One of the most central is **Pharmacie de Paris,** *(73 rue Thiers; Tel 03/21-31-44-37)*.

Bus BCD *(Place de la Gare; Tel 03/21-83-51-51)* runs direct lines to Dunkerque (a 90-minute ride) via Calais for 60F. Schedules are available at the adjacent hostel or by calling.

Trains Boulogne has two train stations, **Gare Maritime** *(Quai Thurot; 03/21-30-27-26)* near the ferry terminal and **Gare Boulogne-Ville** *(Blvd. Voltaire; 03/21-80-48-44)*, about a 1 kilometer walk from the center of town. The **Gare Maritime** offers service to Paris timed for ferry arrivals.

Boats Boulogne has Seacat hydrofoils operated by **Hoverspeed** *(Tel 03/21-80-62-79; Closed Nov 2-Mar 29)* to Folkstone, England that dock across from boulevard Gambetta. The fare is 200F, 40F extra for bikes; the trip is 56 minutes.

Laundry At the self-serve **Lavomatique** *(62 rue de Lille; Tel 03/21-92-71-56; 8am-7pm daily)* in the old town, you can do a load of wash for around 30F.

Postal Located off rue Faidherbe, the **central post office** *(Rue Religieuses Anglaises; Tel 03/21-99-00-33; 8am-7pm Mon-Fri, 10-noon/2-5pm Sat)* has all the usual postal operations, except the *Cyberposte*. The hostel [see *crashing*, above] across the street from the Gare Boulogne-Ville has an e-mail-equipped machine.

LE TOUQUET-paris plage

In the days before WWII, this resort at the mouth of the Canche Estuary was known as the "playground of kings." *Le Figaro* christened the town *"Paris Plage,"* or the "Beach of Paris," and a Yorkshire entrepreneur, John White, looked at its golden sands set against a backdrop of pine forests and decided Le Touquet was just the place to attract wealthy English vacationers and Parisians alike. The architecture looks like some faded French Hollywood from the era of Valentino and Gloria Swanson. With its elegant avenues and invigorating sea air blowing in from the English Channel, Le Touquet still lures many vacationers. The fine sandy beach is still there, as is much of the pine forest, as well as golf courses, a race-track, and a casino. The many retirees from Paris who have decided to relocate here are a greater presence off-season, while a more youthful air prevails in summer, when bikini- and Speedo-clad youths flock here for the beach life. As a result, in July and August the whole place can get very cruisy for both men and women.

neighborhoods and hanging out

Le Touquet's wide streets and avenues lined by monied suburban white stucco houses with tree-and-shrub-lined lawns extend out toward the hard-knocks suburb Le Touquet-Etaples. Between these two districts sits the stately Hôtel Westminister. From the Hôtel, the **rue Saint Jean** the town's main strip runs west to the small beach of imported white sand open to the public. Bring a towel, your most fashionable bathing suit, and a pair of shades so people can't follow your eyes as they linger on the Parisians you previously could only imagine in their swim suits. Other than the beach itself, the place to be is a waterfront park, **Aqualud** *(Blvd. Thierry-Sabine; Tel 03/21-05-90-96; Open Apr, June, Sept 10am-6pm; Jul-Aug 10am-7pm daily; All-day admission 85F, 3 hours 68F)*, right on the beach. It offers the best water sports facilities of all the English Channel ports. Half of the complex is outside and half inside, including a giant pool with a wave machine and three giant slides which can even be enjoyed on rainy days. At the **Casino rue Saint-Jean** *(26 rue St.-Jean; Tel 03/21-05-16-99, Fax 03/21-05-98-95; Must be 18 or over to enter)*, you can lose your money with the best of them. In the casino's stale, smoke-laden air, you can play the slot machines and roulette and practice your poker face in a stiff game of cards. Like all of Le Touquet, the place may leave you with a feeling that the good times started to dry up a long time ago.

bar scene

Le Touquet has various nightlife attractions, all of which seem to leave you aching for a shower the next morning to wash away the nicotine stain of sleaze. Only slightly livelier than a Jimmy Buffet slow jam, **Perroquet Bleu** (60 rue de Metz; Tel 03/21-05-69-79; Closed Sun) is just as you might imagine a bar named after a parakeet would be. The place has an Edwardian look and attracts lots of visiting Brits, young Parisians, and an increasing number of immigrants to France. You'll hear as much English as French among the clients. The umbrella-in-your-drink *tiki*-and-cocktails theme works in Le Touquet as it does in few places outside of the Caribbean.

If you gamble your way into the morning hours in Le Touquet and want to throw your money around in true Las Vegas, open-butterfly-collared-shirt-wearing, hairy-chested fashion, stop by the **Le Doral Night Club** (26 rue St.-Jean; Tel 03/21-05-16-99, Fax 03/21-05-98-95; Tue-Sat 10pm-6am; 60-80F cover) adjoining the **Casino rue Saint-Jean** [see *neighborhoods and hanging out,* above]. It has different house and techno theme parties on the weekends, replete with go-go dancers galore and *ooooh-la-la* interior decoration. Between June and September, the club is likely to have live music every night it is open; it is packed virtually every night with a party crowd. The rest of the year, it's busy on Thursday, Friday, and Saturday nights; the scene is much tamer on Tuesday and Wednesday, with recorded music and some dancing.

eats

A true Le Touquet institution, **Restaurant Perrard** (67 rue de Metz; Tel 03/21-05-13-33, Fax 03/21-05-62-32; 11am-2pm/5-11pm daily; MC, V) in the center of town on the street running parallel to rue Saint-Jean, has some of the best fish soup you'll have in France—so good, indeed, that they package it into jarred 6-packs. Dab in some of their spiced mayo, swirl it around with your spoon, and take a sip of heaven! The interior of the restaurant could best be described as a set piece from "Gilligan's Island," with fishing nets twisted around buoys and other set-sail-sometime-in-the-sixties paraphernalia. To really do it up right on your 3-hour tour of Le Touquet, you'll want to order the hilariously kitschy wooden boat chock-full of fresh seafood, which sails swoopingly to your table, navigated by one of the restaurant's fresh-faced *serveurs.*

Outfitted like a 1930s-style Art Deco brasserie you might expect in Paris, **Brasserie Paris-Plage** (31 rue St.-Jean; Tel 03/21-05-59-59; Main courses 75-120F; Fixed price menus 89-109F; 11am-midnight daily; AE, MC, V), offers a satisfying array of seafood, shellfish, and meats, all served with *bonhomie* and good cheer. Especially succulent is an Atlantic version of *bouillabaisse,* made with variations on the original garlicky version you'd expect on the Mediterranean. There are also steaks of all sorts, some of them garnished with pepper sauce.

Brasserie des Sports *(22 rue St.-Jean; Tel 03/21-05-05-22; Main courses 65-130F; Set-price menus 86-106F; Daily 8am-3am; V)*. The setting is conservatively decorated and relatively modern, except for an Art Deco-era bar usually crowded with young men and women who genuinely enjoy sports. Beneath a beamed ceiling, in a dining area that looks larger than it is thanks to lots or mirrors, you can enjoy dishes that include steaks, an Atlantic version of *bouillabaisse*, fish soup, marinated mussels, and *turbot* with *béarnaise* sauce. The cookery has flavor but no particular flair. It's inexpensive fortification for a night in the cool air blowing in from the Channel.

crashing

For down-to-earth accommodations, the comfortable **Hôtel Red Fox** *(Angle rue St.-Jean et rue Metz; Tel 03/21-05-27-58, Fax 03/21-05-27-56; 420-470F single, 470-520F double summer; 380-430F single, 440-490F double fall; AE, DC, MC, V)* in the middle of the rue Saint Jean, has spacious, comfortable rooms perfectly equipped for the prototypical hotel lounge lizard, from the bow-tied fox emblem to the comfy beds to the TVs with English channels.

Staying in Le Touquet isn't cheap, and not surprisingly, the classiest Le Touquet has to offer is actually quite classy. Fringed in lacy four-star opulence, **Hôtel Westminister** *(Ave. du Verger; Tel 03/21-05-48-48, Fax 03/21-05-45-45; 580-1050F single, 680-1150F double, 85F breakfast; AE, DC, MC, V)* in the heart of town, near the eastern edge of the rue Saint-Jean, has a host of amenities befitting the über-monied classes of England and France. You'll feel like you've finally arrived when you don your argyle socks, slacks, penny loafers, and cardigan and head to the bar to soak up some fine aged whiskey. You'll click your heels together when you see the rooms, let alone the lobby, decorated in turn-of-the-century schmaltz.

need to know

Currency Exchange ATMs are available at **BNP**, *(41 rue St.-Jean, Tel 08/02-35-63-21)* and **Crédit Lyonnais**, *(59 rue St.-Jean, Tel 03/21-06-29-01)*.

Public Transport There are no municipal buses in Le Touquet. Instead, there are buses that service villages and hamlets within the *département*, and some make stops to far-flung points of town on their way out of town. The nerve center of the town's bus routes, and their main depot, is beside the Marché Couvert, near Église Jeanne d'Arc. The company that runs the buses is **Compagnie Dumont Voyages** *(Tel 03/21-09-01-52 for information)*.

Tourist Information The **Office de Tourisme** *(Palais de l'Europe, place de l'Hermitage; Tel 03/21-06-72-00, Fax 03/21-06-72-19; 9am-7pm Mon-Sat, 10am-7pm Sun)* dispenses all the information you could hope for and also will arrange tours, excursions, and other touristy treats. The website, ***http://www.letouquet.com/fnotsi.html,*** also offers lots of info, and if you're traveling by car will even plot out itineraries depending on the speed at which you drive and your point of departure.

Health & emergencies There's no hospital in town, but the **Clinique des Acacias,** in the village of Cucq *(Tel 03/21-94-26-66),* 3 miles (5km) east of Le Touquet. To reach it from Le Touquet, take any of the buses from Marché Couvert marked Trèpied.

Pharmacy Try the **Pharmacie Quatre Saisons,** *(17 rue St.-Jean, Tel 03/21-05-04-66),* in the center of town.

Telephones Area code: 03.

Trains and buses Unfortunately, trains on the Paris-Boulogne-Amiens line stop only in **Le Touquet-Etaples** *(Tel 03/21-94-68-77),* Paris Plage's poorer, underdeveloped cousin, which is 5 long kilometers (3.1 miles) away. However, buses run the 10-minute gauntlet from Etaples to Paris Plage once an hour on the hour every day except Sundays and holidays for 10F. There is daily train service between Paris Gare du Nord and Etaples/Le Touquet Station. The journey takes 2 hours and 15 minutes and costs approximately 150F.

Boat Rentals Try **Base Nautique Nord,** *(Ave. Blériot, Tel 03/21-05-12-77).*

Bike Rental For bike rental, try **Boobaloo** *(38 rue St.-Louis (Tel 06/11-63-46-62),* which runs parallel to the rue Saint-Jean, in the center of town.

Laundry Try **Le Lavorama,** *(Rue de Metz, Tel 03/21-05-82-02),* in the center of town.

Postal La Poste, *(100 rue de Metz, Tel 03/21-90-75-70).*

champagne

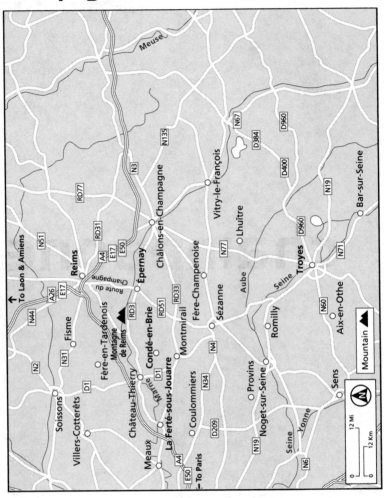

The low-slung, gently trestled vines of pinot noir, pinot muernier, and chardonnay grape plants that hug the chalky soil of Champagne—along with superb marketing and help from the likes of "Puffy" Combs, who feature frothing magnums of bubbly in their videos—have made this region one of the richest in France. But the flashy wealth that is often associated with champagne in the United States and Great Britain could not be more remote from the well-groomed landscape, whose monotony is only occasionally broken by gentle hills, rather modest country homes, and well-endowed châteaux. Unlike the French Alps, the Champagne country is not known for its outdoor activities; most people spend more time in subterranean champagne cellars than outdoors. Hiking and biking are the main activities from April through October. The best place to experience the natural beauty of this vineyard-studded region is Montagne de Reims or "Route de Champagne" [see sidebar in Epernay], a forested plateau south of Reims, where Pinot Meunier or Pinot Noir grapes—used to make bubbly—are grown. Though the champagne industry is dominated by several monster houses, such as Moët, Chandon, and Mumm, located in the towns of **Épernay** and **Reims,** most of the actual grapes are still grown by small farmers on small farms, away from the city and town centers. Unfortunately, both Épernay and Reims suffered serious damage during the Second World War. Only the champagne industry was able to revive the region, and today life around the region still very much revolves around the ground that produces the grapes and keeps the bottles filled with fermenting wine. Kids in Champagne tend to be either quite wealthy, part of the champagne agribusiness aristocracy, or lower-middle class, though small schools and universities in both towns bring in students from other regions of the country. Overall, Champagne lacks the sophisticated youth culture you find further east in places like Nancy or Strasbourg, or in Lille further north, but it is worth visiting if only for a taste of the finest, freshest champagne ever to grace your tender lips.

getting around the region

Centrally located within 150 kilometers of Paris, Champagne is most easily navigated by train. Buses are cheaper and connect most major towns of the region, but are less reliable and less pleasant to ride.

The tiny town of Épernay is the best base of operations in this region. Not only is it much friendlier and more attractive architecturally than the larger Reims, it's closer to Paris. Most of the grapes used in champagne pro-

TRAVEL TIMES

** By car	Épernay	Paris	Reims
Reims	:20**	1:36	-
Épernay	-	1:20**	:20**

duction are still grown on small farms surrounding the pint-sized town. For those with time and energy, biking the lush, hilly Route du Champagne [see **Épernay,** below] between Épernay and Reims is the best way to get a true flavor of the region. The trip winds through the Champagne countryside, and, depending on your route, could stretch the distance between Épernay and Reims from 27 to up to 75 kilometers.

bursting the bubble on bubbly

The French, ever finicky about language, have made it law that only champagne produced in the Champagne region can be truly sold as champagne. Take a tour of a champagne cave in Épernay or Reims and study the size of the bubbles that rise from the bottom of the complimentary glass that you receive at the end of the tour. The size of the bubble is an indicator of the quality of the champagne and the labor-intensive care put into the aging and fermentation processes. The smaller the bubble, the better the champagne.

The French dine with champagne as a complement to food, rather than shaking it up and spraying it around the room at bachelor parties. As the label tells you, champagne is bottled as *brut, sec, demi-sec,* and *doux,* each an indication of how sweet it is. Brut, the driest, is best consumed with meals; it is also the most common, stocked by liquor stores and Monoprix supermarkets alike. The slightly sweet sec is also consumed at meals, whereas demi-sec and doux are served with desserts. Unless you are Bill Gates, you may want to avoid pricey champagne labeled vintage or *milléssime,* the best and most expensive bubbly, made from grapes harvested in one banner year. Other cheaper champagnes are composed from a medley of fermented grapes over several different years, including the not-so-good harvests. Furthermore, champagne is very sensitive to temperature and light. An unopened bottle of bubbly sitting on the room-temperature shelf has a life of less than a week, and refrigeration won't solve your problem either—most refrigerators are too cold to maintain its crisp purity. But as you sip and contemplate whether you've ever had a real unspoiled glass of champagne, don't let the bubbles go to your head. After all, it was the French language that birthed the phrase *faux-pas.*

reims

Reims (pronounced *rahns*) is surrounded by graying suburbs, which unfortunately do not provide much contrast to the graying city center. Rebuilt during the fifties after the devastation of WWII, the city retains a bit of that nascent fifties easy-money feel to it, while falling short on charm and elegance. As opposed to the casualness of Épernay, people wear their wealth more often, and more blatantly, here. Dining and drinking tend toward the expensive side, especially in the more touristy areas. After visiting the cathedral and the town's famous champagne cellars—Mumm, Tattinger, Veuve Clicquot—and tasting the bubbly, you probably won't want to spend more than a couple of days here. Reims offers the best nightlife in all of Champagne, but compared to other regional capitals in France it is mediocre at best.

neighborhoods and hanging out

Reims, like most French towns, is laid out on a highly irregular gridlike pattern. The **Gare Centrale** is on west side of town, located along the boulevard that is **boulevard Joffre** to northeast of the *gare* and **boulevard Roederer** southwest of the gare. **Boulevard Géneral-Leclerc**—which turns into **boulevard Foch** to the northeast—runs parallel to Roederer and Joffre, and the narrow **Parc Driant** runs between them. At the north end of this boulevard-park sandwich lies the **place de la République.** Radiating roughly southeast from the train station across the boulevards and into town is the pedestrian walkway **place d'Erlon,** which intersects with the main thoroughfare **rue de Vesle** and then becomes **rue de Capcines.** Another main road runs southwest from the place de la

reims

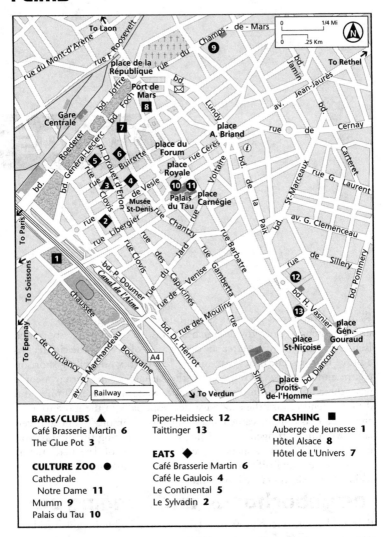

BARS/CLUBS ▲
Café Brasserie Martin **6**
The Glue Pot **3**

CULTURE ZOO ●
Cathedrale
  Notre Dame **11**
Mumm **9**
Palais du Tau **10**

Piper-Heidsieck **12**
Taittinger **13**

EATS ◆
Café Brasserie Martin **6**
Café le Gaulois **4**
Le Continental **5**
Le Sylvadin **2**

CRASHING ■
Auberge de Jeunesse **1**
Hôtel Alsace **8**
Hôtel de L'Univers **7**

République, which starts out as **boulevard Lundy** and becomes **boulevard de la Paix** as it runs away from the place. As you may have gathered by this point, streets in Reims have a tendency to change names after several blocks, so be sure and pick up a detailed map at the office de Tourisme, or be prepared to be very, very patient in finding your way around town.

On sunny days kids sun themselves in the cramped, green **Parc Driant-Estienne,** between boulevard Joffre and boulevard Louis Roederer across from the train station. If you're carrying a heavy pack, it's a nice place to sit and orient yourself before embarking on a walk into the city. **Parc Leo**

Lagrange is the largest park in central Reims, a grassy, tree-dotted haven favored by joggers and anyone looking for a respite from urban (and wine-related) life. A 15-minute walk south of the Cathedral Notre Dame, it's more English in its relaxed layout than French, and has none of the rigid symmetry and sculptures you might associate with formal French landscape design. For one thing, there's an entire section devoted to a children's playground.

bar and cafe scene

Beginning just across the street from the *gare*, the **place Drouet d'Erlon** is a long pedestrian walkway lined with bars and cafes. Walking down its recently renovated pavement, you will see the occasional street musician playing and tourists and *Reimois* alike there to see and be seen—which is not to say that there is much to actually see, besides the numerous bustling bars, brasseries, cafes, and restaurants.

During the summer, **Café Le Gaulois** *(2 place Drouet d'Erlon; Tel 03/26-47-35-76, Fax 03/26-88-16-61; 8am-midnight; MC, V)* has tables lining the corner of rue Condorcet and place Drouet d'Erlon, perfect for people watching. Crowded with people of all ages, it's a nice place to stop and grab a coffee or something stronger to calm shaken nerves after an intoxicating ride on the adjacent merry-go-round, and listen to the running water of the nearby fountain.

The Glue Pot *(25 place Drouet d'Erlon; Tel 03/26-47-36-46; 10am-midnight; MC, V)* is the place to go after a day of dainty champagne-sipping if you seek something suitably proletarian and not necessarily distinctively French. This dark-varnished English-style pub serves decent burgers and club sandwiches to accompany the football game on the telly. Like most English-style pubs in France, it tends toward the expensive side, with 51F burgers and 30F pints of Murphy's Irish Stout.

Just across the street from The Glue Pot, **Cafe Brasserie Martin** *(30-32 place Drouet d'Erlon; Tel 03/26-50-02-02; 7:30am-midnight, closed Sun; MC, V)* also has tables that spill out onto the place Drouet d'Erlon. If your cup of tea is a gigantic mug of beer, they don't get much larger than the hulking liter beers this cafe serves to unsuspecting tourists. Incidentally, artfully prepared entrées and elegantly arranged ice cream are also on the menu. Depending on the time of day, you may be subjected to radio's commercial Euro-trance blast-off while trying to down your fistful of beer.

If you need something to satisfy your sweet tooth, look for the blue awning of the family-run *patissier* and *chocolatier* **Le Sylvadin** *(10 rue Clovis; Tel 03/26-40-66-30; 7:30am-7:30pm Tue-Sat, 8am-1pm Sun)* off rue Vesle. Their house specialty, L'Antilla, a banana flambée tart, can't be beat.

The club scene here is tame and predictable, but if you really feel the need to get your groove on, there are a few options. None of these places have a dress code (jeans are totally acceptable), and the cover is about 50F across the board. They all start filling up around eleven or midnight, and close at 4 or 5am. **Le Boss** *(17 rue Lesage; Tel 03/26-84-95-14)* is probably the best bet, as long as you're into techno.

Aquarium *(93 blvd. General Léclerc; Tel 03/26-47-34-29)* and **Le Tigre** *(2 bis ave. Georges-Clemenceau; Tel 03/26-82-64-00)* attract a slightly older crowd and play more mainstream dance hits; Le Tigre has a funky decor going on, with old cars lining the walls, and is also open in the afternoons as a bar/cafe. **Les Lilas Club** *(75 rue des Courcelles; Tel 03/26-47-02-81)* is a gay and lesbian hotspot.

CULTUre ZOO

Reims' main attractions are the gorgeous Gothic spires of the Cathédrale Nôtre Dame and the mossy cellars of the many champagne houses, which the French call *caves*. After an awe-inspiring, if not spiritual, spin around the cathedral, a visit to one of Reims' **champagne houses** should bring one back to more worldly concerns. Just about all the houses have English-language tours of their cellars, but only some feature a complimentary tasting at the end of the tour. The houses listed below offer tours without appointments; prices range from free to 45F.

Cathédrale Nôtre Dame *(place du Cardinal-Luçon; 7:30am-7:30pm):* Built for the most part during the 13th century, seriously destroyed by fires during the First World War, and then by bombs in the Second, the Cathédrale was finally restored in part by a grant from the Rockefeller Foundation after the Second World War. Solemn saints, snarling demons, and all manner of creation play upon its stone exterior weathered by earth, wind, and fire. Despite the apparent wear and tear, its beautifully ornate spires still soar starkly above the dulled architecture of Reims. The interior, with its 16th-century rose window and 20th-century Chagall stained-glass, is just as dramatic as the exterior. It's best to check out the cathedral either late in the afternoon or early in the morning to avoid the crush of tourists.

Palais du Tau *(2 place du Cardinal Luçon; Tel 03/26-47-74-39; 9:30am-6:30pm July, Aug; 9:30am-12:30pm/2-6pm Mar-June and Sep-Nov; 10am-noon/2-5pm Nov-Mar; 32F):* The Palais du Tau was formerly the Arcbishop's palace, and now contains the sculptures that originally graced the exterior of the cathedral, and tapestries, sculptures, and some of the preserved pomp & circumstance from the French King's coronations that were once held in Reims.

Mumm *(34 rue Champ du Mars; Tel 03/26-49-59-70; 9-11am/2-5pm Mar-Oct; 25F):* Mumm is the word in champagne to many. Millions of bottles pass through their hands every year; 24 kilometers of caves filled with dimly lit cellars also house a small museum of 18th-century bottling equipment. At the end of the free tasting, you are invited to shop at the house store.

Taittinger *(9 place Saint-Nicaise; Tel 03/26-85-45-35; 9:30am-noon/2-4:30pm Mon-Fri, 9-11am/2-5pm weekends and holidays, Mar-Nov; Weekdays only Dec-Feb; Free):* Founded in 1930, this is perhaps the finest *marque* in French champagne and has some of the most picturesque tunnels, built over and inside the remains of a medieval abbey. If you only have time for one champagne cave, make it this one.

Piper-Heidsieck (*51 blvd. Henry Vasnier, Tel 03/26-84-43-44; 9-11:45am/2-5:15pm; Closed Tue, Wed Dec-Feb; piper@ebc.net):* One of the oldest houses, Piper has also taken the leap into the future by installing neat six-person electric cars to scoot you smoothly through the tunnels and soothe your weary feet. After your battery-powered tour, you can soothe your sober head with a free glass of bubbly.

stuff

After touring the cellars, if you'd like to ship some of the bubbly home, you can find good deals, especially if you decide to buy in bulk. The in-house stores generally take Mastercard, Visa, and American Express.

crashing

▶▶CHEAP

Situated next to Parc Leo-Lagrange, **Auberge de Jeunesse/Centre Internationale de Séjour** (*Esplanade André-Malraux; Tel 03/26-40-52-60; Fax 03/26-87-35-70; Reception open 7-11 am; Bus K direction Bezannes to Colin; HI membership required; singles 82F, a bed in a triple 65F; Breakfast 10F)* is a nondescript, bland hostel that thankfully tends to be quieter than most other *auberges.* The reception takes reservations, but as with all hostels you'd better show up early or risk having them given away. The place's two pluses are its park-side location and lack of a curfew. It lies within a 25-minute walk (2 miles) south of the town center. To reach it by public transportation, take bus C, A, or F from the railway station to the stop called "Théâtre." Then change to the H bus and go two stops to "Pont-de-Gaulle." Other cheap-o options include **Hôtel au Bon Accueil** (*31 rue de Thillois; Tel 03/26-88-55-74, Fax 03/26-05-12-38; Singles 100-150F, Doubles, 150-220F; Breakfast 25F; V, MC, EC),* just a five-minute walk from both the cathedral and the train station; **Hôtel Le Parisen** (*3 rue Perin; Tel 03/26-47-32-89, Fax 03/26-86-81-39)*; and **Hôtel St. Andre** (*46 ave. Jean-Jaures; Tel 03/26-47-24-16; Rooms with bath 199F, rooms without bath 119F),* near the city center, a 10-minute walk from the train station.

▶▶DO-ABLE

The one-star **Hôtel Alsace** (*6 rue du GI Sarrail; Tel 03/26-47-44-08, Fax 03/26-47-44-52; 105F single, 240F double; MC, V)* has clean, comfortable, homey rooms and is conveniently located just an 8-minute walk from the train station on a quiet residential street, away from the hustle and bustle of place d'Erlon. Of the hotel's 24 rooms, 18 have full bathrooms; the rest have only sinks. Downstairs is a bar/brasserie that serves tasty and cheap French standards, efficiently run by a kind patron and a squawking parakeet.

Other mid-range options include **Hôtel Crystal** (*86 place Drouet-d'Erlon; Tel 03/26-88-44-44, Fax 03/26-47-49-28, hotelcrystal@minitel.net, www.hotel-crystal.fr; Single with WC and bath 330F, single with WC and shower 300F, double with WC and bath 390F, double with WC and shower 320F, twin with WC and bath 390F, twin with WC and shower 330F; Breakfast 39F; V, MC, AE, EC)* and **New Hôtel Europe** (*29 rue Buirette;*

Tel 03/26-47-39-39, Fax 03/26-40-14-37, reimseurope@new-hotel.com, www.new-hotel.com; Singles 440F, doubles 495F, triples 565F; Breakfast 55F; V, AE), each about a five-minute walk from the train station. All rooms at both hotels have private baths.

▶▶SPLURGE

Though perhaps lacking in character and individuality, the three-star **Grand Hôtel de L'Univers** *(41 blvd. Foch; Tel 03/26-88-68-08, Fax 03/26-40-95-61; www.ebc.fr/hotel-univers; 425F single, 480F double; MC, V)* has modern, quiet, spacious rooms, outfitted with nice bathrooms, desks, extra pillows, cable television, and everything else you need to forget you're traveling. It's also about 100 steps away from the *gare,* just across Parc Driant.

Another option for those willing to splurge is the serene **L'Assiette Champenoise** *(40 ave. Paul-Vaillant-Couturier; Tel 03/26-84-64-64, Fax 03/26-04-15-69, assiette.champenoise@wanadoo.fr, www.chateau-muire.com; Doubles 585F; Breakfast 80F; V, MC, AE, EC),* a ten-minute taxi ride outside of the city center. All rooms have private baths.

need to know

Currency Exchange The best place to change money is at the **post office** [see below].

Tourist Information The easily exasperated workers at the **Office de Tourisme** *(2 rue Guillaume de Machault; Tel 03/26-77-45-25, Fax 03/26-77-45-27; 9am-6pm Mon-Sat, 10am-5pm Sun and holidays; VisitReims@netvia.com, www.tourisme.fr/reims)* dispense maps and information about Reims, but don't count on patience or a friendly face to greet you when you walk in the door of the medieval ruins that house the office. For more information about not-so-happening happenings in the city, you might want to take a peak at ***www.reims-web.com.***

Public Transportation Almost every **city bus** stops in front of the train station, but unless you are heading to the Auberge de la Jeunesse, you probably won't need to wait for one. Tickets are 5F and can be bought from the bus driver or in a *carnet* (book of 10) at the train station. **Taxis** *(Tel 03/26-47-05-05 or 03/26-02-15-02)* are expensive but available all night long.

Health and Emergency Police: *17;* fire: *18;* medical emergency response: *15* or *Tel 03/26-06-07-08.* The largest branch of the Centre Hospitalier Universitaire de Reims, the **Hôpital Robert Debré** *(rue Général Koenig; Tel 03/26-78-78-78; Bus A, N, S; www.chu-reims.fr),* housed in a monolithic building, is most easily accessible by taxi or bus. If you are going to do a walk-in, you might want to check their website to make sure you are going to the correct building. Directions and contact information are listed on the site.

Trains Trains depart from Paris's Gare de l'Est to Reims every two hours, passing through Épernay on the way. Buffeted by the inviting Parc Driant-Estienne, the **train station** *(Blvd. Joffre; Tel 03/26-65-17-07; 5:30am-11:30pm)* is a 15-minute stroll from the center of town.

Postal You can mail letters, check your e-mail, send faxes, and conduct other postal operations at the **post office** *(8-10 place Drouet d'Erlon; Tel 03/26-09-60-67, Fax 03/26-09-88-49; 8am-7pm Mon-Fri, 10am-noon Sat)* located at the northwest end of the Drouet d'Erlon pedestrian area.

Pharmacy The conveniently located **Pharmacie Bride-Charlier** *(36 place Drouet d'Erlon; 03/26-47-23-26; Mon-Sat 9am-7:30pm)* can handle all your over-the-counter medicinal needs.

Telephones Area code: *03*

Laundry The Laundromat at the youth hostel, **Centre International de Séjour** [see *crashing,* above] contains two washers and two dryers, and is open to absolutely anybody who wants to wash a load 24 hours a day.

epernay

The true body and soul of Champagne is Épernay, which is far cozier and more inviting to the traveler than the sometimes-brash wealth and boring modern architecture of Reims, the region's capital. Épernay has stood in the pathway of every main war in France since the 6th century, and the town has been demolished, looted, and burned more than a dozen times. The architectural glory of Épernay, created by champagne money, has gone into the faux-Renaissance mansions along avenue de Champagne and not the drab and dreary buildings found elsewhere in the town. Épernay has remained a true small town—only one-third the size of Reims—and lacks a sophisticated youth subculture, which makes things refreshingly unpretentious. While here, you'll definitely want to explore a champagne cellar or two (though after a while the tours get pretty repetitive) and probably buy a bit of the bubbly afterwards to enjoy on your next picnic.

neighborhoods and hanging out

Épernay is a small, comfortable town, and easily navigable. The train station is located at the place Mendés France, a green space encircled by a car roundabout. Just south of Mendes France is the place de la République, the town's central square. The champagne houses all sit along the predictably named **avenue de Champagne,** which runs south from the place de la République. Just south of République, between avenue de Champagne and **rue de Verdun**—which has its start at Mendes-France under the name **rue P. Sernard**—is the **Parc de Maigret.** A half-block east of the park is the **Marne River,** which cuts a neat little arc through the southest corner of town. The pedestrian zone around place des Arcades and place Hughes-Plomb houses the town's best bakeries and delis, where you can secure the makings of a picnic lunch. To reach these squares, walk west from place de la République along rue Général-Leclerc, turning south along rue Saint-Thibault. You certainly won't need any public transportation here.

On sunny summer days, small groups of kids congregate in the **Parc de la Mairie** to drink and smoke joints on the sly among blossoming flowers and picturesque, well-trimmed trees just yards from the Hotel de Ville, where city administrators doodle and scowl from behind their neat desks.

bar and café scene

Across the street from the **Parc de la Mairie** [see *hanging out,* above] and next to Le Chapon Fin [see *eats and crashing,* below], the laid-back, down-to-earth **Cafe-Bar de L'Hôtel de Ville** *(4 place Mendes; Tel 03/26-55-31-32; 7am-midnight)* plays sixties rock in a relaxed, no-nonsense atmosphere presided over by an understanding, chain-smoking bartender. A word to the wise: The bar's thoroughly tattooed, working-class clientele play smart snooker and pool, so unless you want to be hustled, it's probably better to play it cool than try to front on pool-playing skills.

For more fashionable, cafe-style drinking, sun yourself on the patio tables of **Le Progrès** *(5 place de la République; Tel 03/26-55-22-72; 6am-10:30pm Mon-Thur, till 1am Fri, Sat, and 3-10pm Sun)* at the place de la République. It's not exactly cheap, but the young, cute clientele get more attractive with each fleeting beverage. Note that they also rent cheap rooms *(Single 195F-225F, double 195F-285F; Breakfast 30F extra per person).*

The nerdier, less socially accepted kids hang out at the **L'Icone Cafe** *(25 rue de l'Hôpital Auban Moët; Tel 03/26-55-73-93; 9:30-midnight Mon-Thur, 9:30am-1am Fri, Sat, 3pm-midnight Sun),* where they check their e-mail, play foos ball, shoot at each other in simulated combat video games, and generally act pretty geeky. The space, with its spray-painted walls, resembles a community center or boys and girls club, rather than a real cafe or bar. Internet access costs about 1F a minute. To reach the café from the place de la République, head northwest for four minutes along rue Flodoard which links with rue de l'hôpital Auban Moët.

For concerts and DJ gigs, head to the **La Marmite Swing** *(160 ave. Foch; Tel 03/26-54-17-72; Bar open 10-midnight daily, concert space midnight-4am Tue-Thurs, midnight-5am Fri, Sat, and holidays; Closed Sun, Mon, and Aug).* At a half-mile south of the town center, avenue Foch is a bit of trek, but given Épernay's slender selection of nightlife, it can be worth it. Like all of Épernay, the neighborhood is safe and without incident, and bus 2 will take you right there.

culture zoo

Moët & Chandon *(18 ave. du Champagne; Tel 03/26-51-20-20; 9:30-11:30am/2-4:30pm daily; 40F):* While in Épernay, you should at least

epernay

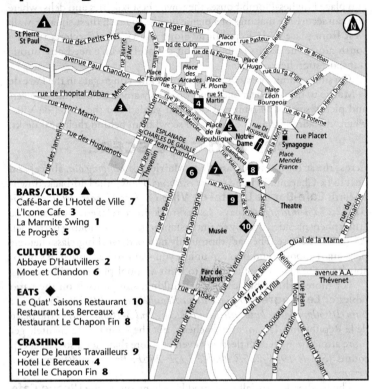

BARS/CLUBS ▲
Café-Bar de L'Hotel de Ville **7**
L'Icone Cafe **3**
La Marmite Swing **1**
Le Progrès **5**

CULTURE ZOO ●
Abbaye D'Hautvillers **2**
Moet et Chandon **6**

EATS ◆
Le Quat' Saisons Restaurant **10**
Restaurant Les Berceaux **4**
Restaurant Le Chapon Fin **8**

CRASHING ■
Foyer De Jeunes Travailleurs **9**
Hotel Le Berceaux **4**
Hotel le Chapon Fin **8**

visit the cellars here. You can practically smell the wealth of this place, founded by Jean Remy Moët in 1743, and a favorite of Napoleon, who, legend has it, used to lug cases of the stuff around for consumption before battle, except of course at his Waterloo, when the ill-fated emperor substituted Belgian ale for the bubbly. The video presentation in stereo-surround-sound is so cheesy it could give you mental indigestion, but the tours are led by witty Englishwomen imported especially for the task, whose anecdotes are sharp and even occasionally cut through the gloss of the Moët marketing strategies. For inquiries about touring other champagne houses in Épernay, inquire at the Office de Tourisme [see *need to know*, below].

From Moët & Chandon, a 10-minute walk to the east takes you to the second most visited house, **Mercier** (*70 ave. de Champagne; Tel 03/26-51-22-22; 9:30-11:30am/2-5pm Mon-Fri; 9:30-11:30am/2-5pm Sat-Sun; Closed Tues-Wed Dec-Feb; 30F*). If you didn't get your fill of bubbly lore at Moët & Chandon, this is the second most visited champagne house, offering a glitzy and commercial 45-minute tour of its 11 miles of tunnels in laser-guided trains. A novelty here is a giant wooden cask holding 215,000 bottles, making it one of the world's largest wooden barrels. Entire oak forests in Hungary were felled to create this 1889 extravaganza. You're rewarded with a glass of champagne at the end of the tour.

The third house of champagne interest is **Castellane** *(57 rue de Verdun; Tel 03/26-51-19-11; 10am-noon/2-6pm daily Apr-Oct; 30F cave tour with tasting).* You can't miss the landmark and ornate tower at the entrance. By now you'll know all about how champagne is made. What's left is the champagne museum here, featuring antique labels and bottles, even paintings depicting wine-making over the centuries. From corks to glitzy ads, it's all here, more than you ever wanted to know about champagne, even posters from the champagne parties of the '20s in Paris attended by those terrors of the flapper era, F. Scott Fitzgerald and his legendary wife Zelda.

Abbaye d'Hautvillers *(Just north of Épernay on D386; Tel 03/26-51-20-20; Open by appointment only; Free):* The faithful will want to visit

route du champagne

Armed with a map from the tourist office in Reims or Épernay, you can set out to explore Montagne de Reims or "Route du Champagne" [see the regional map] along a series of long hiking or biking trails called *sentiers de Grandes Randonnées* (or simply GR's) running along the top of the northern plateau of Montagne de Reims. Since you're not likely to have the time or interest to visit all of them, we recommend routes GR14 or GR141, each of which forms a loop of some 50 kilometers around the plateau's eastern section, taking you past fields of grapes and miniature towns like Verzy and Ay. While the route is a rather winding hilly affair, the frequent *dégustations* (tastings) at the smaller, often much friendlier champagne houses in these charming little villages make it worth it. You'll probably want to make Épernay your base of operations, because of its comfortable atmosphere. You can also store your luggage at the *bagagerie automatique* in the train station in Épernay, which as of the summer of 2000 you could not do at the train station in Reims. There are several train stations along the route as well, including the most convenient one at Verzy, which will take you back to Reims or Épernay should you tire out before finishing the full loop. For a more detailed look at the actual route, see ***www.marisy.fr/cote_des_bar/montagne.htm.***

this beautiful abby to pay homage to the tomb of that visionary monk, Dom Perignon, who helped perfect the art of champagne fermentation by utilizing Spanish cork to seal the bottles. In 1670, at age 28, he was appointed cellar master of the Benedictine abbey, a position which he held until just before his death in 1718. The grave of the innovator who reportedly "saw stars" when he first drank his bubbly invention, is in the church chancel at the foot of the altar, marked with a black marble tombstone. Founded in 660 by Saint Nivard, the abbey has been rebuilt several times over the centuries. The most interesting aspect of its parish church is a series of choir stalls with beautifully carved wood paneling, the work of the school of Philippe de Champagne from the 16th and 17th centuries. The site lies 6 km (4 miles) north of Épernay, and is reachable only by hopping on a school bus that's available only on Tuesday and Thursday mornings, and whose schedule is erratic. For info on this very dubious transit option, call the local bus company **STDM** *(Tel 03/26-65-17-07)*.

Note: The site contains a Church (Eglise d'Hautvillers) and immediately adjacent to it, the larger and more artistically prominent Abbaye d'Hautvillers. The tomb of Dom Perignon is visible within the church. The abbey section, however, is owned outright by Moët & Chandon, and is *not* open to the public.

STUff

Shopping in Épernay centers around the boutique-lined **rue du Général-Leclerc, place des Arcades,** and **place H. Plomb.** Shopping for champagne, it's often easiest to buy from the house store after a generous tasting, and almost all the houses take all major credit cards. Generally, champagne houses prefer that you actually take the tour of their cellars and taste the product before shopping at their boutiques. You can get the best discounts from the cellar boutiques when you buy several bottles at a time.

If you're looking for something sweet to complement a demi-sec champagne, or just to have for breakfast, the triple-threat *patissier, chocolatier,* and *salon de thé,* **Vincent Dallet** *(26 rue du Général-Leclerc; Tel 03/26-55-31-08; 7am-10pm, closed Sun),* serves all manner of mouth-watering pastries and chocolates, and wraps its tasty *tartelettes* in cute pyramidal paper packages.

eats and crashing

The name **Les Quat' Saisons** *(22 rue de Reims; Tel 03/26-51-80-42; Noon-2pm/7-10pm, closed Tue, Sat lunch; Lunch menu 59F)* says just about everything about this small, reasonably priced restaurant. If you can stand the restrained Martha Stewart atmosphere and New Age music, you'll be served dishes that feature simple preparation and deliciously fresh seasonal ingredients. To reach the restaurant, walk northeast from the place de la République, veering to your right at the intersection of rue de Reims, which lies to the southeast of the train station.

Around the corner from Les Quat' Saisons, the hostel **Foyer de**

parc de la forêt d'orient

The city of Troyes is known both as a center of well-preserved medieval and Renaissance buildings as well as home to natural park, **Parc de la Forêt d'Orient,** containing a trio of artificial lakes: **Lac de la Forêt d'Orient,** with its large beach and sailboat rentals; **Lac Temple-Auzon,** which lures fishermen; and the most fun-filled lake of all, **Lac Amance,** where in the summer you can rent boats or take water skiing lessons. To rent a boat, contact: **Nautic Évasion au Lac d'Orient,** *(Parc d'Orient, 10220 Piney; Tel 03/25-41-28-87).* They have sailboats, small putt-putt outboard engines, and larger boats which require a special permit the owners of the company can issue after some lessons are given and basic requirements met.

The **Parc de la Forêt d'Orient,** lying 20 miles east of the city of Troyes and 150 kilometers (94 miles) east of Paris, was created in the 1960s around these artificial lakes to regulate the flow of the Seine. The park sprawls across 170,000 acres of low rolling hills and lush meadows, encompassing nearly 50 small towns dotted with traditional Champenois buildings. In the northeast is a 1,200-acre bird sanctuary, plus an 80-acre animal reserve stocked with stag, wild boar, and deer. Literally hundreds of miles of hiking trails cut through this forest, going past the lakes and heading south to the Valley of the Seine. Along these trails you'll pass dozens of champagne vineyards as well as cider houses, since this is an apple-growing region as well.

At the entrance to the park, the **Maison du Park at Piney** *(Tel 03/25-43-81-90; 9:30am-12:30pm/2:30 to 6:30pm daily)* freely provides basic maps of the park not available at the tourist office in Troyes. Other more elaborate maps, as well as books on birdwatching, botany, and geology, are sold. Some trail maps indicate bus stops, where you can hop aboard and return to Troyes when you've had it with hiking. Buses operated by **Courriers de l'Aube** *(Tel 03/25-71-28-42 for information)* service the forest daily from Troyes, with stops near all three artificial lakes. A one-way bus fare costs 35F. Oh, and hunting season lasts from October to February, so if you go at this time, be sure to wear bright colors like chartreuse or sunflower yellow, and definitely don't show up if you look like a bull moose.

Jeunes Travailleurs (FJT) *(2 rue Pupin; Tel 03/26-51-62-51, Fax 03/26-54-15-60; 72F singles and doubles)* provides slightly small rooms for the cheapest price in town. From the station, it is fairly easy to follow the marked signs to the hostel, easily recognizable for its institutional look. Don't expect to find comfortable mattresses or quiet within its stolid walls.

For those who want ritzier accommodations and the taste of classically complex *Champenois* cuisine, head to the three-star **Hôtel-Restaurant Les Berceaux** *(13 rue des Berceaux; Tel 03/26-55-28-84, Fax 03/26-55-10-36; Fixed menus 220-300F; Single and double rooms 390-450F; Breakfast 50F extra per person)*, just steps away from the place de la République. Though meals tend to be smothered in snooty pretension, they are excellent, showcasing fresh, seasonal, and regional cuisine. Particularly fine are the roast leg of lamb in an herb-wine sauce and the *gallette* of guinea fowl in puffed pastry, served with potatoes. Ask the waiter to help you pick a suitable local wine or champagne to match your meal. Rooms here are spacious and comfortable, with cushy towels and mattresses, private baths, and individually accented with Champagne-related schmaltz.

For those craving more down-home French and *Champenois* cuisine, check the **Hôtel-Restaurant Le Chapon Fin** *(2 place Mendés; Tel 03/26-55-40-03, Fax 03/26-54-17; Closed Jan 1-Feb 9; Menus from 65F; Singles and doubles 230F; Breakfast 30F extra per person)*. This mom-and-pop establishment directly opposite the railway station serves cheap, super-filling, top-notch French classics, while the rooms vary in quality. Those facing place Mendés are bright, clean, standard one-star-hotel fare, with televisions, toilets, showers, and telephones; the cheapest rooms, above the kitchen, lack good ventilation and televisions, and are generally less well-kept. Note that there are slightly cheaper rooms available at **Le Progrés** [see *bar scene,* above]. There is also the **Hôtel St-Pierre** *(1 rue Jeanne-d'Arc; Tel 03/26-54-40-80, Fax 03/56-57-88-68; Singles 118F, doubles 150-200F, breakfast 28F; MC, EC, V)*, right near the St.-Pierre church in the center of town, a 15-minute walk from the train station. All but two rooms have private baths. Another option is the **Hôtel Le Chapon Fin** *(2 place Mendés-France; Tel 03/26-55-40-03, Fax 03/26-54-94-17; Singles 210F, Doubles 232F; Breakfast 25F; V, EC)*, located near the theater in the center of town. All rooms have WC and shower.

need to know

Currency Exchange The most convenient place to get money is from the **automatic teller machine** at the SNVB on place de la République. For the best rates, which often change, check the Tourist Office for a list of banks in town and compare their rates.

Tourist Information The kind folks at the **Office de Tourisme** *(7 ave. de Champagne; Tel 03/26-53-33-00, Fax 03/26-51-95-22; 9:30am-12:30pm/1:30-7pm Mon-Sat, 11am-4pm Sun, holidays Apr 16-Oct 15; till 5:30pm Oct 16-Apr 15; www.epernay.net)* dispense maps and highly complete information about shopping, eating, and staying in Épernay.

They will also reserve space in a town hotel but *only* once you physically show up in the office (no advance phone reservations will be accepted). There is a 20F booking fee (nonrefundable) for each reservation made.

Health and Emergency Police: *17;* fire: *18;* medical emergency response: *15.* The **Centre Hospitalier Auban Moët** *(137 rue Hôpital Auban Moët; Tel 03/26-58-70-70)* is located down the road from L'Icone Cafe, a half-mile south of the town center, at the periphery of the built-up part of the city. From the center, take bus 1.

Pharmacy **Pharmacie Herbet** *(24 place Auban Moët; Tel 03/26-55-32-26).*

Telephones Area code: *03.*

Trains Trains run almost hourly to Reims and several times a day to Paris. Eight trains a day run to Châlons-en-Champagne, the southernmost point of the "golden champagne triangle" whose other two points are Épernay and Reims. The **train station** is a five-minute walk north from the center of town at the place Mendés France.

Buses **STDM Trans-Champagne** *(Tel 03/26-65-17-07)* buses run daily to Chalons-en-Champagne from the parking lot of the train station. The trip takes an hour and costs approximately 30F. Buses also run to Paris and Reims.

Bike Rental You can rent a bike in Épernay at **Royer Cycles** *(10 place H. Plomb; Tel 03/26-55-29-61, Fax 03/26-55-13-57; 9am-noon/2-7pm Tue-Sat).*

Postal Fulfilling all the basic postal operations, as well as providing Internet access with an iMac, Épernay's central **post office** *(1 place H. Plomb; Tel 03/26-53-31-68)* is located off the rue St.-Martin.

alsace-
lorraine

alsace-Lorraine

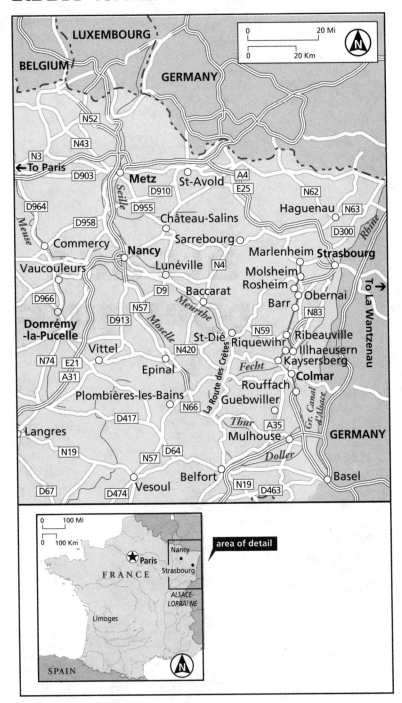

These two often-hyphenated regions are actually as distinct from each other as are their regional dishes. While **Lorraine** also retains a bit of German and Polish influence, it is as quintessentially French, as lean and elegant as *quiche,* the regional dish that has been adopted by the rest of France. As you travel farther east from Lorraine to **Alsace,** you'll notice something about people's proportions. Limbs lumbering. Breasts bulging. Cheeks puffed. Skin pickled white. The people of Alsace begin to resemble the sausages and sauerkraut of their famous Alsatian diet.

What the two regions do share, at least partly, is a long history of on-again, off-again German occupation. After the Franco-Prussian War of 1870–71, Alsace and the northern part of Lorraine were given over to Germany following the Treaty of Frankfurt. Germany gave the land back to France at the end of World War I, only to take up occupancy there again in World War II.

Alsace-Lorraine is somewhat off the beaten path for the average English-speaking tourist, attracting more of a Belgian and German crowd. Strasbourg particularly is practically overrun with plump Germanic day trippers, who have come to see how the sauerkraut and sausage across the border differs from their own.

With large student populations in both **Strasbourg** and **Nancy,** the capitals of Alsace and Lorraine respectively, nightlife thumps here harder than just about any place outside of Paris, and the region's proximity to Germany makes it far more accessible to larger European trends, and ripe for large concerts that draw kids from all over the continent. While certainly Strasbourg wins the heavyweight prize for most-populated, Nancy, given its small stature, boasts a vibrantly bohemian bar culture—you'll probably want to stop over and soak up a few 10F Stella Artois before making your way east to soak up Strasbourg's Alsatian wines. And if things get too pricey in Strasbourg, you can put your wallet on a diet by visiting **Mulhouse** and other small Alsatian towns. But beware of **Colmar:** as cute as it is, it's no bargain. It's worth a day trip, but linger only if you've got plenty of cash to lay down.

getting around the region

Both Alsace and Lorraine have punctual, well-run rail systems. Getting around the regions by train is easy and efficient. Strasbourg and Nancy, as regional capitals, are connected to Paris by trains that run every other hour or so. Metz is on the same rail line. Renting a bike in Strasbourg is fun, but not necessary, as the city is easily walkable; keeping a quick pace, you can cross the city center in twenty minutes. A bike would be ideal for exploring the nearby countryside.

▶▶ROUTES

Strasbourg is the perfect base for exploring Alsace, with day trips or overnight jaunts to Colmar and Mulhouse.

If you're coming from Paris and just want to hit the highlights, take the train to Nancy, soak up some *mojitos,* and party with the slacker students at any of the many bars and cafes. Then train it to Strasbourg for even more debauchery. In Nancy and Strasbourg, as elsewhere in France, the weekend is always more happening than the weekdays.

travel times

** TGV (Fast Train— more expensive * By car	Nancy	Strasbourg	Mulhouse	Colmar	Paris	Metz
Metz	:35	1:30	2:40	2:00	3:00	-
Nancy	-	1:20	2:20**	1:30**	3:00	:35
Strasbourg	1:20	-	1:00	:40	4:20	1:30
Mulhouse	2:15	1:00	-	:30	4:30	2:40**
Colmar	1:30**	:40	:30	-	4:55	2:00

alsace

METZ

Introduction

Metz, Lorraine's second largest city, lacks the vibrant student life, hip bar scene, and sophisticated cultural offerings of Nancy. People will tell you that Metz is the most beautiful city in Lorraine, but whether you believe them depends on how much you appreciate the architecture. The stone for the buildings in Metz's *vieille ville* was cut from the surrounding hills and has a sandy yellow tint, which washes over the city. The city seems to slumber in a lazy daze, and you get the correct impression that not much happens here. Certainly the colossal **Cathédrale St. Etienne** [see *culture zoo,* below] is stunning, but aside from that there's not much going on. Despite the presence of a small regional university, the Université Ile du Saulcy, there isn't a huge youth culture or nightlife scene here. The town is more well-known for its outdoor activities: canoeing, kayaking, and swimming along the Moselle and biking along the river's green banks.

neighborhood and hanging out

Metz's *vieille ville,* built in the 17th century and made up mainly of pedestrian streets, is encircled by **canals.** The central point of the *vieille ville* is the **Place d'Armes,** which contains the gorgeous **Cathédrale St. Etienne** [see *culture zoo,* below]. The principal pedestrian area, located southeast of the Place d'Armes, is the area around **Place St. Jacques** and, just west of that, the three linked squares, **Place St.-Simplice, Place St.-Louis,** and **Place au Quarteau.** All of these squares are lined with bars and cafes.

The canals connect to the **Moselle river,** which runs diagonally across the northwest side of town, and the planned **lake,** also on the west side of town. Between the lake and the Moselle, on its own little island, is the **Université Ile du Saulcy.** Both the lake and the river are about a 15-minute walk from the *vieille ville.* The **Gare Centrale** is on the south end of town, about a half hour walk from the *vieille ville.*

There are several outdoor spots where you'll probably want to hang out for lack of anything else to do: the **Esplanade,** the **Plan d'Eau,** and the **banks of the Moselle.** Like most French parks, the Esplanade, located just off Avenue Robert Schumann, is trimmed, chopped, and cleaned regularly, and has the usual crew of *boule*-playing, cigarette-smoking and lewd remark-making old dudes. At the east end of the Esplanade is the Plan d'Eau, a pond created in the 1960s at the same time bulldozers were channeling the road for the autoroute that flanks Metz's eastern periphery. Set a half-mile southwest of the cathedral, and containing waters channeled from nearby Moselle, it does not have any swimming area. Instead, there's a boat-rental kiosk that rents canoes, kayaks, and small sailboats: **Le Kayak Club,** *(Longeville; Tel 03/87-66-93-18).* The banks of the Moselle, while not exactly beautiful, do offer an escape from the stale atmosphere of the town, especially if you stay at the **Auberge de Jeunesse "Plage"** [see *crashing,* below] and take advantage of the free bikes to rough and tumble around the 22 kilometers (13 miles) of twisting paths.

bar, club, and live music scene

All the cafe-bars on Place St. Jacques (where almost all the cafes are) suffer from bouts of glacial-speed service, especially if you're sitting in the middle of the square. Learn to ignore the slow service and adjust yourself to Metz's speed, and you'll be much happier while you're here. Weekends, the clubs—if not always fun—still bounce with good vibes to the beats of hard techno and booty-booty house.

On the north corner of the square, **Bar St. Jacques** *(12 place St. Jacques; Tel 03/87-75-08-20; 8am-midnight; MC, V),* a city icon since the 1950s, is crowded every afternoon with local office workers, shopkeepers, politicians, and students. 18 year-olds and 50 year-olds alike appreciate the 12F glasses of wine and 11F beers.

Le Tunnel *(Place au Quarteau; Tel 03/87-36-62-99; 5pm-midnight daily, till 2am Fri, Sat; Beers 15F, Mixed Drinks 30F),* on place de Quarteau, has a large-screen TV, occasional drum 'n' bass pouring out of its CD stereo system, and loud, roughneck crowd of local twentysomethings livening up what is otherwise a rather normal bar.

If biker bars are more your thing, head to **O'Carolan's Harp** *(20 ave. Robert Schumann; Tel 03/87-21-03-33; 11am-2am Mon-Thur, till 3am Sat, Sun; 33F a pint of Guinness; MC, V),* between the train station and place St. Jacques. On some nights the bikes line up and down the block and the tough guys and girls down liters of beer before tearing off on their Harleys, Hondas, and Ducatis.

METZ

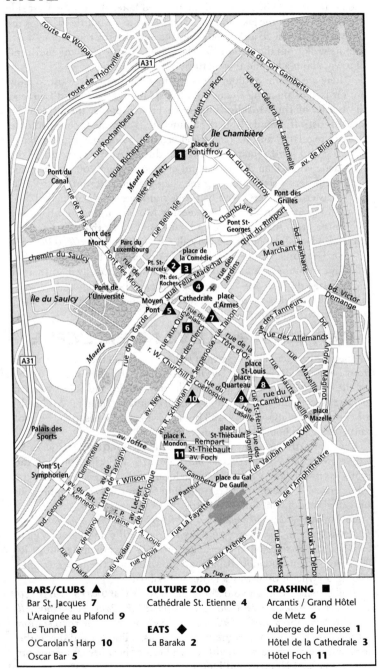

BARS/CLUBS ▲
Bar St, Jacques **7**
L'Araignée au Plafond **9**
Le Tunnel **8**
O'Carolan's Harp **10**
Oscar Bar **5**

CULTURE ZOO ●
Cathédrale St. Etienne **4**

EATS ◆
La Baraka **2**

CRASHING ■
Arcantis / Grand Hôtel
  de Metz **6**
Auberge de Jeunesse **1**
Hôtel de la Cathedrale **3**
Hôtel Foch **11**

Just down the street from Le Tunnel, the club-bar **L' Araigne au Plafond** *(16 rue des Mulliers; No phone; 11pm-5am weekends; 40F cover incl. one drink; No credit cards)* has Gothic techno-futurist aesthetic and plays hard-booty house Fridays and hard-techno Saturdays. It's fun to watch the French dance to hard house with vocals like "I'm a ho, you're a ho, all the ho's get on the dance floor." As a stranger, you'll probably stick out in what's a pretty small, closed scene. Even getting into the club requires a speakeasy-esque slight of hand: You have to knock on a closed door before the bouncer will let you in, even though they have the entrance monitored on closed-circuit TV.

CULTURE ZOO

Cathédrale St. Etienne *(Place d'Armes; 9am-5pm daily, Closed during services):* This hulking cathedral, the third tallest in France, towers over the place d'Armes. It was mostly built between the 13th and 16th centuries, with the entrance built in the 18th century, and has some amazingly beautiful stained-glass by Marc Chagall in the left transept.

Two blocks from the cathedral stands the **Musée d'Art et d'Histoire** *(2 rue du Haut-Poirier; Tel 03/87-75-10-18; 30F adults, 15F students; open 10am-noon, 2-6pm daily).* Set in a former 17th century Carmelite convent, this museum displays some of the most outstanding archeological finds in Eastern France. The relics evoke the Metz of Gallo-Roman times, when it was a major crossroads. Relics from the time of the Carolingian kings, when Metz again became a cultural center, are also displayed. Religious works of art are stored in the Grenier de Chèvremont, a granary dating from 1457. The top two floors of the museum are devoted to a less than impressive Musée des Beaux-Arts focusing on regional artists. There's also a small military museum, with some relics left over from the Napoleonic era.

That's it for museums. But before leaving the city, stop in at the small **St-Pierre-aux-Nonains,** *(rue Poncelet; Tel 03/87-76-35-64; exhibits staged Tues-Sun 2-6:30pm April-Sept; Open 2-6pm daily, closed weekends Dec-Mar; Free admission),* the oldest church in France, built originally by the Romans in the 4th century as part of a series of baths. Since then, the church has been rebuilt as many as four times, each time using parts of

wired

The most convenient place to check your e-mail is the small, but very friendly, **Netcafe** *(Cours St. Etienne; Tel 03/87-76-30-65; 1-6pm Tue-Sat; about 1F per minute),* located in the exact center near the cathedral. Like just about everywhere outside of select locations in Paris, they use the French keyboard on their PCs rather than the English QWERTY keyboard.

the older structures. Temporary exhibits are presented in the church, and a list of monthly concerts are posted on the door.

STUFF

Dreary as it is, Metz has a tiny, gay-friendly record store, **Hotbox** *(64 en Fournique; Tel 03/87-75-55-00; 11am-5pm Mon-Sat)* with a healthy stock of that funky disco house you can't help but tap your toe to—unless your hips start to sway first. It's close to Place St.-Jacques.

For those who like their beats harder, faster, and without vocals (unless they've got horribly mind-convulsing distortion), **Virus 34** *(34 rue Mazelle; No phone; 11am-5pm Mon-Sat)*, just southeast of place St.-Jacques, carries industrial, hardcore, and gabber on vinyl as well as a small assortment of street and skate clothing, CDs, and mix tapes.

EATS

At the foot of the cathedral, the relatively inexpensive **La Baraka** *(25 place de Chambre; Tel 03/87-36-33-92; 11am-2pm/5-11pm, closed Wed; Entrees from 50F; MC, V, AE)* has generous helpings of couscous and succulent lamb and vegetable *tangines,* friendly waiters who speak excellent English, a light, airy, arabesque interior, and a comfortable patio with a beautiful view of the cathedral. La Baraka is the perfect place to go if you're hungry after a day of bike riding. Sip sweet mint tea poured scalding-hot with that aerial precision and contemplate metaphysics as you watch the sun set on the cathedral.

Taverne de Maître Canteur *(22 rue des Clercs; Tel 03/87-75-01-18; Main courses 59-100F, Noon-midnight daily; AE, MC, V)* is the local branch of a nationwide restaurant chain whose goal is to bring the flavors of Alsatian cuisine to as wide an audience as possible. There's a special pride on the part of the staff about authenticity of cuisine. Beneath beamed ceilings in both upstairs and downstairs dining rooms, you can enjoy dishes including sauerkraut, foie gras, grilled steaks, and a local form of pizza, flammaküchs, made from crème fraîche and herbs.

Robe de Champs *(14 Nouvelle rue; Tel 03/87-36-32-19; Main courses 39-115F; 11:30am-3:30pm and 7-11pm daily; MC, V).* Set on the main pedestrian throughfare of town, amid a cluster of shops and other restaurants, this place has emerged as one of the neighborhood's most popular eateries because of the copious portions, rich desserts, and platters that always include roasted potatoes, served with the skins on (the French refer to them as "pommes de terre en robe de champs"). Don't expect appetizers, as they are not offered here. Instead, meals are composed of large platters piled high with foie gras, magret of duckling, smoked salmon, sauerkraut with sausages, or various preparations of fresh fish. Desserts are something of an event here, and include tarte tatin, crème brulée, and various forms of Alsatian pastries.

On the popular pedestrian square place St.-Jacques, **La Fine Mouche** *(2 place St.-Jacques; Tel 03/87-37-35-33; 9am-midnight daily; MC, V)* has expensive, mediocre Continental cuisine—a mix of Italian, French, and Mediterranean foods.

crashing

Surrounding the train station is a wealth of cheap, unsavory hotels, a 29-minute walk from the *vieille ville* and not that much cheaper than ones closer to town. Avoid these losers in favor of something closer to the "action."

Surprisingly, considering the sheer lack of visitors, Metz has two hostels. **Auberge de Jeunesse "Carrefour"** *(6 rue Marchant; Tel 03/87-66-57-33; Minibus A to Place d'Armes, walk three blocks north, turn right at the Place du Chan. Ritz and immediate left onto rue Marchant; Reception open 24 hours; 85F single paper sheets 17F; 3-4 bed dorm rooms also available MC, V; No curfew)* is the more centrally located of the two, only four blocks from the place d'Armes. It's noisy though, and has a horribly 1970s government-institution feel to it. Its only redeeming quality, depending on your state of mind and sexual preference, is the large number of girls who stay here, as it doubles as a center for young working women.

You'll definitely enjoy staying at the **Auberge de la Jeunesse "Plage"** *(1 allee Metz Plage; Tel 03/87-30-44-02, Fax 03/87-33-19-80; Bus 3, 11 to Pontiffroy; 7-10am/5-10pm; 85F bed, 100F single, free bicycles; MC, V)*, whose rooms and bathrooms are cleaner, more recently renovated, and better kept than the Carrefour's. At the Plage, you can sit and sunbathe or go for a bike ride along the Moselle, and you also have a better chance of meeting other travelers. If you're unused to sparse accomodations, the Plage is probably one of the better introductions to the hostel style of travel. It's also one of the only, if not the only, place you can conveniently rent a bike in Metz, and certainly the cheapest (it's free). From the Plage, you're about 15 minutes by foot from the place d'Armes.

Hôtel Foch *(8 Ave. Foch; Tel 03/87-74-40-75, Fax 03/87-74-49-90; 168-200F single, 200-310F double, breakfast 30F; MC, V, AE)* is ideally located, almost equidistant from the *gare* and the *vieille ville,* and has clean, standard, bland rooms, all with TV and basic cable. The two cheapest rooms, one with just a toilet (168F) and the other with just a shower (178F), face the Place Raymond Mondon. With the window open, the cool sounds of the fountain in the deserted square will soothe the budget-weary to sleep.

Arcantis/Grand Hôtel de Metz *(3 rue des Clercs; Tel 03/87-36-16-33, Fax 03/87-66-29-91; Minibus B to place d'Armes; 260F single, 520F double; MC, V)* is rather overzealously decorated with cheap wallpaper, fake potted plants, and neon lights in the foyer. The beds are comfortable, but the window panes are too thin to keep out the sounds from the raucous Rue des Clercs and adjacent Place St.-Jacques area. Like the Hôtel Foch, the rooms have basic cable as well as the excellent Canal+ channel. All the bathrooms are splendidly new, even while adhering to the rather invasive color scheme of the place.

The most romantic place to stay in Metz is the **Hôtel de la Cathédrale** *(25 place de Chambre; Tel 03/87-75-00-02, Fax 03/87-75-40-75; Minibus B to Place d'Armes; hotel-cathedrale.metz@wanadoo.fr; 300F single,*

560F double). With charming antique furniture, gold-leaf angelic flourishes, plush bedding, and beautiful cathedral views, all the rooms breathe rustic comfort, and the front desk will bend over backwards to ensure your stay is comfortable. Rooms with numbers ending in 02 or 03 have cathedral views.

need to know

Currency Exchange The best place to change money is at the **post office.**

Tourist Information The folks at the **Office de Tourisme de Metz** *(Place d'Armes; Tel 03/87-55-53-76, Fax 03/87-36-59-43; 9am-7pm Mon-Sat Mar-June, Sept-Oct; 9am-6:30pm Mon-Sat Jan, Feb, Nov, Dec; 9am-9pm Mon-Sat July, Aug; 11am-5pm Sun and holidays all year long; tourisme@ot.marie-metz.fr, www.mairie-metz.fr)* are remarkably helpful and knowledgeable about just about everything in Metz, dispensing brochures and maps. Though sometimes overburdened and understaffed, they admirably maintain their cool and kindness. They will make hotel reservations for you, but only if and when you physically show up at the office.

Public Transportation The only time you'll need to take the **bus** is to get from the train station to the Place d'Armes or to get to the **Auberge de Jeunesse "La Plage"** [see *crashing,* above]. Buses 3 and 11, direction Pontifroy, go to both places. The minibus B also goes to the place d'Armes. Stops, lines, and times are listed at most stops. The fare for bus or minibus is 4.50F.

Health, Emergency, and Pharmacies Police: *17;* fire department, *18.* Emergency medical service, *15;* ambulance service, *03/87-55-00-04* or *03/87-76-37-37.* **L'Hôpital Bonsecours,** *(Place Philippe Vigneulles; Tel 03/87-55-31-31) is the closest hospital to the center of town. For minor ailments or basic amenities, try* **Pharmacie Bisschop,** *(5 rue Serpenoise; Tel 03/87-75-04-75).* For information about **on-call hospital services** and **pharmacies:** *03/87-36-97-97.*

Trains Metz's *gare* is three hours from Paris-Est at a cost of around 240F. Metz is 40 minutes from Nancy; trains run hourly between the two cities, and a ticket costs around 50F. The train station is about a half-hour walk from the center of town.

Bus The **Gare Routiere** *(place Coislin)* is just east of the train station. From here, **Les Courriers Mosellans** *(Tel 03/87-34-60-06)* and **Les Rapides de Lorraine** *(Tel 03/83-32-34-20)* run buses to departmental cities as well as Nancy.

Laundry There are 24-hour laundry facilities at the **Auberge de la Jeunesse Carrefour,** in which you can wash and dry for 20F. There is a **Lavomatique** *(22 rue Pont des Morts; Tel 03/87-63-49-57; 7am-7pm daily; 30F per load; coin only)* just north of the university and west of the *vieille ville.*

Postal There is the **post office** *(8am-7pm Mon-Fri, 8am-12 Sat)* in the shopping center just off place St.-Jacques.

Internet [see *wired,* below]

nancy

If you visit only one city in Lorraine, it should be the capital. Nancy is a university town with a lot of cool student bars, the beautifully designed **Musée des Beaux Artes,** and the **Musée de l'Ecole de Nancy** [see *culture zoo,* below], a museum dedicated to the supple organic forms and designs of Art Nouveau. The city's architectural details—window gates, doors, and cornices—often pick up the themes of Art Nouveau, one of the most imaginative artistic movements of the late 19th and early 20th centuries.

Kids in Nancy may not be *chic* in a Parisian or Strasbourgian way, but, unused to overwhelming numbers of tourists, they're very kind and refreshingly unpretentious, and there is a bar in town to suit just about every taste in décor and music. Things are generally less happening in July and August, when the students clear out of town.

neighborhoods

Cultural life in Nancy is centered in the charming *vieille ville* centered around the Grande Rue north of the **place Stanislas,** a golden-gated square that was named after the last Duke of Lorraine, Stanislas Leczinski, and is just 10 minutes by foot from the train station. To reach Place Stanislas, turn right immediately as you walk out of the station. Head straight through the **place Thiers** and **place André Maignot,** and stroll up **rue St. Jean** to **rue St. Georges** through Nancy's shopping district, turning left on **rue des Dominicans.** The rigidly straight rue St. Jean and rue St. Georges in Nancy's *ville neueve* (new city) were designed and built by Stanislas in the 18th century, along with the square that bears his name, in order to bring Nancy up to speed with other European capitals.

nancy

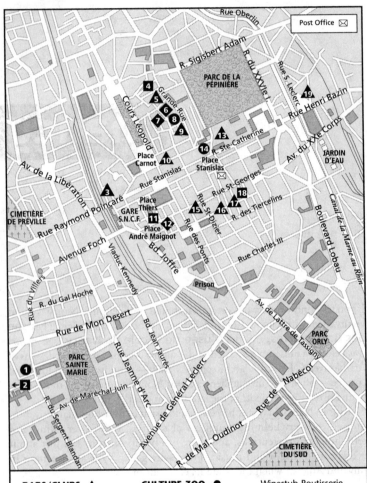

Post Office ⊠

BARS/CLUBS ▲
Blitz Cafe **16**
Kilo What's Bar **5**
Le 5eme Elemen **3**
Le Vertigo **15**
Les Caves du Roy **13**
Les 2 Palmiers **10**
Les Pietons **9**
Ó Circo **17**
Terminal Export **19**

CULTURE ZOO ●
Musée des Beaux-Arts **14**
Musée de l'Ecole
de Nancy **1**
Musée Historique
Lorrain **8**

EATS ◆
Cafe Pinnochio **7**
Restaurant Cam Ranh **12**

Winestub-Routisserie
Le Petit' Cuny **6**

CRASHING ■
Auberge de Jeunesse **2**
Grand Hôtel
de la Poste **18**
Hôtel American **11**
Hôtel de Guise **4**

hanging out

On pretty days, the place Stanislas is a good bet for a cup of coffee at one of the outdoor cafes, but the steady stream of German adolescents on school trips and senior tour groups during the summer will probably make you want to seek shelter elsewhere. Check out the gorgeous gold and iron gates on the square before you flee. Even if you're not interested in art, the **Musée des Beaux-Arts** [see *culture zoo*, below] is so gorgeous that you may want to pay just to stroll around its air-conditioned

wired

Nancy's Office de Tourisme operates the multilingual site *www.ot-nancy.fr*, offering everything from virtual walks around town to tasty recipes for *quiche lorraine*. The actual content of the site is more virtual than real, not updated very often, and in desperate need of copyediting by a native English speaker.

Linked to the Office de Tourisme's page, *www.2st.fr/Nancy*, a project by university students in Nancy, lets you take a virtual, albeit slow, walk down Grande Rue and see the interiors of many of the establishments located on the famous street.

Another website, *www.toutnancy.com*, has four modules, *"tourisme," "etudiant," "cyber,"* and *"cultural,"* but is really just a glorified yellow pages. Under the *"tourisme"* module you'll find a handy listing of hotel addresses and telephone numbers and a listing of the concerts you'll probably want to skip.

The best site for nightlife is *www.nancybynight.com*, which is slicker, if a bit slow-loading. It also has more complete concert listings, if fewer actual listings of bars and clubs.

If you're in eastern France for any length of time and looking to travel to any of the big European festivals, the cyber travel agency *voyages4a.com (2 Mgr Trouillet [place St.-Epvre]; Tel 0/83-37-99-66, Fax 03-83-37-65-99; voyages4a@voyages4a.com, www.voyages4a.com)* is located in Nancy. The website sells bus trips to just about every major festival in Europe for decent prices that include accommodations.

When the main post office [see *need to know*, above] is closed, you can check your e-mail at **Voyager** *(57 rue St. Jean; Tel 0/83-32-71-07; 9am-midnight Mon-Sat; 2-11pm Sun, holidays; 1F per minute Internet access)*, if you don't mind the constant background of video games, clanking pool balls, and table hockey slamming. Otherwise, the main post office's **Cyberposte** unfailingly offers the best rates for Internet usage.

galleries or take a seat in the room of your choice. Incidentally, the art on display is excellent as well.

The university infrastructure is scattered over about a half-dozen sites, divided by courses of study. The densest concentration of students—i.e., those studying literature, history, and economics—is in and around 23 bd. Albert 1 er, a contemporary looking university "campus" ten minutes walk north of Nancy's historic core—come and pretend to be studying abroad.

If you want a taste of nature—albiet tamed, manicured, and primped—go to the **Parc de La Pepiniere** *(Place Stanislas; 6am-9pm),* formerly the gardens of the Duke of Lorraine's palace. You'll find charming rose gardens, nattily dressed geezers playing *boule* (lawn bowling), jogging paths, and surely the most depressing display of caged animals being teased by annoying adolescents you'll see in all of France.

bar and live music scene

Nancy's charmingly unpretentious cafe and bar scene is basically sustained by the large student population, so as you might expect, the scene dies down a bit when students go home for the summer. While barhopping you may get the feeling that different bars are competing to have the strongest or strangest interior design; at first, you may feel like someone slipped something in your drink.

Giant ants crawl up the tapestry-covered walls of the **Blitz Cafe** *(76 rue St. Julien; Tel 03/82-83-77-20; 11am-9pm Mon, Tue, 11am-2am Wed-Sun; Shows 8pm; www.nancybynight.com/pages/blitz.htm; No cover),* in the center of town near the place Stanislas, where a mixed crowd of blacks, whites, straights, gays, scruffy types, and cool cats come to chill on the couches and occasionally hear a live *indé* (indie) band play. The friendly bartenders slap 15F brews down in front of you before you ask for them.

Just across from the Blitz Cafe is **O Circo** *(25 rue St-Julian; No phone; opens 11pm Wed-Sun; 1st and 3rd Wed of each month, cocktails with food and live music from 7pm; www.nancybynight.com/pages/circo.htm; No cover),* is a smoking live jazz "Ritmo Bar" ("rhythm bar", in the local parlance) that packs 'em in till there's hardly room to breathe. The bar is hot and smoky. With a faux vine-covered ceiling that seems like it's about to descend and devour the audience like a hyperactive flesh-eating orchid, but the 15F cocktails du jour and extremely live music keep the natives from getting restless and fan the fires of desire. Check the web or schedules available around town for show listings.

For those about to rock, **Les 2 Palmiers** *(64 rue Stanislas; No phone; noon-2am Tue-Thur, noon-5 Fri, Sat)* salutes you. Metallic fly creatures emerge from the harsh, exposed-brick walls of this otherwise no-nonsense, rowdy rock 'n' roll joint a few blocks east of place Stanislas. Kids play pool, and hard rock, heavy metal, and alternative rule. Wink at the cute indie rock girls, whose rocker boyfriends are too busy flexing their muscles to talk to them.

About two blocks from Les 2 Palmiers, **Le Vertigo** *(29 rue de la Visitation; Tel 03/83-32-71-97; 11am-midnight Mon-Wed, 6pm-2am Thur,*

five things to talk to a local about

1. ***Starsky and Hutch:*** This TV show was the introduction to American culture for a shockingly large number of French kids in the 18 to 30 age group. You'll be able to impress locals with your off-the-cuff impressions of David Soul as the steely, calm Detective Kenneth Hutchinson and Paul Michael Glaser as the tough-yet-vulnerable Detective David Starsky.

2. ***Friends:*** Believe it or not, this show is an underground hit in France, and whether you like watching television or not, sticking to such soft subjects maximizes the time you'll actually get to speak.

3. ***Racism and police brutality in America:*** Okay, maybe you always laughed so hard at *Friends* that you never noticed there aren't any black people on the show and that it could possibly be the whitest show on earth. The French notice, and they also notice when they see our boys in blue beating down suspects on the nightly news. Whatever your position, the French will want to discuss it.

4. ***The difference between northerners and southerners:*** Yet another chance to be lectured, but thankfully this lecture is often more humorous and good-natured than the previous. Open up the discussion by comparing stereotypes of northerners and southerners in the U.S. and France.

5. ***The mythology of New York City:*** More than any other city, New York has a firm hold on the collective cultural imagination of the French, so even if you've never been there, talk about how your grandma wept the first time she saw the Statue of Liberty. Your new French friend will probably remind you that it was France's backhanded gift to the United States.

till 5am Fri, Sat) is run by the Terminal Export crew [see *club scene,* below]. The interior, crowded with tables, couches, and chairs, is decorated in a sub-continental Asian-on-acid theme. There are intensely painted ceiling hangings and papier-mâché sculptures to trip out to, and plenty of cheap beer and crazed people to help speed along alcohol-induced hallucinations.

Another cluster of bars and cafes is north of the place Stanislas in the area around the place St. Epvre and Grande Rue. Decorated with tattered skateboards and skillful graffiti, the bi-level **Kilo What's Bar** *(1 rue St. Michel; Tel 03/83-37-33-09; 5pm-2am Tue-Sat, 3pm-11pm Sun; Happy hour 7-9pm; Drinks 20F www.multimania.com/kilowhat/kilo.htm);* is the only bar in Nancy that regularly features hip-hop, drum 'n' bass, and house and techno, making it a hangout for skaters, hip-hop heads, and assorted cool cats and nutters who regularly keep it packed until closing time. On weekends, the super-friendly bartenders keep things popping downstairs while local DJs drop tunes on the turntables upstairs.

club scene

While boozing in Nancy is indubitably a pleasure for many, whether you enjoy the club scene depends on your state of drunkenness and related finickiness about the kind of music you're willing to listen to. Located in a harsh, industrial, metallic basement space on Place Stanislas, **Les Caves du Roy** (*9 place Stanislas; Tel 03/83-35-24-14; Hours vary; Cover varies*) plays a French mixture of pop, electronica, and just about everything else you haven't heard since the late eighties. On the upside, the place fills up with pretty young things, and the dance floor lights up like the "Billie Jean" video. If you're traveling in a group or feel you cannot stand any more Euro-trash dance without heavy drinking, it's probably best to tell the beefy doorman that you and your friends (imaginary or not) intend to buy a full bottle of liquor to avoid paying the cover; after enough vodka, you'll definitely feel like Michael Jackson on the dance floor—and might even start to dance like him, too.

Next to the gare, **Le 5eme Element** (*4 rue Piroux; Tel 03/83-32- 20- 30; 11pm-4am Wed, Thur, 11pm-5am Fri, Sat; Cover 30F plus drink Wed, Thur, Cover 50F plus drink Fri, Sat, 30F plus drink after midnight*) features a futuristic neoclassical theme, plays slightly more respectable mixes of house and techno, and has a slightly older crowd of twentysomethings. In place of the frenetic, youthful "I don't care if I don't know how to dance" attitude of Les Caves du Roy, the Le 5eme Element substitutes a more sophisticated state of "I'm going to sit here and look cool" attitude. If you burn out at Les Caves du Roy, drop by the Le 5eme Element after hours to cool down.

Clubbers who are serious about their grooves should probably wait for a well-promoted and advertised DJ gig at **Terminal Export** (*2 rue Sebastian Leclerc; Hours vary; Closed July, Aug; Cover 50F*) is east of the Parc de la Pépinière. While the style of music varies from gig to gig, their reggae-dancehall-zouk-raggae-R'n'B-jump-up music nights rock as steady as you'll get in eastern France. The French love ragga, the cool cousin of réggae and dancehall, and ragga and dancehall have undeniably heavily influenced rap in France. You'll probably be the best dancer in the place: The French tend to dance rather unself-consciously, which is simultaneously refreshing, frustrating, and generally humorous.

arts scene

A couple of blocks north of the place André Maginot, the large warehouse-like arts space of **Le Garage** (*14 rue de Serre; Tel 06/09-88-65-74; 2-7pm Tue-Sun; www.legarage.aero.fr; Free*) blurs the lines between the plastic arts, the literary arts, and the visual arts. A seasonally themed program of talks by authors, poets, and artists; video and film screenings; and exhibits by conceptual, multimedia, and visual artists dissolve the traditional boundaries between the arts. Programs are available around town. They also have some cool permanent interactive multimedia installation art, a bookstore selling books on art and book arts (with a focus on marginal artists), and a hip cafe where you can sip coffee and discuss I. M. Pei's architecture or the sociology of the family fridge.

gay scene

Nancy's gay scene is pretty well-integrated into the other scenes and communities. Only one bar, the tiny but cute **Les Pietons** *(7 Grande Rue; Tel 03/83-37-32-08; 10am-2am Tue-Sat, 7pm-2am Sun; Happy hour 6-9pm; www.nancybynight.com/pages/pietons.htm; No cover)* is pretty much exclusively gay (male and female), and their occasional theme parties are hopping. The Keith Haring-esque interior and choice chilled-out techno and house make it the place to meet and greet like-minded girls and boys.

While not specifically gay, there are several places that are quite gay-friendly, such as the **Blitz Cafe** [see *bar scene,* above] and the pastel-colored **Cafe Pinnochio** *(9 place St. Epvre; No phone; 8am-midnight daily)* on place St. Epvre. It's a cool spot to grab a cup of espresso, sit in the sun, and admire the neighboring church, the beautiful people sitting next to you, or the cute guy serving your coffee.

CULTURE ZOO

The three must-see museums that should be included on any visit to Nancy are the Musée des Beaux-Arts, the Musée de l'Ecole de Nancy, and the Musée Historique Lorraine. They each offer several hours worth of wandering, sitting, and pondering, if not studying.

Musée Historique Lorraine *(64 Grande Rue; Tel 03/83-32-18-74; 10am-6pm Wed-Mon May-Sept; 10am-noon/2-5pm Wed-Mon, till 6pm Sun and holidays Nov-Apr; 20F):* Even the culturally deprived will enjoy this place, housed in a glorious ducal palace that, like the building of the Musée des Beaux-Arts, is almost as breathtaking as the works displayed. The museum features an enormous collection of 17th-century engravings by Jacques Callot, delicate Medieval tapestries, and works by Georges de La Tour, Jacques Callot, and Claude Deruet.

Musée des Beaux-Arts *(3 place Stanislas; Tel 03/83-85-30-72; 10:30am-6pm Wed-Sun, 2-6pm Mon, 30F adults, 15F students;):* Housed in an immaculately well-kept 18th century mansion, the Musée has an interior that's so drool-inducingly pretty, you might be tempted to buy postcards of the building rather than of the art. But after strolling past the calvalcade of Picassos, Modiglianis, Manets, and Utrillos, you'll probably want both. They also have interesting relating exhibits of contemporary artists.

Musée de l'Ecole de Nancy *(38 rue Sergent-Blandan; Tel 03/83-40-14-86; 2-6pm Mon, 10:30am-6pm Wed-Sun; 20F):* Designed and built by Eugene Corbin, the "patron saint" of Art Nouveau, this museum displays all manner of the slickly supple forms of Art Nouveau design, while focusing especially on design for the home. Principally on display are the works of Emille Galle, who basically orchestrated this original "multimedia" movement to counter the Neoclassicism rampant at the end of the 19th century. The museum also has works by other giants of the movement like Vallin, Daum, and Muller. The museum is opposite the Parc Sainte Marie.

STUFF

While Nancy isn't exactly a shoppers paradise, there are some finds to be had. Shops line the streets of the new town, in particular rue St. Georges and the area around place Stanislas. Just off place Stanislas, the *chocolatier* **Pierre Koenig** [see *eats*, below] has a sweet tooth-satisfying array of sensual milk, semi-sweet dark, and rich white chocolates.

On the place Mengin, off rue St. Dizier, there is an **open air market,** open everyday, that has everything from food stuffs to all kinds of cheap clothing and wacky accessories and odds-and-ends.

For those that want the coolest pair of scissors or neatest pen in class, **Número Huit** *(8 place St.-Epvre; 03/83-37-08-88; huit@wanadoo.fr; 10am-noon 2pm-7pm Tues-Fri, 10am-7pm Sat)* has quite a cool selection of Euro-modern-design art supplies and knick-knacks and doodads.

EATS

Two streets in Nancy are particularly good for finding neat spots to eat— **Grande Rue** and **rue des Marechaux.** The latter is closed to cars and lined with restaurants that post their menus on the street to make comparative shopping easy.

Though it has a distinctly sagging-in-the-center, middle-ager-cum-geriatric vibe, the food at **Winestub-Rotisserie Le Petit' Cuny** *(97-99 Grande Rue; Tel 03/83-32-85-94; 11am-2pm/4-11pm Tue-Sat; Piano music on weekend evenings; Entrees 66-150F)* is tasty in a meat-and-potatoes kind of way, and quite in keeping with Lorraine's Germanic-Polish history. A word to the wise: Unless you are of supreme meat-eating blood, order light. You get more than you bargain for here and might unintentionally eat yourself under the table.

For almost alarmingly authentic Chinese-Cambodian-Vietnamese food, try the **Restaurant Phenom Penh** *(16 rue St.-Dizier; Tel 03/83-37-22-75; Noon-1pm/7-11pm, closed Sun; Entrees from 60F)*, on the second floor of a commercial building two blocks southeast of place Stanislas. The relatively new restaurant, still unknown to much of Nancy, has satisfyingly greasy food that arrives sizzling at the table, cute Vietnamese-Thai decor, and mournful Asian synth-pop music that floats around the empty interior.

Cheaper and lighter than Phenom Penh, **Restaurant Cam Ranh** *(5 rue Clodion; Tel 03/83-35-85-19; Noon-2pm/6-10pm Tue-Sat; Lunch menu 67F)* is a small, family-run restaurant just off rue St. Jean that specializes in homey, tasty—if slightly bland—Vietnamese food. It has a

picnicking

For cheap but delicious takeout sandwiches, Nancy has two excellent choices, both within three and a half blocks of the perfectly picnickable tailored gardens of Parc de la Pepiniere [see *hanging out,* above]. People que up all the way down the block for gigantic, super-filling sandwiches and delicious, fresh fruit shakes at **Made in France** *(1 rue St.-Epvre; No phone; Noon-9pm, closed Sun; Sandwiches 20-40F)*. But sensitive eaters beware: You may not be able to finish before your stomach tries to fight the grease of the grill. Unfortunately, there's no toilet in Made in France or the park to which you can run; the closest friendly usable facilities are located in Kilo Whats [see *bars,* above]. Made in France's sandwiches are definitely not vegetarian friendly, and not for the timid.

For a smaller but more refined and tastier sandwich, go around the block to **Aux Delices de Palais** *(69 Grande Rue; Tel 0/83-30-44-19; Noon-3pm/7-9:30pm; Sandwiches 30-50F)* on Grand Rue. There's seating in a cute, kischy Keith Haring-inspired interior of delightful antique tables and chairs.

Because dessert is the most important course in any meal, picnics no exception, head across the place Stansilas to the ritzy chocolatier, **Pierre Koenig** *(42 rue des Dominicans; Tel 0/83-35-18-36; 11am-7pm Tue-Sat; MC, V)*, which has all manner of delicate dark and light chocolates, refined bonbons, and assorted delectables. With the assistance of the sympathetic staff, you can customize your own box to surprise and satisfy even a discriminating sweetheart's sweet tooth.

Finally, pick up wine, water, and other odds and ends for your picnic at the grocery store **Prisunic** *(20 rue St.-Georges; Tel 0/83-32-87-34; 9am-5pm Mon-Sat),* a couple of blocks south of place Stansilas.

small, loyal following of regulars, and you'll probably be won over by the charm of the elderly man who waits tables and by the satisfying feeling in your stomach after your meal.

crashing

Accommodations in Nancy range from budget hostels outside of town to student dormitories scattered around town to romantic, albeit rickety-floored, medieval aristocratic residences in the heart of the old town.

Four kilometers (2½ miles) from the city center in the suburban Villers-Les-Nancy, **Auberge de Jeunesse/Chateau Remicourt** *(149 rue* *de Vandoeuvre; Tel 03/83-27-73-67; Bus 26 to St. Fiacre, after 8pm, Bus 4, direction Brabois to Braschl; Bed in dorm room 82F, double with shower 97F per person incl. breakfast)* provides standard hostel fare out of a converted Medieval château, if you can handle the relative isolation. Buses stop running at midnight, imposing a kind of de facto curfew on those without other forms of transportation. Kids lounge and play soccer and other outdoor sports in the surrounding park.

If you don't mind sparse, thin-mattressed accommodations, Nancy's university student dormitories are located all around town and are empty every July and August. To make necessary reservations, call **CROUS** *(75 rue de Laxou; Tel 03/83-91-88-00; All rooms under 100F)*. The dormitories vary in quality, but all have that drank-too-much-the-night-before air about them. Cité Universitaire Medreville, the dorm where CROUS is headquartered, is the most convenient (within a ten-minute walk) to the center of Nancy.

Nancy has two aged but excellent and affordable hotels located close to the action on Grand Rue and St. Épvre. Resembling the church that sits adjacent to it, the beautiful **Grand Hôtel de La Poste** *(56 place Mgr-Ruch; Tel 03/83-32-11-52, Fax 03/83-37-58-74; 145F single, 255F double)* has a gorgeous interior, tasteful and comfortable rooms, and a pampering staff, and is about four blocks from place Stanislas. But beware of a rude awakening by the nearby cathedral bells, if you sleep lightly.

Located in a quiet, pre-Revolution countess's residence built in 1763, the charming **Hôtel de Guise** *(18 rue de Guise; Tel 03/83-32-24-68, Fax 03/83-35-75-63; 240F single, 390F double, breakfast 35F)* has wide marble staircases, tall mirrors in the hallways, and high ceilings in the rooms. Beds are slightly stiff, floors squeaky, and walls thin in the cheaper rooms; the more expensive, individually named rooms, however, are plush and pretty, with brocade furniture. All told, the hotel's convenient location near the cathedral, five minutes from Place Stanislas, makes up for its shortcomings.

The clean, modern, two-star **Hôtel Americain** *(Place Andre Maginot, Tel 0/83-32-28-53, Fax 03/-83-32-79-97; www.americain-hotel.com; 250-300F single, 350-500F double)* is between the train station and place Stanislas. Although a bit pricey, rooms here are comfortable and furnished with gold-leaf flourish, and there's a rustic stone basement dining room. If you've got a bit of cash to throw around and want a double or expensive single, ask for Room 7, which goes for 300F and has a nice view of the adjacent square and a ceiling-high mirror over a marble fireplace.

need to know

Currency Exchange Currency can be exchanged at the **Crédit Lyonnais** *(10 rue Saint-Georges; Tel 03/83-39-84-00)* recognizable by its magnificent art nouveau facade.

Tourist Information You'll find friendly faces, guided tours, and lots of helpful information at the **main tourist office** *(Place Stanislas; Tel 0/83-35-22-41, Fax 03/83-35-90-10; 9am-7pm Mon-Sat, 10am-5pm Sun and holidays Apr-Oct, 9am-6pm Mon-Sat, 10am-1pm Sun and holidays Nov-March; www.ot-nancy.fr, tourisme@ot-nancy.fr;). They will make hotel reservations for you, but only if and when you show up at their office.*

Public Transportation Nancy's public transportation system, **Allobus** and **Agencebus** *(3 rue du Docteur Schmidt; Tel 0/83-35-54-54; 7:15am-7:15 pm; Buses stop running at midnight, Fare 7F)* is fine for traveling to the suburbs, but totally unnecessary for transportation in the *vieille ville.* All buses stop at the central *gare* and place Stanislas, running down rue Stanislas and up rue St. Georges. **Taxis** *(Tel 0/83-53-20-20 or Tel 0/83-37-65-37)* are available 24 hours a day.

Health and Emergency Police emergency: *17;* **Ambulance:** *15.* For advice, information, and referrals you can go to the **Carrefour Santé** *(14 rue Saint-Thiébaut; 03/83-35-02-98, 9am-5:30pm Tue-Sat)* next to the commercial center Saint-Sébastien.

Pharmacies Pharmacie du Marché, *(89 rue St. Dizier (Tel 03/83-35-52-78).*

Airport Most international travelers opt for arrivals at the larger, better-equipped airports of Strasbourg, Brussels, or Luxembourg. Small aircrafts, most of them originating within France, can land at the regional airport of **Nancy-Metz,** *(Lieu-dit-Guin; Tel 03/87-56-70-00 for information),* which lies midway between Nancy and Metz, about 24 miles from either. Taxis are the only option, as shuttle bus service between the airport and Nancy is not available.

Trains The **central station** *(3 place Thiers; Tel 0/83-22-15-15)* approximately 800 meters from Place Stanislas is open 24 hours a day; the area immediately surrounding the station is, as usual, sleazy at night. Nancy is about three hours from Paris-Est; trains run almost hourly in both directions, stopping in Nancy on their way to Strasbourg. The fare to Paris-Est is about 223F; to Strasbourg, 128F.

Bus Line Out of the City Most buses leave from the **Gare Routière,** *(Porte Sainte-Catherine; Tel 03/83-32-34-20 for information),* within a three-minute walk from the Place Stanislas. Buses are maintained by "Les Rapides de Lorraine" and run to points within small villages of the surrounding département.

Bike Rental The most convenient rental spot is **Cyclotop** *(Central Station; Tel 03/83-22-11-63; 6:45am-9:30pm daily; Bikes 10F/hour, 20F/half-day, 35F/full-day; Mopeds 30F/hour, 300-500F deposit required),* right in the train station; the biggest in **Michenon** *(91 rue des 4 Églises; Tel 03/03-17-59-59; 9am-noon Mon-Sat; Bikes 110F/day; V, MC).* Both places will give you good info on the best local and nearby bike routes.

Laundry A short walk from place Stanislas down Grande Rue and through the Porte de la Craffe, there's a self-serve **Laverie Automatique** *(3 rue Jean Lamour; 7am-7pm daily; 30F per load, coin only)*.

Postal The **main office** *(8 rue Pierre Fournier; Tel 0/83-39-27-10; 8am-7pm Mon-Fri, 8am-12 Sat)* has Internet access as well as telephones, telegrams, and other postal services.

Internet see *wired,* above

Lorraine

strasbourg

Strasbourg is a cosmopolitan place, blending and fusing German and French traditions to create an amazingly interesting bar, cafe, club, and culinary culture. Given Alsace's historical tumult and its capital city's proximity to Frankfurt (two and a half hours by train), it's not surprising that Strasbourg is more Germanic than most of France. German day-trippers come to Strasbourg for the world-famous Alsatian wines, which are actually grown with German grape varieties. During the height of the summer tourist season, the most trodden areas of the city, *La Petit France* [see *hanging out,* below] and the quaint, dark-wood and white-stucco buildings cut by narrow crooked streets surrounding the cathedral, tend to be overrun with German teenagers on organized school trips. Across the L'Ill river to the south, the university neighborhood around Place Zurich [see *hanging out,* below] offers some smart nightlife.

With the headquartering of the European Parliament in the city, Strasbourg considers itself the "capital of Europe," and Strasbourgeois bristle at Paris's self-acclaimed dominance of French cultural life. In fact, nightlife and mass culture flower in Strasbourg and Alsace. Strasbourgers take their cultural clues from a different set of sources than Parisians. Discerning clubbers tend to diss the "French Touch"—the Parisian house sound—as overblown and overplayed. The music in Strasbourg and surrounding towns is more open to influences from European and international trends than the highly centralized, sometimes stratified, always self-absorbed Paris scene. Bossanova, house, down-tempo trip-hop, and even drum and bass can be heard on *Radio Bienvenue Strasbourg* (91.9 FM), Strasbourg's progressive radio station.

12 hours in strasbourg: "s" is for strasbourg

1. Start the day right by waking up early and breakfasting at the Place du Marché Gayot. The normally bustling pedestrian square lined with cafes, off rue des Freres, is peaceful, serene and beautiful in the morning.

2. Reserve a spot on a tour of the Kronenburg brewery [see *bar, club, and live music scene*, below] just outside of town a day, or at least a couple of hours, in advance by telephone. Then rent a bike and zip out to the brewery. The ride back will be twice as much fun after your token two beers. But go easy on the all-you-can-eat pretzels lest your stomach turn into one from the exercise.

4. Surf soundwaves at Soultronik [see *stuff*, above] for a couple of hours until you're forced to empty your wallet on the latest releases of the groovy German bossanova house of Ranier Trüby and funky fusion breakbeats, only pausing to try on some silkily synthetic shirts, chat with the hip cats behind the counter about tonight's most happening DJ gig, or talk to your friends at home (about what you're not missing) on the Web.

5. Stuff yourself (or swear you're becoming vegetarian) with supersized servings of sauerkraut and sausage and get sauced on Alsatian wines at the *winestub* Pfifferbrieder [see *eats*, above]

6. Slipping past the beefy bouncer and down the dark staircase of the Café des Anges [see *bar, club, and live music*, below], sit at the bar and strike up a convo about racism and police brutality in America over a couple of sleek vodka and tonics. *Right on!*

7. Slather your hair with gel until you look like Dieter, don all your best black clothing, and ask someone to pet your proverbial monkey at Le Schutzberger. "And now we dance!"

8. Steam in the sauna at Aux Trois Roses [see *crashing*, above] with your newfound French fling, and impress her/him with the color-coordinated towels and the linens on the super-comfy beds.

neighborhoods

The center of Strasbourg is a tear drop-shaped island, enclosed by canals and the **Ill River.** Many of the streets in the center are quite narrow and still paved in cobblestone. Canals carve up the central neighborhood of **La Petite France,** with its pink pastel buildings and winding streets, at

strasbourg

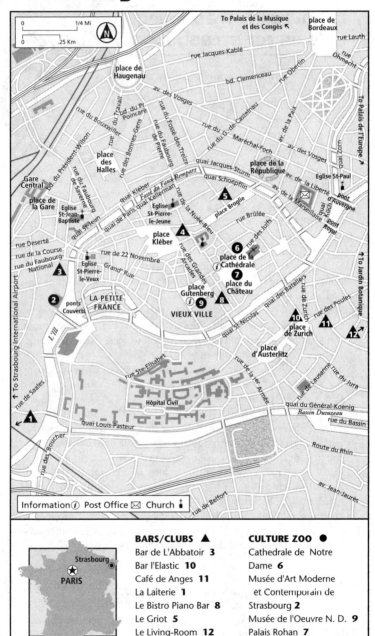

To Palais de la Musique et des Congès

place de Bordeaux

rue Lauth

rue Onmacht

rue Jacques-Kablé

place de Haugenau

bd. Clemenceau

rue Oberlin

av. des Vosges

rue du Travail

rue du Bouxwiller

rue du Pr. Poincaré

rue du Faubourg de Pierre

rue des bonnes Gens

rue du Gl.-de-Castelnau

av. de la Paix

To Palais de l'Europe

rue du Maréchal-Foch

av. des Vosges

rue du Président-Wilson

rue du Faubourg de Saverne

place des Halles

quai Kléber

quai Jacques-Sturm

place de la République

Eglise St-Paul

Fossé du Faux Rempart

quai Schoepflin

av. de la Liberté

pont d'Auvergne

Gare Central

place de la Gare

Eglise St-Jean-Baptiste

quai de Paris

quai Kellerman

Eglise St-Pierre-le-Jeune

rue de la Nuée-Bleue

place Broglie

av. de la Marseillaise

quai Koch

pont Royal

quai St-Jean

⑤

rue Brûlée

rue Deserté

rue de la Course

rue du Faubourg-National

place Kléber

④

rue des Juifs

To Jardin Botanique

Eglise St-Pierre-le-Veux

rue de 22 Novembre

Grand'Rue

rue des Grandes Arcades

place de la Cathédrale

⑥

⑦ place du Château

② ponts Couverts

LA PETITE FRANCE

place Gutenberg

⑨ ⑧

quai des Bateliers

rue de Zurich

rue des Poules

L'Ill

VIEUX VILLE

quai St-Nicolas

⑩ place de Zurich

⑪

⑫

To Strasbourg International Airport

place d'Austerlitz

rue de la 1er Armée

rue de Lausanne

rue du Jura

rue Ste-Elisabet

Hôpital Civil

quai du Général-Koenig

Bassin Dusuzeau

rue du Bassin

rue de Saales

③

quai Louis-Pasteur

① ←

rue des Boucher

Route du Rhin

av. Jean-Jaurès

Information ⓘ Post Office ⊠ Church ⓘ

rue de Belfort

BARS/CLUBS ▲

Bar de L'Abbatoir **3**
Bar l'Elastic **10**
Café de Anges **11**
La Laiterie **1**
Le Bistro Piano Bar **8**
Le Griot **5**
Le Living-Room **12**
Le Schutzberger **4**

CULTURE ZOO ●

Cathedrale de Notre
Dame **6**
Musée d'Art Moderne
et Contemporain de
Strasbourg **2**
Musée de l'Oeuvre N. D. **9**
Palais Rohan **7**

Strasbourg

★
PARIS

the southwestern tail of the island. The central tourist traffic hub of the city center in **place Kléber,** a cafe-lined square a few blocks northeast of *La Petit France.* Students hang out around the **place de Zurich,** a neighborhood of more modern, rather staid architecture, across the river from the easternmost tip of the island. The **Gare Central** is on the western edge of the city. You exit the Gare into the aptly named **place de la Gare;** from here walk southeast on **rue de Maire Kuss** (which turns into **rue de 22 Novembre**) for about five minutes to get into the city center.

Strasbourg has cool almost all-glass trams and a decent bus system [see *need to know,* below], but you won't need them unless you're heading outside of town to the **Auberge de Jeunesse** [see *crashing,* below]. Most people walk around the city—you can easily walk the length of the island in under half an hour—but bike lanes and bike locks everywhere attract the hip set to two-wheeled transportation, and if you stick around town long enough or get into trouble, you'll probably see a large number of policemen on bikes. Bikes can be rented at many different points around the city [see *need to know,* below].

hanging out

On sunny days, sit in **La Petite France** by the banks of **L'Ill,** the river that encircles the eye-shaped center of Strasbourg, and snack on a sandwich. Have a drink in **Place du Marché Gayot,** a pedestrian square with many cafes and brasseries near the cathedral and off the **rue des Freres** near the **Place St. Etienne.** The **ponts Couverts,** literally translated as "covered bridges"—actually a single, uncovered bridge that stretches over the canals which branch out into the La Petit France neighborhood a stone's throw from the **Museé d'Art Moderne et Comtemporain** [see *culture zoo,* below]—is a great place to get a bird's-eye view of the city. To mix and mingle with Strasbourg's student set, head across the river to **Place de Zurich,** filled with funky shops and bars.

The tourist office [see *need to know,* below] gives away free maps showing bike routes that fan from the city out into the countryside, with special emphasis on cycle lanes (the French refer to them as "Les Pistes Cyclables") that prohibit cars. One of these runs along La Route des Vins, a 17-mile southwesterly stretch from Strasbourg to the wine hamlet of Molsheim. You'll have a forest on one side, the banks of the Brûche River (a tributary of the Rhine) on the other, and very little auto traffic to cope with en route.

bar, club, and live music scene

Strasbourg after dark can be a bit dull in summer unless your idea of a good time is sitting in an open-air cafe enjoying the night breezes and endless mugs. During the school year, from September through late spring, the scene livens up considerably. The hottest place to go at night—and the best for live music—is the rowdy section between **place de Zurich** and **place d'Austerlitz** across the canal from the old town (*vieille ville*). The sounds of everything from Cuban salsa to funk fill the night air. As

wired

Www.strasbourg.com: run by the Office de Tourisme, this is a surprisingly smart, hip guide to local nightlife **(www.strasbourg.com/strasbourg-by-night)**, all in English, if at times with stilted grammar. While strasbourg-by-night can give the 18 to 25 set some cool tips, the rest of the site, not surprisingly, is aimed at the middle-aged to senior set traveling *en masse,* and the maps of the city suck. But if you're craving a recipe for such delicacies as "Escalope of Panfried Duck Liver with a Caramel of Muscat Wine" or want to read about the history of cheese by the "Cheese Master," click away.

http://strasbourg.webcity.fr: Lots of practical information can be gleaned from this site, as well as more info on current happenings, festivals, and exhibitions, if you've got a good working knowledge of French and know what you're looking for. The articles are smart and the site is well-indexed and easily searchable. The maps, though better than strasbourg.com's, are still somewhat difficult to navigate.

www.vos-sorties.com: Formerly **www.67bynight.com,** this site offers the hippest guide to Strasbourgian nightlife and the best maps. The site is all in French, so a working knowledge of the language is necessary. Although not as easily searchable as the other sites, it does have an electronic version of the very-well-labeled map distributed by the Office de Tourisme. For the clubber in all of us, they also conveniently scan in flyers for parties around town, arranged by month.

Finding places to use the Internet in Strasbourg is kind of a drag, so you might want to do your online research before you go. The cheapest options are either to ask to use the machine at **Soultronik** [see *stuff,* above] or use the machines at the main **post offices** [see *need to know,* above]. The machines at the **Cyber-Center Gare** *(Galerie à l'En-Verre-place de la Gare; Tel 03/88-22-40-32; 2-7pm Tue, 10am-noon/2-7pm Thur, 9am-noon Fri, 10am-1pm Sat)* are rarely available—they're usually occupied or experiencing network problems. As in the rest of France, you won't be finding any QWERTY keyboards either.

in Paris and larger European cities with active nightlife, clubs get animated after around 11pm. Before then, it's best defined as "restful."

On the Place Kléber, the two-floor brewery-brasserie "for the 21st century," **Le Schutzberger** *(29-31 rue des Grandes Arcades; Tel 03/90-23-66-66; 10am-2am daily, till 4am weekends and holidays; www.palais-biere.com; MC, V),* serves its own delicious brews as well as fresh-squeezed juice in a strangely futuristic setting. Sit outside and watch Strasbourg walk by, or lounge in the bi-level interior on smoke-gray, primary-orange, and yellow couches and chairs. Let your eyes wander over the mirrored walls and imagine you're in a Kraftwerk video experiment.

If you get sick of the pretension to which Le Schutzberger can fall victim, head for the nifty student hangout **Bar de L'Abbatoir** *(1 quai Charles Altofer; Tel 03/88-32-28-12; 11:30am-2:30pm/5:30pm-1:30am daily; No cover),* plop down on a pillow in the corner, and grab a 16F brew or sandwich. Strasbourg's smart student set comes to drink in the sexy Asian-influenced interior. The bar is at the very southern tip of quai St. Jean, near the Musée d'Art Moderne et Comtemporain, and occasionally features concerts on Wednesdays (call for times). Unfortunately, the place suffers from poor ventilation; the air is so thick with smoke you could be in an opium den.

Not far away is **La Laiterie** *(13 rue du Hohwald; Tel 03/88-23-72-37; Hours vary; Cover varies),* perhaps Strasbourg's premier venue for big-ticket DJ acts and live shows. You don't need to be a model or flash a lot of skin to get in, just make sure you've got a ticket ahead of time for shows or a club card for the Friday night DJ parties. The show schedule is available around town, and tickets and club cards can bought at the FNAC on Place Kléber, Bar L'Elastic, and other locations listed in the schedule, or by calling the box office the day of the show.

satiating yourself on alsatian wines

Alsatian winegrowers—surprise, surprise—use German grapes, though eschewing the characteristic German sweetness for sheer brute strength. The famous four "noble" grape varieties are all white: Riesling, gewürztraminer pinot gris, and muscat. Traditionally, the Riesling goes well with fish, seafood, and poultry, while the gewürztraminer, with its high alcohol content and spicy aromatic body, best underscores curries and exotic food. The golden pinot gris adds life to poultry (white meat) and perfectly complements the rich taste of *foie gras*. The dry, light muscat is usually drunk as an apértif. Another variety of grape common to Alsace is the sylvaner, which is generally cheaper than the "noble" varieties, but still a very light and tasty companion to white meat and fish.

The only Alsatian red wine is the pinot noir, which Alsatians drink with red meat, substituting it for the perhaps more pedestrian French burgundy.

The hot spot for live jazz, soul, funk, groove, and even African story-telling is the cellar of **Le Griot** *(6 Impasse de l'Écrevisse; Tel 03/88-52-00-52; 7:30pm-4am Mon-Sat, opens 8pm Sun, 7pm on a storytelling Sun; Show times vary; Cover varies; MC, V),* on place Broglie 2nd across from the Hôtel de Ville. Call for a schedule of concerts or pick one up around town. Le Griot takes the sounds so popular around Strasbourg—fusion jazz and African-influenced drumming—to another level.

For more traditional live jazz, head toward place Gutenberg to **Le Bistro Piano Bar** *(30 rue des Tonneliers; Tel 03/88-23-02-71; 6pm-4am Tue-Sat, 8pm-4am Sun, Mon; Happy hour 6-8pm, 10F drinks; Shows 10pm; No cover).* Though the vibe is more collared-shirt than the jamming drumming at Le Griot, its inexpensive happy-hour drinks and no cover charge make it a sure shot.

Off place de Zurich, **Cafe des Anges** *(5 rue St. Catherine; Tel 03/88-37-12-67; 9pm-4-am Tue-Sat; No cover)* has two floors with two different themes. The 5 rue St. Catherine entrance, often guarded by a heavily muscled, bald, black man, leads to a bar-lounge decked out in '60s Black Power memorabilia, where DJs spin all kinds of jazz, nu-school groove, and trip-hop. Upstairs, salsa reigns king at "The Salsa Lounge" from Tuesday to Saturday, and occasionally reggae, funk, and indie bands play. Come smoothly dressed, order a stiff drink, and dig the groove, man, dig it.

If you're more comfortable hanging out with gutter-punks, assorted nutters, and disreputables, high-step it across the street to **Bar L'Elastic** *(27 rue des Orphelins; Tel 03/88-36-11-10; 5pm-3am daily, till 4am weekends, holidays; No cover),* located just off the place Zurich. You might want to leave your American-flag jacket at home; nationalism and conservatism have infiltrated the punk scene in France, probably as a backlash to the commercial success of hip-hop. There's a fooseball in the back for those who've got game, and behind the bar, rowdy bartenders like to mix flaming B-52 shooters—careful or you might get burned.

Also in the university area, **Le Living-Room** *(11 rue des Balayeurs; Tel 03/88-24-10-10; 11am-1:30am Mon-Fri, 6pm-1:30am Sat; Pastis, beer, and sangria 12F Mon-Wed)* has a dark-red interior, a heavily varnished wood bar, and comfortably overstuffed booths that fill with attractive, good-looking girls and boys. There's also a DJ booth, and Strasbourg's top DJs regularly make appearances to spin groove, house, and funk.

arts scene

Classical drama, ballets, concerts, and speeches are presented beneath the impressive high ceilings of the **Théâtre National,** *(1 ave. de la Marseillaise; Tel 03/88-24-88-00 for tickets),* an imposing building erected under the German régime in what the French refer to as "the Imperial style."

Also of note is the equally grand **Opéra National,** *(19 place Broglie; Tel 03/88-75-48-01 for tickets).* It's one of very few nationally funded Opera houses in France, and the citizens of Strasbourg consider themselves very lucky to have it.

More contemporary and controversial drama (performed in French) appears at the **Théâtre Pole Sud,** *(1 rue de Bourgogne ; Tel 03/88-39-23-40),* a contemporary piece of design set 5 miles south of the center of Strasbourg.

Art galleries in Strasbourg tend to show works by artists hailing from both sides of the Franco-German border. Two of the most visible galleries, both located in the heart of the old town, are **Gallerie Raucher,** *(14 rue des Dentelles; Tel 03/88-32-74-48)* and **Gallerie Aktuaryus,** *(23 rue de la Nué Bleue; Tel 03/88-32-39-38).* Both specialize in contemporary paintings, lithographs, ceramics, and sculpture.

CULTURE ZOO

Cathedrale de Notre Dame *(Place de la Cathedrale; 7-11:30am/12:40-7pm Mon-Sat, 1:30-6pm Sun; 5F for 12:30 show of the horloge astronomique [astronomical clock]):* Soaring above the *vieux ville,* the gorgeous red-brick, single-spired cathedral is definitely worth a visit. Check out the stunning 13th-century stained glass and the mechanical movements of the 16th-century astronomical clock. **Musée de l'Oeuvre Notre Dame** *(3 place du Château; Tel 03/88-52-50-00; 10am-noon/1:30-6pm Mon-Sat, 10am-5pm Sun, closed Tues; 15 F):* If your expert eye happens to notice that most of the exterior's saintly statuettes and grinning gargoyles are not original, then head across the square to the nearby musée, which houses the originals, as well as all kinds of decorative arts, stained-glass, and jewelry.

Palais Rohan *(2 place du Château; Tel 03/88-52-50-00; 10am-noon/1:30-6pm Mon-Sat, 10am-5pm Sun, closed Tue; 15F one museum, 30F all three):* Adjacent to the cathedral, this spread houses three well-put-together museums: **Musée Archeologique, Musée des Arts Décoratifs,** and **Musée des Beaux-Arts;** however, only the seriously culture-starved will have the appetite for all three. For most, the Musée des Beaux-Arts, with its meaty selection of northern European (read Flemish) pre-1870 paintings as well as important Italian Renaissance works will suffice. If you still haven't had your fill, check out the Musée des Arts Decoratifs: Just the thought of dining on that fine china will satisfy.

Musée d'Art Moderne et Comptemporain de Strasbourg *(1 place Hans Jean Arp; Tel 03/88-23-31-31; Bus 2, 3, 10, 15, 20, 23 to Obernai/Musée d'Art Modern; 11am-7pm daily, noon-10pm Thurs, closed Mon; mamcs@sdv.fr; 30F):* Located across L'Ill River on a high hill overlooking La Petit France, this is a sharply designed glass, steel, and pink granite structure that lets natural light filter into its bright airy entrance. The extensive museum collection dates from 1860 to the present day, and the layout allows the visitor to follow the development of modern art. The cafe on the upper level is pricey, but the views of the city make it well worth a visit. For the French-proficient traveler who's bored with bars, or just plain broke, there's also an extensive free library of art and art theory books.

by foot

1. *Gare* to Place Gutenberg to La Petite France: Department Stores and Drug Dealers

To acquaint yourself with the city after arriving by train, proceed across the place de la Gare down ruc du Marie Kuss past the seemingly endless kebab stands to rue du 22 Novembre. Continue on past the Tati [see *stuff*, above] and the ever-homogenous Virgin Megastore. After about seven minutes of walking, you'll reach **place Kléber;** the corporate-fabulous music store, FNAC, will be on your left. On Tuesday mornings there's an open-air market here that sells everything from clothing to cheapo CDs.

At night on place Kléber, North African kids hang out and hiss "hash" at you unless you politely decline and keep walking, or, of course, stop and buy some. (But be beware of such street deals; they are infamously nefarious.) Cross the square, turn right on rue des Grandes-Arcades, and walk until you reach place Gutenberg, a crossroads of sorts. The cathedral is to your left, and La Petite France is to your right. For now, head toward **La Petite France**, whose pastel colors, twisted, narrow streets, and quiet residential vibe contrasts nicely with the slightly edgier areas around Place Kléber. Have fun getting lost (until you realize the city isn't really that big). Grand Rue is particularly neat, with cobblestones, good restaurants, and some smart shopping; if you do indeed get lost, the spire of the cathedral makes a good compass needle. Zig-zag in a southeasterly direction and eventually you'll find yourself surrounded by canals. Stop and rest by

Kronenburg *(68 rte. d'Oberhausbergen; Tel 03/88-27-41-58; Bus 7 to rue Jacob or Tram A to St.-Florent; Hours open Free; Reserve in advance).* Set in the suburb of Cronenbourg (yes, with a "C"), three miles west of the center of Strasbourg, the brewer of that beer with the flashy advertisements all over France, gives free tours, culminating with a two-beer, all-you-can-eat pretzel free-for-all. Don't let the fiesty German couples with matching mullets elbow you out of your share of pretzels!

stuff

▸▸**TUNES**

For a neat selection of both new and old vinyl, including cheap old soul 45s and used and new CDs of all musical genres, check out **L'Occase de L'Oncle Tom** *(119 Grand Rue [corner of Grand Rue, rue des Francis Bourgeois, and rue de la Division Leclerc]; Tel 03/88-37-33-60; 1-7pm Mon, 10:30am-7pm Tue-Fri, 10am-7pm Sat; www.oncletom.com; CDs from 30F; MC, V),* on Grand Rue in the *vieux ville.* CD players are avail-

one for moment, and then retrace your steps back to place Gutenberg.

2. Daytripping to Drum 'n' Bass: Place Gutenberg to place Zurich

From place Gutenberg, walk toward the cathedral on rue des Halle-bardes. If by now you're yearning for a little Alsatian wine and don't mind the crowds, turn right on rue du Maroquin to the place du Marché-aux-Cochons-de-Lait and grab a glass at the Pfifferbrieder [see *eats,* above]. Or, if the crowds of tourists are too much for you, continue straight past the cathedral on rue des Frères to reach the charmingly hidden pedestrian square, place du Marché Gayot [see *hanging out,* above] and grab a glass of wine here. Then head south and cross the river on one of several pedestrian bridges. Continue south on either rue de Zurich or rue des Batelliers to the **place de Zurich.** Even though you have left the narrow, crooked streets behind the cathedral, perhaps Strasbourg's most picturesque part of town, and entered a newer part of the city, you'll find that some of Strasbourg's coolest spots are centered around this rather unassuming square, including the '60s-black-power-themed basement of Café des Anges [see *bars,* above] and the record store *extraordinaire,* Soultronik, whose steady stream of music provides the tunes for Strasbourg's established and still-aspiring DJs alike.

able to preview CDs, but unfortunately there are no turntables to listen to vinyl.

If you want to hang out and listen to records, **Soultronik** (*33 rue de Zurich; Tel 03/88-24-90-99, Fax 03/88-24-90-98; 11-8pm Mon-Sat; soultronik@zapata.fr, www.soultronik.com; MC, V*) has a hot selection of house, drum 'n' bass, techno, bossanova, breakbeats, and European and German jazz re-releases as well, as a small but smart collection of the latest ultra-hip American and European men's and women's urban streetwear. It also offers Internet access and sells trips to Europe's largest music festivals for Nancy's Voyages4A travel agency. [see **Nancy**] You'll find Soultronik off the Place de Zurich.

▶▶KITSCH

If you harbor a burning desire for pseudo-hippy-ethno-kitsch, trinkets, pipes, and other assorted goods, ignore the West African guys in umbrella hats peddling stuff around the cathedral and head straight to the source, the hole in the wall known as **The 70's** (*7 rue de la Division Leclerc; Tel*

strasbourg

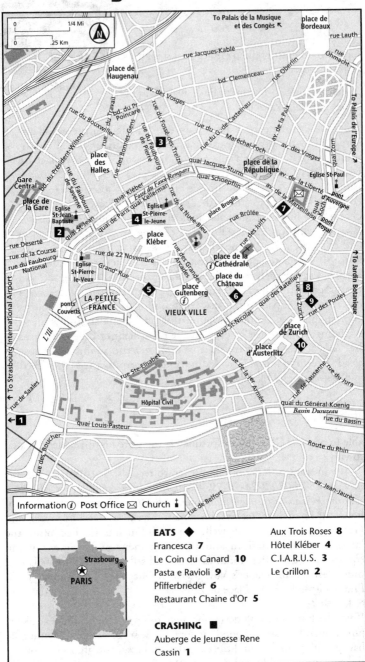

Information ⓘ Post Office ✉ Church ♱

EATS ◆

Francesca **7**
Le Coin du Canard **10**
Pasta e Ravioli **9**
Pfifferbrieder **6**
Restaurant Chaine d'Or **5**

Aux Trois Roses **8**
Hôtel Kléber **4**
C.I.A.R.U.S. **3**
Le Grillon **2**

CRASHING ■

Auberge de Jeunesse Rene
Cassin **1**

03/88-22-20-33; 10am-7pm Tue-Sat) in central Strasbourg and feast your eyes on the dusty clutter.

For the budget minded, there's a venerable **Tati** *(1 rue du 22 Novembre; Tel 03/88-75-77-66, Fax 03/88-75-78-11; 10am-7pm Mon-Sat; www.tati.fr; MC, V),* the kitsch-chic discount department store that took France by storm in the late eighties and early nineties, the mecca of the cheap, the plastic, and the poorly made yet somehow indescribably cool. Be prepared to dig through a lot of crap to find that perfect shirt, then wait in long lines at the cashier. But as they say, it takes a lot of coal to make a diamond. It's not far from the train station, on the main rue du 22 Novembre as you come into town.

▶▶DUDS

If you prefer something more upscale but still young, smart, and feminine, check out **Signe du Temps** *(8 rue Ste. Madeleine; Tel 03/88-25-55-30; 10am-5pm Mon-Sat; MC, V).* Here you can find the latest trends, east of the German border to the western fields to Paris, in *chic* club wear, and sexy street wear. Signe du Temps focuses on smaller, trendier designers, leaving the big names for the department stores.

If you don't have the dough to spring for Soultronik's or Signe du Temps' *prêt-à-porter,* check out the more pedestrian but wallet-pleasing women's fashions at **Kilo Shop** *(6 rue de la Lanterne; Tel 03/88-32-98-84; 10:30-6pm Mon-Sat; MC, V),* off Grand Rue. A sort of Strasbourgian hybridization of the Parisian Kookaï stores, Kilo is more closely focused on girls' rather than women's clothing.

EATS

▶▶CHEAP

For the drunk, or just economically minded, the street across from the *gare,* **rue du Maire Kuss,** is lined with döner kebab (very similar to shwarma) joints. Especially tasty is **Snack Nemrut** *(11 rue du Maire*

EN VELO

The most appealing outdoor activity in these parts is without a doubt biking. The **tourist office** [see *need to know,* below] gives away free maps of the bike routes that fan from the city out into the countryside, with special emphasis on *Les Pistes Cyclables,* designated cycle lanes that prohibit cars. The best of these runs along *La Route des Vins,* a 17-mile southwesterly stretch from Strasbourg to the wine hamlet of Molsheim. You'll have a forest on one side, the banks of the Brûche River (a tributary of the Rhine) on the other, and very little auto traffic to cope with en route. *Bon voyage!*

Kuss; Tel 03/88-23-10-91; 10am-11pm daily; Sandwiches from 25F), whose in-store manufactured flat bread and meat shaved with a large handheld electric saw will easily satisfy your stomach when it cries out for kebab.

▶▶DO-ABLE

In La Petite France, **Restaurant Chaine d'Or** *(134 Grand Rue; Tel 03/88-75-02-69, Fax 03/88-32-11-06; 10am-2pm/6-11:30pm daily; Lunch menus 55F)* serves elegant Alsatian classics like sauerkraut and sausage that are surprisingly light, given the region's reputation for heavy cuisine. The delicious, fluffy fish *terrine pate,* beautifully multilayered and mousse-like, is a near-perfect appetizer. During the day, street musicians serenade you on the outdoor terrace with all manner of music, from classical guitar to accordion polkas.

Near the place de Zurich, the nook-like student hangout, **Pasta e Ravioli** *(23 rue de Zurich; Tel 03/88-36-57-92; 11am-2pm/5-10pm Mon-Sat; Pizza 30F; MC, V),* has only four tables, but you don't have to snag one to taste the fresh pastas and delicious, thin, crispy-crusted pizzas for wallet-pleasing prices; they also prepare food for takeout. You can't sit down if you're not wearing at least a T-shirt, shorts or pants, and shoes, but it's nice to dine in the restaurant, enjoy the homey atmosphere, taste the super-hot pepper olive oil, and commune with the students.

For slightly more upscale Italian dining, try **Francesca** *(14 ave. de la Marseillaise; Tel 03/88-25-50-60; Noon-2pm/5-11pm Mon-Sat; Appetizers from 28F, entrees from 39F),* east of the river near the place de la République, for delicious pastas and antipasto—but beware, they don't serve pizza. They do offer comfortable if not cozy street-side dining in the shade of the tree-lined avenue.

For lovers of waterfowl, **Le Coin du Carnard** *(8 rue Renard Prechant; Tel 03/88-25-03-24; 11am-2pm/6-11pm Mon-Sat; MC, V)* located in the university zone known as "La Krutenau," about a 15-minute walk southeast of the cathedral, serves every possible variety of duck in pleasing portions, while managing to keep things from getting greasy. Try the duck served on noodles in a light white sauce sprinkled with cinnamon; you won't be disappointed. Outdoor dining is available.

The cupcake-cute **Pfifferbrieder** *(9 Place du Marché-aux-Cochons-de-Lait; Tel 03/88-32-15-43, Fax 03/88-32-15-43; 11am-2pm/5-11pm Mon-Sat; MC, V)* offers the authentic Alsatian *winestub* (wine pub) experience. But there's nothing cute about the seriously hearty, sauerkraut-laden portions of pork, strong Alsatian wines, and tasty onion tarts.

crashing

Unfortunately, because the European Parliament has its headquarters in Strasbourg, hotel rooms do not come cheap, and the city's hostels have nightlife-curtailing curfews.

▶▶CHEAP

Auberge de Jeunesse Rene Cassin *(9 rue l'Auberge de Jeunesse; Tel 03/88-30-26-46, Fax 03/88-30-35-16; Bus 3, 23 to Auberge de Jeunesse;*

Reception 7-11am; Curfew 1am Apr-Oct, 11pm Nov-Mar; 69-99F bed, 149F single, 42F camping, 17F sheets, 49F dinner or lunch; No credit cards) offers thin-walled but clean rooms in the Montagne-Vert suburb about 2 miles southwest of the center of Strasbourg. On sunny days, kids kick it in the surrounding park and sunbathe along the canal.

Centre International d'Accueil et de Rencontre Unioniste de Strasbourg (C.I.A.R.U.S.) *(7 rue Finkmatt; Tel 03/88-15-27-88 or 03/88-15-27-90, Fax 03/88-15-27-89; Bus 10 to pl. Faubourg-de-Pierre; Curfew 1am; www.crous.fr; 69-86F bed, 189F single; No credit cards)* offers dormitory-style beds in a slightly worn building constructed in the 1960s, with some renovations as long ago as 1989. But every room is about 9m by 10m and each has its own bathroom; kitchenettes are available, and if you can't cook or don't want to, breakfast is included. There's also a laundromat on the premises. It's a bit more expensive than the Auberge de Jeunesse René Cassin, but it's also a bit more modern and well maintained, and you can stay there even if you're not a member of the international youth hostel organization. The CIARUS is north of L'Ill, a few blocks from the Place de la République.

▶▶**DO-ABLE**

The second-floor **Hôtel Kléber** *(29 place Kléber; Tel 03/88-32-09-53, Fax 03/88-32-50-41; Closed Dec 24-26; www.hotel-kleber.com; 189-351F single, 320-400F double; MC, V, AE)* has narrow hallways but spacious rooms furnished with understated '70s-style German furniture and comfortable beds. If you're a light sleeper, beware of noisy nights on the place Kleber. Even though you can set CNN on the cable system, don't expect it to lull you back to sleep.

Two blocks from the station and four blocks from place Kleber, **Le Grillion** *(2 rue Thiergarten; Tel 03/88-32-71-15, Fax 03/88-32-22-01; grillion@compuserve.com; 180-240F single, 230-280F double; MC, V, AE)* has a light, easygoing atmosphere that pervades the adjacent Bar Perestroika as well. Friendly desk service, a generally young, well-behaved clientele, and easy access to the station and the adjacent bar make this place a winner. Rooms are on the small side but comfortable and well put together, with warm wood furnishings.

If you want to impress your date, take him or her back to **Aux Trois Roses** *(7 rue Zurich; Tel 03/88-36-56-95, Fax 03/88-35-06-14; 298-398F single, 398-470F double; MC, V)*, where romance is definitely in the air. Situated just around the corner from the hot spots on place de Zurich, this hotel has quiet rooms, perfect if you like making a bit of noise but don't like hearing others. The plush rooms are furnished in warm wood furniture with linens that would make Laura Ashley proud. The hotel sauna is ideal for sweating away hours of Alsatian wine- and beer-swilling.

need to know

Currency Exchange Automatic teller machines are probably your best bet for obtaining cash in Strasbourg. They're everywhere, and generally have the best rates. If you need to exchange Canadian or American dollars, head to the American Express office [see below], whose rates are often quite good.

Tourist Information The main **Office de Tourisme** *(17 place de la Cathedrale; Tel 03/88-52-28-28, Fax 03/88-52-28-29; 9am-7pm daily April-Sept, 9am-6pm Mon-Sat, 9am-12:30pm/1-5pm Sun Oct-Easter; www.strasbourg.com)* makes reservations, dispenses information and maps, gives tours, and has a **branch office** *(Place de Gare; Tel 03/88-32-51-49)* on the lower level of the train station. The website is pretty helpful and has lots of neatly indexed information.

Public Transportation The public buses and tram of the **Compagnie des Transports Strasbourgeois** *(Tel 03/88-77-70-11)* are convenient and run from 4am to midnight, but are ultimately unnecessary unless you want to head to the suburbs; even then it's more fun and almost as cheap to rent a bike. Most buses run from the *gare* down rue du Vieux Marché and then on to other destinations. The tram runs from the place de l'Homme de Fer to the suburbs. Tickets are interchangeable, good for one hour, and cost 7F. Maps are available at the Office de Tourisme [see above].

American Express Located just off of place Kleber, the **AMEX office** *(19 rue des Francs-Bourgeois; Tel 03/88-21-96-59; 8:45am-noon/1:30-6pm Mon-Fri)* changes money at good rates and doesn't charge commission.

Health and Emergency police: *17;* **ambulance:** *15;* **fire department:** *18.* If you get into trouble or lose your passport, see the police and then your consulate for help. **Canadian Consulate** *(rue Ried, 67610 La Wantzenau; Tel 03/88-96-65-02);* **American Consulate** *(15 ave. d'Alsace; Tel 03/88-35-31-04 for information, Tel 03-88-35-31-04 for cultural services).* The local hospital is **L'Hôpital Civil de Strasbourg** *(1 place de l'Hôpital; Tel 03/881-67-68.* It lies within a 10-minute walk south of the center of town. It is also reachable by Train A.

Airport Serviced mainly by **Air France** *(0-800-802-802),* Strasbourg's **airport** *(Rte. de Strasbourg, Entzheim; Tel 03/88-64-67-67)* is 15 km (9 miles) outside of town. An airport shuttle (25-45F) picks up passengers at the normal bus stops at the place de la Gare and place de l'Homme de Fer every 30 minutes.

Trains Trains to and from Nancy (1 1/2 hours), Lyon (5 hours), Paris Est (4-5 hours), and Frankfurt (2 1/2 hours) run daily from the **Gare SNCF** *(Place de la Gare; 08/36-35-35-35; Open 24 hours),* about a five-minute walk from the city center. As in most stations, there is a *bagagerie automatique* (baggage lockers) and *consigne* (baggage consignment) where you can stow your stuff for 15-30F for 72 hours.

Bike Rental There are four convenient locations around town and one in the suburb Montagne Verte where you can rent a bike: **Gare** *(4 rue de Maire Kuss; Tel 03/88-52-01-01; 6am-7:30pm Mon-Fri, 8am-noon/2-7pm Sat, 9am-noon/2-7pm Sun),* **Centre** *(10 rue des Bouchers; Tel 03/88-35-11-65; 8am-7pm Mon-Fri, 9am-noon/2-7pm Sat, Sun),* **Points Couverts** *(Impasse de la grande Ecluse; Tel 03/88-22-59-19;*

9am-7pm Tue-Fri, 9am-noon/2-7pm Sat, Sun), **Sainte-Aurelie** *(1 Blvd. de Metz; Tel 03/88-32-20-11; 7am-7pm Mon-Fri, 9am-noon/2-7pm Sat, Sun)*, and **Montagne Verte** *(217 Route de Schirmeek; Tel 03/90-20-47-12; Similar hours)*. Bikes rent for 20F a half-day and 30F full, with a 300F deposit and a photocopy of one form of identification.

Postal The **main post office** *(5 ave. de la Marseillaise; Tel 03/88-52-31-00; 8am-7pm Mon-Fri, 8am-noon Sat)* has all the normal operations including telephones and telegrams, and new blue iMacs for accessing the Internet. For 50F you get a card, your own French e-mail address, and an hour of time. Hour refills of the card cost 30F.

Internet [see *wired,* above]

everywhere else

mulhouse

Mulhouse is in southern Alsace, just across the border from Basel, Switzerland, and Freiburg, Germany, and just 41 kilometers south of Colmar. Why does that matter to you? It matters, dear reader, because Mulhouse's privileged geographical location at the crossroads of so many national borders means that it gets to play host to one of Alsace's largest music festivals [see *festivals and events,* below]. While it's not Alsace's prettiest town (the beauty contest would probably be won by Colmar), Mulhouse has several beautifully kept parks, some quirky museums, and a visitor-friendly population of about 230,000. While a decidedly small town in both size and earnest easy going feel, Mulhouse was once a relatively strong city-state, an early 18th-century industrial center, and the site of interesting turn-of-the-20th-century quasi-utopian urban planning. Before you come to town, you might want to consider booking your hotel room through the Office de Tourisme's web site, *www.ot. ville-mulhouse.fr*, and you'll definitely want to check the website of **Le Noumatrouff,** *www.mulhouse@fede-hiero.com,* [see *bar, club, and live music scene,* below] to see if there any upcoming concerts.

neighborhoods and hanging out

Mulhouse's *vieille ville* centers around the **place de la Réunion,** a medieval craftsmen's and tradesmen's district that's now kept car-free and filled with cafes and bars spilling out onto the streets. The *vieille ville* is where you'll probably spend most of your time. Take a walk around the area and admire the architecture, which has been largely preserved since its conception. After having a cup of coffee in one of the many cafes on place de la Réunion, you should take a stroll down the romantic chestnut-tree-lined paths of **Parc Salvator,** a five-minute walk directly west of the place de la Réunion. During the summer, Parc Salvator hosts concerts in an open-air auditorium. Ask for details about the program at the Office de Tourisme. Or you could take a nap by the flowered beds of **Square Steinbach,** a block and a half southwest of Place de la Reunion.

The streets here are haphazard and bendy—perfect for wandering, not so perfect for getting directions. One of the main streets is **rue de la Siene,** which runs east-west along the bottom edge of the *vieille ville,* about a three-minute walk south of the place de la Réunion. Another biggie, **avenue Clemenceau,** runs pretty much parallel to rue de la Siene, a block to the south. At its east end it meets up with **place de la République.** A number of streets radiate out from République, including **rue du Sauvage** to the north, which forms the eastern border of the *vieille ville.* On the southern edge of the place de la République is the **place de la Bourse,** a green triangular park lined with neo-classical and arcaded brick buildings. The area comprising the place de la Bourse, the place de la République, and the fan of streets below it is Mulhouse's *nouveau quartier,* designed and built in the 19th century as a model for modern urban living. The *Canal du Rhône au Rhin,* a canal connecting the French *Rhône* with the German Rhine, runs roughly east-west across the south end of town, about a ten-minute walk from the *vieille ville.* The train station sits just south of the *Canal du Rhône au Rhin,* almost directly across from the place de la Bourse.

bar, club, and live music scene

There are lots of cafés in Mulhouse, but **Café des Alpes** *(11 rue des Francisques; Tel 03/89-66-04-64)* seems particularly convivial and conducive to meeting locals. Open daily from 7:30am to at least 11pm, it serves not only coffee and tea, but platters of food and—later in the evening—stiff drinks to a busy nocturnal clientele.

Bar Glen Coe *(143 ave. de Colmar; Tel 03/89-43-00-22)* is the most authentic Scottish pub in town, with the kind of battered paneling and rich array of single-malt whiskies (more than 100 varieties) that you'd expect in the Highlands. Have a whisky or a beer (30 varieties) and you could end up talking with anyone from a student to a visiting rock and roll star.

festivals

Le Noumatrouff [see *live music scene* above] hosts a major annual multi-genre music festival, **Bêtes de Scène** *(Tel 03/89-32-94-10; www.fede-hiero.com)* that's definitely worth catching if you're in the area in mid-July. In the summer of 2000, the 10th festival Bêtes de Scène featured Toots and The Maytals, Afrika Bambaataa, the Rollins Band, Sleater Kinney, DJ Krush, the Skatalites, Ranier Trüby, and Jazzanova, who all played over a five-day period at Le Noumatrouff. Be sure to book a room in advance if you're coming at festival time.

Four blocks towards expressway A36 from Hôtel Bristol, **Le Nouma-trouff** *(57 rue de la Mertzau; Tel 03/89-32-94-10, Fax 03/89-42-05-96; mulhouse@fede-hiero.com; Hours vary; Cover varies)* is Mulhouse's coolest venue for all types of live music from house to reggae to rock. It was at Le Noumatrouff that the Hiero Federation, a nationwide organization made up of more than 500 members dedicated to the arts and a progressive cultural agenda was started. At Le Noumatrouff, the foundation hosts and sponsors a literary cafe as well as experimental films, multimedia, and art exhibitions, and holds their super-cool music festival, the **Bêtes de Siène,** every summer [see *festivals and events,* below].

CULTURE ZOO

Mulhouse has several quirky museums, all centered around industry. One chronicles the rise of electricity, another focuses on the railroad, and the third is dedicated to the automobile. All three are located outside of the city center but are still within hiking range. You can probably skip the Electropolis and the French Railway Museum, and head to the National Car Museum.

Electropolis *(55 rue du Pâturage; Tel 03/89-32-48-60, Fax 03/89-32-82-47; 10am-6pm Tue-Sun; 48F admission, 23F students, 60F admission to both Electropolis and Railway Museum, 30F students):* Unless you're 10 years old, scientifically inclined, an engineer, or have a soft spot in your heart for the electric boogaloo, the Electropolis will probably not electrify you. The interactive exhibits on the different forms of electricity are best left for those who brought their graphing calculators with them to France.

Musée National des Chemins de Fer *(2 rue Alfred de Glehn; Tel 03/89-42-25-67, Fax 03/89-42-41-82; 9am-6pm daily Apr-Sept, 9am-5pm Oct-Mar 46F admission, 20F students, 60F admission to both Railway Museum and Electropolis, 30F students):* Guaranteed to thrill those who still have model trains hidden in their basements, this collection of trains from continental Europe includes around 100 steam locomotives, electric locomotives, railcars, luxurious carriages, and wagons, this museum comprehensively chronicles 150 years of French railway history. It is located only steps away from the Electropolis, three miles west of the town center.

Musée National de l'Automobile *(192 ave. de Colmar; Tel 03/89-33-23-23, Fax 03/89-32-08-09; 9am-6pm daily Mar 26-Oct 31; 10am-5pm daily Nov-Feb; Hours change annually; Closed New Year's Day and Christmas; 60F admission, 46F students):* Even if you're baffled by Bill Nye, the Science Guy, you'll probably get a kick out of this place. The collection of more than 600 cars is housed in a vast garage-like space and was put together by the wonderfully named Schlumpf brothers. Admire the sexy curves of the Bugati and the stately grille of the Rolls Royce. This museum is slightly isolated from the other two, set two miles north of the town center.

eats

La Brasserie O'Bryan *(5 place des Victoires; Tel 03/89-56-25-58; Prix fixe lunch 49F, main courses 29-69F, 11:30am-3pm, 6:30pm-midnight daily; AE, DC, MC, V)* bridges Alsatian and Celtic culture more gracefully than any other restaurant. Many customers hang out at a long bar and stare at Irish beer advertisements postered on the wall as they savor their Guinnesses; in some cases, they never move into the dining room at all. If you opt to drag yourself away, the dining room offers an authentic array of the rib-sticking fare for which Alsace is famous, and which usually tastes wonderful with beer. The best examples include sauerkraut, steaks, steamed mussels with fries, trout, and for lighter appetites, an array of meal-sized salads.

Restaurant Pic Vit *(8 rue des Bons-Enfants; Tel 03/89-45-71-17; Main courses 65-130F; 11:30am-3pm, 6:30pm-midnight daily; MC, V)*, the name of which, in French slang, translates to "Fast Eats" (or "eat and run"), which was the mentality of the owners when the place was established in the 1950s by the Bihler family. Since then, a new generation of Bihlers has expanded its premises into three dining rooms on two levels of an Alsatian house built in 1652. Here, beneath beamed ceilings and 17th-century vaulting, you'll enjoy authentic Alsatian cuisine for a lot less than at other places in the neighborhood. Look for everything an Alsatian grandmother might remember from her childhood, including sauerkraut, foie gras, and a savory Alsatian stew made from several kinds of meat, as well as potatoes, onion tarts, and virtually anything that an Alsatian butcher can do with pork.

crashing

Mulhouse's **Auberge de Jeunesse** *(37 rue de L'Ilberg; Tel 03/89-42-63-28, Fax 03/89-59-74-95; Reception open 8am-noon/5-11pm, till midnight in summer; 48F bed, 17F sheets; No credit cards)* is clean, comfortable, and quiet. Though it is a bit far from town (2 kilometers west of the station), the friendly atmosphere extends to the surrounding park, where kids sometimes play soccer. They have rooms of four to six beds and a communal TV room where you can relax.

In the center of Mulhouse, five minutes by foot from the *gare,* **Hôtel Saint Bernard** *(3 rue des Fleurs; Tel 03/89-45-82-32, Fax 03/89-45-26-32; stber@evhr.net; 150F single, 280F double, 35F breakfast; MC, V)* is the best place to stay in Mulhouse for your money, with comfortable rooms and kind folks working the front desk. Internet is available at reception, and bikes are available for two-wheeled touring around town. Both of these services are blissfully, incredibly free.

If more luxury is what you seek, try the **Hôtel Bristol** *(18 Ave. de Colmar; Tel 03/89-42-12-31, Fax 03/89-42-50-57; info@hotelbristol.com; 200F single, 550F double, 40F breakfast; MC, V)*. This comfortably bland, three-star hotel, a five-minute walk north of the town center, has spacious rooms and soft beds.

nEED To Know

Currency Exchange The best place to exchange traveler's checks is the Central **Post Office** *(3 place Gén de Gaulle; Tel 03/89-56-94-11; 8am-7pm Mon-Fri, 8am-noon Sat),* which faces the train station. There is also a **Banque Paribas** *(25 place Réunion; Tel 03/89-45-64-46),* conveniently located directly on the place de la Réunion.

Tourist Information The **Office de Tourisme** *(9 ave. Foch; Tel 03/89-35-48-48, Fax 03/89-45-66-16; www.ot.ville-mulhouse.fr)* is located across the canal from the *gare.* You can get information here about the town and book a hotel room. You can also book a room online at the website. Additional information in French is available online at *www.ville-mulhouse.fr.*

Health/Emergency **Hôpital Émile Müller,** *(20 ave. du Docteur Laennes; Tel 03/84-64-64-64)* lies a mile south of the city center.

Pharmacy Pharmacie Walter, *(9 rue du Sauvage; Tel 03/89-45-28-29).*

Trains Trains leave the **Gare Mulhouse Ville** *(10 ave. du General LeClerc Tel 08/36-35-35-35),* just south of the city center, for the hour-long trip to Strasbourg 14 times daily. Tickets are 85F. Rail lines also connect Mulhouse to Basel, Freiburg, and Colmar. Call for schedules and fares.

Bike Rental Head for **Cycles B.A.,** *(Place de la Concorde; Tel 03/89-45-13-46).*

Laundry Laverie GTI, *(ave. de Colmar 65; Tel 03/89-42-23-25).*

Postal Bureau de Poste PTT, *(3 place du Général de Gaulle; Tel 03/89-56-94-00; Open Mon-Fri 9am-7pm, Sat 9am-noon, closed Sun).*

Internet Café Noumatrouf, [see above, *bar, club, and live music scene*] *(57 rue de la Mertzau; Tel 03/81-32-94-10),* has rooms customers can use for e-mail and Netsurfing.

coLmar

Nestled in the Vosges mountains southwest of Strasbourg, Colmar is the third largest town in Alsace and perhaps the cutest (if not the most expensive), with many of its homes restored to gingerbread and cupcake perfection. It's directly across the border from Freiburg, so the German daytrippers, their fists and pockets stuffed with converted marks, are inescapable—just buckle down and try to blend in if you can. Take refuge from the touristy masses at **Le Kraken** [see *club scene,* below], a French multimedia arts and electronic music collective and Colmar's only lonely outpost of hipster-ism and the sponsor of numerous goings-on around town—it is reason enough to make a trip here. A word to the wise: check their web-site ahead of time to see whether your trip will coincide with any concerts. Knowing is half the battle.

While in Colmar, you should not neglect the quaint canals and cutsy cobblestone of the supremely touristy *vieille ville* and **La Petite Venise.**

Even when the *vieille ville* is crowded with German *volk*, it's fun to navigate the crooked cobble-stoned streets and admire the rickety timber-and-stucco buildings. Cross the **Lauch River** via **Pont St. Pierre** and you'll have a pretty cool view of the *vieille ville*. From there, you'll be set to wander La Petit Venise, whose canals more closely resemble Amsterdam's than Venice's.

As part of the Hiéro Federation [see **mulhouse**], a French multimedia arts and electronic music collective, the superhip **Le Kraken** *(7 rue de la Lauch; Tel 03/89-41-01-81, Fax 03/89-41-19-16; colmar@fede-hiero.com, www.fede-hiero.com/colmar; Cover varies)* hosts a number of events around town—including the annual summer "beach party" in the Parc du Natala—as well as at its own space. The music varies from pop folk to house. See their website for concert listings.

For a different kind of musical experience, come to town in July, when the **Colmar International Festival** *(Tel 03/89-20-68-98, Fax 03/89-41-34-13; Tickets 75-450F)* is happening. It's all about classical here, but they feature mostly young artists, so it is far from staid. Concerts are held in various public spaces, like churches and at the base of monuments, around town. Make sure to reserve a room ahead if you're coming during festival time.

To get the full effect of the long history of Alsatian art and history, you should definitely check out the **Musée d'Unterlinden** *(Place d'Unterlinden; Tel 03/89-41-89-23; www.musée-unterlinden.com; 9am-6pm daily Apr-Oct, 10am-5pm Wed-Mon Nov-Mar; 35F)*, housed in a 13th-century Dominican convent that was converted into a museum around 1850. It includes everything from the fiery Issenheim altar piece painted by German realist Matthias Grünewald, to an ancient armory collection. In *Le Retable d'Issenheim* or the Issenheim Alterpiece, St. Anthony's temptations are framed in the larger scene's of the Cruxifixion, Incarnation, Annunciation, and Resurection. St. Anthony is tempted by twisted evil creatures, pus-faced demons, and grinning goblins—you'd think you were on a New York subway train. You'll probably wind up spending more time here than you would have imagined.

EATS

The food options in Colmar hit both extremes of the spectrum—cheap and expensive—and not much in between. If you just want to grab some supplies, the local **Monoprix** *(place d'Unterlinden; Tel 03/89-41-48-65)* is conveniently right across from the youth hostel.

Housed in the intricately and beautifully sculpted Hôtel des Têtes, **Maison Des Têtes** *(19 rue des Têtes; Tel 03/89-24-43-43; Reservations required; Entrées from 92F; MC, V, AE, DC)* is worth a splurge. The interior of the dining has exposed wood beams, Art Nouveau light fixtures, and stained glass windows. The classic French food, featuring seasonal fresh game, fowl, and trout, is perfectly complemented by delicious Alsatian wines. Try the *foie gras* with truffles or roasted duck with two spices, and send your mouth into ecstasy.

crashing

Located ten minutes from the tourist office, **Auberge de Jeunesse Mittelharth** *(2 rue Pasteur; Tel 03/89-80-57-39, Fax 03/89-80-76-16; Reception open mornings and 5pm-11pm, until midnight during summer; 48F a bed, 17F sheets)* dispenses the fairly predictable hostel fare: antiseptic, on occasion worn, rooms with thin mattresses. There is a midnight curfew.

Behind the attractively flowered exterior of the **Hôtel Turenne** *(10 rue de Bâle; Tel 03/89-21-58-58, Fax 03/89-41-27-64; www.turenne.com; 250Fsingle, 320F double, 48F breakfast; MC, V)* is a charming small hotel with comfortable rooms with color televisions in all and mini-bars in some. Conveniently located right in the Petit Venice area. On-line booking is available on their web site.

Although the **Rapp Hôtel** *(1-5 rue Weinemer; Tel 03/89-41-62-10, Fax 03/89-24-13-58; reservation@rapp-hotel.com, www.rapp-hotel.com; 325-350F single, 395-435F double; MC, V)* is decidedly family- and business-oriented, it has a number of winning amenities that anyone would enjoy, such as an indoor swimming-pool, a training room, a sauna, and bicycles for rent. Located in *Vieille Ville,* the hotel has an elevator and offers clean, comfortable, functional rooms with reasonably new bedding, televisions, and a choice of bath or shower. Adjacent to the hotel are a *winestub* and restaurant.

need to know

Currency Exchange Banque Populaire (Agence Nauban) *(14 route Neuf Brisach; Tel 03/89-41-82-22).* Note that there are ATM's here, as well as along the rue des Clés. Currency exchange is also available at the tourist office and the post office (36-38 ave. de la République).

Tourist Information The **Office de Tourisme** *(4 rue Unterlinden; Tel 03/89-20-68-92, Fax 03/89-41-34-13; Bus 1-4 to Place Unterlinden; 9am-6pm Mon-Sat, 10am-2pm Sun Apr-Jun & Sept-Dec, 10am-7pm Mon-Sat, 9:30am-2pm Sun Jul-Aug, 9am-noon Mon-Sat, 10am-2pm Sun Jan-Mar),* facing the Musée d'Unterlinden, dispenses maps of Colmar and its environs, as well as a lot of other information.

Public Transportation Though you will not need them as the center of Colmar is easily navigable on foot, buses are run by **Trace** *(4a rue Unterlinden; Tel 03/89-20-80-80).* Tickets (5.30F) and *carnets* (packs of 10 tickets) (41F) are available in local *tabacs.*

Trains Nine trains a day leave Paris for the six-hour journey to Colmar. Rail lines also link Colmar with Mulhouse and points in Germany via Freiburg. Colmar's *Gare (rue de la Gare; buses 1-5 to Gare)* is a 20-minute walk to the Office de Tourisme along the ave. de la République.

Bike Rental Bikes can be rented at the **Hôtel Rapp** [see *crashing,* above] and across from the Hostel at **La Cyclothèque** *(31 rte d'Ingersheim; Tel 03/89-79-14-18; 90F a day for a VTT, or mountain bike).*

burgundy

burgundy

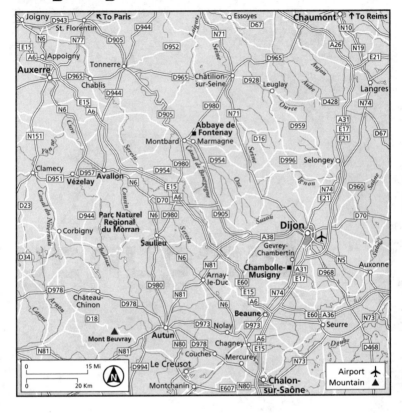

as you meander down the cobblestone streets that wind in a labyrinth through the towns of Burgundy, you may get the feeling that you've gone back in time a few centuries. This region, historically a dukedom separate from the rest of France, was largely unharmed in the World Wars, leaving its architecture remarkably well-preserved. The atmosphere is subdued and slow-paced—you probably won't come across any raging parties while you hang out here. What you will find are charming villages that have remained far enough off the beaten track to be decidedly, thoroughly French.

The medieval architecture may remind you of the Alsace region in northern France: You will see lots of old timbered houses with exposed wood beams. Towns like **Dijon,** from whose Palais du Duc the region was ruled in years past, and **Beaune,** are excellent places to lose your way and yourself in—and small enough that you'll never *really* get lost while you stumble around discovering amazing little buildings and hidden courtyards. But architecture isn't what draws the masses of visitors to this region. Burgundy—or "Bourgogne" as the French call it— is best known for its cuisine and its wines, which are among the best in the country. The reds get the most press, but the whites shouldn't be ignored. Sample a local white as part of the favorite local aperitif, *kir,* which mixes wine with syrup of cassis. The local cuisine complements the wines with meats cooked in delicate sauces, typically made with wine and mushrooms.

For more info about the region, check out ***www.bourgogne-tourisme. com*** or ***www.burgundy-tourism.com.***

great outdoors

The lush countryside of the Burgundy region, which stretches north of the Rhône river valley toward Paris, is of course covered in vineyards. But besides all those grapes, there are also quiet hiking and biking trails. The best place for hiking and biking is the **Parc Naturel Régional du Morvan,** not so much a wilderness as a bucolic section of country roads, vineyards, old farmsteads, and little villages.

The 175,000-hectare park, created in 1970, sprawls across the entire sparsely inhabited region surrounding the towns of Autun, Avallon, and Vénelay. The northern part of the park can be reached by buses from Avallon, the southern part by buses from Autun.

The park has the best marked hiking and biking trails in France—labeled VTT or *vélo tout terrain*. Some of these are quite steep, others roll through relatively flat countryside. Some of the villages in the park exist like Brigadoon in a landscape that hasn't seen much change over the last 50 years (the villagers have TV, but that's about it). Along the way you'll pass gurgling streams, but don't drink the water, regardless of how clean it looks....

The northern section of the park is like a picture postcard of Burgundian hills, valleys, farms, and villages. Avallon or Vézelay make the best bases. Need a goal for your hiking or biking? Make it **Quarré-les-Tombes,** 12 miles south of Avallon. This is Burgundy's most perfectly preserved village, reminiscent of the days when the region was a kingdom unto itself. In the center of the park is a series of four lakes, all ideal for boating or windsurfing. If you prefer steeper mountains to rolling vineyard-studded countryside, head for the southern section of the park, best explored on a day trip from the sleepy town of Autun. The tourist office in Autun *(3 ave. Charles-de-Gaulle; Tel 03/85-86-80-38),* provides free maps and even bike rentals. Lists of campsites are available from all local tourist offices. Note that it's against the law to camp outside designated sites. The tourist office in Dijon (see *need to know,* below) gives away free maps and pamphlets detailing at least a half dozen hiking and biking trails through the park. Excursions last from a few hours to a full day, and some even last several days, with the understanding that clients will camp or stay at hotels en route.

TRaVEL TIMES

* TGV (Fast Train—more expensive)	Beaune	Paris	Dijon
Dijon	:20	1:50 2:50*	-
Beaune	-	2:10 4:00*	:20

wines of burgundy

We don't quite agree with the Burgundian vinter who claimed that he once tasted the finest of Bordeaux and the most sparkling of champagne but had to spit them both out in disgust. "They tasted like vinegar," he claimed. "Only a true Burgundy can satisfy the palate of the connoisseur."

A bit of an exaggeration, but the wines of Burgundy or Bourgogne are indeed among the best in the world. Being able to taste them in their vineyards is reason enough to visit the region. The reds give you an inner glow from their fruity taste and aromatic bouquet, and, of all the world's whites, a white Burgundy is the most preferred by gourmet palates. (But don't worry—even if your palate is far from gourmet, you'll still have a great time tasting these spectacular wines while gazing out at the gorgeous vineyards. Hey, maybe you'll even learn what an aromatic bouquet is supposed to smell like!)

After the Roman conquest, it was actually fat, wine-guzzling church bishops who launched the fiefdom's vineyards. Monuments were built to the glory of God and to Bacchus, who, at least in Burgundy, shares the celestial throne. In time the dukes of Burgundy became known as the "Princes of the best wines of Christianity."

In the years to come, the legends of France sang the praises of Burgundy—Napoléon had a weakness for Chambertin, and Madame de Pompadour claimed she became sex-crazed after drinking Romanée-conti. In 1878, the vines were destroyed by the insect phylloxera, but plants shipped in from the United States were not vulnerable to the pest, and ended up replacing the Burgundian grapes of yore.

Suprisingly, Burgundy, birthplace of Pinot Noir and Chardonnay, produces only two percent of the wines of France. Vineyard acreage is only half of what it was in 1870. Nearly half of the grapes are used to produce Beaujolais. Burgundies beloved by wine-fanciers the world over include Chablis, Pouilly-Fuisse, Chambertin, Nuits-Saint-Georges, Beaune, Pommard, and others.

As you travel through Burgundy, you'll find that some 150 wine producers or wine traders welcome you to their small cellars to sample their products. These vintners have signed a "Welcome Charter" to guarantee you a friendly reception. Look for a sign on their entrance— *"Bourgogne Decouverte"*—to know they're opening a bottle for you inside.

If you're looking for a little hand-holding, **Eurobike** *(4 rue du Faubourg Raines, a half mile southwest of the center of Dijon; Tel 03/80-45-32-32)* will help you plan a self-guided bike trip. The best of these follows D122 south along the **Route des Grands Crus,** first through Beaune (a distance of 25 miles), and then if you're up for it, on to Macon, an additional 68 miles. (Macon is 93 miles south of Dijon.) Traffic is not terribly dense on this secondary highway, which takes you through Burgundy's most legendary wine villages. Eurobike will rent bikes and—if needed—arrange hotel accommodations en route.

If hillclimbing and spelunking among the caves and grottoes of the Morvan sounds more appealing than busting your butt on a bike all day, contact **Dijon Spéléo,** *(35 rue Jean-Baptiste Baudin, Dijon; Tel 03/80-31-86-30).*

getting around the region

Trains are the best and most efficient way to get around the area. You'll most likely see Burgundy on your way south from Paris. It's a great place to get off the train for a day or two to check out the architecture and countryside of this historic part of France.

▶▶**LIST OF SUGGESTED ROUTES**
The best route is from Lyon to Dijon, with a stopover at Beaune, which lies between the two cities. If you're pressed for time, you can cut your stop in Beaune to only an hour or two.

dijon

One of those old, walled towns with winding, easy-to-get-lost-in streets, Dijon (like the mustard) is the capital of Burgundy and one of the larger cities in the region. It was once the home of the Dukes of Burgundy, and its most recognizable feature is the old **Palais des Ducs** [see *culture zoo,* below] in the center of town. There are a number of other medieval buildings with exposed wooden beams that might remind you of Alsace. Dijon's local architectural buffs are proud that, because the town has never been damaged in a war, many medieval and Renaissance buildings are still standing and well-preserved. The tourist office can provide a list of these buildings, which are also marked by brown and white signs throughout town. There is an overwhelming number of beautiful churches and cathedrals here for such a small town, such as **St. Benigne, St. Philibert, St. Jean, Notre-Dame, St. Etienne,** and **St. Michel.** The narrow streets are lined with two- and three-story homes, and around almost any corner you'll find a hidden, ivy-draped courtyard.

Most of Dijon's points of interest are in the center of town. It's more than likely that the only reason you'll have to leave the *centre ville* is if you're staying in one of the hostels on the outskirts of town. Besides, wandering the streets of the old town and getting lost is the best way to explore Dijon. Bring your camera, because you'll stumble upon amazing little corners and approach cathedrals from rarely photographed angles. You shouldn't miss the **Musée des Beaux Arts** [see *culture zoo,* below] in the **Palais des Ducs.** As you wander through the streets of the old town in the afternoon, the best place to stop off for an aperitif is **La Brasserie Déclic** [see *bar scene,* below] on the Place des Cordeliers. Try

dijon

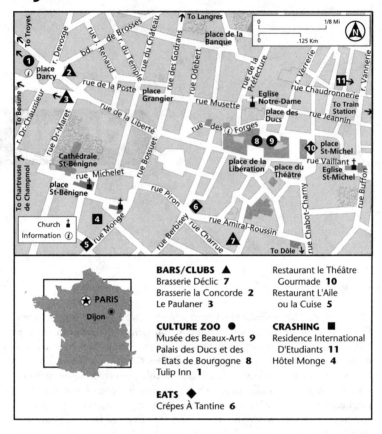

BARS/CLUBS ▲
Brasserie Déclic **7**
Brasserie la Concorde **2**
Le Paulaner **3**

Restaurant le Théâtre
Gourmade **10**
Restaurant L'Aile
ou la Cuise **5**

CULTURE ZOO ●
Musée des Beaux-Arts **9**
Palais des Ducs et des
Etats de Bourgogne **8**
Tulip Inn **1**

CRASHING ■
Residence International
D'Etudiants **11**
Hôtel Monge **4**

EATS ◆
Crépes À Tantine **6**

a *kir,* the local aperitif of choice, which is a mixture of white Burgundy wine and cassis, or get regal with a *kir royal,* which is made with sparkling wine.

The atmosphere of Dijon is pretty relaxed and casual. People are more likely to wear jeans than feature high-fashion threads, and the locals will take their time with you and try to help you with your French. Dijon isn't a wild party town, but there's plenty to do if you're down to hang out. There are several bars and clubs on **avenue Foch,** which you'll pass on your way from the train station to **place Darcy.** For information on local happenings, check *DOC.umentation: Le Guide Culturel,* which lists info on museums, music, theater, and dance, and which you can get at a *tabac* or local bar.

neighborhoods

The center of town has a ton of pedestrian-only streets, including **rue de la Liberté,** which runs on a nearly east/west axis and takes you from the large square by the train station, **place Darcy,** to the **Palais des Ducs** [see *culture zoo,* below] in the center of town. The **centre ville** of Dijon is bordered by wide, tree-lined avenues: **rue du Transvaal** on the south, **boulevard de Brosses** on the north, **boulevard Carnot** and **boulevard Thiers** on the east and rue de l'Arquebuse on the west. The maps of Dijon make it look deceptively easy to navigate; in fact, the streets are so old and curvey that it's easy to get lost. This makes the town fun to cruise around in, though, because you constantly feel like you're discovering things and can be proud of yourself when you start to know your way around.

Since Dijon is so small and most of the sights are on or near the pedestrian streets, buses aren't really necessary unless you're staying on the outskirts of town.

bar scene

Dijon's bars are the main hangouts for its young people. There are a few karaoke clubs and piano bars, but they're usually pretty deserted except for some older tourists. In the bars, it's easy to meet the local kids—they're less involved in their own scenes than kids in bigger cities. A good spot for happy hour or late night is **La Brasserie Déclic** (*2 place des Cordeliers; Tel 03/80-50-03-35; 8-2am Mon-Sat; average drink 15F; V, MC*), right in the old town. It has a few tables outside and a bigger space indoors, decorated with murals, with a pool table and a couple of dart boards. Order some snack grub and listen to French radio, unless you're lucky enough to be here for a night of live music, starting at around 10pm.

Back toward the train station and place Darcy, the avenue Maréchal Foch is lined with bars and pubs. The busiest, most popular one is **Le Paulaner** (*1 ave. Foch; Tel 03/80-43-57-60; 6:30-2am daily; drinks 15-30F; V, MC*), where the light wood bar is always jammed with locals and the crowded tables are packed with students and tourists. There's a different fruity drink on special most nights of the week. Things start picking up in this corner of town at around 11pm.

wired

The Tourist Office's web site is *www.ot-dijon.fr,* and there are general web sites on the Burgundy region in both French and English at *www.bourgogne-tourisme.com* and *www.burgundy-tourism.com.*

Dijon offers a couple of places to check e-mail: the **Cyberposte** in the post office [see *need to know,* above] and **Port Cyber** (*4 Quai Nicolas Rolin; No phone; Bus stop Hopital Général; 9am-9pm daily; 40F an hour; No credit cards*), just west of the *centre ville.*

For an older, more mellow, and decidedly local crowd, go to **Brasserie La Concorde** (*2 place Darcy; Tel 03/80-30-69-43; 7-1am daily; food 25-100F, drinks 15-20F; V, MC, AE*). There's a dining area where you can hide in a big black booth as well as a bar section both downstairs and upstairs where you can peer though the big windows at the passers-by outside. A largely local crowd has dinner here after work, but it's also a good happy hour spot.

arts scene

Dijon has a popular performing arts scene. The **Opéra** and the **Théatre** are traditional and conservative for the most part, while the big annual May theater festival includes more experimental and modern pieces.

The **Opéra** (*Place du Théatre; Tel 03/08-68-46-40; Ticket office open 10am-7pm Mon-Sat; Tickets 100-250F; No credit cards*) is a large, beautiful building in which well-established French and Italian operas are staged.

The **Theatre National Dijon Bourgogne** (*Venues vary; Tel 03/80-30-12-12; 35-150F; No credit cards*) hosts the big theater festival in May, and more traditional fare during the rest of the year. Although it's not a regular occurrence, the theater does have occassional performances in English. The festival in May presents various forms and styles from all over the world nad is thus the best time to catch a performance in English. You and all the hip kids in town can catch alternative French and foreign films at **Cinéma Eldorado** (*21 rue Alfred de Musset; Tel 03/80-66-12-34; Show times 2-10pm; 40F; No credit cards*).

culture zoo

In addition to the famous Palais des Ducs, the main cultural attractions of Dijon are its medieval and Renaissance buildings, which you see on

notre dame

The **L'Église Notre Dame** (*place Notre Dame; Tel 03/80-74-35-76; Open year-round; No admission charge*), one of Dijon's many old churches, is located a block north of the enormous **Palais des Ducs.** On one of the central columns, just above eye level, is a softened stone about the size and shape of a cupped hand. According to tradition, if you place your palm on the stone and close your eyes, your wish will come true. Right near that spot, there's a little salamander carved into the cathedral wall. We haven't heard that he has any magical powers, but he sure is cute.

your walks about town; get a more detailed map with explanations from the tourist office [see *need to know,* below].

Check out the exterior of the **Palais des Ducs et des Etats de Bourgogne** *(place de la Libération)* at night as well as during the day—it has a very different look and feel depending on the hour.

The **Musée des Beaux-Arts** *(Palais des Ducs; Tel 03/80-74-52-70; 10am-6pm daily except Tue, modern art section closed 11:45am-1:45pm; 25F, free for students, free on Sunday; No credit cards)* is an eclectic museum housed in the Palais des Ducs that offers a great collection of art and artifacts along with a glimpse of parts of the stunning interior of the palace. The museum has everything from Egyptian artifacts and old Ducal tombs to tapestries and paintings of the French and Flemish Renaissance. There are also some fine examples of Impressionism and modern art (including a few Picassos). Don't go during lunchtime because you really won't want to miss the modern art section upstairs, which is closed from 11:45am to 1:45pm.

The austere interior of the **Cathédrale St-Bénigne** *(Place St-Bénigne; Tel 03/80-30-14-90; No entrance fee for the cathedral, entrance to the crypt 10F; Visiting hours 9am-5pm Mon-Sat, services Sun)* rests under a brightly tiled roof that forms one of the most distinctive landmarks on the Dijon cityscape. Built on the site of a Romanesque basilica, the church was constructed in a pure Burgundian and Gothic style after it collapsed in 1271. The west front is held up by towering buttresses, and the façade is marked by two great towers resting under conically shaped roofs. The crowning architectural glory here is the eerie crypt left over from the 11th century—a forest of pillars and columns surmounted by a rotunda which evokes the tomb of the basilica, *Christ in Jerusalem,* constructed in the 4th century. This rotunda is one of only eight of its kind left in the world. Some of the columns are decorated with grotesque animals and kneeling figures, some of the rarest examples of pre-Romanesque sculpture in France.

STUff

Many of the town's most interesting shops line either side of the rue de la Liberté. Three shops that typify the Dijonnais interest in food and things culinary include:

Boutique Grey Poupon *(Rue de la Liberté, corner of rue du Chapeau Rouge; Tel 02/80-30-41-02).* Here, within a Dijonnais monument to its own gastronomical ideas, you'll find everything that the city most concerned with mustard can possibly do with mustard.

The theme of **Boutique Vedrene** *(1 rue Bossuet; Tel 03/80-49-98-52)* is blackberries *(les cassis),* which grow in profusion in the surrounding forests. Come here for blackberry brandy, digestifs, and aperitifs, as well as candy, pastries, jams, marmalades, and confections made from the distinctive berry.

Gingerbread, a local specialty, comes in every conceivable shape, size, and degree of sweetness at **Boutique Mullot et Petit Jean** *(13 place*

Bossuet; Tel 03/80-30-07-10), a cozy reminder of France's grandes-mères from years past.

EATS

Burgundy is famous not only for its wines, but also for its food. You might see *boeuf Bourguignon* on menus outside of Burgundy, but in Dijon you can try the real deal. The region is also known for its ham, fish, and lamb dishes, and of course you should try something served with the famous Dijon mustard.

A great, small restaurant serving traditional Bourgogne cuisine is **Restaurant L'Aile ou la Cuisse** *(2 rue Monge; Tel 03/80-44-97-59; 11am-2pm/7-10pm daily, closed Sat at lunchtime and Sun evening; Average meal 50-70F; V, MC)*. Near the St. Jean cathedral, this little hole-in-the-wall has small, closely packed tables, rickety stairs down to the wine cellar, and an old interior of stone and beams. The chef said he'll offer you a free *kir* if you show him this book!

Along the pedestrian streets are lots of good little places to eat, such as **Les Crepes à Tantine** *(35 rue Admiral Roussin; Tel 03/80-49-99-36; 11am-2pm/7-10pm Tue-Fri, 7-10pm Sat; 20-45F; V, MC)*, which has terrace seating perfect for people-watching and serves simple and tasty crepes and salads.

For some local cuisine near the old theater in the center of town, try **Restaurant le Théatre Gourmand** *(31 rue Chabot Charny; No phone; 11:45am-2pm/7:15-10pm Mon-Fri, 7:15-10pm Sat; set menus 60-100F; V, MC)*. It has a central location, serves all the local specialties, and is decorated in the traditional blues and yellows of the region.

crashing

The cheapest places to stay are in the two hostels listed below, which are unfortunately both a 20-minute bus ride outside of town and force you to depend on the buses, which stop running at 8pm. If you need transportation later than that, the best place to find taxis is near place Darcy. In the old town you'll find some friendly, quirky hotels, such as **Hotel Monge** [see below], which are fun because they give you a first-hand view of some of the little courtyards and spiral staircases of the old buildings.

The **Residence International D'Etudiants** *(6 rue Maréchal Leclerc; Tel 03/80-71-70-00; Bus 4 or 6 to Vélodrome; 90F; V, MC, AE)* has dorm rooms with hall showers and toilets, an international crowd (including many long-term student residents) that likes to socialize, and no curfew. Built in the 1970s, its two five-story buildings contain 300 fairly stark rooms, 296 of which are single rooms with sinks. There's always room for anyone with a student ID. There's a cafe on the premises as well as a kitchen for guests who want to prepare their own food.

Centre de Rencontres Internationals de Dijon *(1 blvd. Champollion; Tel 03/80-72-95-20; Bus 6 to place du Republique then transfer to bus 5 to Epiray; Closed Jan; Singles, doubles, and triples 140-155F, dorm quads 78F per bed, dorm for eight 72F per bed; V, MC)* also built in the

1970s, consists of two four-story buildings. Some double rooms have showers but not WCs, while dorm-style rooms, suitable for either four or eight occupants, have neither. There's a patio, a terrace, a community swimming pool literally next door, a microwave for guests, and a 24-hour reception desk— which means no curfew.

The woman who runs **Hotel Monge** *(20 rue Monge; Tel 03/80-30-55-41; Reception open 7am-10pm; 125-210F singles, 145-230F doubles; V, MC)* will serve you breakfast at noon if you want to sleep in, and loves to befriend bedraggled travelers. The hotel is on the western end of the town center, near the St. Jean cathedral. The dark rooms are clean and have an antique feel; the hall showers in the storage room can be a fun—if harrowing—experience.

Near the train station, the **Tulip Inn** *(14 ave. Foch; Tel 03/80-41-61-12; 200-460F singles, 450-660F doubles; V, MC, AE, DIN)* has modern rooms with bathtubs or showers, and a big breakfast buffet is included.

need to know

Currency Exchange The **tourist office** can change money for you, as will many of the **banks** nearby on **place Darcy.**

Tourist Information Dijon's **Office de Tourisme** *(Place Darcy; Tel 03/80-44-11-44; 9am-8pm daily)* is just a block east of the train station if you walk down avenue Foch. They change money, and also provide town maps, bus maps, telephone cards, souvenirs, and brochures.

Public Transportation The **STRD** buses have a central stop at **place Grangier,** near the Tourist Office. They run until 8pm Mon-Sat with very limited Sunday service. The fare is 8F.

Heath and Emergency Emergency: *15;* police: *17.* The local **hospital** is at *3 rue du Faubourg-Raines (Tel 03/80-29-30-31).*

Pharmacies Most of the pharmacies in town, identifiable by their **green neon crosses,** are open 8am-noon/2-7pm.

Telephone Local area code: *03.* Telecartes can be purchased at newsstands and Tabacs.

Airport Dijon-Bourgogne airport *(Tel 03/80-67-67-67)* is around 3 miles from the town center. Bus 1 from rue de la Liberté will drop you off at Longvic Mairies, a ten-minute walk from the airport.

Trains The SNCF train station, **Gare de Dijon** *(Ave. Foch; Tel 08/36-35-35-35),* is just a block from the Tourist Office at place Darcy and a 5- or 10-minute walk from downtown.

Bus TRANSCO bus station *(rue des Perrières; Tel 03/80-42-11-00; Info desk open 6:30am-7:30pm weekdays, 12:30-7:30pm Saturday, 11am-12:30pm/5 to 7:30pm Sunday)* is in the same building as the train station.

Bike/Moped Rental Riding a bike around the countryside of Burgundy is a great way to explore the area. You can rent one from **Euro-bike** *(4 rue du Faubourg Raines; Tel 03/80-45-32-32; www.euro-bike.fr; 8am-12:30pm/1:30-6:30pm Mon-Fri, 9am-noon/2-6pm Sat; bikes*

100F per day, motos 270F per day; V, MC, AE), a half mile southwest of the city center.

Laundry Laverie Automatique is at 17 rue Pasteur near the place des Cordeliers *(No phone; 7am-9pm daily)*.

Postal The main branch of **La Poste** *(Place Grangier; Tel 03/80-50-62-19; 8am-7pm Mon-Fri, 8am-noon Sat)* is right by the big bus stop.

Internet See wired, above.

beaune

The quaint but very touristy village of Beaune makes a great stop for a couple of hours, though you likely won't want to spend the night here. It has the steep prices of a tourist town, and you'll probably run out of things to do after a few hours. You can take a half-hour train ride from Dijon, or make it a midway stop on your way from Lyon to Dijon.

Beaune is well known for its *caves,* wine cellars where you can take a tour and taste that famous Burgundy wine. Its other main selling point is the medieval architecture of the **Hospices de Beaune** and the adjacent **Musée de l'Hotel-Dieu** [see *culture zoo,* below]. The architecture here is similar to that of Dijon, with a lot of wooden beam-framed buildings on winding, cobblestone streets.

Beaune is a tiny town enclosed by old ramparts, and unless you decide to rent a bike and tour the vineyards in the surrounding area, you'll stay within those walls during your visit. To get into town from the train station, walk down the main street, **avenue du 8 Septembre,** which will take you straight into town just past the ramparts. To get to the very center of Beaune, follow the signs to the **Tourist Office** and the **Hotel-Dieu,** which will lead you through the twisty, narrow streets. These two buildings are in the middle of town, on **place de la Halle,** and they're also the center of the action. The rest of Beaune, consisting mainly of small medieval buildings and old wine cellars, continues on tiny pedestrian streets (and other streets that are so small you'd *think* they were pedestrian streets), out toward the ramparts. The ramparts are where the local young people hang out to have a cigarette or a beer or to kick a soccer ball around.

beaune

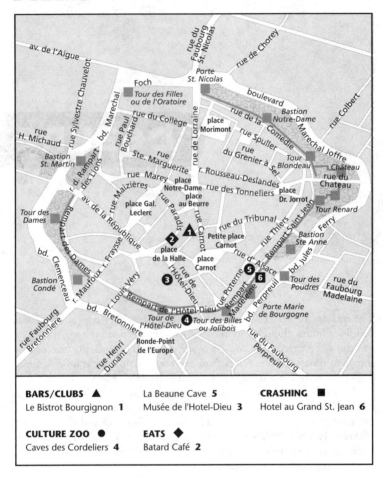

BARS/CLUBS ▲
Le Bistrot Bourgignon **1**

La Beaune Cave **5**
Musée de l'Hotel-Dieu **3**

CRASHING ■
Hotel au Grand St. Jean **6**

CULTURE ZOO ●
Caves des Cordeliers **4**

EATS ◆
Batard Café **2**

bar scene

There's not much of a bar scene in Beaune apart from the wine tasting at the local *caves* (wine cellars) so that may be where you choose to stop for a drink while you're here.

There are some good wine bars, like **Le Bistrot Bourgignon** *(8 rue Monge; Tel 03/80-22-23-24; 5-10pm Tue-Sat; Drinks 20-40F, dinner 80-200F; V, MC, AE),* which also serves dinner and jazz shows on Saturday night beginning around 9pm. It has some outdoor seating on the pedestrian street, which is just off the central place de la Halle. The interior is predictably decorated with wine pitchers and old green wine bottles. The **Batard Cafe** [see *eats,* below], is more of a traditional, smoky bar/cafe/brasserie.

CULTURE ZOO

It's all about the architecture and the wine. You can cruise around town to see all the old buildings and wander into any *cave* you see, but here are a few places you won't want to miss.

Musée de l'Hotel-Dieu (*rue de l'Hotel-Dieu; Tel 03/80-24-45-00; 9-11:30am/2-5pm Jan 1-Mar 24; 9am-6:30pm Mar 25-Nov 19; 9-11:30am/2-5:30pm Nov 20-Dec 31; 32F, 25F students; No credit cards*): Arguably the main attraction in Beaune. This 15th-century hospital founded by Nicolas Rolan in 1443 boasts beautiful architecture, particularly its intricately tiled roof, which you can see best from the center courtyard. Inside is a museum that displays the history of the hospital, which until recently continued to admit new patients. The collection includes the famous painting *Le Jugement Dernier,* by Roger van der Weyden.

La Beaune Cave (*3 rue Poterne; Tel 03/80-22-92-43; 10am-7:30pm daily; Free; V, MC, AE*): This is actually more of a shop than a traditional wine cellar, but has free admission and free tastes, and therefore makes a great start to your wine-tasting.

Caves du Couvent des Cordeliers (*6 rue de l'Hotel-Dieu; Tel 03/80-25-08-85; 9:30am-7pm daily; 30F; V, MC, AE*): The streets near the Hotel-Dieu are full of *caves,* but this is one of the best. You can see the big barrels and bottles of fermenting wine and smell that stale, cold, earthy, penicillin-y smell that is the mark of any wine cellar.

EATS

The only really cheap options in town are the little sandwich stands on the pedestrian streets such as **rue Monge** and **rue Carnot,** or a picnic on the ramparts. Most of the restaurants are fancy dinner spots, but we're not recommending that you spend the night in Beaune anyway.... A mid-range, busy, central lunch place is **Batard Cafe** (*14 place de la Halle; No phone; 7-2am daily; 30-50F dishes; V, MC*), just across from the Office de Tourisme and the Hotel-Dieu. It has a stone interior, blue neon lights, tables decorated with old newspaper clippings, and seating upstairs, downstairs, and on the patio. There's a mixed crowd of locals and tourists. The smoky cafe is also a bar and serves basic fare like pizzas, quiches, and salads.

crashing

There's no youth hostel in Beaune and the little hotels are quick to fill up in the summertime, so, uh...good luck!

If you do decide to spend the night, the **Hotel au Grand St.-Jean** (*18 rue du Faubourg Madeleine; Tel 03/80-24-12-22; 255F doubles, 315F quads; V, MC*) is one of the largest hotels and more likely to have rooms available. The place is clean and otherwise pretty standard for a mid-range hotel.

NEED TO KNOW

Currency Exchange There are a few **banks** on **place de la Halle,** near the Tourist Office, that will change money for you.

Tourist Information The **Office de Tourisme** *(rue de l'Hotel-Dieu; Tel 03/80-26-21-30; 9:30am-7pm Mon-Thur, 9:30am-8pm Fri & Sat, 9:30am-6pm Sun)* has maps and complete information on the museum and wine cellars, and makes hotel reservations.

Health and Emergency Emergency: *15;* police: *17.* The local hospital is **Centre Hospitalier SMUR** *(Ave. Guigogne de Salin; Tel 03/80-22-07-08).*

Trains The train station is around a half mile east of the city center at the end of avenue du 8 Septembre. There are two trains per hour going each direction between **Beaune** and Dijon *(ave. du 8 Septembre; Tel 08/36-35-35-35).*

Bike Rental You can rent a bike to tour the vineyards in the surrounding countryside from **Bourgogne Randonnées** *(7 ave. du 8 Septembre; Tel 03/80-22-06-03; 9am-noon/1:30-7pm Mon-Sat; 10am-noon/2-6pm Sun; V, MC),* which is right between town and the train station and will give you a map of the wine country.

Laundry The only place in town is **La Lavandière** *(rue Faubourg St. Jean; No phone; 7am-8pm daily).*

Postal La Poste is located just north of the ramparts *(7 blvd. St. Jacques; Tel 03/80-26-2- 50; 8am-7pm Mon-Fri; 8am-noon Sat).*

the massif central and the auvergne

тhe massif central

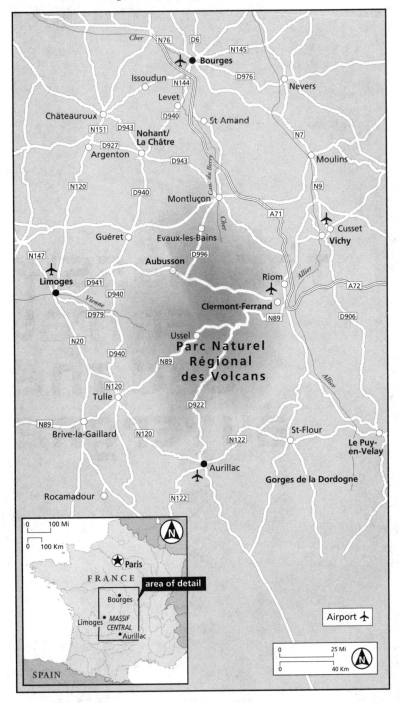

hundreds of years ago, before modern buildings and cars and tourists with camcorders, France must have looked something like the Massif Central of today. If you take the train west from Lyon or south from Paris, you won't need a map to know when you've arrived: You'll sense it as soon as the scenery unfolds into a distinctly green, undisturbed mountain range.

The country's rural heartland, the Massif Central is a rugged landscape of open valleys, extinct volcano ranges, forests, and small mountain villages in central France. Past volcanic activity has created a bizarre landscape: The *puys* (volcanoes) are now softly rolling green hills, lakes fill what used to be craters, and little villages perch on old lava flows and volcanic spires. In many towns, even the buildings are made from volcanic stone, giving them a somber, earthy look against the grassy green *puys* in the background.

In the heart of the Massif Central is the Auvergne, which stretches from the awesome old volcano range known as the Mont Dômes in the north to the Mont Cantal in the south. It's the most rural and isolated part of the region, is one the poorest parts of France, and is filled with volcanoes and wild open spaces. It's also home to some of France's famous cheeses: St. Nectaire, Cantal, Fourme D'Ambert, Blue d'Auvergen, and Roquefort.

The train will take you past tiny stone villages that will make you feel like you've stepped back in time. Even in the bigger, more accessible towns, the people remain less cosmopolitan and Americanized than in other parts of France. Food here is simple and relies on the area's fresh veggies for its unique flavors, like *potée auvergnate,* a cabbage soup that's often served with pork.

The Massif-Central (and especially the Auvergne) is perfect for hiking—the local sport of choice—as well as skiing, rafting, hanggliding, and mountain biking. From scaling the heights of the **Puy de Dome,** the highest and most awesome old volcano in the Mont Dômes volcanic range, to exploring the wilds in the **Parc Naturel Régional des Volcans d'Auvergne,** you'll have your pick of beautiful places. Unfortunately for the budget traveler, the area is hard to navigate if you don't have a car. Your best bet for exploring the outdoors is to go to a larger city like **Clermont-Ferrand,** where you'll have easy access

travel times

	Le Puy de Dome	Le Puy en Velay	Bordeaux	La Rochelle	Paris	Clermont-Ferrand
*TGV (Fast Train—more expensive **By car						
Clermont-Ferrand	:15**	1:15**	5:25**	5:15**	3:30	-
Le Puy de Dome	-	1:30**	5:10**	5:00**	4:15**	:15**
Le Puy en Velay	1:30**	-	5:00**	6:30**	5:15**	1:15**
Bordeaux	5:10**	5:00**	-	1:15	5:20*	5:25**
La Rochelle	5:00**	6:30**	2:15	-	3:30* 5:15	5:15**

to the mountain trails and parks in the surrounding region. Or, if you're more of a townie, stick to one of the smaller towns, such as **Le Puy en Velay,** with its medieval buildings and (sometimes campy) religious shrines.

getting around the region

Trains are the second-best way to get around, and the countryside near any of the towns is an awesome place to explore by bike. You can visit Le Puy en Velay as a day trip from Lyon; it's only about a 2- to 2-1/2-hour train ride. Getting from Le Puy to Clermont-Ferrand should take you about another two hours; from there, you can explore the countryside around the "big city" by foot, by bike, or by shuttle. From Clermont-Ferrand, you can shoot back over to Lyon in just less than three hours, and Lyon's busy train schedule can link you to anywhere else in France you might want to go.

▶▶ROUTES

Although it doesn't let you get into the wilds of the country, the train is still the best cheap way to get around the Massif Central. If you're coming from Paris or Lyon, the best loop to take is through Clermont-Ferrand and Le Puy en Velay and back to Lyon or down to Provence.

If you're lucky enough to have access to a car, you can make a similar loop. Be sure to take your time and stop at some of the smaller towns and trailheads along the way.

clermont-ferrand

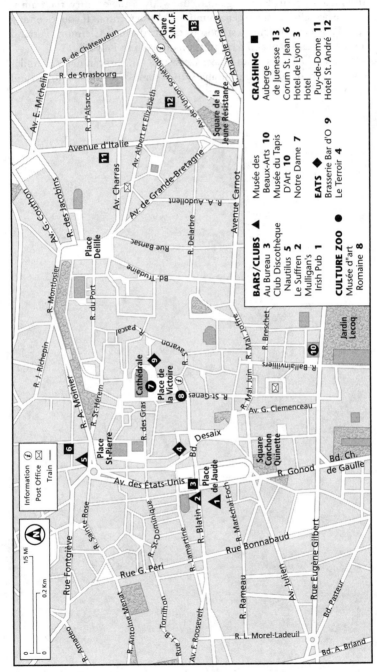

CRASHING ■
Auberge
de Juenesse **13**
Corum St. Jean **6**
Hotel de Lyon **3**
Hotel
Puy-de-Dome **11**
Hotel St. André **12**

Musée des
Beaux-Arts **10**
Musée du Tapis
D'Art **10**
Notre Dame **7**

EATS ◆
Brasserie Bar d'O **9**
Le Terroir **4**

BARS/CLUBS ▲
Au Bureau **3**
Club Discothèque
Nautilus **5**
Le Suffren **2**
Mulligan's
Irish Pub **1**

CULTURE ZOO ●
Musée d'art
Romaine **8**

Information (i)
Post Office ⊠
Train —

CLERMONT-fERRAND

The spooky architecture of Clermont-Ferrand would make a great backdrop for a horror movie. The huge cathedral, city hall, and fountains are all built out of a smoky black volcanic stone that's impressive almost to the point of being oppressive—the somber, charcoal-colored Gothic cathedral looms against an often stormy sky, and the inside feels even more darkly grandiose and empty than most cathedrals in France. After a few days in the area, however, the buildings seem less gloomy, and you'll see that they suit the city perfectly, linking it to the nearby countryside and its range of extinct volcanoes. The dark colors contrast beautifully with the rolling green *puys* (volcanoes) that you keep glimpsing beyond the narrow, cobblestone streets that wind downhill from the cathedral.

Although it's Auvergne's capital, Clermont-Ferrand lacks the cosmopolitan feel of a big city. The people seem more like small-town folk: They take their time, and they like to be outdoors. Although they have a reputation for being cold and can seem somewhat reserved, they're friendly when you approach them, and this is one place where the locals still seem very decidedly French: It's unlikely you'll hear a lot of English, and you'll probably see your fair share of folks sporting matching top-and-bottom shiny jogging suits and maybe a beret or two.

Like most towns in the Auvergne, Clermont-Ferrand is surrounded by nature. If you wander along its outskirts, you'll run into dozens of hiking paths. It seems that every local's favorite activity is taking a hike or bike ride up one of the old volcanoes nearby. Contact the **tourist office** or the sports outfitter **Espace Massif Central** for more information [see *need to know*, below, for both]. The best hikes can be found in the Parc Naturel

Régional des Volcans d'Auvergne [see *everywhere else,* below]. But despite its medieval appearance and outdoorsy locals, Clermont-Ferrand is mainly an industrial city. In fact, it's the birthplace of the Michelin tire company, founded in 1889 by Scotsman Charles Mackintosh. In recent years, production has slacked off and some of the old factories have closed.

Thanks to the student population at the city's two major universities—the Université de Clermont-Ferrand 1 (also called the Université d'Auvergne), and the Université de Clermont-Ferrand 2 (also called the Université Blaise Pascal)—there are some spots to hang out at night, although you probably wouldn't call Clermont-Ferrand a real hopping party town. You can check the latest cultural attractions in *Le Mois à Clermont-Ferrand,* a free monthly magazine that's available in most hotels and at the Tourist Office. The cosmopolitan students of Paris are sometimes dismissive of university students in the Massif Central, viewing them as the "hillbillies" of France, based on an old perception that the region is cut off from the rest of the world. Generalizations are wicked and dangerous, but young people here still tend to be more religious, conservative, and family-minded than elsewhere in France. Universities in the area have been much improved in the last quarter of a century, especially the school of fine arts and the business school, which is turning out some of the country's movers and shakers.

neighborhoods and hanging out

When you arrive at the train station at the eastern end of town, you'll want to hop right on a bus (you can take 2, 4, 8, or 14) to the center of town, about a five-minute ride rather than a thirty-minute walk; the area around the station is pretty run-down, and there's not much to see or do down there. If you get off the bus at **place de Jaude,** you can walk easily around the main areas of town, and you'll probably only use the buses to get back to the station or to get to a hiking trail on another end of town. Place de Jaude is the largest and most central square in town, with several restaurants, bars/brasseries, a large shopping center, and the central bus stop. **Le Suffren** [see *bar and club scene,* below] is the best cafe to stop for a cup of tea in the afternoon and watch the bustle of the town. The square is on the edge of the largely pedestrian *centre ville,* an area bordered on the north by **rue Andre Moinier,** on the west by **avenue des Etats-Unis,** on the east by **Cours Sablon** and **boulevard Trudaine,** and on the south by **boulevard Leon Malfreyt** and **boulevard Lafayette.** In the center of this pedestrian area, and basically at the top of the hill, is **place de la Victoire,** where you'll find that large and spooky cathedral, **Notre Dame** [see *culture zoo,* below], as well as the Tourist Office and a great fountain.

The main walking streets, which are lined with little shops and cafes, are **rue des Gras,** which runs straight up to the cathedral from place de Jaude, **rue du 11 Novembre, rue St. Barthelemy,** and **rue de la Boucherie.** Locals and the visitors spend a lot of time browsing these shops and hanging out in the cafes and brasseries nearby on **place de la**

wired

There are two places to check your e-mail in town. One is in the main branch of the Post Office at the **Cyberposte** *(60F for the first hour, 30F each additional hour);* the other is **Cybercafé** *(34 rue Ballainvilliers; Tel 04/73-92-42-80; 1-10pm Mon, Sat, 8am-10pm Tue-Fri; 50F per hour; V).* Before heading into town, you can check out the city's website at *www.ville-clermont-ferrand.fr.*

Victoire, and there is always a big group of local kids skateboarding on the wide, slanty steps in front of the cathedral. The *centre ville* also houses a quiet little park called **Square Blaise Pascal** and the large, imposing, volcanic rock **Préfecture,** as well as a lot of smaller houses and buildings built out of that same dark stone. In the middle of the rue St. Barthelemy, and contrasting remarkably with the older feel of the *centre ville,* is the large, modern, blue-and-yellow covered market called the **Marché St. Pierre.** The streets stretching away from the center of town are mainly industrial or residential, depending on which direction you head. The buildings of Clermont-Ferrand's universi You'll find the densest concentration of students within three separate neighborhoods: the suburb of Les Cézaux, 2 miles south of the center, and accessible by bus 3, 8, and 13, the closest section in town to a definable "campus," most of which is bureaucratic-looking, functional architecture from the 1970s; the inner city area around the corner of **boulevard François Mitterand** (still known by many residents as **avenue Gergovia**) and the **Boulevard Lafayette,** about a half-mile southeast of the place de Jaude, where you'll find students of "sciences and liberal arts"; and **avenue Carnot** near the corner of the **rue Paul Collomp,** about a half-mile east of place de Jaude, which attracts students studying foreign languages, including dozens willing to practice their English on you.

bar and club scene

The bars are really where most of the action is in town; the clubs that are *branché,* or "in," are in the suburbs, which are too far to walk to and not served by the buses. You can only get there if you've got a ride with a local who knows where to go. But if you're just looking for a few drinks, there are a lot of young people hanging out at the bars around place de Jaude. The scene is pretty mellow, and this is where the reserved attitude of the locals really shows itself. You won't see people getting really hammered or loud and raucous, but they do enjoy meeting up with their friends and hanging out.

For dinner and happy hour, **Au Bureau** *(16 place de Jaude; Tel 04/73-34-36-34; 7am-1am daily; 15F average drink; V, MC, AE, DIN)* is both a local and a tourist venue. It's on one of the corners of place de Jaude, right in the middle of most of the action at night. Have a beer on the patio while you wait for your friends to show up, then head into the smoky dark-wood interior, which has that look of a French place that thinks it looks American—decorated with old license plates and lined with vinyl booths where you can try out the pizza menu.

On another corner of place de Jaude, directly across from the mall and movie theater, are the two busiest bars in the center of town. It's hard to find a town in France without a popular Irish pub, and Clermont-Ferrand is no exception. **Mulligan's Irish Pub** *(1 ave. Julien; Tel 04/73-93-36-70; 8-1am Mon-Sat; 20F average drink; No credit cards)* is probably the loudest and most frequented drinking hole in town. Don't let all the green chairs, shamrocks, and Guinness signs fool you, though, because the crowd is strictly French. People show up in big groups starting at happy hour, and the place stays crowded till closing. From the street seating, you can hear the laughter echoing inside and see the neon lights on place de Jaude.

Just across the street from Mulligan's is another popular bar that doubles as a *salon de thé* during the day. **Le Suffren** *(48 place de Jaude; Tel 04/73-93-40-97; 7-1am daily; 15F average drink; No credit cards)* has patio seating that stretches around the corner, overlooking both place de Jaude and the crowd at Mulligan's. The daytime patrons are a mix of old and young, but as it gets later, the crowd gets younger, and people show up in couples and big groups getting ready to go barcrawling in the area.

One of the downtown nightclubs is **Club Discothèque Nautilus** *(9 rue Sainte Claire; Tel 04/73-31-05-55; 11pm-dawn Tue-Sat; Cover varies; No credit cards)*. Only about a block off of place de Jaude, it's a pretty typical small dance club—it's dark and smoky, plays all the hit dance tracks, and has theme nights several times a week.

CULTURE ZOO

Clermont-Ferrand's most impressive "culture" is its architecture: If you want to see what makes this town unique, take a walk around to check out the cathedral and the public buildings. If it's a rainy day, there are also some museums to keep you dry, all of which are located in the center of town.

Musée d'Art Romain *(in Office de Tourisme, place de la Victoire; Tel 04/73-98-65-00; 8:45am-6:30pm Mon-Fri, 9am-noon/2-6pm Sat, 9am-1pm Sun; Free admission):* This museum is a good place to check out when you first cruise into town—it's free and small, and it provides an interesting introduction to the area and its art and architecture. There are exhibits on the old volcanoes and the stone that was used to construct the city.

Câthédrale Notre Dame *(Place de la Victoire; No phone; 8am-dusk daily; Free admission):* The imposing Gothic cathedral is, as we mentioned above, one of the most remarkable sights of Clermont-Ferrand.

Musée des Beaux-Arts *(Place Deteix; Tel 04/73-16-11-30; 10am-6pm Tue-Sun; 23F, 13F students; No credit cards):* Home to a large collection of primarily medieval paintings.

Musée du Tapis d'Art (*45 rue Ballainvilliers; Tel 04/73-90-57-48; 10am-6pm Tue-Sun; 23F, 13F for students; No credit cards*): A unique collection of Asian and Middle Eastern carpets.

EATS

The local cuisine [see *Auvergne cuisine,* below] is simple, hearty, and known especially for its sausages and cheeses. Dishes often use cabbages and other green vegetables from the countryside. As a relatively large town, Clermont-Ferrand has restaurants that serve the local cuisine as well as a selection of brasseries with the typical fare you'll find all throughout France—pizzas, quiches, chicken, French fries—and, of course, the inescapable kebab stands.

For good brasserie fare before going out, **Au Bureau** [see *bar scene,* above] on place de Jaude has a big menu, specializing mainly in Italian-style pizzas.

The more local, campy **Brasserie/Bar d'O** (*5 place de la Victoire; Tel 04/73-91-43-14; 8-1am Mon-Sat, lunch served 11am-2pm; Average entrée 30-65F; V, MC*) is located between the Tourist Office and the cathedral. The place fills up with local professionals every day at lunchtime, when they serve a couple of *plats du jour.* The loud, busy restaurant is two stories high, with tables and chairs crowded onto the landing of the steps. Old-school French food advertisements and pencil drawings crowd the walls in the stairway, and the innumerable cigarettes that have been smoked by the regulars after their meals have begun to dull the red wallpaper.

You can order some local specialties at **Le Terroir** (*16 rue de la Prefecture; Tel 04/73-37-47-13; Noon-2pm Mon, 7:30-9:30pm Tue-Sat;*

auvergne cuisine

The local food is very rich and hearty, and furthers the impression that the locals spend a lot of time outdoors—you'd *have* to do some serious hiking to burn off all the calories. The Auvergne is best known for its meats and sausages, and the most famous dish of the region is *la potée Auvergnate,* a sort of stew full of locally grown cabbages, potatoes, and other vegetables with pork, bacon, and sausages, all cooked in a salty bouillon sauce. There are, of course, many locally made cheeses—the ones that you'll probably recognize are the Cantal and the Auvergne Bleu. Local bakeries usually have a good selection of mountain breads and grainy wheat breads in addition to the traditional white baguettes.

TO MARKET

If you're really sticking to your budget, you can get great produce at the market. The big covered market, **Marché St. Pierre** *(Espace St. Pierre; 7am-7:30pm Mon-Sat),* has vegetables, breads, meats, cheeses, and wines. The best fresh produce markets are **Halle St. Joseph** *(rue de Courpière; 7am-1pm Fri, 4pm-8pm Tue),* which sells vegetables from Puy-de-Dome; **Neuf-Soleils** *(rue des Chambrettes; Tue, Thur, Sat mornings);* and **Littré** *(place Littré; Tue, Thur, Sat mornings).* You can eat on the sloped steps outside the cathedral on place de la Victoire, or in Square Blaise Pascal, the small and secluded park just east of the pedestrian streets of the *centre ville.*

Menus 71F, 82F, 107F; MC, AE), a small restaurant whose stone interior has a very basic, no-frills decor. The place is hidden behind the big Prefecture building, close to place de Jaude.

crashing

The youth hostel and student housing dormitory are the best bets for a cheap place to crash here. The budget hotels in town are really cheap, and it shows. Though you might not pay a lot, you don't feel like you're walking away with a great deal.

The **Auberge de Jeunesse** *(55 ave. de l'Union Sovietique; Tel 04/73-92-26-39; Mar-Oct, reception open 7-9:30am/5-11pm; closed Nov-Feb; 48F; V, MC)* is a small hostel, with only 58 beds, a guest kitchen, and a small common room/TV room. Rooms contain 4 beds. Located very close to the train station, it's convenient when you arrive but a little out of the way when you want to hang out in town. To reach the center, take bus 2, 4, 18, or 14 from the train station. Access to the rooms is possible only during the hours of 7am–9:30am and 5–11pm. If you're not back before 11pm, you're locked out for the night. The entire place is closed between Nov 1 and Feb 28.

Some of the rooms at the dormitory-style student housing facility, **Corum St. Jean** *(17 rue Gaultier de Biauzat; Tel 04/73-31-57-00; Reception open 24 hours; 80-100F for a bed in a double room; No credit cards),* have their own shower, and the price includes breakfast, so it's a pretty good deal. Although the architecture is kind of unwelcoming—the design of the place somehow doesn't cater to meeting fellow travelers—the reception is friendly and helpful, and it's very close to the center of town (only a block north of the *centre ville* and a couple of blocks from place de Jaude).

The blocks around the train station are full of cheap hotels that are pretty run-down and pathetic looking. Typical is **Hôtel Puy-de-Dome** *(49 ave. Charras; Tel 04/73-90-74-38; 100F single, 200F double; No credit cards)*, with its steep, dark stairwell and cold linoleum floors. Registration is at the bar downstairs.

A couple of blocks away (and more than a couple of steps up) is the **Hôtel St. Andre** *(27 ave. de l'Union Sovietique; Tel 04/73-91-40-40; 230F single, 260F double; breakfast 30F; V, MC)*. All the rooms have a toilet and either a bath or a shower, and the place is cleaner and better kept than most of its neighbors. The reception is very friendly.

Directly upstairs from Au Bureau is **Hôtel de Lyon** *(16 place de Jaude; Tel 04/73-93-32-55; 285-335F single, 335-380F double; V, MC, AE)*. The spacious, high-ceilinged rooms have big windows, and some rooms have terraces. There are tubs or shower stalls and cable TV in the somewhat stark but very tidy rooms, and it's the most central, conveniently located hotel you could pick.

need to know

Currency Exchange You'll find a great number of **banks** concentrated in the area right around **place de Jaude,** and you'll probably get the best exchange rates there. **ATMs** *(distributeurs des billets)* are everywhere-in the railway station and along the major boulevards. Place de Jaude (the town's main square) has three of them: Crédit Lyonnais, Banque Populaire, and Société Générale.

Tourist Information There are two branches of the city's tourist office: the smaller **Office de Tourisme** *(Gare SNCF de Clermont-Ferrand; Tel 04/73-98-65-00; 9:15-11:30am/12:15-5pm Mon-Fri, same hours on Sat June-Sept)* is right in the train station, and the main **Office de Tourisme** *(Place de la Victoire; Tel 04/73-98-65-00; 8:45am-6:30pm Mon-Fri, 9am-noon/2-6pm Sat, 9am-1pm Sun)*, on the same square as the big cathedral, has maps, information on local happenings, and a hotel reservation service. It also houses the **Musee d'Art Romain** [see *culture zoo,* above] and the **Espace Massif Central** *(Place de la Victoire; Tel 04/73-42-60-00; 9am-6pm Mon-Fri, Tue open at 10am, 9am-noon/2-6pm Sat, Oct-May; 9am-6:30pm Mon-Fri, Tue open at 10am, 9am-12:30pm/1:30-6:30pm Sat, June-Sept)*, which has information on sports and activities nearby and will rent you a bike.

Public Transportation The bus system is called **T2C** and is useful for going to and from the train station and for occasional longer trips, although you probably won't need to use it much while you're in town. The central bus stop is on **place de Jaude,** and there is a **T2C office** *(17 blvd. Robert-Schuman; Tel 04/73-28-56-56; 9am-noon/2-6pm Mon-Sat)* close to the center of town. Tickets are 7.50F, and you can buy them on the bus or in the office. The buses run Mon-Sat from 5:30am to 9pm, with very limited Sunday and holiday service.

Health and Emergency SAMU: *15;* **police:** *17.* The local hospital is **Centre Hospitalier Universitaire,** or **CHU** *(Blvd. Winston Churchill; Tel 04/73-75-07-50).*

Pharmacy There are pharmacies all over, of course, marked as usual by the big neon green crosses. **Pharmacie Ducher** *(1 place DeLille; Tel 04/73-91-31-77; V, MC)* is open 24 hours.

Trains **Gare SNCF** *(Ave. de l'Union Soviétique; Tel 04/73-30-12-79 or 08/36-35-35-35; Bus 2, 4, 8, or 14)* is on the east side of town, at least a 20- or 30-minute walk from the center.

Bike/Moped Rental You can rent some wheels to discover the area (and this is probably the best way to explore while you're in town— that way you can get to the nearby countryside and see what makes Clermont-Ferrand such a beautiful place) at **Troc 2 Roues** *(46-bis ave. d'Aubiere; Tel 04/73-69-82-27; 2-7pm Mon, 9am-noon/2-7pm Tue-Sat; 60-150F for bike/moped rental; V, MC).* You need to be at least 16 and have a license for moped rental.

Laundry There is a Laundromat in the *centre ville* called **Lavomatique** *(2 rue Gregoire de Tours; Tel 04/70-29-57-70; 7am-8pm daily).*

Postal The main branch of the post office is **Poste St. Eloy** *(17 rue Marechal de Lattre-Tassigny; Tel 04/73-30-63-00; 8am-7pm Mon-Fri, 8am-noon Sat).*

Internet [see *wired,* above]

everywhere else

parc naturel régional des volcans d'auvergne

Many moons ago, the area in and around the Massif Central was a mass of teeming volcanoes and gigantic glaciers ripping through the land. Thanks to geographical evolution, we now have the Parc Naturel Régional des Volcans, a 946,000-acre park that stretches almost the entire length of the Massiff Central's western border. A beautiful mixture of dense forest, massive hollowed-out volcanic craters and beautiful meadows used for goat farming, the Parc Naturel Regional des Volcans is a shining example of the diversity and power of nature.

Composed of three distinct volcano ranges—the smooth **Mont Domes** in the north, **Monts Dore** and the craggy **Monts du Cantal** to the south—the Parc works its way down the western border of Masiff Central enveloping numerous cities and towns in its path, the largest of which is Clermont-Ferrand. You could skip a visit to this spot, but you'd miss your chance to get an up close and personal view of a geographical phenomenon that has given this region its truly unique appearance. Besides seeing these genuinely stunning volcanoes, you'll also find your share of old stone villages, as well as acres of beautiful, undisturbed nature.

The park is enormous, towns are spread throughout, and, unfortunately, there is little to no public transportation. So if you want to make a trek to the Parc, it's extremely helpful to have a car. Or, if you're of the athletic variety, you may want to try biking.

An excellent place to begin your exploration of the Parc is right in Clermont-Ferrand, home to the Puy-de-Dome, the most well-known and visited peak in the area. It's an important landmark in Clermont-Ferrand—postcards of the city include it in the background, and the locals do their hiking and biking there.

You can pick out the Puy-de-Dome volcano from its neighbors by the big weather/radio receiver that pokes out of the top of it. At the summit is the *Centre d'Acceuil* (information center), which has an exhibition on local volcanic activity, a gift shop and cafe, and maps and information on the plethora of hiking trails that wind around the mountain [see *need to know*, below]. You don't actually need to buy a map in order to find a good hike—the trails are clearly marked, and it's easy to explore them on your own. You can get great views of Clermont-Ferrand and the surrounding countryside, and you'll find plenty of peaceful, quiet places to have a picnic during your hike.

The locals not only love to hike here, but also consider it an excellent place to go bike riding. And they love their biking trails here for good reason—the Puy-de-Dome is an important hill on the course of the Tour de France, and you may have seen footage of the cyclists pushing their way up the 12-percent-grade hill. If you want to join the biking craze, rent your wheels in Clermont-Ferrand and start the ride from town, since you can't a rent a bike from the mountain. You can also make arrangements to go biking or hang-gliding from the summit through the **Espace Massif Central,** a company housed in Clermont-Ferrand's tourist office that arranges outdoor activities and excursions.

About 20km to the south of Clermont-Ferrand on D90 is the town of **Montlosier,** which contains the Parc's main tourist office [see *need to know*, below]. There's an exhibition on volcanoes and local wildlife there, and you can pick up one or several guides to local trails, although you'll have to pay for them.

Beginning at the southern end of the Parc, around 90 km south of Clermont, a bit of a trek down road D922, is the town of **Aurillac,** home to another helpful information center, **Musée des Volcan** [see *need to know*, below]. Located at Château St-Etienne, the Musée fills all of your guide book needs and offers useful exhibits on the cultural and geographical history of the region.

need to know

Hours/Days Open On the whole, the park is a bit too large to have actual hours—you could probably wander onto a part of it without really knowing—however, all of the tourist and organizational offices do keep specific hours, so look below for the ones that apply to you.

Tourist Information There are three information centers in the park: the **main park headquarters** (*Montlosier 63970 Aydat; Tel 04/73-65-64-00; www.parc.volcans@wanadoo.fr; 10:30am-12:30pm/1:30pm-7pm May to Nov 2; Afternoon hours 2:30pm-7pm July and Aug. Dir: Take N89 south-east 20km*) and the **Aurillac Musée des Volcans** (*Tel 04/71-48-07-00; 10am-noon Mon-Sat Feb-Oct; 10:30am-6:30pm Mon-Sat, 2pm-6pm Sun mid June-mid Sept. Dir: N89 to D922 south 90 km*). The ***Centre d'Acceuil*** (*04/73-62-21-46; 9am-8pm daily July, Aug; 10am-6pm weekends Apr-June, Sept, Oct*) on the summit of the Puy-de-Dome, has hiking maps, souvenirs, and an informational exhibit on local volcanic activity and the Tour de France.

Directions/Transportation Unfortunately there's no public transportation to the Parc from any of the nearby towns, so you'll either have to bike it or make friends with a local with wheels....To reach the Puy-de-Dome by car, follow the signposts from place de Jaude; the mountain is about 15 km from the city. Once you get there, a **shuttle service** *(11am-6pm daily in summer, 12:30-6pm weekends in spring and fall; 21F)* will cart you up from the base of the volcano to the Centre d'Acceuil. Access to the summit via the road is reserved for cyclists on Sunday and Wednesday mornings from 7 to 8:30am. Convenient, huh?

Rental Rentals aren't available in the Parc itself, so you should make arrangements ahead of time at one of the outdoor offices in Clermont-Ferrand, such as the **Espace Massif Central** *(Place de la Victoire; Tel 04/73-42-60-00; 9am-6pm Mon-Fri, Tue open at 10am, 9am-noon/2-6pm Sat, Oct-May; 9am-6:30pm Mon-Fri, Tue open at 10am, 9am-12:30pm/1:30-6:30pm Sat, June-Sept)* or the **Comite Departemental du Tourisme** *(Place de la Bourse; Tel 04/73-42-22-50; Same hours).*

Eats Pack a picnic, or drop by the pricey **Le Mont Fraternite** *(Tel 04/73-62-23-00; 11am-9pm daily, April 15-Nov 2; V, MC)* at the summit of the Puy-de-Dome to refuel. It has a pretty fancy restaurant overlooking the valley and an overpriced cafe and sandwich area.

Crashing If camping under the stars is your thing, you've got a few options. There's year-round camping in Couron, a small town 10 km southeast of Clermont-Ferrand on road D21 *(Tel 04/73-84-81-30).* For more information on nearby camping spots, contact the **main park headquarters** in Montlosier [see above].

Le Puy en Velay

Le Puy en Velay, often shortened to "Le Puy," is a hilly Auvergne village with cobblestone streets that are so narrow, old, and windy that they look like they belong in an "old village land" at Disneyland. Many of the streets turn into stairs without any warning, as they twist and turn past Medieval, Gothic, and Renaissance houses. From its highest point, the plug of a former volcano, the town spills down the hills into a valley that's sheltered by the rolling green mountains of the countryside.

An old pilgrimage town, second only to Lourdes, Le Puy was built up around the worship of the Virgin Mary, and has three main religious sites: the **Cathedral Notre Dame,** the **Rocher Corneille,** and the **Dyke St. Michel,** [see *culture zoo,* below, for all three]. All are built on steep volcanic spires, and they continue to draw religious pilgrims even today. But the town is pretty enough to warrant a visit by even non-pilgrims, especially since it's such a great base for exploring the volcanoes. The buildings here are predominantly old but not run-down, and almost every one of them has colorful red, blue, green, or yellow shutters. There

le puy-en-velay

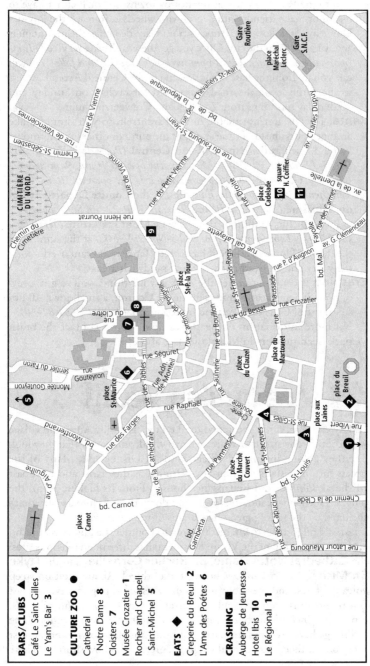

BARS/CLUBS ▲
Café Le Saint Gilles **4**
Le Yam's Bar **3**

CULTURE ZOO ●
Cathedral
Notre Dame **8**
Cloisters **7**
Musée Crozatier **1**
Rocher and Chapell
Saint-Michel **5**

EATS ◆
Creperie du Breuil **2**
L'Ame des Poétes **6**

CRASHING ■
Auberge de Jeunesse **9**
Hotel Ibis **10**
Le Régional **11**

are old stone fountains everywhere you turn, and despite a few tourists and people on pilgrimages, Le Puy en Velay remains quaint and natural. The town is also famous for its traditional lace, and you'll find a large lace display at the **Musée Crozatier** [see *culture zoo,* below], as well as women making lace outside the little shops in the center of town.

neighborhoods and hanging out

As you come out of the train station on the southeastern end of town, walk straight along **avenue Charles Dupuy** and you'll come to the main post office. From there, turn left on **boulevard Marechal Fayolle** to get to the main square of town, **place du Breuil,** a short walk away. The Tourist Office is here, and so is the small, shady park **Jardin Henri Vinay** and the **Musée Crozatier** [see *culture zoo,* below]. There are often old men in the park playing *pétanque* and young moms watching their kids playing in the playground. Young people meet here or at **Le Yam's Bar** [see *bar scene,* below] on **place aux Laines,** which adjoins the central place du Breuil. North of this central square is considered the old town, and consists of narrow shopping streets that thread past small squares, such as **place du Plot,** all eventually winding up the hill to the cathedral, at the top of the town's main volcanic spire. On the spire just north of the cathedral stands the Rocher Corneille; this enormous statue of the Virgin Mary and the baby Jesus, which is visible from all over town, is the main monument used to identify Le Puy. North of that is the third spire, the Dyke St. Michel, which has a winding path leading up to a tiny stone chapel. There's a beautiful cemetery on the sloping hill on the north end of town, which is full of flowers in the warmer months, and offers views of the hills and valleys of the surrounding countryside year round.

bar scene

Le Puy is a pretty quiet town, and the bar scene is equally mellow, as there is not a large population of kids in their twenties in town. The people who *do* hang out tend to end up for happy hour and drinks at one of the bar/cafes that surround the two smaller main squares of town, place aux Laines and place du Plot.

A couple of bars offer terrace seating out on place aux Laines, with views of the big main square, place du Breuil. Although it disappointingly has no sweet potato/yam decorations, or even an orange color scheme, **Le Yam's Bar** *(1 place aux Laines; Tel 04/91-09-72-36; 7:30am-1am daily; Average drink 10-15F; No credit cards)* offers some great people-watching in the busiest and most central area of town. Big groups of people meet up here in the afternoons and evenings, and the noisy street gives you the feeling that more is going on in town than there actually is.

If you walk from place aux Laines into the old town, up toward the cathedral, you will reach place du Plot, the biggest open square in the narrow and windy village streets. It is lined on all sides with cafes whose terrace seating is jumbled together inside the square. **Cafe Le Saint Gilles** *(Place du Plot; No phone; 7am-8pm daily; average drinks 15F; No* *credit cards)* is on the southern end of the square, so you can sit on the edge of things and watch the action on the streets as well as on the square.

CULTURE ZOO

In addition to its three hilltop pilgrimage destinations, Le Puy also has a campy, fun, small-towny museum. A 45F ticket that covers admission to all four major sights is available at any of Le Puy's monuments/museums—it's a pretty good deal if you plan to see them all.

Cathedral Notre Dame *(No phone; Open sunrise to sunset daily; Free):* North of the old town, this grand old cathedral is especially famous for its statue of the 17th-century Black Virgin at the altar. The statue is disappointingly small, but it's still interesting to see—or at least, it's interesting to watch all the people on their pilgrimages who are stunned and awed to see it.

Cloister de Notre Dame *(Cathedral Notre Dame; 9:30am-6:30pm daily, July-Sept; 9:30am-noon/2-6pm Apr-June, till 4:30 Oct-Mar; 25F, 15F for students; V, MC):* Once you've reached the cathedral, you should stick around for a visit to its cloister. Meditate in the peaceful old stone-pillared square, then check out the collection of the cathedral's treasures: paintings, bibles, chalices, etc. It's worth going in, if just for the awesome photos you can take of the pillars of the cloister rising against the spires of the cathedral and the sky.

Rocher Corneille and **Statue de Notre Dame de France** *(9am-7:30pm July, Aug; till 7pm May, June, Sept; till 6pm Mar, Apr; 10am-5pm Oct-March; 20F, 10F for students):* Topping the spire north of the cathe-

FESTIVALS

Le Puy has a number of cultural festivals featuring music and folklore in the spring and summer months. Contact the Tourist Office by phone or via the web for current information on all of them.

The **European Music Street Festival,** held on a weekend in mid-March, involves a number of street musicians to welcome the spring.

The **Music Festival of Le Puy en Velay** takes place during the second week of July, and has primarily Latin and world music at stages set up in town.

The **International Folklore Festival,** during the third week of July, has dance, music, song, shows, and costumes from cultures throughout the world.

In the third week of September, Le Puy hosts a **Renaissance Festival,** with parties, costumes, and actors to recreate the magic of Renaissance life.

pedaling to polignac

A gorgeous three-mile bike ride to the northwest of Le Puy is the **Forteresse de Polignac** *(43000 Polignac; Tel 04/71-02-46-57; Entrance fee 15F for adults, 5F for students and children under 12; April-May, October, 2-6pm daily; June-Sept, 10am-7pm daily)*, sometimes ambiguously referred to as the Château de Polignac. To reach it, follow the N102 in the direction of Polignac; there is no bus service. Dating from Romanesque times, the fortress was the headquarters of a cult of Apollo, whose priests used an echo chamber to divine, then reveal the wishes of the God, which was delivered with pomp and circumstance, often whispered, in an echo chamber that was designed to terrify the recipient. Apollo's answer was artfully delivered, through the echo chamber, to a huge depiction of the God's face carved into the rock. The site even received a visit from the Roman emperor Claude in 47A.D. Today, the château is partially ruined, but its church is in better shape and worth a visit to check out its Romanesque interior and a Gothic porch.

In the same village is the much more elegant and elaborate baronial home of the Duc de Polignac, the family seat of one of the most glamorous names in France (ooo-la-la!), **La Voulte Polignac** *(Voulte-sur-Loire; Tel 04/71-08-50-02; visit by appointment only Easter-late October, 9am-noon, 2-5pm daily; Entrance fee 27F, 13F for students or children under 12)*. During a visit here you get a *very* detailed history of the Polignacs—wait! Don't run away! It's actually pretty fascinating: They were a robber-baron family who gained their prestige and wealth because and only because they had friends in high places. Yolande de Polastron, wife of one of the Polignac boys, was good buddies with Marie Antoinette. But what brought them up also brought them down—they ended up fleeing the country during the Revolution because of their ties to Miss Let-them-eat-cake, amid rumors that there was more to Yolande and Maries "friendship" than met the eye (wink, wink). See, and you thought history was dull....

dral, these big ruddy statues are visible from anywhere in town. If you're not religious, you'll find it a little campier than the cathedral. To get here, you climb up a windy path through gardens of flowers and cacti, enjoying great and then better views the higher you get. Don't miss the climb up the spiral staircase inside the statue, where you can reach out and touch the Virgin Mary's gold crown.

Dyke Saint-Michel *(Same hours as Rocher Corneille and Statue de Notre Dame; 15F):* This is on the third spire of town, reachable by another steep garden climb, this time through mossy stones and wild iris, up to an old stone chapel with an asymmetrical floor plan and simple stained-glass windows. Below the chapel is a small museum on the chapel's history as a pilgrimage site.

Musée Crozatier *(Jardin Henri Vinay; Tel 04/71-09-38-90; Open daily except Sun morning and Tue, 10am-noon/2-6pm May-Sept; 10am-noon/2-4pm Oct-April; 20F, 10F for students; No credit cards):* Just south of the place de Breuil, Le Puy en Velay's campiest attraction hosts a collection that includes Roman artifacts, old lace, paintings, old-fashioned stuffed birds and mammals with fierce expressions, bones, and a volcano display. There's also a changing exhibit that often features contemporary art.

EATS

The local specialties in Le Puy are similar to those in Clermont-Ferrand: Restaurants serve the same big pot of Auvergne stew, and many of the dishes have bacon, pork, or sausages. Le Puy is especially famous for its green lentils. If you're buying picnic supplies to eat in the gardens or on some of the hidden steps all over the old town, be sure to try some *Pain des Volcans,* which is hearty and seedy and a nice change from the standard baguette.

If the religious sights of Le Puy don't inspire you, **L'Ame des Poètes** *(16 rue Seguret; Tel 04/71-05-66-57; 7-10:30pm Tue-Sun; Average entrée 70-100F; V, MC)* hopes to be your muse. Right at the foot of Cathedral Notre Dame's *grand escalier* (the stairs that lead up to the side entrance), the restaurant is small and unassuming, with warm orange frescoed walls and sturdy wooden tables. It serves mainly Le Puy specialties, which often use the local green *lentilles.*

Creperie du Breuil *(10 place du Breuil; Tel 04/71-05-71-67; Noon-2pm/7-10:30pm daily; 30-60F entrées; No credit cards),* right on the main place du Breuil, is so narrow that there's barely enough room for the little row of tables and the waitress. The family-run place is very friendly, and you can see right into the kitchen to watch your crêpes being cooked. They have a 40F lunch menu including a drink, which is a great deal.

WIRED

The Tourist Office of Le Puy has a website at *www.ot-lepuyenvelay.fr.*

You can check your e-mail at the **Cyberposte** in the post office. Le Puy also has one of the cheapest Internet cafes in all of France: **Au Forum Café** *(5 rue Lafayette; Tel 04/71-04-04-98; 1-7pm Tue-Sat; No credit cards)* charges only 10F for an hour on the Internet.

crashing

Most of the places to stay in Le Puy (and there aren't many to choose from) are small and have something old or quaint about them. If one place is full, the people will usually direct you to another place in town. Also, since the village is so small, the people who work at the reception desk are often good local guides and almost as helpful as the Tourist Office.

▶▶**CHEAP**

The **Auberge de Jeunesse** (*9 rue Jules Valles; Tel 04/71-05-52-40; Reception open 7am-noon/1:30-7pm daily; 42F; Breakfast 11.50F; V*) has four-person rooms with bunk beds as well as an old-school large dormitory. It's in a good location, in the same building as the youth and cultural center of town and right next to the cathedral, so you can hear the church bells chiming. There's a kitchen and an 11:30pm curfew.

▶▶**DO-ABLE**

Le Régional (*36 blvd. Marechal Fayolle; Tel 04/71-09-37-74; 130F single, 210F double; V, MC*) is also pretty central, but it's down by the main square and out of the old town, so the street traffic gets a little noisy. It's in a funny-shaped little corner building and has an old spiral staircase and clean rooms.

Or you can be like the rest of the tourists and head to the standard French chain **Hotel Ibis/Centre Ville** (*47 blvd. Marechal Fayolle; Tel 04/71-09-20-97; 295F single, 330F double; V, MC, AE*). This place has an elevator, showers and toilets in every room, and a restaurant with room service, but nothing especially quirky or unusual.

need to know

Currency Exchange There are no specific change bureaus, but the main **banks** of Le Puy, clustered around **place du Breuil,** can change money for you.

Tourist Information The **Office de Tourisme** (*Place du Breuil; Tel 04/71-09-38-41; 8:30am-noon/1:30-6:15 daily, closed Sun afternoon Oct-Easter; open 8:30am-7:30pm July, Aug; www.ot-lepuyenvelay.fr*) is located right on the central place du Breuil. It has information on hotels, museum passes, and nearby walks and day trips. They will make reservations for you, but only if you show up at their office; advance phone reservations are not possible.

Health and Emergency **Medical Emergency: 15; police: 17.** The local hospital is **Centre Hospitalier Emil Roux** (*Blvd. Docteur Chantemesse; Tel 04/71-09-87-00*).

Pharmacies Even in this small town, there are pharmacies everywhere, and they are always marked by the familiar **green neon crosses.**

Trains and Buses The **buses** around the Auvergne are not highly recommended, so you should stick to **trains.** To get to town from **Gare SNCF** (*Place Marechal LeClerc; Tel 04/71-07-71-63 or 08/36-35-35-35*), walk along avenue Charles Dupuy to place du Breuil.

Bike Rentals Rent bikes and get biking advice from **Vitaform,** a squash club and health club (*Espaly, Le Puy en Velay; Tel. 04/71-02-22-*

97). Bikes rent for between 80 and 120F per day, depending on the model. The outfitter lies _ of a mile from the town center.

Laundry The most central Laundromat is **Laverie** (*24 Portail d'Avignon; Tel 04/71-02-64-20; 8am-8pm Mon-Sat, 9:15am-6:30pm Sun*).

Postal The main post office is on the corner of avenue de la Dentelle and avenue Charles Dupuy: **La Poste** (*8 ave. de la Dentelle; Tel 04/71-07-02-05; 8am-7pm Mon-Fri, 8am-noon Sat*).

Internet [see *wired*, above]

The Rhône
Valley and
the French
Alps

The rhône valley and the french alps

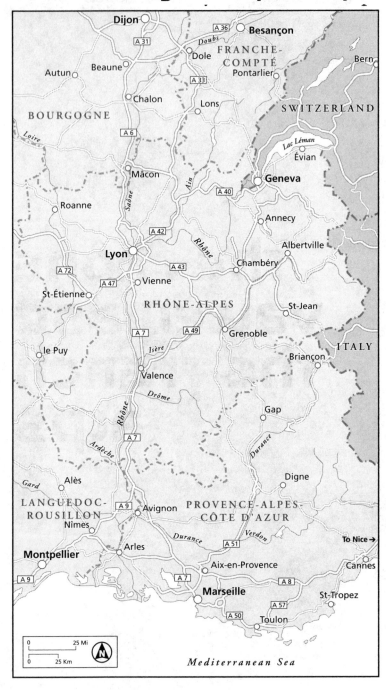

Dijon
A 31
A 36
Besançon
Doubs
FRANCHE-
Dole
COMPTÉ
Bern
Beaune
Pontarlier
Autun
A 33
BOURGOGNE
Chalon
Lons
SWITZERLAND
Loire
A 6
Lac Léman
Évian
Mâcon
Ain
A 40
Geneva
Saône
Roanne
Annecy
Rhône
Albertville
A 42
Lyon
Chambéry
A 72
A 43
Vienne
St-Jean
A 47
RHÔNE-ALPES
St-Étienne
A 7
A 49
Grenoble
le Puy
Isère
Briançon
ITALY
Valence
Drôme
Rhône
Gap
A 7
Ardèche
Durance
Digne
Gard
Alès
A 9
Avignon
PROVENCE-ALPES-
LANGUEDOC-
Nîmes
CÔTE D'AZUR
ROUSSILLON
Durance
Verdon
To Nice →
Arles
A 51
Montpellier
Cannes
A 9
Aix-en-Provence
A 7
A 8
Marseille
St-Tropez
A 57
A 50
Toulon

0   25 Mi
0   25 Km

Mediterranean Sea

from the awesome powdery peaks of the Alps to the lush vineyards and rivers of the Rhône Valley, you'll find plenty to do in these two very distinct regions. With its network of tiny Alpine towns, icy mountain lakes, and drop-dead gorgeous views, the region of the Alps promises to be an unforgettable experience, especially if you're into mountain sports. Bordering these dramatic peaks and valleys is the Rhône Valley, the perfect place to check out some vineyards, explore the old-but-new-city of Lyon, and—what else?—sample the valley's much touted *Beaujolais Nouveau.*

The Alps are just as amazing as you might imagine them to be—mountains jut up in every direction, and it's not unusual to see glaciers or at least glacial streams and waterfalls running into clear mountain lakes. Both the locals and the people who visit this region tend to be outdoorsy and adventurous, and there's no end to the adventures you can have: Ski, hike, mountain-climb, swim, dive, or hang-glide before you take a break in the evening to stock up on one of the region's famous filling cheese-and-potatoes dishes, then hang out for late-night drinks and share your day's stories with fellow adventurers.

The area that we now call the **French Alps** is actually made up of several different political *départements,* which are divided roughly along the lines of the ancient dukedoms that once ruled the area. **Grenoble,** an important city under Emperor Gratien's rule, has long been the capital of the Dauphiné region, which became part of France in the 14th century. Savoie and Haute-Savoie, the two *départements* that are home to many of the small lake towns of the Alps, including those on Lake Annecy and Lake Geneva, were ruled by the dukes of Savoy until the 16th century.

Beneath, on, or near the towering mountain peaks are the Alps' small towns, each with its own distinct sense of place. **Annecy,** on its own lake, is known as an artist's town—in addition to the ever-present emphasis on sports, there is a focus on the artistic beauty of the landscape. **Evian-les-Bains,** a traditional resort destination of the old dukes of Savoy, is still famous for its spa and water source, and is so tiny that it conveys the quiet, slow-paced lifestyle of the local Alpine folk. **Chamonix,** the ski resort town at Mont Blanc, is perched up in the mountains that you keep craning your neck to see from down below. Its proximity to dramatic cliffs and glaciers will make you catch your breath in that unmistakably thin mountain air—as will careening down its world-famous slopes. The

Travel Times

*TGV (Fast Train— more expensive) **By car	Grenoble	Annecy	Chamonix	Evian	Paris	Lyon
Lyon	1:15	2:05	5:00	1:50**	2:10*	-
Grenoble	-	1:45	4:10	1:45**	5:15**	1:15
Annecy	1:45	-	2:30	:50**	4:00* 5:00	2:05
Chamonix	4:10	2:30	-	1:05	7:00**	5:00
Evian	1:45**	:50**	1:05**	-	3:30* (from Geneva Station)	1:50**

only real city in the region is **Grenoble,** and even there you'll find a strong sense of the mountains, with fashion-conscious theatergoers rubbing elbows with laid-back hikers and bikers.

The Alps border Switzerland and Italy, and some aspects of Alpine culture may remind you of Switzerland—from the Swiss chalet-style buildings with their sloping roofs and plain interiors to the locals' familiarity with the mountains they grew up in. Like those traditional pictures of Switzerland, you'll probably also see lots of cows with big bells grazing in the fields. Even the foods are similar—don't leave without trying the local specialties, all of which seem to involve a lot of cheese: *fondue* (which you haven't really had until you've had it in the Alps), *raclette,* a dish with boiled potatoes and raclette cheese that you melt yourself on a special little grill, and *tartiflette,* a casserole of cheese, potatoes, and bacon.

The Alps border the **Rhône Valley,** an area composed mainly of countryside surrounding the Rhône and Saône rivers and home to the cosmopolitan center of Southeastern France, **Lyon.** Just a short train ride from the Alps and the third largest city in France, Lyon has less of a rushed, overwhelming feel than Paris, but it's decidedly more fast-paced and urban than the laid-back environment you'll find in the Alps. In addition to seeing several universities, renowned theaters and live music venues, outstanding cuisine, excellent museums, and beautiful architecture, you'll also get to dip into a rich history that spans from Roman times through to the 20th century; today it's a modern, progressive, and fun city. As you travel through the southern regions of France, from the Alps to the Rhône Valley to Provence, Lyon's train station is a central hub—and the city itself is certainly worth a visit as well.

getting around the region

The trains in the Alpine region are very good and will get you anywhere you want to go. There are also buses that connect the smaller towns, but they usually take longer than trains and aren't all that much cheaper. In the lakeside towns, you can usually hop a ferry to get to the neighboring towns. Even if you don't use the ferries for transportation, they're usually lovely rides, and a lot less touristy than those narrated rides on the Seine in Paris.

As the biggest town in the Alps, Grenoble has the best train schedule, so to see the most of the Alps in a limited amount of time, you might want to head there first and then make a circle around the smaller towns. With two large train stations and hundreds of arrivals and departures daily, Lyon has quick routes to both Geneva and Grenoble: the trip to Grenoble takes about an hour and 15 minutes, going to Geneva takes just less than 2 hours, and getting to Annecy takes two to two and a half hours. The trips from Grenoble to Annecy and Annecy to Evian take less than two hours each, so your travel days should be pretty easy. Chamonix is the only place in the region that will take longer to get to: You usually have to take a train to Saint Gervais les Bains first, and then take a smaller, slower mountain train up the steep, snowy hill. Allow around four or five hours to get to Chamonix from Lyon.

▶▶**ROUTES:**

From Grenoble, which is the largest hub and train station of the Alps, a nice five- or six-day trip would be to head up to Annecy, loop around to Evian via Geneva and a boat ride on Lac Léman, and finish up in Chamonix.

To see the most in a short period of time, you might cut Evian out of your journey and head straight to Chamonix from Annecy.

the rhône valley

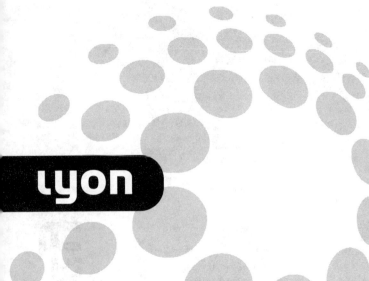

lyon

Lyon is one of those great cities that manage to be hip and progressive without completely chucking their history in the face of bigger and better things. The Lyonnais are very cosmopolitan and progressive, but they're also proud of their customs and the texture that their history adds to modern-day life. Even though Lyon now has popular club, bar, and live music scenes, some of the biggest parties are the traditional festivals of *Beaujolais Nouveau* [see **beaujolais nouveau,** below] and the **Fête des Lumières** [see **ville lumière,** below]. Modern apartment buildings and skyscrapers stand next to old bridges, cathedrals, cobblestone streets, and ancient ruins. The key to falling in love with Lyon is to get to know both sides of its personality: its modern lifestyle and its rich history.

In Lyon you get the big-city feel without the overwhelming feel of Paris, which makes it a great place to get acquainted with French cosmopolitan culture. Its stature as a large city and its two major universities—the imaginatively named Lyon I and Lyon II, whose buildings are scattered along regular city blocks—keep Lyon hip and with-it. However, unlike some other French cities, the University in Lyon is very, very slow (i.e., virtually closed down) between mid-June and mid-September—student life, in most cases, hibernates. Many students depart Lyon in summer, taking summer jobs or, if they're well-heeled, vacations. But when school is in session, the youth scene here is pretty big, and bars, live music, and clubs abound. In addition, the arts scene, which includes a lot of contemporary art and modern theater, is well-established without being staid or conventional. There are three good sources for info on local cultural and nightlife happenings: *Lyon-Poche,* a weekly sold at newsstands for around 7F; *La Progrescope,* a bi-monthly available at the tourist office; and the *Guide du Petit Pammé,* and harder-to-find, student-written guide—ask at your hotel.

Lyon has always been at the center of the action, from its beginnings as a major ancient Roman capital, then as a busy publishing center, later as the capital of Europe's silk industry, and today as one of the best food cities in France. Today you can visit the silk museums and factories and explore the city's *traboules,* little passageways that were used to bring silk from the hilltop factories to the trading posts down by the rivers. During WWII, French Resistance fighters used them as secret hiding places [see *culture zoo,* below].

Lyon was also home to the Lumière brothers, who get props for inventing the first motion picture ever, in 1895. Today, the locals are big movie buffs, and there are tons of movie theaters to choose from. At night, Lyon's public buildings are illuminated, furthering the city's claim to the title *Ville Lumière,* or City of Light, from its big sister, Paris [see **lyon: ville lumiere,** below].

TWELVE hours in lyon

Look around for the legendary buried Golden Head at the **Parc de La Tête d'Or.** If you're going to visit just one museum in Lyon, don't miss the **Centre d'Histoire de la Résistance et de la Déportation** [see *culture zoo,* below]. It's one of the most well-assembled museums in town, informative without feeling like school; it's also arguably one of the best, most poignant museums on its subject matter.

Eat at **L'Empika** on rue des Marronniers or **Les Pavés St. Jean** in Vieux Lyon for a taste of the gastronomic capital's *bouchon* specialties [see *eats,* below, for both].

Walk up the **Jardin des Rosaires** to **Fourvière** [also in *culture zoo,* below for both], and don't forget to walk around the side of the church to the big overlook of the city. Test yourself and see if you can find the statue of Louis XIV on Place Bellecour and the big dome of the **Opéra.**

From the pedestrian bridge that crosses the Saône, watch as the sunset turns the sky pink against the ruddy rooftops of Croix-Rousse, and then watch Lyon transform into the *Ville Lumière* as the lights come up on the public buildings and glisten on the river.

lyon

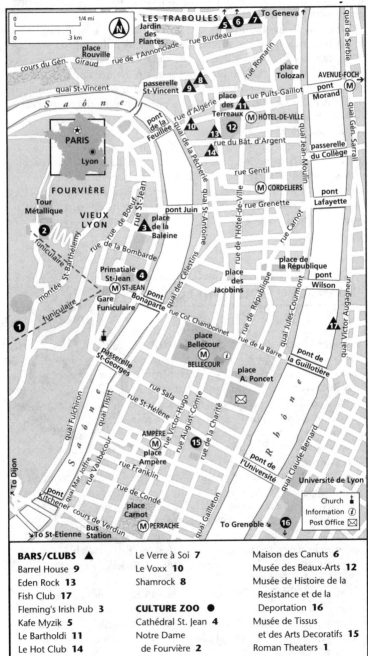

BARS/CLUBS ▲

Barrel House **9**
Eden Rock **13**
Fish Club **17**
Fleming's Irish Pub **3**
Kafe Myzik **5**
Le Bartholdi **11**
Le Hot Club **14**

Le Verre à Soi **7**
Le Voxx **10**
Shamrock **8**

CULTURE ZOO ●
Cathédral St. Jean **4**
Notre Dame
 de Fourvière **2**

Maison des Canuts **6**
Musée des Beaux-Arts **12**
Musée de Histoire de la
 Resistance et de la
 Deportation **16**
Musée de Tissus
 et des Arts Decoratifs **15**
Roman Theaters **1**

neighborhoods

The defining geographical features of Lyon are its two rivers, the **Rhône** and the **Saône.** The main downtown area is in the peninsula between the two rivers called the **Presqu'ile.** The Presqu'ile stretches from **Gare de Perrache,** the train station on **place Carnot** at the southern end of town, to the north along the pedestrian street **rue Victor Hugo,** which runs through the small public square called **place Ampère** into the central public square, **place Bellecour.** The Presqu'ile continues through the pedestrian shopping district of **rue de la République** ("Rue de la Ré") and the public square **place des Terreaux,** which is at the base of the **Croix-Rousse** hill on the northern end of town. Lyon's medieval old town, **Vieux Lyon,** is on the west side of the Saône; from there you can hop on a *funiculaire* to reach **Fourvière Hill,** where you'll find the ancient excavated Roman theaters (built way back in 17 to 15 B.C.) and a panoramic view of Lyon. The university district is just east of the Rhône, where you'll also

walking tour

From the **Louis XIV statue** in the center of place Bellecour, walk toward the Office de Tourisme and continue to the Post Office at **place Antonin Poncet.** (You should be on the opposite side of the square, so you can look across to the Post Office.) Midway down place Antonin Poncet, you will find the little street called **rue des Marronniers,** which turns off to the left. Sit down for an espresso at one of the little cafes on the corner before you meander slowly down the narrow street. If you happen to be there at lunchtime, you'll have singing and joking waiters soliciting you with their menus and their specials, and the colorful terrace tables will be jammed with locals and tourists.

When you reach the end of the street, turn right on **rue de la Barre** and continue to the end of the block before turning right on **quai Docteur Gailleton.** Walk down the quai, checking out the six-story buildings on either side of the Rhône with their wrought-iron railings, so typical of Lyon's architecture. Continue until you get to the green bridge, which is called the **Pont de L'Université.** Cross the Rhône to the opposite quai, turn right, and check out the large buildings that house the **University of Lyon II.** You can poke your head into one of the lobbies to see the tiled floors, and wander inside like you know what you're doing. You'll quickly come to one of the central courtyards, where students hang out between classes, and where you can try to meet some French or international kids.

wired

There are lots of places to check e-mail in Lyon. The main branch of La Poste [see *need to know*, above] has a **Cyber-poste** station, and cybercafes abound. **Espace Connectik** *(19 quai St. Antoine; Tel 04/72-77-98-85; 11am-7pm Mon-Sat; 60F for an hour; V, MC, AE)* is right along the Saône on the Presqu'ile. You'll find similar prices at **Le Cybar** *(50 Montée du Gourguillon; Tel 04/78-36-60-09; 11am-7pm Mon-Fri; V, MC),* which is in Vieux Lyon and has some food, and **Raconte Moi La Terre–Mundo Café** *(38 rue Thomassin, at the corner of rue Grolée; Tel 04/78-92-60-20; 9:30am-7:30pm Mon-Sat; V, MC),* on the Presqu'ile, which is a conglomeration of traditional cafe, bar, Internet cafe, bookstore, and venue for music and art shows.

You can check out Lyon's local newspaper at ***www.leprogres.fr.***

find Lyon's second and less centrally located train station, **Gare de la Part-Dieu.** Lyon's modern and industrial districts extend further to the south.

Like Paris, Lyon is organized into ***arrondissements,*** with the numbers beginning just below the Croix-Rousse district and continuing down the Presqu'ile before finally circling around the edges of town. The main neighborhoods where you'll find yourself hanging out are in the **1st** and **2nd** arrondissements on the Presqu'ile, as well as Vieux Lyon and Fourvière Hill in the **5th** arrondissement and the university district in the **7th.**

The 1st arrondissement includes the central Place des Terreaux, where you'll find the Hôtel de Ville and the **Opéra,** and the 4th arrondissment comprises the ruddy, tiled roofs of Croix-Rousse, which stretches up the hill. Croix-Rousse was originally the center of the silk-weaving industry in Lyon; today, the area is one of the best places to explore the old *traboules.*

You are likely to find yourself making plans to meet your friends at the **statue of Louis XIV** in the middle of place Bellecour in the 2nd arrondissement, arguably the most central and often-used *point de rencontre* (meeting point) in town. The rest of the neighborhood is a busy maze of walking streets such as rue de La Ré and rue Victor Hugo, as well as heavily trafficked streets and open squares, all lined with shops, cafes, and theaters.

Across the Saône, Vieux Lyon in the 5th arrondissement has the narrow, twisting, cobblestone streets of a medieval village. The buildings are colored with the warm pinks and oranges of a Botticelli fresco, and the area is also famous for its *traboules.* Vieux Lyon is sandwiched between the **Cathédral St. Jean** [see *culture zoo,* below], an old Gothic cathedral, and **Fourvière Hill,** home to a modern 19th-century cathedral built near the excavated **Roman Theater** [see *culture zoo,* below]—the oldest theater in all of France.

On the *quais* of the Rhône just opposite the area of the Presqu'ile where you'll find the place Ampère are the buildings of the **universities, Lyon I** and **Lyon II.** There are some reasonably priced cafes and restaurants in this neighborhood, as well as the impressive **Centre d'Histoire de la Résistance et de la Déportation** [see *culture zoo,* below]. If you continue strolling down this side of the Rhône, you'll come to the **Parc de La Tête d'Or** [see, *city sports,* below], one of the most beautiful city parks in all of Europe, as well as the modern **Part-Dieu** [see *stuff,* below], where the big shopping mall and Lyon's second train station are.

With its network of four metro lines, two funicular railway lines, and buses, Lyon is relatively easy to get around, and you can pick up your tickets (good on any mode of transport) at the nearest metro station.

hangıng ouт

You can join the people-watchers as soon as you step off the train at the Gare de Perrache; **Brasserie L'Espace Carnot** [see *eats,* below] has tables under the shady plane trees, reminiscent of Paris, that are perfect for spying on the tourists coming out of the station or the locals cruising down rue Victor Hugo. From here to Place des Terreaux, the Presqu'ile is full of pedestrian streets lined with benches and squares lined with cafes, and the locals and students spend much of their time alternating between being the watchers, sitting in the cafes, and being the watchees, window-shopping through town.

Arguably the best place to kick it for an afternoon of eavesdropping, writing in your journal, or listening to the sounds of French voices, fountain water, and skateboard wheels is **Le Bartholdi** [see *bar scene,* below], in the center of place des Terreaux.

The cafes near the university and the sandwich stands around **place Ampère** are prime places to meet local students at lunchtime. Although people don't really hang out on the steps outside of the university build-

down and ouт

One great thing about the art, architecture, and history of Lyon is that a lot of it is not enclosed in museums. You can troop around town and see the depth of Lyon's history, from the Roman ruins to the old medieval town to the modern buildings along the rivers to contemporary architecture like the **Musée d'Art Contemporain** [see *arts scene,* below]. Going for a tour of the painted walls is free, and so is a peek into the *traboules* [see *culture zoo,* below, for both], where you can imagine the old caches of silk being trundled downhill to the trading posts, and the secret activity of the Resistance.

lyon

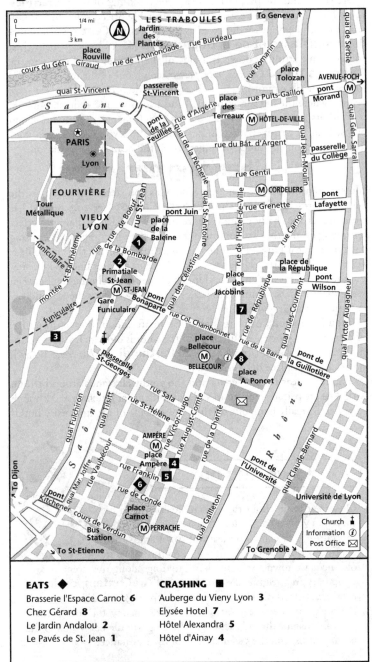

EATS ◆

Brasserie l'Espace Carnot **6**
Chez Gérard **8**
Le Jardin Andalou **2**
Le Pavés de St. Jean **1**

CRASHING ■

Auberge du Vieny Lyon **3**
Elysée Hotel **7**
Hôtel Alexandra **5**
Hôtel d'Ainay **4**

ings, you can poke your head inside and look for one of the courtyards with lawns and benches where you can park yourself for a while and try to blend in [see *walking tour,* below]. Or, if you'd rather meet other travelers, take your picnic to the steps of **St. Jean** in Vieux Lyon or up to the old **Roman theater** on the Fourvière hill—there are plenty of sunny lawns when the weather is pleasant [see *culture zoo,* below, for both].

One of Lyon's most beautiful spots is the enormous **Parc de la Tête d'Or,** where you can run, walk, bike, skate, pick up a game of soccer, Frisbee, or *pétanque,* visit the rose gardens or the zoo, or take a nap. The park is so big that you could get lost as you escape the sound and feel of the city.

bar scene

There are bars all over Lyon—almost anywhere you go, there is likely to be a good spot to sit down and have a beer on a hot day, as the locals do. At night, most young people, locals and students alike, hang out near Place des Terreaux, where, according to the Lyonnais, *"ça bouge"*—literally, "it moves." Most bar/brasserie combinations, which are bars serving meals in the evenings, are open till 1am, while the traditional bars stay open till 3am. There's a heavy international pub scene here—you can take your pick of Irish, English, or Australian pubs. All of the bars listed here are within walking distance of each other.

The bars lining place des Terreaux have their tables set out in the middle of the square near the Bartholdi fountain, with its rearing horses. From your table at the best of these, **Le Bartholdi** (*6 place des Terreaux; Tel 04/72-10-66-00; Metro to Hôtel de Ville; 7:30am-1am daily; Drinks 15-5F; V, MC, AE*), you can hear the splash of the fountain and gaze at the illuminated facades of the Hôtel de Ville and the Musée des Beaux-Arts. Concerts are held here several days a week, and on occasional cultural evenings. On nights of big soccer matches, the cafes on place des

five-o

Lately there are more and more police in town (and the locals roll their eyes at this), because Interpol, the center of police for the Rhône-Alpes department, has its headquarters in Lyon. Be as cautious of the police as the locals are—and that means be pretty responsible. When it comes to waiting in line or slowing down for pedestrians, the French hate to follow the rules, but you'll notice that they do not blatantly disregard laws. In general, France doesn't look very kindly on smoking pot, so definitely do not smoke in the open, especially in Lyon with all the police around; the rumor is that they often make arrests just to meet their quotas. So do as the French do: Exercise caution and be discreet.

Terreaux set up an enormous outdoor TV screen, and practically all of Lyon fights for seats at the tables, with most having to settle for plopping down on the ground.

The most popular place to hit up the bars—among locals, students, and travelers alike—is on rue Sainte Catherine, just a block past place des Terreaux toward the Croix-Rousse hill. Most of the numerous bars here are Irish, English, or Australian pubs.

A great Irish pub is the **Shamrock** (15 rue Ste. Catherine; Tel 04/78-27-37-82; Metro to Hôtel de Ville; 5pm-3am daily; Drinks 15-30F; No credit cards), whose Irish bartenders will pour you a Guinness with a shamrock in the foam or will (reluctantly) serve you a cocktail. The two dark wooden rooms are usually crowded and smoky, and you can count on some U2 on the stereo. They show old movies on Sunday nights, usually around 8 or 9pm.

Just next door is the **Barrel House** (13 rue Ste. Catherine; Tel 04/78-29-20-40; 5pm-3am daily; Drinks 15-20F; AE), which is longer and narrower than the Shamrock but decorated in much the same manner. There is a stage area in the rear, and the live music varies night to night from folk to blues to TV-theme-song cover bands to local French rock groups. English/Irish pub grub is available, along with a few different Irish beers on tap and some drink specials.

On the edge of the Saône, just a few blocks from place des Terreaux, is **Le Voxx** (1 rue d'Algérie; Tel 04/78-28-33-87; Metro to Hôtel de Ville; Tue-Sun 11-3am; V, MC), a bar with a more French atmosphere. It's also more modern than the bars on rue St. Catherine, with its sleek neon lights and metallic lines. The students who hang out here tend to be a bit more sleek and sophisticated as well, although the place does get more raucous into the night, especially at the ever-crowded tables on the sidewalk terrace.

The best late-late-night option is **Road 66** (8 place des Terreaux; Tel 04/78-27-37-42; Metro to Hôtel de Ville; 8pm-3am Sun-Tue, 9pm-3:30am Wed, 9pm-4am Thur, 9pm-5:30am Fri, 3pm-5:30am Sat; 20F cover on weekends after 11pm, plus one drink minimum; V), which has the questionable French take on America—it's full of old license plates, road signs, and pool tables, and serves burgers and beers.

In Vieux Lyon, **Fleming's Irish Pub** (2 rue de la Loge; Tel 04/78-39-43-49; Metro to Vieux Lyon; 3pm-2am daily; Shows Tue and Sun at 7:30 or 8pm; Average drink 20F; V, MC) is a tiny joint with a dark red interior and some couches that are good for lounging. With a crowd of young students and older regulars, it's a good happy-hour spot where you can hear traditional Celtic music.

For rock or reggae or cover bands, cruise by the **Barrel House** [see bar scene, above], where shows generally start around 10 or 11pm and there's rarely a cover charge.

An upscale cocktail bar known for its rock shows is **Eden Rock** (68 rue Mercière; Tel 04/78-38-28-18; Metro to Cordeliers; 11:30am-1am Mon-Sat, Thur till 2am, Fri till 3am; Show times vary; No cover; V, MC), a fairly large space decorated with an Art Deco/Modern art theme. Eden Rock's Thursday, Friday, and Saturday night concerts include rock, blues, and country, and it claims to have American décor—there are TVs all over the place. Rue Mercière, at the midpoint between place des Terreaux and Vieux Lyon, is also close to a lot of restaurants and cafes.

Lyon's famous jazz club is **Le Hot Club** *(26 rue Lanterne; Tel 04/78-39-54-74; Metro to Cordeliers or Hôtel de Ville; 9pm-1am Tue-Sat; Cover charge varies; No credit cards)*, a dark, cellar-like building on a street just off of Rue Mercière that plays host to small jam sessions and larger jazz combos featuring both local greats and recognizing international players. The crowd is a fun, laid-back mish-mash of old and young, tourist and local—*everybody* comes here.

LIVE MUSIC SCENE

Live salsa, reggae, jazz and rock music can be found nightly at the bars and pubs in town. Sting, Blondie, and other big international touring bands have played up at the **Roman theater** [see *culture zoo,* below] which also sponsors a series of classical music concerts every summer. There are also often big shows in other theaters near Lyon. Concert schedules are in *Le Petit Bulletin* and the *491,* which are both free cultural papers that you can find in the hotels, in CD shops, or in the Tourist Office; you can also find a list of local shows at the ticket counter in the local **FNAC** or at either of the **Boul'dingue** record stores [see *stuff,* below, for all].

The local Irish pubs have a lot of live music, both traditional Irish tunes and your basic rock/reggae shows [see *bar scene,* above].

CLUB SCENE

The ultra-hip clubs in Lyon like to be a little bit elusive and exclusive—they almost always have two-way mirrors at the entrances and doorbells to ring for admission. It's best to dress up a little (certainly no jeans, and wearing all black and bringing your cell phone can't hurt either) and to

RULES OF THE GAME

The closing time of the bars in Lyon varies somewhat. As a general rule, a bar connected to a brasserie will close at 1am, while traditional pubs/bars stay open till 3am. The metros stop running between midnight and 5am, so if you stay out past midnight, you might as well head to one of the clubs, which are open until dawn. You should be careful walking around at night, especially in the metros and near the rivers. Girls: Try not to walk anywhere alone after dark, and don't be surprised to get some comments and catcalls when you go out at night.

have at least one female in your group if you want to get in. As everywhere, the cool kids don't show up till midnight, but you'll have a better chance of getting in if you show a bit earlier. These clubs are constantly moving and changing, so your best bet is to make friends with a native in the know who can lead the way.

For those of us without the right connections, there are countless clubs and discothèques lining the edge of the Saône, but these places tend to be close quarters, sweaty, and too easy to find to be *really* cool but are nonetheless fun if you're in town for a night or two and just want to shake your butt. We're giving you the best of the bunch.

On the opposite end of town, the **Fish Club** *(opposite 21 quai Victor Augagneur; Tel 04/72-84-98-98; Metro to Bellecour; 10pm-5am Thur-Sat; 50-60F cover, Admission free before 11pm; V, MC)* is a boat-turned-dance club with DJs and house/dance music. The crowd varies from students to people in their twenties and thirties, and they have the occasional disco theme night. A happy hour with reduced price drinks goes from 10 to 11pm, although if you get there that early you'll miss out on making a fashionable entrance.

One of Lyon's cooler, more unusual clubs is **Kafé Myzik** *(20 Montée St. Sebastien; Tel 04/72-07-04-26; Metro to Croix-Paquet; 9pm-3am Wed-Sat; 1F cover; No credit cards)*. Located up the Croix-Rousse hill only a couple of blocks from Place des Terreaux, Kafé Myzik has wild murals downstairs by the bar where you'll pay your funny little 1F cover, and an open upstairs room that turns the place into a club when the rock/dance music comes on for the crowd of young students and international travelers.

ARTS SCENE

Lyon has a fairly strong arts scene. Locals are especially proud of the cinema, as the Lumière brothers, who are credited with the creation of movies, were from Lyon. In addition to the cinema, there is a well-established contemporary art scene and a variety of more traditional performing arts venues.

▶▶VISUAL ARTS

The contemporary art gallery **Le Rectangle** *(Place Bellecour; Tel 04/72-41-88-80; Metro to Bellecour; Noon-7pm Tue-Sun; 10F; No credit cards)*, housed in a little building opposite the Tourist Office, has an ever-evolving display of paintings, sculptures, and video art.

The **Musée d'Art Contemporain de Lyon** *(81 Cité Internationale, Quai Charles de Gaulle; Tel 04/72-69-17-18; Hours and admission charges vary; www.moca-lyon.org; No credit cards)* is in an impressive modern glass building near Parc de La Tête d'Or, and is open only when there is a show installed. Check the website or the Tourist Office for information.

The **Institut d'Art Contemporain** *(11 rue Docteur Dolard, Villeurbanne; Tel 04/78-03-47-00; Metro to République; Hours and admission charges vary; No credit cards)*, outside the center of town in the area known as Villeurbanne, has the same deal as the Musée d'Art Contemporain; again, check at the Tourist Office for show information.

five things to talk to a local about

1. Ask "In the last five years, what was the best Beaujolais Nouveau?" The locals are very proud of their region's wine, and everyone has an opinion about the best vintages.
2. Love and sex...or love vs. sex. This is one of their favorite debates.
3. The latest movies, and preferably not the blockbuster ones—it's cooler to know something about an art film or a foreign film.
4. The weather. It sounds dumb but you can actually start a lively conversation about weather predictions. The locals are obsessed.
5. Ask a waiter to describe some Lyonnais specialties. If your stomach can handle hearing about them, you'll expand your French vocabulary to include things like pig's feet.

▶▶PERFORMING ARTS

The main traditional theater is in the center of the Presqu'ile, in the direction of the Saône from place des Terreaux. **Théâtre des Célestins** *(4 rue Charles Dullin; Tel 04/72-77-40-00; Metro to Cordeliers or Hôtel de Ville; Show times and prices vary; No credit cards)* is a large, old theater that presents more conservative plays, all in French. For you non-French-speakers, there are also opera and classical music performances here at Célestins.

The modern theater is **Le Point du Jour** *(7 rue des Aqueducs; Tel 04/78-15-01-80; Bus 42, 46, 49, 66 to Point du Jour; Ticket info 1pm-6:30pm Mon-Fri; Show times and prices vary; No credit cards)*, which is smaller than Théâtre des Célestins but has more experimental and avant-garde performances, also in French.

You can find modern as well as traditional dance at **Maison de la Danse** *(8 ave. Jean Mermoz; Tel 04/72-78-18-00; Metro to Grange Blanche to Bus 34; Ticket office 11:45am-6:45pm Mon-Fri, 2pm-6:45pm Sat; Show times and prices vary; V)*. The dance company goes on vacation July 20-August 20.

The **Opéra National de Lyon** *(Place de la Comédie; Tel 04/72-00-45-45; Metro to Hôtel de Ville; Ticket office 11am-7pm Mon-Sat; 50-420F; V, MC)*, separated from place des Terreaux by the Hôtel de Ville, is a widely debated structure. The bottom half is an old, classical-style theater, with columns and statues of the muses, while the new glass-and-iron dome with its nightly red illumination is so modern that it's a cause of resentment among many locals. You can find a schedule of the opera season at the Tourist Office or at **FNAC** [see *stuff*, below]. The concerts and operas, like the building itself, range from the traditional to the modern and experimental.

For English-language films, the best place to go is **Ambiance** *(12 rue de la République; Tel 08/36-68-20-15; Metro to Hôtel de Ville; 30-50F admission; No credit cards)*, which is right on the main walking street and shows all the American movies currently released in France in V.O., or *version originale.*

gay scene

While there is no particular gay quarter in Lyon, the city is much more gay-friendly than it has been in the past. There are a number of exclusively gay and lesbian bars, and as their numbers increase, other places in town are becoming more accepting of the scene. The Tourist Office has a complete list of gay bars, and there is a San Francisco-style gay pride parade in late June.

Near the pubs on the rue St. Catherine and place des Terreaux is **Le Verre à Soi** *(25 rue des Capucins; Tel 04/78-28-92-44; Metro to Croix-Pacquet; 11am-3am Mon-Sat; Drinks 15-30F; V, MC)*, a good happy-hour place for both gays and lesbians that stays hopping late into the evening. The narrow stone interior is dark, and you'll pass the ever-present big rainbow flag on your way back to the plain tables and chairs in the rear. They have a special 100F admission on the second Friday of every month, which includes drinks at an open bar.

Le Village *(8 rue St. Georges; Tel 04/78-42-02-19; 8pm-3am Tue-Sat; Drinks 20-30F; No credit cards)* is a lesbian-only piano bar.

CULTUre ZOO

Thanks to its long and varied history, Lyon has a rich culture that's celebrated today in its many museums. The city's architecture dates from Roman, medieval, and modern times, and the art museums have displays ranging from conventional fine arts to decorative arts and traditional silks. The historical museums focus on specific cultural events throughout Lyon's history, such as the Resistance, the silk workers, or the creation of the first motion picture.

Place des Terreaux is home to some of the most interesting architecture of Lyon, namely the traditional buildings of the **Hôtel de Ville** and the Musée des Beaux-Arts, the **Bartholdi fountain,** and the nearby conventional-meets-experimental style Opéra.

The *traboules* are series of secret passageways through Vieux Lyon and Croix-Rousse. Originally designed to safely transport silk down the hill to be exported, they became an essential part of the WWII Resistance movement. Check out 24-28 rue St. Jean, or ask at the Tourist Office for a complete listing.

There is a series of painted walls throughout Lyon, especially in Vieux Lyon and at the Croix-Rousse end of the Presqu'ile. If you wander around and keep your eyes open, you'll start noticing the huge murals, fake facades, and *trompse-l'œil.*

On the east side of the Rhône, Lyon's museum of film history, the **Institut Lumière** *(25 rue du Première-Film; Tel 08/36–68–88–79;*

VILLE LUMIÈRE

Lyon is often referred to as the *Ville Lumière* not only because it was the home of the Lumière brothers, originators of the cinema, but also because every night, it truly becomes a City of Light. Everyone in town sets candles out on their balconies and windowsills, and all of the public buildings in town are illuminated with gorgeous electric lights—**Notre Dame de Fourvière** and the Hôtel de Ville most dramatically. On December 8, the night of the famous **Fête des Lumières,** things get even brighter. The Fête des Lumières honors the Virgin Mary and the Immaculate Conception, as well as the construction of the statue of the Virgin Mary on top of the Fourvière hill. There are candles floating down the river, fire and light shows at place des Terreaux, and fireworks exploding over Fourvière hill. Everyone goes out walking around town to drink *vin chaud,* eat roasted chestnuts and other yummy vendor food, and look at the lights—it's like a city-wide block party. If you don't mind cutting a path through dense crowds of people, it's a fun and breathtaking night.

Metro to Montplaisir-Lumière; www.institut-lumière.org; No credit cards) is housed in the former home of—you guessed it—the Lumière family. There's a replica of the huge workshop they used, and other displays highlighting dad Antoine and sons August and Lois's first flick, *La Sortie des Usines Lumières* (The Exit of the Lumières Workshop). Today you can see old black-and-white classics like *Casablanca* and new artsy films that you might find at the Cannes film festival. Films are screened outside in the summer.

Musée des Beaux-Arts *(20 place des Terreaux; Tel 04/72-10-17-40; Metro to Hôtel de Ville; 10:30am-noon/2-6pm, closed Tue; 25F, 13F for students; No credit cards):* A great collection of fine art with an especially impressive Impressionist collection. Don't miss the sculpture garden in the center courtyard.

Centre d'Histoire de la Résistance et de la Déportation *(14 ave. Berthelot; Tel 04/72-73-33-54; Bus 11, 26, 32, 39, or Metro Perrache and a short walk across the Rhône; 9am-5:30pm Wed-Sun; 25F, 13F for students; No credit cards):* Lyon was the capital of the French Resistance during WWII; the city is still proud of the Resistance leader Jean Moulin, for whom a few streets and a university are named. This museum is housed in the former SS office buildings and is a very informative, well-put-together, and poignant take on Lyon's role in the resistance. The display markers are in French only, but there are free English-language headsets available for self-guided tours.

Maison des Canuts *(12 rue d'Ivry; Tel 04/78-28-62-04; Metro to Croix-Rousse; 8:30am-noon/2-6:30pm Mon-Fri, 9am-noon/2-6pm Sat; 25F; V, MC):* A small museum in Croix-Rousse that focuses on the silk weavers of Lyon. It shows examples of the silks that were traditionally spirited down the *traboules.*

Musée des Tissus et Musée des Arts Décoratifs *(34 rue de la Charité; Tel 04/78-38-42-00; Metro to Bellecour; Musée des Tissus 10am-5:30pm Tue-Sun; Musée des Arts Décoratifs 10am-noon/2pm-5:30pm Tue-Sun; 30F for admission to both; V):* You can see the silks in use at this museum, which is actually two joint museums with one admission price. The Musée des Arts Décoratifs has antique furniture and tapestries; the Musée des Tissus has beautiful old clothing, costumes, and fabrics.

Roman Theaters *(On the Fourvière hill; No telephone; Metro to Vieux Lyon, then funiculaire to Minimes; 9am-dusk daily; No admission charge):* Perched on beautiful Fourvière hill, the most ancient theaters still standing in France are not only an in-the-flesh history lesson, they're also a good spot for picnics! Although they were built way back in 15 to 17 B.C., you can still see the huge pillars of the sanctuary that was dedicated to the goddess Cybele in A.D. 161. Concerts are held here in the summer [see *live music scene,* above].

Cathédral St. Jean *(Place St. Jean; Metro to Vieux Lyon):* Lyon's Gothic cathedral, which sits in the center of the cobblestoned old town, was built from 1180 to 1480. Its most unique feature is the old astronomical clock inside, which chimes and has little dancing figures that pop out hourly from noon to 4pm—stop in then for a look, there's not much other reason to dawdle.

Notre Dame de Fourvière *(Fourvière Esplanade; Metro to Vieux Lyon and then funiculaire to Fourvière; Open dawn to dusk; No admission charge):* The big white church, Lyon's most prominent landmark, has an eclectic merging of architectural styles and a remarkably ornate interior, including a large golden sculpture honoring the Virgin Mary. The Jardin des Rosaires, a winding, shady path linking St. Jean to Fourvière, is lined with small statues and sites for prayer.

modification

The most reliable haircut in town is **Jean Louis David** *(6 place Ampère; Tel 04/78-38-27-28; Metro to Ampère, 9am-7pm Tue-Fri, 8:30am-6:30pm Sat; 120-225F; V, MC),* which is a chain but much more upscale than American chains like Supercuts. They have a few other salons throughout town (this one is conveniently near Place Ampère), no appointment is necessary, and the stylists serve a primarily young, student clientele.

You can get tattoos and body piercing at **Acolor Trip** *(1 rue Constantine; Tel 04/78-30-43-93; Metro to Cordeliers; 2-7pm Mon-Sat; name.worldnet.re/incubus; V, MC), near quai de la Pecherie,* or at **Franck**

Tattoo *(2 rue Fernand Rey; Tel 04/78-27-73-50; Metro to Cordeliers; 2-7pm Tue-Sat; V, MC)*, near the Jardin des Plantes. Both are small, cramped places, as the tattoo parlors in France tend to be.

CITY SPORTS

Parc de la Tete d'Or *(Main entrance at the corner of blvd. des Belges and ave. Grande Bretagne; Bus 4, 41, 47, 36, or 59; Open dawn-dusk)* is one of the largest city parks in Europe, and legend has it that the golden head of an ancient sculpture of Christ is buried somewhere on its grounds. The park has a lake, a large rose garden, a botanical garden, a zoo, puppet shows and a playground, walking paths, and a lot of grassy areas—some with *pelouse interdite* signs, meaning you're not allowed on the lawn, but others where you're likely to find groups of kids playing soccer or Frisbee.

The Quai along the Rhône, on the side opposite the Presqu'ile, has a long running/biking/in-line skating path that runs the length of the city and ends up at the park [see *need to know*, below, for skate and bike renting info].

The indoor climbing gym, **Gym** *(11 rue Lortet; Tel 04/72-71-83-84; noon-10:30pm Mon-Fri, 9:30am-6:30pm Sat, Sun)*, has a big climbing wall to practice on. It is down at the south end of town, on the eastern bank of the Rhône near the university.

STUFF

The best places for shopping are along the pedestrian streets rue Victor Hugo and rue de la Ré, as well as rue du Président Edouard Herriot, which runs parallel to rue de la Ré and tends to have more expensive

fashion

The fashions of Lyon are very similar to those of Paris; the city has a very cosmopolitan flair, and the locals want to be up to par with the Parisians. The women most often wear very slim-fitting pants, Capri pants, or mid-length skirts. They love the same chunky-heeled shoes that Americans do, and they still wear platform sneakers a lot. Perhaps because they've been able to shop for silk scarves all their lives, the women of Lyon know how to look elegant in a scarf like no one else in the world. Messenger bags have yet to become popular with women; they still carry smaller purses, and everyone, but everyone, has a cell phone. The male fashion is a little less set—you'll see guys in jeans or slacks (but very rarely shorts, even in hot weather), and almost all of them are carrying messenger bags now.

shops. These streets have all the typical chains with moderately priced French styles. There are also lots of expensive silk shops where you can buy traditional Lyonnais gifts.

▶▶MALL RATS

Lyon has one big indoor shopping mall, **La Part-Dieu** *(17 rue du Docteur Bouchut; Tel 04/72-60-60-62; 10am-7pm Mon-Sat),* home to department stores and chains. If you can handle all the recycled air and bad lighting, La Part-Dieu is worth a trip so you can check out the enormous Carrefour, a store that seems to sell literally everything on the planet—food, clothes, music, computers, garden hoses, etc.

▶▶DUDS

One of the French chains with the biggest selection of current fashions is **Zara** *(71/73 rue de la République; Tel 04/72-41-41-15; Metro to Cordeliers; 10am-7pm daily; 100-300F; V, MC),* which has especially bright, stylish women's clothing. Similar chain stores abound along rue de la Ré and rue du Président Edouard Herriot.

▶▶FOOT FETISH

Just off rue de la Ré, you'll find inexpensive shoes for men and women at **Pêle-Mêle** *(21–23 rue d'Algérie; Tel 04/78-39-55-56; Metro to Hôtel de Ville, 8:45am-7:15pm Mon-Sat; 200-400F; V, MC).* You have to rummage through stacks of boxes to find your size, but they have a large selection.

France Arno *(30 rue de la République; Tel 04/78-37-39-26; Metro to Cordeliers; 400-800F; 10am-7pm daily; V, MC),* just down the way, has nicer, more stylish leather shoes for men and women, as well as sneakers, flats, and sandals.

▶▶BOUND

The area around place Ampère is full of antique stores and used bookstores specializing in leather-bound books and first editions. One of the many is **Salvador Miraglia** *(24 rue des Remparts d'Ainay; Tel 06/07-27-53-32 or 04/78-42-14-62; 9am-noon/2-7pm daily; www.livre-rare-book.com/miraglia.htm; V, MC, AE),* which has that floor-to-ceiling look and the smell of leather and aging paper.

A Plus d'un Titre *(8 rue Platière; Tel 04/78-27-69-51; Metro to Cordeliers; 10am-7pm Mon-Sat; V, MC),* back in the Presqu'ile shopping district, has both used and new books, with some foreign language and travel literature, lots of children's books, and often little sidewalk sales.

▶▶TUNES

In Vieux Lyon, **Boul'dingue 1** *(8 rue du Palais du Justice; Tel 04/78-38-03-97; Metro to Vieux Lyon; 10am-noon/2-7pm Mon-Sat; V, MC)* is the place to go for used comics and used rock, rap, reggae, and techno CDs, while **Boul'dingue 2** *(16 rue du Bœuf; Tel 04/78-42-90-50; Metro to Vieux Lyon; 10am-noon/2-7pm Mon-Sat; V, MC)* carries used jazz, classical, world music, and vinyl. Both places have information on local live shows, and both are crowded and well-stocked.

Lyon's **FNAC** *(85 rue de la République; Tel 04/72-40-49-49; Metro to Bellecour; 10am-7:30pm Mon-Sat; www.fnac.com; V, MC, AE)* is enormous, and has a lot of listening stations as well as concert tickets and a smallish section of English books.

▶▶OTHER STUFF

Voisin Chocolates *(38 rue Victor Hugo; Tel 04/78-37-42-40; Metro to Ampère; 2-7:30pm Mon, 9am-7:30pm Tue-Sat; V, MC, AE)* is well-known in town. Try the specialty, the *cousin,* a little green or pink candy made of chocolate and almond paste.

EaTS

Lyon has long been considered a center of gastronomic expertise. One of the most famous chefs in France, Paul Bocuse, has an incredible restaurant here. Specialties of Lyon include *quenelles,* fish dumplings that look like plump little hot dogs and taste something like gnocchi; *salade Lyonnais,* which has lettuce, a poached egg, croutons, and bacon; and lots of meat dishes, often using pork or seafood. The little restaurants called *bouchons,* which serve the local specialties, are concentrated in three main areas of town: Vieux Lyon; on rue Mercière, just between place des Terreaux and the Saône; and on rue des Marronniers, off of place Bellecour.

▶▶CHEAP

Le Jardin Andalou *(44 rue St. Jean; Tel 04/78-42-77-11; Metro to Vieux Lyon; 11am-midnight daily; Sandwiches 20-25F, plates 30-75F; No credit cards)* is a tiny restaurant with a street-side stand that serves up great falafel sandwiches you can take to eat at the Roman theater just up the hill.

Rue Victor Hugo has a number of food stands, especially near place Ampère; you can grab a bite to sit down with there, or go across the Rhône by the university.

TO MarKET

La Halle de Lyon *(102 Cours Lafayette; Bus 3; Tue-Thur 7am-noon/3-7pm, Fri, Sat 7am-7pm, Sun 7am-noon)* is the city's covered fresh vegetable and food market.

On the **boulevard de la Croix-Rousse** *(Metro to Croix-Rousse),* there is an open-air market every morning except Monday, and since the Croix-Rousse is still a largely residential area, the market feels more small-scale and local, like a market in a smaller town.

The **quai St. Antoine** along the Saône *(Metro to Vieux Lyon or Bellecour)* is the site of another food market every morning except Monday; produce and flowers are sold here.

le beaujolais nouveau est arrivé

Beaujolais Nouveau, a light red wine released just a month or two after the harvest and intended for consumption before it ages, is the most popular of the Rhône Valley wines. It is so popular, in fact, that the local joke is that there are actually three rivers in Lyon: le Rhône, la Saône, and le Beaujolais! The release of Beaujolais Nouveau, each year on the third Thursday of November, is the occasion for one of the biggest festivals in Lyon and the surrounding Rhône Valley. The French are a bit jealous that the first release of Beaujolais Nouveau happens in Japan, since the date changes there first, but they make up for that with their enthusiasm and pride at their own parties.

The big, organized festival happens nearby in **Beaujeu,** the old capital of the Beaujolais region, easily accesible from Lyon by train [see *need to know,* below]. Go and watch the local winemakers roll their barrels down the street in the annual race, sample some of the goods, and party with the rest of the wine-lovers who have made the trek.

In Lyon, the party is more informal, less planned. For the weeks of November following the release, every bar puts out a big sign reading "Le Beaujolais Nouveau est arrivé!" and pours the wine directly out of barrels, at *very* fair prices. It seems that everyone in town is out on the streets or in the bars—and they *all* have a friend with a vineyard that makes Beaujolais, and everyone wants you to try a glass of *their* wine. Who are you to refuse such hospitality?

▶▶DO-ABLE

Brasserie L'Espace Carnot *(4 place Carnot; Tel 04/72-41-98-40; Metro to Perrache; 7am-1am daily; Set menus 65F, 85F, 110F; V, MC, AE)* serves up the traditional brasserie fare (quiches, pizzas, and salads), as well as daily specials and local cuisine. The terrace seating is on the square beneath lovely light-filtering shade trees, and the waiters run back and forth across the street from the restaurant to the square to take orders and carry food.

Pavé St. Jean *(23 rue St. Jean; Tel 04/78-42-25-13; Metro to Vieux Lyon; 11am-2:30pm/7-11:30pm daily; Set menus 68F-100F; V,)* is one of the little bouchons in Vieux Lyon. Try the *quenelles,* one of the restaurant's best Lyonnais specialties. The waiters are particularly friendly, and it's usually crowded on the terrace in the warm summer months. The set menus include wine, making them an especially good deal.

On the rue des Marronniers, amidst another cluster of bouchons, is **L'Empika** *(7 rue des Marronniers; Tel 04/78-37-13-90; Metro to Bellecour; noon-2pm/7-11pm daily, till 11:30 Fri, Sat; Set menus 50-100F; V, MC).* The waiters are funny and full of song, and the mirrored walls make the tiny restaurant seem only slightly bigger than it is.

Across the street, **Chez Gérard** *(6 rue des Marronniers; Tel 04/78-42-76-02; Metro to Bellecour; 11am-2pm/6:30-10pm daily except Wed; Set menus 85F, 99F, 115F; V, MC, AE)* has great seafood, terrace seating, and tiny upstairs and downstairs seating areas.

▶▶**SPLURGE**

One of the most famous restaurants in France, **Restaurant Paul Bocuse** *(40 rue de la Plage, Collonges-Au-Mont-d'Or; Tel 04/72-42-90-90; open daily for lunch and dinner; 200-800F; V, MC, AE, DIN),* helps Lyon live up to its reputation as the gastronomic capital of the country. It will be your splurge of splurges if you decide to go, and if so, you absolutely need reservations in advance and dress in your best (at least try for not wrinkled...). Their best-known specialties are truffle soup and *loup en croûte* (lamb).

crashing

The best places to stay in Lyon are on the Presqu'ile or in Vieux Lyon, so you can be close to the cultural attractions and shopping during the day and within walking distance of the bars and clubs, as the metros stop running at midnight. The hostel in Lyon is a great one, and there are a number of reasonably priced hotels.

▶▶**CHEAP**

The **Auberge du Vieux Lyon** *(41-45 Montée du Chemin Neuf; Tel 04/78-15-05-50; Metro to Vieux Lyon to funiculaire Minimes; Reception 7am-noon/2pm-1am 72F per bed incl. breakfast, 17F for sheets; V, MC, AE)* is arguably the best hostel in France. It's in the modern, remodeled style, with two- to six-person rooms and sturdy, new bunk beds. The rooms have showers and sinks, and the garden has awesome views overlooking the city. There is a kitchen and laundry, a bar, music all night, and a staff that won't let you escape partying with them. It's a steep walk up the hill from Vieux Lyon, or you can take the funicular up to the Minimes stop and walk right down the hill to the front door.

Or try the **Hôtel de Vichy** *(60-bis, rue de la Charite; Tel 04/78-37-42-58, Fax 04/78-37-42-58; Singles 165-200F, Double: 220F, Triple 260F, Quad 280F, all with separate bath; V, MC, AE),* a 5-minute walk from train station near Bellecour.

▶▶**DO-ABLE**

The **Hôtel Alexandra** *(49 rue Victor Hugo; Tel 04/78-37-75-79; Metro to Ampère; 180-250F single, 250-280F double; V, MC, AE, DIN)* is right near place Ampère. The reception area is one flight up from the entrance, and the rooms are pretty standard, except for the slanty-roofed and sky-lighted garret rooms. The low roofs and low-to-the-ground furniture can make you feel a bit like Alice in Wonderland after she ate too much of the Caterpillar's mushroom. All the rooms have showers, and the more expensive ones have toilets as well. You can usually squeeze extra people into the rooms; an extra bed is 30F.

Right around the corner is **Hôtel d'Ainay** (*14 rue des Ramparts d'Ainay; Tel 04/78-42-43-42; Metro to Ampère; 165-225F singles, 175-235F doubles; V, MC*), whose linoleum floors may not be homey but are always clean. Most rooms have their own bathrooms; the cheapest have hall toilets. The reception desk is one floor up from the entrance, and the staff is friendly and helpful.

Other decent relatively affordable options include **Hôtel du Theater** (*10 rue de Savoie; Tel 04/78-42-33-32; Fax 04/72-40-00-61; Single w/out bath 195F, Single w/ bath 275-320F, Double w/ bath 300-360F; V, MC*), a five-minute walk from the city center; and **Grand Hôtel Château Perrache** (*12 cours de Verdun; Tel 800-MeRCURE or 04/72-77-15-00, Fax 04/78-37-06-56; Single 780-880F, Double: 880-980F, Suites 1400-1500F; V, MC, AE*), in the city center.

▶▶**SPLURGE**

Elysée Hotel (*92 rue Président Edouard Herriot; Tel 04/78-42-03-15; Metro to Bellecour; 340-360F single, 360-380F double; V, MC, AE*) is a gracious, upscale place with an elevator. There is plush red décor in the lounge, and the rooms all have toilets and a bathtub or shower. The floral-themed rooms are bright and cheerful. Conveniently near rue de la Ré, this is one of the most central places to stay in Lyon.

Another big-wallet option is the lovely **Cour des Loges** (*6 rue du Boeuf; Tel 04/72-77-44-44; Fax 04/72-40-93-61; contact* 2250-2400F; V, EUR, MC, AE, DIN*), in the heart of Old Lyon.

need to know

Currency Exchange There are **banks** all along rue Victor Hugo and surrounding place Bellecour; these will probably get you the best rates. You can also change money at **AOC** (*20 rue Gasparin; Tel 04/78-38-12-00; Metro to Bellecour; 9:30am-6:30pm Mon-Sat*).

Tourist Information The **Office de Tourisme** (*Place Bellecour; Tel 04/72-77-69-69; 9am-7pm Mon-Sat, 10am-7pm Sun*) is in the middle of place Bellecour and provides maps, show schedules, a hotel reservations service, an SNCF office, and day-trip information. There are also **SOS Voyageurs** offices in the *Gare de la Part-Dieu* and the *Gare de Perrache* that will make hotel reservations for you.

Public Transportation The bus/Metro system is run by **TCL** (*43 rue de la République; Tel 04/78-71-70-00; 8am-6:30pm Mon-Fri, 9am-noon/1:20-5pm Sat; V, AE*). The four **metro** lines and two *funiculaires* are really easy to navigate and make traveling around the city easy. There are also a lot of **buses,** which are a bit more confusing if you're only in town for a couple of days. Tickets for both buses and metro are 8F each, or you can buy 10 for 68F, and you can get them in any metro station. Be sure to validate your ticket in the orange machine because they *"controle"* a lot. The metro runs daily from 5am to midnight.

American Express The local **American Express** office *(6 rue Childebert; Tel 04/72-77-74-50; 9:30am–noon/2-6:30pm Mon-Fri)* located near the quays of the Rhône, off place Bellecour, no longer changes money but does provide other American Express services.

Health and Emergency Medical emergency: *15;* Police: *17.* The local **Hôpital** *(5 Place d'Arsonal; Tel 04/72-11-73-11)* has emergency services.

Pharmacy There are pharmacies absolutely everywhere you turn, and they're all marked by the big flashing **green neon crosses.**

Telephone City code: *04;* You can buy phone cards from France telecom at any *tabac* (they are identifiable by the red diamond symbol). You can also buy a card at the **post office.**

Airport The **Lyon Satolas Airport** *(Tel 04/72-22-72-21)* is about 40 minutes from town on the bus, **Cie Satobus** *(Tel 04/72-68-72-17; 49.50F).*

Trains There are two main SNCF stations: **Gare de la Part-Dieu** *(Part Dieu station, Tel 08/36-35-35-35; Metro to Part-Dieu)* and **Gare de Perrache** *(Place Carnot; Tel 08/36-35-35-35; Metro to Perrache).* Perrache is the more central station, so if you are given a choice, get off at Perrache. However, Perrache doesn't usually handle TGVs. Often the trains only stop in Part-Dieu, and that's okay, too—you can get right on the metro and go straight to Bellecour, which is the metro stop in the center of town, right by the Tourist Office.

Bike/Moped Rental The best place for rentals is **Holiday Bikes** *(8 Quai Lassagne; Tel 04/72-07-06-77; Metro to Croix Paquet; 9am–noon/2-7pm daily; Must be 18 and have a license to rent a moped; V, MC)* which sits on the east bank of the Rhône near the Hôtel de Ville.

Laundry There is a central Laundromat on the Presqu'ile, **Laverie** *(7 rue Mercière; Tel 04/78-38-21-19; Metro to Bellecour; 6am-9pm daily)* and another closer to the youth hostel, also called **Laverie** *(18 rue de Trion; No telephone; Metro Vieux Lyon to funiculaire Minimes; 7am-9:30pm daily).*

Postal The main branch of **La Poste** *(Place Antonin Poncet; Tel 04/72-40-63-03; Metro to Bellecour; 8am–7pm Mon-Fri, 8am–12:30pm Sat)* is right off place Bellecour.

Internet See *wired,* above.

the french alps

grenoble

When you emerge from one of France's most beautiful art museums, the **Musée de Grenoble,** [see *culture zoo,* below] you'll find yourself standing in the shade of 15 contemporary sculptures made of metal and stone, looking up at the Bastille fortress on the city's famous hill—and also within earshot of a drum circle and in view of a rehearsing university theater group.

The largest city in the Alps, Grenoble is the region's center of music, art, education, and politics, while the nearby mountains and hiking trails give it a distinctly alpine vibe. Two of France's most highly respected 18th-century literary figures, Jean-Jacques Rousseau and Stendhal, lived here, and Grenoble continues to enjoy a lively arts and literature scene even today. This is thanks in large part to the **Université de Grenoble,** whose students flock to the cafes hosting literature and philosophy discussion groups and to the French and foreign-language bookstores. And how could a town call itself cultured without a strong music scene? Grenoble's corners and parks are always peopled with street musicians, and the bars host a number of local up-and-coming bands, most of them rock and reggae groups.

Locals and students get along here, so you'll thankfully miss that wonderful town-gown tension that divides so many American college towns. In fact, the university and its students are such an integral part of the town's culture that it's often hard to distinguish between student and local. The full flower of student life is best experienced from May to September, although the University of Grenoble has the largest summer-session program in Europe. Even so, you won't see as many of those shaggy eco-political party radicals—called Les Verts (The Greens)—or as many walking sex symbols as you do when autumn leaves start to fall. For some reason, Grenoble has been known for attracting some of the sexiest students in Europe—the budding French versions of a young Cindy Crawford or the young Brad Pitt. Photographers from Paris come here in their search for new faces.

Grenoble has the fastest pace of any of the alpine towns you'll visit, and it's the closest you'll come to cosmopolitan in this neck of the French woods. Locals are as fashion-conscious as any other city-dweller—there are lots of small boutiques along the pedestrian streets where you can find chic duds, and you will see your share of the French city uniform: slim Capri pants, sparkly sandals, and cell phones. The city's modern, nearly silent, above-ground tramways whisking commuters to and fro remind you that you're not in the backcountry Alps anymore.

But even with all this city-esque movement, you won't ever forget that you're still close to the mountains that ring the city. The locals tend to be outdoorsy types who enjoy hiking, biking, climbing, canyoning, and paragliding as much as a night at the opera. Forget about taking a walk in the city park: Grenoble's bike lanes go straight from city streets up into the mountains, and the hiking trails start right at the edges of town. It's one of the only cities in France where you'll see the local guys wearing shorts and hiking boots (usually that's a sure way to spot an American backpacker!).

As in other towns in the Alps, people take their time here—nothing seems to be too rushed or harried. Generally they're willing to help you out and tell you more about the town and the region. Don't be afraid to strike up a convo with salespeople in shops, waiters in cafes, and people on the hiking trails—they'll definitely respond to your friendliness. Although Grenoble has its share of tourists in the summer, they never overrun the city; the locals favor their native French here, and probably won't instantly answer your struggled *"Bonjour"* with an English response as they do in Paris and other big, touristy cities.

But if your French is rusty (or non-existent), don't fret—you'll get your share of English, Spanish, and German from the international university students who dominate Grenoble's population. Seek these students out! They are your link to the youth scene, which comes alive after dark in the busy cafes and bars. The emphasis is on live music rather than on clubbing, and you can usually check out the local bands without dropping too much dough. Of course, like every town in France, Grenoble has its *boîtes de nuit* (night clubs), but locals and students alike seem to favor hanging out with their friends over gyrating to mainstream dance tracks. Perhaps that's why the clubs are often filled with older tourists. You can find a listing of local cultural events in the weekly **Le Petit Bulletin,** which is available at the tourist office [see *need to know,* below] and almost any music store or cafe.

grenoble

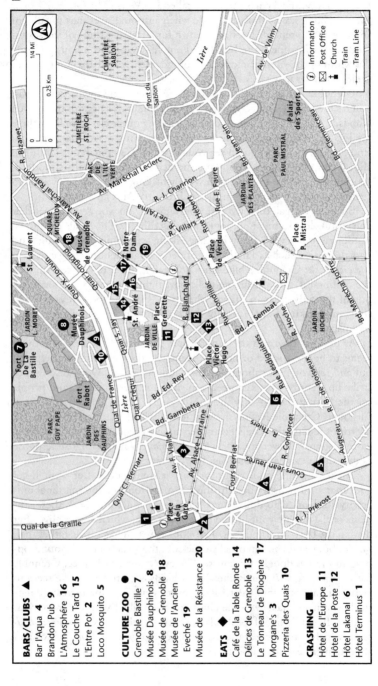

BARS/CLUBS ▲

Bar l'Aqua **4**
Brandon Pub **9**
L'Atmosphère **16**
Le Couche Tard **15**
L'Entre Pot **2**
Loco Mosquito **5**

CULTURE ZOO ●

Grenoble Bastille **7**
Musée Dauphinois **8**
Musée de Grenoble **18**
Musée de l'Ancien
  Eveché **19**
Musée de la Résistance **20**

EATS ◆

Café de la Table Ronde **14**
Délices de Grenoble **13**
Le Tonneau de Diogène **17**
Morgane's **3**
Pizzeria des Quais **10**

CRASHING ■

Hôtel de l'Europe **11**
Hôtel de la Poste **12**
Hôtel Lakanal **6**
Hôtel Terminus **1**

neighborhoods

The main downtown area of Grenoble doesn't have the pronounced neighborhoods or districts that you'll find in Paris, Lyon, and Marseille.

The **place aux Herbes** and especially the **place St. André** stand in the very heart of the *centre ville.* To miss these famous old squares would be like a visit to London without a stopover at Piccadilly Circus. Of the two, place St. André, dating from the Middle Ages, is the most photographed and evocative of old Grenoble, graced on one side with the Palais de Justice and on the other by the Église St. André. Two main streets for strolling and seeing what the shops are selling include rue de la Poste, within the city's medieval core, and rue Jean-Jacques Rousseau, a mostly pedestrian walkway that's within a somewhat newer section that's a five-minute walk to the southwest.

The main streets of town, which are lined with bigger department stores, chain hotels, bakeries, and hair salons are **avenue Alsace-Lorraine,** a wide street running east/west for cars as well as the tramway tracks, and two streets that cross the avenue, **Cours Jean Jaurès** and

walking tour

Start out on **place Grenette,** then leave the busy shopping district by way of the quiet **rue Jean-Jacques Rousseau** for some window-shopping in the little boutiques and bookshops. Be sure to look up and notice the window boxes, garret windows, and chimneys on every building. Follow rue Jean-Jacques Rousseau until you spill out onto the place Sainte Claire; here you can go into the **Halles Sainte Claire,** where there is a daily food and fruit market, to pick out a picnic. Leaving the market, continue walking north on **rue Carnot** until you hit **place Notre Dame;** you will be heading straight for the **mountains** that loom over the city. Sit down for a coffee at **Le Tonneau de Diogène** [see *eats,* below]; pay for your drink inside so you can look at the huge collection of little porcelain owls over the bar, then go upstairs and check out the bookstore. Continue along place Notre Dame, passing the **Musée de l'Ancien Eveché** and turning right on **rue du Vieux Temple.** Take an immediate left to ease your way onto **avenue Maréchal Randon,** a busy street that passes the **Musée de Grenoble.** Turn left into the **Parc A. Michalton,** which curves behind [see *culture zoo,* below, for both museums] the *musée* and has a sunny lawn area and sculpture garden. There are lots of shade trees, so it's a nice spot for a picnic, and there are often drum circles or solo sax, flute, or guitar players.

wired

To check your e-mail, you have a few options. There is the usual **Cyberposte** at La Poste [see *need to know,* below], which charges 50F for the first hour and 30F to recharge your card. You can also go to **Espace Culture Multimedia** *(Place St. Laurent; Tel 04/76-44-88-80; 9am-noon/2-6pm Mon-Fri, 2pm-6pm Sat, Sun; 30F an hour; No credit cards),* or you can hang out at **Le New Age Cyber Café** *(16 place Notre Dame; Tel 7am-midnight daily; 25F per half hour, 40F per hour).* Grenoble's official website is *www.grenoble-isere-tourisme.com.*

boulevard Gambetta. Another happening area of town is the **place Condorcet** area, which is southwest of the center toward the train tracks and has a number of budget hotels, bars, and *boulangeries,* although fewer shops and boutiques. The river Isère flows up from the southeast end of town, runs up along the university area, continues along the north end of town, and flows out to the northwest. The *banlieu,* or suburbs, spread to the south, and you reach residential and industrial areas fairly quickly as you move out of the center of town. Except for a few less visible branches, most of the University of Grenoble lies within the industrial-looking suburb of St. Martin d'Heres, a 20-minute tram ride via tram B southeast of the city's center. Don't expect architecture that's historic or avant-garde—the concern here is the brutal winter weather and cost-efficient construction. The result looks bland and rather bureaucratic, relieved only by the vivacity and sex appeal of the students. Grenoble's two speedy train lines and 20 bus lines will get you where you need to go; just keep in mind that the bus service stops running in the early evening.

hanging out

You are likely to meet the locals in the parks—either the large **Parc Mistral**, located south of the *centre ville,* or the smaller sculpture garden behind the **Musée de Grenoble** [see *culture zoo,* below]—or on the hiking trails [see *city sports,* below], where they're just hanging out themselves, and are probably the most friendly and open. In town, **L'Atmosphère** [see *bar scene,* below] is arguably the best place to park yourself for an afternoon of espresso and eavesdropping—the university students spend a lot of time in the cafes on the main squares, drinking coffee or beer, discussing philosophy, studying, or surfing the net.

bar scene

The student-heavy bar scene in Grenoble is all about cafe/happy-hour joints and bars that get louder and more crowded as the evening goes on. To get to most of the action, just head into the old town, mainly around place St. André, place Claveyson, place aux Herbes, and rue du Palais.

There are a number of bar/brasseries on the main squares where people begin gathering in the late afternoon for an *apéritif* or a coffee. These places are fun at night, too, and they generally give you a better chance to hang out and talk than some of the louder bars.

One of the coolest of the bunch is **L'Atmosphère** *(1 place Claveyson; Tel 04/76-44-27-84; Mon-Sat 9am-1am; No credit cards),* just around the corner from Place aux Herbes, which hosts a largely young French crowd, both students and locals. It has terrace seating and serves reasonably priced food at lunchtime, when the indoor seating is pleasant in a light, bright, but cool tiled room. Drinks will run you between 15 and 20F.

For a more upscale, pricier spot, come feel the history at **Café de la Table Ronde** [see *eats,* below], Grenoble's oldest cafe and the former hangout of Rousseau and his buddies. A pretty wide variety of people assemble here—students, locals, and tourists alike—although the younger crowd tends to clear out after dinner, leaving an older and more mellow crowd.

Later in the evening, young French and international students, hangs out at **Le Couche Tard** *(1 rue du Palais; Tel 04/76-44-18-79; 5pm-2am daily; Average drink 20-30F; V, MC),* which is on the street between place aux Herbes and place St. Andre, only about a block from L'Atmosphère. There's a happy hour Monday through Thursday between 7 and 8pm with 12F beers, but the place usually doesn't pick up until later in the night, when the dark, two-story bar blasts rock, rap, or reggae, and the red neon lights shine from the stairwell.

On the southern end of town near Place Condorcet is one of Grenoble's best happy-hour joints. The **Loco Mosquito** *(56 rue Thiers; Tel 04/76-85-03-16; 6pm-1am Mon-Sat; V, MC)* has a happy hour from 7 to 8:30 nightly, offering 5F *pastis* and 8F beers. It attracts a young, French student crowd, and the graffiti-covered walls are hung with concert and cult

festivals and events

Grenoble has a number of music and theater festivals. The biggest music festival is the **Musiques Nomades,** featuring a variety of folk music periodically from September through June. A yearly **Jazz Festival** takes place in March. The **European Theater Festival** is held in the first week of July, and there is a **Film Festival** featuring films about nature each November. For complete and up-to-date information about these festivals, contact the Tourist Office or check out Grenoble's festival website at **www.esc-grenoble.fr/vf/Envt/festivals.htm.**

movie posters *(Pulp Fiction, Reservoir Dogs)*. Folks come to meet their friends after school or work and to listen to the evening's selection of rock, reggae, salsa, or ska. You can count on Thursday night salsa and the occasional '70s disco night.

LIVE MUSIC SCENE

Grenoble is arguably one of the best places in France to catch some live local music, from the live rock, reggae, and ska music in the bars and pubs to the street musicians and kids playing in drum circles in the parks. You'll find ads for local shows in most of the numerous CD/record shops in town. Even the large chain music stores have a good-sized selection of CDs by local bands.

You can usually count on live music at the popular Irish pub **Brandon Pub** *(8 quai Perrière; Tel 04/76-85-01-75; Average drink 20F; 5pm-1am Tue-Sun; V, MC)*, on the northside of the Isère River, across from the old town and the **Couche Tard** [see *bar scene,* above]. You'll recognize the pub by the tell-tale Guinness sign in the doorway. Inside, amid the barrels set up as tables and chairs, and the wildly colorful murals on the walls, you'll hear a large variety of sounds, mainly local. The music ranges from classic rock cover bands to reggae to dance music; there's also live Latin music every Thursday night starting just after 9pm.

Across the train tracks from downtown, the popular **L'Entre-Pot** *(8 rue Auguste Genin; Tel 04/76-48-21-48; 9pm-2am Wed-Sun; www.entre-pot.fr.st; Occasionally free, otherwise 30-100F; V, MC)* hosts a variety of rock and reggae shows, with local as well as some larger touring bands. You can check the schedule at their website; the music usually starts between 10 and 10:30pm.

Fans of virtually anything Irish—rugby, shamrocks, leprechauns, and blue-eyed Celts—gravitate to **Murphy's** *(5 place Vaucauson; Tel 04/76-85-30-30; 5:30pm-2am daily)*. Guinness, Irish whiskey, and all kinds of suds, both French and imported, flow freely. There's recorded music (always) and often the best Irish music in the Alps. Come here for the music and to mingle, but know your soccer scores in advance before you begin a sports dialogue with a local.

Less sports-oriented and more attuned to cutting-edge music from such centers as London or Los Angeles, is **Le Styx** *(6 place Claveyson; Tel 04/76-44-09-99; drinks from 12F; 10am-1am daily)*. Expect a standard mix of hip-hop, R&B, soul, techno, but anticipate anything. The dance floor is too small, but used anyway. The art deco-style coffeehouse scene here in the morning is the most laid-back in town. Young office workers head here after 5pm to sample one of 80 different cocktails featured, with beer and pastis being the drinks of choice.

Le Summum *(ave. d'innsbruck; 04/76-39-63-63; www.summum grenoble.com)* packs 'em in to its 3,000 seats for about 80 shows a year. It's mostly jazz and world music, like Third World, mixed with some pop, like the lovely Vanessa Paradis.

arTs scene

▶▶VISUAL ARTS

There isn't much of a happening gallery scene here. To find the best visual arts in Grenoble, head for the contemporary art in the **Musée de Grenoble** [see *culture zoo*, below]. There's also the occasional local exhibit in the Tourist Office [see *need to know*, below].

To enjoy an inexpensive brasserie-style meal and an insight into contemporary art in Grenoble today all in one fell swoop, visit the **Galerie Rome** *(1 rue Très Cloîtres. Tel 04/76-42-82-01)* where oversized, ultra-contemporary paintings line the walls. Virtually anything displayed here is for sale.

Newer, smaller, and less time-tested is **Galerie Voltaire** *(3 rue Voltaire. Tel 04/76-51-19-51.)* whose repertoire is changed frequently. Here, you'll see a parade of some of the most creative alpine statements being made in painting, ceramics, and sculpture.

▶▶PERFORMING ARTS

The performing arts are a big focus for both locals and students. They love and appreciate innovative, contemporary plays and alternative, artsy movies—even the main theater hosts student performances. They are, for the most part, only in French.

For indie flicks, go to **Cinéma le Melies** *(3 rue de Strasbourg; Tel 04/76-47-24-33; Show times noon-10pm; 30-40F; Reduced prices on Wed; No credit cards)*. In summer 2000 they were running the Cannes Film Festival winners, some animated shorts, and an English version of *Oliver Twist*. Matinee prices are good till 7pm, and Wednesday is cheap night. The cinema is in the old town area, near the pedestrian shopping streets.

The **Office de Tourisme** [see *need to know*, below] can give you a schedule for the popular **Théâtre de Grenoble** *(4 rue Hector Bérlioz; Tel 04/76-44-03-44; Show times and prices vary)*, near the Isère River just east of the *centre ville*. Everyone—the locals, the students, and the tourists—comes here for a variety of traditional and nontraditional theater.

The **Théâtre de Rue** *(Tel 04/76-01-21-21)* is a mobile alternative theater company that sets up for free shows in the parks and on the street. Call and see where their next stage will strike.

There is an amateur theater week in May, and there are university theater groups that perform in various places—sometimes at the main theater, sometimes at an alternative amateur theater called **Le Cargo** *(4 rue Claudel, Tel 04/76-25-91-91, Tram A to Maison de la Culture)* located in the *centre ville*.

gay scene

The one area to check out for any signs of gay life—over beyond place Condorcet and further toward the railroad tracks—is sort of out of the way, which seems to sum up Grenoble's gay scene: it's not very big or well-known, but then again there isn't any open hostility either. The **Bar l'Aqua** (*3 rue Étienne Marcel; Tel 04/76-87-55-89; 5pm-1am Tue-Sat; Average drink 20F; V, MC*) hosts a largely gay male crowd and a few lesbian females in its small, blue-neon-lit bar.

CULTURE ZOO

Grenoble's museums aren't as famous as the museums in Paris, but they're still impressive. You can buy a pass good for a year at all the museums in and around Grenoble. Available at the Tourist Office [see *need to know*, below] and at the museums, it costs only 50F, so if you plan to visit a number of museums, it's a pretty good deal.

Grenoble Bastille (*Quai Stéphane Jay; Tel 04/76-44-33-65; 9am-12:30am daily, opens 11:30am Mon, July-Aug; 9am-midnight Tue-Sat, 11am-7:30 Sun-Mon, spring and fall; 10:30am-6:30pm daily, opens 11am Mon, winter):* There is a *téléphérique (leaves from Quai Stéphane Jay between Pont Marius Gontard and Pont St. Laurent; Tel 04/76-44-33-65; Apr-Oct: first trip up 10:30am, last trip up 11:30pm Tue-Sun, first trip up 11am, last trip up 7:15pm Mon; Nov-Mar: first trip up 10:30am, last trip up 6:30pm Tue-Sun, first trip up 11am Mon; 22F one way/33F round trip adults, 17F one-way/26F round trip students),* which resembles an enclosed ski lift, that takes you up to the Fort de la Bastille, just north of the old town across the Isère. At 475 meters (1,558 feet), the view of the city and nearby Mont Blanc is amazing. If you don't like the *téléphérique,* you can also hike up the path across the river. You can walk up to the Bastille in an hour or so, if you're an Olympic athlete; the entrance is signposted immediately to the west of place St. André. However, we'd suggest you take the téléphérique to the top, then stroll *down* the mountain along the footpath, *Montée de Chalmont,* which winds its way through the alpine flower gardens and past old ruins before reaching a cobblestone walkway that finally empties into the streets of the Old Town. The Grenoble Bastille dates from the 16th century, and was strengthened in the 19th century, but it saw so little battle action that there's virtually no story to tell. The fort itself isn't all that happening (the main attractions are a cafe and a gift shop)—it's all about the view.

Musée de Grenoble (*5 place de Lavalette; Tel 04/76-63-44-10; 11am-7pm daily, closed Tue; 25F, 15F for students; No credit cards):* Grenoble's bright and open fine arts museum houses a collection ranging from 17th-century Flemish, French, and Italian paintings to Modern art, including a great collection of Matisse—His *Intérieur aux Aubergines* alone is worth the trek over here—and some works by Picasso, Chagall, Miro, and Kandinsky. The museum also has several rooms of contemporary art and a shady sculpture garden.

Musée de La Résistance et de la Déportation (*14 rue Hebert; Tel 04/76-42-38-53; 9am-6pm daily, closed Tue, summers open till 7pm; 20F, 10F for students; No credit cards):* A well-put-together and informative display, focusing on the Resistance movement in the region during WWII, near place de Verdun. All displays are in French, English, and German.

Musée Dauphinois *(30 rue Maurice Gignoux; Tel 04/76-85-19-01; 10am-6pm daily except Tue, till 7pm in summer; 20F, 10F for students):* If it's a roll of the dice between Musée Dauphinois and the one below, make it the Dauphinois. No museum in all the Alps gives such a detailed view of the artifacts of the alpine people, often forced to struggle against ferocious weather to eke out a living. Furnishings, tools, and artifacts recreate the life here, and miniature replicas of alpine settings, both outdoor and indoor, bring daily mountain life into focus. Before heading out on a ski trip, check out their special exhibition on skiing, tracing the earliest development of the sport to the high-tech innovations of the 21st century. The museum also stages exhibitions—sometimes controversial—on contemporary French life, such as a recent show exploring the effect of massive immigration on French society. The museum is north of the Isère, opposite the *centre ville.*

Cathédrale Notre Dame et l'Ancien Eveché *(2 rue Tres Cloîtres; Tel 04/76-03-15-25; 10am-7pm daily, till 9pm Wed, closed Tue; 20F, 10F for students):* Housed in Grenoble's first baptistry and the old bishop's palace in the *centre ville,* this museum covers the history of the Isère region and actually does a pretty good job of making it interesting even to non-history buffs with a focus largely on the people and their crafts and artwork. It is actually made up of three museums: the *Crype Archéologique,* which showcases the Roman-era (4th-10th century) walls of the baptistry; the *Musée d'Art Sacré,* featuring liturgical and other religious objects; and the *Centre Jean Achard,* which showcases the art of the Dauphine region. The highlight here is a stunning scripted door panel from the 1400s depicting Jacob and his sons.

modification

There is no shortage of hair salons in Grenoble—in fact, it seems like there's one on every corner. In addition to the usual chains, like Jean Louis David, you'll find a bunch of smaller, more intimate salons, such as **L'Aterlier à Tifs** *(24 rue Barnave, Tel 04/76-54-87-37; 9am-7pm Tue-Sat; Average haircut 100-150F; V, MC),* near Place St. André. It offers student discounts and draws a generally young and hip crowd, both men and women.

The best place to go to add another hole to your head is the little boutique **Opale** *(15 rue Jean-Jacques Rousseau; Tel 04/76-51-50-15; 1-7pm Mon, 10am-7pm Tue-Sat; Prices vary; V, MC),* which is on a pedestrian street right in the center of the old town. Even if you're not going under the needle, it's worth stopping in to browse the silver jewelry, glass-beaded rings and necklaces, which are just elegant enough to escape classification as costume jewelry.

For other types of body piercing, you'll want to check out the nearby **Espace Musik** *(5 Grand Rue; Tel 04/76-42-15-82; No credit cards),* which has a big selection of hard-rock CDs and concert tickets and sells some ear- and body-piercing jewelry and T-shirts imprinted with the names of '80s heavy metal bands.

And if you want lots and lots of tiny little holes in your body, take a trip to **Tattoo Land** *(9 rue du Vieux Temple; Tel 04/76-42-33-20; 11am-7pm Tue-Sat)*, also in the central part of the old town. Its artistically decorated design space is so small that you might want to call ahead and make sure they have time for you.

great outdoors

The savage beauty of the landscapes around Grenoble provide outdoor enthusiasts with lots of opportunities for exposure to the great outdoors. And because of the region's popularity with sports fans of all kinds, the same staffs who promote snow sports in winter change their costumes, and priorities, in summer, and adapt their personae to hiking, canoeing, and cycling.

▶▶CYCLING

The French refer to mountain biking as VTT (Vélo Tout Terrain) and devote enormous energy to it. Consult the sports division of Grenoble's Tourist Office [see *need to know,* below] where you can buy topographical maps, priced at 100F, of the region around Grenoble, with bike trails clearly marked. Their list of biking itineraries is extensive, usually packaged in the form of guidebooks, priced at around 30F each. The most useful is *La Traversée des Alpes à VTT du Lac Léman à la Méditérranée.* Published by Didier-Richard, it details 35 itineraries of varying degrees of difficulty that stretch between Lake Geneva and the Mediterranean seacoast. The city's best rental outfit is **Bike Sensations** *(130 rue de Stalingrad; Tel 04/76-49-54-99; 100-150F per day).*

▶▶SNOW SPORTS, HIKING, AND ROCKCLIMBING

The sports department of the Grenoble Tourist office devotes enormous energy to promoting the allure of the Alps in midwinter. Otherwise, your best resource is an organization sponsored and endorsed by the local government, **Bureau des Guides de Grenobles** *(14 rue de la République; Tel 04/76-03-28-63),* which will provide information, advice, booklets, itineraries, descriptions of local chair lifts and gondolas, and insights into the degrees of difficulty of virtually every ski or hiking trail within the region. They will also provide an experienced guide, for warm weather (all kinds of hiking and canyoning) or cold weather (snowshoeing, cross country or downhill skiing, ice climbing) exploration of the region, for around 1,550F per day for supervision and guidance of between one and eight people. They'll sell topographical maps of the Savoy, clearly marked with hiking trails, for around 100F each. Even specialty winter sports such as Canadian-style snowshoeing is pursued here.

▶▶PARAGLIDING

You'll find lots of professional sports people proclaiming the physical and spiritual advantages of jumping off a Savoyard cliff with a da-Vinci-style paraglider strapped on. The French refer to the sport as *Le Parapente,* and it can be arranged during warm weather months only, through **Particul** *(11 route de Grenoble or 38300 St. Pierre de Chartreuse; Tel 04/76-45-07-*

79). The location is a mountain hamlet perched atop the Massif de Belle-donne, about 20 miles east of Grenoble. Expect to pay between 250 and 400F for a 90-minute high-vertigo experience.

STUff

The maze of pedestrian streets in the center of Grenoble serves up great shopping, which includes some of the usual French chains, but mainly smaller, more specialized boutiques. The stuff isn't too expensive, either, and there's good selection of used music shops and bookstores. All of the stores mentioned below are in the old part of town, either on one of the pedestrian streets or just outside of them.

▶▶DUDS

You'll find a selection of upscale casual clothes and cool hats at **Atmosphère** *(15 rue Lafayette; Tel 04/76-54-04-64; 2-7pm Mon, 9:30am-12:30pm/2-7pm Tue-Thurs, 9:30am-7pm Fri-Sun; V, MC)*, where you can outfit yourself in that Grenoble mix of outdoor gear and cosmopolitan flare.

▶▶FOOT FETISH

Vans and other skater gear are for sale just around the corner from Atmosphère at **Turbulences** *(5 rue Vicat; Tel 04/76-51-28-44; 10am-noon/2-7pm Tue-Sun; V, MC)*.

▶▶JEWELRY

There are a lot of fancier jewelry stores with engagement rings and stuff like that, but for jewelry hunters with a more earth-bound budget, **Opale** [see *modification,* above], right near the large covered market, is the place to be.

▶▶TUNES

The best place for used CDs is **O'CD** *(5 rue Sault; Tel 04/76-43-38-86; 10:30am-7:30pm Tue-Sat, 3-7:30pm Sun, 2-7pm Mon; V, MC)*. It has a big selection of used CDs and a few new ones, and you can listen to anything in the store at the listening stations.

fashion

The local fashion has a sort of city-meets-outdoors theme. Shoppers downtown sport the city fashions that you'll see in Paris and other big cities, but you'll also see more laid-back, mountaineer attire, like khaki pants and shorts, fleeces, hiking boots, and Vans. The local students look a lot like American students, so your backpacker gear will likely blend in better here than anywhere else in France!

You can also find used CDs at **Espace Musik** [see *modification, above*], which carries mainly old-school hard-rock CDs and does not offer listening stations.

▶▶BOUND

There are tons of bookstores with foreign-language sections in Grenoble. You'll find one of the best selections at **Librairie La Strada** (*1 place St. Claire; Tel 04/76-54-66-47; 9:30am-noon/2-7pm Mon-Sat; V, MC*). It's small and crowded with bookshelves full of almost exclusively foreign-language literature. The staff is, as you might expect, very bookish and eager to help.

Another used bookstore, with stuffed-full shelves, corners, and staircases, is the 2nd-floor **Librairie Le Sphinx** (*6 place Notre Dame; Tel 04/76-44-55-08; 9:30am-7pm Mon-Sat; V, MC*), which is just upstairs from **Le Tonneau de Diogène** [see *eats*, below] and specializes in philosophy and poetry.

EATS

As a cosmopolitan city, Grenoble offers a variety of cuisines, not just the traditional cheese-and-potatoes dishes that dominate the menu in other alpine towns. Also, thanks to the poor student population, there are a gazillion pizza places and cheap sandwich joints to choose from.

▶▶CHEAP

One of the cheapest sandwich/crêpe joints in town is **Morgane's** (*36 ave. Alsace-Lorraine; 06/85-33-40-25; 8am-10pm Mon-Fri; Sandwiches 15-25F; No credit cards*), which is over toward the train station away from the center of town, on the main drag. You can eat here or take your food to go and eat in one of the squares or on a park bench.

For a very reasonably priced breakfast or lunch right in the shopping district, try **Délices de Grenoble** (*1 rue Millet; Tel 04/76-43-27-55; 7:30am-7:30pm daily; Meal menus for around 25F; No credit cards*). This place is a step up from your average sandwich stand; and you can sit at a table without paying steep restaurant prices. Try their *paninis* for lunch, or come here for a breakfast pastry.

▶▶DO-ABLE

There are pizzerias galore along quai Perriere. One with lots of personality (or lots of personalities, maybe) is **La Pizzeria des Quais** (*48 quai Perriere; Tel 04/76-87-67-12; 11am-2pm/6-11pm daily, closed on the weekends at lunchtime; Menus for 48F or 78F; single dishes for 35-50F; V, MC for amounts over 50F*). The decorations are a strange conglomeration of Grenoble memorabilia and foreign trinkets, including nautical décor and some foreign license plates. American country is the music of choice, and the place glitters year-round with colored Christmas lights. Check out the ancient massive mound of candle drippings—always with a new candle burning its way to eternity on top—back by the kitchen area.

Another fun place in the old town is the cafe/restaurant **Le Tonneau de Diogéne** (*6 place Notre Dame; Tel 04/76-42-38-40; 7am-midnight daily; Dishes for 20-50F; V, MC, DIN*).

TO MARKET

You will find fresh vegetables, breads, meats, and cheeses at various markets any day of the week except Monday.

The covered market, **Les Halles Ste. Claire** *(Place Ste. Claire; 6am-1pm Tue-Thur, Sun; 6am-7pm Fri, Sat)* is right in the old town, very close to place St. André and place aux Herbes. There is an overflow vegetable market on **place Ste. Claire,** just outside the covered market *(6am-1pm Tue-Sun, 3-8pm Fri).* The vegetable market at **place aux Herbes** is open Tue-Sun from 6am to 1pm. The **Marché Hoche** at **place André-Malraux** *(7am-1pm Sat)* has organic foods as well as artisan stands.

Try the daily special menu, which is usually the best thing the kitchen has to offer. There is patio seating, and lots of students gather there to study—they have periodic book discussion groups, and every Thursday evening there are philosophy discussions.

▶▶**SPLURGE**

For a fancy meal in a restaurant you can brag to your parents about, try **Café de la Table Ronde** *(7 Place St. André; Tel 04/76-44-51-41; 9am-midnight Mon-Sat; Entrées 80-150F; V, MC).* Founded in 1739, this is Grenoble's oldest cafe, also known as Rousseau's favorite hangout. It has set menus serving regional specialties, like fondue and local salads, and an extensive wine list. There is indoor as well as patio seating. Set in the heart of the city's oldest section, **La Cour des Miracles** *(7 place Paul-Valier; Tel 04/38-37-00-10; noon-3pm/7:30-11:30pm daily; set menus 98-124F; AE, DC, MC, V),* doesn't exactly deliver miracles, but it serves solid and filling portions of food. The chefs roam Europe and Asia for inspiration, and also serve Old Town's best couscous, as there are North African members on the staff. The décor of flamboyant colors is jarring. If possible, try to go on Tuesday or Wednesday beginning at 7:30pm for the live entertainment. It's corny and fun, and might include either a strolling magician or a five-member circus act.

crashing

Since Grenoble is less overrun by tourists than the other towns in the Alps, it's much easier to find a reasonably priced place to stay here. During the busy summer months, you might want to call ahead for reservations, but it's not completely necessary.

▶▶**CHEAP**

The youth hostel, **Grenoble-Echerolles** *(10 ave. du Gresivaudan; Tel 04/76-09-33-52; Bus 1 to La Quinzaine; Reception open 7:30am-11pm;*

70F incl. breakfast; V, MC), is a 10- to 15-minute bus ride outside of town. The rooms are locked between 10am and 5pm, but there is no curfew. There is a kitchen and laundry, and the staff will strongly encourage you to visit the bar. There are wild murals all over the walls, and a pretty mellow atmosphere.

Hôtel Lakanal *(26 rue des Bergers; Tel 04/76-46-03-42; 110F single, 120F double; V, MC)* is just southwest of the center of town, in the place Condorcet area. It's a bit shabby and loud—you can tell that it's a budget hotel from the rickety furniture and old carpeting—but the beds and bathrooms are clean. There is also the unremarkable **Hôtel Alize** *(1 rue Amiral Courbert; Tel 04/76-43-12-91, Fax 04/76-47-62-79; Single/double w/shower 202F, w/out shower 162 F, breakfast 23F; V, MC, AE, DIN),* but a 1-minute walk from the train station.

▶▶DO-ABLE

Centrally located on one of the pedestrian streets of the old town, **Hôtel de la Poste** *(25 rue de la Poste; Tel 04/76-46-67-95; 130-150F single, 160F-200F double; V, MC)* is a small, clean, family-run hotel with dark hallways and bright rooms. The higher-priced rooms have showers, and hall showers are free for the rooms with only a sink. If you have a big group, you can make the place really cheap—they'll let four people sleep in a room for 220F. The hotel does not serve breakfast, but **Délices de Grenoble** [see *eats,* above] is just across the street.

The oldest hotel in Grenoble, and still one of the nicest, the **Hôtel de l'Europe** *(22 place Grenette; Tel 04/76-46-16-94; 140-190F single, 160-220F double; V, MC, AE)* overlooks the central place Grenette and has some rooms with a view of the Bastille. It is clean and has a bright stairwell with a skylight and also an elevator. You can get a room with a private bathroom if you're willing to lay down the extra bucks.

If these are full, try **Hôtel Bellvue** *(corner of rue Belgrade and quai Stéphane Jay; Tel 04/76-46-69-34, Fax 04/76-85-20-12; Single 245F, twin 295 F, double: 270F, triple 300F, quad 360F (all with private bath); Breakfast 34 francs; hotel.bellvue@wanadoo.fr, www.hotel-bellvue.fr; V, MC, AE, DIN),* **Hôtel Victoria** *(17 rue Thiers; Tel 04/76-46-06-36, Fax 04/76-43-00-14; Single w/ shower 180F, single w/ shower and WC 205F, double with shower 210F, double w/ shower and WC 235F, triple 280F, quad w/ shower and WC 300F, breakfast 35 francs; AE, V, MC, D, DIN),* or **Hôtel Trianon** *(3 rue-Pierre-Arthaud; Tel 04/76-46-21-62, Fax 04/76-46-37-56; Single 279-390F, double: 249-350F (all rooms have private bath); breakfast 38F info@hotel-trianon.com, www.hotel-trianon.com; V, AE, DIN)* all conveniently located in the center of town.

▶▶SPLURGE

You can splurge on a nice place close to the train station, but you'll miss out on the personality of some of the older places downtown. **Hôtel Terminus** *(10 place de la Gare; Tel 04/76-87-24-33; 350-500F single, 450-550F double; Breakfast 45F; V, MC, AE, DC)* is big and pleasantly clean, and every room has a bathroom with tub or shower as well as a TV with English channels.

need to know

Currency Exchange You can change money at any of the **banks** along **rue Alsace-Lorraine;** most are open 8:30am-12pm/2-7pm Mon-Sat., and have **ATMs.**

Tourist Information The **Office de Tourisme** *(14 rue de la République; Tel 04/76-42-41-41; 9am-7pm Mon-Sat, 10am-7pm Wed, 10am-1pm Sun)* has maps and information on museums, shows, and outdoor activities.

Public Transportation The bus/tramway system, called **TAG,** runs a network of buses and two above-ground tramways, which run on the same ticketing system. The trams run from 5am till midnight; regular buses stop running around 8pm, but there is a limited night service that runs till midnight. Sunday service is very limited. You probably won't need to use the public transportation very much unless you're staying at the youth hostel. For bus information, go to the **Espace TAG** *(Square Docteur Martin, 7:30am-6:30pm Mon-Fri, 8am-noon/2-5pm Sat; 7.50F per ticket, or 10 for 56F).* Tickets for Grenoble's trams and buses can be bought from automated machines (coins only) placed strategically beside each tram stop. Once you buy a ticket from one of the coin-operated machines, stick it into a special slot of another, nearby machine (it's a small blue box prominently posted near the larger machines that actually sell the tickets) to show the local authorities where and at what time you used it. For information about bus or tram lines, contact either the tourist office or call Tel 04/76-20-66-66.

Health and Emergency SAMU, the emergency number: *15.* The hospital is **MGEN: Hôpital de Jour** *(Tel 04/76-86-63-63).*

Pharmacies There are pharmacies on practically every corner in town; each is identified by a **big green neon cross.**

Telephone Area code: *04.* You can buy a *télécarte* at any **tabac,** or from the post office

Airport The **Grenoble Airport** *(Tel 04/76-65-48-48)* is about 25 miles outside of town. There is a bus to town *(Tel 04/76-87-90-31; 65F one-way, 98F round trip)* that takes about 45 minutes and will drop you at the Gare Routière (bus station).

Trains The **Gare SNCF** *(1 Place de la Gare; Tel 04/76-47-50-50 or 08/36-35-35-35)* is just west of downtown. To get to the center of town from the station, take Tram 1 or 2 to Alsace-Lorraine, where the Tourist Office is located, or just walk down Avenue Alsace-Lorraine—it's only eight blocks.

Buses The **Gare Routière** *(Tel 04/76-87-90-31; information booth 7:20am-6:30pm Sun-Fri, 8am-noon/2-5pm Sat)* is right next to the train station. It serves the following bus lines: **Intercars** *(Tel 04/76-46-19-77),* which serves international destinations, and **VFD** *(Tel 04/76-47-77-77),* which runs to other towns in the Alps.

Bike/Moped Rental You can rent bikes from **Vèlos d'Isere** *(14 rue des Arts, Tel 04/76-46-12-24; 9am-noon/2-7pm Tue-Sat)* or **Mountain**

Bike Grenoble *(6 quai de France; 10:30am-12:15pm/2:30-7:15 Tues-Sat; V, MC)*. The Tourist Office also rents bikes.

Laundry In the downtown area, there is **Lavomatique** *(14 rue Thiers; Tel 04/76-96-28-03; 7am-9pm daily)*; across the river toward the Bastille is **Laverie La Saponaire** *(10 quai Perriere; Tel 04/76-00-90-23; 7am-9pm daily)*.

Postal The main branch of **La Poste** *(7 blvd. Maréchal Lyautey; Tel 04/76-43-51-69; 8am-7pm Mon-Fri, 8am-noon Sat)* is right next to **Parc Mistral** [see *city sports,* above].

Internet See *wired,* above.

everywhere else

annecy

The streets along the canals in Annecy are so beautiful, they could be straight out of a painting. So it should come as no surprise that the town—along with the lake and mountains that surround it—has a large artist's community. Walking around, you'll always find street artists painting, drawing, and photographing the scenery, and their art is usually for sale on the street or in one of the open-air markets where farmers and antique dealers also gather several times a week. You'll find these markets in Annecy's old town, or *vieille ville,* where colorful houses, cafes, and shops line cobblestone walking streets and the canals that give Annecy its nickname, "Little Venice of Savoy."

Annecy's bohemian artists' community gives the town a relaxed and laid-back vibe, and the slow pace of the Alps makes it a quiet place in the off-season, namely the fall and spring. At the same time, French and foreign tourists bring energy and diversity to the town, drawn not only to Annecy's scenic beauty but also to the nearby hiking, swimming, cycling, boating, and paragliding. The locals tend to hang out in the smaller, more bohemian cafes, which sometimes host live music or little art shows, while in the summer the larger pubs draw big, noisy crowds of kids getting together after a day in the mountains.

Right on the northern shore of **Lac D'Annecy,** the town also has its share of grassy lakeside beaches and swimming pools, and it's close to the forested **Semnoz Mountains,** including the 2,351m **La Tournette.**

neighborhoods and hanging out

Annecy's *vieille ville* is so captivating that you'll quickly forget about the more modern part of town where you get off the train. To get to the center of town from the train station, walk southeast on **rue de la Poste,** then turn left on **rue Royale** toward the enclosed mall called the **Centre Bonlieu,** where the **Office de Tourisme** is. Or stay on **rue de la Poste,** which later turns into **rue de la République,** to get to the streets of the old town. These

annecy

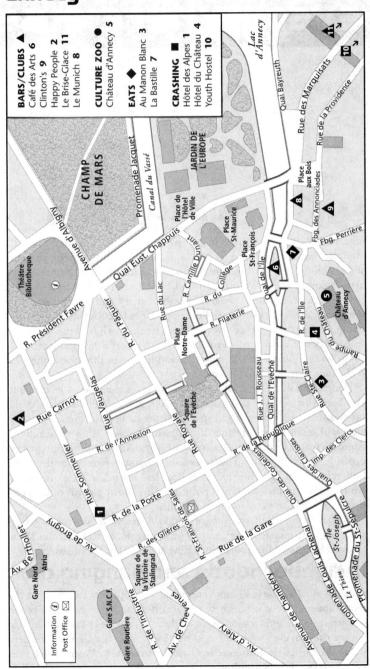

BARS/CLUBS ▲
Café des Arts **6**
Clinton's **9**
Happy People **2**
Le Brise-Glace **11**
Le Munich **8**

CULTURE ZOO ●
Château d'Annecy **5**

EATS ◆
Au Manon Blanc **3**
La Bastille **7**

CRASHING ■
Hôtel des Alpes **1**
Hôtel du Château **4**
Youth Hostel **10**

narrow and winding central streets, such as **rue Sainte Claire, quai de L'Ile,** and **quai Perrière,** are lined on one side with pink, green, yellow, and blue buildings and old stone archways, and on the other with the slowly flowing **Canal du Thiou,** which reflects the same colors. There are bright little flower boxes and window shutters, art easels, and street musicians everywhere you turn. Touristy shops line the main streets on the canal, and some of the fancier boutiques and shops extend into the surrounding pedestrian streets, such as the **rue Carnot** and the **rue du Paquiner.**

If you follow the main part of the Canal du Thiou east toward the lake, you'll come upon the large lakeside area called the **Jardin de l'Europe,** which links the town to **Lac D'Annecy.** Locals and tourists alike swarm this park, having picnics, throwing Frisbees, rollerblading, or watching the paragliders descend from the mountains that rise dramatically up from the lake on all sides. Crossing the **Canal du Vassé,** you'll reach another popular park, the grassy **Champ de Mars.** The lake is also lined with a walking, biking, and blading path; it's busy all day, especially from late afternoon until dusk. One of the more famous spots is the **Pont des Amours** (Lovers' Bridge), which spans the Canal du Vassé at the edge of the lake. The lake and mountains are popular spots for outdoor activities, and there is a huge variety of things to do near Annecy; visit the **Sport Information** office [see *city sports,* below] for more information.

There is local bus service in Annecy, but unless you're planning an out-of-town excursion or are staying at the **Auberge,** [see *crashing,* below] it's unlikely you'll need one: Most sites are within walking distance.

bar, club, and live music scene

Most of Annecy's locals stop off at one of the small, bohemian cafes on the canals for an afternoon coffee or a drink at happy hour, when local guitarists and singers often perform. The bigger bars along the quais of the canals pick up as the tourist season sets in, and you'll encounter the typical alpine scene of active tourists and locals gathering after a day of hiking, biking, or swimming in the mountains to share their stories. There are a few clubs in Annecy, but they tend to cater to an older crowd.

One of Annecy's best little cafes, **Café des Arts** (*Cour des Vieilles Prisons; Tel 04/50-51-56-40; 9am-1am daily, Sun till 8pm; Drinks 12-*

wired

There are websites on Annecy in both French and English: go to *www.lac-annecy.com* or *www.lake-annecy.com.*

The best place in town to check your e-mail is at the **Cyberposte** in the Post Office.

15F; V, MC), is right smack in the middle of the old town, on a cobble-stoned passageway across from the Palais de l'Ile, a little island on the Canal du Thiou. Its tiny rooms seem even smaller than they are, with dark wood walls and the clutter of art and old, science experiments on the shelves. A crowd of locals shows up for live jazz every Monday night from 7:30 till 10. Other local musicians also play there, but on a very unpredictable schedule, so if you're interested in live music, you kind of have to show up and hope for the best.

You'll find a rollicking Saturday night crowd at **Le Munich** *(Quai Perrière; Tel 04/50-45-02-11; 9am-1am daily; V, MC, AE)*, which offers at least 20 kinds of beer (mostly German) on tap, priced at 20–30F. It has a big terrace right on the main canal, a busy indoor bar, and a large open upstairs room. Typical brasserie/pizzeria-style food is served at lunchtime and dinnertime; it's fun to have dinner here and hang out into the evening and watch as the younger late-night crowd moves in on the older dinner-time crowd.

The biggest club is **Clinton's** *(8 Fanborg des Annonciades; Tel 04/50-45-32-89; 10pm-5am Tue-Sun; Average cover 50-60F, No credit cards)*, which has karaoke, pool tables, and dancing. There's a dress code and a doorman, so don't wear jeans or anything grungy, but other than that you probably won't have too much trouble getting in. It's fun for dancing, but the scene is more geared toward an older crowd and the drinks are kinda pricy, 30–50F. For a more energetic dance scene and a younger crowd, check out the gay-friendly **Happy People** *(48 rue Carnot; Tel 04/50-51-08-66; 6pm-5am daily; Cover varies; No credit cards)*, a smallish club a few blocks from the Centre Bonlieu that can get crowded and sweaty. There's a different DJ each night playing house, techno, and dance music. There is usually no cover, although the occasional theme nights might cost a few francs. Doors open at 6pm, but no one gets there for another five hours.

The big live music venue is called **Le Brise-Glace** *(54 bis rue des Marquisats; Tel 04/50-33-65-10; Ticket window 9:30am-12:30pm/2-7pm Tue-Sat, closed Thur afternoon; Shows at 9pm, doors open 8:30pm; Average ticket price 30-100F; V, MC if over 100F)*, near the lake on the southeast side of town. It has rock, rap, and reggae played by lots of local bands and some bigger French bands.

You can get a schedule of shows and other events going on in the little towns throughout the region in *L'Officieux*—pick one up at a *maison de la presse* (book and newspaper shop), the Office de Tourisme, or the local used CD store, **O'CD** *(2 rue St. Francois de Sales; Tel 04/50-45-10-59; 10am-7:30pm Tue-Sat, 2pm-7:30pm Mon; www.ocd.net; V, MC)*, in the *vieille ville*, where you can listen to used CDs and get the most complete local concert info.

arts scene

Annecy's arts scene focuses exclusively on visual arts. You can find the most up-to-date contemporary art right on the streets and canals in town, and you can probably buy a wet oil painting directly from the artist. In addition, the Office de Tourisme, which promotes Annecy as a *ville d'art*, can give you a full list of local contemporary galleries to visit [see *need to know*, below].

Galerie Nadir (*15 rue Filaterie; Tel 04/50-45-20-60; Tue-Sat 10am-noon/3-7pm; www.nadir-gallery.com*) is one of Annecy's larger and more visible art galleries, it focuses mainly on blown glasswork, ceramics, and sculpture by well-known artists, some of them living in the French, Swiss, and Italian Alps. There are very few paintings here, but local trendies assume that whatever's on exhibit here represents the cutting-edge in art.

The fine-arts section of the museum in the **Château d'Annecy** [see *culture zoo*, below] also exhibits contemporary art.

CULTURE ZOO

Some of the most important cultural sights are the colorful old buildings and stone archways in the old town. Some of the old buildings have entrance fees, but they are really just as interesting to see from the outside as you walk along the canal or window-shop on the pedestrian streets.

Château d'Annecy (*Place du Château; Tel 04/50-33-87-30; 10am-noon/2-6pm daily, closed Tue, open inclusively 10am-6pm June–Sept; Admission 30F adults, 10F students; No credit cards*): Annecy's main cultural attraction. The beautiful old castle sits atop the hill just behind the old town and has incredible views of the rooftops of Annecy as well as a fine arts museum and some local cultural and contemporary art exhibits.

annecy—VILLE FLEURIE and VILLE d'ART

Annecy is designated as both a "Ville Fleurie" (town in bloom) and a "Ville d'Art." It has received numerous awards for its flowers, which you'll see everywhere you go in the town: spilling from window boxes, on bridges, planted around fountains, and hanging near the canals. Annecy won France's grand prix for flowered towns several times in the 1990s. Maybe it's the beauty of the flowers that contributes to Annecy's reputation as an art town. In addition to just wandering around and taking in the beauty you can visit all kinds of art galleries and check out the work of street artists throughout Annecy. The Tourist Office also provides guided tours of the most "artistic places."

Musée du Palais de L'Ile *(Ile du Canal du Thiou; Tel 04/50-33-87-30; 10am to 6pm daily June-Sept, 10am-noon/2-6pm Wed-Mon Oct-May; Admission 30F adults, 20F students, and those under 18):* This old structure resembles a stone-built prow of a ship in the way it sits atop a serpentine island that rises from the center of the Canal du Thiou. It's had quite a history: originally built as the residence of the local feudal lord in the 1100s, it was later transformed into the headquarters of power of Annecy (home of the Châtelaine d'Annecy) when that potentate reported to the Counts of Geneva (not to the French kings), then functioned as a mint for the fabrication of coins, then a prison. It was almost razed to the ground during the late 19th century, but saved by popular appeal and made a historic monument. Today, it showcases a changing series of temporary exhibitions, usually focusing on the history of the town and its culture. Incidentally, the bridge that connects it with the "mainland" of Annecy is the resort's best photo-op.

CITY SPORTS

If you're looking for something low-impact, the path along Lake Annecy is one of the best places in France for a twilight walk, bike ride, or in-line skating trip. The scenery is unbeatable, and it's a great place to meet people. The **Sport Information** office *(Centre Bonlieu; Tel 04/50-33-88-31; 3-7pm Mon-Fri)* in Annecy's central shopping mall can also provide information on group activities.

Paragliding lessons for beginners and package deals are given by **Vols Decouvértes** *(10 rue du Pre. Felin; Tel 04/50-45-16-00).*

You can find more hikes and bike rides in the hills above Annecy. The tourist office distributes free pamphlets showing about a dozen easy hiking and biking excursions from Annecy to points in the environs, especially the surrounding hills. They're designed for families and not terribly experienced hillclimbers. A detailed set of walks for more experienced hikers is described within a map (with notes) that sells for 20F. Walks within both of these categories last for between 2 and 6 hours each. Some of them begin in the center of Annecy, but others require a trip by private car or by bus from one of several towns in the environs of Annecy. There are really great spots up in **Semnoz,** just above town past the youth hostel. In the summertime, Bus 1 will take you from the center of town up to the trail entrances, and for an extra ticket you can bring your bike along [see *need to know,* below, for bike rental info].

Hiking and mountain-climbing trips are organized by **Takamaka et Bureau des Guides** *(17 Raubourg Ste. Claire; Tel 04/50-45-60-61)* and by a great local travel agent, **Agence Crolard** *(Place de la Gare; Tel 04/50-45-08-12)* that sells bus tickets to all the destinations around Annecy and Léman. They also arrange excursions by minibus to sites of panoramic interest, but only for departures during July and August.

At the lake, you can rent pedalboats or motorboats for 70-150F an hour from the nice old men who have set up shop down by the lake. It's all very DIY—none of the shops have official names or hours of operation—but if you're down by the lake, you can't miss them. If you'd rather relax, you can take a tour boat from the **Compagnie de Navigation du Lac d'Annecy** *(2 Place aux Bois; Tel 04/50-51-08-40; 61F; www.annecy-croisières.com; V, MC).*

EATS

Alpine cheese-and-potatoes dishes are the specialty in Annecy. Most of the restaurants have *tartiflette,* a casserole of cheese, potatoes, and bacon, and are especially proud of their *fondue* recipes.

The cheapest option (as usual) is to buy some picnic supplies at the grocery store or at one of the local markets [see *to market,* below] and take it to a bench by the lake or the grass at the Jardin de l'Europe.

Right in the center of town on a mini-island on the Canal du Thiou sits the tiny **Café des Arts** [see *bar, club, and live music scene,* above]. It serves a breakfast menu, snacks, and the usual inexpensive cafe fare of sandwiches, fries, and salads. Jockey with all the other cafe-goers for the best position at the tables laid out on the terrace.

You'll find lots of crêpe and ice cream stands with terrace seating underneath the stone archways of the pedestrian streets in the *vieille ville.* An especially quaint little restaurant is **Au Manon Blanc** *(21 rue Ste.-Claire; Tel 04/50-45-47-37; 11am-9pm Tue-Sun; Average entrée 15-45F; V, MC).* It serves dinner crêpes *(salé)* and dessert crêpes *(sucré),* which you should eat with a *bollée de cidre,* a little ceramic bowl of apple cider. The tiny restaurant is crowded with tables, and you can see the kitchen at the back. Au Manon Blanc is run by a nice young couple and patronized largely by their friends as well as tourists, so you get a nice blend of the laid-back local culture and excited, wide eyed visitors.

For some typical pizzeria- or brasserie-style food, there are lots of places lining the canals, such as **Brasserie le Munich** [see *bar scene,* above].

On the south banks of the Canal du Thiou, **La Bastille** *(3 quai des Prisons Vieilles; Tel 04/50-45-09-37; Noon-2:30pm/7-10:30pm Wed-Sun; Average entrée 60-80F, set menus 80-120F; V, MC)* serves up *Savoie*-fare in a setting that captures Annecy's bohemian style. Off the small dining

TO MARKET

The main **food market** is in the old town, along **rue de la République, rue Sainte Claire, Pont-Morens,** and **quai de L'Eveché,** on Tuesday, Friday, and Sunday mornings from 8am to noon. The same streets host an antique market on the last Saturday of each month, from 8am to 7pm.

room you'll find terrace seating amid a wild throng of trees that hides diners from the cobblestoned streets; the interior is painted dark red and decorated with pictures of old locals, military figurines, and the like. You should try the *Savoie* specialties such as *tartiflette, raclette,* or *fondue.* The laid-back waiters love to advise you on what sort of alcohol you should drink with each dish, and it's an easy place to spend the whole evening.

crashing

Although it's tourist season practically all year long in Annecy, the busiest summer months can pose problems for travelers looking for lodging. The youth hostel is a large one, however, and the hotel reservation service at the Tourist Office can be helpful. The old town is the coolest place to be, but also tends to be the most expensive. You'll want to find something that puts you pretty close to the center of town, but far enough away from the *vieille ville* to escape the monstrous room rates.

▶▶CHEAP

The **Auberge de Jeunesse** *(4 rte. du Semnoz; Tel 04/50-45-33-19; Reception 7am-10pm; 72F incl. breakfast; V, MC)* is one of the nicer youth hostels, with new, sturdy furniture, four-person rooms with bunk beds, a shower and sink in each room, and no curfew or lockout. There's a laundry room and a kitchen, and you can sign up for a 50F-dinner if you like. The picnic tables outside have a stunning view of the green mountains, and although the hostel is just a short (1 km) walk from town, it is isolated enough to be quiet and peaceful.

▶▶DO-ABLE

The **Hôtel des Alpes** *(12 rue de la Poste; Tel 04/50-45-04-56; 238F double; V, MC)* is just across the street from the train station, so it's an easy stop if you're only going to be in town for a little while. It is close to the *vielle ville,* although actually located in the less interesting, more modern area of town. The reception desk is one floor up, and each of the clean, small doubles has a shower, toilet, and TV.

On the road up the hill to the Château d'Annecy, you'll find the quaint **Hôtel du Château** *(16 Rampe du Château; Tel 04/50-45-51-74; 260F single, 290-320F double; closed mid-Nov-mid-Dec; V, MC).* The small, family-run, alpine-style hotel has clean and cozy rooms with private baths, and breakfast is served for 38F on a gorgeous terrace, with views of the château and the rooftops of the *vieille ville.*

If those are full, try the centrally located **Hôtel du Nord** *(24 rue Sommeiller; Tel 04/50-45-08-78, Fax 04/50-55-90-81; 228-318F single, 248-338F double, 338-438F triple or quad (all rooms have private baths); 38F breakfast; annecy.hotel.du.nord@wanadoo.fr, www.annecy-hotel-du-nord.com; V, MC, DIN).*

need to know

Currency Exchange You can change money at the **Post Office,** or at the 24-hour change machine at the **Crédit Lyonnais** *(Centre Bonlieu, 1 rue Jean Jaurès),* just outside the large enclosed mall called the Centre Bonlieu.

Tourist Information The **Office de Tourisme** *(Centre Bonlieu; Tel 04/50-45-00-33; 9am-6:30pm Mon-Sat, 9am-12:30pm/1:45-6:30pm Sun May–Sept; 9am-12:30pm/1:45pm-6:30pm daily in winter, www.lac-annecy.com)* has information on hotels, art exhibits, and other local events. They'll also help you book a hotel room.

Public Transportation The local buses are called **Bus Urbains,** and their main office is at the **Espace Sibra** *(Centre Bonlieu; Tel 04/50-10-04-04; 9am-7pm Mon-Fri),* in the center of town, where you can pick up schedule and route information. The buses run 7am-8pm Mon-Sat; but you'll probably only need them to go longer distances such as up to the mountains or to another of the little towns along the lake. The tickets are 7.5F, and you buy them from the driver.

Health and Emergency SAMU emergency: *15;* Police: *17.* The local hospital is **Centre Hospitalier** *(1 ave. de Trésum; Tel 04/50-88-33-33).*

Pharmacies Pharmacies are identifiable by **big neon green crosses,** and you'll find them on practically every corner. None are open 24 hours.

Trains and Buses The **SNCF Gare d'Annecy** *(08/36-35-35-35)* is just north of the center of town, and the local **Gare Routière,** which has SNCF buses to the nearby towns, is right next door. From the station, it's just a 10-minute walk southeast into the center of town.

Bike/Skate Rental You can rent bikes and in-line skates to try out the trails along the Lac d'Annecy from **Little Big Shop** *(80 rue Carnot; Tel 04/50-67-42-13; 8:30am-noon/2-7pm Tue-Sat, 9am-noon Mon; 70F a day for bikes, 60F/day for blades; V, MC).*

Laundry The Laundromat closest to downtown and the train station is **Lav'Confort Express** *(6 rue de la Gare; Tel 06/07-30-21-57; 7am-9pm daily).*

Postal La Poste *(4 rue des Glières; Tel 04/50-33-68-00; 8am-7pm Mon-Fri, 8am-noon Sat)* is between the train station and the old town.

Internet [see *wired,* above]

chamonix

In Grenoble you're in the cultural center of the Alps, and in Annecy and Evian you're close to the famous alpine lakes. But it's in Chamonix that you'll begin to feel as though you've finally arrived in *the* Alps. The mountains rise dramatically above you on all sides, the air is noticeably thinner, and the glaciers look close enough to touch.

Set in the cleft of a deep mountain valley, Chamonix is close to not one but nine ski resorts, making it a skier's paradise in the winter. Even if you don't ski, you'll appreciate the views: Bordered on the east by the glacier-streaked 4807m Mont-Blanc and on the west by the awesome Aiguilles Rouges range, Chamonix is surrounded by some of the most amazing scenery you'll see. Mountains of awesome magnitude can be

chamonix

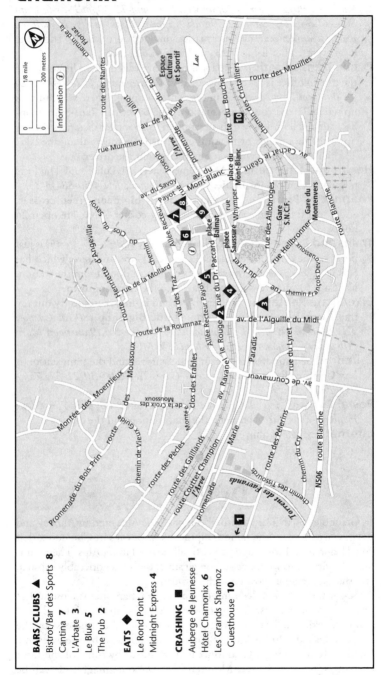

BARS/CLUBS ▲

Bistrot/Bar des Sports **8**

Cantina **7**

L'Arbate **3**

Le Blue **5**

The Pub **2**

EATS ◆

Le Rond Pont **9**

Midnight Express **4**

CRASHING ■

Auberge de Jeunesse **1**

Hôtel Chamonix **6**

Les Grands Sharmoz

Guesthouse **10**

seen in every direction: from west to east, **Les Grandes Jorasses** (4208m), the **Aiguille du Géant** (4013m), **Mont-Blanc du Tacul** (4248m), and **Dôme du Gouter (4304m).**

When it's not overrun with tourists, Chamonix has a relaxed, laid-back vibe, unlike the fast-paced ski resorts nearby. There are Swiss chalet-style buildings everywhere, jewel-green gardens, and the glacier-cold **Arve River,** which flows through the middle of town. In contrast to the little poodles you see all over Paris, Chamonix is full of big dogs, especially St. Bernards. Most of the locals are active, outdoorsy types, enjoying a deep connection to the mountains nearby, and you'll get a real sense of the pace that is unique to this area of France—and so different from the pace of life in the U.S. But you may have to look for the locals: Chamonix's population on any given week will be mostly made up of tourists (at least half of them twentysomethings and thirtysomethings), especially at the height of the winter ski season.

The town of Chamonix is tiny: You won't have to walk far to get to where you're going. Only three or four streets comprise the main downtown area, which is centered around **place Balmat** and the pedestrian street **rue du Docteur Paccard,** which runs north through the center of town before turning into **rue Joseph Vallot.** You'll quickly realize that the main focus here isn't the town; it's the mountains. Locals and tourist alike spend most of their time there, meeting up later in the day at one of Chamonix's bars or restaurants to swap their stories of the day.

bar, club, and live music scene

Several bars in town, popular among both locals and visitors, are Swiss mountain-style chalets with exposed wood beams and big roofs designed to stand up to heavy snowfall. Open until 2am, they all host a young, active crowd.

The Pub *(215 rue Paccard; Tel 04/50-55-92-88; 4pm-2am daily; Drinks 10-20F; V, MC)* is full, loud, and hopping every night of the week. It has patio tables in the summertime and a large but crowded indoor area where you can warm up in the wintertime. This place plays the important European sports matches on TV and classic rock or basic pop radio music other times.

wired

You can check e-mail at **Cyberposte,** in La Poste [see *need to know*, below] at **Cybar** *(81 rue Whymper; Tel 04/50-53-64-80; 10am-5pm daily; 60F/hour),* or at the **Cantina** [see *bar, club, and live music scene,* below]. The official website of the village is **www.chamonix.com.**

Bistrot/Bar des Sports [see *eats*, below] is another popular spot. Come for dinner, then stay on into the evening. You'll probably find more locals here than at The Pub, but the two places have similar interiors (heavy on the wood) and atmospheres (heavy on the sports).

The Mexican-style **Cantina** (*37 Impasse des Rhododendrons; Tel 04/50-53-64-20; 5pm-2am daily; Average drinks 10-15F; V, MC*) is equally loud and popular. The décor is pretty unusual in France—but with the crowd and the surroundings, you still definitely feel like you're in the Alps. Mexican food is served, and a cybercafe is attached. As in most Mexican restaurants in Europe, the food is pretty forgettable—most folks come just for the margaritas....

The main disco in town is **Le Blue** (*32 rue du Docteur Paccard; Tel 04/50-53-63-52; 11pm-4am daily; Average cover 50-100F; No credit cards*), which calls itself a jazz club but often has DJs spinning rock/disco/dance music. It's decorated to live up to its name—everything is blue!—and admission is free for women mid-week. The crowd can sometimes be older, so it's a good idea to hang out at The Pub or Cantina first and see if anyone is really going dancing.

You can often catch live shows at **L'Arbate** (*80 Chemin de Sapi; Tel 04/50-53-44-93; 6pm-2am Thur-Sat; No cover, beer 30-40F, mixed drinks 40–50F; Call ahead for a schedule of live shows; V, MC*), a bigger version of the exposed wood-beam chalet bar. Don't be too excited about the lack of a cover—they more than make up for it with the steep drink prices. Try to catch happy hour between 8 and 9pm, when they serve two-for-one drinks.

great outdoors

Hands down, the mountains win as the most popular reason people come to Chamonix. In warmer weather, you can go hiking, biking, mountain climbing, or whatever else you can think of—there are beautiful trails and spots to hang out all over. If you want to take the DIY route, the tourist office sells a hiking map (25F) showing all the nearby hiking trails. If you'd like a little guidance, call the ***Club des Sports*** (*Tel 04/50-53-11-57*), located in the **Centre Sportif** (*214 ave. de la Plage; Tel 04/50-53-09-07*). The Centre is about 500m outside of town, and is open every afternoon. (They also offer swimming, ice-skating, tennis, squash, and a weight room, if you'd like some indoor activity.) There are some serious hikes in this area, so don't think you can just strike out for any of the mountains on your own without a map from the tourist office. For a pleasant, less-crowded trip, try hiking from the smaller town of Argentiere to Chamonix along a trail called "Le Petit Balcon Sud". It should take the average walker about 2 hours to complete and involves only very minimal climbing.

There are six main ski areas in the Chamonix-Mont-Blanc area, and the hours for all six are the same (*8:30am-4pm daily, half-day passes begin at 1pm*). The ski season lasts from about December through April; the Tourist Office always has an up-to-date listing of which trails are open. Each of them is accessible by the Chamonix bus, so it's easy to get to them all from town. Unfortunately the bus system is not so convenient for getting from one area to another, so you might want to plan on picking one and staying there for the day.

If you're going to be hanging around for a longer period of time, though, it makes more sense to buy one of the two multiple-day passes, which you can get at the tourist office. **Cham'ski pass** *(4-day pass 819F; 7-day pass 1,164F)* includes access to all the resorts in the Chamonix valley except Les Houches and free rides on the shuttle ski bus. The more comprehensive **Ski Pass Mont Blanc** *(7-day pass 1,332F)* includes access to all the ski lifts within all the resorts of the Mont Blanc region. Both passes also allow access to the lifts in the resort of Courmayeur Val-Veny on the Italian side of the Franco-Italian border.

Advanced skiiers should spend their time at **Les Grands Montets** *(Full-day adult pass is 193F, half-day adult pass is 155F)*. The adventurous and highly-skilled can try one of the three "pistes" that come down from the top of Grands Montets: one that goes straight down, one that skirts the Glacière D'Argentiere, and a famous off-piste run called Le Pas de Chèvre that leads straight to the Glace de Mer (NB: this trail can be *extremely* dangerous—we're talking multiple past deaths—and should only be attempted by master skiers with a guide). Another run, La Herse, offers 5km of moguls, and there is also a snowpark with a half-pipe for snowboarders.

Le Brévent *(Tel 04/50-53-13-18; Full-day adult pass is 142F, half-day adult pass is 103F)* would be a good pick if you're with a group of people with varying levels of slope skills—they have slopes ranging from beginner to intermediate-advanced. It's known for the Charles Bozon Trail (named for the 1962 slalom champion), which gives a panoramic view of the Mont Blanc range.

Le Tour *(Tel 04/40-54-00-58 Full-day adult pass is 148F, half-day adult pass is 111F)* is the place for beginners. At a top elevation of 2,150 meters, the La Tour area is one of the sunniest places in the valley in winter, and is known for its exceptional snow cover, usually coming early in the ski season (mid-December) and lasting until May. The area is open and gentle, with panoramic views at the top of the valley. Though the majority of the trails here are strictly beginner material, there is one much more complicated route, really only for experts, that stretches from Col de Balme into Switzerland, with a return trip by a small mountain train.

La Flégère *(Tel 04/50-53-18-58; Full-day adult pass is 160F, half-day adult pass is 119F),* an intermediate's delight, is now linked with Le Brévant by cable car, so you can "jump" from one area to another. From the mid-station down, a ski run crisscrosses the face of the ski slopes, dropping steeply in places before opening up into mogul fields near the bottom. The gullies in the area make for generally good skiing, especially behind the rocks east of l'Index, but the snow can be icy and slush— call ahead and check conditions.

Close to the center of the Chamonix valley, the very family oriented **Les Planards** *(Tel 04/50-53-98-97; Full-day adult pass is 86F, half-day adult pass is 67F)* is more of a year-round resort area, attracting skiers in winter and general outdoorsy types in summer, who flock here to go sliding on its famous toboggan. The ski school here can help you improve your technique. The snow, aided by big "snow guns," is usually plentiful and fluffy all winter long.

Known for having plenty of winter sunshine, **Les Houches** *(Tel 04/5 0-55-50-62; Full-day adult pass is 153F, half-day adult pass is 119; people un der 20 pay 138F for a full-day, 107F for a half-day)* attracts families with young children as well as novice skiers. There are 67 snow-making machines to guarantee a good snow cover. The slopes here have been cut through copses of pine and birch forests, a nice change from slopes set above the tree line. Tranquil Les Houches is less crowded than the other resorts, even in the height of ski season, because access to its ski lifts isn't included in most of the valley's ski passes.

You can rent any gear you might need (skis, climbing equipment, backpacks, etc.) at **Locamarché** *(200 ave. de L'Aiguille du Midi; Tel 04/50-53-38-25; 8:30-7:30 daily; V, MC)*.

If you're not a rock jock or a ski bunny and you just want to check out the damn mountains without breaking a sweat or possibly your neck, check out one of the *téléphériques* (cable cars) around the area.

A *téléphérique* will take you from Chamonix up to the **Aiguille du Midi,** a huge glacier standing at 3842m (12,605 ft). *(Tel 04/50-53-30-80 for reservations)*. Once there, catch the Mont-Blanc cable car *(Tel 04/50-53-40-00 for reservations)*. The highest of the car's three stops is Pointe Helbronner on the Italian border, so you might want to bring your passport just in case you decide to stroll into Italy! Also remember to bring your sunglasses, because it gets really bright up there among all the snow and the glaciers. Plan on standing in line for awhile; it's a very popular diversion and gets extremely crowded. If you don't feel like crossing borders, consider getting off at the second stop, Plan de l'Aiguille, which is a good starting point for hikes. You catch the téléphérique at a station south of town at the end of the Avenue de l'Aiguille du Midi. (It runs from 8am to 3:45pm and from 6am to 4:45pm between July 5 and August 24). Prices vary depending on how far you go. A return ticket from Chamonix to Aiguille du Midi is 194F. From there, a return ticket to the téléphérique's halfway-point (Plan de l'Aiguille) is 82F. A return ticket to Pointe Helbronner (on the Italian border) is 96F.

La Mer de Glace *(35 Place de la Mer de Glace; Tel 04/50-53-12-54; Trains run daily every 20 minutes; 10am-4pm winter, 8:30am-5:30pm spring, and 8am-6pm summer; closed Nov 15-Dec 15; Combined ticket good for train, téléphérique, and cave 105F; No credit cards)*, is the largest French glacier. To see it, first catch a train from Chamonix at the Gare du Montenvers, which is behind the Chamonix-Mont-Blanc train station and is used only for the cogwheel trains that go up to the téléphérique. It's roughly a twenty-minute ride. From Montenvers, take the *téléphérique,* up to see the *grotte.* There are ice sculptures on view inside; outside are some easy hiking trails.

And if you're more into indoor sporting activity, the **Centre Sportif** *(214 ave. de la Plage; Tel 04/50-53-09-07)* is just outside of town, and is open every afternoon. They offer swimming, ice-skating, tennis, squash, and a weight room.

eats

While you'll still find the cheese-and-potatoes dishes characteristic of the Alps here, the typical fare is a bit healthier than in other alpine towns: you'll find hearty soups and pastas for the active crowd, and from the local bakeries, some awesome grainy mountain bread for your picnics in the mountains.

There are a few stands around town that fit the bill when you need a quick bite to go, serving the typical French fare of crêpes, sandwiches, etc. One of the better ones is the centrally located **Midnight Express** (*21 rue Docteur Paccard; No phone; 8am-2am daily; Sandwiches 20-30F; V, MC, AE*), which is almost as cheap as a picnic.

Right on the main drag, **Bistrot des Sports** (*182 rue Joseph Vallot; Tel 04/50-53-00-46; 11am-1am daily food served noon-2pm, 7-9:30pm; Entrées 20-40F, set menus 70-80F; V, MC*) is one of the most popular local bars, and it's also a great place to grab a bite before you go out. Try one of the set menus, which always feature the daily special, such as a fish filet with potatoes or a big salad.

Also in the very center of town, **Le Rond Pont** (*50 rue Docteur Paccard; Tel 04/50-53-03-73; 8am-9pm daily; Entrées 50-80F; V, MC*) is a more touristy spot, but it's got an upstairs room with a gorgeous panoramic view. There is also a bar/cafe downstairs, with outdoor seating in the summertime. They serve average sandwiches, salads, meats, and pastas—come for the atmosphere and view, not the food.

crashing

If you're excited about being outdoors in the mountains, Chamonix is a great place to meet kids from all over who feel the same way. And you're likely to meet them wherever you stay, be it at the popular youth hostel or one of the local homes that rent out dormitory-style rooms.

The local **Auberge de Jeunesse** (*127 Montée Jacques Balmat; Tel 04/50-53-14-52; Check-in after 5pm only; Open to individuals from Dec 10-May 10, May 18-Oct 1; 72F for bed in 4-6 person room incl. breakfast, private double w/shower 81F; V, MC*) is a new, big, clean, and comfortable hostel, plus it has a laundry room and no curfew—you can't ask for much more. The only slight bummer is that during the winter months, you can only stay here as part of a weekly ski package—but why would you be in Chamonix in the winter if you weren't skiing, right? A bit outside of town (about a 20-minute walk), it's set against a beautiful green (or white, depending on the season) hillside. To get there, walk directly out of the train station into town. If you're too pooped to walk, the main bus stop is just a block or two from the station; take the bus to the Pélerins École stop.

The other hostel in town is **Le Vagabond** (*365 Ravanel-le-Rouge; Tel 04/50-53-15-43; 65F per bed in 6-bed rooms*). It's an easy walk from the train station, up avenue Michel Croz, then left onto place Balmant, which becomes Ravanel-le-Rouge. Its rooms are simple but bright, and there's a cozy bar with a late-night snack menu, perfect for when you're too worn out from skiing to leave the hostel.

Les Grands Sharmoz Guesthouse (*468 Chemin des Pélerins; Tel 04/50-53-45-57; 200F double, 80F dorm bed; No credit cards*), a small place run by a friendly American couple (the guest house is located on the bottom floor of their home), has a guest kitchen and stunning views of the mountains. If all the rooms are booked, they're nice enough to call the other guesthouses nearby and give you directions if there are any open rooms.

The center of town has more traditional—and more expensive—hotels, such as the **Hôtel Chamonix** (*58 Place de l'Église; Tel 04/50-53-11-07; 300F single, 330-380F double; V, MC*). The building is in the quaint local architectural style, and the rooms are very pleasant and clean.

need to know

Currency Exchange A 24-hour change machine that takes any currency of cash is located at **21 place Balmat,** just across from the Post Office. There are actually tons of change places everywhere you turn, but since it is a pretty heavily hit tourist area, you want to be careful of steep commissions.

Tourist Information The local **Office de Tourisme** (*85 place du Triangle de l'Amitie; Tel 04/50-53-00-24; 9am-12:30pm/2-7pm daily; www.chamonix.com*) has information on hotels, hiking, skiing, and other outdoor activities. They'll also make hotel reservations for you, upstairs in the **Centrale de Réservation** (*Tel 04/50-53-23-33, Fax 04/50-53-58-90; reservatione@chamonix.com*).

Public Transportation To get to all the different ski stations, you can take the **Chamonix Bus** for 8F daily between 7:30am and 6pm, and from 10F till 11:45 pm.

Health and Emergency The **Centre Hospitalier** (*509 rte. des Pélerins; Tel 04/50-53-84-00*) is in the nearby village of Les Favrands.

Pharmacies The main pharmacy is **Pharmacie du Mont-Blanc** (*9 rue Vallot; 24-hour emergency number 04/50-53-36-79; 9am-12:30pm/2:30-7:30pm daily*).

Trains and Buses The local **Gare SNCF** (*Facing ave. de la Gare; Tel 08/36-35-35-35*) is just a block from the center of town. Most trains connect to the station in **St. Gervais-les-Bains;** from there, you take the red **Mont-Blanc Express** on a slow, beautiful ride up the mountains past glacial streams and either lush gardens or piles of snow and ice. There are also buses from Annecy, Grenoble, and Geneva arriving at the Chamonix train station.

Bike Rental You can rent bikes from **Chamonix Mountain Bike** (*138 rue des Moulins; Tel 04/50-53-54-76; 30F an hour or 95F a day*)—maps are provided—or from **Trajectoire** (*91 ave. Ravanel-Le-Rouge; Tel 04/50-53-18-95; 60F for 3 hours or 105F a day*).

Laundry You can wash your clothes at **Miele Laverie** *(Galerie Alpina; Tel 04/50-53-30-67; 8am-noon/2:30-7pm daily).*

Postal Send postcards from the local branch of **La Poste** *(Place Balmat; 8:30am-noon/2-7pm Mon-Fri; 8:30am-noon Sat).*

Internet See *wired,* below.

Evian

Known universally for its spring water, Evian-les-Bains is a sleepy little alpine town on the edge of **Lac Léman** (or **Lake Geneva**), and just a short boat ride from Switzerland. With its fancy spa, upscale casino, great lakeside beaches, and picturesque trails that wind through the surrounding countryside, Evian-les-Bains has long been a popular vacation spot for rich French tourists. Yet it probably offers the least excitement of any of the towns covered in this region: Except for July and August, when it's mobbed with tourists, it's a great place to escape the hustle and bustle of the larger ski towns. Even if you do come at the peak of the season, the locals manage to remain welcoming and friendly.

The downside of visiting in the off-peak months is the weather. Evian is directly across the lake from Lausanne, and the local joke is that if you can't see Lausanne, it's raining—and if you can, that means it's going to rain! But the weather is nice in the summer, and there are lots of local *plages* with swimming pools, diving boards, slides, and grass, both in Evian and in the neighboring villages along the lake.

Aside from walking and window-shopping, strolling along the edge of the lake, or hopping a boat to a nearby town, there's not a whole lot to do here. In fact, Evian is so tiny that its main street, **rue Nationale,** is only about three blocks long, and you'll probably get to know your way around in a day or two. The rue Nationale runs parallel to a beautiful path along the lake, where there seems to always be at least one group of old men fishing, and plenty of ice cream stands to choose from. You should also check out the local *Savoie* architecture, with its sloping roofs and sturdy window boxes and terraces. You'll find lots of little gardens; old, mossy

wired

Before you come, you can check out Evian's website at **www.eviantourism.com,** or the casino's site: **www.casino-evian.com.** Unfortunately, there's no place in town to check your e-mail.

evian

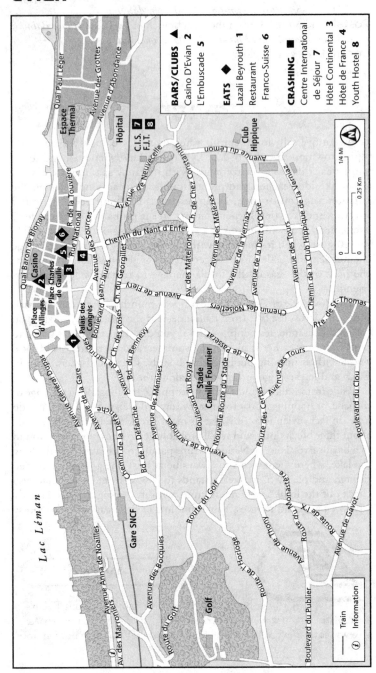

BARS/CLUBS ▲
Casino D'Evian **2**
L'Embuscade **5**

EATS ◆
Lazali Beyrouth **1**
Restaurant
Franco-Suisse **6**

CRASHING ■
Centre International
de Séjour **7**
Hôtel Continental **3**
Hôtel de France **4**
Youth Hostel **8**

◇—— Train
ⓘ Information

fountains; and geranium-filled window boxes. While in Evian, don't miss a trip to one or several of the quaint, even-smaller villages in the hills above town, each with their own central fountain, large gardens, orchards, and animals [see *great outdoors,* below].

Evian's nightlife is centered around the **casino,** which is primarily for the richer tourists, but you'll find a younger crowd in the adjacent disco, as well as a couple of bars along the rue Nationale [see *bar and club scene,* below].

bar and club scene

The bars are frequented mainly by locals at happy-hour, before they get crowded with tourists. There are a few places along rue Nationale with terrace seating where you can sit and watch the world go by while you have a drink. The options are limited, but you didn't come to Evian to party, did you? Get a bottle of wine, sit by the lake, and philosophize with some fellow travelers.

One bar with particularly cool *Savoie* architecture and a really friendly, laid-back staff is **L'Embuscade** *(82 rue Nationale; Tel 04/50-75-02-08; 8:30am-1am Tue-Sat; Drinks 8-15F; No credit cards).* It has the typical dark, exposed ceiling beams both inside and on the facade of the building, and an open, sunny terrace area on the pedestrian street. The crowd is mainly local and doesn't change much from night to night.

Another place to hang out at night is the **Casino D'Evian** *(Rive Sud du Lac de Genève; Tel 04/50-26-87-87; 10am-2am daily, till 3am Fri, Sat; www.casino-evian.com; Must be 18 years old),* which is right on the water. Entrance is free if you just want to be a slot jockey, but there's a 70F

that sitting-in-a-cafe attitude in france

You probably aren't starting your trip in Evian, so by now you know that the French love to sit and people-watch in the afternoons, and you also know that you can sit in a cafe from dawn till dusk as long as you've paid your 7F for one tiny little espresso. But it's still funny to notice that even the ice cream stands along the lake in Evian have chairs and tables—buy an ice cream cone, you've bought your right to a lakeside table for the afternoon and you can watch the fishermen, the young couples, and the people walking their poodles. It's another example of the extra-relaxed attitude in the Alps—you get the sense that people here really, *really* like to take their time.

admission fee and a strict dress code if you want to play cards with the big boys. The adjacent disco (11pm-2am) has a 60F admission fee and a dress code—read: "no jeans"—and is where you'll find the younger crowd.

great outdoors

Outdoor activity here is, of course, centered around the lake and the Evian springs. The big **steamboats** that link the towns along the lake's perimeter, both in France and Switzerland, are organized in Evian by the **Bureau CGN** *(c/o Office des Baigneurs, place du Port, Lac Léman; Tel 04/50-70-73-20),* and you can get info and schedules at the Tourist Office [see *need to know,* below]. A particularly lovely trip is out to **Yvoire,** where you can enjoy a picnic lunch among the perennial flowerbeds of the tiny, walled town. Board any of the two or three mid-summer boats from Evian to Yvoire, a travel time of 90 minutes, at a round-trip price of 150F. In the winter, there is only one boat per day.

Famous for its drinking water as well as its healing spas, Evian's natural spring has a chic spa called the **Thermes Evian** *(Place de la Libération; Tel 04/50-75-02-30; Mon-Sat 9am-12:30pm/2:30-7pm; 350F a day; V, MC).* The day pass gives you access to the club, the natural baths, a Jacuzzi, and the hot springs. Unfortunately, you can't visit the actual springs.

Evian's swim center is **Evian Plage** *(ave. du General Dupas; Tel 04/50-75-02-69; 9:30am-7pm daily, till 8pm July, Aug; 22F; No credit cards).* The "beach" is a grassy, sloping hill, and there is a long waterslide into the pool. There is also a large swimming area roped off in the lake. To find the beach, head toward the lake on the western edge of town. If you can't find it, you should probably have your eyes checked.

pétanque

So you're strolling through town when you notice all these dirt courts crowded with groups of old men hurling colored balls. Is it bocce? Lawn bowling? *Au contraire, mon frère.* It's **pétanque,** a very popular French game that's particularly hot in the Alps and in Provence. A little "jack" ball is thrown out, and the object is to get your team's metal balls closest to the jack ball. Favored strategies include gently rolling the balls into place or blasting the opposition's balls out of the way. There are courts in peoples' yards as well as in the local parks, and if you show up and look interested in the game, they'll probably be more than happy to teach you the rules and invite you to embarrass yourself in your first attempt to play a game.

eats

Most of Evian's restaurants serve regional specialties like fondue and other dishes featuring the famed alpine cheeses, and the daily special is likely to be *filet de perche,* locally caught fish prepared according to the house recipe.

The traditional *Savoie* restaurant **Restaurant Franco-Suisse** *(Place J. Bernex, in the center of rue Nationale; Tel 04/50-75-14-74; 6-10pm daily; Menus from 75-200F; V, MC, AE, DIN)* has a large terrace seating area smack-dab in the square at the center of rue Nationale, and the friendly staff serves all of the local specialties, as well as locally caught fish and mussels.

Locals are excited about the Middle-Eastern and African restaurants that have been springing up all over town, evidence of an increasingly diverse population. One to try is the Lebanese **Lazali Beyrouth** *(13 ave. de la Gare; Tel 04/50-70-76-54; 6-10pm Tue-Sat; Entrées 30-50F; V, MC),* which is on the continuation of the rue National as it heads out west of the central downtown area. It's a casual place as far as dress code goes, but the décor is authentically lavish and the service is excellent; the waiters take great care of you, and they serve tasty hummus, grilled vegetables, and soothing mint tea.

crashing

Evian is the sleepiest place imaginable until July and August, when the tourists descend in hoards and hotel prices escalate. If you plan to stay in one of the hotels downtown during the summer, you really need to plan ahead and make reservations—they fill up quickly.

The local youth hostel, **Centre International de Séjour** *(ave. de Neuvecelle; Tel 04/50-75-35-87; 24-hour reception; www.cur-archamps. fr/mjc-evian; 125F single; V, MC),* is up on the hill overlooking the lake, halfway between the train station and the center of town (about a 10-minute walk to either). It has single rooms with private bathrooms (!), and there's no curfew—truly a god among hostels.

If you can't get a room at the hostel—or would like something a little nicer—head to one of the small hotels on rue Nationale. One of the best options is **Hôtel de France** *(59 rue National; Tel 04/50-75-00-36; Hotel-France-Evian@wanadoo.fr; 260-300F single, 280-360F double; Breakfast 30F; V, MC, AE, DIN),* which has TVs in every room, private bathroom, a great breakfast terrace in the garden, and clean rooms decorated by someone who likes flowers (maybe a little too much...).

Just down the street, the **Hôtel Continental** *(65 rue Nationale; Tel 04/50-75-37-54; 220F single, 260F double; V, MC, AE)* has a cute green facade, lots of flowers in the stairwell, and clean, simple rooms with private baths. Breakfast is 30F and an extra bed is 60F.

need to know

Currency Exchange The best place to go is one of the banks along **rue Nationale.** Most are open 9am-noon/2-7pm Mon-Fri, and have **ATMs.**

Tourist Information The **Office de Tourisme** *(Place d'Allinges; Tel 04/50-75-04-26; 8:30am-noon/2-6:30pm Mon-Fri, 9am-noon/2-6pm Sat, 10am-noon/3-6pm Sun)* is housed in a big glass building by the lake. They have maps and information on hotels, restaurants, and boats, and will even make hotel reservations for you.

Health and Emergency Health emergency: *15;* police emergency: *17.* The local hospital is **Hôpital Camille Blanc** *(ave. d'Abondance; Tel 04/50-83-20-00).*

Pharmacies There are several along the rue Nationale, identified by their **green crosses,** but none are open 24 hours.

Trains The train station, **Gare SNCF** *(ave. de la Gare; 08/36-35-35-35; 8:30am-7:30pm daily)* is just up the hill from town about a 20-minute walk from rue Nationale.

Boats You can arrive by boat from Geneva or Lausanne; the port is almost directly across from the casino and a two-minute walk from the main downtown area. For information, contact **Bureau CGN** *(c/o Office des Baigneurs; Tel 04/50-70-73-20).*

Laundry **Laverie Libre Service** *(5 rue Folliet; Tel 04/50-75-33-45; 8am-8:30pm daily).*

Postal There is only one **Post Office** *(rue Nationale, 8am-noon/2-6pm Mon-Fri, 8am-noon Sat).*

Internet See *wired,* above.

côte d'azur and the french riviera

the french riviera

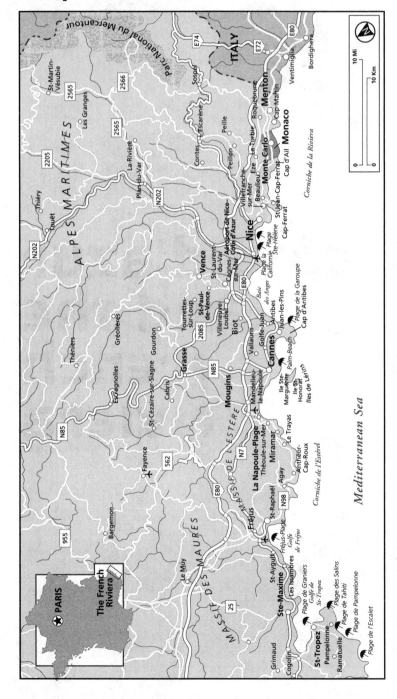

I f the words "French Riviera" conjure up images of baccarat and 007, you're not far off. Casinos are still a big deal even outside **Monaco,** and there's no quicker way to win enough for dinner or lose enough to have to live off crusty baguettes for the remainder of your stay. Cherries spin and coins drop by the bucket in practically every town along the coast, be they glamorous or not. It's part of the "cultural" draw.

The French definitely don't do it Vegas-style. Though you may feel at home here mingling with men in plaid jackets from Toledo and busloads of women from Jersey, you ain't getting the Vegas treatment. There're no free drinks or comped continental breakfasts; you get what you pay for. While the front rooms are filled with gum-smacking tourists in Bermudas, there's a pride of high rollers in the private back rooms. Some of these pros make it out to the main floor, but they won't appreciate your inexperience mucking up their blackjack game. (Don't forget: In Monte Carlo, getting blackjack means squat if the dealer gets it too. Unlike in Vegas, you don't automatically win.)

Acting cool after dropping a thou will let you blend in with the big-timers, but it could also force an early return home. Don't let the gambling high carry you off into debtland! Even if you're just playing the slots, those whirling cherries can get totally mesmerizing—and before you know it, you're dialing C-A-L-L A-T-T for help. Imagining the look on Dad's face when you do should inspire self-restraint.

Another Riviera draw is the vision of barren beaches and buff bodies glistening in the sun. Don't be surprised if your dreams *á la Baywatch* turn out to be a wash. *Les plages* along the Côte d'Azur are well-trodden by millions of star-seeking foreigners, and you'll have to look at your share of saggy bods before finding the hot ones. What's worse, the sand in **Cannes** and Monaco looks like it came from a hotel ashtray: once smooth and powder white, now dirty and filled with butts. If you want comfort, you'll have to buy it in the form of a rented chair, available all along the Côte.

The best beaches can be found around **St. Tropez,** where the pace is a little more relaxed. **Nice** is also more laid-back, but don't be surprised if you find a pile of rocks where the sand should be. Arranging the pebbles so that you don't get a crick in your neck is tricky, but could be worth it, since it's a little more pleasant here than in star-stained Cannes. Whichever beach you're on, if you're a woman, there's no longer a reason to envy guys for taking their shirts off. Why not take this opportunity to liberate yourself and do as the French?

Even if your dreams of perfect Mediterranean beaches are disappointed, your fantasies of ocean-liner-sized yachts and fast cars won't be—from the glitz of high-profile Cannes to the movie-set port of St. Tropez. Real gamblers will dig Monaco, a principality that's independent of France and ruled by Prince Rainier III, where rich geezers (and young-uns) fling about wads of cash at the **Monte-Carlo Casino.** The sea beyond the beaches offers up its own wealth of opportunities: Jet ski or scuba dive or sail the azure waters to your heart's content—if you've got the bucks.

Finding a bed is easiest and most economical in Nice, which can be a good base for zipping around the rest of the Côte d'Azur. Cannes, Monaco, and Nice are only 20 to 40 minutes apart by train, and staying

12 hours on the french riviera

1. In Monte Carlo, check out the Casino [see *casinos* in *Monaco,* below], gardens [see *culture zoo* in **monaco,** below], and the royal palace.
2. Have a nice cappuccino and play some slots at **Cafe de Paris** in Monte Carlo [see *hanging out* in **monaco,** below].
3. Go to the beach in Nice [see *hanging out* in **nice,** below]; the crowd is larger and flashier than in Monaco or Cannes.
4. Trip out at the **Musée National Message Biblique Marc Chagall** [see *culture zoo* in **nice,** below] on the mind-blowing mural-size paintings of biblical scenes.
5. Ditto the **Musée Matisse** [see *culture zoo* in **nice,** below]; it's worth the short trek to Cimiez to check out the great one.
6. Vieux-Nice [see *hanging out* in **nice,** below] is a lovely neighborhood of charming squares and quaint cafes.
7. Groove to tunes at **Neil's Club** or get funky at **Le Duke** [see *bar, club, and live music scene,* in **nice,** below].
8. Take a flight on the wild side and go parasailing at the Monaco, Nice, or Cannes beaches.
9. Celeb-watch while you walk along **La Croisette** in Cannes.
10. Check out the ever-cookin' **Jimmy'z** [see *bar, club, and live music scene* in **cannes,** below] and the **Palais des Festivals** in Cannes.

Travel Times

* TGV (Fast Train—more expensive)
**By car.

	Monaco	Cannes	St. Tropez	Paris	Nice
Nice	:20	:40**	3:00**	8:00 8:30	-
Monaco	-	1:05	3:30**	7:00* 11:30	:20
Cannes	1:05	-	2:30* :20†	7:00* 10:00	:40**
St. Tropez	3:30**	2:30**	-	7:00* 10:00††	3:00

†2 hr. 30 min.—train to St. Raphael (20 min.), then bus to St. Tropez (2 hr. 10 min.)

††10 hr—in both cases, train to St. Raphael, then bus to St. Tropez (2 hr. 10 min.)

in Nice will save you a few francs that you can wile away in Monaco's casinos by night or the stargazing cafes of Cannes by day. But if you're dead set on sampling the nightlife in Monaco or Cannes, you'll have to sleep over. Trains stop running by midnight, just when the doormen at clubs are turning their first trainer-clad visitors away. In St. Tropez the clubs are even harder to sneak into, and budget hotels are nowhere in sight.

In terms of relating to the natives, remember: Money turns the gears here, and it's all about how you look and who you know—or pretend to know. It's hard for some locals to decide whether they love us or feel invaded. In the big scheme of things, though, if you find yourself lost and alone, and your French sucks or is nonexistent, don't worry. The Riviera is used to an international crowd who have turned the place into a mythic, starstruck playground.

Finding someone who speaks English is not a problem. However, it's best to learn at least a few basics, like *"Bonjour, parlez-vous anglais?,"* before belting out your English request at the speed of light. People here tend to get annoyed at assumptions, and even if they do speak English, they're more apt to pretend that they don't. And, given the prosperity here, you may feel uncomfortable walking around in your scrubs. It's all about attitude in the long run. Assess the situation, work with what you've got, try to be a polite representative of your country, and f—k 'em if they've still got a problem with your smelly Tevas.

getting around

The Côte d'Azur is pretty self-contained and easily covered, with little travel time between Nice, Cannes, and Monaco. The SNCF trains connect all three, and the conductors checking tickets are unpredictable. On a good day, catching a free ride is easy; on a bad one, you'll spend your trip eyeing the next car to see if the conductor is coming. Home-base yourself in Nice, where the cheapest, easiest accommodation is found. There's also an airport in Nice, which, along with the trains and buses coming in from other French regions, makes it a good place to begin your Riviera adventure. Take day trips out to Monaco and Cannes, or spend a night in these towns to catch some nightlife. If you're on your way to St. Tropez, check out Nice and Monaco first, then stop over in Cannes on your way down to the peninsula. St. Tropez doesn't have a train station, so from Cannes you train it to St. Raphaël, then bus it to St. Tropez. The distance on the bus isn't that far, but the winding, traffic-choked road makes for a long, nauseating haul.

▶▶ROUTES

Nice to Monaco, then back to Nice.
Off to Cannes, then continuing to St. Tropez (via St. Raphaël).

nICE

Nice is nowhere near as glitzy and starstruck as its neighbor Cannes; it's a big city with an old-fashioned Provençal heart. Blocks of achingly beautiful pale-golden buildings sit like medieval townhouses on the narrow, cobbled streets of Vieux-Nice, the city's Old Town. This, as well as in the center of town, around Place Masséna, is where you'll find most of the nightlife in Nice.

neighborhoods

Between wall-walker vendors and musicians who make up in heart what they lack in talent, the **rue des Piétons** [see *hanging out,* below] is tourist central. Walk the street, and try to avoid having anything to do with any of the American food-wannabe restaurants—they're overpriced, and the food sucks. At the end of Piétons sits the fountained **place Masséna** [see *hanging out,* below] with its rib-cage sculptures and saturated green lawn. Technically a park, this oasis also functions as the center of town, where people love to eat lunch or read the morning paper. The surrounding neighborhood houses the **Opéra de Nice** [see *arts scene,* below] and the **Museum of Modern and Contemporary Art** [see *culture zoo,* below] as well as the souvenir street market selling products of the Provençe region [see *stuff,* below]. On Sundays, the over-60 crew takes over the best shaded area in place Masséna, so be polite and don't haggle over a chair with somebody's *grand-mère.*

A block or two south of Masséna, you hit the old part of Nice—aptly called **Vieux-Nice**—that's filled with enough bars and pubs to fit anyone's taste and galleries and shops to visit in the daylight hours. The

nice

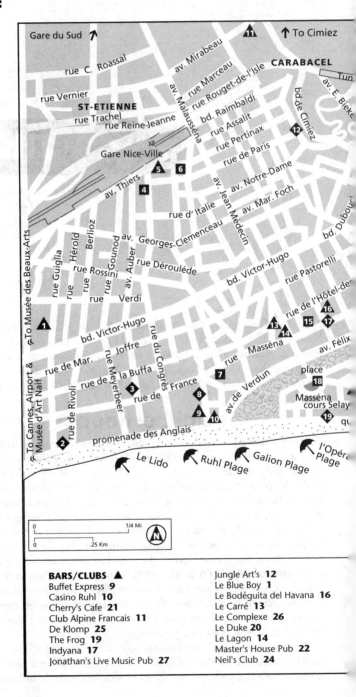

Gare du Sud ↗   ↑ To Cimiez

rue C. Roassal   av. Mirabeau
                        rue Marceau   CARABACEL
rue Vernier   rue Rouget-de-l'Isle   av. E. Bieke
ST-ETIENNE   av. Malausséna
rue Trachel   bd. Raimbaldi
        rue Reine-Jeanne   rue Assalit
                        rue Pertinax
Gare Nice-Ville   rue de Paris
        5   6
            4   av. Notre-Dame
av. Thiers   av. Jean Médecin   av. Mar. Foch
        rue d' Italie
rue Guiglia
rue Hérold
rue Berlioz   av. Georges-Clemenceau   bd. Dubouc
rue Rossini   av. Gounod rue Déroulède   bd. Victor-Hugo
rue Verdi   av. Auber   rue Pastorelli
                                    rue de l'Hôtel-de-
1   16
bd. Victor-Hugo   13   15   17
        rue Joffre   14
rue de Mar.   rue   Masséna   av. Félix
rue de Meyerbeer rue du Congrès   place
    rue de la Buffa   rue de France   av. de Verdun   18
3   7   Masséna
        8   cours Selay
        9   10   19
promenade des Anglais   qu
    Le Lido   Ruhl Plage   Galion Plage   l'Opéra
                                       Plage
2

To Musée des Beaux-Arts
To Cannes, Airport & Musée d'Art Naïf

0   1/4 Mi   (N)
0   .25 Km

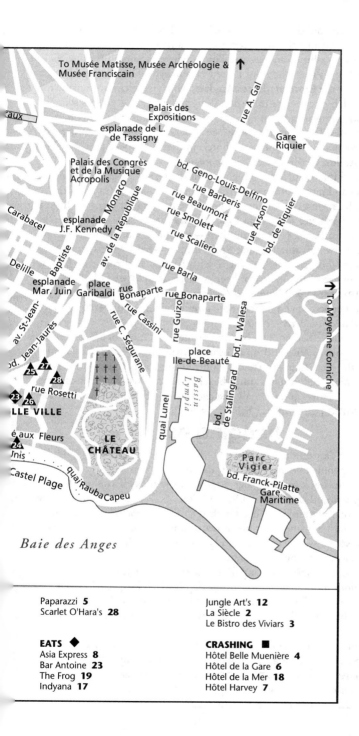

To Musée Matisse, Musée Archéologie & Musée Franciscain

Palais des Expositions

Gare Riquier

esplanade de L. de Tassigny

rue A. Gal

Palais des Congrès et de la Musique Acropolis

bd. Geno-Louis-Delfino

rue Barberis

rue Beaumont

rue Smolett

rue Scaliero

Monaco

av. de la République

Carabacel

esplanade J.F. Kennedy

Baptiste

Delille

esplanade Mar. Juin

place Garibaldi

rue Bonaparte

rue Bonaparte

rue Barla

rue Cassini

rue Guizo

bd. L. Walesa

rue Arson

bd. de Riquier

av. St-Jean-

bd. Jean-Jaurès

rue C. Ségurane

place Ile-de-Beauté

To Moyenne Corniche

25   27

28

23   26

rue Rosetti

LLE VILLE

é aux Fleurs

24

Jnis

Castel Plage

quai Lunel

quai Rauba Capeu

Bassin Lympia

bd. de Stalingrad

Parc Vigier

bd. Franck-Pilatte

Gare Maritime

LE CHÂTEAU

Baie des Anges

Paparazzi **5**
Scarlet O'Hara's **28**

Jungle Art's **12**
La Siècle **2**
Le Bistro des Viviars **3**

EATS ◆
Asia Express **8**
Bar Antoine **23**
The Frog **19**
Indyana **17**

CRASHING ■
Hôtel Belle Muenière **4**
Hôtel de la Gare **6**
Hôtel de la Mer **18**
Hôtel Harvey **7**

medieval-style buildings are human-sized and charming: No building in Nice is overwhelmingly tall, except for the flashy Casino Ruhl [see *casinos,* below] tower, a bit of an eyesore. This is where the nightlife is in Nice. Minutes from Vieux-Nice and Place Masséna, you'll see the big blue sea bordered by the **Promenade des Anglais,** which is a glamorous name for the wide slab of concrete that runs along the water and gets its share of rollerbladers, musicians, and people lunching or stopping for coffees at outdoor cafes. The **Gare Routière** [see *need to know,* below] is just east of Place Masséna, convenient to the hotels in the Vieux-Nice area. The bus station **Station Centrale** [see *need to know,* below] is here, too.

With all the resources of a big city but the feel of a beach town, Nice is warmer and more homey and intimate than Monaco or Cannes. It's the type of place you can settle into if you have the time. If you only have a couple of days here, you'll want to stick to the Vieux-Nice and the beach. You're sure to find a party somewhere—and don't worry about the etiquette involved in nursing one drink forever—bar owners prefer that their places look crowded. If you're with friends, and counting francs, take advantage of the "meter of beer" specials at **Scarlet O'Hara's** and **Jonathan's** [see *bar, club, and live music scene,* below, for both]. The trust-fund crowd can enjoy the more rarefied vibes at **Le Carré** [see *bar, club, and live music scene,* below].

When you've had enough of city life and want more of a beach experience, get out of Nice and zip to nearby towns of Cap d'Ail and Juan les Pins on the local train. You're only a nice (no pun intended) walk away from Cimiez, which has a quiet beach area, and where the museums devoted to Matisse and Chagall [see *culture zoo,* below] and the **Fondation Kosma** [see *arts scene,* below] await you.

hanging out

During the day, outdoor cafes in the the old town's squares are popular places for people to congregate. But the most obvious hangout spot here is the beach. Look for the paler bodies on the rocks if you're trying to hook up with other travelers. Oh, and don't expect golden sand, or any sand for that matter. The Nice beach is rocks, just rocks. Wear a pair of good sandals. This beach is no snobatorium like those at Monaco and Cannes, so you won't feel out of place without a cell phone. Families, travelers, locals, young people, and old-timers mix it up at the beach, and you'll have no problem making friends with your neighbors, especially in the summer months when towels overlap for lack of space. To beat the tourist crowds, follow the locals—you'll know them by their bare chests and portable umbrellas—who prefer the less-populated strips of beach to the west.

If you're starting to get crispy, the park at Place Masséna is a great shady place for lazing around. Cool off in the nearby **Musée d'Art Moderne et d'Art Contemporain** [see *culture zoo,* below], where more than one weary soul has napped on the leather couches without being rudely awakened by a security guard.

Not much stays open on Monday and Tueday nights, so people meet on the steps of the Palais de Justice in Vieux-Nice. Young scholarly types and scholar wannabes sip wine at the cafes that line the Place du Palais de Justice until they close at 11pm. Come in—watch the human zoo go by. After 11pm, there are plenty of nighttime choices: Locals love **Le Carré** and the Dutch pub **De Klomp** [see *bar, club, and live music scene,* below, for both]. And Nice's **Casino Ruhl** [see *casinos,* below] stays open late-night to service the gambling addicts. It shuts down from 5am till 10am, just long enough to clean up.

Any of the Vieux-Nice pubs that stay open till 4am can satisfy your after-hours chow needs. But the only true 24-hour joint to hit after a late, late night is a little hole-in-the-wall takeout joint right off the water called **Buffet Express** *(Promenade des Anglais & Rue Halevy; Tel 93/825-455; Bus 3, 6, 7 to Congrès; Open 24 hours daily; No credit cards),* an annex of the larger **Cafe Promenade** next door. Grab a greasy croque-monsieur or a pain au chocolat and head to the Promenade.

There's no actual château, but the **Parc du Château** *(Top of Castle Hill; Tel 93/856-233; Any bus to Masséna; 10am-6pm daily, 9am-8pm Aug; Free admission)* is still a great place to kick back, with its fountains set in lush gardens, miniature golf, and a human-scale chess board. Get a group together and play some putt-putt, or just sit next to the waterfall and catch some rays. "La Cascade" is a refreshing spot on a hot summer day, especially after the uphill march to the top, where you can see all of Nice. You'll run into large groups and families—the park has made it onto the must-see list of the "Tourist Trolley." These obnoxious little yellow trollies lumber around town at like, 2 mph, full of pointing people with sunburned faces. But don't let that stop you from enjoying the scenery—after all, you may be one of those tomato-faced pointers.

bar, club, and live music scene

Nice lacks what you would call a real club scene. Most bars and live music spots have dancing, too, so even the idea of clubs is different here. There are a bunch of sketchy places around town that have cartoonlike windows on the doors and require a "password." Never mind where to get the password, these places never even seem to be open. Ignore them. Also, don't be fooled by bouncers who usher you in, claiming "no money, no money"—cover charges are cleverly disguised by sky-high drink prices like draught beer for 100F. When it comes to entrance standards, Nice clubs adhere to the standard form: Male bouncers shepherd the ladies in and give fellas a hard time. Clubs vary in their levels of snobbery, but dressing well always helps your case.

Bars are a different story—there's no shortage of watering holes in Nice, and most of the ones worth going to are conveniently packed into Vieux-Nice, so barhopping is easy. Everyone migrates from place to place, and drunken fools pack the area late at night. For a slightly less "party time!" scene, try one of the many hip restaurants not in Vieux-Nice that transform into bars later at night: People tend to come and

mec meets nana

Unlike the Italians, the French aren't con-
vinced that it's their mission to pursue every female visitor no matter
what "get lost" vibes you might be giving off. Ladies, for a fling with
a local boy, head to any of the bars they frequent: in Nice, **De
Klomp** and **Masterhouse;** in Cannes, **Carling's Pub;** and in
Monaco, **Flashman's English Pub** [see *bar, club, and live music
scene* in respective cities]. Guys, it's best to use a purposeful approach
when wooing the women in France. It may be tempting to cruise
the beach for victims, but don't go in for the kill if the sight of a girl
with no top on leaves you fumbling for words.

In Nice, **Neil's Club** [see *bar, club, and live music scene,* in Nice,
below] is a good spot to meet local gals, **Jimmy'z** [see *bar, club,
and live music scene,* in Cannes, below] is the place to scout them
out in Cannes. In Monaco, try **Cherie's Cafè** [see *bar, club, and
live music scene,* in Monaco, below].

plant themselves in one such spot for the night. Those in the know take
root at **Indyana** [see *eats,* below], but you'll be expected to order some
tapas with that drink, bub. For a change of pace, immerse yourself in the
pre-Castro Cuban vibe at La Bodéguita del Havana [see below].

Live music is definitely a part of the culture, and it pops up in even the
most unassuming places. A guitar duo plays at **The Frog** [see *eats,* below]
on weekend nights, and you even have a choice of karaoke spots. Jazz aficionados should plan to hit Nice during the **Jazz Festival** [see *festivals &
events,* below] in July to hear jazz bigs such as pianist Herbie Hancock. The
festival packs 'em in, so plan to make hotel reservations well in advance
and check on the main Nice website [see *wired,* below] for ticket availability. For concert info on jazz and rock bands—and everything else,
really—look on the wall outside of Neil's Club [see below]. And then stick
around—Neil's has all kinds of shows that span the gamut from jazz to
indie rock.

Master Home Pub *(11 rue de la Préfecture; Tel 93/803-382; Any
bus to Masséna; 11am-2am Mon-Sat, 2pm-12am Sun)* could easily trans-
plant itself into any college town. Take away the French waiters, and
you're left with a bunch of baseball-capped boys in khaki shorts. Beer
lovers should get off on the 50 or so ales from a dozen countries. The
creamy, cherry-flavored Belgian Krieke Bellvue (45F) lacks the yuck-
factor of most fruit beers. Have a seat on the outdoor patio and watch
the people go by.

Everyone gets the occasional urge to belt out some tunes off-key, and
Jonathan's Live Music Pub *(1 rue de la Loge; Tel 93/625-762; Any bus*

to Masséna; 8pm-2:30am Tue-Sat; No credit cards) understands this need. They host the Wednesday Night Singing Challenge, which means karaoke sung to all kinds of international sounds. Push it—try Jamiroquai. There's a definite par-tay atmosphere, with loads of Americans, and best of all, no cover. Before you jump onstage, build some confidence with some 10F beers at the 8 to 9:30pm happy hour. On Tuedays, happy hour lasts all night, with a "meter of beer" at 150F. Live music (usually rock/pop-oriented) moves in on weekends in the "Cellar Cave" downstairs.

Even if it's not Wednesday, don't give up your dream of singing in the spotlight. With 1,600 titles and a mostly American crowd, **Le Lagon** *(2 rue Masséna; Tel 93/877-685; Bus 7, 9, 10 to Jean-Médecin; 11pm-4am daily; V)* gets its karaoke going by midnight nightly. Bathe yourself in the strobe lights, order up one of their specialty cocktails named after exotic cities of the world (45F), and belt out "Karma Chameleon." The purple-and-green disco decor in the big circular main room takes you back to a more polyester time, and the staff of large men with gelled hair add to the we're-still-living-in-the-early-'80s atmosphere. There's no cover, but they do charge two francs to pee.

A boisterous collegiate crew hangs out at **Scarlet O'Hara's Tavern and Ale House** *(Corner of rue Droite and rue Rossetti; Tel 93/804-322; Any bus to Masséna; 5pm-2am daily, V, MC, AE)*, whose motto reads: "a pint of plain is your only man," whatever that means. O'Hara's is a traditional pub complete with a dart board and televised sporting events and is one of the few night spots open seven days a week. Hit happy hour for the 15F pints, or come later for dancing on the tables—yes, dancing on

RULES OF THE GAME

It's pretty rare to see someone openly smoking a joint on the street in Cannes, Nice, or Monaco. Monaco clubs don't see much drug use, at least not openly—that's too 1985 here. Gay clubs tend to have more of a drug thing going on, usually some E. Keep in mind that the penalty for being caught with even a joint is stiff. The French government cracked down on hash smoking about 10 years ago, and the penalty is jail time (like...seven years!!). Still, you don't see cops hanging around waiting to capture offenders. Note: Travelers should definitely refrain from carrying any sort of mind-altering substance on the train. As for booze, you're pretty safe having a drink on the beach or on the streets of Vieux-Nice or Cannes, but it's just not done in Monaco. In general, the French like their wine as much as you do, and as long as you don't cause trouble, there shouldn't be a problem. Getting rowdy at a bar or cold-cocking the casino dealer who just dealt himself blackjack is definitely a bad idea.

the tables. Live music sessions happen Thursday–Saturday at 10pm, and Celtic grub gets served up pretty much all night.

Only in Nice for a couple of hours? You could run across the street from the train station to **Paparazzi** *(26 ave. Durante; Tel 93/885-968; Bus 12, 30 to Gare; 10am-1am daily, No credit cards)*, the billiards-pub-restaurant joint on the corner, which clearly survives on the merits of its...location. The whole place has a Planet Hollywood-wannabe feel, with a giant movie camera, a plastic statue of Marilyn Monroe, and a jukebox full of the tired pop titles you'd expect: Nirvana, Madonna, Elton John, etc. On the up side, a game of pool or pinball is 10F, the owner plays music videos on the bar TV, and there's decent live music at night, usually rock or jazz. There's no cover per se, but drink prices are jacked up by 10F on live music nights. Then again, just hanging out in the train station isn't such a bad way to pass the time either....

Odd that the only Dutch pub in Nice is run by a couple of Brits, but that's the case at **De Klomp** *(6 rue Mascoïnat, Vieux-Nice; Tel 93/924-285; Any bus to Masséna; 5pm-2:30am Mon-Sat, 8:30pm-2:30am Sun; V, MC)*. They like to watch "footy" on the telly, so expect it to be packed during the World Cup or any other big match. De Klomp, jammed with guys of all ages, is a man's place and its hefty wooden furniture and wood paneling give it a sort of bachelor-pad feel. The 5:30 to 9:30pm happy hour brings in the students, local and foreign. It's a chill place during the day but energized later on, with live music every night and jazz on Thursdays at 10pm. Expect a mainly local all-age crowd of expats and French alike. The bass player (if he's still around) is good news, as are the 18 beers on tap and 40 types of whiskey.

The très sophistiqué **Le Carré** *(6 passage Emile Negrin, pedestrian zone; Tel 93/883-882; Any bus to place Masséna and then ya gotta walk; 8pm-midnight Mon-Sat; No credit cards)* reels in the cool, black-clad Euro types. Le Carré throws lots of parties in the summer, and anything goes with the DJs: funk, soul, salsa, jazz, whatever. The decor mixes zebra-striped couches with a Casablanca-esque feel. Tasty tapas of salmon tartare and a martini runs about 100F. Le Carré is a restaurant, too, but you can definitely feel comfortable just having a drink. Come after 10pm to mingle with the artsy crew and pick up a party invite or two.

Neil's Club *(10 Cité du Parc, Vieux-Nice; Bus 6, 11, 16 to Gare Routière; 10pm-5am Tue-Sat; 30-50F; No credit cards)* has jazz every Tuesday night and by far the most live shows of any club around. Look next to the door for the schedule of weekly concerts, ranging from the Pixies to nameless electronic groovers. Indie rock theme nights move into the cavernous underground space twice a month, where DJs blast the likes of Pavement and Superchunk. This no-nonsense place doesn't bother with any fancy-schmancy decor, and the crowd depends totally on who's playing. The cover includes one drink.

The **FNAC** ticket outlet [see *arts scene,* below] has tickets for and info on bigger jazz events around the area. Check for big rock concerts, too.

The over-glitzed **Forum** (*45 promenade des Anglais; Tel 93/966-800; Bus 6 to Meyerbeer; 11pm-6am Thur-Sun; 100F drink minimum; No credit cards*) comes complete with a red carpet out the door and an army of beefy, suit-clad bouncers. The neon-lit interior is an electrifying mix of purple-and-red carpet with fuchsia lights. Cheesy? Perhaps. Disco? Definitely. The twentysomething touristos fill this baby up, though Forum does have a local following. Smile pretty at the four knuckleheads who stand with crossed arms outside the door—being or showing up with a girl in a tight dress doesn't hurt, either.

Le Duke (*11 rue Alexandre Mari; Tel 93/804-050; Any bus to Masséna; 12-5am Wed-Sun; No credit cards*) doesn't really get started till about 1am, so be fashionably late and get here at 2. There's supposedly no cover, but plan to pay 100F for a drink. The mirror-clad space is pretty small, so make reservations by phone to ensure a place on the dance floor, where you can get down to the hip-hop/funk grooves of DJ Bruno with go-go dancers Krishna and Vishnu. Dress with panache—tight is the operative word here.

Wild nights also begin after dinner at **The Jungle Arts** [see *eats*, below], when the lights dim and the restaurant becomes a mini club.

If you're feeling smooth—and coordinated—**La Bodéguita del Havana** (*14 rue Chauvain; Tel 93/926-724; Any bus to Masséna; 6pm-2am Tue-Sat; No credit cards*) holds salsa dancing classes Sunday–Wednesday nights from 8 to 10pm for 35F. This is a hardcore dancing arena, so the lessons are definitely a good idea.... The interior is what a happenin' Cuban dance club in Havana should look like: timbali and bongo drums everywhere and an upstairs that looks like a cockfighting pit.

casinos

There's nothing lit-up like the **Casino Ruhl** (*1 promenade des Anglais; Tel 93/879-587; Bus 6, 2, 12 to beach; No credit cards*), Nice's homage to gambling, complete with twinkling lights and singing slot machines. The *salon des jeux* (gaming room) stays open from 8pm till 4am and charges a 75F fee to enter. Bring your passport—they require photo ID—and mind the dress code: no shorts, jeans, or untucked shirts for men; no pants for the ladies, and no sandals for anybody. They do play 21 and American craps, but some rules differ, so ask before laying down those chips. The *machines à sous* (slot machines) are open from 10am till 4am. They close for a few hours, so the house can count the money or something. Here you can walk in wearing anything but a bathing suit, and slots start at 2F.

arts scene

▶▶VISUAL ARTS

Where there are galleries there is inevitably a cigarette-smoking, champagne-sipping, fashion-clad following. The classy Manoir Cafe [see below] has its own gallery space in addition to being a restaurant and bar.

festivals and events

There are over 30 festivals yearly in Nice, but these are the most fun:

Triathlon International de Nice *(late June):* World-class athletes high-tail it to Nice for this endurance test that takes over the city.

Nice Jazz Festival *(early July):* The best from the jazz world: Herbie Hancock, among others. The festival's website *(www. nicecoteazur.org/francais/culture/jazz)* is in French, but the schedule is easily decipherable.

Fête de la Vigne *(early Sept):* A wine-filled celebration of the grape harvest.

Bain de Noël: Skinny-dipping in the Mediterranean the Sunday after Christmas.

The starving artists blow their patronage checks at **Indyana** [see *eats*, below], and get pumpin' at night at **Le Duke** [see *bar, club, and live music scene*, above]. Vieux-Nice cafes [see *hanging out*, above] are sure bets for catching a bleary-eyed artist by day. The exhibitions at the galleries below change almost monthly to showcase a variety of fresh talent. None costs to get in.

The **Galerie Municipale Renoir** *(8 rue de la Loge; Tel 93/174-046; Any bus to Masséna; 10:30am-1pm/2-6pm Tue-Sat)* is far from stodgy, showing pomo-cubist work like Paul Pacatto's Light Sculptures.

Galerie des Ponchettes *(77 quai des Etats-Unis; Tel 93/623-134; Bus 1, 2 to Gare Routière; 10:30am-1pm/2-6pm Tue-Sat)* and **Galerie de la Marine** *(59 quai des Etats-Unis; Tel 93/623-711; Any bus to Masséna; 10:30am-1pm/2-6pm Tue-Sat)*, probably the two most revered galleries in Nice's small art world, often cohost international group shows. In summer months expect to see young Italian painters and sculptors like Luisa Rabbia and Enrica Borghi. Hit one of the openings, usually Fridays at 6pm, for some free grub. Such offerings as Van Gogh exhibitions (in Marine) and poetry illustrated on canvas (at Ponchettes) give these galleries the feel of scaled-back museums.

Manoir Cafe *(32 rue de France; Tel 93/163-616; Bus 6, 2, 17 to Meyerbeer; 7pm-midnight daily; 98-150F prix-fixe menus; V, MC, AE)* has a whole different thing going on. This subdued gallery/restaurant/lounge boasts a stained-glass ceiling, leather chairs to sink your butt into, and a circular staircase that leads upstairs to the couches, coffee tables, and fashion mags. Shows include local artists' 2-D works that are enjoyable if not exceptional. Come for the atmosphere—the art is just a bonus. And chef Frank Huneau serves up a mean lobster and a savory artichoke salad. Now, *there's* art for ya.

▶▶PERFORMING ARTS

Theater here is in French without exception, and it's pretty commercial. Big productions at Théâtre de Nice and the Opéra [see below] include old favorites like *Hansel and Gretel* (the opera, dummy). The big-deal **Nice Jazz Festival** [see *festivals & events*, above] hits town in July. Tickets for this and most other performing arts event can be picked up at the **FNAC** *billeterie (Centre Nice Etoile 2nd floor, 30 ave. Jean Médecin; Tel 92/177-774; Any bus to Place Masséna; 10am-7pm Mon-Sat; MC, V)*. A few movie houses show films in English—look for the magic phrase "original language." Your best bet is the homey **Cinéma Le Mercury** *(16 place Garibaldi; Tel 08/36-68-81-06; Bus 30 to Garibaldi; Shows nightly, times vary; 42F, 28F w/student ID)*, which showcases at least two pictures in English, about a year behind their opening abroad. Their phone line is an automated listing in French, so you may need to make the trek to Mercury for showtimes.

The **Nice Opera and Acropolis** *(4-6 rue Sainte Françoise de Paule; Tel 92/174-040; Any bus to Masséna; Closed Mon)* hosts six operas each season along with concerts and lectures. Tickets range from 100F for a nosebleed seat to 700F for Placido Domingo's spitting range. Pick up info on shows at FNAC [see above] or the **Theater Box Office** *(9 rue de la Terrasse; 10am-6:30pm Mon-Sat)*.

There are free concerts Monday nights at **Fondation Kosma** *(Conservatoire de Nice, 24 blvd. de Cimiez; Tel 92/267-220; Bus 15, 17 to Cimiez)* from October to April. They usually tend to be symphony-type affairs with a student following. Hey, it's music, and it's free.

Bimonthly jazz concerts are on offer at **Cédac de Cimiez** *(49 ave. de la Marne; Tel 83/538-595; Bus 15, 17 to Cimiez; Call for times)*—a more formal setting than the clubs. Tickets can be as cheap as 25F.

Théâtre de Nice *(Promenade des Arts; Tel 93/805-260; Any bus to Masséna; 1-7pm Tue-Sat; 75F, 50F if under 25)* showcases experimental works by smaller companies including *L'Etat de Siège*, a mix of dance, performance art, and music that deals with (what else?) the human condition.

Cinéma Rialto *(4 rue de Rivoli; Tel 93/880-841; Bus 9 to Rue Rivoli; Hours vary; 54F, 35F students)* shows a lot of indie flicks, and once in a while they have one in English. Films are only a few months old when they hit the Rialto, so you won't be seeing *Fargo* for the sixth time.

If you're a film student or just a buff, call up **Cinémathèque de Nice** *(3 esplanade Kennedy; Tel 92/040-666; Bus 25 to Acropolis; Tue-Sun)*. They know how to treat starving film junkies, charging 12F for students and 20F for the masses.

gay scene

You don't see Gay Pride flags flying on every corner, but the attitude in Nice toward men who like men and women who like women is casual and unassuming. Plenty of cafes, lounges, and dance spots cater to gay visitors and residents. Websites give out good info on gay hangouts. Local publications like **Hyzberg** and **Lesbian & Gay Pride Côte d'Azur** are free at local newsstands and at the tourist office.

The annual **Festival of Gay and Lesbian Film** takes place at **Cinéma Le Mercury** [see *arts scene*, above] in mid-June. You can also always find fliers for gallery shows by gay artists, and restaurants and bars that service gay clientele, at Mercury.

Le Blue Boy *(9 rue Spinetta; Tel 93/446-824; Bus 38 to Rue Maréchal Joffre; 11pm-6am Tue-Sun; No credit cards)* is one of the oldest gay clubs on the Riviera. Gay men of all ages show up at Blue Boy, located in a residential neighborhood between the promenade and the train station, but it's not all about sugar daddies. Disco down with the best of 'em on the multi-level, blue-neon dance floors. Plan to stay up late—Blue Boy doesn't get groovin' till well after Cinderella was due home. Spinetta is a teeny side street, so ask if you get lost. The cover varies depending on business, but is usually between 40 and 70F.

Not your average bar/eatery, **Cherry's Café** *(35 quai des Etats-Unis; Tel 93/138-545; Any bus to Masséna; 7pm-midnight daily; V, MC)* loves its theme nights. Shake a leg at the Soirée Espagnole and Soirée Paris Nuit. They've also got live music, eats, frothy cocktails, no cover charge, and an outdoor patio facing the ocean where most of the action happens. Dress casual-cool and you'll fit right in with the local groovies.

CULTUre ZOO

Paris it ain't. Still, Nice has some great cultural treats. Musée Matisse and Musée National Message Biblique Marc Chagall in Cimiez are both worth the trip (the Chagall is really a must). The 40F Art Pass gets you into any museum in Nice for seven days. You could also go all-out for the 130F version that provides access to every cultural sight in town, but you really need to be into sightseeing.

Musée Matisse *(164 ave. des Arènes, Cimiez; Tel 93/810-808; Bus 15, 17, 20, 22 to Arènes; 10am-5pm, Wed-Mon, closed Tue; 20F, 15F if under 25):* Over 400 permanent works spanning the career of the famous color-saturated Henri.

Musée National Message Biblique Marc Chagall *(16 ave. Docteur Ménard; Tel 93/538-720; Bus 15 to Cimiez; 30F, 25F if under 25, discount rate for all on Sundays):* Chagall's mural-sized paintings make you just stand and stare and keep on staring. Go!

Musée d'Art Moderne et d'Art Contemporain *(Promenade des Arts; Tel 93/626-162; Bus 3-10, 16, 17, 25 to Promenade des Arts; 10am-6pm Wed-Mon; 20F, 15F if under 25):* The exterior of this steel structure alone should whet the palate for the Warhols, Lichtensteins, and installation pieces inside.

Musée des Beaux Arts *(33 ave. des Baumettes; Tel 92/152-828; 10am-12pm/2-6pm Tue-Sat; 15F, 25F):* The most classic collection in town, with works from the 17th to the 20th centuries, including Degas paintings and Rodin sculptures.

down and out

Oh, what to do when the cask runs dry. Well, for starters, don't sit down at a table to eat—food to go will always save you a centime or two. Try the cheap local specialties [see *eats*, below], or do like the truly hard-up and buy a baguette and fruit in the morning to munch on all day, then have a decent dinner.

You can lie on the beach all day for nothing, and you won't work up an appetite on your towel. Galleries won't put a dent in your wallet, nor will strolling about the **Parc du Château** [see *hanging out,* above]. And of course you can always nurse a coffee over the course of an afternoon spent people-watching at a cafe, in traditional cheapskate fashion.

modification

So you want to come back from Europe looking like a whole new person? Well, eating French pastries til you drop will do it, and so will getting a freshly cut tattoo! The world-renowned **House of Pain** *(32 rue de la Préfecture; Tel 93/800-041; Any bus to Masséna; 11am-7pm Mon-Sat, 9am-midnight in Aug; No credit cards)* hasn't considered changing its name, despite the implications. The shop is as antiseptic as you can get, with no eating, drinking, or smoking allowed. Too bad—getting a tattoo is one time you'd want a shot of anything within reach. Prices start at 400F for tattoos, or 200F for body piercing, and soar from there. These guys are pros, with a wide selection of designs, and they're not averse to improvising if you want something a little bit special.

great outdoors

If the hard work of tanning your front and back evenly becomes too much for you, take a breather with some water sports. All the Nice beach clubs offer the usual parasailing, water skiing, tubing, and jet skiing. Prices are basically the same everywhere. A standout is the **Plage Beau Rivage** *(107 quai des Etats-Unis; Tel 06/03-02-63-66),* where Lionel or one of his other bronzed buddies will set you up during daylight hours with an ocean kayak (70F/hour), a paddle boat (100F/hour), or a jet ski (300-400F/half hour). You have to prove you're 17 to ride the jet ski, preferably with a driver's license. Have the guys explain how to ride in English, Spanish, Portuguese, Italian, or even a broken Russian.

If you're bent on diving in the Mediterranean, there are plenty of places dying to take you out on a boat. The **Centre International Plongée de Nice** *(Quai Lunel at the Port; Tel 92/004-386; Bus 1, 2, 9, 10 to Port; 9am-6pm Mon-Sat; www.poseidon-nice.com, poseidon.nice@*

wanadoo.fr; No credit cards) takes out first-timers and experienced divers. Their first-time dive, called a "baptism," will put you back 140F; regular dives are 190F. Boats leave at 9:30am and 3:30pm. If you have any doubts about your comfort or safety underwater, don't do the slightly unnerving, no-certification-required "introductory dives" that are standard in Europe and totally illegal in the U.S.

If it's a particularly hot day and your skin is just too red to lay on the beach, stroll up the rue Rosetti to enter **Le Parc Château** (*Tel 04/93-85-62-33; 10am-5:30pm daily Oct-Mar; 9am-7pm daily Apr, May, Sept; 9am-8pm Jun-Aug*). From this entrance you have to hike a little, take a right after going up the stairs and follow signs for La Cascade, the waterfall. It's the most refreshing moment, looking out at Nice's tile roofs, cafe awnings, and stretch of beaches while the man-made falls sprinkle your back.

Not a beach bum? Came here in the winter? Find out about alpinism, rockclimbing, mountain biking, canoeing, paragliding, skiing, and snowshoeing possibilities at the **Club Alpin Français** (*14 ave Mirabeau; Tel 04/93-62-59-99; Any bus to Masséna; 4-8pm Mon-Fri*). They have a changing calendar of events and excursions, and in ski season they have Sunday outing/lessons. A little tricky to find: If you leave from the train station, walk away from the shore up avenue Malausséna, then take a right on Mirabeau. You may not have thought it, but 60–90km from Nice there are quite a few ski spots: Mercantour, Aurón, and Isola. For general info on skiing in the area, call the **Comité Régional Cote d'Azur** (*39 rue Pastorelli; Tel 04/93-80-65-77; Bus 1, 2 to rue Pastorelli*).

If you can tear the sales boys away from their televised boarding competitions, the aptly named **Space Cadet** (*5 ave. Gustave V; Tel 93/825-066; Any bus to Masséna; 10am-7pm daily; V, MC*) is a convenient place to rent blades—45F will get you four hours of blading pleasure; a full day is 75F. If you're into the skating thing, this is a cozy little hangout with plenty of puffy/shiny gear and info on the scene. To show off your skills, skate down the Promenade des Anglais, where beginners stumble on cracks and old pros twirl on a franc. The promenade is also the best place for a jog any time of day. If you'd rather move a little faster, you can rent a bike or moped from **Nicea Location Rent** [see *need to know,* below]. For a scenic ride, nothing beats the beach for views. For a shadier locale, pedal into the hills of Cimiez and gaze at the grand old villas.

STUff

Rue Masséna has all the designer shops you can sink your little teeth into, if you have cash to burn. Skip the street vendors selling African art, pick up a wacky wall-walker or two, and check out these more offbeat buys.

Head for the **main flea market on Cours Saleya** in Vieux-Nice from 8am till 5pm on Mondays and pick up anything from old cameras to junk jewelry. The daily **vendors' market on rue Jean Médecin** is so-so, mainly cheap perfume and stuff made from Laura Ashley–esque fabric. There are Provençal goodies aplenty, but most of these throw-aways, like quilted toilet seat covers and milkmaid skirts, might not even qualify as kitsch.

If you thought wacky wall-walkers got left behind in the '80s, think again. A new and improved weighted version has popped up on the streets of Nice that is far more advanced in its ability to successfully crawl down a wall or window: better, faster, stronger! Have a go.

▶▶BOUND

There's nothing worse than needing a good read and finding nothing but shelves of Harlequin Romances. That's not the case in Nice. There are three stores—count them—right around place Masséna. English books are notoriously expensive everywhere in Europe, so expect to pay 30 percent more than you normally would.

The Barnes & Noble–ish **FNAC Book and Record Store** *(Centre Nice Etoile, 2nd Floor, blvd. Jean Médecin; Tel 92/177-738; Bus 1, 2, 4, 5 to rue Pastorelli; 10am-7pm Mon-Sat; V, MC)* is the biggest. Though most of their stock is in French, they carry a bunch of books, maps, and guides in English. You can find *Bridget Jones's Diary* alongside Faulkner.

Librairie Masséna *(55 rue Gioffredo; Tel 93/809-016; Any bus to Masséna; 9am-7pm Mon-Thur, till 7:30pm Fri, Sat; V, MC)* has a decent selection of books—better than a newsstand, but no Chekhov or Bukowski. There are a rather astounding number of Agatha Christies, though.

The Groupe Sorbonne *(23 and 37 rue Hôtel des Postes; Tel 93/137-797; Any bus to Masséna; 10am-7pm Mon-Sat; V, MC, AE)* has a few college-bookstore shops around the place Masséna. Look for *The Pillars of Hercules* by Paul Theroux—it's set in this very same region. The number 37 location opens a half-hour earlier and has paper supplies too.

▶▶HOT COUTURE

If you plan on hitting the *salon des jeux* at **Casino Ruhl** [see *casinos,* above] you'll have to dress the part. If, like most travelers, you sacrificed the dressy stuff when you packed, pass by **Zara** *(10 ave. Jean Médecin; Tel 93/137-610; Bus 1, 2, 4, 5 along Jean Médecin; 10am-10pm Mon-Sat; V, MC, AE)* for chic men's and women's wear. Sexy little dresses run about 350 to 450F, and suave linen pants for men are 400F.

If you need to accessorize, the Parisian jewelry shop **Agatha** *(17 rue de France; Tel 93/887-644; Bus 3, 6, 7 to Meyerbeer; 10am-7pm Mon-Sat, closed Sun; No credit cards)* has fun faux rhinestone and cut-glass pieces. Handmade beaded headbands are 150F, and all sorts of jewelry and hair stuff range from 30 to 600F. Check out the great nail polish colors.

For the best, softest tees you'll ever wear, sail on down to **Petit Bateau** *(13 rue Masséna; Tel 93/820-500; Bus 3, 6, 7 to Meyerbeer; 10am-7pm Mon-Sat; V, MC, AE)*. Okay, it's actually a kids' store—so what? Grab the hip packaged shirts (30-90F) that sell for nearly twice as much in the States.

At **Rubber Way** *(6 rue Rosetti; Tel 04/93-80-38-50; Any bus to Masséna; 3-7:30pm Mon-Sat)* you can choose from some *really* hot couture that you may *have* to have to give you that added boost of confidence when you walk into the casino. The steel cup and chain bras, dog collars, and leather cat suits may be too much, but there are some more, um, *concealable* items on the racks as well.

eats

It's easy to scrimp in Nice and live off food from vendors and markets. Try the *socca*, a chickpea pancake-type thing with pepper. Anytime you sit your ass down in a chair it will cost you, so if you need to save change, take food to the promenade instead. A whole rotisserie chicken is yours for the bargain price of 20F at almost any food stand on rue des Piétons. Lunch and dinner hours can be strictly adhered to, so plan to eat on the local schedule—it's damn hard to find a sit-down lunch after 2:30pm.

▶▶CHEAP

The cheapest sit-down places don't serve Niçoise cuisine. The aptly named **Asia Express** (*5 rue Halevy; Tel 93/383-313; Bus 14 to Halevy/Promenade des Anglais; 10am-11pm daily; 18-36F per entrée; V, MC*) is an ugly cafeteria serving yes, Asian cuisine, but don't let the ambience steer you away—it pulls in a Chinese clientele, which is always a good sign. Walk right by the nasty sandwiches in the front window, head to the counter, and pick from about 30 different Chinese entrees. Ginger chicken has just the right bite to it, the egg rolls are a must, but maybe skip the scary balls of paste labeled "dessert."

In the center of Vieux-Nice, **Bar Antoine** (*27 rue de la Préfecture; Tel 93/852-957; Any bus to Place Masséna; 7am-8:30pm daily; 20-25F sandwiches; No credit cards*) stays open all day. The *panini Antoine* has tapenade (a tasty olive spread), mozzarella, and bacon all melted together in a gooey-but-delicious greasy treat. Take your food to go, or park it at the tables outside for a sit-down affair.

▶▶DO-ABLE

Try not to wear leopard print or your friends won't be able to find you in **The Jungle Art's** (*6 rue Lépante; Tel 04/93-92-00-18; Any bus to Masséna; Food served noon-2pm/7-10:30pm Mon-Sat, bar open till 1-3am Fri-Sat; Entrées 65-95F; V, MC*). Nights eating kangaroo and ostrich get a little savage once the cave-like downstairs opens. Resident DJs cue up dance and ambiant vinyl during dinner and continue through the night, when dancing can burn off calories for the chic 20s–30s herds.

The Frog (*Rue Milton Robbins; Tel 93/858-565; Bus 11b to Gustave; 5:30pm-midnight Mon-Sat; 68-85F per entrée; V, MC, AE*), a little Tex-Mex restaurant on the outskirts of Vieux-Nice, with its stucco walls and heavy wood furniture with big cushions, looks like the kind of place you could hang out in for hours, and many people do. There's live music on weekends and enough flavored margaritas to keep you sippin' all night. A little questionable on authenticity, the cuisine is sort of like Mexican food that someone's grandma might cook up: easy on the spices and with a salsa that's missing an ingredient or two.

Do the tapas thing at the hipster hideaway **Indyana** (*13 rue Gustave Deloye; Tel 93/806-769; Any bus to Masséna; 8pm-midnight Mon-Sat; 28-*

110F tapas; V, MC). Pasqual owns this groovy little eatery with glowing orange chandeliers and "tree of life" sculptures on the wall, where the 20-to-35 artsy crowd munches on Italian ravioli and spiced polenta. Wine flows all around and everyone glances at the door every few minutes to make sure no one important arrives unnoticed. The music is loud, so don't expect to whisper words of love to your sweetie.

▶▶SPLURGE

For the true French bistro experience, head to the charmingly informal **Le Bistrot des Viviers** *(22 rue Alphonse Karr; Tel 93/160-048; Bus 38 to Alphonse Karr; Noon-2:30pm/7-10:30pm; 75-200F per entrée; V),* a few blocks just northwest of the place Masséna, where you read the menu off a chalkboard and the owner sits down with you to discuss anything from the food to politics. The house foie gras is excellent, if you're into pâté, and the salmon tartare is fresh and tasty. There's even a tank of lobsters in the front so you can choose your own critter.

A totally different type of splurge is to be had at **La Siècle** *(31 promenade des Anglais; Tel 92/144-400; Bus 6 to Magnan; Noon-2:30pm/7-10:30pm; 180-250F prix-fixe menus; V, MC, AE),* a chic brasserie that looks out on the water. Careful you don't fill up on the great dense sourdough they start you off with—you definitely want to leave enough room for the cod in citrus butter and the artichoke risotto. Waiters are dressed formally, so this might not be the best place to show off your favorite cutoffs, and if it's summer, a reservation wouldn't hurt.

crashing

▶▶CHEAP

If you're in Nice for a one-night party followed by an early-morning train ride, get some melatonin and try to stay close to the station—it may be worth an extra 15 minutes of sleep in the morning. **Hôtel de la Gare** *(35 rue Angleterre; Tel/Fax 04/938-875; Any bus to Masséna; Desk hours 7am-8pm; 115-175F single, 155-220F double, 240-260F triple, 320F quad; V, MC)* dishes up a hostel-type atmosphere at good prices. The cheaper rates are for rooms without showers, but if the grunge has accumulated to an alarming level, pay the 13F and have yourself a wash, dammit. For non-scrimpers, a room complete with bath runs about 60F more. They speak English at the desk, and rooms are basic: clean and smallish, no AC. Breakfast (bread and coffee) is yours for 20F extra.

Hôtel Belle Meunière *(21 ave. Durante; Tel 93/886-615, Fax 93/825-176; Bus 38 to Ave. Durante; Desk open 24 hours; 76F dorm beds, 120F single w/shower, 160-240F double w/shower; V, MC)* is a converted villa even closer to the station and a bit prettier to look at. Lots of folks head to the outdoor courtyard to meet fellow travelers or just to kick back with a book. Check-in is 10:30am. There's a TV in the breakfast room, and no lockout or curfew to kill your buzz. For the best deal, ask about the apartment behind the hotel that has three shabby-but-clean double rooms (190F/each) with a shared bathroom and kitchenette.

If those are full, try **Hôtel Baccarat** *(39 rue d'Angleterre; Tel 04/93-88-35-73, Fax 04/93-16-14-25; 184F single, 227F double, 280F triple, 360F quad, 425F 5-person, 85F dorm, all with private bath; V, MC)*, next door to the train station.

▶▶DO-ABLE

Right on place Masséna is Madame Feri's **Hôtel de la Mer** *(4 place Masséna; Tel 93/920-910, Fax 93/850-064; Any bus to Masséna; Desk open 24 hours; 300-380F double; V, MC, AE)*. Madame Feri becomes your second mom; she takes care of her guests and gives discounts for stays of more than two nights. Rooms vary in size, but all have minibars and TV, and five have AC. The big rooms overlooking the park are simple and airy. Three people can squeeze into one room for a slightly increased price.

Closer to the beach and right on the rue des Piétons, the slick **Hôtel Harvey** *(18 ave. de Suède; Tel 93/887-373, Fax 93/825-355; Bus 6 to Congrès; Desk open 24 hours; 330-450F double; V, MC, AE)* has a more formal atmosphere with a polished look: brass beds, glass coffee tables, etc. The rooms have satellite TV, minibars, and AC that works well. It seems like Harvey could charge a lot more and get away with it, but bless him for not doing so. You can't get rowdy at 4am here, but falling into these beds after a late night is worth it.

Also doable are **Hôtel du Centre** *(2 rue de Suisse; Tel 04/93-88-83-85, Fax 04/93-82-29-80; www.nice-hotel-centre.com; 220F single, 270F double, peak season; 140F single, 180F double, low season; kitchen open for use, breakfast 25F; V, MC, AE)*, a 5-minute walk from the train and 10-minute walk from the beach; **Hôtel Plaisance** *(20 rue de Paris; Tel 04/93-85-11-90, Fax 04/93-80-88-92; 340-350F single, 450-465F double, 450-465F twin, 520-560F triple Apr-Oct, all with private bath; 290F single, 360F double, 360F twin, 435F triple, Nov-Mar, all with private bath; breakfast 25F; V, MC, AE)*, also a 5-minute walk from the train station (in the center of town); **Hôtel de la Buffa** *(56 rue de la Buffa, bus 23 to Buffa-Gambetta; Tel 04/93-88-77-35, Fax 04/93-88-83-39; www.hotel-buffa.com; 380-400F single or twin, small double 280-320F, 420-450F double, 400-500F triple, peak season, all with private bath; double or triple for 1 person 220-300F, for 2 people 250-350F, for 3 people 400F, for 4 people 450F, low season, all with private bath; breakfast 35F; V, MC, AE, DC)*, in the center of town near the Promenade des Anglais; or **Hôtel l'Oasis** *(23 rue Gounod; Tel 04/93-88-12-29, Fax 04/93-16-14-40; www.hotel-oasis-nice.com.fr; 350-390F single, 420-490F double, 550-630F triple, all with private bath; Breakfast 48F; V, MC, AE, DC)*, in the center of the city near the ocean (10-minute walk from the train station).

▶▶SPLURGE

Hotel prices in Nice go from reasonable to ridiculous with not much in between. That said, **Hôtel Masséna** *(58 rue Gioffredo; Tel 93/854-925, Fax 93/624-327; Bus 4 to Gioffredo; Desk open 24 hours; 650-890F double; V, MC, AE)* has prices that are less appalling than those of its beachfront peers. Right in the center of things, just off place Masséna, this is a luxury hotel with its own restaurant, room service, and rooms that would be considered suites in other hotels. The terraces have great views of Nice.

Also consider **Hôtel Gounod** *(3 rue Gounod; Tel 04/93-16-42-00, Fax 04/93-88-23-84; www.gounod-nice.com; 655F single, 780F double, 1115F triple, Apr-Oct, all with private bath; 425F single, 560F double, 765F triple, Nov-Mar, all with private bath; Breakfast included; V, MC, AE, DC),* just a couple of steps from the sea and, of course, the shopping district.

need to know

Currency Exchange You can buy **French francs** (F) at **Thomas Cook Bureau de Change** *(3 locations: 13 ave. Thiers; 2 place Magenta; Gare S.N.C.F. de Nice, 12 ave. Thiers),* but it charges a rip-off commission of 8 percent; competitors charge 4 to 6 percent.

Tourist Information There are two offices in town, one right at the main train station *(Gare Nice Ville; Tel 93/870-707; 8am-7pm Mon-Sat)* and one right on the water near the center of town *(5 promenade des Anglais; Tel 92/14-48-00; 9am-6pm Sept-June, 8am-8pm July, Aug).*

Public Transportation All local buses start and stop at the **Station Centrale** *(10 ave. Félix Faure; Tel 93/165-210)* in place Masséna. Rides are 8.5F each way, and you pay on the bus. Most lines run until 12:15am.

wired

www.nice-coteazur.org: General info, plus up-to-date lists of sporting and cultural events.

www.alpix.com/nice/: Unofficial site by former Nice resident—good maps and links.

http://rivieragay.interspeed.net: Listings of gay hot spots in Nice and around the Riviera.

The one-person cubicles at **WEB Nice** *(25 promenade des Anglais; Tel 93/88-72-75; 10am-8pm Tue-Sun; 30F per 30mins; V, MC)* make socializing a bit difficult, but you'll still run into English speakers who are far from home.

There's a new Internet spot in town every time you go back to Nice. An easy one to get to with a fast connection, **Free Internet** *(16 rue Paganini; 04/93-168-981; Bus 38 to rue Durante, or any bus to Gare or Masséna; 9am-10pm daily; planetcyber@wanadoo.fr; 39F per hour, 15F coffee and quarter hour, 29F Bfast and half hour, 39F snack and half hour; No credits cards)* is down the street from the train station and isn't exactly free. Signs will lead you to it. Nautical theme and organic coffee brighten the morning up with American keyboards (important here if you took typing in high school).

Bike/Moped Rental Nicea Location Rent *(12 rue Belgique; Tel 93/824-271; Bus 12, 30 to Gare; 9am-6pm Mon-Sat, till 2pm Sun; Bikes 120F/day, mopeds 290-340F/day; MC, V)* is near the train station, and true to their name, they rent mopeds and bikes.

American Express *(11 promenade des Anglais; Tel 93/165-353; 9am-9pm daily in summer, till 8pm daily rest of year)*.

Health/Emergency Ambulance: *15*. **Hôpital Saint Roche** *(5 rue Pierre Devoluy; Tel 92/033-375)* has 24-hour emergency service, and **Nice Médecins** *(Tel 93/524-242)* is a 24-hour on-call doctor service.

Pharmacies Pharmacie de la Place Masséna *(56 blvd. Jean Jaurès; Tel 93/856-545; V, MC)* is centrally located and open 24 hours daily, except 8am to 7pm Sun.

Telephone City code: *4*. For local calls buy a phone card at the post office.

Airports Nice Côte d'Azur Airport *(Tel 93/213-012)* is 5 miles west of Nice. Buses run from 6am till 10pm. A direct 10-minute bus ride into the city center costs 21F; a bus ride to the Nice S.N.C.F. train station costs 8.5F. Cabs into the city cost 120 to 200F.

Airlines Air France *(Tel 93/188-989)*, **British Airways** *(Tel 93/21 4-701)*.

Trains The main station is **Gare Nice Ville** *(Ave. Thiers; Tel 36/353-535)*. If you know that you're staying near the center of town, get off at **Gare Routière** *(5 blvd. Jean Jaurès; Tel 93/800-870)*.

Bus Lines To skip town on the bus, go to **Gare Routière** *(5 blvd. Jean Jaurès; Tel 93/800-870)*. Bus depart from the Intercars Terminal.

Laundry Laverie du Mono *(8 rue Belgique)* is a self-service laundry. Wash and dry for 40F/load. **Le Panier à Linge** *(8 ave. Durante; Tel 93/887-840)* will do the work for you, 50F/4 kilos. Both laundries are within a few blocks of the Gare Nice Ville.

Internet See *wired*, above.

everywhere else

monaco

It's hard to tell who's native to Monaco and who's just visiting—the hip spots are the hip spots whether you live here or are just dashing through. Also, if people have jobs here (other than serving tourists), they certainly seem to keep odd hours: Cafes are full at all times of day with groups of locals who sit for hours smoking and ordering after-lunch drinks in dizzying succession. The Monaco scene is pretty old-school, with large numbers of middle-aged partyers from all over Europe crowding in. No one will look at you funny if you're 18 and in Monaco for the first time, but you might not fit the Monaco standard of sleek and sophisticated.

Despite its über-hyped rep of being the cleanest and most polished city around, Monaco ain't pretty. The roads and ramps on the ocean side screw up the harmony of Monaco and Monte Carlo, the buildings in town are big and ugly, and the gorgeous villas set far back in the hills aren't accessible unless you have a car and plenty of time. Still, that doesn't take away from the spectacularly lush parks that lead to the **Place Casino** [see *down & out,* below], with their fountains, statues, and lakes, or the royal-looking exterior of the **Monte Carlo Casino** [see *casinos,* below]. And in general, Monaco is notoriously well-organized. You can count on times being accurate for any event and the **Direction du Tourisme** [see *need to know,* below] has more information than you'll ever use.

Try to avoid descending on this little principality during the second week in May when **Le Grand Prix de Monaco** takes over the town. It's a big hassle to compete for your dinner—not to mention a place to sleep—with all of Europe's racing fans.

The glamour and glitz of Monaco are only a 20-minute train ride from Nice, but keep an eye on the time, since trains stop running around midnight.

monaco

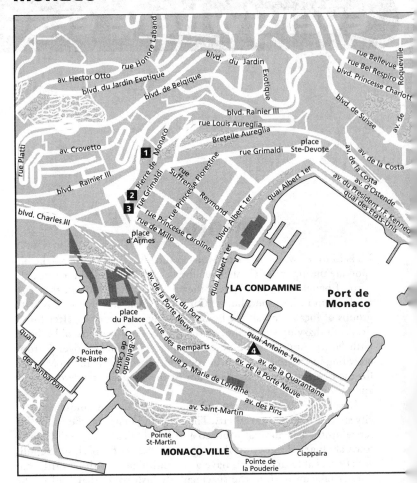

neighborhoods

There's no visible division of areas in Monaco. **The Port** is a central point, equidistant from **Monaco Ville,** the train station, and the town of **Monte Carlo.** To get to the sea, walk south from the train station and stop when you see the big yachts. Up the hill from the Port lies Monte Carlo, a coil of streets that all lead back to the famed **Monte Carlo Casino** [see *casinos,* below]. The in-town **Direction du Tourisme** [see *need to know,* below] is located nearby on boulevard des Moulins, so it's not a bad idea to make this an early stop.

The medieval town of Monaco Ville is situated on "the Rock," on the southwest side of the Port. Built atop the Rock, the **Palais de Monaco**

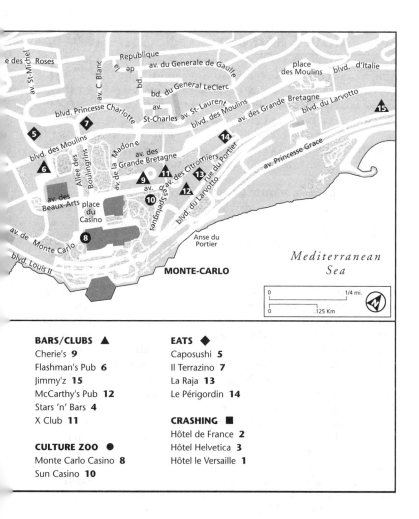

BARS/CLUBS ▲
Cherie's **9**
Flashman's Pub **6**
Jimmy'z **15**
McCarthy's Pub **12**
Stars 'n' Bars **4**
X Club **11**

CULTURE ZOO ●
Monte Carlo Casino **8**
Sun Casino **10**

EATS ◆
Caposushi **5**
Il Terrazino **7**
La Raja **13**
Le Périgordin **14**

CRASHING ■
Hôtel de France **2**
Hôtel Helvetica **3**
Hôtel le Versaille **1**

[see *culture zoo*, below] rises an imposing 200 feet above the sea. The Port has a few good night and day spots like **Stars 'n' Bars** [see *bar, club, and live music scene*, below]. Take a gander at the ridiculous collection of yachts and ships that drop anchor in Monaco. To the west of the port, a 10-minute walk takes you to Fontvieille, the less-visited sports complex area of Monaco. **Fontvieille** hosts the **Saturday Flea Market** [see *stuff*, below] and is home to the **Princesse Grace Rose Garden**.

hanging out

Regular Joes and Josephines who don't want to pay 300F per person to sit at the **Monte Carlo Beach** play at the sandy public and private stretches of **Larvotto Beach.** Though not huge, and no better than decent, Lar-

down and out

If you're out of dough, Monaco's a little rough, but you can still go to **Larvotto Beach,** where the sun will make you drowsy. Take along some water and treat yourself to a cheap game of ping-pong or fooz.

To beat the heat, **Fontvieille** and **Princesse Grace Rose Garden** (to the west side of the port), open sunrise to sunset, have no entry fee and, in season, over 4,000 roses to sniff [see *hanging out,* below].

Hanging out at **Monte Carlo Casino** [see *casinos,* below] may not be something to do all day, but between the slots room, the gardens outside, and Häagen-Dazs on the corner, you can make an afternoon of it.

votto is a great place to meet fellow travelers. "Crowded" is a word that comes up often when describing it, especially in the summer, when crowds can get overwhelming. There's usually a friendly mix of families, students, and travelers all looking forward to a dip in the ocean. The requisite topless ladies and Speedo'd lads strut their stuff here, but there are plenty of modestly clad beachgoers as well, so you won't feel out of place if a thong is not your thing. When hunger strikes, there's no need to go far: Larvotto is lined with cafes that actually serve decent non-junk food. **Miami Plage** *(Larvotto; Tel 93/509-416; 8am-7pm daily; No credit cards)* has crispy pizzas for 40F and a hollowed-out pineapple fruit salad for 35F. On the public end, they've got ping-pong, fooz, and volleyball courts for rent. You can use the outdoor showers and bathrooms for free, but indoor showers and changing rooms will run ya 10F.

To stay out of the sun but in the spotlight, head to the notoriously unsnobby **Stars 'n' Bars** [see *bar, club, and live music scene,* below], where Hard Rock Cafe meets boardwalk arcade/boat club by the port, to nosh on some passable "good old American food." It's a bit on the cheesy side, with a Western Americana theme in hot competition with Formula 1 racing paraphernalia, but the outdoor cafe stays open all day—a plus, since most eating establishments like to shut down at 2 pm, just when midday hunger sets in, and stay closed to 7 pm. If you happen to meet up with fellow wanderers, there's nothing like a "bucket of beer" (100F) to waste the day away.

Professional people-watchers will take to the overpriced **Cafe de Paris** *(Place du Casino; Tel 92/162-124; Bus 1 to place Casino; 9-3am daily; V, MC, AE)*, perched right in front of the **Monte Carlo Casino** [see *casinos,* below]. Sip pricey mimosas for hours at an outdoor table amid the Monte Carlo gentry and sink into the cushioned chairs like you're right at home. The giant olives they give out free with drinks make for a nice little snack. Cafe de Paris and the Casino are planted on the manicured place Casino, a good spot for a photo op or meeting up with friends.

bar, club, and live music scene

Monte Carlo is probably the only place around where clubs outnumber restaurants. Dressing well is pretty much customary across the board— funky club gear loses out to the more tastefully sleek all-black. Ladies can be spotted in gravity-defying backless tube tops. Jeans are generally scoffed at, even though they're "technically" pants (as opposed to the truly declassé shorts). Best to drag out that one pair of wrinkled dress pants and steam them in the shower before you hit town. In the summer it's tough to side-step cover charges, and drink prices increase by 30 percent. Drink at a pub in the evening and head to the clubs about 1:30 or 2am when things get started. After-hours junkies will meet their match in Monaco—all the clubs stay open past 4am, so chances are you'll run out of energy before they do.

Avenue des Spelugues is home to five or six bars/clubs—if you want variety it's a good place to plant yourself on. This street is right off place Casino [see *hanging out,* above], so you can do a pre-club warmup at the slot machines. But don't come to Monaco expecting to see the latest in indie rock. There's not a whole lot on the live music tip that's worth men-tioning; lots of bars advertise "live rock" that turns out to be the kind of background noise you can deal with only after many drinks. **Bienvenue à Monaco,** which you can pick up at the **Direction du Tourisme** [see *need to know,* below], lists all the nightspots in town and tells you if they've got live sounds.

Cherie's Cafe *(9 ave. des Spelugues; Tel 93/303-099; Bus 1, 6 to Ave. des Spelugues; 7pm-6am daily; No credit cards)* is a cafe by day and bar/club by night. Live rock, dance, or jazz music moves in several nights a week, usually around 11pm—call or stop by to see what nights have live stuff. Tons of rich-looking twenty- and thirtysomethings come in to dine on the Italian-French-Asian fusion cuisine, then stay planted on the terrace until the wee hours ordering bottle after bottle of wine. This is definitely one of the hipper nightspots in town, so it's worth going to, whether there's music or not. Champagne is 60F a glass, but you can opt for 20F beers instead.

McCarthy's Pub *(7 rue du Portier; Tel 93/258-767; Bus 1 to Portier; 5pm-5am daily; AE, V, DC)* attracts more backpackers and beer lovers than locals, as most Irish pubs abroad do. It's kind of a cookie-cutter ver-sion of every Irish pub you've ever been in, with traditional Irish tunes and rock happening on Friday and Saturday nights. Try a big ole Guin-ness (30F), or an Irish Eyes, Irish Kiss, or Michael Collins (all 50F), and sink into the green vinyl pub cushions with a smile.

Flashman's English Pub *(7 ave. Princesse Alice; Tel 93/300-903; Bus 1 to Casino; 11-5am daily; No credit cards)* isn't in any of the Monaco brochures, so it tends to be a more low-key, local hang. The interior has that seedy-bar feeling, but there's an outdoor deck if you need some air.

fashion

Monaco is a place where you'll need to break out the fancy duds. Next to Yves Saint-Laurent and Chanel, shorts and Birks will look decidedly out of place. It's like putting a sticker on your head telling the world that you're new in town and have no idea how to behave. Even during daylight hours, Monégasques are ready to transform themselves from beachgoers to club/casino-goers in the blink of an eye, so be sure to have some versatile clothes on hand. You can be more casual in Nice and Cannes. Nice favors cyborg-esque stretch-fabric club gear and anything black for nighttime. Cannes requires a mix of Nice and Monaco fashions. More upscale spots like **Jane's** [see *bar, club, and live music scene* in **cannes,** below] will make you feel like you're in Monaco, but you can wear shorts to local bars and not be snubbed.

The beaches in these three Riviera cities are all about wearing as little as possible. As a somewhat bizarre alternative to losing that bikini top, many women wear a one-piece and roll it down until it's nothing more than a bottom. Strange as that sounds, they think nothing of it. The men here love them Speedos, even thongs. If you choose to go native, don't forget to apply sunscreen to those areas that haven't seen the sun in a while.

All types congregate here, from twentysomething businessmen popping in after work to a younger crowd later at night. There are live shows on Friday and Saturday nights, a decent mix of British/American pop. Fosters draughts are 20F and a "big" whiskey is 50F.

On avenue des Spelugues, along with a string of bars and clubs, lies the strobe-light-and-disco-ball scene at **L'X Club** *(13 ave. des Spelugues; Tel 93/307-055; Bus 1, 6 to Ave. des Spelugues; 11pm-4am daily; No credit cards)*. Get over the purple-and-green carpet and get down with the disco/techno vibe. Wait till the outdoor terrace opens for drinks at 9pm; you'll pay less than you do inside. One of the more down-to-earth places here, the club is not into turning away good business, so there are no worries about having the door barricaded by bouncers. On weekends, 70F is supposedly the cover, but they charge at their discretion, so dress nice and hope for the best.

One of the two clubs in the Sporting d'Eté complex, **Jimmy'z** *(26 ave. Princesse Grace; Tel 92/162-277; Bus 4, 6 to Larvotto; 11:30pm-5am daily in summer, closed Mon, Tue in winter; No credit cards)* takes the vibe of X Club, modernizes it, and serves it up on a much larger scale. Along with the attached **Paradise Club,** this complex can handle hundreds of people. If you don't know where to go late-night, search no longer; everyone under 50 heads out here after midnight. Again, it doesn't hurt to look nice; you'll fit in better wearing black pants than jeans, and it might get you out of the 100F cover charge.

The club at **Stars 'n' Bars** (*6 quai Antoine I; Tel 93/509-595; Bus 1, 2, 6 to Princesse Stephanie; 11pm-5am daily; www.isp-riviera. com/starsnbars*) is 99 percent attitude-free: There's no dress code, and they won't even look at you funny for wearing flip-flops. The floor upstairs, above the bar, is devoted to all-night dancing, with plenty of space to groove the night away to a mix of techno, hip-hop, and dance vibes. When you get sick of dancing, try your skills in the game room downstairs, or sneak off for a late-night e-mail session at the club's terminals. The 100F cover charge gets you one drink; after that you'll pay 45F for beer and 60F for cocktails. At more reasonable hours, this is the place to watch World Cup soccer or whatever Grand Prix is on that week—the picture wall of sports heroes should put you in the mood. During the day, draughts are still 25F, so the 100F bucket (six mugs' worth) is a deal.

casinos

One glance at the glamorous, Rococo **Monte Carlo Casino** (*Place Casino; Tel 92/162-000; Bus 1 to Place Casino; Slots from 2pm, salon des jeux from 8pm; No credit cards*) makes Casino Ruhl [see *casinos* in **nice,** above] look like the Holiday Inn. To catch a piece of the action here, you'll need to dress well (no shorts, jeans, or sandals) and be over 21, with a passport ID to prove it. It's 50F just to enter the *salon des jeux* where the exotic dancer/convicted spy Mata Hari performed in the early 1900s.

If you're looking for a more laid-back scene, try the **Sun Casino** (*12 ave. des Spelugues; Tel 92/162-123; Bus 1 to Ave. des Spelugues; Slots from 11am, salon des jeux from 5pm; No credit cards*). There's no dress code until 8pm, and even after that it's just a no-shorts policy.

Cafe de Paris [see *hanging out,* above] also has a slots room with no dress requirements, located below the cafe.

arts scene

The *Major Events* brochure at the **Direction du Tourisme** [see *need to know,* below] lists all the goings-on around town. *Bienvenue à Monaco,* also at the well-stocked Direction du Tourisme, gives a rundown of movie theaters and nightly opera/theater events. The **FNAC** ticket outlet (*Centre Commercial "le Metropole," 17 ave. Ligure; Tel 93/108-199; Bus 1 to Casino; 10am-7:30pm Mon-Sat; V, MC*) has tickets to everything that matters.

The **Théâtre Princesse Grace** (*12 ave. d'Ostende; Tel 93/253-227; Bus 2 to Ostende Supérieur; Office open 10am-12:30pm/3-6:30pm Mon-Sat*) offers everything from plays to symphonies to variety shows. Go to their ticket office to find out the details, or check in *Major Events*. Tickets are 115F for students and 230F for everyone else.

festivals and events

For details on the following events, check *www.monaco.mc* or *www.visiteurope.com/Monaco/Monaco03.htm*.

International Fireworks Festival *(end of of July):* Takes place at the Port, but you can see the fireworks from anywhere. Find a smooching partner, and make your own.

International Circus Festival *(held yearly, often in Feb; Tel 92/05-23-45):* The best of the clowning and acrobatics world comes to Espace Fontvieille. Call for details.

Formula 1 Grand Prix *(second week in May; Tel 93/15-26-00)* is one of a handful of coveted Grand Prix titles. Testosterone-pumped racing fans flock to Monaco for it.

Monte Carlo International Tennis Open *(Apr):* It's a hard-court tournament that players use as a warmup for the main season.

Film freaks can get their fix at the outdoor **Cinéma d'Eté** *(Le Sporting d'Eté, 26 ave. Princesse Grace; Tel 93/258-680; Bus 4, 6 to Larvotto Plage; 9:30pm daily June-Sept).* Films are shown in their original language, so call ahead to make sure that language is English.

If air conditioning's more your thing, the **Cinéma Le Sporting** *(Sporting d'Hiver, place Casino; Tel 93/308-108; for program and info, Tel 08/36-68-00-72; Bus 1 to Place Casino; 6:15pm Fri, 6:15, 9:15pm Mon, Thur, 9:15pm Sun)* shows films in their original languages.

culture zoo

Palais Princier *(Place du Palais; Tel 93/251-831; Bus 1, 2 to Monaco Ville; 9:30am-6:30pm daily, 10am-5pm in Oct; 30F admission):* Its architectural magnificence gives you a glimpse of how Monaco's royal family, the Grimaldis, live.

Jardin Exotique *(Blvd. du Jardin Exotique; Tel 93/152-980; Bus 2 to Jardin Exotique; Open daily May 15-Sept 15, 9am-7pm; open daily Sept 16-May 14, 9am-6 pm or sundown; 40F admission adults, 19F students):* One of the world's greatest cactus collections, as well as caves of stalactites and stalagmites, 60 meters down.

The **Monte Carlo Casino** [see *casinos,* above] is to Monaco what the Eiffel Tower is to Paris.

the great outdoors

If water sports are what you crave, go down to the east end of **Larvotto Beach** and look for a sign...specifically, the one that reads, in French, "Water Sports." There's no phone, so just show up between 8am and

7pm. Pedal-boat rentals are 100F an hour, jet skis are 600F an hour, and parachuting is 350F.

Aside from the beach, Monaco isn't really an outdoorsy or fitness-focused place. You never see joggers here. If you really need a workout, try the **Columbia Tonus Center** *(7 ave. Princesse Grace; Tel 93/250-327; Bus 1 to Portier; 9am-9pm Mon-Fri, till 2pm Sat; No credit cards)*, a small gym/spa with cardio equipment, weights, and plenty of body-pampering treatments. A one-day gym pass is 130F, and a half-hour massage is 190F.

Ambitious walkers can go for the pretty 90-minute walk along the coast to Cap Martin. If you'd rather stay in the city, hike around the **Exotic Gardens** [see *culture zoo,* above] or traipse through the olive groves in **Parc Princesse Antoinette** *(Entrance at blvd. de Belgique or blvd. du Jardin Exotique).*

STUff

If you've been rereading the same novel for several weeks now, **Scruples** *(9 rue Princesse Caroline; Tel 93/504-352; Bus 1, 2 to Place des Armes; 10am-5pm Mon-Sat; No credit cards)* can help. It's right near the train station, and they carry fiction and those oh-so-helpful phrase books for non-French speakers.

The bizarre **Boutique Formula 1** *(13 rue Grimaldi; Tel 93/158-244; Bus 1, 2 to Place Sainte Dévote; 10am-6pm Mon-Sat)* is a kick. You probably won't be purchasing authentic race car suits, or a car-shaped coffee table, or a full-size Formula 1 car/sculpture, but it's fun to look.

Cheap but chic outfits for the ladies can be grabbed at **Morgan** *(5 rue Grimaldi; Tel 93/256-358; Bus 1, 2 to Princesse Florestine; 9:30am-7:30pm Mon-Sat; V, MC, AE)*. Put together a quick casino-worthy ensemble from Morgan's own fashions that range from 100F to 400F.

The Monaco Stroll

You can case this joint in a couple of hours, easy. Start at the train station and walk downhill, following signs to the **Palais de Monaco** on "the Rock." Hike the steps and take a tour of the royal palace, or bypass it and walk down the **avenue du Port** to **boulevard Albert I** and check out the **Monaco Port.** From the Port take **boulevard Albert I** to **avenue d'Ostende.** Hang a left up **avenue de Monte Carlo** to the **place Casino.** The curvy **avenue des Spelugues,** right past the casino, hits **avenue Princesse Grace,** which is the coastal road running along all beaches. **Larvotto Beach** will be on your right. Hang out on the beach and rest your tootsies.

The only flea market worth a visit is **Les Puces de Fontvieille** *(Bus 5, 6 to Fontvieille; 9am-6pm Sat)* at Espace Fontvieille, an open-air venue near the heliport in Fontvieille.

eats

If you've tired of the regional cuisine, **Stars 'n' Bars** [see *bar, club, and live music scene,* above] has burgers and American-style breakfasts. For cheap eats, the pickings are slim. There are no vendors selling *socca* (a crêpe made of chickpea flour sold on the streets of Nice), but the beach cafes like **Miami Plage** [see *hanging out,* above] do have simple fare that won't bust your wallet.

▶▶DO-ABLE

A sandwich place by day and sushi restaurant by night, **Caposushi** *(6 Impasse de la Fontaine; Tel 93/255-952; 8am-8pm Mon, till midnight Tue-Sun; No credit cards)* is a good pit stop for breakfast, lunch, or dinner. They offer giant platters of sushi for 130 to 170F and, for those who like their meals cooked, pressed sandwiches for 39 to 74F. At night the bar gets going with 65F bottles of sake and a more obvious Japanesey atmosphere.

It doesn't look like much from the outside, but the secluded patio at **Il Terrazzino** *(2 rue des Iris; Tel 93/502-427; Bus 1 to Place Casino; Noon-2:30pm/7:30-11pm Mon-Sat; 60-80F per entrée; V)* has flowers and grapevines hanging overhead and an Italian peasant decor. Choose from 30 varieties of tea: Marco Polo is a Chinese mix of fruit and flowers, pharoan is perfumed by the fruits of the Nile delta. Graze at the tasty antipasto buffet, or go for one of the Italian-country-cookin' entrées.

La Raja *(27 rue du Portier; Tel 93/50-7-14; Bus 6 to Portier; 70-95F per entree; Noon-2pm/7-11pm; V)* dishes up some damn fine Indian cuisine. The vegetable samosas and the spicy chicken vindaloo are both excellent. Beeline past the Italian joints on this street straight for Raja. Indoors, Raja is plain but nice; the outdoor balcony is fine, too, if you don't mind noise.

▶▶SPLURGE

Gourmet palates will appreciate Gérard Baigue's **Le Périgordin** *(5 rue des Oliviers; Tel 93/300-602; Bus 1 to Ave. des Spelugues; Noon-2pm/8-10:30pm, closed for lunch Sat, closed Sun; 78-168F per entrée; gbaigue@monaco.mc; V, MC, AE).* The business card features a dead duck, and, lo and behold, duck is the dish of choice. The duck pâté, the filet of duck cooked in crisp pastry on a bed of apples, and the foie gras are all excellent. There are seafood and other meat dishes, too, but this is not a place for vegetarians. The three-course 60F prix-fixe lunch is one of the best deals in Monaco. Ask Gérard for a recommendation from his excellent wine selection.

crashing

Monaco does have a few hotels whose prices won't make you cringe. But, as in Nice, room rates go from do-able to unreal with not a whole lot in between.

beat the system

Those in the know visit Monaco but stay in nearby Beaulieu Sur Mer, less than 10 miles west. Beaulieu's beach is a hell of a lot less crowded than Monaco's, and it's much easier to find cheap lodgings. And don't think that Beaulieu is some dingy suburb—far from it. Gorgeous villas along the ocean and manicured parks in town make it a much more inviting place than Monaco, with a following of Europeans who know that.

Be sure to check train times: trains from Beaulier Sur Mer to Monaco and back are limited and run at limted times. Less than a five-minute walk from the train station is the quaint **Hôtel Marcellin** *(18 ave. Albert I; Tel 93/01-01-69, Fax 93/01-37-43; Desk hours 7am-10pm; 180-360F double; V, MC)*, where you follow a winding staircase up to the rooms in this villa-turned-hotel. Madame Rostaldo is a doll—she'll practice French with you and loves to serve up cocoa with breakfast. The doubles range in price because some have baths and others don't—either way, they're much cheaper than in Monaco. If Marcellin is booked, ask Madame Rostaldo to recommend an alternative.

▶▶CHEAP

Bunking up with 4 to 10 people isn't exactly living with the princess. But this clean youth hostel will leave you extra francs to play the slots with a French, Brit, or Japanese buddy you meet at **Centre de Jeunesse Princesse Stephanie** *(24 ave Prince Pierre; 377/ Tel 93/508-320, Fax 377/93-25-29-82; reception & curfew 7am-midnight Sat, till 1am Jul-Aug; info@youthhostel.asso.mc, www.youthhostel.asso.mc; HI card not required, ID required, age restriction 16-31 years; 80F bunk breakfast included; no cards)*. Thank god there's a five-night limit, otherwise you'd break the bank at the casino.

▶▶DO-ABLE

Hôtel Helvetica *(1 rue Grimaldi, 1st floor; 377/Tel 93/302-171; 42-04-70F double; hotelhelvetica@monte-carlo.mc, www.monte-carlo.mc/helevicta.fr; V, MC, AE)*, near the train station, is a cute little pink hotel with balconies in front and a lovely salon du thé inside. The plain rooms are totally sufficient, with AC and TVs, and the price includes breakfast. For Helvetica, definitely book ahead; it's a hell of a lot nicer than most of the cheapish hovels and fills up fast. They can also do triples and singles, so ask about pricing.

Right down the street, **Hôtel de France** *(6 rue de la Turbie; Tel 93/302-464, Fax 92/161-334; Bus 1, 2 to Place Sainte Dévote; 370F single,*

480F double, 590F triple; hotel-france@monte-carlo.mc, www.monte-carlo.mc/france; V, MC) is a lot more modern and Holiday Inn–looking than Helvetica. It's big, with 26 track-lit rooms and plenty of amenities, like cable TV and AC. Breakfast—if you call bread and butter and coffee breakfast—is included.

Still in the same one-block radius of reasonable-hotel-land, **Hôtel le Versailles** *(4-6 ave. Prince Pierre; Tel 93/507-934; Bus 1, 2 to Place Sainte Dévote; 400-600F double; V, MC, AE)* has similar decor to Hôtel de France. The desk attendant wears a suit, and the furnishings are modern. There's an elevator, and rooms have a TV and mini fridge, and all have showers.

▶▶SPLURGE

If you just can't resist dropping a wad of dough to sleep next door to the rich (if not famous), make a reservation well in advance at the **Hôtel du Louvre** *(16 blvd. des Moulins; Tel 04/93-50-65-25, Fax 04/93-30-23-68; www.monte-carlo.mc/louvre; 740-840F single, 830-930F double, 1200F triple, regular season; 840-940F single, 930-1030F double, 1300F triple, July-Aug; V, MC, AE, DC),* where plush linens, luxurious private baths, minibars, color TVs, direct phone lines, air conditioning, and attentive—but always discreet—service will remind you why most people give up backpacking the minute they can afford fancy hotels. The location, 10 minutes from the beach, appeals to those who love the whole Riviera scene but prefer to get away from the madding crowd when the sun goes down. Don't get too excited about the possibility of spying on any reclusive celebs, though; the walls here are specially soundproofed to protect guests' privacy.

need to know

Currency Exchange Though independent, Monaco uses the **French franc (F). Crédit Foncier de Monaco** *(11 blvd. Albert 1 and 6 rue Felix Gastaldi)* is a trustworthy spot to change money.

Tourist Information Direction du Tourisme *(2a blvd. de Moulins, Tel 92/166-116)* will supply all the info you need.

Public Transportation There are five bus lines running through Monaco from 7am till 9pm. You can pick up a bus schedule at the train station or Tourist Office (see above).

Bike Rental Auto Moto Garage *(7 rue du Millo; Tel 93/501-080).*

American Express *(35 blvd. Princesse Charlotte; Tel 93/257-445; 9am-6pm; Closed Sat afternoon and all day Sun).*

Emergency Ambulance: *18;* Police: *17.* For medical emergencies, call **Centre Hospitalier Princesse Grace** *(Ave. Pasteur; 97/989-769).*

Pharmacies After hours, call *93/253-325* for doctors and pharmacists on call. **Pharmacie Ferry** *(1 rue Grimaldi; Tel 93/392-196; 8am-12:30pm/2-7:30pm Mon-Sat).*

Telephone Country code: *377.*

Airports The **Nice-Côte d'Azur International Airport** is 22km (13 miles) northwest of Monaco. A shuttle service operates daily between the airport and Monaco (8am-7:30pm).

wired

Monaco hasn't caught on to the whole concept of Internet cafes/bars as a social prospect. You basically have two options:

The Aussies who run **Gale Force Computing** *(13 ave. Saint Michel; Tel 93/50-20-92; 9:30am-12:30pm/2-5:30pm Mon, Tue, Thur, Fri, 9:30am-11:30am Wed; gfc@monaco.mc)* have only one terminal yet, but they're thinking of expanding. It's right near the **Direction du Tourisme** [see *need to know,* above], so they get traffic from visiting travelers wanting to "phone" home.

The other e-mail option is back at good old **Stars 'n' Bars** [see *bar, club, and live music scene,* above]. Along with having almost everything else you need to sustain yourself, Stars has two Internet terminals.

For info about the city, go to: ***www.monaco.mc*** or ***www. visiteurope.com/Monaco/Monaco03.htm.***

Trains Monaco is served by express trains from Paris and Rome that stop at **Gare SNCF** *(Ave. Prince Pierre; Tel 36/353-535)* and **Gare Routière** *(Place des Armes; Tel 93/856-181).* Buses 4 and 5 stop at the **Gare SNCF,** and taxis *(Tel 93/505-628)* hang out there, too.

Bus Lines Out of City Buses leaving Monaco only travel to the Nice airport. From there you can transfer to a bus to downtown Nice. Fare from Monaco to Nice is 80F one-way, with stops at Monaco's **tourist office,** the **Monte Carlo Grand Hotel,** and the **Meridian Hotel.**

cannes

Nice is an ancient city that absorbs its visitors; Cannes is a chic resort town that exists for them. Yes, there are the absurdly glitzy beachfront shops and hotels, but most evidence of film-festival splendor is gone by the time that last private jet splits. What remains is a classy, expensive Riviera town with amazing ocean views, narrow village streets, and plenty of good food and drink. Speaking of the infamous **Cannes Film Festival,** unless you somehow finagle a ticket to the screenings (which, by the way, is close to impossible), don't expect to schmooze with movie stars strolling down La Croisette. If you're not above star-worship, you can pick up celebrity glamour shots in local camera shops and maybe pass them off as your own. For most of us though, it's best to skip the festival.

cannes

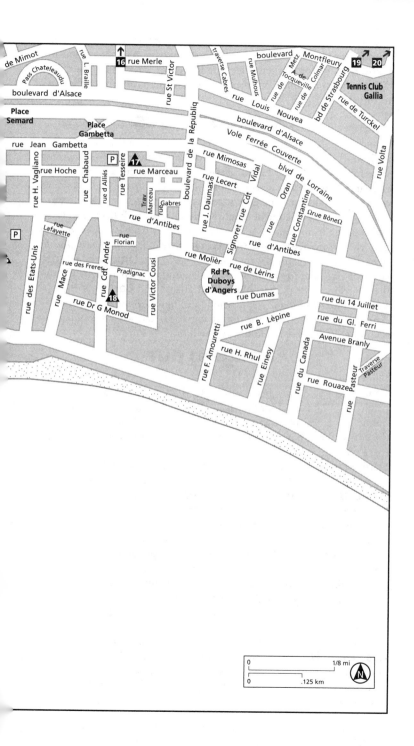

When locals leave town, they often rent out their apartments—that's how serious the hotel shortage is. Business travelers sometimes even end up in Nice for lack of lodging in Cannes. In case you're the walk-around-in-a-bikini type, be forewarned: Fines are doled out for inappropriate attire. The beach is one thing, but they prefer that you have your clothes on in this town.

neighborhoods

The part of Cannes you'll want to see is relatively small. A five-minute walk south of the train station puts you at the beach and the sweeping waterfront promenade, **La Croisette.** Basically all the restaurants, bars, etc., are along the five streets between the station and the beach. You could take it all in in one action-packed day, on foot. Along the water-front are the out-of-control expensive hotels and the **Palais des Festivals,** home to the better of two tourist info offices [see *need to know,* below], and the **Casino Croisette/Jimmy'z** [see *bar, club, and live music scene,* below]. You'll want to come here to visit **Limelight Records** [see *bar, club, and live music scene,* below] and pick up a week's worth of fliers for local/area parties. **Midnight Blues** and **Carling's Pub** [see *bar, club, and live music scene,* below] are right around the corner. The center of town—between the station and the beach—is a mix of bars and boutiques with a few restaurants thrown in.

hanging out

Life here revolves around the beach by day, and Le Suquet and **Casino Croisette** [see *casinos,* below] by night. The beach is so-so, with a small patch of public sand alongside umbrella-covered, hotel-owned sand. The public beach sees mostly tourists and families who want a few hours in the sun without having to pay the all-day fees at beach clubs. Despite space constrictions, it's still the most popular spot to laze the day away. **Eden Plage** (*La Croisette; Tel 93/946-436; Bus 8 to Henri IV*) is the most reasonable in price. It has simple umbrellas and chairs and a friendly staff. **Plage du Martinez** (*73 La Croisette; Tel 92/987-422; Bus 8 to Miramar*), with its cotton-candy pink umbrellas, is the crème de la crème of beach clubs, with the ritziest clientele.

You could easily miss **Cafe Poet** (*15 rue Félix Faure; Tel 04/93-39-59-58; Bus 8 to Gare Maritime; 7:30am-midnight daily; No credit cards*) were it not for the celeb photos hanging outside the store next door, glossy finishes gleaming. Poet is a people-watching coffee shop/bar with a *cave à bières,* serving up 30 beers from a handful of countries (20-36F). It's also a busy little joint where locals stop in for morning coffee and travelers plop down for a beer.

The only park-ish area is the **Square Maritime** in front of **Palais des Festivals.** It's good for picnicking or nursing a beer at night while you wait for **Jimmy'z** [see *bar, club, and live music scene,* below] to open its doors. Older locals spend their days here, and students from abroad have picnic lunches on the grass.

bar, club, and live music scene

The live music scene in Cannes is sort of lacking—train it to Nice if music is your thing—but a few worthy bars and hoppin' dance clubs make you want to stick around. **Limelight Records** (*13 rue Saint Antoine; Tel 92/991-664; Bus 8 to Mairie; 1:30pm-midnight daily; vedrenn@aol.com; No credit cards*) has the word on concerts, parties, and shows for the hip-hop and house crew. It's kind of a frightening place at first, but the staff will answer any questions you have about the invites or flyers stacked on the windowsill.

Midnight Blues (*Ave. Georges Clemenceau; Tel 93/396-626; Bus 8 to Mairie; 9pm-2am daily; No credit cards*) is plastered with black lights that don't quite mesh with the old-style bar decor. There's no cover, even for the Wednesday live rock nights, which often feature British bands doing a blues-rock mixture. Live shows sometimes show up on other nights too, so ask.

At **Carling's Pub** (*7 rue Georges Clemenceau; Tel 93/383-406; Bus 8 to Mairie; 7pm-2:30am daily; No credit cards*), the mostly local crowd spills out the door to sip drinks on the sidewalk outside. This tiny pub is packed, but if you push through to the bar, you'll be rewarded with 30F whiskeys. Girls, be prepared to be shamelessly scoped out by boys who lean on the bar waiting for their next victim. Reggae is the music of choice, and they also do live stuff on Thurday nights—usually rock or reggae played by a local band.

five things to talk to a local about

1. The **Nice Jazz Festival** is always a popular topic. Most locals have something to say about the new and old schools of jazz.
2. **How much money you lost** at the casino last night and how you can't figure out why you're going back tonight....
3. Ask about the **Monaco Grand Prix** and feign some knowledge of Formula 1 racing. Mention Williams/Renault and BMW and nod a lot.
4. Express disgust at all the **packed cafes** that cater to people-watchers (do this preferably in a cafe while people-watching).
5. Insist that **French art** died with Manet and see whether anyone will contradict you (a good way to get tips on contemporary shows—or a cold shoulder).

Studio 13 *(233 ave. du Docteur Picaud; Tel 93/062-990; Bus 9 to Beausite; Hours and days vary; No credit cards)* is home to jazz concerts, films, techno parties, and even *Flamenco Dancing Nights.* There's something going on four or five nights a week at this classy culture house that likes to feature fresh sounds from young musicians. Tickets are usually 20 to 35F. Monthly "jam sessions" are free, and anyone can pull up a chair and rock out. Pick up Studio 13's schedule at the **tourist office** [see *need to know,* below].

There are Irish pubs and there are Irish pubs. This one is the real thing, with a hefty wooden bar and plenty of taps flowing—the bouncer even has an Irish accent. **Morrison's** *(10 rue Teisseire; Tel 92/981-617; Bus 17 to Gare; 5pm-2am daily; AE, V, MC)* kicks up its heels to traditional Irish music (excellent) on Wednesdays and rock, blues, and jazz (not so excellent) on Thurdays. The party starts early with lots of backpackers wandering in for a before-dinner mug of draught, and the medium-sized space gets packed by midnight as more locals stop by. Beers are 30F, and seven different Irish whiskeys run 28 to 45F. Happy hour is between 5 and 8pm, when *all* beers, plus selected wines and spirits, are half price.

For the ultimate club experience, you have to hit **Jimmy'z** *(Casino Croisette, Palais des Festivals; Tel 93/381-211; Bus 8 to Palais des Congrès;*

festivals and events

It goes without saying that the big event in Cannes is the **International Film Festival** that takes over the city in mid-May. To catch a glimpse of celebrities walking down the red carpet to a screening that you can't get a ticket for, loiter outside the **Palais des Festivals** *(Esplanade Georges Pompidou, La Croisette, on the east end of Cannes Harbor; Tel 93/39-01-01).* A very few passes are up for grabs at Palais de Festivals. If you can somehow produce evidence of being a film student, they might take pity on you. *Might.*

The more accessible **Festival International d'Art Pyrotechnique,** where you'll see the best that video animation has to offer, takes place at the Palais des Festivals over seven days in July and August. Go to *www.cannes-on-line.com* to find out exact dates.

There are also various two-day music festivals throughout the year, but the dates change annually, so it's best to check the aforementioned website.

The Cannes leg of the **Miss France Competition** is held in mid-June. Tickets are 100F and you can call *93/90-37-97* for more info. Yeah, we're kinda kidding.

10pm-5am Wed-Sun, daily July, Aug; No credit cards), where the bouncers are big and the dresses are tight. The cover charge of 100F with drink is waived for groups of ladies. People of all ages head to Jimmy'z, so expect to party with 18-year-olds and divorcees alike—as well as a large Arab contingent. Groove on the disco atmosphere: bars, mirrors, strobes, the whole bit. Music varies within the pop/'80s range with the occasional techno beat surfacing. You enter Jimmy'z via elevator inside the casino.

The women at **Jane's** *(Hôtel Gray d'Albion, 38 rue des Serbes; Tel 92/997-959; Bus 8 to Hôtel Gray d'Albion; 11pm-whenever Thur-Sun, daily July, Aug; No credit cards)* tend to like their fellas older and loaded. Jane's has its share of pretty people dressed in the latest designer duds lounging on cushioned seats and chaises and getting up for the occasonal twirl. It's 100F to mingle with this exclusive crew. Thurdays are theme nights, and Sundays are free for girls. You should call and make a reservation before showing up.

With plenty of velvet couches and curtains, it's easy to sink into **The Loft** *(6pm-2am daily; No cover),* above **Le Saloon** *(13 rue Docteur Gérard-Monod; Tel 93/394-039; Bus 8 to Gray d'Albion; 11am-2pm/7pm-whenever daily; No credit cards).* Drinks are 40F, and the DJ kicks it with a little house and hip-hop. Cool it with the twenty-to-thirty crew and bust a move on the dance floor. Le Saloon downstairs is a Tex/Mex theme party with sombreros on the wall alongside cowboy hats. They serve up some tasty tostadas (63F) and a mean margarita (40F). You can start off at Le Saloon and head up to The Loft around midnight.

casinos

Good news—you don't have to travel to Monaco for a gambling fix! **Casino Croisette** in the Palais des Festivals is open for business daily from 5pm till 3am. Don't dress like a schmuck—no shorts, no sandals— and do plan to shell out the 70F entry fee for the gaming room. If you're just a slots player, the coin room is open from 10am till 4am, and there's no entry fee.

arts scene

The art galleries in Cannes are all business. Most of them are part of a hotel, with longer hours than those other galleries, and everything is marked with a price tag. As a rule, the work isn't too interesting, and several galleries sell nothing but copies of Renoirs, Picassos, and other big names. If you want art, make the 20-minute train trip to Nice. A hangout tip: **Jane's** tends to attract the fashion/artsy people at night, and **Studio 13** [see *bar, club, and live music scene* above, for both] has a little bar/cafe where the younger artists hold court.

There are festivals throughout the year that spotlight the performing arts [see *festivals & events,* above]. The **Palais des Festivals** *(Tel 92/986-277; Bus 8 to Palais des Congrès; Ticket office 10am-7pm Mon-Fri)* is where you should go to find out specifics and buy tickets for theater, music, or dance. The brochure *Le Mois à Cannes*—pick it up at the **tourist info**

office [see *need to know,* below]—gives a day-by-day account of the cultural goings-on.

It's a little disheartening to walk past three or four theaters in the heart of town and find that they have no movies in English. **Cinéma de Valbonne Sophia Antipolis** *(Salle des Fêtes du Village; Tel 93/129-188; Hours vary)* breaks the rule, showing mainstream films in English about once a week. Look for the telltale *VO* (original language) mark. Call ahead for scheduling, or get their flyer from the tourist office [see *need to know,* below].

gay scene

Cannes is the place to go on the Riviera if you're gay. The **tourist info office** [see *need to know,* below] has all kinds of flyers and 'zines on gay living on the Riviera including a little free one called *le zoom—le guide de la vie gay and lesbian,* which lists some hot spots. To get a head start, visit **Le Groupe Action Gay Côte d'Azur** at ***www.services.worldnet. fr/gagca*** and see what's happenin' during your stay, or call **Centre Gay Associatiff** *(Tel 04/93-60-03-00).* For info on the June *Festival du Film G&L,* call *Tel 04/93-92-42-00.* By the way, the French here seem to think that gay = male: All the gay posters, flyers, etc. feature pictures of gay men—not a lady in sight.

Le Zanzibar *(85 rue Félix Faure; Tel 93/393-075; Bus 17 to Maréchal Joffre; 6:30pm-dawn daily; No credit cards),* near the Palais des Festivals, has a really laid-back cafe atmosphere in the evening, both on the outdoor patio and in the indoor bar area. The music is on, but it's not overwhelming—this is the kind of place where you could actually have a conversation. Later in the night it's more barlike, but there's still no cover, and drinks run 20 to 50F. Zanzi is sort of the "must-go" gay bar in Cannes; it's been around forever. A few women are on the premises, but this is a mostly male joint.

At **Twiggy Records** *(3 rue des Suisses; Tel 04/939-91-32; Bus 8 to Mairie; 3pm-12:30am Tue-Sat; no cards)* you could be in a comic book, sitting in furry zebra chairs, looking at Spiderman on the ceiling and Barbie in a fan cage. The shop is a cafe that offers more than house, techno, acid jazz, and easy-listening vinyl. You can munch on a John Steed salad (35F) and a banana milkshake (25F), and view plenty of guys with piercings and plastic frame glasses for hours.

modification

If you decide to commemorate your trip to Cannes with a brand-new tattoo, Danny at **Black Star Tatoo** *(39 rue Georges Clemenceau; Tel 92/992-055; Bus 8 to Mairie; 10am-7pm Mon-Sat; No credit cards)* will advise you on *tatouage* and cut some skin if you decide to go for it. But be prepared to wait—Danny is a man in demand. His mom hangs out and chats with customers to the wail of country music in a shop filled with skull & crossbones paraphernalia. Tattoos are 200F and up; piercings are 50 to 400F.

The great outdoors

Scan the beachfront for the pink umbrellas of **Plage du Martinez** [see *hanging out,* above] and walk out on their dock to the water sports arena. Here you can choose from water skiing (150F), parachuting (350F), or tubing (200F). They're open for business from 8am to 8pm.

For runners or speed walkers, **La Croisette** [see *hanging out,* above] is wide enough to get in a workout while you take in the ocean view. City streets are not such a good option; they're narrow and fairly crowded at all times of day.

If you're feeling *Top Gun* (you know: you feel the need, the need for speed), bikes and mopeds can be rented at **Alliance** [see *need to know,* below].

stuff

Bypass the cheap stands on rue Maréchal Joffre and stop at the **Saturday Flea Market** *(Across from the Palais des Festivals; 9am-6pm daily).* It's a mess of booths overflowing with used books, furniture, geodes, and jewelry. For photo buffs, there's a pretty amazing used camera section. If you know what to look for, you could make out big. Down the pedestrian street **rue Meynadier** sit rows of vendor stands, shops, a bakery, a deli, and a big fresh produce stand at number eight. The souvenir, accessory, and clothing goods you can buy here aren't outrageously priced, and it's a fun, colorful walk to meander along.

▶▶**IMPULSE BUYING**

The designer gadgets at **Davis** *(50 rue d'Antibes; Tel 04/93-99-09-05; Bus 7 to Rue des Serbes; 10am-7pm Mon-Sat; V, MC, AE)* are the types of things you can pretend you need. Metal bean-shaped lighters that mimic Elsa Peretti designs are only 50F. One of the best trinkets is a bullet-shaped key chain that unscrews to reveal a tiny plastic vial for storing pills or a pair of earrings. You can buy some of the cooler Film Festival Shirts here too.

For perfumes and all sorts of accessories, head for **Reminiscence** *(56 rue d'Antibes; Tel 93/394-076; Bus 7 to Rue des Serbes; 10am-7pm Mon-Sat; V, MC).* Add to your club gear with their modern and funky, glitzy earrings and rings *(300-400F).*

▶▶**DUDS**

Do you have a hard time finding that perfectly fitting pair of jeans? Maybe you'll have luck at **Liberto** *(Rue Tony Allard; Tel 04/93-38-62-09; Bus 17 to Gare; 10am-1pm/2:30-7:30pm Mon-Sat; AE, V, MC, DC),* a denim and sportswear store for men and women. They have a small but groovy stock of urban wear, Miss Sixty, and Liberto jeans, or perhaps you need a new pair of No Name sneaks (490F) to warm up those dancing feet.

Bill Tornade *(Galerie Gray d'Albion; Tel 93/689-891; 9:30am-12:30pm/2:30-7:30pm Mon-Sat; V, MC, AE)* serves up original designs that add a funky flair to modern styles for guys and gals. Men's pants go from casual to dressy to rubberized, for 800 to 1,000F. Embroidered chiffon chemises are a hot pick for women at 395F.

An inconspicuous shop, **Le Grand Bazar** (*90 rue d'Antibes; Tel 04/93-39-13-13; 9:30am-7:30pm Mon-Sat; V, MC, AE*) is filled with the works of hip French designer Isabelle Marant, along with Paul and Joe and Stella Cadente. Cotton skirts with paisley trim (650F) can easily go from the beach to a club, and summery silk dresses are 500 to 2,000F. Bazar also has beaded handbags, jewelry, and outrageous bikinis.

▶▶BOUND

There aren't a whole lotta English bookstores in Cannes, but there is the **Cannes English Bookshop** (*11 rue Bivouac Napoléon; Tel 93/994-008; Bus 8 to Gray d'Albion; 10am-1pm/2-7pm Mon-Sat; No credit cards*). They have posters for museum exhibits on the door and a selection of English titles, from Martin Amis to Jean Genet in translation.

Eats

▶▶CHEAP

Sifting through the typical markets for decent food can be a chore. An inconspicuous bread shop named **Paul** (*572 rue Meynadier; Tel 93/381-559; 8am-7:30pm Mon-Sat, 8-1:30pm Sun; No credit cards*) sells tasty sandwiches (15-20F) and all sorts of breads. Several doors down on the walking-only rue Meynadier, there's a big fruit market open daily from 9am till 5pm.

Pizzeria (*9 place de l'Hôtel de Ville; Tel 92/986-080; Any bus to Mairie; Noon-2:30pm/7pm-Midnight daily; piazza@iname.com; 54-78F per entrée; V, MC*) is a pretty big place, with tables clad in—what else—

down and out

Technically, it won't cost anything to take a peek inside the **Casino Croisette** [see *casinos*, above] slots room. If you don't trust your immunity to gambling fever, get some 2F chips and try your luck at slots or video poker.

Walk along **La Croisette** [see *hanging out*, above] and try not to be envious of the luxury clientele in their luxury hotels. If it gets too hot, duck into one of said establishments and amble around their shopping arcade.

For more of an exercise, head up **rue Montfleury,** northeast of the **Gare SNCF.** You'll be on tree-lined streets that wind uphill and make you think Cannes might not be a bad place to own a house—the villas in this neighborhood will make you drool. What could be more cathartic when you're broke?

red-and-white-checked vinyl. The pasta is made fresh on the premises, the pizza crusts are perfectly crisp, and the spaghetti à la Fellini, with tomatoes, olive oil, pimentos, and basil, is extra tasty.

▶▶**DO-ABLE**

Even if you're a meat eater, the vegetarian dishes at **Montgard** *(6 rue Maréchal Joffre; Tel 93/399-838; Bus 27 to Maréchal Joffre; Noon-2pm/7:30-10pm Mon-Sat; 118F, 160F prix-fixe menus; V, MC)* make it worth a visit. Mustard-colored walls and Provençal furniture provide a cozy little atmosphere, and the veggie-filled ravioli with thyme butter is super.

Le Stratège *(16 rue de Suquet; Tel 04/93-99-92-93; Bus 8 to Mairie; menu 125-170F; V, MC)* is a tight squeeze of tables inside through the red curtains and out on the terrace, where you can enjoy French dishes of beef and tuna, some with a international flavor like curry. The guys from **Limelight Records** [see *bar, club, and live music scene,* above] run the restaurant and bring their hip-hop and cool house over.

crashing

▶▶**CHEAP**

Cannes has two youth hostels that are close to town and curfew-less. The hike down to the beach for either is 10 to 15 minutes—to the train station is maybe five minutes. **Le Chalit** *(27 ave. Gallieni; Tel/Fax 93/992-211; Bus 4 to Gallieni; Desk hours 8:30am-1pm/5-8:30pm; 85-90F dorm beds; No credit cards)* is the more homey of the two, but they do have an 11am to 5pm lockout. Rooms have a maximum of four people with shared bathrooms, and the price includes a shower. Chalit is in the suburbish neighborhood above the train station, which is not the most visually stimulating, but Internet access [see *wired,* below], laundry, and groceries are close by. Ask about discounts on cruises, mopeds, and cars.

Centre International de Séjour et de la Jeunesse *(35 ave. de Vallauris; Tel/Fax 93/992-679; Bus 6V to Sardoux; Desk hours 9am-12pm/5pm-8pm; 70-80F dorm beds; http://perso.wanadoo.fr/hostellingcannes; No credit cards)* is bigger and slightly closer to town, with a nice garden outside for playing cards or whatever, and a living room with a TV if the heat gets unbearable. Rooms sleep four to six people with shared bath facilities, and the friendly staff will help you get oriented.

▶▶**DO-ABLE**

If you like the idea of a cheap hotel in the hip part of town, **Hôtel Chanteclair** *(12 rue Forville; Tel/Fax 93/396-888; Bus 5 to La Ferrage; Desk hours 9am-7pm; 140-170F single w/o shower, 170-230F single w/shower, 200-260F double, 240-330F triple, 280-440F quad; No credit cards)* is for you. There are no cockroaches crawling around—at least I didn't see any—and there's a pretty courtyard with orange trees, but all 15 rooms are small and the beds are narrow. Monsieur Déflene is down with travelers' needs: If you're leaving late on the day you check out, he lets you leave your bags in a locker so you can come back and shower, and he has no problem with two people squeezing into a single if they can't afford anything better.

• Can't hack carrying that pack? Stay right across from the train station at the quirky **Hôtel du Nord** (*6 rue Jean Jaurès; Tel 93/384-879, Fax 92/99-28-20; Bus 17 to Gare; Desk hours 7am-1pm; 180-250F single, 270-300F double, 360F triple, 430F quad; No credit cards*). Rooms are unpredictable in this place; you might find that your bathroom is bigger than the bedroom. Most rooms have TVs, but be prepared to sweat in summer, this baby isn't air conditioned.

▶▶**SPLURGE**

If you have the means, staying in a quiet villa with its own pool is always nice. **Villa Toboso** (*7 Allée des Oliviers; Tel 93/382-005, Fax Tel 93/68-09-32; Bus 4 to Pont République; 350-740F double rooms/suites; V, MC, AE*) is a 10-minute walk from town, but so worth it. You won't find a party here—and they won't be too thrilled if you make one—but it's definitely nice to come back to rose-scented sheets and antique furniture after a night on the town. Some of the suites and rooms have kitchenettes and terraces or balconies, and all have cable TV and AC.

To have the fairy-tale Cannes experience, stay right on the water at **Hôtel Bleu Rivage** (*61 blvd. de La Croisette; Tel 93/942-425; Bus 8 to Malmaison; www.cannes-hotels.com; 500-1,000F double; V, MC, AE*), the only oceanfront hotel whose per-night prices are relatively bearable. You'll pay more to get an ocean view, but every cool, whitewashed room has a breezy feel, with AC, TV, and phone.

need to know

Currency Exchange Office Provençal (*17 ave. Maréchal Foch; 8am-7pm daily*) will exchange your money without charging a rip-off fee.

Tourist Information Two offices: one at the **Gare SNCF** train station (*Tel 93/991-977; 9am-6pm Mon-Sat*), the other in the lobby of **Palais des Festivals** (*Tel 93/392-453; 9am-6pm Mon-Sat*). In July and August these offices are open on Sundays, too.

Public Transportation The bus depot is at **Place de l'Hôtel de Ville** (*Tel 93/39-18-71*), and tickets for local buses are 7F.

Bike/Moped Rental Alliance (*19 rue des Frères; Tel 93/386-262; Bus 8 to Palais des Congrès; 9am-7pm daily*) has bikes for 80F per day, mopeds for 250F per day, and cell phones for 99F per day.

Emergency Police emergency: *18;* medical emergency: *Tel 93/383-938.* **L'Hôpital des Broussailles** (*13 ave. des Broussailles; Tel 93/697-000*).

Pharmacies AS Cannes (*9 rue Louis Braille; Tel 93/39-35-85; 8:30am-12:30pm/2:30-7:30pm Mon-Sat, closed Sun*) is open during regular pharmacy hours. On Sundays or after 7:30pm, call the main pharmacy hot line at (*Tel 93/683-333*).

Telephone Country code: *33;* city code: *4.* For local calls buy a phone card at the post office. **AT&T:** *Tel 00/990-011;* **MCI:** *Tel 08/00-99-00-19;* **Sprint:** *Tel 08/00-99-00-87.*

Airports The **Nice Airport** (*Tel 93/213-030*) is only 20 minutes to the northeast and is serviced by a bus that runs every 40 minutes (48.50F). Or take a cab for about 350F.

wired

Cannes is a bit behind on the cyber tip. There's only one place to e-mail friends back home. **Microbasik** *(18 rue Mimont; Tel 93/38-82-32; Bus 17 to Gare; 2:30-7:30pm Mon, 9:30am-12:30pm/2:30-7:30pm Tue-Sat; seywert@infonie.fr)* is close to the youth hostels and about a five-minute walk behind the train station. They charge about a franc a minute.

www.cannes-on-line.com has everything on the city, plus links to other related sites.

Airlines Air France *(Tel 93/393-914 or 08/02-80-28-02).*

Trains Most people reach Cannes by train. Most hotels are walkable from the station, but if you have a lot of baggage, take the bus for 9F or a cab for 30 to 50F. Nice is about 20 minutes away and trains leave hourly. Call *(36/353-535)* for rail information or stop by the main station, **Gare SNCF,** from 9am to 6pm.

Bus Lines Out of the City For cities east of Cannes (Nice, Monaco, etc.), buses leave from **Gare SNCF.** For points north or west, you'll need to go to **Gare Routière.**

Laundry Laverie Club *(36 rue Georges Clemenceau; Tel 93/380-668; Bus 8 to Palais des Congrès; 8:30am-6:30pm Mon-Fri, 8:30am-12:30pm Sat),* is near Le Suquet. Drop-off is 70F per load and self-service is 40F per load.

ST. TROPEZ

Even if you're too young to really know what all the fuss is about, you'll still be able to appreciate St. Tropez for its super-glitzy clubs, clean sand beaches, and movie-set harbor. But since you're probably not the only twentysomething who needs a historical briefing, let's just say that the town was first made famous by the 1956 flick starring sex symbol Bridget Bardot, *Et dieu créa la femme (And God Created Woman).* Thanks to that movie, which was filmed here, the joys of St. Tropez and its secret peninsula paradise were revealed to the world: a culture of baring breasts to salt water and the Riviera sun, of a fortunate glamorous few stripping down and getting carried away in a sea of hedonism. In its wake came bohemians, wanna-bes, Hollywood émigrés, and yacht owners, followed by tourists, all searching for excess at an affordable price. Yes, the wealthy still live here, but they're hidden away in their villas.

ST. TROPEZ

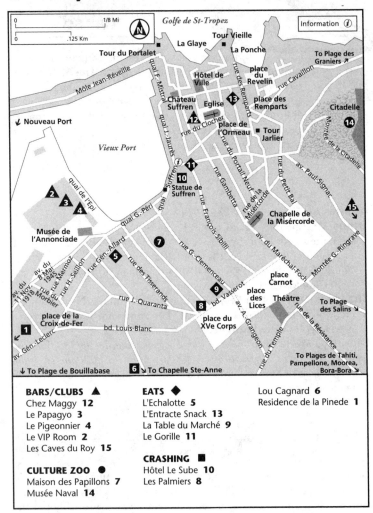

BARS/CLUBS ▲	**EATS** ◆	Lou Cagnard **6**
Chez Maggy **12**	L'Echalotte **5**	Residence de la Pinede **1**
Le Papagyo **3**	L'Entracte Snack **13**	
Le Pigeonnier **4**	La Table du Marché **9**	
Le VIP Room **2**	Le Gorille **11**	
Les Caves du Roy **15**		
	CRASHING ■	
CULTURE ZOO ●	Hôtel Le Sube **10**	
Maison des Papillons **7**	Les Palmiers **8**	
Musée Naval **14**		

Almost isolated from reality, the St. Tropez peninsula offers good times to those with bulging pockets and plenty of plastic melting in their wallets. Spending a day at the beach where bikinis and topless bathing were invented may leave guys with a bulging pocket but not a buck left in it. It's easy to dive into the sea of debt by eating well, drinking a lot, sleeping on a cushy bed, or skipping sleep to party in the clubs till dawn. Pleasure seekers, you are welcome to forget all woes during your stay. Pretend it's Monopoly money, and welcome to Fantasy Island.

Besides sunning yourself to a crisp, you can find plenty of water sports here, including sailing and scuba diving. Crash pads are on the pricey side, and the VIPs-only clubs are hard to get into, but hey, isn't that part of the thrill of club hopping? Bring your best duds and hope for the best. If you tire of the beach, which you may, you can tour the 400-year-old walled fortress of the **Citadelle,** or drop by the **Maison des Papillons,** home to 20,000 different kinds of butterflies [see *culture zoo,* below, for both].

neighborhoods and hanging out

Whether you're looking to hang with yachters, yuppies, or yankees, the town is small enough for you to rub shoulders with anyone and everyone. Sure, you can always wiggle sand through your toes at *les plages* and bask in the rays as you scan the crowd for someone to rub suntan lotion on your back or other hard-to-reach places, but St. Tropez is more than just beaches. In fact most are a ways from the center, **Vieux Port** (the old port), and can be a bit difficult to get to. Strolling its quays to scope the fast cars and the yachts affords a picture that's half movie set, half tourist mania. To the east of the docks is the **Citadelle,** a mound topped by a fortress and a dry, dusty park [see *culture zoo,* below]. Between the port and the park lies a street grid of cute little pastel-colored houses and small squares. Here you find boutiques, churches, and your occasional "starving" artist painting watercolors. They are "starving" in the nature of being bohemian, yet somehow make enough duckets to live on the peninsula and peruse the **place des Lices** with other Tropéziens. The long, rectangular, tree-spotted common on the south end of the grid has some restaurants, a cinema, and an area for *petanque* fanatics to play a pick-up game of *boule.* Although there are buses around the greater peninsula area, St. Tropez is small enough that there's no need for them in town. If you must, find a cab stand on the quai H Bouchard in front of the Musée de l'Annonciade, or call for one *(Tel 04/94-97-05-27).* They may be handy to get to the hotels if you're loaded with bags.

beaches

The only public beach close to Vieux Port, **Plage des Graniers,** is invariably crowded with nude sunbathers (which, of course, is why it's so popular) in summer. It takes about 15 minutes to walk to it along Chemin des Graniers (past the Citadelle). From there you can walk 2.5 miles along the Cap de St. Tropez, a path that will give you an up-close view of the rich-and-famous summer homes, to get to the next public beach, **Plage de Salins.** But some of the best beaches are even farther away, so you may want to go by bike or moped (see *bike/moped rental,* below), or go beach-hopping on the minibus shuttles *(les navettes)* that depart from place des Lices in the center of St. Tropez several times a day during the summer. That way you can easily check out the long, wide **Plage de Pampelonne** and the most famous beach of all, the notoriously decadent **Plage de Tahiti** at the northern stretch of Pampelonne's sands. If there's a Bardot of the 21st century, she'll be seen flaunting it here. The gay beach here is **Plage Neptune.** If you don't want to take the shuttle, you can catch a SODETRAV bus from the **gare routiére.**

Les plages

Ladies, if you've brought your bikini, leave the top at the hotel and grab some 30 spf 'cause the beaches here are the best place to liberate yourself. *Naturisme* is a common practice so don't feel shy. People are more apt to stare at you if you're shifting around uncomfortably covering up your breasts with your hair, your towel, or if you lie on your stomach all day. Bare it on one of the most celebrated beaches—where Bridget Bardot took it off—on the **Baie Pampellone,** southeast of the center. Pampellone is home to the beach clubs **Tahiti** *(Tel 04/94-97-18-02)* and **Club 55** *(Tel 04/94-79-80-14),* where yachters and the sort can afford lunches at the *club* for 300F and everyone rents chaise lounges so as not to get sand on their tush. The rest of us bring a picnic and park our butts on our towels. There are also cafes and concessions along the strip that offer more reasonably priced lunch menus. The **Plage des Salins,** a tad north, is more crowded, with bathers tangled in seaweed. To reach these *plages,* take a SODETRAV bus from the *gare routière,* or rent a bike from **Holiday Bikes** or **Lois Mas** [see *need to know,* below]. The bike ride takes only 15 minutes, but if you'd rather not pedal—and have to keep track of a rented bike while you work on your full-body tan—take the shuttle bus that departs from the place des Lices four or five times a day throughout midsummer (5F). It takes about 20 minutes. The **Plage de la Bouillabaisse** is another option closest to the center city; head west down the avenue du 15 août 1944. You can easily walk here in about 15 minutes from the center of town, or bike it in about 5 minutes. For even quicker access (about 2 minutes), take a bus from the station on ave. General Léclérc; the buses are marked "St. Raphaël" or "Toulon."

clubs

Don't hate them because they're beautiful, rich, famous, and can get into any club on the coast. St. Tropez didn't get its reputation for nothing. The stars still come out at night, which means you have to have a glimmer in your eyes as well as in your Versace pockets. Money flies when you're having fun.

    Le VIP Room *(Résidences du Nouveau Port; Tel 04/94-97-14-70; midnight till the rooster crows daily 15 Jun-15 Sept, weekends only 1 Apr-14 Jun, closed 16 Sept-Mar; www.the-vip.com; obligatory consumption 120F; AE, V)* is appropriately named. You can check the web site for the party program, but unless you're name is Jack Nicholson, Robert DeNiro, or

Naomi Campbell, you're going to have to look like one of their friends to slide through the cracks in this club. Relatively new, Le VIP has quickly become one of the hottest dance floors in town to shake your groove thang. Techno and hip-hop bend around the corners of the low red booths where your Magnum Champagne Roederer for 5,000 francs chills in a bucket of ice.

You can't stand around with your finger in your nose at **Les Caves du Roy** (*Avenue Paul-Signac; Tel 06/12-77-73-31; 11pm-dawn daily Jun-Sept, 11pm-dawn Fri-May; www.byblos.com; obligatory consumption 140F; AE, V, MC, Din);* you have to be busy looking cool and acting like the legends who tromp through this playground. Les Caves, on the lower level of the ritzy Hôtel Byblos, is a classic on the club list.

Le Papagyo (*Résidences du Nouveau Port; Tel 04/94-97-07-56; 11:30pm-5am daily Apr-Nov; cover with consumption 110F)* has helped St. Tropez gain party fame since the sixties, and the decor makes you trip back to that time, too. Although the three bars and two floors give you plenty of roaming space, you can't use pub etiquette to pick up a sexy someone. High class and glitz reside here, often overflowing from Le VIP.

If you'd rather sit in a cafe and drink a bottle of wine than hang out at the glitz-and-tits clubs for the rich and famous, try **Kelly's Irish Pub** (*Sur le Port, at the end of Vieux Port; Tel 04/94-54-89-11),* a casual tavern with an international crowd. Or if you're looking for a more Parisian atmosphere, check the resolutely old-fashioned **Café des Arts** (*Place des Lices; Tel 04/94-97-02-25),* where homesick Left Bank types gather to pout and pose at the zinc bar. The drinks are less expensive—and therefore far more appealing to the younger party crowd—at **La Bodega** (*Quai de l'Epi; Tel 04/04-97-76-70),* just downstairs from another fun drinking spot, **Papagayo** (*Tel 04/94-97-07-56),* a mostly straight bar that also attracts a scattering of gays.

Topless beaches have always been a part of the scene around here, but flashing bare breasts at a bar or café was a major *don't* until Bardot publicly ripped off her bra "to wake up sleepy St. Trop" at **Café Sénéquier** (*Sur le Port, at the center of the port; Tel 04/94-97-00-90).* Make the trip as part of your Bardot pilgrimage and stay on to drink at least a bottle of Provençal wine. An equally irreverent, skimpy-clothed bunch hangs out nearby at **Café de Paris** (*Sur le Port; Tel 04/94-97-00-56),* which also has a long, zinc, Parisian-style bar. This is one place where the richest of the yachties mingle with travelers doing Europe on $10 a day. Live it up—you may end up spending the night on your new best friend's yacht.

gay scene

I'll take the Provençal and Italian cuisine, sautéed with a few *petits garçons* on the side. Start the evening in the restaurant of **Chez Maggy** (*5 rue Sibille; Tel 04/94-97-16-12; 8pm-3am daily, closed Nov-Mar; fixed menu 145F; V, MC)* for chicken curry with coconut milk, capers, and cucumbers, or regional produce stuffed with savory meat. After dinner, make

festivals

There seems to be a holiday for every saint, and Monsieur Tropez is no exception. He was the inspiration for the **Fête de la bravade** or **les Bravades** celebrated on May 16–18. Townies dress up for processions and parade about the streets singing and dancing. But if it takes getting tortured and beheaded for declaring myself Christian to get people to pay me a tribute, I think I'll stick to anonymity.

your way to the bar that takes up much of the venue's space, where cruising male bodies overflow into the streets.

At **Le Pigeonnier** (*Résidence du Nouveau Port; Tel 04/94-97-36-85; open daily midnight-5am; disco daily in summer, weekends in winter; cover with drink 70F*), get out your binocs to scope out the fine gentlemen along the bar. Listen for different accents so when you start up the conversation by asking "Where have you been all my life?" you're not surprised to hear that it's somewhere in Europe. Mostly gay men fill the joint in summer and in the winter, when the disco is open on weekends.

culture zoo

Chapels and a couple of museums are the sum of cultural activities available on the peninsula. Most folks aren't here to sightsee anyway—they're here to go boating, play tennis, golf, or be on the beach.

Musée Naval (*Mont de la Citadelle; Tel 04/94-97-59-43; 11am-6pm Wed-Mon Apr-Oct, 10am-noon/1-5pm Wed-Mon Nov-Mar; 25F adults*): Come here to brush up on nautical terms and the maritime history of St. Tropez to impress the crowd on the quays. Entering the museum also leads you to the **Citadelle.** Climb to the top for views from this 400-year-old walled fortress; peacocks strut at your feet, ocean waves sound in your ears, and the town sits in the distance. The museum is worth a brisk walk-through, but the Citadelle is the real reason to come here.

Maison des Papillons (*9 rue Etienne Berny; Tel 04/94-97-14-96; 10am-noon/3-7pm Apr-Oct, 2-6pm Oct-Apr*): If you've been pinned to the beach all week and are looking for some colorful distraction, come on down. This *tropezienne* house—which, like most of the homes on the peninsula, reflects soft pastel colors off plastered walls—displays over 20,000 kinds of butterflies from all over the world.

sports

The crew at **Octopussy** (*Parking du Nouveau Port; Tel 04/94-56-53-10; open year round, call for reservations*) takes you diving into the crystal blue Med around St. Tropez and out to Ramatuelle, a neighboring town. You don't necessarily have to have 007 skills to go deep—they have excursions at various levels of skill. A novice *baptème* (baptism) includes a few hours of orientation and a dip 15 feet down for 250F. The veteran diver packs a one-tank dive for 230F. The scuba diving organization is based in Gassin in the Quartier de Berteau, southwest of St. Trop's Vieux Port.

STUff

Stall after stall of clothes, sunglasses, lotions, sarongs, and beach mats to sit on so you don't get sand in your crotch junk up the **Quai Jean Jaurès** among a few classier boutiques. More classy *mode* from each and every designer you're looking for can be bought on **rue Sibille** and **rue Georges Clemenceau**. Count the days, and nights, you're planning to stay in St. Tropez and make sure to buy a new outfit for each. God forbid someone sees you wearing the same thing twice.

▶▶DUDS

For *prêt-à-porter femmes*, stop at **Claire L'Insolite** *(1 rue Sibille; Tel 04/94-97-10-74; 10am-1pm/4-10pm daily, mid Jun-mid Sept; 10am-1pm/3-8pm daily, mid Sept-mid Jun; AE, V, MC, Din)*, shi shi c'est chic. Try on a Versace, Yves St. Laurent, or Christian Lacroix affair for this evening's stroll along the port. Other famous designer rags include Gianfranco Ferré and Escada.

Douyou Douyou *(9 quai Jean Jaurès; Tel 04/94-97-37-62; 10am-10pm; No credit cards)* is younger fashion along the port. Three-inch platform sneaks, leopard print everything, and glimmering sandals to go with the pink panther-print pants, and crocheted sweaters for chilly sea breezes. As you view a shimmering rack of bikinis, you realize we all need glitz and sparkle in our lives.

fashion

Bring socks to match your polo or go barefoot in your docksiders as you loaf past the yachts pretending you're on your way to your own for an afternoon excursion. A lot of people here look like they just stepped off a cruise ship and most of their tags read dry-clean only. You may also want to consider waiting to buy that travel iron till you get to France. Blowing a fuse at the hotel is always embarrassing when you plug in the wrong wattage. If you're planning to hit the town at night, remember that it's hard enough to get in anywhere if you're not on the A-list, so looking your dazzling best can only help.

eats

Kebab stands grill it up and crêpe griddles flip it over throughout St. Tropez. Snacks for between 30 and 55F will fill the tummy, but eating lamb and pancakes the whole trip may inspire a splurge on a menu, from around 130 to 300F and up. Rue Georges Clemenceau provides take-out options to eat as you sit in the squares. Also, **L'Entracte Snack** *(14 rue de Remparts),* where a sandwich and a coke are 35F, is a good option of the cheap panini jobbies.

▶▶CHEAP

Put a little meat on your bones at **Le Gorille** *(1 quai Suffren; Tel 04/94-97-03-93; 24 hours daily summer, 6am-8pm daily winter; No credit cards).* Greasy grub anytime of the day or night. A four-in-the-morning burger and fries never hurt anyone, except my neighbor Don who had double bypass surgery. Go straight for the jugular, you only live once.

▶▶DO-ABLE

L'Echalotte *(35 rue Allard; Tel 04/94-54-83-26; 12:30-2pm/8-11:30pm Fri-Wed, 8-11:30pm Thur, closed Nov 15-Dec 10; 7-5-140F entrée, 98-160F menu; AE, V, MC)* dishes out southwestern and southeastern French food, including some things PETA wouldn't approve of and you'd rather not know the source of while you're eating them (like grilled veal kidney). Swimming and flying animals, like duck and sea bass, also land on the plate. Gourmet critters, eaten outside on the terrace, never tasted so good.

▶▶SPLURGE

Managing to both go with the trends and stick to the traditional, **La Table du Marché** *(38 rue Georges Clemenceau; Tel 04/94-97-85-20; 7:30am-10:30pm Tue-Sun; 330F menu, 89-290F entrée; AE, V, MC)* turns the tables. Downstairs, Japanese and Thai are served for eating in or

to market

This little piggie went to **Place des Lices** on Tuesday and Saturday mornings to stock up on regional produce, meats, and wine. Amid the trees on the square he saw some ham and decided to move on to the other daily market, on **Place aux Herbes,** instead. There, behind the Quai Jean Jaurès, he found the catch of the day at the fish market, veggies, and fruit more appealing. He also picked up a bunch of flowers sure to spruce up any house, be it straw, wood, or brick.

taking out. The first floor specialty: Thai bouillabaisse. Upstairs, regional dishes and wines are oohed and aahed over in the antique-filled room. Second-floor specialty: *tarte à la tomate fraîche et basilic,* for a taste of tomato and basil. The tea salon and the deli/pastry shop in the front of the cute provincial pink building are open all hours, but you can feast only between noon and 2:30pm and dine from 7 to 10:30pm; Sundays the place is open only for lunch.

crashing

Good luck to the travelers arriving with dirt under their fingernails and cheese crud on their Swiss army knives. Lodging is pricey, the nearest hotel is 23 miles away, and there's no sleeping on the beach. The tourist office [see *need to know,* below] has some full-color listings of your options, some of which are also on their web page *(www.nova.fr/saint-tropez).*

▶▶CHEAP

Lou Cagnard *(18 ave Paul Roussel; Tel 04/94-97-04-24, Fax 04/94-97-09-44; 280-440F low season, 310-550F high season; MC, V)* looks a tad rough from the outside, but it's about as cheap as you're gonna get for something decent here on fantasy island. You ain't getting an ocean view, but Louie Louie is in the center near the Place des Lices, so you're in a prime location. And there's another plus: 14 of the hotel's 19 rooms have complete private baths, while the remaining five have showers and sinks in the room, with toilets in the hallways.

▶▶DOABLE

A nightcap at the terrace bar overlooking the port is a must at **Hôtel Le Sube** *(15 quai Suffren; Tel 04/94-97-30-04, Fax 04/94-54-89-08; closed 3 weeks in January; www.nova.fr/sube; 390-590F single, 590-1500F double; AE, V, MC, Din)* before heading up to your cozy, fully stocked room. As evening sets in, lounge in the nautical decor and discuss sailor knots with the yacht owner drinking a brandy next to you. If you're lucky you'll be having breakfast with them at the bar in the morning, their treat (65F).

Les Palmiers *(26 blvd. Vasserot; Tel 04/94-97-01-61, Fax 04/94-07-10-02; 350-800F low season, 440-1050F high season; AE, V, MC)* is painted pink and topped with a Spanish tiled roof to let you know you're on the Riviera. Private bathrooms, of course, cable TVs, and climate control make for comfortable lodging. Some rooms look onto the patio/backyard/garden that you can sit in. Have your *petit dejeuner* for 55F there, or sit at the hotel bar to comment on the *petanque* game you saw on the Place des Lices near the hotel.

▶▶SPLURGE

Flash some plastic at **Residence de la Pinede** *(Plage de la Bouillabaisse; Tel 04/94-55-91-00, Fax 04/94-97-73-64; closed mid Oct-mid Apr; 715F-2350F low season, 1900-4750F mid-season, 2050-5400F high season; AE, V, MC, Din)* and you can get anything you want. I know my rent isn't pricey, but one night in the cheapest room here would cover me for a month. But what the hell! If you've got it, money can buy you a private beach, pool, and a patch of the greener grass on the other side of the fence for a day.

need to know

Currency Exchange Plastic or paper, ma'am? Money, they take any form, and you'll be spending plenty of it. Change it at any bank, use the ATMs, and above all lose your attachment to it. The most centrally located currency exchange and ATM machine is at **Master Change** *(18 rue Allard, Vieux Port; Tel 04/94-97-80-17; 10am-8pm daily May-Sep; 6F commission fee)*.

Tourist info The team at the **tourist office** *(Quai Jean Jaurès; Tel 04/94-97-45-21, Fax 04/94-97-82; tourisme{nova.fr, www.nova.fr/saint-tropez; 7:30am-1/2-7pm Mon-Sat summer; 9am-noon/2-6pm Mon-Sat rest of the year)* wear cute outfits and offer detailed brochures and maps with a smile.

Public Transport SODETRAV Var tours *(Avenue du 8 Mai 1945; Tel 04/94-97-88-51, Fax 04/94-97-88-58)* runs buses around the peninsula and the region. Find a cab stand on the quai H Bouchard in front of the Musée de l'Annonciade, or call *Tel 04/94-97-05-27.*

American Express Havas Voyages is the AmEx rep office *(17 blvd. Louis Blanc; Tel 04/94-56-64-64)*.

Health and Emergency Emergency: *15;* fire: *18;* police: *17.* The local hospital is **Clinique de l'Oasis** *(Tel 04/94-79-07-07, night emergencies Tel 04/94-79-07-20, hospital Tel 04/94-79-47-00, daytime emergencies Tel 04/94-79-47-30)*.

Pharmacies Green crosses flash you to the pharmacy where you often don't need a prescription for simple ailments. Call 04/94-07-08-08 for the pharmacy on night duty *(pharmacie de garde)*.

Telephone Area code: *(0)4,* city: *94;* national operator: *12;* international operators: *00-33-12* plus the country code; *0/800* numbers are free, *0/836* charge you a "premium" rate. To use most public phones in France, you need to buy a *télécarte* (phone card) at newsstands and tobacconists. The lowest denomination is 50F. Cafes and bars often have coin phones.

Bus Lines Out of the City The *gare routière* **SODETRAV Var tours** *(Avenue du 8 Mai 1945; Tel 04/94-97-88-51, Fax 04/94-97-88-58)* has routes from St. Tropez to Toulon, Nice, Ramatuelle, Gassin, Grimaud, and St. Raphaël (via Fréjus).

Boats Boats are definitely the best way to reach St. Tropez. From April to November **MMG** *(Tel 04/94-96-51-00; 32F one way, 6F round trip)* zips to and from St. Maxime, a town across the cove. The boat ride takes about 20 minutes. Boats depart hourly in both directions during midsummer; about four times a day April-June and September-October. There's no service at all November to late March. Farther north up the coast, boats travel frequently throughout the day, year-round, to and from St. Raphäel. The trip on **Les Bateaux de St.**

Raphaël *(Tel 04/94-82-71-45, 04/94-95-17-46; 70F one way, 110F round trip)* takes about 50 minutes.

Bike and Moped Rental Land dwellers can bike or motor around the star-studded jungle with **Louis Mas** *(5 rue Josef-Quaranta; Tel 04/94-97-00-60; 9am-7pm Mon-Sat, 9am-12:30pm Sun Jun-Sept; 9am-12:30pm/2-7pm Mon-Sat 9am-12:30pm Sun Oct-Apr, closed holidays; bikes are 48F per hour, scooters are 190-275F per hour; AE, V, MC)* or rent bikes from **Holiday Bikes** *(14 ave. Général Leclerc; Tel 04/94-97-09-39, Fax 04/94-97-25-90; 8:30am-12:30pm/2-8pm Mon-Sat Apr-Oct; 8:30am-noon/2-6:30pm Tue-Sat Nov-Mar; hb.tropez{wanadoo.fr, www.holidaybikes.com).*

Laundry Get the sand out of your britches at **Le Lavoir** *(1 rue François Sibilli; Tel 04/94-97-04-28; 6am-12:30pm/3:30-7:30pm daily; dedéé@club-internet.fr).*

Postal La Poste is on rue de la Poste *(Tel 04/94-55-96-50)*. If you need to mail something *rapide*, **FedEx** has an info line *(0800/12-38-00)*.

Languedoc-Roussillon and the Pyrenees

Languedoc-Roussillon

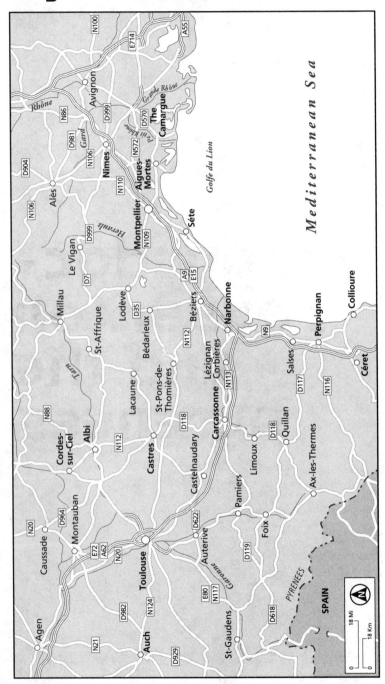

Sure, Paris is the most romantic city in the world, but they also speak the language of love in the south of France, and often more so to *you*. Running along the Mediterranean coast, Languedoc-Roussillon serves up a sunny southern hospitality that helps redeem France from the bad rep that its bad ol' sister city of lights in the north sometimes gives it.

If you've heard one too many stories about haughty saleswomen in boutiques who eye your every move while refusing to speak with you (in English—or French); if you've met freaked-out travelers who didn't get a shred of help or sympathy when they were obviously lost, confused, and hungry; or if you've just come off the snooty-nosed boulevards of Paris and find you can't take it anymore, you can either head home weary and bitter, or come here.

Like most Southern locales, the warmth here comes not only from days of sunny skies but also from the people sheltered by them. For the most part, the people here really *do* seem much happier and more open. And it offers proof that there's life beyond the Riviera's Côte d'Azur, which tends to be slammed with tourists. (Funny how we're always trying to get away from ourselves.)

The Languedoc-Roussillon region offers a lot and has a million hidden secrets, so don't hesitate to do some exploring on your own. We've chosen a few highlights: **Toulouse** and **Montpellier** because of their raging student life and picturesque architecture, and **Foix** for a moment of peace and quiet in the mountains after you've visited these cities. You can also detour to a town further south for some fun in the sun.

With its low cost of living and good universities, Languedoc-Roussillon is particularly attractive to college students. Both Montpellier and Toulouse have long-established schools and are taken over by more and more academic folk each year. Each town paints a distinct picture. Montpellier's 17th- and 18th-century architecture reflects classic styles, with Corinthian columns and statues of round-hipped women. The city is close enough to the coast for visitors to spend a day at the beach. Toulouse, further inland where the Midi-Canal and the Garonne River converge, used to be one of the wealthiest cities in France. Today it is known as the *Ville Rose* because of its rose-tinted Renaissance architectural gems. Foix sets a medieval scene, complete with châteaux. Here you

Travel Times

*TGV (Fast Train— more expensive) **By Car	Toulouse	Foix	Paris	Montpellier
Montpellier	2:30**	2:00**	4:20* 8:30	-
Toulouse	-	:50**	5:20* 7:30	2:30**
Foix	:50**	-	6:10* 8:30*	2:00**

are technically in the Midi-Pyrénées, just barely south of Languedoc-Roussillon's defined border.

As far as the region's traditional cuisine goes, game, trout, lamb, and seafood are flavored with enough garlic, olive oil, and herbs to ward off a vampire. You'll also find truffles, rare mushrooms, escargots, and a lot of *foie gras,* insides of ducks or other animals smashed into a lovely paste for spreading on bread or crackers. Around Toulouse you'll find *cassoulet,* a sort of stew consisting of goose, pork, lamb, or partridge and white beans cooked in an earthenware dish.

Even with all these local delights, McDonald's has managed to make an appearance. Recent disgust for the franchise and a nationalist movement to keep it in the family has inspired people to burn a McDonald's just outside of Toulouse, and since that incident there has been much debate. Meanwhile, the line of locals waiting to order fries and a Coke continues to reach the door.

For more details on the region, look up ***www.cr-languedocroussillon. fr/tourisme/, www.sunfrance.com,*** or drop a line at ***www.contact. crtlr@sunfrance.com*** *(Tel 04/67-22-81-10, Fax 04/67-58-06-10).* To get brochures, write to the **Languedoc Routage** *(Tourisme Languedoc-Roussillon, BP 279 344 35 St. Jean de Védas, France).*

getting around

SNCF train lines cover the area well, so you have little reason to hop on a bus. Unfortunately one downside of taking the train is that they run late more often than not. Double- and triple-check schedules, especially on the timetables that have a million codes and special conditions. Look out especially for notes indicating Saturday only, or from such and such a date to the next. It can get confusing, so don't be shy about asking whether you're on the right track. Also, the French SNCF employees like to go on strike at the first signs of pleasant weather in the spring and summer or when there's a major holiday. Perk up your ears to learn of any potential hold-ups. During strikes there could be no trains running, or only one per day. It's possible to get stuck in one place for a couple of nights, forcing you to rearrange your grand itinerary.

There are a lot of people hanging around the *gares* in the south, many of whom have *chosen* this nomadic lifestyle. They often travel with dogs and approach you to ask for cigarettes or sometimes *une petite pièce*, or spare change. Since the train conductors often don't come by to check tickets, many people with and without homes catch free rides. Keep this in mind when you're planning on taking a late train, which is not recommended especially if you're alone or female. Always have your zipped-up stuff in sight.

Of course, one can spin the roulette and not buy a ticket, but those who do this most often end up paying the fare, plus an additional percentage, if the conductor makes the rounds.

art + architecture

Languedoc-Roussillon is so diverse in art and architecture it's hard to put all the styles into one neat package. Each town—Toulouse, Montpellier, and Foix—paints a distinct picture. Intellects young and old can't survive without stimulation, and the art in both Toulouse and Montpellier's museums ranges from Rubens to Matisse to poster and contemporary, offering a taste of everything.

Housing the intellectuals in each town gets eclectic too. Toulouse grew rapidly in the Renaissance period, when it was one of the wealthiest cities in France. The typical building material was a pink-colored brick, which still paints the town red (er—*almost* red) and adds dimension to the facades of mansions and hotels. Historical buildings include the largest Romanesque church in France, the Basilique Saint Serin, and the Gothic churches poking out here and there around town.

Montpellier's more classical 17th- and 18th-century architecture and its abundance of fountains and statues make for a very civilized bubble that you can tell has been an academic environment for quite some time. The new, very symmetrical part of town, Antigone, adds an eerie contemporary neoclassic flair. Small and out-of-the-way Foix, on the other hand, sets a medieval scene, and your main concern is how they manage to keep that huge castle-fortress on its hill.

▶▶SUGGESTED ROUTES:

To get into Languedoc-Roussillon by train from the Riviera, you'll pass through Marseilles and may have to change trains there. Be careful: This station is especially sketchy, and Marseilles is known for its thieves.

Continue on to Montpellier for your first stop in the region. From there, taking the city buses from above the train station to the beach, Palavas les Flots, is easy, and you don't have to get up super early to make a good day out of it. An afternoon is sufficient to dip your toes since travel time is about a half-hour.

For the longer run from Montpellier to Toulouse, take the train inland, which passes through Narbonne and Carcassonne.

From Toulouse to Foix, head south on those easy trains (when they're running...), or take a bus for a mountain excursion.

If you want to go from Montpellier to Foix, you'll probably end up going south by train along the coast, then taking a bus from Perpignan inland. You could shoot up to Toulouse from Foix, making the loop in the other direction, but the transfer of transport makes this route less direct and more time-consuming.

MONTPELLIER

If you're on a three-week European tour between semesters, you'll feel right at home here. And if you're long past those hectic, unforgettable years, this is a great place to relive them. Most of the people out and about in Montpellier aren't locals, nor are they necessarily French—they're students at the University of Montpellier, making the average age here about 25 years old. The university was established in 1289 as a medical school. Today, 65,000-plus students arrive yearly to be enlightened, not only in the world of sciences, but also in literature, flirting, and liberation from *les pères*. The mix of kids is international—French, Americans, Brits, Swiss, Swedes, Germans, North Africans—and adds dimension and life to the picturesque streets. If you come in July or August, when most students leave for summer break, it's almost like a different town. College is a time of expression and lazy days wondering how you can improve the world, how you're going to live, love, laugh, and be happy. Get back into that frame of mind in Montpellier and don't let it go when you leave. Cruise the endless packed outdoor cafes before you pick one, spend hours over a coffee and a long journal entry, or eavesdrop on the students chattering around you—before you strike up your own convo, that is.

If you walk around Montpellier's old center, past the Grand Opéra Théâtre, the place de la Comédie, and the gardens, you'll see old buildings being polished to a shine. You'll wonder if the people here have time to do anything else but restore, especially in the warmer months when all they seem to do is socialize, strolling or enjoying cafe life on the many squares. Surely the people of the 10th to 12th centuries, when Montpel-

Montpellier

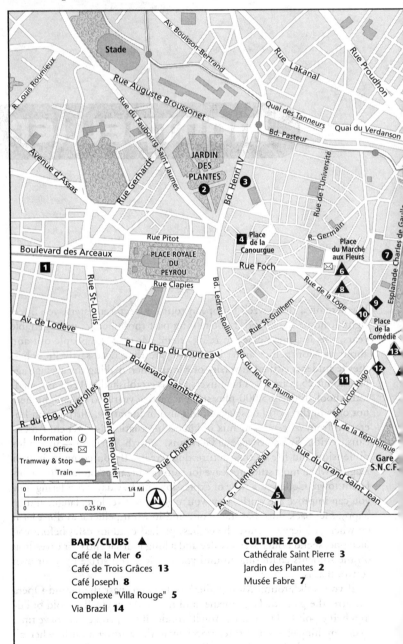

BARS/CLUBS ▲
Café de la Mer **6**
Café de Trois Grâces **13**
Café Joseph **8**
Complexe "Villa Rouge" **5**
Via Brazil **14**

CULTURE ZOO ●
Cathédrale Saint Pierre **3**
Jardin des Plantes **2**
Musée Fabre **7**

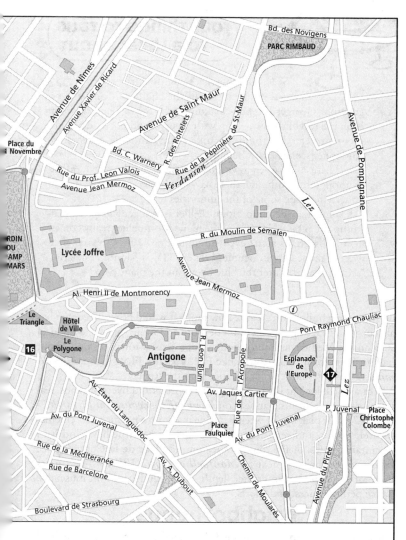

EATS ◆

Cappadoce **15**
Crêperie des deux Provences **10**
El Cuba Café **17**
Taco Mexican Food **12**
Tripti Kulai **9**

CRASHING ■

Hôtel des Arceaux **1**
Hôtel des Étuves **11**
Hôtel des Touristes **16**
Hôtel du Palais **4**

four things to talk to a local about

1. So...uh, what's your major?
2. Talk about all the changes Montpellier's governor Georges Frêche is making to the town: The new tram is on the top of the list, along with plenty of other city development projects like building bike paths, and the completed Antigone [see *only here,* below].
3. Race relations between townies, foreigners, and the recent influx of immigrants. Although there have not been major crises, it's an underlying issue some of the minorities feel.
4. Ask someone where the Mount Pellier is and get a giggle. Then stump them by asking where the name Montpellier really comes from. Historians aren't even sure, but one of the "town's" first written names, in a document dated 985, is Monte Pestelario, "Mount Pastel," after the blue dye from the plant *pastel.*

lier was being built, didn't realize how much it would grow. The town has also begun attracting the attention of more and more tourists as an ideal stop on the Mediterranean. Although not a coastal town, it's only about half an hour from beach towns like **Palavas les Flots** [see *within 30 minutes,* below], and it's a lot cheaper than the Riviera.

For a quick look at life in Montpellier, posters and flyers of expos, festivals, shows, and music appear on ***www.affichezvous.com*** *(Tel 04/67-02-70-25).* Or pick up the weekly freebie mag, ***Sortir,*** which lists cinema, theater, music, and restaurants not to miss in Montpellier. Find it in restaurants, cafes, or the tourist office on the **Place de la Comédie** [see *need to know,* below], next to ***Montpellier Notre Ville,*** which carries more of the same but in greater depth, and includes info on museums, dance performances, and sports.

neighborhoods

Small, walkable, and self-contained, Montpellier's old center is defined on the eastern edge by straight line of the **esplanade Charles de Gaulle,** which runs north-south to form the western edge of the **Jardin du Champ de Mars**. To the west of the esplanade, the streets fan out until they run into the western boundary of the old center, what appears to be one semi-circular boulevard whose name changes from the south to the north: Jeu de Paume, Ledru-Rollin, Prof Vialleton, Henri IV, Pasteur, and Louis Blanc. Just west of this semicircle are two green spaces, the **place Royale du Peyrou,** a garden square, and, north of that, the **Jardin des Plantes,** a peaceful spot for sunset walks with new-found crushes. Within the fan, streets jumble up, with periodic open squares that are cluttered with cafe tables in better weather. One of the few big, straight avenues within the fan is **rue Foch,** which runs east-west down the center of the old town and ends, to the west, at Montpellier's **Arc de Triomphe.** Although the **place de la Comédie** lies on the southeastern side of the fan, it's the center of attention; Montpellier's soul resides in this square. The magnificent **Grand Opéra** is located on Comédie, but there's probably more of a show outside the theater. Following Comédie through the large **Polygone** mall takes you to the surreal new section of town, **Antigone** [see *only here,* above].

You'll hardly use, or even notice, TAM city buses or the new single-line tram. They serve the residential hoods surrounding the old center and their stops closest to the action are on place de la Comédie. This is the best thing about all the center streets: you own them. No cars puttering out exhaust in your face, no horns tooting into your headache—it's fabulous!

hanging out

I think the students here are issued a woven chair, a cup and saucer, and a bag of grinds when they sign up for their first classes. Life is best lived in and viewed from a cafe. Choosing which one is often hard to do; at first glance they all look more or less the same, so you need to take some time to observe. Scoping out the scene, ages, and style of the night takes concentration. The best cafe on Comédie is **Trois Grâces** [see *bars,* below], where cool (but not too cool) intellectuals mull over their recent

only here

In Montpellier you get the strange feeling that they are trying to make it too perfect. So much effort is put into improving and cleaning up the town that the new parts almost seem sterile, especially in **Antigone.** Once the site of military activity, this district, about a 10-minute walk east of the old center, was converted in the '80s into a little shopping, housing, and office district in an effort to extend the city's old center. Antigone's vertebrate ped walkway reaches down to the Lez River and draws a line down the symmetrical design in what architects call *la perspective:* Vision from one end to the next isn't obstructed. You probably won't see people wearing Mickey Mouse logos sweeping up after every crumb you drop, but Antigone's empty, Postmodern, Neoclassic architecture will remind you of Epcot Center. It's cool to look at, but you'll wonder when the park closes...

wired

A young staff works the machines at **Station Internet** (*6/8 place du Marché aux Fleurs; Tram to Comédie; 2-8pm Mon, 10am-8pm Tue-Sat; montpellier@station-internet.com; 40F per hour, 30F per hour under 26 and students; No credit cards*), a link in the national chain of computer access centers. I can't imagine how the French and foreign students manage to compose their term papers with 20 computers, big open windows overlooking the square next to the Préfecture, and funky music. My study habits certainly couldn't handle serious transactions here, but e-mailing buddies in Seattle was straight and to the point.

Down in Antigone, the more rudimentary Net connection **Cybersurf Cafe** (*22 place du Millénaire; Tram to Antigone; Tel 04/67-20-03-50; 10am-8pm Mon-Fri, 10am-6pm Sat; 25F half-hour, 35F hour; No credit cards*) only has about six computers and is a bit more expensive. They're trying to go for that fifties diner look with pink neon and a billiard table but don't quite make it. It's a decent place to check the score at home while the kid next to you finds the golden orb.

discovery of Camus or the cutie they sit next to in class. In the morning, it's not unusual, either, to make a stop at the bakery then go to a cafe to eat your pastry with a coffee. Any time of the day, you can sit in a cafe till your butt goes numb. When it does, you can always motivate to sit on stairs or a nearby curb. The circular fountain Trois Grâces in front of the opera house is smack in the action and definitely a people-watching perch.

If you don't smoke, you're out of luck: You'll miss the opportunity to queue up with the local smoking population—which ironically seems to be nearly every young person studying medicine at the *faculté*—to buy cigarettes at **La Civette** (*8 rue Boussairolles; Tel 04/67-58-17-15; 10am-11pm tram to Comédie*), two steps south off Place de la Comédie. It's truly a social experience.

cafe, bar, and live music scene

Montpellier's fun, young energy comes from the carefree university life which allows week nights to be as busy as the weekend. Some of the French kids go home for the weekend, so they take advantage of the scene starting on Wednesday or earlier. The best time of year to go out in Montpellier is when the weather is bright and warm. July and August, however, mean no more teachers, no more books, and students jet, leaving the streets much less animated. Winters are worse, though, as the cold forces everyone inside the bars or their homes.

Cafes are open for after-dinner digestive espressos (thicker than a mud slide), and often till 1 or 2 am for drinks and conversation. That's also the closing time for most bars, which open around ten. You may go from a cafe to a bar as the night ticks on, but other than that the scene stays pretty still. Drinks can be expensive, so if you're bar-hopping on mom and dad's 100-franc-a-week allowance, you'll call it a night early. Once you order, you usually plant your feet. Unlike their Mediterranean cousins to the south who party till lunch the next day, the Montpelliers' night life is strangely short-lived. Bodies don't heat up till around 11:30 or midnight, compacting party time to a few hours. Just as you're warming up, doormen sweep the crowd to the door and pluck the half-filled cup out of your hand. So you may want to consider drinking up early, perhaps before heading out for the night.

The few clubs, mostly outside of the center, provide diversion to the night owls if you have transportation. **La Ville Rouge** [see *gay scene*, below] is the biggest one; crowds are gay, but straight stragglers are welcome. Without a car, grab a cab or call the 24-hour companies **Taxi Tram** *(Tel 04/67-58-10-10)* or **Taxi Bleu** *(Tel 04/67-03-20-00)*.

Some of the best seats in the house to view Comédie action are at **Café de Trois Grâces** *(14 place de la Comédie; Tel 04/67-58-43-59; Tram to Comédie; No credit cards)*, named for the fountain on the Place de la Comédie of the three Graces spewing water and turning green. You'll find better company and better prices here than at Cafe Riche across the way, whose name says it all. A jolt of caffeine will cost you nine francs, and soda or beer start from 18F. Find the open woven chair and table with your name on it. Don't sweat it if you have to circle the square a few times to score; waiters serve till one or two.

Everyone has spent at least a night or two on the **Place Jean Jaurès,** a 5-minute walk northwest from Place de la Comédie, where bars cluster together and their music intertwines as you pass from one to the next. **Café Joseph** *(3 place Jean Jaurès; Tel 04/67-66-31-95; Tram to Comédie; 9 or 10am-1am daily; 14F beer, 40F cocktail; No credit cards)* is one of the best, and almost all foreign students frequent the patterned velvet chairs in the cool red illumination at the edge of the dance floor. The evening

fIVE-O

Two kinds of cops roam the streets: the municipal police, who wear all blue and are serious about restrictions and violations, and the CRS, a special branch of police more like public security. The CRS would probably give some young ruffian causing trouble a good talkin' to, and the municipal police would take them downtown.

boy meets girl

Off discovering the world, studying French lit or biology...ahh, youth. They also happen to be single, vibrant, and above all, away from the confines and restrictions of the 'rents. Girls, you've got the power to lure any man if you make some eye contact. It's like the Price is Right. Simply scan the audience and say *come on down* by flashing those baby blues, greens, or browns at your chosen man. Guys, hope for the best and wait for some innocent glances—you may be the next contestant. Keep in mind that you can't go to the grocery store to pick up condoms; you have to either ask for them in the pharmacy, or have enough change for the vending machines on the street.

begins with an electronic mix and, as the crowd arrives, moves into Top-40 dance music and radio tunes to sing along with. They also host occasional amateur jam session nights.

Montpellier's Latino community is small, but people can't get enough of its culture, especially at **Via Brazil** *(7 rue de Verdun; Tel 04/67-58-63-33; Tram to Comédie; 6pm-1 or 2am daily; V, MC)*, a Caribbean restaurant, bar, and stage for live performers just southeast of Place de la Comédie. They have a busy week: Cabaret Monday gets sexy, Tuesday and Wednesday host the salsa band Son del Corazón, Thursday through Sunday DJs spin R&B and Ragga Zouk, and theme parties are held on weekends. If you come early to dine, you don't have to gussy up or say *"Bon soir"* to the doorman, who really isn't too picky about what you're sporting but likes to see something decent. Drink prices before he arrives are 12F a beer and 25 a whiskey. They go up from there.

If you're not confident on the dance floor, **El Cuba Café** [see *eats*, below], east of the old center in Antigone, hosts beginner's classes Thursday to Friday from 6 to 8pm and Saturday from 3 to 4:30pm. Just need to brush up? The advanced sessions are on Saturday from 5 to 6:30. Practice here with Cuba Café's own salsa bands dropping in on Wednesday and Sunday evenings. Call *04/67-15-17-17* for info.

arts scene

▶▶PERFORMING ARTS

Montpellier is proud of the annual international dance festival sponsored by the city's choreographic center. It takes place at the end of June through the beginning of July [see *festivals*, below].

At **Jam** *(100 rue Ferdinand de Lesseps; Tel 04/67-58-30-30, Fax 04/67-58-30-30; Bus 12 to Les Alizès, info@lejam.com, www.lejam.com; concerts free-120F)*, concerts on Thursdays at 9pm are followed by an open jam session. If you are looking for a reason to stay in Montpellier that makes more sense than the fact that you like life in a cafe, you can sign up for a course at their music school in jazz theory and technique, learn to play the flute, sax, piano, drums, or just about anything you can get your hands on.

gay scene

The Montpellier gay community is visible and welcoming, especially at the **Centre Gai and Lesbien** *(30 rue Cardinal de Cabrières; Tel 04/67-60-37-34; Tram to 3rd stop after Comédie, on Blvd. Pasteur; 5-8pm Mon-Sat),* located on the north side of the old center. Although they were only open a few hours a day during renovations in 2000, it continues to maintain strong connections to the Montpellier scene. On location, get together for theme discussions, debates, and *soirées surprises* on Friday at 8pm to play games, watch videos, and eat pizza. Off location, the group

festivals

Dansons! You'll wish you'd listened to your mother when she told you to keep up those ballet classes. You'll probably end up in a classroom with 20 kids in tights and tutus when you're back home after seeing the inspirational festival of dance, **Montpellier Danse** *(Hôtel d'Assas, 6 rue Vieille Aiguillerie; Tel 04/67-60-83-60; info@montpellierdanse.com; www.montpellier.com).* This celebration of creative movement can be seen in various venues downtown from the end of June to the beginning of July. The festival has risen to fame after 20 years of inviting international companies. In 2000, the young performers included some from Loyola Marymount University in the states, as well as some Portuguese improv troops. There are also get-togethers with choreographers, dancers, and producers to discuss hot topics like breaking through the triteness of current classic and contemporary styles into new forms of expression, or the relationship between the audience and performers. Tickets for most of the shows are from 35 to 260 francs. There's also a long list of freebie performances, shows, and films of equally high quality and creativity. "Body, Little Body on the Wall" and "I'm Sitting in a Room Different from the One You Are in Now" were a couple of the titles that caught my eye.

"Beaujolais" isn't a festival, it's a wine from the Montpellier region. The vineyards harvest in the fall, and with the first pickings of the grapes, Beaujolais is everywhere. During this time, it is sold cheap and drunk fast. Keep your ears and palate perked for this happening but don't be afraid to drink the Beaujolais no matter *when* you're here.

Rules of the game

Scant enforcement of open-container laws allows university kids or street roamers to have a coupla brewskies on the curb—in fact it's a good way to save a buck if the goal of the night is to get drunk, not to soak up atmosphere and some *Français*. Get-togethers, however, don't tend to grow into block parties or loud beer brawls. Hash drifts in and out of the night and isn't in plain sight; after all, it *is* illegal, punishable with seven years in the slammer. It's especially noted by the powers-that-be if you're laughing loudly and not speaking French or any other comprehensible language. So keep it low-key if you don't want to hear "Book 'em Dan-O!"

breaks out to go on picnics, to the beach, and to parties organized with local cafes and bars.

What did I see, I saw the sea. **Café de la Mer** *(5 place du Marché aux Fleurs; Tel 04/67-60-79-65; Tram to Comédie; 8am-1am daily; 20-30F beer, 35F cocktail; No credit cards)* floats among the other outdoor cafe/bars on the "square of the flowers'" at the eastern end of Rue Fochs. The painted palm trees and big mosaic boat set the mood in the spacious indoor bar where you can find out just about everything about the gay scene from the flyers, publications, and sailors waiting for you to come to shore.

At **Complexe "Villa Rouge"** *(Route de Palavas; Tel 04/67-06-52-15; Club 11pm-5am Thur-Sun, restaurant and complex 8 or 9pm till 4 or 5am; www.villa-rouge.com; Cover 50-100F; menu 79-140F; No credit cards)*, special "Girls and Co." and "E-M@LE" parties take place with Asian themes and gold and red decor. There are various areas, including techno, disco, and show rooms, and some back rooms which I didn't get to, but can only imagine. Unfortunately, it's a good 15-minute drive from Place de la Comédie, and there's no public transportation to get here while the place is open, so you're stuck flagging a cab or finding someone with a car. Fortunately, Villa Rouge is a one-stop venue. The summer and winter patio is refreshing whether you're chilling those dancing shoes, letting your dinner settle, or looking to flaunt your new tattoo or hair style. The food specialties are grilled and wood-fired, and the salads are good complements.

CULTURE ZOO

The cultural check list in Montpellier is short if you only count the places where someone takes a ticket. Some of the best sights here are seen while walking through the squares and parks where spring cleaning, beautifying, and rehabbing are in progress. In the old center, classic French architecture dating from the 16th to the 18th centuries is getting buffed with the help of the current council. Places to snap some shots: Place de la Comédie and the theater bordering the square, of course, all along Rue Foch to the **Arc de Triomphe** and the Place Royale du Peyrou, a park promenade [see *by foot,* below]. Don't get confused about the Arc de Triomphe; you're not in Paris. There seem to be a million of these in France to boast of victories. They're like big trophies, only there's no figurine in a frozen backhand serve.

Jardin des Plantes *(163 rue Auguste-Broussonnet;Tel 04/67-63-43-22; Tram to 3rd stop after Comédie on Blvd. Pasteur, bus 2, 5 to Place de Peyrou or Boulevard Henri IV; 10am-7pm Tue-Sun Apr-Sept, 10am-5pm Mon-Fri Oct-Mar; Free admission):* Famed for being the oldest botanical gardens in France. Would you believe some of the plants are direct descendants from 1563, when this place opened?

Cathédrale Saint Pierre *(place St. Pierre;Tel 04/67-66-04-12; Tram to 3rd stop after Comédie on Blvd. Pasteur; 9:30am-noon/2:30-7pm daily; Free admission):* This is hardly one of the grand cathedrals of France, and it suffered badly in centuries of religious wars and revolutions. For a long time after 1795 it wasn't a cathedral at all but was occupied by a medical school. Today in spite of its lack of pretension, it is the town's spiritual centerpiece. Once associated with a Benedictine monastery, a church was founded on this spot in 1364. The cathedral's greatest architectural achievement is its unusual canopied porch, supported by two conical turrets. The best artworks inside are 17th-century canvases in the transepts—notably the work of a Huguenot, Montpellier-born Sébastien Bourdon, who painted himself among the "heathens" in *The Fall of Simon Magus.* Also worth seeing is Jean Troy's *Healing of the Paralytic.*

Musée Fabre *(39 blvd Bonne-Nouvelle; Tel 04/67-14-83-00; Tram to Comédie; 9am-5:30pm Tue-Fri, 9:30am-5:30pm Sat-Sun; 20F adults, 10F students and under 20; No credit cards):* This fine collection of paintings spans the centuries, from the Flemish in the 19th century to the modern era. The titles say a lot about the progression of history through art: from *The Curing of the Man Possessed by a Demon,* to *Portrait of Van Wyck Coklers,* to *Untitled.* Trying to go in chronological order gets confusing on the various floors of different shapes and sizes.

modification

Seeing patterns, pictures, and designs in palaces and churches from the Middle Ages inspires a desire to decorate your skin. The artists at **Monkey Studio** *(20 rue de l'Université;Tel 04/67-60-62-98; Tram to 2nd stop after Comédie on Blvd. Louis Blanc; 10am-noon/2-7pm Mon-Sat; No credit cards)* have sterile, new equipment. You'll be thankful later that appointments are required because if you're not sure, that $10,000 laser surgery could put a dent in college loans.

The mind always gets the attention, but now it's time to take care of the body and soul. Zoning out in a meditation course with **Centre de Méditation Sri Chinmoy** *(Bureaux du Polygone, 8ème Étage;Tel 04/67-40-01-59; Tram to Comédie; 7pm Tue; Free)* can help you see the light. OHM la, la, la...Have the urge to participate in chanting? Go directly to **Yoga Shakti** *(18 rue de l'Université;Tel 04/67-27-36-52; Tram to 2nd stop after Comédie on Blvd. Louis Blanc; shakti.om@fnac.net, www.chez.*

com/shakti) where classes of all levels are offered Monday to Saturday from as early as 9:45am to as late as 9pm. Class fees start at 200F a morning for non members, 150 for members, and go up depending on the class, hours, etc. Stretching is the key to longevity, so reach your body into positions that could be illegal in some countries in a yoga class. To get the goods on more crunchy info and events like these, go to **Tripti Kulai** [see *eats,* below] for directions.

Right, so you don't want to let your underarm hair get so long it tangles like that of the hippie chicks. **L'Occitane** *(26 grand rue Jean Moulin; Tel 04/99-51-40-50; Tram to Comédie; 10am-7pm Tue-Sat, 2-7pm Mon; AE,V,MC)* has a small salon for waxing and facials starting at 150F. You too can smell delicious and emanate beauty like the French with products from the relaxing atmosphere in the front. Cosmetics, essential oils, and perfumes for women, and colognes and shaving products for men, range from 40 to 150F. Treat yourself, or buy a little something *Français* for that someone special.

sports

Thanks to a large and youth-conscious population, and a setting within easy reach of many regions of ecological and panoramic interest, Montpellier provides ample choices for Escapades de Nature.

People who jet around town on wheels don't have "No skating" or "No biking" signs to deal with, resulting in a remarkable skating and biking community. As a matter of fact bikes are strongly promoted. *Montpellier á Velo: Vill'á Vélo* is the city's project to construct bike trails and promote bikes as a means of transport. They're setting up more and more trails and will rent cycles for cheaper than other places. Info on the project is at the bus station, which is upstairs from the **train station** [see *need to know,* below]. Rent bikes there for 10F an hour, 20 a half day, and 40 a full day. Also on Sundays at 10am there are 3-hour city tours *á vélo* with a guide who speaks some English—a fun way to see things without wearing out your sneaker soles. You must reserve your place and pay 80F by 5pm the Friday before by contacting **Vill'á Vélo** *(Ste. TAM, Gare*

down and out

Find the best viewpoint on Place de la Comédie and make that 9F cafe last for hours or at least till dusk. Get up and walk through the lovely **Esplanade Charles de Gaulles** gardens to the **Corum-Palais des Congrès Opéra**. Climb as many stairs as you can and you'll reach a roof-terrace where the view as the sun fades into the distance is priceless, yet takes nothing out of the coin purse.

Routière de Montpellier, Place de la Comédie/Rue Jules Ferry; Tel 04/67-92-92-67), or the **tourist office** [see *need to know*, below].

Borderline *(19 rue du Pila Saint-Gely; Tel 04/67-60-60-70, Fax 04/67-60-26-42; Tram to Comédie or to 2nd stop after Comédie on Blvd. Louis Blanc; www.boarderline.net)*, established in the mid-1990s by entrepreneurs and skateboard enthusiasts Bruno and Nadine, is a travel agency and school that specializes in anything non-motorized that slides or rolls, whether on ice, snow, or concrete. Most of their energy is dedicated to organizing week-long courses in skateboarding, which attract the hyper-fit from throughout the region, who arrive, with their skateboards and (hopefully) their headgear, to be video-taped and coached in the fast-rolling life of a skateboard enthusiast. The company has a firsthand knowledge of most of the skateboard parks and obstacle courses in the south of France, and can send you to any of several sporting goods stores to buy the appropriate boards, helmets, and protective clothing. (Alas, they don't rent, but in the trend-conscious world of French skateboarding, personalized equipment takes on some of the aspects of a personal fetish for their users.) A week of coaching (i.e., seven days of six-hour lessons in a skateboard park) begins at around 2,300F. Add-ons for lodgings in two-star hotels and supplements for full board can also be arranged. Regrettably, no hourly or half-day lessons are available, as the company's spokespersons value a more complete exposure to the sport than a short-term lesson can provide. The company also offers weeklong exposures to snowboarding in the Alps, and wave-surfing along France's Atlantic seacoast.

Safari Nature en Camargue Gitan *(6 rue des Alliers, 30240 Grand du Roi; Tel 04/90-97-89-33)* specializes in four-wheel drive explorations of secondary, sometimes marshy back roads. A worthy competitor, handling roughly the same visions and itineraries and style, is **Camargue Aventure** *(Pierrot-le-Camarguais. Tel 04/66-51-90-90)*.

Play *gardian* (cattle-keeper, cowboy-style) for an hour, a half-day, or a day at the **Domain Paul Ricard** *(Mijanes en Camargue, 13200 Arles; Tel 04/90-97-10-10)*, where a corral of horses stamps and snorts, waiting to be exercised.

Some geologists compare the **Gorges of the Hérault** to the gorges of the U.S.'s Grand Canyon, albeit on a smaller, gentler scale. For access to a company that specializes in rides, by canoe or raft, down the lazy river, contact **Canoe le Moulin** *(B.P. 14, 34190 Saint-Bauzille de Putois; Tel 04/67-73-30-73)*. Equivalent excursions along France's strategic Canal du Midi can be arranged through **Sainte Camargue Plaisance** *(B.P. 8, Carnon; Tel 04/67-50-77-00)*. Set within a hamlet about 6 miles southeast of Montpellier, their specialty is barge tours that begin on a Saturday, end on a Monday, include lots of single participants, and expose you to loads of scenery and culture en route.

Though Montpellier is landlocked, about four miles inland from the sea, lots of yacht-minded entrepreneurs operate from bases within the region. An outfitter that will provide sailing lessons, or which will rent from a flotilla of sailboats by the half-day or by the week, is **Mr. Ruby**

(Route de Nîmes, Le Cres; Tel 04/67-70-45-10). He operates from a base about 3 miles north of Montpellier.

The **tourist office** [see *need to know*, below] is a great source for sports and the outdoor scene. Ask to see the "sports" three-ring binder, a listing and compilation of excursion courses, organization addresses, and flyers and brochures for adventures in and around town. Horseback-riding, rock-climbing, dancing...hey, if you sweat and breathe heavy, it's a sport—'nough said.

STUFF

The **grand rue Jean Moulin** is the main artery of the cutesy shopping district. Prime window-browsing for *prêt-à-porter* women's and men's clothing is found in this pedestrian zone and down a few of the smaller streets. **La rue de l'Université,** beginning from the **Préfecture** continuing north, sports more student-geared *magasins,* like little book, used clothing, and artisan stores. Finally, if the favorite jeans you packed on this trip have seen their last day and your butt doesn't fit into anything but Gap jeans, never fear. The **Polygone** mall is here, open from 9:30am to 7pm Monday through Saturday. If you must, it's in sight of the tourist office on the Place de la Comédie.

▶▶FRIPES

A used clothing store, **New Puces** *(10 rue de l'Université; No phone; Tram 2nd stop after Comédie on Blvd. Louis Blanc; 10:30am-7pm Tue-Fri, 2-7pm Mon & Sat; No credit cards)* has lots to choose from, but like a trip to Goodwill, expert sorting skills are required to find treasures. The ultimate retro combinations can be discovered with patience. You too can be charged 150F for a leather jacket or old shoes the owner probably wore in the days when she was hip.

▶▶TUNES

Right off the Grand Rue Jean Moulin, **Wool Music** *(4 rue en Gondeau; Tel 04/67-66-62-83; Tram to Comédie; 11am-7:30pm Tue-Sat;*

fashion

Basic university rules apply. Everyone comes from different directions and brings a little bit of their own wardrobe taste with them. A lot of people who don't have anything more comfortable to slip into will walk around in jeans-and-tee uniforms while others pick up some Paris fashions and worry about displaying the designer tag. There aren't too many super-freaks though. Piercing and spiked green hair come in moderation.

MC, V, AE) is *the* choice independent record store. New imports arrive regularly in all shapes and sizes on vinyl and CDs—lots of electronic music, deep house, trip hop, drums n' bass, techno, reggae, funk, ska, rock, jazz, and the beat goes on.

▶▶BOUND

They got creative with the name, **Bookshop** *(4 rue de l'Université; Tel 04/67-66-09-08; Tram to 2nd stop after Comédie on Blvd. Louis Blanc; 9:30am-1pm/2:30-7pm Mon-Sat, Jul-Aug closed Mon; V, MC)*, possibly to highlight the considerable collection of books in English. They say they've got the best selection in the region. If you've finished your train book already, get a new bestseller here. The reference shelves are lined like a library with language studies, teaching English material, French-English dictionaries, and travel guides. Wonder when they'll get this one in.

▶▶DOO-DADS

The **Zoo** *(Place Jean Jaurès; Tel 04/67-60-24-34; Tram to Comédie; 10am-8pm Mon-Sat; V, MC)* is an open, colorful space that sells silly Wallace and Gromit tub stoppers and key rings, 3D wallets, mobile phone covers, and mouse pads picturing birds, butterflies, farm animals, and the Virgin Mary (50-120F)—a lot of fun stuff. Later you'll wonder what possessed you to buy it.

▶▶CLUB GEAR

Get decked for strutting around town in the loads of stylin' tight shirts and pants by the big ones, Moschino, CK, etc., from **Le Village** *(3 rue Fournarié; Tel 04/67-60-29-05; Tram to Comédie; noon-7pm Tue-Sat, 3-7pm Mon; MC, V, AE)*. This men's store helps you accent your finest features, and the guys behind the counter can direct you to the flyer and info piles by the cash register to see what's hot tonight besides your pants.

EATS

This whole European eating schedule, I swear it must change in every country. Fortunately for Yanks, Montpellier works on an eating schedule more similar to the U.S., with restaurants open between 11:30am and 2pm for lunch and from 7 to 10pm for dinner. Finding somewhere to eat in any price range isn't a problem, from cheap artery-clogging food on the run for students to sit-down meals for people with an income. Head to just about any square to find nourishment, especially Jean Jaurès and Comédie. If fast is the motive, the **Polygone** mall has food-court grub and McD's. Golden arches also shine in the Place de la Comédie along with a **Quick burger** French McDonald's imitation. And what college town would be complete without take-out pizza? **Domino's** *(19 quai des Tanneurs; Tel 08/02-85-09-50; 04/67-79-26-20; Tram to 3rd stop after Comédie on Blvd. Pasteur)* is on the northern edge of the old quarter.

▶▶CHEAP

Going to France to eat Mexican food? I know, but **Taco Mexican Food** *(22 blvd. Victor Hugo; Tel 04/67-58-79-30; Tram to Comédie; 11am-10pm Mon-Sat; No credit cards)* comes in handy when the thought of another panini makes you want to vomit and your budget is still tight. A Tex-Mex place that's not a five-star restaurant by any means, it's still not quite as nasty as Taco Hell. You'll probably have to order up a few of the small tacos to fill up, or grab some extras with the standard combo of a single burrito, fajita, or taco, a drink, and salad (average 35F).

While dancing to R&B, workers at **Cappadoce** (*9 rue Boussairoues; No phone; Tram to Comédie; 11am-1am Thur-Sun; 25F kebab; No credit cards*) find a sec to slide up to the counter and take kebab orders. Flat traditional bread wraps around juicy cuts of lam...mmmm, just another delicacy to cover with fries and loads of condiments. On the lighter side, the chicken or tuna salads (22-30F) are fresh and crispy. The guys trying to hit Mariah Carey notes will take 35-60F off your hands for a combo meal including a drink.

▶▶DO-ABLE

Tripti Kulai (*20 rue Jacques Cœur, Tel 04/67-66-30-51; also 3 rue Massillian, Tel 04/67-66-36-94; Tram to Comédie; noon-9:30pm Mon-Sat; menu 65-89F; No credit cards*) is the central veggie hangout with two locations. Veggie pate, fresh-pressed juices, and milkshakes are good for snacking; the rest of the menu, including Greek and Asian salads at 52F, or the plate of the day at 39 to 46F, offers more substantial rabbit food. Lunch gets crowded with more than just granola heads, but don't worry— if you keep getting distracted by the aura of your dining company, takeout is available. *Namaste.*

Crêperie des deux Provences (*7 rue Jacques Cœur; Tel 04/67-60-66-80; Tram to Comédie; 11:45am-2:15pm/6:45pm-midnight Mon-Fri, 11:45am-midnight Sat; 30F and up; V, MC*) is a crepe-o-rama, like a factory with a million choices. The menu on display outside the restaurant takes up the whole sidewalk. Stuff crepes with cheeses, mushrooms, ham, chocolate, sugar, or whatever your pleasure.

Walk to the end of *la perspective* walkway in Antigone, the new part of town, and reward yourself with a refreshing piña colada or margarita (35F) at **El Cuba Café** (*Esplanade de l'Europe, 6 rue de Rhodes; Tel 04/67-15-17-17; Bus 2 to Antigone direction Faculté des Sciences Économiques; cubacafe34000@webfrance.fr, www.webfrance.fr/cuba-cafe.htm; V, MC, Din*). The restaurant is new, with a covered patio and rooms decorated like Caribbean beach shacks. It looks out to a narrow bit of the river **Le Lez,** which seems more man-made than a work of Mother Nature. I'm guessing they didn't catch the 60F *poisson Yucatan* there, a fish accompanied by onion, lemon, pepper, and mushrooms. Chicken fajitas at 75F go well with extras like chips, guac, or quesadillas.

crashing

You can throw down your pack at your hostel on the way to town because most places to hit the tree are located between the train station and the old center. You're bound to find something on or between the three roads that converge off the Place de la Comédie and run south down to the station: rue de Verdun, rue Magueione, and boulevard Victor Hugo. The **tourist office** [see *need to know,* below] has plenty of publications that list names and num-

by foot

You'll probably already be here, but get yourself to **place de la Comédie** to circle around the fountain of *les trois grâces.* To the east you can look up the Corinthian columns, bounce your eyes over the arches of the grand theater **L'Opéra,** and slide around on the open marbled floor space. Start moving up **rue de la Loge** going ever so slightly uphill. Try not to get in the way of the shoppers flowing up and down the street, each with destinations unknown and urgent. The shoppers themselves are just as entertaining as some of the prêt-á-porter clothing boutiques and chausseurs shoe shops, but don't stand a chance against the yummy Godiva chocolatier and lingerie. La Loge continues through **place Jean Jaurès,** where more café culture resides and entertains, breaking the shopping monotony momentarily. When you reach the end of La Loge take a left onto **rue Foch** and window-shop more, plan your next trip at the travel agency, or check the time in the jewelry-watch *bijouteries.* Run to the end of Foch with your arms in the air and your fingers in a "v" for victory, and go under the **Arc de Triomph**e monument that's smaller than the one in Paris. Come out to cross Boulevard Prof. Vialleton to reach Place Royale du Peryou, your reward. The **Promenade du Peyrou** is the park where all *les garçons* take their sweeties to view an aqueduct, old church steeples, and roofs stretching out from above. Here the **Château d'eau du Peyrou** looks like a Roman temple surrounded by a *petit* pond (no swimming!) and marks the best lookout.

bers of accommodations. For a quicker run down the list, with ratings, addresses, and phones, the (**Montpellier, Matin, Midi et Soir Map** can simplify your life when setting out to find your bed: it has every local hotel spotted on it. Pick one up in the tourist office [see *need to know,* below]. The tourist office will also make a hotel reservation for you, without charge, but only if you physically show up. Folks who phone find themselves out of luck.

▶▶CHEAP

Hôtel des Étuves *(24 rue des Étuves; Tel 04/67-60-78-19; Tram to Comédie; hoteldesetuves@wanadoo.fr; 140-160F single, 150-170F double, breakfast 27F; No credit cards)* couldn't be in a better location—about two blocks from the Place de la Comédie, but not smack in the middle of the commotion. It gives you time to hop in your shower—all of the hotel's 15 rooms have private baths—to clean up and get out there for a night in the cafes. If you're arriving late to Montpellier, make sure you let them know; they don't like waking up to check you in much past midnight.

Hôtel des Touristes (*10 rue Baudin; Tel 04/67-58-42-37; Tram to Comédie; reception 9am-8pm; 150F single, 180-200F double, 260F triple, 300F quad; No credit cards*) is not classified by the rating system, but is a decent old lodging. The best advantage of staying here is the possibility of cramming everyone into a room for four. Aren't you glad you used Dial? And don't you wish every hostel had a shower in each room, like this one? Another perfectly acceptable option is **Le Mistral** (*25 rue Boussairolles; Tel 04/67-58-45-25, Fax 04/67-58-23-95; Single with toilet 160F, Single with shower and WC 225F, Single with bath and WC 240F, Double with shower and WC 235F, Double with bath and WC 260F, Triple with shower and WC 295F; Breakfast 33F; V, MC, AE*), a three-minute walk from the train station in the city center.

▶▶DO-ABLE

Hôtel des Arceaux (*33-35 blvd. des Arceaux; Tel 04/67-92-61-76, Fax 04/67-92-05-09; Bus 6 to Ave. de l'Agriculture; 300-355F double; AE, V, MC*) has been around awhile, west of the old town's hubbub and the Place Royale du Peyrou Promenade. Set a good half-hour walk from the train station, it's a family-owned, intimate place that looks like a house and has a *petit* garden to sit in. Walk through the gate up the porch stairs to check into rooms with bathrooms and simple furniture. The staff speaks English.

Hôtel du Palais (*3 rue du Palais; Tel 04/67-60-47-38, Fax 04/67-60-40-23; Tram to Comédie; 330-400F double; AE, V, MC*) feels like a palace all right. Its 26 large rooms are fat with A/C and a *telly*, and complete with bathrooms. The place is funny, though: From the outside it's an 18th-century building with wrought iron balconies, awnings, and outdoor cafes nearby. The inside was redecorated in the '80s with painted-on marble and big curtains. Conveniently located in the old center, just a couple blocks north of Rue Fochs.

within 30 minutes

Going to the beach for the afternoon from Montpellier takes a little planning. A bus to **Palavas les Flots** leaves from the **Gare Routière**, just outside the upper level of the train station. There are several lines running to the shore (17, 22, and 28 are a few); check the listings, or ask the guy with suntan lotion in his pocket which bus goes to Palavas. It takes about half an hour to get to the soft, desirable, beige sand, which has none of the pretentiousness or glitziness of the Riviera beaches and is rather down-to-earth and lined mostly with condos and apartments. There is a harbor full of sailboats and a stretch of seawall to walk along. In summer, it's *extremely* crowded, as are all the beaches stretching along the nearby coast. Most of the year taking a splash in the sea is quite nipply, but it's a fun, refreshing wake-up on a scorching day. Palavas could be any Ocean City, U.S.A., back in the day before the boardwalks were jammed with fudge, T-shirts, and shells glued in the shape of animals. If you're low-maintenance and need a beach fix, this is the easiest place to find it even if it's just for the afternoon. The buses run regularly till 8:25pm, then hourly till 1am.

need To Know

Currency Exchange There are **ATMs** and **banks** all around town, a safe bet is always near shops. One ATM is inside the **Polygone** mall, east of Place de la Comédie, and the tourist office will also change bills for you.

Tourist Info One stop at the **tourist office** (*East end of place de la Comédie; Tel 04/67-60-60-60; Tram to Comédie; 9am-1pm/2-6pm Mon-Fri, 10am-1pm/2-6pm Sat, 10am-1pm/2-5pm Sun*) and you'll know everything about theater, music, sports, culture, and anything else you're interested in. Plenty of employees wait for questions. You can sit for hours at the tables and flip through the literature they offer.

Public Transport The **buses,** the main transport in town, run less frequently after 8pm; thereafter they run on the hour from 9pm to 1am. A spanking new **tram** runs often till 1am. Both the buses and tram start from the *gare.* The **TAM** transport system office is at *27 rue Maguelone Tel 04/67-22-87-87.*

American Express The AmEx representative office is at **Havas Voyages** (*2 place de la Comédie; Tel 04/67-91-31-70; Tram to Comédie; 9am-6:30pm Mon-Fri, 9:30am-12:30pm Sat*).

Health and Emergency Emergency: *081;* Ambulance (SAMU): *15;* Fire: *18* (firefighters here are trained paramedics too); Police: *17;* Euro emergency: *112;* "SOS" doctors: *04/67-72-22-15.*

Pharmacies Pharmacies are marked by flashing blue crosses, and there's a big one on Place de la Comédie. For late night drugs (past 8pm), there's usually one that's open till morning. Its address will be posted on the window of pharmacies. If you don't see a posting, ask a cop.

Telephone City code: *04/67* if you call within France, *467* if you're calling from any other country; National operator: *12;* International operators: *00-33-12* plus the country code.

Airport Aéroport Montpellier-Méditerranée (*Tel 04/67-20-85-00*) is 8km southeast of the center, and you can get into town from here on a shuttle bus (*Tel 04/67-06-03-67; 30F*) leaving from the **Gare Routière.** The first airport bus leaves at 5:15am Mon to Fri and 5:50am on weekends; the last is at 8:15pm.

Trains Trains come and go from the **Gare SNCF** (*Place Auguste Gilbert; Tel 08/36-35-35-35, 04/67-34-25-10; Tram to Gare*), located south of the center about a 5-minute walk from Place de la Comédie. It's pretty sketchy late at night, with a lot of people hanging around with their dogs. You can take the new tram from the station to Place de la Comédie if you can't manage the short hike.

Bus Lines Out of the City Skip town on a **bus** from *Gare Routière* (*Place du Bicentenaire; Tel 04/67-92-01-43; Tram to Gare*). It can be reached by going upstairs in the train station. Buses from the *Gare* head down to the coast to Carnon, La Grand Motte, la Grau du Roi, Port Camargue, Aigues Mortes, Sête, as well as destinations further inland.

Bike Rental Pedal pushers can rent bikes at **Vill'à Vélo** *(Gare Routière; Tel 04/67-92-92-67; Tram to Gare; 9am-8:30pm Mon-Fri, 9am-7pm Sat-Sun and holidays Apr-Sept, 1-7pm daily Oct-Mar; 1000F deposit or credit card required; 10F an hour, 20F a half day, 40F a full day; V, MC).*

Laundry Rub a scrub scrub, wash your clothes at the self-serve **Lavosud** *(Rue de l'Université; No phone; Tram to 2nd stop after Comédie on Blvd. Louis Blanc; 7am-9pm daily; 19-40F wash, 2F per minute dry; No credit cards).*

Postal Of the four main Postes, the convenient location of the one on Place de la Comédie *(Tel 04/67-60-07-50; Tram to Comédie; 9:30am-6:30pm Mon-Sat)* can't be beat.

Internet See *wired,* above.

everywhere else

TOULOUSE

After Paris, the University of Toulouse takes second in having a population of, count 'em, 110,000 knowledge-thirsty, or just plain thirsty, youth—a number that's constantly growing. But if the college vibe makes you jittery and only reminds you of last semester's freak-out cram sessions, relax: Students don't flood *every* corner and cafe in Toulouse. The city also attracts lots of travelers (like you) and people from the sprawling suburbs and industrial regions just outside its historical center.

Nicknamed *Ville Rose* for its pink- and red-brick architecture, Toulouse is a gateway to the Pyrénées to the south. You'll find most of the action in the old center, tucked between the Garonne River and the 17th-century Midi-Canal, which remains the oldest working canal in France and connects Toulouse to the Mediterranean.

Thanks to the sheer number of people passing through, a tourist is not going to feel too out of place here. A city with outside influences and comings and goings, there's no particular look or Toulousian uniform, which makes it a cinch for any young whippersnapper of student age to sit down in a cafe with a French magazine and pretend to be skipping class. To really pull off the student disguise, here's a mini history lesson: During the 2,300 years it's been around, Toulouse established itself more than once as an important center of commerce. The Celts and Romans had it out in the fifth century when the Visigoths busted in to make it their capital. Then the Middle Ages came along, and Toulouse prospered from rich travelers and pilgrims on their way to Spain. But the big-time money started coming in with trading of natural dyes for wool in the 16th century, from which sprouted all the mansions in town [see *culture zoo*, below]. Taking a huge leap to the 1920s, Toulouse's aviation industry took off. Even today, it remains a major aeronautical site for France and Europe.

12 hours in Toulouse

1. Get lost wandering the streets of the *centre ville* and discover the hidden architectural gems. Look for bright, freshly sprayed graffitti art too [see *arts scene*, below].

2. Sit for a *petite creme* (a coffee with milk) at **Le Florida** [see *bars*, below] on the Place du Capitole and savor blending in with the locals. This should take up at least four of the 12.

3. Walk circles around the Place Saint Sernin, following all the arches, up to the steeple of the **Basilique Saint Sernin** [see *culture zoo*,].

4. Cross the Pont-Neuf to the **Prairie Filtres** park and the **Hôtel Dieu Saint Jacques** [see *by foot*,] to see why Toulouse is called the *Ville Rose*.

5. While you're over on the west bank of the Garonne, check out the photo exhibition at **Château d'Eau** [see *visual arts*,] and buy a poster for the empty space on your wall at home.

6. Dine on the best crêpes in town at **La Sherpa** [see *eats*,]; try the *Cabecou champignon* if you like mushrooms, and tell the new friends you're sharing a table with what you think.

Knowing which cafe to frequent and getting in on the Toulousian scene takes little effort when you have a few entertainment and culture guides. *Intramuros* (Tel 05/61-59-98-01; omg.toulouse@wanadoo.fr), a free weekly paper you can pick up in the tourist office, gives you all the cinema, theater, music, and cultural listings. *Flash* is not a superhero but another weekly magazine with much of the same info, but for 6F gives you extra show, restaurant, and cafe reviews; pick it up at any newsstand. And *Culture Toulouse,* a free monthly magazine you can pick up in museums, publishes articles on what's going on in the theater, art, and cinema worlds, going into more depth and including lots of photos.

If you can't decipher *any* French, go to **Books and Mermaids** [see *stuff,* below], which publishes a fabulous monthly magazine called *Doings in Toulouse* for English-speaking visitors. The publication lists places to eat, shop, and drink, as well as current festivals, theater, art, and music happenings. It includes showtimes of films in original-version cinemas. Because most travelers probably come by bus or train, it recommends venues reachable by foot. Sometimes there's a pile at the tourist office.

neighborhoods

The **centre ville** of Toulouse, the central nucleus of activity and historical sightseeing, lies along a bend in the **Garonne River** like a big elbow macaroni, bounded to the southwest by the river and on the northeast by a contiguous series of big boulevards and roads that bends along and follows the shape of the river. The main landmark and reference point is the **place du Capitole,** which is equidistant between the river and the boulevard, pretty much in the center of the *centre ville,* where the town hall sits next to half the coffee-drinking local and visiting population. You'll be walking through this square quite often, as most of the small streets radiating off it are full of restaurants and shops. A few blocks east of the place du Capitole is the **place Wilson,** another mini-heart of action, with plenty of cinemas and bars surrounding it. Running north-south right between these two *places* is **rue d'Alsace- Lorraine,** a commercial shopping road. About five blocks due south, it intersects with **rue de Metz,** another major thoroughfare that runs all the way over to the river. This intersection is the closest you'll get to grid blocks in the *centre ville;* the windy streets here meander all over the place, hitting small squares here and bumping into randomly placed churches there.

At the north end of the *centre ville,* industrial university buildings and their inhabitants crowd your vision. Kids studying too hard to walk *all* the way to Capitole hang out around the **place Arnaud Bernard,** perched on the boulevards at the northernmost edge of the *centre ville,* for afternoon coffees and cheap eats. Venture southwest across the river, and you'll find the throughways, bars, restaurants, and shops aren't so condensed. But there's a nice park, **Prairie des Filtres,** to stroll along. It's directly to your left if you cross the river on **Pont Neuf,** the extension of Rue de Metz. The bus system and one metro line are extensive in the

down and out

Since all the museums are free to students, the **Musée Augustins** [see *culture zoo,* below] is a great, cheap—not to mention peaceful—visit. It's especially cool because it's like a little maze: You get to the end of one section, go up some stairs to another, find more stairs or doors that open onto courtyards, patios, or the chapel. After going through the rooms of battle scenes, martyrdom, and Roman column capitols, you can smell the fresh well-kept gardens of the main courtyard. Lilies, squash and grapevines weave in and out of the garden paths. Then let the row of gaping gargoyles escort you out.

TOULOUSE

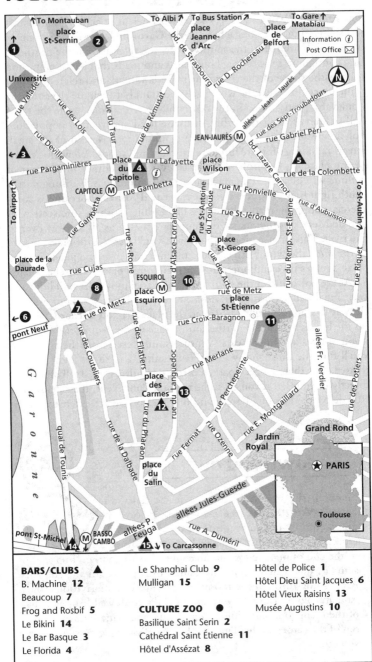

BARS/CLUBS ▲
B. Machine **12**
Beaucoup **7**
Frog and Rosbif **5**
Le Bikini **14**
Le Bar Basque **3**
Le Florida **4**
Le Shanghai Club **9**
Mulligan **15**

CULTURE ZOO ●
Basilique Saint Serin **2**
Cathédral Saint Étienne **11**
Hôtel d'Assézat **8**

Hôtel de Police **1**
Hôtel Dieu Saint Jacques **6**
Hôtel Vieux Raisins **13**
Musée Augustins **10**

center, but you probably won't need it unless you're feeling beat; Toulouse is very walkable.

hanging out

The cafe culture in Toulouse makes people-watching and sitting around for hours an acceptable habit to acquire. Most squares, like **place du Capitole** and **place Arnaud Bernard,** are lined with cafes and bars that have outdoor seating in the summer so fresh air can complement your conversation. On the Place du Capitole, each bar, brasserie, or cafe has its own regular clientele. **Le Florida** [see *bars,* below] is the hippest place to check out the pick of the young, good-looking students. As the night progresses and midnight munchies attack, the **Épicerie de Nuit** *(60 rue de la Colombette; Tel 05/61-99-09-48; Bus 14, 15, 19 to Colombette, Metro to Jean Jaurès; 7pm-2am Mon-Thur, till 3am Fri-Sat, 3-9pm Sun; No credit cards),* about 2 blocks west of Place Wilson, gives you a good opportunity to meet someone reaching for snacks on the shelf. It's like a convenience store, but much better, and serves up couscous and cassoulet, a hot dish with beans and duck or goose meat.

bar, club, live music scene

The huge and growing student population calls bars and clubs *boites,* which means boxes in English, perhaps 'cause you get boxed into bars and find yourself unable to get out. Beer is the drink of choice, especially Heinies and a brand called Desperado. You can find a Bud out there now and then, which seems more exotic with francs on the bill.

Friday is the night to hit the town and mingle with the locals at their best. Closing time for bars tends to be around 2 or 3am most of the

wired

A couple of good Net cafes are frequented by Internet users for e-mail and chatting, but there's quite a rage of gamers even on late-night weekends! For those hooked on Starcraft Broodwar, you can get regular status making local friends at either **Resomania** *(85 rue Pargaminières; Tel 05/62-30-25-62; Bus 10, 22, 24, 38, Metro to Capitole; 11:30am-midnight Mon-Sat; resomania@wanadoo.com; 30F per hour; No credit cards),* where they have a happy-hour from noon to 2pm (when one hour is only 15F), or **Blodstation** *(42 rue Pargaminières; Tel 05/34-45-09-99; Bus 10, 22, 24, 38, Metro to Capitole; noon-midnight Mon-Sat, 2-8pm Sun; blodstation@wanadoo.com; 25F per hour; No credit cards)* down the street, where happy-hour (at 15F) is between 8pm and midnight.

festivals

Summer is the time for festivals, when Toulouse's **tourist board** [see *need to know*, below] puts on **Musique d'Été** (July and August) and **Festival Garonne** (late June to early July). At Musique d'Été jazz, Cuban rhythms, tango, and gospel continue through the night, both months, about every two to seven days. You pay about 85F for each concert or show and purchase tickets at the tourist office. Same story with the Festival Garonne, which has a broader spectrum of activities compacted into a shorter time. Every year there's a different theme that threads through the theater and dance performances, cinema, and art shows you experience in various galleries, theaters, parks, and gardens throughout the city.

week, till dawn on Saturdays, making Saturday morning an excellent time for viewing the true, uninhibited side of Toulousians. Though a night out in Toulouse hardly ever cuts off at midnight, most public transportation does. If you're walking like you just spent a month on a boat, taxis will be the vehicle of choice—flag 'em down, or call 05/34-250-250.

The classic **Le Florida** (*12 place du Capitole; Tel 05/61-21-87-59; Bus 10, 22, 24, 38, Metro to Capitole; 7am-2am daily; 18F beer on tap, 9F coffee; V, MC*) has been here on the Place du Capitole forever. The marble, brass, wood trim, and waiters in white smocks remain the same, but the regular student crowd transforms the cafe into a legendary hangout for discussing the Functionalist theory they learned in philosophy class this week. The intellectual chats die down after a couple of minutes—then you can talk over a beer about how your dreads are coming along or if your new tongue piercing will get infected if you eat too much ice cream.

Try to swing by for happy-hour between 7 and 8pm at the **Le Bar Basque** (*7 place Saint Pierre; Tel 05/61-21-55-64; Bus 24, 25 to Barcelone; 11am-2am daily, till dawn on Sat; 15F beer on tap, 7F coffee; No credit cards*), but plant yourself for a while to watch as the bar starts chanting and chugging. With the recent additions made, you now have more room to shake your money maker, or just down one for the home team. Of course the *Basque* in the bar brings on the tapas and Spanish wine for those who want to hang on the terrace outside on the square along the Garonne.

A lounging neon frog lures you down the street to **Frog & Rosbif** (*14 rue l'Industrie; Tel 05/61-99-28-57; Metro to Jean Jaurès; 5:30pm-2am*

Mon-Fri, 2pm-4am Sat, 2pm-2am Sun; www.frogpubs.com, rosbif.toulouse @frogpubs.com; 30F pint), the only pub in town to brew its own because they know just how important a pint and a match of football (soccer) are to the soul. Three screens show live matches so you'll never miss your team, and Sundays are quiz nights when you can win prizes for attempting to be bilingual. Come for a 25F pint during happy-hour, 5:30-9pm, to get the live acoustic music program, which isn't held on any fixed night.

If you want to be assured of a couple of jigs, **Mulligan's** *(39 grande rue St-Michel; Tel 05/61-14-04-21; Bus 38, 54 to Notre Dame or Prisons)* is the answer—with a name like that, how could it not be an Irish pub? There's a regular music program with groups like Scotch Mist, Paddy in the Smoke, and Skippy and the Bush Kangaroos, which despite the name, is Celtic! It's hard not to hook up with someone, especially when the student crowd packs in for the 20F pint and Mad Tuesday Night Quiz.

Live music blasts and DJs occasionally spin at **Le Bikini** *(54 chemin des Etroits; Tel 05/61-55-00-29; Bus 53 to Lacroix-Falgarde; 10:30pm-dawn Thur-Sat; 20F cover & a beer, 50F+ shows, 20-40F drinks; No credit cards),* well known by young Toulousian rock 'n' roll fanatics as the one and only. In the summer they open up an outdoor patio and have shows veering away from rock toward dance music, mixing funkadelic DJs with percussionists, or live techno-house performances from the UK or even Detroit.

arts

Keep your eyes peeled down Toulouse's narrow streets and alleys for exceptional graffiti art. Of course you'll see the usual scribbles and tagging, but it's apparent that some of the artists take their time. I first noticed the bright colors of urban scenes on rue Saint Pantaleon; after that they seemed to be around every corner. On one side of rue Saint Pantaleon there's a devilish temptress named *Fofi* in pink lace-up leather, ironically facing a pristine bridal shop. *Truskool et Fils,* the creator of *Fofi,* made another stop on rue Baour-Lormain. By the Place Arnaud Bernard on Rue Gramat there is some mural art on the front of an apartment building, painted with a brush, not an aerosol can, depicting roof-top parties.

CAN'ART *(28 rue des Polinaires; Bus 24, 38, 54 to Esquirol Rouaix; 3-7pm Tue-Sat; art 250F and up)* is a little storefront art gallery with the motto *"Ouvert aux createurs, ouvert aux passions,"* meaning "open to creators and passions." Exhibits here come with a twist, like photos of adults from a child's point of view, or rusty wiry sculptures of everything from creatures to candelabras. The work here includes both functional art like furniture and lighting, as well as objects of purely aesthetic functions.

Walking across the Pont Neuf to the west bank of the Garonne you'd never guess that the old water tower, **Le Château d'eau** *(1 place Laganne; Tel 05/61-77-09-40; Bus 2, 12, 52, 54, 53, 56, 62, 78-80 to*

Cours Dillon, Metro to St Cyprien République or Esquirol; 1-7pm Wed-Mon, closed some holidays; 15F; No credit cards), has been converted into a prestigious international photo gallery. The exhibits change frequently, although some themes stay constant throughout the year.

The sign above the entrance to the **Centre Municipal de l'Affiche** *(58 allées Charles-de-Fitte; Tel 05/61-59-24-64; Metro to St. Cyprien République; 9am-noon/2-6pm Sun-Fri, closed holidays; 14F adults, students and under 18 with ID)* looks like it leads to a circus tent or a fun house. Its bright colors are a taste of the poster and graphic art awaiting you inside.

▶▶**FILM**

The collection of some 20,000 films at the **Cinématèque** *(69 rue du Taur; Tel 05/62-30-30-10; Bus 10, 22, 24, 38, Metro to Capitole; Sessions 6:30pm and 8:30pm Tue-Sun, extra sessions 2:30pm Wed and Sat, 3pm Sun; Admission 28F adults, 25F students; No credit cards)* spans the history of film, from one of Toulouse's Place du Capitole in 1896, to American indie films of today. It's a little theater that has a deal with other European cinémathèques to exchange films, almost all of them undubbed so you won't have to watch Kung Fu fighters' mouths move when you've already heard what they said.

An original-version cinema, where you can view the latest Hollywood hits and lots of tourists is **ABC** *(13 rue Saint-Bernard; Tel 05/61-21-20-46; Bus 10, 59, 60, 61 to Arnaud Bernand, Chalets, or Concorde; Admission 42F adults, 32F students; No credit cards)*. Expect a line on Wednesdays when everyone pays just 32F.

Théâtre du Fil a Plomb *(30 rue de la Chaîne; Bus 10, 59, 60, 61 Stop Arnaud Bernand, Chalets or Concorde; Reservations Tel 05/62-30-99-77; Admission 40-60F; No credit cards)* was founded by three friends with the idea of opening a theater for one and all. Performances (in French) consist mostly of home-grown comedies like *Le Directeur des Mouches*, in which we follow (or don't follow) the warped meaning of time, and pencils and erasers turn into ghosts in the lives of two workers. If you're a young upcoming artist but haven't achieved showing status, bring your works here and they'll put them up in the theater for free!

gay scene

The Toulousian gay scene (bars, restaurants, shopping, clubs, plenty of sex shops, and a couple of saunas) is scattered throughout the center, but you can contact **GELEM** *(34 rue Paul Decamps Apartment 530; Tel 06/11-87-38-01)* for information. It may be easier to make an appearance at the Monday 9pm meetings at the bar/club **B. Machine** to find out what's happening around town and to meet people. There's also a complete Southwest regional guide called ***Factory*** *(abo@neopresse.com)* for 10F that can be found in the region's gay establishments (including some of the ones below), with venue listings and event reviews along with monthly political or humor articles (in French only).

There's *beaucoup* of everything—food, music, parties, and guys—at **Beaucoup** *(9 place du Pont Neuf; Tel 05/61-12-39-29; Bus 52, 12, Metro* *to Esquirol; noon-2am-ish daily, Sat from 11am; 15F beer on tap, 8F cafe, 58-69F lunch menu, 80F brunch; No credit cards)*, a restaurant by day. The mostly male customers do lunch out on the corner terrace between noon and 3pm. At night the scene turns to excess, with 25- to 40-year-old bodies squeezed in the lower level of the bar.

The all-gay, predominantly masculine **Le Shanghai Club** *(12 rue de la Pomme; Tel 05/61-23-37-80; Bus 10, 22, 24, 38, Metro to Capitole; midnight-dawn Wed-Sun; No credit cards)* vibrates the techno beats as you work up a sweat dancing. Nudge up against a new acquaintance and take him to the bar in the back for a drink, where you can scope out the people scoping you out.

B. Machine *(37 place des Carmes; Tel 05/61-55-57-59; Bus 24 to Carmes; 10:30am-2am daily, till all hours Sat; 15F beer on tap; No credit cards)* invites all the ladies (and gents) who stick to their own kind for Thursday theme nights like costume or '80s parties, or to watch go-go dancers work it. Special ladies-only nights include strip teases starting at 7pm on Tuesdays; guys have their turn on Sundays around 5pm. Flirt by the blue glowing bar or head downstairs for more pickings.

CULTURE ZOO

In the museums in Toulouse, all of which are free to students with a valid ID card, you can discover natural history or old watches and china, but the best cultural exploration can be done walking and observing. Toulouse's architecture is unique in that it is a brick-built city, whereas most cities of the Middle Ages were constructed of stone. Because in Toulouse the nearest stone quarries were some 50 miles distant, local builders learned to fashion red bricks from readily available Garonne clays. They were cheap, robust, and rosy, earning the city the appellation of *La Ville en Rose,* or "the city in pink." Because of the clay, these rose-colored bricks were lighter in tone than those within other nearby cities such as Albi. For extra grandeur, the builders of Toulouse trimmed their bricks in white marble, giving the city a touch of architectural elegance and splendor. The *hôtels particuliers* include some Renaissance townhouses that are more like mansions. The wealth from wool-dye commerce poured in and traders reaped the profits, building houses with comfort and style. There are a few you can see (but won't be able to enter) as you walk around the *centre ville* town: **Hôtel d'Assézat** *(Place d'Assézat; Metro to Esquirol),* **Hôtel Dieu Saint Jacques** *(just over Pont Neuf bridge; Bus 14 to Olivier Hôpital la Grave, metro to St Cyprien République),* **Hôtel de Police,** and the **Hôtel Vieux Raisins** *(Rue Ozenne off Place des Carmes; Bus 24 to Carmes).* They helped Toulouse establish itself at the height of its grandeur and paint part of the *Ville Rose.*

Musée Augustins *(21 rue de Metz; Tel 05/61-22-21-82, Fax 05/61-22-34-69; Bus 14, 22, Metro to Esquirol; 10am-6pm daily, till 9pm Wed; www.augustins.org, courrier@augustins.org; 14F adult, free students and under 18 with ID):* An outstanding array of Romanesque and Gothic sculpture and religious paintings are displayed in the old sacristy, chapter house, and cloisters of this former Augustinian monastery. The sculptures romanes—mostly from the 12th century—are enough to merit a visit. Much of it in gray marble from the Pyrénées, this collection of anonymous Romanesque sculpture is among the greatest in Europe. Sculpture displayed spans the Gothic period to the Renaissance era. You'll find lots of saints, martyrs, and baskets of plums in the paintings here, and there are enough gargoyles to give you a fright.

After Augustins, you will have viewed the best of the museums of Toulouse. But if it's rainy and you're bored for something to do, check out the **Musée du Vieux Toulouse** *(7 rue du May; Tel 05/61-13-97-24; Bus 14, 22; 3-6pm, Mon-Sat, June-Sept only; 15F)*, lying off Rue Saint Rome. This is a kind of dusty attic of Toulouse memorabilia, with a little bit of everything locals felt worth saving, from religious paintings to sculpture and rare documents. There's even a model of the gym used by Jules Leotard, the inventor of the flying trapeze.

Of minor interest, **Musée Saint Raymond** *(Place St. Sermin; Tel 05/61-22-21-85; 8am-noon and 2-6pm Wed-Sat, noon-6pm Sun; 12F; Metro to Capitole)*. Next to the Basilica of St-Serin, this museum has one of Southwest France's best collections of Gallo-Roman artifacts, from busts of Caesar and other imperial lords to ancient coins, vases, and an impressive array of Roman jewelry. There are also some prehistoric artifacts to bring out the archaeologist in you.

Basilique Saint Serin *(13 place St. Serin; Tel 05/61-21-80-45; Bus 10, 59, 60, 61 to Arnaud Bernand, Chalets or Concorde; church 10am-noon/2-6pm daily, crypt 9am-noon/2-6pm Mon-Sat, noon-6pm Sun; church free, crypt 10F; No credit cards)*. Enter the crypt here, if you dare...Relics of 128 saints are said to be kept here, along with a thorn from *the* crown of thorns. The Romanesque church itself has an odd five naves, and from the outside the steeple looks like a waffle cone upside down.

At **Cathédrale Saint Étienne** *(Place St. Étienne; Tel 05/61-52-03-82; Bus 1 to Étienne; 7:30am-7pm daily)*: The big yellow doors of the Cathédrale contrast with the Gothic spires, stained glass windows, and cannon domes that reach towards the heavens. Bits look like they're crumbling on some of the massive columns, but restoration is in progress, as you can tell from the white smooth plaster and brick-work. Gregorian chants are pumped through mini-speakers; their echoes, and the flaking paintings and dusty wrought iron, make for a medieval effect.

modification

Find **Fetish Tattoo and Piercing** *(2 rue Cujas; Franck Tel 06/14-14-67-56, Tel 06/72-15-56-27; Bus 10, 22, 24, 38, Metro to Capitole; 1-8pm Wed-Sat, 3:30-8pm Tue; No credit cards)* a few blocks south of the Place du Capitole, by the graffiti-painted girl lounging in lavender and puckering up. Makes you wonder what she has tattooed on her butt. The waiting area is as comfy as a New York loft apartment. Look at the tatt mags and books or the Marlon Brando poster—maybe they'll give you ideas of what you want to print permanently onto your body.

sports

Toulouse isn't a crazy, tense city, but the park **Prairie des Filtres** on the west bank of the Garonne, and the **Promenade Henri Martin,** a walkway that extends along the river's east bank, provide refuge for runners, rollerbladers, strollers, and picnickers.

Feeling a little antsy from sitting on all those trains and buses? Get back control of the wheel at **Circuit Indoor de Toulouse** (165 route de Revel; Tel 05/62-16-32-00; Bus 78 to St. Orens Église; 2pm-midnight Mon-Sat, till 8pm Sun; 50F five minutes; No credit cards). It's a little pricey to drive a go-cart wildly around the indoor track, but if you come in a group and call ahead of time, you can organize races and the winner gets showered with Champagne.

Climbing the walls with all the damn culture and 16th-century art your traveling companion is making you see? **Altissimo** (5 rue Jean Rodier-Z.I. de Montaudran; Tel 05/61-54-32-00; Bus 80 Stop Rodier or Villet; noon-11pm daily; No credit cards) is a wall-climbing gym that will work out any tensions between you two. With 1,400 square meters

by foot

Before setting out, get some picnic fare for your day pack [see *to market,* below]. Find the **Hôtel d'Assézat** [see *culture zoo,* below], on the Place d'Assézat after you hop off the metro at Esquirol. (Note: When crossing the Toulousian streets, that's not an alarm clock you're hearing, it's just the cross-walk signal.) Take a peek at the grandeur of the old mansion you'll never live in. In the courtyard sits an awkward sculpture of a musician playing the guitar which confirms that if you're rich enough, you can do what you want. Return to the Place, go down rue Metz, and cross the Pont Neuf to reach the other bank of the Garonne. Take a left down Cours Dillon, which leads to **Prairie des Filtres,** a long park where you can sit, graze on the nibbles you brought, and watch the river flow. Then back up toward the bridge to see the huge oyster shell in the gardens of the **Hôtel Dieu** [see *culture zoo,* below], bigger and better than one you just saw. Take a right on rue Viguerie, a back street of little interest, till you get to the *Pont Saint Pierre.* From this bridge the famous pink city stretches out in front of you for prime viewing.

(4,667 square feet) of surface and over 200 routes of all levels, it's one of the largest gyms in France and has all the gear available to rent. You could be in the Pyrénées, the Rockies, any mountain range in the world.

STUFF

Follow that mob with their arms full of shopping totes down rue Alsace-Lorraine! They know where to find sexy little dresses (mostly for adolescent girls or women who think they have to look like one), accessories, and chain stores like the Spanish **Zara** *(25 Alsace-Lorraine)*, similar to Banana Republic. On **rue Pomme** (Apple Street), which crosses Alsace-Lorraine, and on nearby **Place Wilson** is where to hunt for more chic shopping. Brands like DKNY, Jeans Couture, Hugo Boss, Kenzo, Givenchy, CK, and Versace make their presence known on Place Wilson. Time for a French lesson: *"Acceptez-vous Visa?"*—or you can just flash the plastic and smile and hope for the best.

▶▶DUDS

You could probably find a cheaper pair of jeans at home, but the men's and women's collections at **WHD Présente GAS** *(14 Alsace-Lorraine; Bus 10, 22, 24, 38, Metro to Capitole; 10am-7pm Tue-Sat, 10am-noon Mon; www.gasjeans.it; V, MC)* can outfit you for the city. The GAS denim clothes aren't dudded with sequins and glitter; they are stylin' simple. Most jeans or pants leave your wallet 400 to 600F thinner, but, hey, that'll just make your butt look smaller.

Chevignon *(13-15 rue Pomme; Tel 05/61-22-61-25; Bus 10, 22, 24, 38, Metro to Capitole; 10am-7pm Tue-Sat, 10am-noon Mon; AE, DIN)*, a three floor *prêt-à-porter* men's, women's, and children's clothing store,

only here

The French are known for their perfume—OK, so maybe they used to be so popular 'cause people didn't shower quite so often, but don't think about that. Toulouse is famous for violet and lavender scents in perfumes, potpourris, bath oils, and overall olfactory seduction. If you're looking to draw that Frenchman from across the room, you have to get a move on it and go to **Violettes et Pastel** *(10 rue Saint-Pantaléon; Tel 05/61-22-14-22; Bus 10, 22, 24, 38, metro to Capitole; 10am-7pm Tue-Sun; AE, V, MC, DIN)*. It's like an old apothecary full of love potions and tubes of herbs, spices, and fragrances (around 30F), made expressly for you man-eaters. Get some before he gets away.

outfits you in its own brand-name sportswear. Come on in and get that I-just-threw-this-on-but-don't-I-look-great-and-didn't-you-notice-it's-*Chevignon?* look. A simple tee costs you 115F.

The crazy woven straw hats complete with daisies and spiraling tops at **Idée en Têtes/Mapie des Vignes** *(29 rue Pharon; Tel 05/61-25-68-88; Bus 12, 38, 52, 53, 54 to Salins; 10am-7pm Mon-Sat)* look like they're out of a Dr. Seuss book. Examples of the colorful clothes designed in the shop and custom tailored to your womanly form are displayed in the window next to the *prêt-à-porter* wear at this *très chic* boutique.

▶▶BOUND

Booksellers set up stalls, stocked with old and new editions, at a couple of book markets, one on Thursdays in the **place Arnaud Bernard,** and the other on Wednesdays right in the heart of the city, on the Place du Capitole.

If you're not here on market day, the absolute best for buying and trading used books in English is **Books and Mermaids** *(3 rue Mirepoix; Tel 05/61-12-14-29, Fax 05/61-23-66-14; Bus 10, 22, 24, 38, Metro to Capitole; 10:30am-noon/2-7pm Mon-Fri; No credit cards),* on a street parallel to the Place du Capitole. You have 15,000 volumes to choose from if you want to settle down in a cafe or need a train book. The people working at the shop are also an excellent source of info to meandering English speakers who need help getting set in the right direction.

▶▶THRIFT

Guys, your girlfriend may shriek at the new Hawaiian print shirt and bowling shoes you sport strutting out of the dressing room at **Le Grenier d'Anais** *(54 rue Peyrolières; No phone; Bus 10, 22, 24, 38, Metro to Capitole; 10am-1pm/3-7pm Mon-Sat; No credit cards),* but you can distract her by buying her the lime-green cat suit or '70s patterned poly dress. City event flyers are also scattered about the store—you need to debut those threads, man!

▶▶TUNES

For the indecisive, the 3,000 vinyl and 10,000 CDs at **Armadillo** *(32 rue Pharon; Tel 05/62-26-28-57; Bus 12, 38, 52, 53, 54 to Salins; 2-7pm Mon-Wed, 11am-7pm Thur-Sat; V, MC)* may cause high stress. Of course you have to like garage, reggae, ska, or good old-fashioned rock and roll. If you really want to experience everything French, they also have some national and local bands' albums too. They're not too pricey with CDs at around 60F and vinyl 70F.

▶▶BAZAAR

Tourists crowd the main flea market, Sunday mornings on **place Saint Serin,** *(Bus 10, 59, 60, 61 to Arnaud Bernand, Chalets, or Concorde)* hunting for deals that used to be easier to find in the day when finding a bargain in other people's old junk wasn't "discovering *vintage* treasures." Plenty of vendors lure you into buying with their practiced English sales tactics. To find even bigger price tags and bigger items, check out the **Antique Market** *(Bus 1 Stop Jardin Royal, 24 Stop Ozenne)* on Allées Jules Guesdes near the Grand Ronde the first weekend of every month.

TOULOUSE

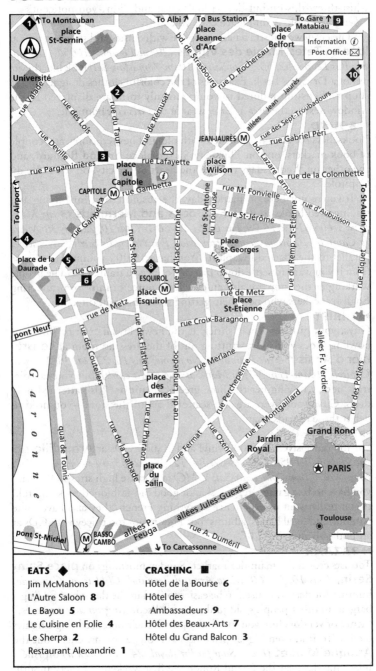

EATS ◆

Jim McMahons **10**
L'Autre Saloon **8**
Le Bayou **5**
Le Cuisine en Folie **4**
Le Sherpa **2**
Restaurant Alexandrie **1**

CRASHING ■

Hôtel de la Bourse **6**
Hôtel des
 Ambassadeurs **9**
Hôtel des Beaux-Arts **7**
Hôtel du Grand Balcon **3**

Go home with musty books, old (or stolen) cameras, or prints, if you don't have room for the rocking chair.

Eats

Unemployed students with time on their hands means a variety of cheap eats in town. But as one of the bigger cities in the region, Toulouse also offers high-end and international dining as well. Of course, part of being a student is procrastinating your studies and reflecting on life, pensively sitting with your pen and paper in cafes and putting on your best bohemian blues. For daytime eating and lolling about with the best of them, head to the Place Arnaud Bernard. Try one of the array of restaurants situated on the many streets radiating off the Place du Capitole, like rue des Gestes (one block south), rue de Taur, and rue Gambetta, which also has a few falafel/sandwich shops and bakeries. Still haven't found what you're looking for? Head a tad east to Place Wilson or across Boulevard Lazare Carnot to rue Colombette. You'll find something to suit your taste on at least one of the central streets in Toulouse.

▶▶CHEAP

The absolute cheapest exotic food, Egyptian and Moroccan, is at **Restaurant Alexandrie** *(20 place Arnaud Bernard; No phone; Bus 10, 15, 16, 59-61, 70, 71 to Arnaud Bernard; 10am-1am daily; 35F student menu; No credit cards)*. For 35F, a starving student can stop the suffering with a falafel or kebab sandwich and fries or a tabouli salad washed down with a cup of mint tea. Both the fresh food and the waiters have made the local papers for being so popular with students, local bohemians, and the North African population.

The victuals at **Le Bayou** *(20 rue Peyrolières; Tel 05/61-23-91-74; Metro Stop Esquirol; open noon, last orders 10:30pm Tue-Sat; Dish of the day 45F, menu 85F; No credit cards)* are dee-licious. Louisiana flavors

TO MARKET

At the food market in Place Victor Hugo, where produce and fruit stalls surround you, you can also eat on a budget at lunchtime—around 60F will leave not an inch of room in your trousers. The market restaurants are down-to-earth and only deal in food, no velvet couches or changing art exhibits. On Sundays there's a farmer's market selling cheese, veggies, etc. at the Place Saint Aubin. They also have birds and farm animals for sale in case you decide to plant your roots in Toulouse.

spice up the food and photos of the Creole State paper the walls. However, as the real Bayou is a jambalaya of cultures and influences, so is the restaurant. You can take your pick of Creole, Indian, Chinese, Cajun, Spanish, or French dishes here while they filter in a little blues or jazz.

▶▶DO-ABLE

There's cool lighting and cool music drowned out by friends chatting and laughing at crêperie **Le Sherpa** (*49 rue du Taur; Tel 05/61-23-89-29; Bus 10, 22, 24, 38, Metro to Capitole; Noon-midnight daily; average crêpe or salad 30F; No credit cards*). The twentysomething crowd doesn't mind sharing a table when the place gets slammed. You can strike up conversation about the pastel classic-style paintings and read the poetry on the walls to get started while choosing what you want in your sweet or savory crepe—or maybe you'll want to share a soybean salad and sip exotic teas. If things go well, invite new friends to the theater, cinema, or a dance party you found out about on one of the posters bordering the walls or flyers lying on the table.

The French classics like *foie gras,* duck, and *croque monsieur* all get a twist as chef Nicolas Favrot turns traditional into innovative at **La Cuisine en Folie** (*15 rue des Blanchers; Tel 05/61-22-13-13; Bus 24, 25 to Arsenal; dinner served till 1am; Menu 105F; No credit cards*). Crazily colored tables, chairs, and old objects hanging on the walls augment the other not-so-traditional dishes, like ostrich and kangaroo. You can also sit on the terrace to take in the colors of the people walking by.

Eating poor little ducks and rabbits (who somehow seem more like victims than cows) or crepes 24/7 can make you sick of provincial *haute-cuisine.* Get your butt over to **Jim McMahons** (*6 blvd. de Strasbourg; Tel 05/61-62-19-50; Metro to Jean Jaurès; 11:30am-2am daily; Sunday brunch 110F; No credit cards*), a good old American diner for when you just want a f—ing burger. The Sunday brunch from noon till 3pm is as breakfast should be: good, greasy, and so much more substantial than a dinky *pain aux raisins,* you probably won't have to eat the rest of the day.

▶▶SPLURGE

They pull out the good china at **L'Autre Salon** (*45 rue des Tourneurs; Tel 05/61-22-11-63; Bus 2, 12, 52, 54, 92, Metro to Esquirol; 10am-7pm Tue-Sat, 10am-6pm Sun; Menu 129F; V, MC*), a tea room where you must put on your dining-with-the-queen manners if you lunch on little salads and provincial plates. Or discuss the weather and taste the yummy homemade cakes at high tea time. You have to treat yourself once and while, and you might as well do it properly!

crashing

In any French town if the *gare* is set away from the center squares, there tends to be a seedy strip or two of flashing lights and grime out near the station, and Toulouse is no exception. We recommend only one hotel near the station. The rest are clumped around the center, where you'll find a range from reasonable budget spots mingled with the hoity-toity joints. The hotels overlooking the main squares can sometimes be noisy, but there are plenty on tucked-away streets where you can find some peace and quiet. It's up to you to make reservations, but the tourist office provides handy booklets of hotels and their telephone numbers with an attached map to get you to your bed. The usual norms hold true for hotel hunting in Toulouse: Call at least a day or two ahead for the weekends or during the summer. Check-out is around noon, so if you don't come into town with a reservation, either arrive early or call immediately after noon to see if there have been any cancellations.

▶▶CHEAP

A little old, but on a quiet street in a central area, the family-run **Hôtel de la Bourse** *(11 rue Clémence-Isaure; Tel 05/61-21-55-86,; Bus 2, 12, 52, 53, 54, 56, 62, 78-80, 92 to Pont Neuf, Metro to Esquirol; 90-160F singles or doubles)* has 17 decent rooms, all furnished with a washbasin and bidet, and none with a shower or WC—this is Old France. You're a block away from the Garonne River and about five blocks from Place du Capitole, which makes trotting around town easier.

▶▶DO-ABLE

For you out there with the 80-ton pack, a perfect location near the train station is **Hôtel des Ambassadeurs** *(68 rue Bayard; Tel 05/61-62-65-84, Fax 05/61-62-97-38; Bus 14, 19, 21, Metro to Marengo SNCF; 150-260F single or double; V, MC)*. It stands above the rest in this area for its shiny spic 'n' span bathrooms where you can take a bath without having to worry about foot fungus. The proprietors are very welcoming to all their international guests. All 32 rooms here have bathroom (WC, sink, shower) plus TV and Tel.

The historic facade and decor of the **Hôtel du Grand Balcon** *(8 rue Romiguières; Tel 05/61-21-48-08, Fax 05/61-21-59-98; Bus 10, 22, 24, 38, Metro to Capitole; 160-210F sink, 210-230F shower, no toilet, 230-270F full bath, single or double)* take you back to a different time, and even though keeping up-to-date on things like central heat and elevators, the place is a little tired. When no one was around I had the feeling I was in *The Shining* and blood was going to start flowing out of the walls. Nevertheless, you couldn't be more central than this, and for the money it's great. Of the 52 rooms in this hotel, 21 have full bathrooms; the remainder have sinks and showers in the rooms, with WC in the hallways. The building's corner faces the Place du Capitole; if you try, you might get a grand balcony.

▶▶SPLURGE

If you sleep at **Hôtel des Beaux-Arts** *(1 place du Pont Neuf; Tel 05/61-23-40-50, Fax 05/61-22-02-27; Bus 2, 12, 52, 53, 54, 56, 62, 78-80, 92 to Pont Neuf, Metro to Esquirol; www.internetclub.fr/hotel-des-beauxarts/ acceui/htm, hba@internetclub.fr; 480-1000F double; AE, V, MC, DC)*, go for the top (floor, that is). Ask for one of the rooms with a terrace overlooking the Garonne and maybe you'll get lucky. The building helps paint the city's landscape pink as a historic brick villa. The inside has nothing to do with history though, with its modern facilities and contemporary art-work in each room. A tad pricey—you might as well enjoy the rooms, which are apparently soundproof, in case things get a little wild.

need to know

Currency Exchange C2E Capitole Echange Estimation *(30 rue Taur; Tel 05/61-13-64-25; Bus 10, 22, 24, 38, Metro to Capitole; 9am-7pm Mon-Sat Jun-Aug, 9am-12:30pm/2-6pm Mon-Sat Sept-May)* is the most central and easiest exchange point, right off Place du Capi-tole. There are also ATMs, known as *distributeurs automatiqies,* located everywhere in the center. The most visible is operated by Banque Pop-ulaire, rue Alsace-Lorraine, adjacent to the Place du Capitole.

Tourist Info The **Tourist Office** *(Donjon du Capitole, Place Charles de Gaulle; Tel 05/61-11-02-22; Bus 10, 22, 24, 38, Metro to Capitole; 9am-7pm Mon-Sat, 10am-1pm/2-6:30pm Sun May-Sept; 9am-6pm Mon-Fri 9am-12:30pm/2-6pm Sat, 10am-12:30pm/2-5pm Sun Oct-Apr; ottoulouse@mipnet.fr; www.mairie-toulouse.fr)* for Toulouse and the Haute-Garonne region is right behind the Place du Capitole and provides maps and guided tours of museums, churches, and the city (in English). It also has a ticket desk for selected city festivals and events.

Public Transportation Toulouse runs mostly on **SEMVAT buses** *(49 rue De Gironis; info Tel 05/61-41-70-70; Bus 52 to Gironis)* and has one **metro** line resembling the tram at Disney World, except you hear jazz or Bob Marley while you wait! The system covers the city and out-skirts thoroughly. You'll be buying red tickets, one ride 8F, return 15F, which can be used for an hour on both buses and the metro and are sold on board and at machines in the stations. Unfortunately, most buses stop running around 8pm and the few night buses run only till about 11:30pm. The last metro leaves the end of the line at midnight, 12:40am on Friday and Saturday. This hardly gives you enough time to get going for the night, so if you're going somewhere that's not in walking distance from your hotel, you'll have to flag a **taxi** or order one by calling *05/34-25-02-50.*

Health and Emergency Emergency: *081;* Ambulance (SAMU): *15;* Fire: *18* (firefighters here are trained paramedics too); Cops: *17;* Euro emergency: *112;* SOS doctors: *05/61-50-10-80.* With med schools galore, there are a handful of hospitals here, the most central being **Hôpital de la Grave** *(Place Lange; Tel 05/61-77-78-33; Bus 14 to Olivier Hôpital la Grave, Bus 1, 3, 66, Metro to St. Cyprien République),* with a couple of clinics surrounding it.

The other main hospitals, further out, are **CHR de Purpan** *(Place du Docteur-Baylac; Tel 05/62-77-22-33; Bus 14, 64, 70 to Place Baylac)* and **CHR de Rangueil** *(ave. Jean-Poulhes; Tel 05/61-32-25-33; Bus 2, 92 to CHR Rangueil).*

Pharmacies Look for flashing crosses to find a *pharmacie.* A **Pharmacie de Nuit,** open from 8pm-8am, is at **13 rue Sénéchal** *(Tel 05/61-21-81-20; Bus 10, 22, 24, 38, Metro to Capitole).*

Telephone City code: *05/61* or *05/62,* if you're calling within France, *561* or *562* if you're calling from another country; National operator: *12;* international operators: *00-33-12* plus the country code.

Airport There's an **airport shuttle** *(Tel 05/34-60-64-00; 5:20am-9pm Mon-Fri, 6am-8:20pm Sat-Sun; from the airport, shuttles run until a half-hour after the last flight, around 11-11:50pm; 23F one way, 36F round trip adults; 18F one way, 27F round trip students)* from the main hangar, **Aeroport de Toulouse-Blagnac** *(Chambre de Commerce; Tel 05/61-42-44-00; www.toulouse.aeroport.fr),* that runs to the **Gare Routière** *(Bus 22 Matabiau Gare SNCF, Metro Marengo SNCF),* **Allées Jean-Jaurés** *(Metro Jean-Jaurès),* and **Place Jeanne d'Arc** *(Bus 40, 42, 70, 71, 59-61, 73-76 Stop Jeanne d'Arc)* every 20-30 minutes.

Trains From the main station, **SNCF Matabiau Gare** *(Blvd. Pierre Sémard; Tel 08/36-35-35-35, 08/36-35-36-15; Bus 14, 19, 21, metro to Marengo SNCF, bus 41, 22 to Matabiau Gare SNCF),* you can get to Paris, Bordeaux, and Marseilles on the high speed trains.

Bike Rental Rent bikes from **Rêves Moto** *(14 blvd. de la Gare; Tel 05/62-47-07-08; 90-125F per day).*

Bus Lines Out of the City Take a bus to towns in the 200km (125-mile) radius of Toulouse from the **Gare Routiére** *(68 blvd. Pierre Sémard; Tel 05/61-61-67-67; Bus 38, 40, 41, 42, 73-76 to Pont Matabiau; 7am-7pm),* right next to the train station.

Laundry Wash your dirty drawers at **Laverie Place St. Pierre** *(17 place St. Pierre; Tel 06/81-03-46-25; Bus 24, 25 to Arsenal; 8am-7pm daily; No credit cards).* Closer to Place du Capitole is **Hallwash Laverie** *(1 rue Mirepoix; No phone; Bus 10, 22, 24, 38, Metro to Capitole; 7am-9pm; No credit cards)* Both have detergent, and you gotta do it all yourself.

Postal The main **La Poste** is at 9 rue Lafayette *(Tel 05/62-15-33-51; Bus 10, 22, 24, 38, metro to Capitole).*

Internet See *wired,* above.

foix

Close to tons of underground caves and rivers, and right in the midst of the awe-inspiring eastern Pyrénées, the quiet mountain village of Foix, about 82 km (50 miles) from Toulouse, is more than your average gateway to outdoor excursions. If you're coming from a big city, you'll be surprised to learn that it's also the center of a lot of the state administrative activities for the *Ariège* department, even though it seems too small to be the seat of any action.

But other than touring the quaint medieval buildings, narrow alleys, and nearby **Château de Foix** [see *culture zoo,* below], there isn't a huge amount to do here—don't expect any rockin' nightlife. Foix *is* tiny, and most of the real action lies outside of town. Trip out on pre-historic drawings in the underground caves, or hop on a boat to drift down Europe's longest navigable underground river [see *great outdoors, below,* for both]. You may also want to consider skipping town altogether and planning an overnight stay in one of the **gîtes** that dot the mountains outside of town [see *gîtes for mountain men and women, below*].

The people in Foix will include a few like yourself, also wandering around in awe snapping pics of the breathtaking surrounding. Otherwise it's mostly locals, who are busy running errands and getting things done.

neighborhoods and hanging out

The Ariège River forks and encloses the town in a triangle. Coming from the *gare,* you exit to the right and walk along the river. Before crossing the **Pont Vieux** (old bridge), stop and get the camera out. Foix's gem, the **Château de Foix** [see *culture zoo,* below], hangs there in the mountains above the rooftops and rushing river. It'll seem silly to have to keep looking at your map as you walk around the tiny blocks of the town center, but believe us—if you don't you'll end up passing the same pharmacy seven times.

The **place Halle aux Grains** is a central square perfect for drinking coffee or eating outdoors. A seasonal market full of produce or regional specialties are held under the gazebo. Another nice stopping point is the **place Saint Volusien** at the point of this triangular town, where you can gaze at the **Préfecture** and the **St. Volusien Abbey.** Both buildings originated around the cult of St. Volusien, former bishop of Tours, who was exiled from the Loire Valley by the Visigoths in 495 AD. After settling near what is now Foix and founding a church, he was beheaded by the Visigoth king, Alaric II (a.k.a Eric II). **Église Saint Volusien** *(Rue St. Volusien, Tel 05/61-65-02-17; 10am-Noon, 2-6pm daily; Free guided tours (in French) in July and August, 11am-noon, 4-6pm)* is the center of his legend today, and site of his relics, such as his skeleton, which during the Middle Ages were reputed to have magical powers. The church and the monastery associated with it (now functioning as the Préfecture of Foix, or the seat of government) were begun in the 1100s, enlarged in the 1300s, partially demolished during the Wars of Religion (mid-1500s), then rebuilt in a less coherent style in the 1700s. After the revolution, what had been the monastery was transformed into the Préfecture, one of the only ones in France that enjoys direct access to a church, supposedly so that the occupants could observe the Mass without going out into the cold. Today, only the church's crypt and the church's main portal remain from the original 12th century construction, with most of the Préfecture and the rest of the church coming from a mishmash of later styles. The Préfecture is a government bureaucracy, and only its main vestibule (which is not medieval) can be entered during business hours by the public, unless they have official business to conduct.

The parking lot next to the Halle des Grains is the place to catch a game or two of *boule* or *pétanque* with the fellas...or maybe just watch. And best of all, if you want a great view of the Château and the river, the parking lot on the **rue des Moulins** is right at the foot of the craggy rocks that support the fortress along a breaking flow of water. A little picnic table at the edge of the lot is a favorite for wanderers of the world. Ariège has attracted these types as far back as prehistoric times; you can see their evidence in the many regional caves [see *great outdoors, below*].

CULTUre ZOO

At **Château de Foix** *(9:45am-noon/2-6pm daily; tours 10am, 11am, 2:30pm, 3:45pm, or 5pm; entrance 25F adults, 12F students; Free tours; No credit cards)*, you can follow the guide around some of the best-conserved architecture of the Middle Ages or just wander around the turrets by yourself. How much money have you spent in Europe paying to climb stairs? What's another 25 francs? The mountain village view alone is worth it.

Here in late July and August? Ask the tourist office, the guys over at the *pétanque* court, or consult **Conseil Régional Midi-Pyrénée's** festival guide page *www.cr-mip.fr,* about the medieval festivities when the town converts to a history book with an old-time market, street performances, and concerts topped off with a light-and-sound show on the chateau.

Great outdoors

The rugged Pyrénéen foothills around Foix provide lots of panoramas for anyone fit enough to indulge in a hiking experience of between two and five hours. The tourist office will provide a free leaflet describing two

legend has it ...

Bet you never really thought much about why places have the names they do. As for the mountain range dividing Spain and France, I can tell you this: Stowed away in one of the largest caves around, called Lombraves, was a clan of mountain folk. Pyrène, the beautiful princess, caught the eye of Hercules himself who was just passing through. Back in the day when there was no Planned Parenthood, things got a little complicated when he knocked her up. What else for Hercules to do but take off? Pyrène tried to skip town too, high-tailing it to the woods. She didn't get too far, though, on account of a bear who slashed her up. Hercules, hearing cries, ran back to his Pyrène, but too little, too late, buddy. So to cope with his guilt, he named the mountain range for her: the Pyrénées.

foix

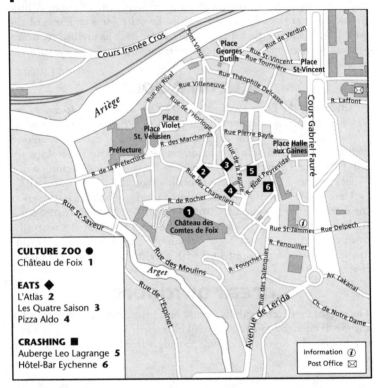

CULTURE ZOO ●
Château de Foix **1**

EATS ◆
L'Atlas **2**
Les Quatre Saison **3**
Pizza Aldo **4**

CRASHING ■
Auberge Leo Lagrange **5**
Hôtel-Bar Eychenne **6**

Information ⓘ
Post Office ✉

themed walks of medium difficulty, both of which depart from the Church of St. Volusien/the Préfecture, in the heart of Foix. The first themed walk leads you, after an hour's uphill climb, to a masonry and metal cross planted into a panoramic hilltop—supposedly the site from which a medieval hermit, St. Sauveur—prayed for the souls of the citizens of Foix. The second themed walk leads you, after about an hour, to the site of a since-destroyed fortress that was built by the much persecuted heretical group, the Cathares, but where absolutely nothing—other than the legend and the panorama—remain today. Keep in mind that either of these themed walks can be extended on to other panoramic, even higher-altitude, outposts, depending on your energy level and time. Terrain is rocky, pine-strewn, and generally rather arid so don't expect a lot of interesting flora and fauna. It's wise to wear sturdy hiking boots and warm clothing, and to carry some bottled water and snack food for energy bursts.

Getting under the surface, go on a *grottes* expedition in one of the many caves. The biggest group of caves in the region, the **Niaux** *(Tel 05/61-05-*

88-37; 8:30am-11:30am/1:30-5:15pm every 45 min. Jul-Sept, 11am, 2:30pm, 4:30pm Oct-Jun; 60F), are about 25 km (15.5 miles) from Foix, south of Tarascon, and can only be visited by reservation. Due to deterioration of the 13,000-year-old cave paintings caused by too many visitors, only 20 visitors are allowed inside at a time. For an appointment, call 48 hours in advance. The grotto begins halfway up the mountainside, beneath a contemporary-looking porch built directly into the cliff's side. Walk through some anteroom-style caves, through long corridors, to a natural rotunda named "the black salon" by archeologists. Here, the edges are painted with remarkable depictions of herds of bison in profile. Prehistoric

gîtes for mountain men and women

If you are planning on hiking in the Pyrénées, Ariège, or Haute-Garonne regions, *refuges*— primitive, bare-bones shelters—spot the mountainsides and approximately 110,000 miles of trails called **Gîtes d'Etape et Rondo 'Plume des Pyrénées.** Refuges can be reserved by calling each place, as they are individually run. There are different kinds of accommodations depending on what each area has to offer. There are *gîtes* geared for hiking, horseback riding, kayaking, mountain biking, skiing, or cultural activities. The rates run from 45 to 120F a night and 50 to 120F for meals. For general info, contact **Centre d'Information Montagne et Sentier (CIMES-Pyrénées)** *(4 rue Maye Lane BP 24 65421 Ibos Cedex; Tel 05/62-90-09-92, Fax 05/62-90-67-61; www.cimes-pyrenees.com, cimes@RandoPyrenees.com),* or call **Vacances en Gîtes de France Ariège Pyrénées** *(Tel 05/61-02-30-89).* You can also request a guide with all the nitty-gritty from la **Confédération Pyrénéenne du Toulouse** *(57 blvd. de l'Embouchure, BP 2166 31022 Toulouse Cedex; Tel 05/61-13-55-88).*

An afternoon hike from Foix takes you to the closest *gîte* in **Roquefixade** *(Tel/Fax 05/61-03-01-36; open year round; roque fixade@mail.dotcom.fr; 65F summer 70F winter per person, 165-200F per person meals included; No credit cards),* which can set you up for mountain biking, rock climbing, skiing, or a visit to the nearby Château Cathare. Stay the weekend (1390F) or a week (3900F) to enjoy nature and meet some mountain man or woman who has extended their stay due to weather and has been on the trail just a little too long. E-mail or call for reservations and information.

painters used a mixture of bison fat and manganese oxide to create the cave paintings, which show a remarkable purity of line and design, marking the pinnacle of Magdalenian Art. The caves are...tricky. Tricky to get to—you can either take the bus [see *need to know,* below] heading towards Auzat with a limited schedule, or hook up with the **Auberge Leo Lagrange** [see *crashing,* below] to set up a day's journey.

Closer to town, six km (about 4 miles) away, the Leo Lagrange will also take you to the **Rivière Souterraine de Labouiche** (*Tel 05/61-65-04-11, Fax 05/61-02-90-77; 2-6pm Mon-Fri, 10am-noon/2-6pm Sun Apr-May 24, Sat May 25-Jun 30, 9:30am-6pm daily Jul-Aug, 10am—noon/2-6pm Sun Oct-Nov 11; 42F*), an underground river you float along in a wooden boat. Kinda cheesy, visited by school groups a lot, but still, an hour and a quarter on the longest European river of stalagmites, 'tites, and a waterfall is cool enough to write home about. Renting a bike or calling a cab are other possibilities for getting there. [see *need to know,* below, for both]

Want to check out some caves—the ones without any prehistoric drawings? Contact **Pyrène Voyage** (*6 place du Maréchale Leclerc, Mirepoix; Tel 05/61-68-83-84*). In addition to hardcore spelunking, the organization offers informal lectures on the region's architecture and historical treasures.

For active hill-climbing, mountain-biking, canyoning, and river-rafting excursions, the best and most versatile outfitter is **L'Association Pyrénevasion** (*6 route de Ganac, Foix; Tel 05/61-65-01-10*).

The best outfitter for watercrafts in the region is the **Comité Départemental Canoe and Kayak,** (*Tel 05/61-65-20-65*), in the hamlet of Ferrières, a mile south of Foix. Here, you can rent canoes, kayaks, and rowboats, and participate in any of the frequent rafting expeditions along the region's most visible river, the Ariège.

You can ride horseback, either within a rink or in the open air, at the **Centre Equestre Cantegril,** in the hamlet of St. Martin de Caralp, 4 miles west of Foix (*Tel 05/61-65-15-43*).

STUFF

▶▶**LOCAL PRODUCTS**

To take home regional smooshed duck in *pâtés* and *foie gras,* or wines, cheeses, and hams set out in lovely country kitchen displays, taste the products from **Les Terroirs du Plantaurel** (*3 rue Préfecture; Tel 05/61-65-05-00; 9:30am-12:30pm/3-7pm Tue-Fri, till 6:30pm Sat; V, MC*). You choose the products and the store wraps up gift packages to lug around. There may have to be an emergency picnic to get rid of the weight on your way.

EATS

▶▶**CHEAP**

The smell of cheap pizza dough drifts down the street from **Pizza Aldo** (*24 rue des Chapeliers; Tel 05/61-65-64-96; noon-1:30/7-9:30pm Mon-Fri, 7-9:30pm Sat; Pizza 25-33F; No credit cards*). Lady and the Tramp eat spaghetti on the window of this restaurant, which is more like a takeout with tables. Veggie toppings don't come from a can, but the dough is a tad floury. Locals can't get enough of it—probably 'cause they never had a Chicago or New York slice.

▶▶**DO-ABLE**

The menu is translated so hungry English speakers can easily fill empty stomachs in the creperie **Les Quatre Saison** (*11 rue de la Faurie; Tel 05/61-02-71-58; 11:45am-2pm Mon-Sat, 7-10pm Fr-Sat; 45-65F lunch, 85-105F dinner; V, MC*). Gather round the small wooden block tables for "salted" crepes with all kinds of cheese and other creamy artery-clogging ingredients, fresh salads to lift that feeling of guilt, and dessert crêpes for that sweet tooth. Open all four seasons, but the outdoor tables are only out in spring and summer.

Eating who-knows-what duck parts mashed into a paste isn't what you feel like for dinner? **L'Atlas** (*Place Pyrène; Tel 05/61-65-04-04; 11:30am-3pm/7-10:30pm Tue-Fri, Sun, 7-10:30pm Sat; Entree 50-70F; AE, V, MC, DIN*) has North African dishes that don't quack. Order up vegetable or chicken couscous and tagine. The latter is a stew served hot and delicious in a clay pot that looks like a party hat and will make you want to get up and bellydance.

crashing

This town, about 15 blocks wide, surprisingly has at least ten places to bunk up for the night. Most are closed between November or December through January and cost from 160F to no more than 450F with bathrooms (but no matching shampoo and shower caps).

A stay at the youth hostel in Foix, **Auberge Leo Lagrange** (*16 rue Nöel-Peyrevidal; Tel 05/61-65-09-04, Fax 05/61-02-63-87; open year round; leolagrange-foix@wanadoo.fr; 80F bed, breakfast included; AE, V, MC*), is like escaping to summer camp. They make it easy to canoe, kayak, rock climb, raft, and get to the caves and underground rivers because Monsieur Curbieres has connections with the local companies running trips and can also help you arrange week-long trips. Not to mention that they rent bikes on location for 50F. Not only is it in the heart of town, in the shadow of the landmark Château de Foix, but it's the cheapest option in town, and you don't need an HI card, but it fills up in the high season with French, Belgians, and close-by Catalan neighbors. Pile in for clean rooms with one to four beds, some with showers, and a big cafeteria where you can bring in food and sit in front of the *telly*. There is no mandatory curfew, since the managers give out keys to the front door, allowing their guests to wander in at any time.

The **Hôtel-Bar Eychenne** (*11 rue Nöel-Peyrevidal; Tel 05/61-65-00-04, Fax 05/61-65-56-63; Open year round; 180-230F double, 280F quad; AE, V, MC*) is right across the street from Leo LaGrange and offers comfy refuge. It's a bit old, the bathrooms are a little tainted—the hotel has a mishmash of bath styles, with some full bathrooms and others woefully incomplete—and the beds a little soft, but construction is underway to expand and put televisions and phones in the rooms, with a hike in prices. The owner will break from serving his buddies at the bar to check you in.

Another option is **Hôtel Lons** (*6 place G. Duthil; Tel 05/61-65-52-44, Fax 05/61-02-68-18; hotel-lons-foix@wanadoo.fr; Doubles 280F, Singles 310F; MC, V, AE, EC*), conveniently located in the city center.

need to know

Currency Exchange Local **banks** are open Monday to Friday till 5pm if you need to change money. The **post office** [see below] will also swap your cash.

Tourist Info The Foix **tourist office** (*31 bis avenue du Général de Gaulle; Tel 05/61-65-17-34; 9:15am-7pm Mon-Sat; ariègepyrénées.com*) is in the courtyard of the town hall and has info on outdoor adventures and clubs in the area. The Foix booklet they provide is complete with various local activities. There's also an office for Ariège-Pyrénées (*45 Cours Gabriel Fauré; Tel 05/61-65-12-12*), which can give you more outdoors-y info.

Public Transportation There's really no need, but perhaps to go outside Foix, call *05/61-65-12-69* for taxis.

Health and Emergency Emergency (SAMU ambulance): *15;* Police: *17,* Fire: *18.*

The hospital is across the street from the tourist office: **Centre Hospitalier** (*18 esplanade de Villote, Tel 05/61-05-40-40*).

Pharmacies One of the pharmacies is on **Place Freycinet** at the corner of **Rue des Merchands.**

Trains and Buses The **SNCF Gare** (*Ave. Pierre Semard; Info and reservation Tel 08/36-35-35-35, station Tel 05/61-02-03-60*) is on the east bank of the Ariège River, a few blocks out of the center. The coach company **Salt** (*Allées de Villote; Tel 05/61-65-08-40*) serves the region from **Ax-les-Thermes** to **Toulouse** and **Pas de la Case** to **Toulouse** (both through Foix), and from **Foix to Auzat.** To travel to **St. Girons,** take a **Denamiel** bus (*5 rue du Sénateur Paul Laffont; Tel 05/61-66-24-37, 05/61-65-06-06*) that leaves from behind the post office. Leaving from the same place, **Sovitours** (*Tel 05/61-01-02-35*) runs from **Pamiers** to **Foix** to **Perpignan.**

Bike Rental The **Sport Expert** (*40-42 rue Declassé; Tel 05/61-65-00-41; 75-90F half-day, 90-110F full day, 200F weekend, 300F week*) will get you on wheels to bike around the area and recommend great day trips.

Laundry Wash your muddy socks at **Laverie la Lavandiere** (*32 rue la Faurie; Tel 05/61-01-72-15; 7am-9pm daily*).

Postal The **main post** is at 4 allées de Villote (*Tel 05/61-02-01-02; 8am-7pm Mon-Fri, 8am-noon Sat*).

basque
COAST

the basque coast

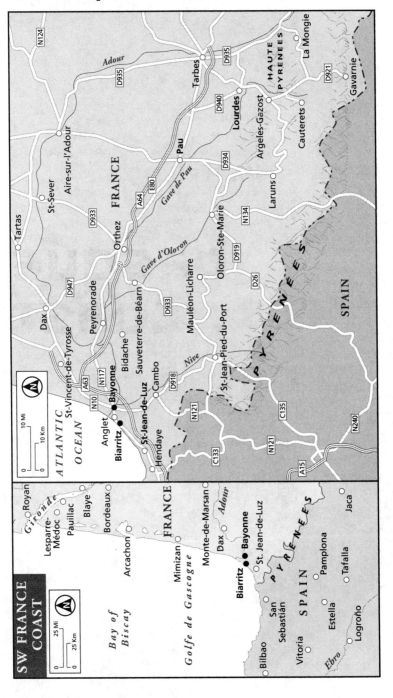

beaches, bikinis, surfboards, mountains...what more could you ask for? The French Basque country is a mix of berets and Sex Wax, surfers on a shoestring and rich guys with Rolexes. The coast draws young energy to ride the waves, wealthy geezers to drop some pocket change, and both to toast in the sun. More traditional Basque culture can be found away from the Atlantic in small towns surrounded by the blues, greens, and reds of the nearby rivers, forests, and mountains. Whichever way you go, the French Basque Country has been opening eyes and attracting visitors for a very long time.

The best seaside romping grounds are clustered around **Biarritz** and **Anglet.** Biarritz is the kind of place that lives up to its full-color travel brochure image, with blossoming hydrangeas, luxury hotels, and perfect terrace cafes overlooking the ocean. But you won't pay as high a price for the wild perfection on the other side of the point in Anglet, where surfer dudes have invaded the beach. Basque's capital city of **Bayonne** and eensy-teensy **St.-Jean-Pied-de-Port** are *tranquiles,* with more culture and tradition, which include mountain walks along the *Chemin de St. Jacques,* a famous pilgrim route that leads to Santiago de Compostela in Spain.

The origin of the Basque people and their language is puzzling. It is known that people have lived here for tens of thousands of years. Traces have even been found from the Paleolithic and Neolithic periods. Then the Romans traipsed in around 202 B.C., the Visigoths followed in 484 B.C., and so began the establishment of the Pays Basque. *Euskara* is spoken in close to one-third of the region's provinces; although it's mainly used by the older generations in larger towns, many folks speak it in smaller villages. *Euskara* may sound like Russian to an outsider, but in fact it has no link to any other language in the world. Possibly the oldest European language, it is certainly the oldest still in use. The Basque terrorist group, ETA (Euskadi ta Azkatasuna, or Basque Nation and Liberty) originates in Spain and maintains a low-key presence in this part of France, but few people in Pays Basque support the group and it presents little threat.

The Basques are some of the best cooks in the south of France. They take simple, fresh food and stir up tasty dishes starting with olive oil, as in every good Mediterranean cuisine, then adding spices, especially black pepper and garlic. On the coast, seafood and shellfish are pulled out of the sea by the bucketful, and you can get a pail of spiced mussels with fries on the side at most restaurants. But if you're a vegetarian who eats fish, you might find yourself questioning whether fish might have feelings: The chewable delight called *chipirones* is prepared by beating cuttlefish, then stuffing them with surprise herbs. Even though the cuttlefish is dead when it gets flogged, it *still* sounds vicious to us.

getting around the region

Bayonne is the first whistle-stop in the French Basque Country from any direction in France. If you're crossing the border from northern Spain, you'll take the "*petit tren*" (a metro-like train) to Irun or Hendaye (France), then a regular SNCF train to Biarritz.

Once you're here, Bayonne, Anglet, and Biarritz are so close together they are best reached by bus; the ride between towns takes 2½ hours or less. In fact, the same local bus system links all three. The buses have different summer schedules and routes (some run *only* in August), so make sure the schedule you're looking at corresponds with the season. Bus schedules and maps are found in each town's tourist office or in the **SNCF** train stations in Biarritz and Bayonne. Individual bus routes and times are also marked at each stop. It's 7.50F for a ticket you can use for an hour. (If you stay at the youth hostels, you can get them for 6.20F.) The 11-line system is easy to follow and pretty extensive throughout the Basque coast region, and drivers will even drop you off at the youth hostel door in Anglet. You can't take bikes on the buses, but you're permitted a surfboard of up to two meters.

To get to the Pyrenees there's a train line or buses to St.-Jean-Pied-de-Port. Both have limited schedules, which means you can't just pop into the station hoping the next departure is in an hour. It helps to plan your day the night before.

▶▶SUGGESTED ROUTES

Bayonne is a good place to start because its train station is close to the center of the region you'll be exploring. From here you can hit the beaches of Biarritz and Anglet or head down to the Pyrenees. Note that Bayonne is some 6 kilometers from the ocean.

Hopping from Bayonne to Biarritz or Anglet is super-easy on the city buses and can be done in 10 or 30 minutes respectively. It's really up to you

rules of the game on the basque coast

Beach bars can get rowdy, and sometimes the alternative, a night of drinking and chilling out on the beach, is more appealing anyway. Biarritz seems to be more low-key than Anglet; at either place you'll likely find informal beach parties, sometimes with a drum circle that passersby can join.

basque architecture

Away from the glitter and glitz of Biarritz, traditional Basque architecture calls attention to the landscape and looks the way good ol' farmhouses should. People created the design out of necessity, using whatever construction materials were available. The whitewashed houses have red or green timber frames of exposed beams, indicating country solidarity with the colors of the Basque flag. Back in the day, poor oxen had to prove their patriotism and by giving blood to stain the wood for these frames and window shutters.

Also back then, the ground floor was a covered entrance leading directly to the stable. The first floor was where you bunkered down and said Goodnight, John Boy. The attic was used to store hay and help insulate the house. On modern houses you may see little triangular windows painted where the attic is. They are purely stylistic now, but the real windows once served to let a breeze pass through the hay.

Rolling in that hay made for larger families, which meant that additions were built onto the sides of houses, and as no one worried about symmetry, roofs on one side often extended further out than on the other. This lopsided lodging tended to stay in the family, and houses today have names that sound like pets or grand estates.

as to how you take on the region: You can go from glitzy Biarritz to the natural beauty of the Anglet beach or vice versa, depending on your mood.

Even though trains connect Bayonne and Biarritz, it's easier on the city bus unless you're already at the *gare*.

Bounce back to Bayonne to get down to St.-Jean-Pied-de-Port, best reached by train, for a little fresh mountain air. (From here you're about 8 kilometers from the Spanish border.)

Travel Times

* TGV Fast Train—
  more expensive)
** By car

	Biarritz	Anglet	St.-Jean-Pied-de-Port	Paris	Bayonne
Bayonne	:10	:15**	1:00	7:30	-
Biarritz	-	:20**	1:00**	5:00* 8:00	:10
Anglet	:20**	-	:50**	7:20**	:15**
St.-Jean-Pied-de-Port	:40**	:50**	-	8:00	:35**

bayonne

Don't make the mistake of thinking Bayonne is on the beach. It's close, but no cigar—actually it's about a 10- to 30-minute bus ride away. Bayonne is situated right at the fork of two rivers, the Adour and the smaller Nive, making it the Basque Country port. Although it's the capital city, it really doesn't have much to offer in the way of parties or beaches, and it feels more like a quiet fishing village.

Bayonne can be a pleasant little stopover on your way to or from the beach. When you turn the narrow corners, you'll happen upon typical Basque architecture, and you may see Spanish immigrants playing flamenco guitar out on the streets. The white, red, and brown buildings have exposed beams and thatching, and you can spend a day sitting in the hidden squares or watching the swirling waters of the rivers. Make sure to catch Mom Nature's show at dusk, when the light reflects the rows of Basque houses on the river. That may be your best shot at nighttime entertainment, though—the bar scene isn't exactly wild, and you may get the feeling that a lot of people go to Biarritz or elsewhere to cut loose.

Bayonne can be an okay base if you want to spend your days at the beach in Anglet or Biarritz (it's cheaper and rooms are much easier to come by in the summer), but keep in mind that the last buses back to Bayonne leave around 8 or 8:30pm. On the other hand, crashing here is a bit cheaper than in Biarritz. It's up to you to decide whether to pay the extra francs for convenience. Buses between Bayonne and Biarritz or Anglet are efficient and frequent [see *need to know,* below].

The rivers going out to the ocean create boundaries for the different sections of town: **le Grand Bayonne,** around the cathedral, is the historical center, has a small shopping district, and is most active during the day; **le Petit Bayonne,** resting between the two rivers, is best for getting the feel of an old Basque town or for hitting the bars; and finally **St. Esprit** is where the train station is, but where there's not much worth seeing.

bar scene

Le Petit Bayonne runs along three parallel streets: **rue des Tonneliers, rue Pannecau,** and **ruc des Cordeliers.** It seems like the locals find nothing of interest in Bayonne and take off to Biarritz or Anglet, or even go down to San Sebastian in Spain to party (an hour and 15-minute train ride away). Then some of the kids in Biarritz or Anglet make little excursions out to Bayonne to chill out. As in any small town, people get ants in their pants sitting around the same places weekend after weekend. I was told there was a club in Bayonne, but that it was really too lame and dead to even look for.

An Irish pub right on the edge of le Grand Bayonne on the river Nive, **Katie Daly's** *(3 place de la Liberté; Tel 05/59-59-09-14; Bus 1, 2, 4 to Mairie; 8:30am-2am daily; pint of Guinness 33F; AE, MC, V, DC)* is complete with Irish bartender who swears the Guinness here is just as good as it is at home. You won't miss televised football (soccer) matches here—they turn on the big screen TV no matter which teams happen to be playing. You probably won't miss the other small, dark, and dingy Basque bars in town either.... At 10 pm on Thursdays, Fridays, and Saturdays, traditional Irish or local rock, pop, and funk bands accompany you and your pint.

It's slightly cheesy, and the crowd is slightly older, but if you've had enough of French Irish bars, check out **Cabaret La Luna Negra** *(Rue des Cordeliers; Tel 05/59-25-78-05; 6pm-2am daily; cover 30-60F).* There are two bars, and frequent live entertainment in the form of floor shows, dancing, and live bands that range from jazz and blues, to French pop.

festivals

Twice a year Bayonne hosts a festival and lets its hair down. Traditional Basque bands come in for 10 hours of music on June 21, the first day of summer, during **La fête de la musique,** which takes place all over France. The **Fêtes de Bayonne** are the town's own festivities, held from the first Wednesday in August till the following Sunday. Every day people play music, drums, and *pelote* (see *only here*). To top it off, there's a bullfight on the final Sunday, when you take to the streets and pretend you're in Pamplona.

Culture Zoo

Bayonne only has a few cultural highlights, making it an easy town to conquer and giving you time to downshift from mega-Euro touring. Strategically speaking, Bayonne is a handy chunk of land to hang on to, so over the years it's been a significant port. The ancient Romans established a garrison here, medieval Bayonne was under French and British rule, and then Spain tried to get its nose in things. With all this tug-of-war, Bayonne became a fortification. It's rampart-like walls—which could almost be overlooked because they lie out on the edge of town—the great 17th-century engineer Vauban designed the walls we see today, parts of which you can walk along on the Avenue F. Forgues.

Cathédrale St. Marie and its cloisters *(Place Pasteur/rue d'Espagne; Tel 05/59-59-17-82; Bus 1, 2, 4 to Mairie; 7:30am-noon/3-7pm Mon-Sat, 3:30-6:30pm Sun & holidays; free):* The spiny 19th-century steeples of this cathedral are the most characteristic landmark in Bayonne. The cathedral is worth half an hour of your time and is a good retreat on a hot day. It was begun in 1258 when Bayonne was under British control, falling to the French in 1451. That explains the cathedral's curious ornamentations, mixing such elements as the English coat-of-arms (three leopards) with the famous fleur-de-lis, most characteristic symbol of France. Some of the stained glass dates from the Renaissance, but the best statuary was smashed during the French Revolution. The gem of the complex—and reason enough to visit—are the wonderful cloisters that have survived since the 14th century. They're like a secret garden from the Middle Ages, the most tranquil place in Bayonne to get in touch with your "spiritual" side.

Musée Bonnat *(5 rue Jacques Laffitte; Tel 05/59-59-08-52; Bus 1-6, 8, 10, 72 to Reduit; 10am-noon/2-6pm Wed-Mon; 20F adults, 10F students, free first Sunday every month):* It's pretty impressive that this amazing collection actually *belonged* to someone (The M. Bonnet for whom the museum is named, of course). It's hardly the Louvre, but its collection encompasses hundreds of canvasses, far too many to display in its limited space. Some of the greatest European old masters are on parade here—not their masterpieces, of course, but still a decent sampling of their work. If anybody's the star, it's Rubens, with an entire salon devoted to his paintings. The collection's strongest point is its 19th-century art. Otherwise, it's like an introduction to art history 101, with works by David, Degas, Goya, Ingrés, da Vinci, El Greco, Tiepolo, and Rembrandt—a preview of European art from the 13th to the 20th centuries. Check out the often overlooked collection of antiquities in the basement, a kind of museum within a museum, with everything from amulets from Egypt to Greek vases.

Eats

Restaurants are found all over town, but travelers passing through often enjoy the ones along the river. At several seafood places along the river

wired

Cyber Net Café *(9 place de la République; Tel 05/559-557-898; 7am-2am daily; Bus 2, 6 to Gare, Bus 1 to Alsace Lorraine; cyber-net-café@wanadoo.fr; 1 hour 45F; No credit cards)* is a bar first, with two pool tables, a TV, and some local men having their morning dose of caffeine. The side room has seven computers to get on line. It's the place closest to the train station, if not the only place in Bayonne, to e-mail home.

Nive on the A. Jaureguiberry, Galuperie, and Corsaires quais, you can get a decent sit-down meal for a reasonable price that includes the mellow scenery. Give the pub **Kate Daly's** [see *bars*, above] a go between noon and 3pm for the plate of the day, dessert, and beer or cider for 69F. The restaurant serves up French dishes with Irish names, like the Limerick salad with duck and cheese.

▶▶**CHEAP**

Café du Théâtre *(Place de la Liberté; Tel 05/59-59-09-31; Bus 1, 2, 4 to Maririe; 7am-11pm daily; daily special 44F; V, MC)* serves up a filling, well-rounded meal of basic French cuisine for pretty cheap. Chicken and rice with a light tomato and pepper sauce *(poulet a la Basque)* is a good plat du jour. The best thing about the cafe is that it's open all day and you can get a sandwich anytime day or night.

▶▶**DO-ABLE**

At the aptly named **L'Italien** *(56 quai des Corsaires; Tel 05/59-59-48-31; Bus 1-6, 10, 72 to Reduit; noon-1:45/7-11pm Mon-Fri, 7-11pm Sat; entrees 50-70F; V)*, the decor is bright and colorful, the waitresses wear black, and the food is indeed Italian. A Madrian red highlights the fresh pasta while you sit along the river.

Xurasko *(16 rue Poissonerie; Tel 05/59-59-21-77; Bus 1, 2, 4 to Mairie; 8am-11pm Mon-Sat; tapas 30-45F; No credit cards)* brings Spanish flavor across the border. The little bar (if you can pronounce it right, I'll buy) serves tapas any time of the day—Spanish ham and chorizo, calamari, cheeses, and octopus. Snack and then play a little pool in the back.

crashing

Right outside the train station, **Hôtel Paris Madrid** *(Place de la Gare; Tel 05/59-55-13-98; Bus 2, 6 to Gare; 95F single, 170F double, 250F triple-quad; V, MC)* is kept clean and comfortable by a well-traveled, knowledge-able couple who are a fountain of local insight. There are only three rooms at the 95F price and they fill fast but have no toilet; when you go down the hall to pee, you can hear the loudspeaker announce the arrival of trains.

Hôtel Monbar *(24 rue Pannecau; Tel 05/59-59-26-80; Bus 1-6, 8, 10, 72 to Reduit; 149-200F singles and doubles)* is in Petit Bayonne among the narrow streets and old buildings. The rooms are furnished with classic furniture, and some have toilets and showers.

Other do-able options are **Hôtel des Basques** *(4 rue des Lisses; Tel 05/59-59-08-02; Fax 05/59-59-08-02; tourador.com/TOWNS/bayonne/hotel/des basques.asp; Single (there is only one) 120F, Twin 140-180 F, Double w/o WC and shower 140-170F, Double w/ WC and shower 180-240 F; MC, DIN, AE)*, a cheaper option in the center of the city; **Hôtel des Basses Pyrénées** *(12 rue Tour des Sault; Tel 05/59-59-00-29, Fax 05/59-59-42-02; tourador.com/TOWNS/bayonne/hotels/desbassespyrenees.asp; Double 250-310F (most have private bath); No Credit Cards)*, also in the city center; **Hôtel Adour** *(13 rue Sainte Ursule; Tel 05/59-55-11-31, Fax 05/59-55-86-40; adour-hotel@yahoo.fr; Rooms for 1-4 people from 250F (all with private bath); MC, V, AE)*, a 5-minute walk from historic city center; and **Hôtel Loustau** *(1 place de la République; Tel 05/59-55-08-08; Fax 05/59-55-69-36; Loustau@aol.com; Single 410F, Double 450F, Triple 510F; MC, V, AE)*, in the city center.

need to know

Currency Exchange The *bureau de change* with the most convenient hours is near the tourist office—**Comptoir Bayonnais d'or et de change** *(Résidence Elgade-1 rue Jules Labat; Tel 05/59-25-58-59; Bus 1, 3, 4, 5 to Pl. des Basques; 10am-12:30pm/1:30-7pm Mon-Sat)*. There are also ATMs all over town.

Tourist Info General tourist maps and Basque coast info are found at the **Place des Basques** tourist office *(Tel 05/59-46-01-46; Bus 1-8 to Pl. des Basques; 9am-6:30pm Mon-Sat, 10am-1pm Sun high season; 9am-6:30pm Mon-Fri, 10am-6pm Sat low season; bayonne.tourisme @wanadoo.fr)*, which also organizes guided tours of Bayonne for 30F. They'll also make hotel reservations for you (in person only) at no charge. During July and August the train station has a little information stand *(Tel 05/59-55-20-45; 2-6:30pm Mon-Sat)*.

Health and Emergency Emergency: *112;* paramedics(SAMU): *15;* fire: *18;* police: *17,* Tel 05/59-59-75-52; medical service: *0/59-52-33-52.* **Centre Hospitalier** *(13 ave. de l'Interne Jacques Loeb; Tel 05/59-44-35-35; Bus 3-5 to Hôpital, Bus 7 to Cassin)* is the main hospital for the region.; it is right in the center of town, accessible via bus 3 or 5.

Pharmacies A **green** or **blue neon cross** indicates a pharmacy. There's one located conveniently right across from the train station at **14 place de la République** *(Tel 05/59-55-03-52; Bus 1 to Alsace Lorraine; 8:45am-12:15pm/2:15-7:15pm Mon-Sat)*.

Telephone City code: *0/559* if you call from within France, *559* from any other country; national operator: *12;* international operators: *00-33-12* plus the country code; *0/800* numbers are free, *0/836* charge you a "premium" rate.

To use most public phones in France, you need to buy a *télécarte* (phone card) at newsstands and tobacconists. The lowest denomination is 50F. Cafes and bars often have coin phones.

Airport Aérogare de Parme-Biarritz-Anglet-Bayonne *(off Blvd. Marcel Dassault; Tel 05/59-43-83-83; Bus 6 to Aéroport)* is between Anglet and Biarritz, close to the Biarritz train station. To get into town from the airport, take bus 6 (7.50F). Because of frequent stops, the ride takes 40 minutes.

Trains The **SNCF** station is on its own square, **Place de la Gare** *(Tel. 08/36-35-35-35. Bus 2, 3, 5, 6, 8, 10 to Gare; Bus 1 to Alsace-Lorraine)*, just north of Place de la République.

Buses Out of the City Hiruak buses *(Tel 05/59-65-73-11)* serve a few nearby towns, including Bayonne (which is easier to get to by train), St. Palais, and Hasparren. Get more info from the tourist office.

Laundry Laverie Hallwash *(6 rue d'Espagne; Tel 05/59-50-01-87; Bus 72 to Pont du Génie; 7am-9pm daily)*.

Postal The **main post** is on rue du 49 *(Bus 2, 8, 7 to Nouvelle Poste/Jorlis)*.

Internet (See *wired*, above.)

everywhere else

biarritz

Half the population of the Basque Coast seems to have been born in Quicksilver apparel and flip-flops (those of us just passing through get them issued). The other half doesn't want to muss their hair or ruin their Rolexes by getting in the ocean. The *ritz* in Biarritz is for the loads of well-heeled visitors who come here, creating a strange mix of swank and scruffy: Barefoot surfers brush up against couples who look like they're ready to be chauffeured to their yacht.

As you enter Biarritz, you'll see that the architecture matches the people. Modern apartment buildings rise next to the luxe hotels and old pink and cream mansions that serve as a backdrop to Biarritz's six main beaches. **Plage de la Milady** is farthest from the center, followed by **Plage Marbella, Côte des Basques, Plage du Port Vieux,** and **Grand Plage.** Finally, **Plage Miramar** ends at the lighthouse on the point that closes off the Biarritz coast.

The minute you sink your bare feet into the silky-smooth, beige sand on Biarritz's beaches, you'll know why life here revolves around them. The most popular beaches are Grand Plage, Plage du Port Vieux, and Côte des Basques simply because they're the closest to the center of the town. Port Vieux is the most relaxing because it's set in a nook where the ocean isn't as rough and there's no surfing. On the other beaches, flags mark the swimming and surfing areas, so surfers (green) and bathers (blue) don't crash into each other. Red means stop: no swimming, no surfing. The Grand Plage and Côte des Basques host all kinds of surfers, but the former is mostly populated by visitors. The occasional natives come around, but they're either hotshots here to let it be known just how well they can ride the waves, or guys here to watch girls in skimpy bikinis—it's their prime viewing place, apparently. Despite the resident peeping Toms, there are some advantages to hanging out at La Grande Plage: It's the only beach in the area that rents out towels, beach chairs, parasols, and cabanas. That's a

biarritz

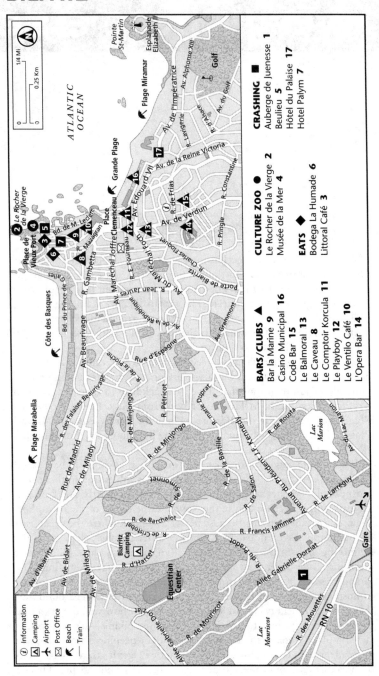

CRASHING ■
Auberge de Jeunesse 1
Beulieu 5
Hôtel du Palaise 17
Hotel Palym 7

CULTURE ZOO ●
Le Rocher de la Vierge 2
Musée de la Mer 4

EATS ◆
Bodega La Humade 6
Littoral Café 3

BARS/CLUBS ▲
Bar la Marine 9
Casino Municipal 16
Code Bar 15
Le Balmoral 13
Le Caveau 8
Le Comptoir Korcula 11
Le Playboy 12
Le Ventilo Café 10
L'Opera Bar 14

huge plus when you want to bask all day and all you have is a tiny face-towel you stole from a cheap hotel somewhere along the way. (Plus you can change into your party clothes right there in your rent-a-cabana if you want to head straight from the beach to happy hour.)

Landlubbers can find shopping, eating, and drinking between the central square just south of the Grand Plage, **place Clémenceau,** and the **Vieux Port,** which forms a point separating the Côte des Basques and Grand Plage. As at most seaside resort towns in France, you get a side of gambling with your order at the **Casino Municipal** [see *bar and club scene,* below]. The somewhat pricey clubs tend to steer the down-and-out crowd to the bars instead, or to an impromptu drum circle out on the beach. For cinema, concert, and show listings, and practical info on the Basque Coast, a little bimonthly magazine called ***Info 7 (Tel 05/59–93-93-56)*** has it all. You can find it in most stores in town, but it's in French only. If you don't speak French, pick up a copy of *The Basque Country,* a 142-page publication that offers similar information in English. It's free at the tourist office in Biarritz (and in some other offices in the area) but it'll cost you 45F at any bookstore.

hanging out

You ask where to hang out? Basically, anywhere there's sand or ocean. Summer isn't necessarily the best wave season, but it's when everyone has vacation so the city is more crowded both in and out of the water. The beaches are full of anyone and everyone, and no matter where you plant yourself for the day, when evening approaches, your skin is either tanned or matches your bloodshot eyes and your throat is dry from salt water. Come here to risk money on the slots, eat fresh seafood, stroll the beach

five things to talk to a basque coast local about

1. **Weather.** You'll be amazed how on top of the forecast surfers are. They can probably predict better than a TV weatherman.
2. **The Surf.** Get in tune with nature and talk about which direction the waves are coming in today.
3. **Wet Suits.** Compare notes on which leave you less chafed in the most crucial areas.
4. **Guys'n Gals.** Critique the exposed bodies passing by your beach towel.
5. **The Biarritz Surf Festival.** Talk about who will win at this summer's rides.

walkways edged with pink and blue hydrangeas, or bask in the sun feeling the ocean mist spraying your toes as you watch the surfers play in the waves. Grandeur awaits those who seek it.

bar and club scene

Nightlife in Biarritz revolves around the commercial center, the streets radiating from the square Place Clémenceau. The area is pretty small, which puts most options within a short walk. If you're not happy in one place, it's easy to skim the streets for something more to your taste. Hit the bars first and get a little drinkie before they close between 2 and 3am. Going to a club afterward empties the wallet with cover charges of 50 to 70F, so not many young locals go to clubs, choosing bars instead. Not to mention that clubs require shoes, so if you can't get the Reef surf sandals unstuck from your feet, your best bet is to follow the native instinct and stay away. To find out about big nights, stop by **Happiness** [see *stuff*, below] to pick up flyers. A lot of people also leave town—and the country—and skip down to San Sebastian for Spanish fiestas.

Most surfers who have run out of money, or who didn't come with any in the first place, head to **Bar La Marine** (*28 rue Mazagran; Tel 05/59-24-87-71; Bus 9, 11 to Clémenceau; 9am-3am daily; V, MC*) where you can engage in some good old-fashioned drinking and swaying in a circle as you sing with your buddies. The music is loud, the crowd is boisterous, and the beer comes by the liter for 45 to 60F. For that beer-induced hunger, they'll fix you up some good omelettes, fries, mussels, or a sandwich for 20 to 40F. You couldn't ask for a better time.

Le Ventilo Café (*30 bis rue Mazagran; Tel 05/59-24-31-42; Bus 9, 11 to Clémenceau; 9am-3am daily; V, MC*) is right next door to La Marine but doesn't have such sticky floors and is a bit more spacious, with red velvet couches and chairs and a terrace. Crowds tend to sip more than slam, but the electronic music and mellow vibe keep it hip and busy.

Set directly on the sands of the beach, **Bar Salsa** (*Grande Plage; Tel 05/59-24-38-34; 5pm-2am daily in summer*) and the attached **Disco Ibiza,** offer an appealing combination of hot music, patrons in artful stages of undress, stiff drinks, and an ongoing reminder of midsummer pleasures, regardless of the season.

five-o

La police don't have a lurking presence, although they do occasionally wander up and down the beach walkways eyeing you. If you skate or play soccer too close to the civilized world, they may come and take away your toys, but eventually they give them back.

Getting a little medieval in decor with tapestries and candelabras, **Le Balmoral** (*Château du Helder-2 rue du Helder; Tel 05/59-22-07-61; Bus 2, 9 to Larralde; 6pm-2am Fri-Sat winter, till 3am daily summer; no cover, 15F beer on tap, 35F cocktails; No credit cards*) is known for its theme soirees when the place and people get made over for the night and the crowds arrive around midnight in their loincloths for jungle night, or their grass skins for hula night. Themes change, but DJ Shapes stays the same, spinning techno, house, and funk. Look for flyers announcing this week's flavor.

Le Balmoral is tight with **Le Playboy** (*Résidence Grand Hôtel-15 place Clémenceau; Tel 05/59-24-38-46; Bus 9, 11 to Clémenceau; midnight-5:30am daily; 70F cover, 50F drink; No credit cards*), so you can get passes to drop the club cover if you start at Le Balmoral and take advantage of the lax door policy at Le Playboy around 2 or 3am when everyone's shifting from the bars to the discos. The club is a bit commercialized, but there's more variety in the style of beats they queue up.

Not ready to call it a night at 2am? One "coverless" option does exist: **Le Comptoir Korcula** (*13 rue Gardères; Tel 05/59-24-46-46; Bus 9, 11 to Clémenceau; midnight-4 or 5am Mon-Sat*). The inside is a simple bar with a pool table, and the drinks—as well as the people—are from the same menu as La Marine. The late-night hours pack in all the local sea drifters.

Ok, so it's not a bar, but you can drink while you gamble at the **Casino Municipal** (*1 ave. Edouard VII; Tel 05/59-22-77-77; Bus 2, 6, 11 to Biarritz Mairie; 6pm-3am daily game room, 10pm-3am daily slots, weekends till 4-5am; 18 and older*), where people drop money like there's no tomorrow. The slots downstairs are a more casual affair. At the fruit machines (slots), old folks wander around trying to decide which slot will bring them fortune, or they stay glued to one station. The gaming rooms upstairs require a little gussying up and a lot more chips in the bag. Minimums are 5F for the slots, 75F in the gaming salons.

gay scene

The gay scene in Biarritz is relatively small, concentrated on one street: **Avenue de Verdun.** There's a strip of a few bars for both guys and girls to hit, but you'll find mostly guys.

As far as clubs go, **Le Caveau** (*4 rue Gambetta; Tel 05/59-24-26-17; Bus 9, 11 to Clémenceau; midnight-5 or 6am Mon-Sat; cover 50-70F; No credit cards*) has a straight and gay pack of dancers and is smaller than **Le Playboy** [see *bar and club scene* above]; it pumps up the house music and fills up around 2am. For monthly updates on gay happenings and articles, flip through the mini-mag *Factory,* which covers the southwest region of France. You can find it in the bars listed below, or e-mail them at *abo@neopresse.com.*

The owner of the **Code Bar** (*36 ave. de Verdun; Tel 05/59-24-28-75; Bus 9 to Frias; 6pm-3am daily summer, till 2am winter; codebar@ wanadoo.fr; 15F beer, 30F mixed drink; No credit cards*) must be a kid at heart—his bar is full of toys to play with. You can space out on Play Station for free, or on the lava lamps surrounding the toy rocket and giant *Playmobil* figure, or surf the Internet for hours (at a price, of course: 50F/hour.) Come around 11pm. The co-ed crowd of gays and lesbians gets a special techno and house DJ treat from Thursday to Saturday.

On the first Friday of the month, the Code Bar plans a party with its neighbors at **L'Opera Bar** *(31 ave. de Verdun; Tel 05/59-24-27-85; Bus 9 to Frias; 6pm-5am daily; MC, V)*, which at 6pm looks like a small, relaxed bar with a few neon lights and paper cut-outs on the walls. That's when it's empty. After midnight, things get pumping and the heavy beats of DJ Ducky start vibrating. It's then you realize that there's another bar in the back room with wall-to-wall gay men, and more space to dance and scope out the guy or girl who you'd like to buy a beer (16F) or mixed drink (29F), cause they don't serve anything fancy—in other words no cocktails with umbrellas.

CULTURE ZOO

The idea of the coast isn't really to see priceless works of art or monuments, so suggestions here are short and sweet. You're really here to sit back, dive in, or bake under....

Musée de la Mer *(Esplanade du Rocher de la Vierge; Tel 05/59-24-02-59; Bus 11 to Rocher de la Vierge; 9:30am-12:30pm/2-6pm daily low season, 9:30am-6pm daily high season, till midnight July 14-Aug 15; 45F adults, 30F students; AE, V, MC):* come check out the pickled cuttlefish and turtle mating video! You also get to watch the main attraction: seeing the sharks and seals torpedo past the window of the tank while they're being fed at 10:30am and 5pm. (Don't worry—they're in separate aquariums.) This is not a must-see attraction if you have only a day or so in the area, but it's a fun diversion for an hour or so if you get sick of baking and posing on the beach.

Le Rocher de la Vierge The Rock of the Virgin *(Bus 11 to Rocher de la Vierge):* This big ol' rock juts out from the Vieux Port, right outside the

FESTIVALS

The **Biarritz Surf Festival** is the biggest event of the year, held from the middle to the end of July. Ever since 1991, competitors and audiences from all over Europe, the U.S., and Australia have come to witness men, women, and kids in longboard competitions (boards 2.74 meters or more). Reggae, funk, acoustic, country, and rock ring in your ears, and special club events are held every night. To those who make it to the festival, "live to ride, ride to live" takes on a whole different meaning.

down and out

There's nothing cheaper than sitting on your ass in the sand and roasting your flesh, but if you want to get up, take the hike up to the old port, **Vieux Port**, and see the **Rocher de la Vierge** [see *culture zoo*, above]. Deeply breathe in the fresh air and have a Zen moment. Scan the place for a native, and ask about the names of all the island-like rocks facing the lighthouse in the distance.

Musée de la Mer. Stroll along the promenade and listen to the waves crashing against the rocks just like the five men whose ship went down on them. Pay homage to their cross, and hope the Virgin's watching over you today.

sports

If Biarritz is only a two-day stop for you and you're not going to become an expert surfer in that time, why not pick up a little bodyboard to mess around on at one of the tourist shops? Don't get me wrong, pro bodyboarders do ride the waves. But unless surfing is the only reason you came to France, you probably won't have your board with you. There are plenty of surf shops to choose from, and most places rent surfboard or bodyboards for 100F a day. The **Jeff Hakman Surf School-École de Surf Quicksilver** *(Casino Municipal; Tel 05/59-22-03-12, Fax 05/59-24-52-44; Bus 11 to Grand Plage; 10am-7pm daily, extended hours in July-Aug, depending on demand; no age restrictions; ID, check deposit, or credit card number required; bodyboard and surfboards 30F/hour, 70F/half day, 100F/day; AE, V, MC)* is located right on the Grand Plage, which is convenient since you'll be carrying your board plenty on the water.

If you want to ride but waves aren't your thing, go to **Sobilo** *(24 rue Peyroloubilh; Tel 05/59-24-94-47; Bus 11 to Port Vieux)*, where you can rent all kinds of wheels by the day: bikes (70F), scooters and mopeds (200–450F, depending on power), or roller skates (80F). Careful though—the cafe-goers on the sidewalks may glare if you get too close. In fact, many locals are far from bike- or blade-friendly, especially since a few older residents were run over (or into) by skaters during the past few years. There are no bike or skate lanes on city streets, and in-line skating is expressly forbidden along the promenade (Blvd. De la Plage) that flanks the beaches of Biarritz and Anglet.

stuff

On the streets just behind the shore is where you'll find Biarritz's commercial center. It's a strange mix of beach junk stores where you can buy sarongs, painted shells, and bodyboards. Other shops sell surfwear that has to cost less than the tag sewn into it and yet others are high-brow fashion boutiques. From the Grande Plage, head up rue Gardères to Place Cleménceau and take a window-shopping stroll on the handful of streets branching off the square toward the Port Vieux: rue Gambetta, rue Mazagran, ave. Victor-Hugo, and in the other direction, ave. Edouard VII, ave. du Maréchal-Foch, and ave. Verdun.

▶▶DUDS

France is divided into *départements,* and the Basque country is depart-ment 64. These people are proud of where they come from, and they show it with T-shirts, key chains, and trinkets from **64** *(16 rue Gambetta; Tel 05/59-22-31-79; Bus 9, 11 to Clémenceau; 9:30am-12:30pm/2-7pm Mon-Sat; V, MC),* Slap a "64" sticker on your board and you're almost a local.

▶▶FOOT FETISH

They marched you out of the restaurant for not wearing shoes? Get some espadrilles at **Les Sandales d'Eugénie** *(18 rue Mazagran; Tel 05/59-24-22-51; 10am-12:30pm/2-7pm; No credit cards).* Choose from a dozen or so styles, from basic (50F) to patterned and strappy (180-200F).

▶▶BOUND

Maison de la Presse *(Esplanade du Casino; Tel 05/59-24-20-85; Bus 2, 6, 11 to Biarritz Mairie; 8am-12:45pm/2-7:30pm Mon-Sat, 9:30am-12:30pm Sun; AE, V, MC)* has international newspapers, travel guides, and novels in a few languages, good for beach reading as you burn your skin to a crab-colored crisp.

▶▶TUNES

Looking for happiness? You'll find it on rue du Helder. Vinyl, CDs, and event flyers scattered on shelves and tables at **Happiness** *(13 rue du Helder; Tel 05/59-22-07-18; Bus 2, 9 to Larralde; 10:30am-noon/2:30-7pm Mon-Sat; V, MC)* bring dance music to your life. Take a load off in the plastic chairs that cling like Saran wrap to the back of your legs and enjoy the lava lamps and mini-mirror balls. It's like a mini-discotheque! And if you have any room in your bags for some take-out tunes, this is a great place to buy CDs. They have a huge selection, including used CDs for 60 to 90F (new CDs cost 139 to 149F).

▶▶REGIONAL JUNK

You need to bring something home to the fam that proves you've done something besides warm your bum on the beach. The **Ligne Basque** *(5 rue Gaston Larre; No phone; Bus 11 to Port Vieux; 9:30am-12:30pm/2:30-7pm Mon-Sat, 9:30am-12:30pm Sun; V, MC)* has everything Basque, or at least everything with Basque symbols on it, such as kitchen towels and pot holders. You *can't* leave without one of the beanie caps all the old Basque men wear!

eats

She sells sea shells by the sea shore—and Biarritz serves them up in a bucket. You'll see a lot of restaurants with mussels and shellfish on the menu along with other seafood, like perhaps cod and squid. During the week most restaurants have a *menu*, which is an all-inclusive price for first and second courses and a drink. In the Vieux Port, down rue Mazagran off the Place Clémenceau, or lining the Grande Plage, you can find *brasseries* and other eateries serving seafood and tapas, with the Spanish influence stretching across the border.

▶▶CHEAP

Right around the bend from the **Musée de la Mer** (see *culture zoo*) is a good Mexican burrito place, **Bodega La Humade** (*5 rue du Port-Vieux; Tel 05/59-24-91-83; Bus 11 to Port Vieux; 6pm-3am daily; 50F avg entree; V, MC*). Old port photos, boxing posters, and a Corona with a lime shoved down its neck go great with mountains of rice and enchiladas or tacos. The tables get a little tight—and the food tastes better—in the late night hours.

▶▶DO-ABLE

Crack into a bucket of mussels with a beer and fries for 58F on the terrace at **Littoral Café** (*3 esplanade du Port Vieux; Tel 05/59-24-17-70; Bus 11 to Port Vieux; 9am to between midnight and 2am daily; 90F menu; V, MC*). You'd expect to shell out big bucks for the fresh white fish prepared Basque style (in a light, fresh tomato and white wine sauce) and these perfect ocean views, but even the more substantial menu of appetizer, main dish, dessert, and coffee is only 90F. Not looking for a big meal? They also have *crêpes*.

crashing

If you're on your own, finding a dirt-cheap place to stay here is almost impossible. The best you can do is the Youth Hostel, which is near the train station and can be a little tricky getting to and from if you want to cruise around or stroll the beaches at night. A double, on the other hand, doesn't always break the bank. Most hotels are in the old center.

▶▶CHEAP

The **Auberge de Jeunesse** (*8 rue Chiquito de Cambo; Tel 05/59-41-76-00, Fax 05/59-41-76-07; Bus 2 to Bois de Boulogne; Reception 8:30am-10pm daily, no curfew; aubergejeune.biarritz@wanadoo.fr; 76F bunk and breakfast, 25F sheets, HI card available for purchase or 20F per night on a temporary card; AE, MC, V*) is an easy hop away, only 500 meters (about 550 yards) from the train station, and 2km from the center. Only two years old, this place is fat with amenities like laundry, a big-screen TV, Internet access (30F/hour), and only three or four bunks to a room, but that also makes it pretty dead compared to the youth hostel in Anglet.

▶▶DO-ABLE

The rooms at **Hotel Palym** (*7 rue du Port-Vieux; Tel 05/59-24-16-56; Bus 11 to Port Vieux; Closed Jan; 230F single or double, 300F triple with shared facilities (no quads with shared facilities); 300F single or double, 400-420F triple, 500F quad with private bath; breakfast 28F; AE, V, MC*) look like the photos in country living magazines—you're likely to see lemon yellow wallpaper printed with blue anchors. To get to half of the 20 rooms you have to walk through someone's living room, which can be entertaining. The hotel is on a perfect little street lined with restaurants and bars, leading out to the sea and the **Rocher de la Vierge** [see *culture zoo*, above] on the Port Vieux.

A couple other reasonable options are **Hôtel de la Marine** *(1 rue des Goëlands; Tel 05/59-24-34-09; Rooms (all with shower, some with toilet) 205-220F; No Credit Cards)*, right next to the casino; and **Hôtel du Rocher de la Vierge** *(13 rue du Port Vieux; Tel 05/59-24-11-74; Single w/ shower and WC 230F, Double (some w/ shower and WC) 265-270F; Triple (depending on size and WC and shower) 310-330F; MC, V, DIN, AE)*, right next to the beach.

▶▶SPLURGE

Beaulieu *(3 esplanade du Port Vieux; Tel 05/59-24-23-59, Fax 05/59-24-93-69; Bus 11 to Port Vieux; Open year-round; 290-320F with shower, TV, 325-380F with full bath, TV; AE, V, MC)* means beautiful place, and it sure is—especially if you pay a little extra for the rooms with balconies overlooking the ocean. There are only 28 of these, so it's best to call ahead and ask specifically for an ocean view.

▶▶REALLY SPLURGING

Go to the top, baby—use that money you won at the casino to sit in the lap of luxury at **Hôtel du Palais** *(Ave. de l'Impératrice; Tel 800-223-6800 in the US or Canada, Local 05/59-41-64-00, Fax 05/59-41-67-99; Bus 1, 2, 6, 11 to Le Palais; email palais@cotebasque.tm.fr; www.cotebasque.tm.fr/palais; 2,600-6,350F; AE, DC, V, MC)*. Okay, so it's totally unrealistic for 90% of us, but it's fun to dream. You won't believe the set-up here, with silk and elegance dripping from every corner. It's easy to see why Napoleon III wanted it to be his private villa. (Bet *he* didn't pay a thousand bucks a night for a suite with a view of the ocean....)

need to know

Currency Exchange Money can be changed at any bank in Biarritz to be deposited right back into the casino's pocket, or you can use ATMs for a good rate. There's also **Change Plus** *(9 rue Mazagran and place Clémenceau; Tel 05/59-24-82-47; Bus 9, 11 to Clémenceau; 9am-12:30pm/2-7pm Mon-Sat Sept-Jun, 9am-8pm Mon-Sat, 10am-1pm Sun July-Aug)*. The most accepted plastic is Visa.

Tourist Info Visitors Bureau *(Square d'Ixelles; Tel 05/59-22-37-10, Fax 05/59-24-97-80; Bus 1, 2, 6, 9, 11 to Biarritz Mairie, Clémenceau; 8am-8pm daily high season, 9am-6:45pm low season; biarritz.tourisme@biarritz.tn.fr)*.

Public Transportation Biarritz is so compact you can easily walk just about everywhere around town (including the beaches). You can catch a bus to Anglet (#9) or Bayonne (#1) in front of the Town Hall *(La Mairie)* on ave. Edouard VII for 7.50F each way.

Health and Emergency Emergency: *112;* paramedics(SAMU): *15;* fire: *18;* police: *17, Tel 05/59-59-75-52;* medical service: *Tel 05/59-52-33-52;* emergencies on the water: *Tel 05/59-31-45-00* (24-hour daily line).

There's a very small clinic in Biarritz, **Polyclinique d'Aguiléra** *(21 rue de l'Estagnas; Tel 05/59-22-46-22, Fax 05/59-24-63-04; Bus 2 to Polyclinique).* The main hospital for the Bayonne-Anglet-Biarritz region is **Centre Hospitalier de la Côte Basque,** in Bayonne *(13 ave. de l'Interne Jacques Loeb; Tel 05/59-44-35-35; Bus 3-5 to Hôpital, Bus 7 to Cassin).*

Pharmacies A **green** or **blue neon** cross indicates a pharmacy. If you need something in the middle of the night, call the **police station** *(Tel 0/55-90-22-22)* for the chemist on duty.

Telephone City code: *Tel 05/59* for calls within France, *559* if you're calling from another country; national operator: *12;* international operators: *00-33-12* plus the country code; *0/800* numbers are free, *0/836* charge you a "premium" rate. To use most public phones in France, you need to buy a *télécarte* (phone card) at newsstands and tobacconists. The lowest denomination is 50F. Cafes and bars often have coin phones.

Airport **Aérogare de Parme-Biarritz-Anglet-Bayonne** *(off blvd. Marcel Dassault; Tel 05/59-43-83-83; Bus 6 to Aéroport)* is between Anglet and Biarritz. The bus ride from the airport to town (#6 Mon-Sat 7:30am-10:30pm, #C Sun 7:30am-10:30pm) takes 15-20 minutes and costs 7.50F each way.

Trains The **SNCF** station **Gare de Biarritz la Négresse** is on the Allée du Moura to the south *(schedule and info: 08/36-35-35-35; Bus 2-9 to Gare de la Négresse).* The station is 3km (2 miles) south of Biarritz, so it's better to take the bus than to walk, unless for some reason you're turned on by the idea of a 45-minute stroll alongside a busy road, sucking up fumes from bumper-to-bumper cars and buses. Bus fare is 7.50F each way; it takes 15-20 minutes to get to the center of Biarritz. You can also take a taxi, but it'll cost you, 75-90F.

wired

Hopefully you'll have no need to be sitting inside in front of a machine when you could be basking in the sun. But if you are truly hooked, **Jeux Video-Génius Informatique** *(60 ave. Edouard VII; Tel 05/59-24-39-07; Bus 2, 6, 11 to Biarritz Mairie; 9:30am-7:30pm Mon-Sat Sept-Jun, 9am-8pm July-Aug; 50F/hour, 1F/minute; No credit cards)* has a few computers with Internet access. This place is more a gaming central with Pokémon paraphernalia at the counter, but it's right off the Grande Plage. Remember, if you plan to stay in the Youth Hostel, you can plug in for 30F per hour.

Laundry Laverie du Port-Vieux *(7 rue Perspective Côte de Basques; Tel 05/59-24-56-98; Bus 11 to Port-Vieux; 8:30am-9pm daily)* is a self-service laundromat with one of the best vantage points for beach views.

Postal Found a board you just have to buy? Mail it home at the **main Poste** *(17 rue de la Poste; Tel 05/59-22-41-10; Bus 9, 11 to Clémenceau; 8am-6pm Mon-Fri, 8am-noon Sat)*.

anglet

Early in the morning, nappy heads begin to turn and blankets stir in the rows of VW vans parked along the beach in Anglet. You see them rolling out of their makeshift van beds for another day of surfing, because that's the way of life here. Some say it's like the sixties in California. This is pure beach, no rent-a-cabanas or beach boys bringing you fresh towels. If you want that, you'll have to go back to La Grande Plage in Biarritz, 2 miles south. During July and August, French kids make the trek here and crowd the water. You can almost see their hair getting blonder and their skin bronzer as they bob up and down, waiting for waves, which are actually not the best of the year—but summer's when they have vacation.

Because life here is reduced to beach and surf—there's no real town—your mentality switches channels when you enter Anglet. Life becomes all about hanging out. Meeting people is not difficult because your interests will probably be the same, at least when you're standing at the edge of the sand looking off into the early morning mist. Stay at the **Auberge de Jeunesse** [see *crashing*, below] to hook up with new friends. Those who stay for the long term come to consider themselves locals and become a tad cliquey—you have to be outgoing to break into their circle. Overall, relations with the natives usually go smoothly, but some locals feel invaded by travelers and are protective of their open space by the sea.

Anglet sits on a little point of land formed by the Atlantic and the Adour River, between the towns of Biarritz and Bayonne. There are a couple of golf courses and a town center, which you have no need to visit because the action (or lack of action) is on the beach called **Chambre d'Amour,** the first beach you come to as you drive, walk, or bike north from Biarritz into Anglet. Other beaches, starting with **Sables d'Or,** stretch up to the mouth of the river, but Chambre d'Amour draws the most people. Legend has it that this strip of beach also drew two lovers who met here secretly and were caught up by the tide and swept to their deaths. Hence the name, which means "bedroom of love." It can be your bedroom, too, if you want to chance sleeping discreetly along the seven or eight beaches that extend past Anglet and offer more down-to-the-roots surfing. But before you unroll your sleeping pack, be sure you don't mind being arrested if you get caught—sleeping on the beach is forbidden by Anglet's municipal police and they enforce the rule. Check out the scene with locals before you crash by the waves.

bar and live music scene

The strip of restaurants, cafes, and bars along the Chambre d'Amour beach is where you want to be, and as it's only a few blocks long, there's not much moving around to do at night—good news if you're beat from fighting the sea all day. There's no live music scene in Anglet, so unless you want to go back down to Biarritz to party, you'll have to settle for a slightly quieter beer-at-the-beach scene here. Almost all of these places have terraces and stay open until between midnight and 3am during the summer.

La Chope *(7 esplanade de Gascons; Tel 05/59-03-82-53; Bus 6, 9 to Chambre d'Amour; Beer 15-18F; V, MC)* is the premier spot for friends to sit around and have a beer in the middle of the terrace cafes on the ocean. If you venture inside the bar, the kayaks and boards hanging on the walls tip you off even further to the fact that the place caters to beach bums—not to mention that shoes aren't required.

The pub at the **Auberge de Jeunesse** [see *crashing*, below], open from 7:30pm–2am, is only for lodgers, but it's no hole in the wall. It's an Irish-looking pub, although on the surreal side, as it's filled with beach bums and lacking Guinness. Grab a Heinie for 12F instead and try to make it here for one of the mostly local bands they bring in on Fridays and Saturdays. You can also get some good eats for cheap (average dinner 27F). Place your order early because the wait is forever, but the surfing videos playing on the TV will keep your mind off your grumbling tum.

beach sports

Okay, so you got to the beach, now what? To the surf shop! Rent some gear from **Rainbow Planète Surf** *(Plage de la Chambre d'Amour; Tel 05/59-03-35-62; Bus 6, 9 to Chambre d'Amour; 10am-7pm Mon-Sat; 60-70F/half day, 100-130F/full day, 500-650F/week surf/long/bodyboards, you must leave ID; AE, MC, V)*. It also has a surf school if you're not sure you know what you're doing.

Another cool water sport to try your hand at is ocean kayaking or canoeing. You can get yourself strapped into a little pointy-nosed boat at **Anglet Olympique Canoe Kayak** *(Plage de la Chambre d'Amour; Tel 06/09-27-31-02; Bus 6, 9 to Chambre d'Amour; 10am-noon/2-6pm Mon-Sat high season, 2-6pm Wed & Sat low season; Canoes and kayaks 50-60F/hour, 70-100F/half day, 130-180F/full day; Under 18 need a parent signature)*. It's right down there with Rainbow Planète Surf. If you're not feeling adventurous you can swim, but only in a few marked areas and you have to be careful—the undertow is powerful. There's plenty of good strolling along the ocean. Some say it is the best on the Basque coast. At night, spotlights along the walkway often cut through the rising, invigorating ocean mist.

eats

Fly girls and rip curls satisfy the munchies with salads, pastas, pizzas, sandwiches, and stuffed baked potatoes at **Mama Nature** *(Chambre d'Amour-19 ave. du Rayon de Vert; Tel 05/59-03-37-21; Bus 6, 9 to Chambre d'Amour; Noon-3pm/7pm-midnight daily; All dishes under 50F; MC, V)*. They're used to granola crunchers, and can fix you up with veggie lasagna, pizzas, and potatoes. A posted sign warns "Please no buzz. Respect." Translated into English: No bud allowed.

Havana Café *(Chambre d'Amour-Ave. des Vagues; Tel 05/59-03-77-40; Bus 6, 9 to Chambre d'Amour; Lunch & dinner daily; Plate of the day 48F; MC, V)* is the oldest restaurant on the beach and dishes out traditional French cuisine for a heartier meal than pizza or sandwiches. The food, rum cocktails, and ocean view draw young crowds that fill the terrace for lunch.

crashing

Quote from bathroom walls up and down the Basque Coast: For a good time, stay at the **HI Youth Hostel-Auberge de Jeunesse** *(19 route de Vignes; Tel 05/59-58-70-00, Fax 05/59-58-70-07; Bus 4, 9 to Auberge de Juenesse; Reception 8:30am-10pm daily, no curfew; aubergejeune. anglet@yhbiarritz.org; 76F bunk and breakfast, 48F on-site camping, 25F sheets, HI card available for purchase or 20F per night on a temporary card; AE, MC, V)*. It's like a budget traveler's resort with all that it offers: sand-filled rooms of 5 to 7 bunks, co-ed bathrooms, Internet access *(50F/hour)*, camping on site, the cheapest board rental on the beach *(55F/day)*, the oldest surf school in France, and best of all, a pub [see *bar and live music scene,* above]. You almost don't have to leave the compound. They also organize excursions to nearby towns like St. Jean de Luz and the caves in Sare.

The camping area down the way from the youth hostel, **Fontaine Laborde** *(17 allée Fontaine Laborde; Tel 05/59-03-48-16; Bus 4, 9 to Fontaine Laborde or Les Corsaires; Open Easter to Sept; 27F per camper, 25F per site, 18F per car)*, is another little hangout, with a bar set up and a mini-mart where you can buy things like cereal when you need them most. The campground has showers, toilets, and room for 99 campers. There are no tents for rent here, so you'll need to bring your own—unless, of course, you strike up an impromptu tent-sharing alliance with a fellow camper. The management here is pretty loose, so whatever arrangement you come up with will probably be fine.

If these two spots are full, try the slightly less budget **Hôtel Arguia** *(9 ave. de Crêtes; Tel 05/59-63-83-82; Single 160F, Double 180F, Triple 220F; No Credit Cards)*, which is right on the beach, a short walk from the train station.

need to know

Currency Exchange There aren't any banks along the Anglet beach and only one ATM—which isn't always reliable. The best idea is to come here with enough cash for a couple of days.

Tourist Info There's the main **Office de Tourisme** *(1 ave. de la Chambre d'Amour; Tel 05/59-03-77-01; Bus 6, 9 to Chambre d'Amour; 9am-7pm Mon-Sat summer, 9am-12:15pm/1:45-6pm Mon-Fri, 9am-12:15pm Sat winter; anglet.tourisme@wanadoo.fr, www.anglet.fr),* and a separate small tourist info annex, conveniently located on the beach. It looks like it could be a concession stand selling ice cream and hot dogs and it's not always open when the sign says, but hey, how much do you really need to know about chilling on the beach? If you show up at their door, the tourist office will help you reserve a place to stay. They don't view themselves as a hotel booking service, but if you need help, they'll do whatever they can. There's no charge for this service.

Public Transportation Anglet is so small you won't need a taxi or a bus until you're ready to head out for the next excellent adventure (see *Bus Lines Out of Town*, below).

Health and Emergency Emergency: *112;* paramedics (SAMU): *15;* fire: *18;* police: *17, Tel 05/59-59-75-52;* medical service: *Tel 05/59-52-33-52;* emergencies on the water: *Tel 05/59-31-45-00* (24-hour daily line). The closest clinic is in Biarritz, **Polyclinique d'Aguiléra** *(21 rue de l'Estagnas; Tel 05/59-22-46-22, Fax 05/59-24-63-04; Bus 2 to Polyclinique).* The main hospital for the Bayonne-Anglet-Biarritz region is **Centre Hospitalier** *(13 ave. de l'Interne Jacques Loeb; Tel 05/59-44-35-35; Bus 3-5 to Hôpital, Bus 7 to Cassin)* in Bayonne.

Pharmacies There's one pharmacy on the **Chambre D'Amour** beaches, **Pharmacie Venturini** *(23 ave. du Rayon Vert; Tel 05/59-03-95-01; Bus 6, 9 to Chambre d'Amour; 9am-8pm Mon-Sat summer, 9am-12:30pm/2-7:30pm Mon-Sat winter).* If you have late-night needs, call the **Services Medicaux de Garde** at *Tel 05/59-52-33-52.*

Telephone City code: *Tel 05/59* if you call within France, *559* if you're calling from another country; national operator: *12;* international operators: *00-33-12,* plus the country code; *0/800* numbers are free, *0/836* charge you a "premium" rate. To use most public phones in France, you need to buy a *télécarte* (phone card) at newsstands and tobacconists. The lowest denomination is 50F. Cafes and bars often have coin phones.

Airport **Aérogare de Parme-Biarritz-Anglet-Bayonne** *(off Blvd. Marcel Dassault; Tel 05/59-43-83-83; Bus 6 to Aéroport)* is between Anglet and Biarritz.

Trains The nearest train stations are in **Bayonne** and **Biarritz**. You can reach them via the **STAB buses** (see *below*).

Bus Lines Out Of Town To get to Biarritz or Bayonne, take **STAB** *(Tel 05/59-59-04-61),* the local bus which runs about every 15 minutes throughout the day to both places. From Anglet, it's about a 10-minute ride on the 4, 7, or 9 to Biarritz (7.50F one way). The 7 also goes to Bayonne (15-20 minutes, 7.50F one way). There's no bus station in Anglet, but the stops are clearly marked along the way, including the place des Cinq Cantons (within Anglet's commercial district) and all along the Plage des Sables d'Or (within the beach district). Buses are silver and white, and buses tends to depart at 15-minute intervals.

Bike/Moped rental If you want to ride but waves aren't your thing, go to **Sobilo** *(Place des Docteurs Genthil; Tel 06/80-71-72-88; Chambre d'Amour; Tel 05/59-03-37-56; Bus 6, 9 to Chambre d'Amour; 10am-7pm Mon-Sat year-round)*, where you can rent all kinds of wheels by the day: bikes *(70F)*, scooters and mopeds *(200-450F depending on power)*, or roller skates *(80F)*. The flat and sandy landscapes of Anglet make it fun and easy to bike between neighborhoods and along the seafront without too much physical effort.

Laundry Laverie automatique *(21 ave. du Rayon Vert; Tel 05/59-03-50-88; Bus 6, 9 to Chambre d'Amour; 7am-10pm daily)* is down in Chambre d'Amour, in case you're wearing anything else besides your swim trunks or bikini.

Postal You can pick up stamps and mail your postcards (or letters home asking for more cash) at the post office *(7 rue de 8 mai; Tel 05/59-58-08-40)*.

St. Jean-pied-de-port

The official brochure of St.-Jean-Pied-de-Port outlines a tour of the town that takes only an hour to do. Okay, so it's obviously a small place, but this welterweight town packs in an impressive amount of Basque culture and architecture. St. Jean is a popular day-trip destination from the coast, so the big buses truck 'em in. But even the herds of fanny-pack-wearin' camera-toters can't diminish the charm of this ancient, walled-in town. Here you can bump into little old ladies speaking that Basque language, *Euskara,* which has nothing to do with any other language in the world, and watch the traditional game *pélote* [see *only here,* below].

Perched up in the Pyrenees along the **Nive** and **Laurhibar** rivers just 8 km from the Spanish border, St.-Jean-Pied-de-Port is a gateway to dozens of cycling and hiking trails, including the well-trodden pilgrimage path, **Chemin de Saint Jacques** [see *great outdoors,* below]. The important streets to know (not that you'll ever lose your way here) are **rue de la Citadelle,** which turns into **rue d'Espagne.** Connected by a bridge that runs over the Nive, these two grand old streets form a line through the two central sections of town to create St. Jean's main street. One block northwest of the Nive is the **place Charles de Gaulle,** the town's center, and just northeast of that is the **place du Trinquet** the town's second-most-important square. **Avenue Renaud,** which leads to the train station, branches out from here. The tourist office on Place Charles de Gaulle puts together *Décrouvrez Saint-Jean-Pied-de-Port,* a complete guide to the town's history, restaurants, and hotels, including practical info as well as a festival calendar every couple of months—get your hands on one (it is in French). Especially in the

ST. JEAN-PIED-DE-PORT

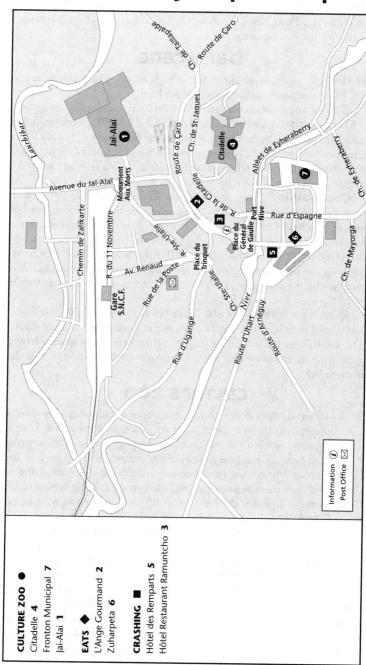

CULTURE ZOO ●

Citadelle **4**
Fronton Municipal **7**
Jai-Alai **1**

EATS ◆

L'Ange Gourmand **2**
Zuharpeta **6**

CRASHING ■

Hôtel des Remparts **5**
Hôtel Restaurant Ramuntcho **3**

Information ⓘ
Post Office ⊠

summer the streets are packed with tourists and travelers, but when the day-trippers leave, you can spend one of those tranquil evenings sitting on the bridge **Pont Nive,** watching the reflections of old Basque homes fade with the setting sun.

bar scene

The bar selection here is limited, but of high quality. Drink prices are reasonable throughout town, about 30F per beer.

The best and most central bar, where the local young guns congregate, is **Chez Louis** *(Place de Gaulle; Tel 05/59-37-02-91; 10am-midnight daily).* It is, esentially, the center of life on the right bank in the old town. Locals call the bar's style American, which we guess means it's not overwhelmingly French. A fellow student told us, "This is where to find a coquette or a Basque loverboy—take your pick." You heard it here.

Chocolainia *(Place de Trinquet; Tel 05/59-37-09-34; 10am-midnight daily),* is packed to overflowing during the pelote matches [see *only here,* below] but lively almost anytime. The neighborhood around here is called the Les Halles of St.-Jean (after the famous open-air markets in Paris), so it's no surprise that you'll often find produce merchants hanging out here, feasting on its reasonably priced *plats du jour.* They may not be the youngest or hippest inhabitants of St-Jean, but they're often the most fun.

Over on the left bank is **Café Tipia** *(Place Flouquet; Tel 05/59-37-11-96),* a cool little haunt that gets exponentially more fun the later it gets. The crowd here ain't sophisticated, but they sure know how to have a good time. If you're getting a jones for some table dancing, this is the place to be.

culture zoo

St.-Jean-Pied-de-Port doesn't house masterpiece sculptures, nor does it have independent theaters, cinema, or art galleries. What it does have is a lot of history, as it is a starting point for the pilgrimage route known as *Chemin de Saint Jacques* [see *great outdoors,* below]. You can go into the little churches, but culture here is mostly outside, in the architecture of the houses with their beamed facades, tiled roofs, and red brown color. Crossing the bridge over the Nive under the clock tower and walking up to the **Citadelle,** an old fortress that sits high above the town, and along the mountain slopes is a fun visual and cultural experience without time schedules or entrance fees.

You can also watch *pelote,* a game like jai-alai, for free on Fridays at 5pm down at the **Fronton Municipal,** a large open-air field. In the style they play here, called *cesta punta,* the ball is served with a hooked, woven mitt at lightning speed against the *fronton* (wall). The audience is mostly local fans who come to watch their neighbors. Flyers let you know they're not just the guys next door. Up at the **Jai-Alai stadium** on Mondays at 5pm you have to pay to see the professionals (40-50F), perhaps because they use their bare hands instead of a mitt to serve and return.

great outdoors

▶▶WALKING

The *Chemin de Saint Jacques,* (the *Camino de Santiago* in Spanish) a pilgrimage route that has been followed for hundreds of years, has recently been inundated with walkers and cyclers from Italy, France, and Portugal making the spiritual journey to the final destination, Santiago de Compostela, in Spain. Shirley MacLaine "discovered" the route in her book, *El Camino.* The **tourist office** [see *need to know,* below] is the best place to get trail maps.

The *Chemin de Saint-Jacques* has been called the longest and culturally and scenically richest art museum in the world. The best place to begin the trail is in St.-Jean-Pied-de-Port. Although some middle-aged people walking the trail are devout pilgrims, many younger and non-religious travelers make the trek just for the fun of it—some 20,000 people walk this trail every year. From St.-Jean to Santiago de Compostela in northwest Spain (Galicia), the distance is 480 miles, a journey likely to take 45 days if walked, half that if biked, and 4 to 5 days if driven, allowing plenty of time for stopovers. You should only travel between April and October, as the route over the Pyrenees from France is difficult-to-impossible in winter. The ideal time to go is in late spring or early autumn—that way you avoid both the blistering summer heat of Spain and the crowds.

Pilgrims often stay in *refugios,* or shelters, along the trail. It's suggested that you leave five dollars or so (this is purely voluntary, but seems like the right thing to do when you're on a pilgrim route, no matter what your reli-

only here

Don't strain your neck turning left and right as men play **pelote Basque,** a game sort of like jai-alai (if you don't know what *that* is, it's like racquetball). Instead of a paddle, the players use a woven wicker and leather hook, called a *chistera,* to wing the ball against a *fronton* (wall) found in most Basque towns. There are 21 variations of the game, including a few in which players use their hands to return the ball instead of the *chistera.* You may not be able to figure out what's going on due to the crazy scoring system. The points keep going up and down. So try to sit with the locals and watch the ball zip by like a bullet. Even the professional matches are rather jovial.

gious beliefs). Some of these shelters are a little, um, *unkempt,* but most are clean and with showers and soft beds. A sleeping bag is recommended, as *refugios* don't come with bedding. There are also a bunch of guest houses and small inns along the trail, with prices starting at $30 a night.

Before setting out from St.-Jean-Pied-de-Port, visit the office of **Bureau d'Acceuil du Chemin de St.-Jacques** *(39 rue de la Citadelle; Tel 05/59-37-05-09)*. This office maintains a list of private homes along the routes, which take in pilgrims for a modest fee. Be sure to ask for an ID, called a Crédential, identifying yourself as a genuine pilgrim walking all the way to Santiago—it's your ticket into those houses.

For day hikers there are trails from 1.2 to 13km in the immediate area of the town, and the maps tell you the trailheads, the level of difficulty, and the approximate hiking time for each.

On the outskirts of town, if you go down Avenue du Jaï-Alaï and cross a bridge over Le Laurhibar, you'll find the **Txik Txak-Club Sport Loisir: école francaise de canoë kayak** *(Base, tournant ISPOURE/ave. du Jaï-Alaï; Tel/Fax 05/59-37-87-80, Info line: Tel 05/59-37-12-20; Open year-round)*. It's about a half-mile walk—if you're not up to it, you can just call to make reservations for an outing of rafting, canoeing, kayaking, or hydrospeeding down the Basque country river—they often organize a free shuttle bus to pick up the folks going on the trips. You must know how to swim, but beginners can start to learn paddling skills here. Rafting or hydrospeeding, which is going down the river on a high-tech kickboard, costs 130F for a half day and 220F for the whole day; canoe and kayak initiation is 100F for a half day.

▶▶CYCLING

To rent a bike for a nice jaunt through nearby mountain towns, go to **Cycles Garazi** *(Ave. du Jaï-Alaï; Tel 05/59-37-21-79, Fax 05/59-37-25-88; 9:30am-noon/2-7pm Mon-Sat; Jean-Jacques. ETCHANDY@wanadoo.fr; 30F hour, 80F day; ID required; MC, V)*. They'll point you in the right direction. (Remember, the tourist office also has some bike route guides.) It's also a huge sporting-good store in case you get chilly at night and forgot your fleece, or in the event you decide to chuck it all and spend a month riding or walking to Spain and need some new gear. The shop is about a 10-minute walk outside town, across Le Laurhibar.

EATS

Restaurants are everywhere here, and they tend to be pricey. A lot of the best dining options are the hotel restaurants, which serve *menus* with a few courses, desserts, and coffee. There are regional food specialties like the Basque cake *(gâteau basque),* which is buttery and filled with a light almond or cherry cream, *fromage de brebis* (ewe's cheese); *Irrouleguy* red or rosé wine; and fresh honey. The few bakeries in town offer the honey and cakes you need to get some sugar in your system before a day of walking.

The cheapest and most down-home restaurant in town is **Zuharpeta** *(Rue de Zuharpeta; Tel 05/59-37-35-88; 7am-9pm daily, closed Tue Oct-Nov; 50-60F per entree; No credit cards)*, where they serve up basic regional dishes of duck, chicken, paté, blood sausage, and white fish. Get a glass of cider to wash it down. Omelettes go for 30 to 45F; the 55F menu will get you a no-nonsense meal of salad and chicken with fries. It's about a 5-minute walk south of the Hotel de Ville.

You can also try the restaurant at **Hotel Restaurant Ramuntcho,** [see *crashing*, below], which has menus for 66F, 79F, or 99F featuring such dishes as chicken, squid, and veggies, all topped with regional sauces that chef André Bigot cooks up in the back to go with the *Irrouleguy* wine. On the main road up from the Pont Nive, just behind the tourist office, feed your face by going down the stairs to the cozy **L'Ange Gourmand** *(3 bis rue de la Citadelle; Tel 05/59-37-09-18; Noon-9pm daily, closed mid Nov-mid Dec, and Jan; avg. entree 60F; V, MC)* for a midday or evening meal. Make it one of the stages in your hike to eat heavenly crêpes as snacks or dinner.

crashing

There are quite a few options for sleeping in St.-Jean-Pied-de-Port, which is surprising considering it's such a small town, but that doesn't mean they have small-town prices. Along **rue de la Citadelle** are a few homes that open up to backpackers and pilgrims taking on the *Chemin de St. Jacques.* They charge around 160F for two people and you must arrange your stay through the **Bureau d'Accenil du Chemin de St.-Jacques** *(39 rue de la Citadelle; Tel 05/59-37-05-09).* If you have your cosmetic bag attached to your full-sized rolling suitcase, however, they may doubt your backpacking and devotional status....

▶▶**CHEAP**

If you have a tent and sleeping bag, head to **Municipal Camping** *(Plaza Berri; Tel 05/59-37-11-19; reception 8-10am/5-8pm daily, campground end of May-end of Sept; 13F adults includes shower, 8F tent/caravan, 15F camping car, 8F car; No cards),* a lovely expanse lined with sycamore trees and nestled along the wooded edge of town. The facility is clean and has showers and toilets that you can sit down on.

▶▶**DO-ABLE**

The cheapest hotel you'll find is **Hôtel des Remparts** *(16 place Floquet; Tel 05/59-37-13-79, Fax 05/59-37-33-44; Closed mid Oct-beginnning of Jan; 205F single, 220-250F doubles; V, MC),* a typical Basque-style house located on the left bank of the Nive that dates to 1643. Rooms have bathrooms and TVs, and there's a restaurant downstairs serving up decent food. The menu of the day is 70F.

Hôtel Restaurant Ramuntcho *(1 rue de France; Tel 05/59-37-03-91, Fax 05/59-37-35-17; Closed Wed Sept-Jun; 275-360F doubles, 305-380F triple, 340-410F quad; AE, V, MC, DC)* is run by a good French woman who walks her poodle and speaks English if you don't speak French. The house squeezes itself into the rows of Basque half-timbered houses off the road leading to the **Citadelle.** All of the rooms have private baths, and some have views of the mountains.

If those two are full up, try **Hôtel Itzalpea** *(5 place du Trinquet; Tel 05/59-37-03-66, Fax 05/59-37-33-18; Singles and doubles 220F, Triple*

300-330F, all rooms have private bath; V, MC) ten minutes from the train station on the main street; or **Hôtel Central** *(1 place Charles de Gaulle; Tel 05/59-37-00-22, Fax 05/59-37-27-79; Single 330-370F, Double 340-398F, all rooms have private bath; MC, V, AE),* which is right in the city center and has the added bonus of a kitchen that guests can use.

need to know

Currency Exchange Change money at one of the few banks in town, like **Banque Michel Inchauspé** *(13 place Floquet; Tel 05/59-37-99-20; 9am-12:15pm/1:50-5:45pm Mon-Fri),* or get cash out of the ATM there.

Tourist Info The **small tourist office** at 14 place Charles de Gaulle *(Tel: 05/59-37-03-57)* provides you with maps of the town and walking or cycling paths in the surrounding areas as well as information on regional activities like caving, rafting, and kayaking, and clubs that make excursions. They'll also make hotel reservations for you.

Public Transportation St.-Jean is way too small for public transportation, but there are some handy cab companies. Call *05/59-37-13-37, 05/59 -37-02-92, 05/99-37-05-70,* or *05/59-37-05-00.*

Health and Emergency Emergency: *112;* paramedics (SAMU): *15;* fire: *18;* police: *17;* ambulance: *Tel 05/59-37-05-00 or 05/59-37-05-70.* There's only a clinic here, **Fondation Luro** down ave. du Jaï-Alaï across the river Laurhibar *(Tel 05/59-37-00-55).* To get here you have to walk or take a cab.

Pharmacies There are a few in town, including **M. Larrègle Pharmacie** *(Tel 05/59-37-02-81),* right on the Place Charles de Gaulle near the tourist office.

Telephone City code: *05/59* if you call within France, *559* if you're calling from another country; national operator: *12;* international operators: *00-33-12* plus the country code; *0/800* numbers are free, *0/836* charge you a "premium" rate.

Trains Whistle-stop station **SNCF Gare de St.-Jean-Pied-de-Port** *(info and reservations: Tel 0/836-35-35-35, station: Tel 05/59-37-02-00)* is a couple of residential blocks from the center. Only a few trains go to Bayonne daily (it takes about an hour), so make sure you check the schedule.

Bus Lines Out of the City The local **bus station** is sandwiched between place de la Liberté and place de Gaulle in the center of town close to the L'Adour River. **STAB** buses running to Anglet and Biarritz leave from here daily: Bus lines 1, 2, and 6 run to Biarritz. Bus line 4 also goes to Biarritz but stops off in Anglet. Departures in summer are every half hour or so. You can grab a bus map at the tourist office, and get information about schedules by calling *05/59-59-04-61.*

Postal La Poste *(Rue de la Poste; Tel 05/59-37-90-00)* provides your basic mail and parcel services in case you need to lighten your pack for the long hike ahead.

bordeaux
and the
mid-atlantic
coast

bordeaux

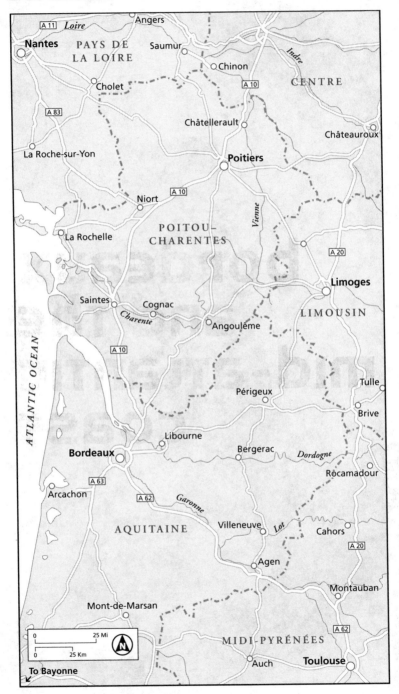

Perched right on the almighty Atlantic, this part of France packs a happening scene that's more vibrant than you might expect: You definitely won't go to bed bored. From **La Rochelle** to **Bordeaux,** both university cities, you can party all night if you want to, then take five to explore the miles of rugged Atlantic seashore or flat vino country outside of town the next day.

From twilight on, the nightlife on the coast revolves around the ocean air, in a way that's comparable to Mediterranean cities like Cannes, but not quite so, well, glam. There's no movie stars here (and no real tourists either)—just Who tribute nights where they don't play any Who songs, and French karaoke nights where everyone sings along and shakes sloshing pints to the beat. The people here definitely party more than some of the more laid-back folks to the east, keeping a plethora of clubs, discos, and theme bars noisy and full.

Look both ways before you cross in La Rochelle, where the kids zip through the narrow streets on their neon Ninja crotch rockets and gusts from the Atlantic cyclone between buildings. It isn't so much the physical force of the wind that could sweep you away, but the overwhelming energy of the city instead. It's filled with enough bright colors to make Martha Stewart cringe, creating a foil to the pale gray buildings and the greenish-brown of the nearby water. During the day, streets bustle with the clamor of outdoor brasseries and cafes that fold into themselves as the sun goes down. When the chairs and tables disappear, they suck townies into the dark bellies of adjoining bars and clubs. But the quays along the water stay bright and hopping with outdoor cafes and restaurants into the wee hours.

The seaside towns here reflect the region's history, and tend to hold on to time-honored traditions. As you wind south along the Atlantic coast, you'll be bombarded with chunky fisherman's sweaters and delicious seafood restaurants everywhere you look. Most ports have kept the original fortresses and towers that protected their cities hundreds of years ago, serving as an obvious reminder of the historic importance of the western seafront. Not only did these towns protect greater France from the threat of invasion, but they also served as points of commerce—in the exchange of both goods and ideas from across the globe. As a result, you'll find that today's Mid-Atlantic region has a worldwide appeal and cosmopolitan flair.

Moving further south along the coast, you'll find yourself in vineyard country, known as the Aquitaine region, along the west of France. It's

the perigord

If you're looking for a more interesting view of France than what's on offer from the window of a tour bus, then time spent biking through the region the French call **Perigord** (the British insist that it's the **Dordogne**) or canoeing along one of its rivers could be the ticket. Composed of small, old-fashioned towns and villages, the area is known for its gently rolling hills, lush valleys, acres of forests, and picturesque ruined fortresses. Numerous rivers, such as the **Dordogne, Garonne, Dronne,** and **Vezere** run through the area, and most travelers choose to bike, hike, and/or canoe along one of them. Campsites are plentiful, and there are B&B's and inns for those who aren't charmed by rusticity. Spring and autumn are the best times to plan a cycling or canoeing trip to avoid traveling hordes or inclement weather; be advised that August is traditionally France's vacation time, so plan accordingly for both crowds and business closings.

ONE IF BY LAND...

The roughly 37-mile bicycle ride from **Bergerac,** in the wine country in the south of the region, to **Le Bugue** makes an ideal day trip. After a ramble around Bergerac's restored *vieille ville* and a stop at the **Tourist Office** *(97 Rue Neuve d'Argenson, Tel 05/53-57-03-11),* you can pick up a bike at **Guy Barbier** *(31 Rue Candillac, Tel 05/53-27-29-40)* or **Perigord Cycle** *(11 Place Gambetta, Tel 05/53-53-57-07)* and head out on your adventure. If you end up staying in Bergerac on either end of your trek, the **Family Hotel-Restaurant Le Jardin D'Epicure** (Place du Marche-Couvert, Tel 05/53-57-80-90; Doubles 180-230F; entrees 45F, menus 84-160F), located near old town center, will take care of you. It's a relaxed little spot, with a young feel (probably due to all the young cyclers passing through). You can also get excellent seafood and local game at **Restaurant La Sauvagine** *(18-20 rue Eugene-Leroy, Tel 05/53-57-06-97. Menus from 80F to 180F; Closed Mon, Sun).* They also serve kick-ass dessert—don't worry, 37 miles of biking should work off those calories!

On the trip up to Le Buge you'll pass through small towns such as **Lalinde, Mauzac,** and **Tremolat,** but don't miss a stop at the fortified town of **Limeuil,** which is considered to be one of France's most beautiful medieval villages. Between Limeuil and Le Buge are the **Caverne de Bara-Bahau,** caves that contains a variety of animal engravings done by hand and flint on the cave walls. It's a popular attraction, and roughly 40-minute guided tours are offered *(Tour information Tel 05/53-07-27-47)* daily. Once in Le Bugue, you can check in at the **Tourist Office** *(Porte de la Vezere; Tel 05/53-07-20-48).* Like all good

French villages, La Bugue has a twice-weekly market, though with a twist—due to a royal decree issued in 1319, the weekday market is on a Tuesday as opposed to the standard Wednesday. Wacky!

If you have another day to explore, consider biking on from Le Bugue to **Montignac,** about 30 miles away. Along the way are the **Grottes de Font-de-Gaume** *(Tel 05/53-06-90-80; closed Tuesdays)* in **Les Eyzies-de-Tayac.** Guided tours of the spectacular caves are available by reservation, but it's essential to book well in advance during peak times like July and August. If you can't get a reservation (or don't want to bother), you can make do with a visit to **Lascaux II** *(Tel 05/53-06-30-94; closed Mondays except in July and August),* a replica of the **Grotte de Lascaux.** The original Lasceaux boasts some of the best extant prehistoric art, featuring many drawings dating from 17,000 years ago, but a heavy flow of visitors caused damage to the images. Lascaux II, opened in 1983, is a painstaking reproduction of the original done by modern artists in the same manner as their Cro-Magnon counterparts. Guided tours are available but tickets must be purchased through the tourist office in Montignac *(Place de Bertran-de-Born, Tel 05/53-51-90-78).* If you want to rest up in Montignac, the **Hotel-Restaurant de la Grotte** *(65 rue du 4-Septembre; Tel 05/53-51-80-48, Fax 05/53-51-05-96; Doubles 180-210F; Menus 60-195F)* will house and feed you.

For more information on biking in this region, contact the **Federation Francaise de Cyclotourisme** *(Tel 01/44-16-88-88) in Paris.*

...TWO IF BY SEA

Another way to see some of the landscape is to canoe down the Vezere or Dordogne rivers. Both are generally shallow and calm in the summer months, so even novice boaters should feel comfortable. Canoes and kayaks can be rented by the hour, but you should try to take at least a half-day if possible. There are numerous companies that you can rent the equipment from, and rates hover around 60-110F per day. In general, operators are open daily in July and August and as demand dictates in May, June, and September. Sorry polar bears, no fall and winter canoeing!

In Dordogne, contact **Canoe Dordogne** *(Tel 05/53-29-58-50),* **Copeyre** *(Tel 05/65-37-33-51),* or **Kayak-Club** *(Tel 05/53-29-40-07).* In Vezere, try **L'Animation Vezere** *(Tel 05/53-06-92-92)* or **Randonnee Vezere** *(05 53 51 38 35).*

here that the Romans planted their first vineyards, beginning the region's tradition of producing much of France's best-known and best-tasting wines. Following the Romans, the bourgeoisie and aristocrats played their part in developing magnificent estates on the geographically diverse lands, showing off their good taste not only in the wines they made, but also the homes they built. Today these châteaux feature prominently in the area's color brochures, which seduce you with scenes that look like happy endings to fairy tales. As you dream of these perfect castle-mansions in the distance, try not to let reality sink in: Pretend that you're the one sipping the contents of your precious barrels of liquid pleasure, rather than the harvester whose hands are all calloused from picking grapes!

Last but not least, don't skip a visit to the capital city of Bordeaux, a cosmopolitan pocket of culture that's surrounded by lush, grape-laden land. You're guaranteed to find a place to cater to your nighttime needs, whether it be a '70s dance club or a gritty dive bar. You'll also find great shopping and plenty of other daytime diversions. The city lies on the **Garonne River,** at the point where the shores begin to widen stretching out to the Atlantic.

getting around the region

The entire Mid-Atlantic region is served by a major rail-line running from Bordeaux in the south to Nantes on the northern end, as well as smaller lines which feed off to the adjoining towns. Once in a particular town, you can often take boat rides or tours to the islands off the coast, which serve as cozy getaways or historical points of interest.

TRAVEL TIMES

* TGV (Fast Train— more expensive)	La Rochelle	Paris	Bordeaux
Bordeaux	2:15	3:00* 6:00	-
La Rochelle	-	3:30* 4:30	2:15

bordeaux

Perhaps because of its wealth, size, and appearance, Bordeaux, the capital of the Aquitaine region, is sometimes called the petit Paris. The name may also refer to Bordeaux's nearly spiritual status in the world of wines: First a Roman city, and later an English one, it gradually got a good rep for its red wine, and now a bunch of wine lovers truly could not live without it.

As you arrive in Bordeaux, you'll pass through squares and tree-lined garden medians leading you to the old center, where the buildings look like the France in your high school textbook: gray slate-tiled rooftops, turrets, and rows of columns and white stone below, following along the flowing Garonne River.

Bordeaux has two distinct groups: the *Bordelais* and the students. It's a well-dressed, well-off town that looks a little like a movie set. The major buildings have been cleaned up and at night are beautifully lit—but look around the corner and down the side-streets and you'll see the soot built up from years of traffic. The students give this staid setting a bit more character and variety. Without them it would probably feel like a big monument—a pretty one, but a monument nonetheless. Anywhere you find the collegiate crowd, you'll find their energy influencing the city, and Bordeaux's three universities and 60,000 thirsty youth are no exception. They're what make a visit to Bordeaux a fun time—from the cool bar and club scene to the shopping, where you can find everything from cowboy boots to retro threads. Just watch where you're going when you're out and about—self-propelled modes of transport are *de rigueur* here, and you'll find yourself sidestepping bikes, boards, and blades everywhere you go. You may want to rent your own set of wheels while you're here.

bordeaux

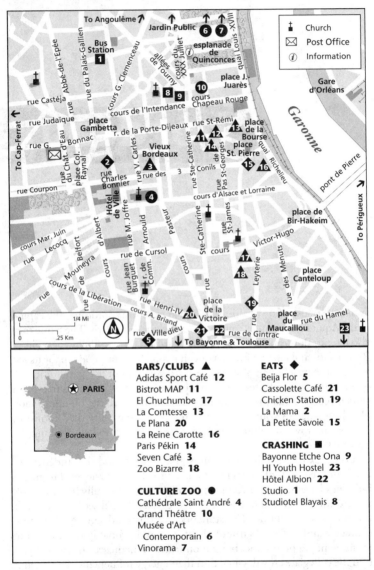

To Angoulême ↗

Jardin Public

esplanade de Quinconces

Bus Station **1**

Gare d'Orléans

Garonne

place J.-Juarès

place de la Bourse

place St. Pierre

place de Bir-Hakeim

pont de Pierre

To Périgueux ↗

place Gambetta

Vieux Bordeaux

Hôtel de Ville

place Canteloup

place de la Victoire

place du Maucaillou

To Cap-Ferrat ←

To Bayonne & Toulouse ↓

- ✝ Church
- ⊠ Post Office
- ⓘ Information

0 — 1/4 Mi
0 — .25 Km

⭐ **PARIS**

● Bordeaux

BARS/CLUBS ▲
Adidas Sport Café **12**
Bistrot MAP **11**
El Chuchumbe **17**
La Comtesse **13**
Le Plana **20**
La Reine Carotte **16**
Paris Pékin **14**
Seven Café **3**
Zoo Bizarre **18**

CULTURE ZOO ●
Cathédrale Saint André **4**
Grand Théâtre **10**
Musée d'Art
  Contemporain **6**
Vinorama **7**

EATS ◆
Beija Flor **5**
Cassolette Café **21**
Chicken Station **19**
La Mama **2**
La Petite Savoie **15**

CRASHING ■
Bayonne Etche Ona **9**
HI Youth Hostel **23**
Hôtel Albion **22**
Studio **1**
Studiotel Blaysis **8**

To get in on the scene, check out *www.clubs-et-concerts.com,* the online version of a free mini-magazine that's found in bars and stores. Information from the **tourist office** [see *need to know,* below] will fill your daypack, and it's not *all* diagrams of architectural styles and historical walking routes. They have a good free magazine called (ready?) *Bordeaux Magazine,* with articles and tidbits about the lay of the land and what's happening each month in sports, theater, dance, and cinema. It's in French, but the listings are decipherable times and addresses. There are also listings in the local paper, *Sud-Ouest,* found at newsstands.

neighborhoods

The name says it all: *Bord*=border, *eaux*=water. Bordeaux lies along the west bank of the curving Garonne River, and the *quais,* the riverside roads, form a big "C" shape that you can walk along for five miles, passing right through Bordeaux without actually going into the city. Bordeaux is a rather large, sprawling city, but the *Vieux Bordeaux,* the old center where most of what you want to see and do is concentrated, is pretty compact.

At the north end of *Vieux Bordeaux,* are the **Jardin Public** and the **esplanade de Quinconces,** two garden- and fountain-laden sites. The V-shaped district just south of these urban oases, bounded on the northwest by the **cours Clemenceau** and on the south by the **cours de L'Intendance**, is full of high-brow cafes, fat-wallet shopping, where you pay for the name on the tag on the dress and a coffee will run you twice the

12 hours in bordeaux

1. Get dizzy looking up at the two spires of the **Cathédrale Saint André** [see *culture zoo,* below].
2. Chill out in **place de la Victoire,** perhaps have a *petit-crème* or *bière* at **Le Plana** [see *bar, club, live music scene,* below].
3. Rent a bike or blades at **Bord'Eaux-Velos Loisirs** [see *city sports,* below] and speed along the *quais* of the Garonne or risk your life taking on the inner streets of the city.
4. Discover the latest in contemporary art movements at **Musée d'Art Contemporain** [see *culture zoo,* below].
5. Pretend you're in Rome while gawking at the splendor of the rows of Corinthian columns of the **Grand Théâtre** opera house.
6. Promenade royally through the **Jardin Publique** as if you had nothing in the world to worry about.
7. Squeeze in at a table and dine on the **rue Saint Remi** in the **quartier Saint Pierre.**
8. Last, but not least, you have no excuse leaving without tasting some wine.

by foot

Ready, set, go. Start, at dusk or later, from the **esplanade des Quinconces,** where a fountain of proud naked women pay homage to Gironde (the region you're in). Go around the semicircle and down **cours XXX Juillet,** passing through **place de la Comédie,** and take a right onto **rue Mautrec.** At the end of this small street you'll see the vibrant colors of the arched stained-glass window lit up, the swirling designs, columns, and stone figures of the **Notre Dame** church at night. With not too many people around it's eerily peaceful. Bolt outta there and to the left, down **rue Martignac,** then take another left at Cours de l'Intendance and follow it till you get to **rue Saint Catherine.** Start down Saint Catherine and it seems like you'll never reach the end, as if you're walking down a conveyor belt the wrong way. So many streets that lead to other destinations for dining and drinking intersect it that you're bound to cross paths with just about anyone: a rastaman, a theater-goer, a skater.... Look up the street, where most stores will be shut down, and you'll see voyeurs leaning out of the apartments above pumping out music. As you finally reach the end of the street, pizza and kebab stands fill the view and most operagoers have gone to bed. Build up speed and bust through the big archway straight ahead, and you've won. Welcome to the **place de la Victoire!** Sit down and have a beer, you deserve it.

usual price. South of here is the heart of the old town, which takes the shape of an old-fashioned kite: The top (northern) point is the **place de la Comédie,** which sits on the **cours de l'Intendance** about two and a half blocks south of the **esplanade des Quinconces.** Running south from the place de la Comédie and forming the spine of the kite is the **rue Saint Catherine,** the main pedestrian shopping drag that isn't so out of control, price-wise. The **place Gambetta,** which uses the cours de L'Intendance as its northern border, forms the western point; the **St. Pierre church** and its surrounding square form the eastern point. The bottom point of the kite is the **place de la Victoire,** a half-hour walk south of the place de la Comédie, where students circle around the bars and cafes. This area of the old town has an authentic, quaint feel. You'll find a concentration of boutiques, and tons of dining options, especially near Saint Pierre where there's a complimentary bar scene.

hanging out

You'll notice how many times I say it's happening in the **place de la Victoire.** Things start up here and radiate off the square. Cars and buses circle the roundabout, and people sit along the edges, hanging out, waiting for buses, friends, or something to happen. You never know, it may be *you* that they're waiting for.... Even if you're not in the habit of going up to someone without a reason, coming up with an opening line late at night after a few is always easier.

Up in the quartier **St. Pierre**, **Cafécito** *(7 rue du Parlement St. Pierre; Tel 05/56-48-08-90; Bus 1, 22, 23, 28, 91, 92 to Douane; 9am-2am Mon-Sat; Beer 12F, coffee 7F)* is known as a local rendezvous, especially because it sells tobacco after the tobacconists have closed for the night. Never has smoking been so social.

To meet up with other travelers, you can't go wrong on the **wine tour** organized by the tourist office [see *only here,* below]. Leave an empty seat open next to you on the bus—you never know, the cute blonde who just spent the semester in Rome might just want to accompany you for the ride.

four things to talk to a local about

1. Read up a little bit about wines before starting up a conversation, and show off your new-found knowledge. You can also go blindly into it in hopes that someone will want to take you out to dinner to show you just how good that young red *Graves* served chilled goes with beef *carpaccio.*

2. "Mutations" could be the name of a Wes Craven movie, but here it's the name Bordeaux chose for the fast and furious urban development project. They want to restore everything—squares, pedways, lighting, facades—and they're working on a tramway. Ask around to see how people are dealing with the growing pains.

3. Bring up the French law "1901," named after the year in which it was passed. It was written to protect the rights of individuals involved in non-profit projects, which include cultural, artistic, social, religious, etc. activities. The law also supports new enterprises. Because of this, it was recently dug up in the 1990s when a surge of nightlife spots in Bordeaux were established, like Zoo Bizarre [see *bar, club, and live music scene,* below].

4. Gironde is the name of the estuary connecting the Garonne and Dordogne rivers to the ocean. It's also the name of the fertile vineyard lands surrounding Bordeaux. You can impress the locals by telling them another meaning of *Gironde:* a gorgeous woman, who also has curves and a richness of the earth.

down and out

How much does tranquility cost these days? Two hundred a month for yoga classes, eighty an hour for reiki...Here it's free! The chirping birds and fresh flowers almost drown out the city's traffic and allow you to compose yourself in the **Jardin Publique** *(Bus 7, 8, 14, 15, 25, 27, 29, 31, 94, Citi U bus to Jardin Publique; 7am-6:30pm Feb, till 7pm March, till 8pm Apr-May & Sept, till 9pm Jun-Aug, till 7:30pm 1-15 Oct, till 6pm mid Oct-Jan).* Like the rest of the architecture in Bordeaux, the gardens really make you feel royally French. The entrance to the botanical gardens, inside the Jardin Publique, is a long set of archways that lead you to gently jetting sprinklers, lilac vines, a lily-pad pond, and wandering swans who get awfully close. If you're a student, you can take advantage of another freebie: no-cost admission to most museums [see *culture zoo,* below].

bar, club, and live music scene

In Bordeaux, as in many larger cities, people are out and about both on weekends and during the week, eating, strolling, or meeting up with friends. In warmer weather, tables are set out in almost every square in town. There are a few nightlife areas in the center, most of which blend together and are adjacent to rue Sainte Catherine. So a night out in Bordeaux, even if you like to hop from one place to the next, can be easily done on foot. To the east of Sainte Catherine, branching off from the place Saint Pierre, is a circuit of bars and restaurants where regulars have their favorite spots, tables clutter the pedestrian walkways, and a few students weave through the sweater sets and mobile phones. To the west, from the place Gambetta down to the **Cathédrale Saint André,** is another pedestrian area sprinkled with nightlife. Finally, the younger population emerges from the place de la Victoire, where you get more student character and a variety of folks. The pacers with mobiles you find here might have pierced eyebrows and be scarfing down some McDonald's.

Most bars stay open till 2am (3am in spring and summer); then the flow continues to clubs, and perhaps to an after-hours. The action often lies behind closed doors armed with doormen and sometimes even door buzzers, but they are mostly for the sake of keeping the noise down and avoiding complaints from the neighbors—there don't seem to be super-snooty restrictions and the fashion police don't patrol either. A tiny bi-monthly free magazine with the creative name *Clubs & Concerts* can be picked up free in bars and shops around town—try **Maori's Concept** [see *modification,* below]—or look up the page *www.clubs-et-concerts.com.*

▶▶AROUND SAINT PIERRE...

La Comtesse *(25 rue Parlement St. Pierre; Tel 05/56-51-03-07; Bus 15 to Comédie, buses 13, 14, 17, 19, 20, 21 to place Jeans Jaurès; 6pm-2am Mon-Sat; No credit cards)* buzzes jazz (acid and non), world music, and funky electronic remixes to help you sink into the red velvet and wooden chairs. Telling you about the chandelier, fireplace, and paintings on the walls makes it sound stuffy, but really it's a classic arty bar to chill in and start the evening with twenty- and thirtysomethings. No cocktails are served, just liquor (30-40F), beers (13-25F), and hot drinks; after 9pm the prices go up a few francs.

Not quite so artsy-fartsy, the **Adidas Sport Café** *(7 rue du Parlement Ste. Catherine; Tel 05/56-44-11-66; Bus 15 to Comédie, buses 13, 14, 17, 19, 20, 21 to place Jeans Jaurès; 10am-2am Mon-Sat, 5pm-midnight Sun; beers 16-25F)* is your ultimate sports bar, and in Europe sports means football—soccer to you Yanks. Jocks and team flags fly everywhere. Run into international football fans, beer in hand, or zone out one of the many screens seen from any table. Polos and dockers not required, but they may make you feel more at home.

The mini-club/big bar, **Paris, Pékin** *(10 rue de la Merci; Tel 05/56-44-19-88; Bus 15 to Comédie, buses 13, 14, 17, 19, 20, 21 to place Jeans Jaurès; 6pm-2am daily; www.parispekin@free.fr; No credit cards)* has a decor that is more Peking than Paris, with its red-lantern lighting and dragons climbing the walls. Perhaps the six mirrored balls are from gay

wired

The **Net Zone** *(209 rue Ste. Catherine; Tel 05/56-590-125 Bus A, B, G, L, N, P, 12, 34 to Ste. Catherine or Bus 5, 6 to Ravez; 10am-8pm Mon-Sat; 1 hour 35F, student 30F; No credit cards)* isn't really a hangout to meet folks, unless you approach kids in caps and Tevas. There are about 10 to 15 computers to game and surf on, and the location is most convenient: right on the main artery of the pedestrian streets. You can't miss it.

Another connection, one a little more appealing to the senses, is **@rt.obas** *(7 rue Maucoudinat; Tel 05/56-442-630; Bus 15 to Comédie, Bus 1, 22, 23, 28 to Douane; 11am-1am Mon-Sat, 3-11pm Sun; E-mail: art.obas@wanadoo.fr; Connection 1 hour 35F, each subsequent hour 30F; No credit cards)*. Good music is on the menu along with some simple 20F food: sandwiches, quiche, brownies, and drinks, too. You're paying for the time you spend here, so don't get too distracted by the little soldier toys or Ken dolls painted white and glued onto a canvas in various designs. General Bordeaux sites also include ***www.bordeaux-online.com*** and ***http://bordeaux.webcity.fr***.

rules of the game

There's low-key boozing and puffing in Bor-
deaux—not quite sloshing around with a forty and a joint in the
great wide open. Most of the action is inside or overflowing onto a
terrace, but you won't get carded by any bar or club bouncers either.
Cigarette smokers, who are banished from society in the U.S., can
kick back and enjoy the freedom of smoking in bars, restaurants, or
clubs. Anti-tobacco campaigns and awareness of the harms of
second-hand smoke are spreading like wildfire, there's still the courtesy of asking your companions if they mind.

Paris, but most of the people are from Bordeaux, the university, or
abroad. You can look cute, but don't have to be decked to sip coolly on
a Bacardi Mojito (35F) as resident DJ Andy spins drum and bass, jungle,
or deep pumpin' house. Happy-hour's from 6 to 10pm, and Thursday
is ladies' night.

▶▶AROUND PLACE VICTOIRE...

You can walk in circles on the place de la Victoire with abundant possibilities, but a favorite and well-known meeting place is **Le Plana** *(22
place de la Victoire; Tel 05/56-91-73-23; Buses 7, 8, 20, 21 to Victoire;
7am-2am Mon-Sat, 2pm-2am Sun)*. This cafe-by-day, bar-and-live-music-
stage-by-night sets out plenty of tables on the square for the overflowing
student crowd, which on most nights gathers around 10 or 11:30pm. On
Sundays live jazz, and on Mondays and Tuesdays other pop and rock
beats resound around 10pm.

At **Zoo Bizarre** *(58 rue du Mirail; Tel 05/56-91-14-40; Bus 7, 8,
20, 21 to Victoire; 10pm-4:30 or 5 am Wed-Sun; zoobi@enfrance.com,
www.zoobizarre.free.fr; No credit cards)*, DJ Alex is the resident, while a
changing monthly program of visiting DJs and performers amplifies the
menu. The two-floor, minimally decorated club (apart from the ducky
inner tube on the wall) brings on the electronic and experimental music:
trip-hop, house, funk, disco, jungle, free-style jazz, and cabaret rock and
roll. To enter the realm, wait till about 1am, look casual, and shell out
30F (more or less) for each show. Drinks aren't too bad though, at 10F
for what's on tap.

Right around the corner from Zoo Bizarre you can get a little closer and
sweat a little more, sliding up to your salsa partner at **El Chuchumbe** *(6
rue Causserouge; Tel 05/56-31-25-88; Buses 7, 8, 20, 21 to Victoire; 10:30pm-
2am Tu-Sat; No credit cards)*. If you don't know the moves, Cecilia gives
lessons on Thursdays and Liz on Wednesdays at 9pm, free with consumption! Or simply try the sweet house "Che" rum and things will go more
smoothly, especially with Xavier cuing up his neverending collection of
musicians, half of whom he's met. If your hips are in perpetual motion after
things get cut off, ask around to find out where the dancing continues.

arTs scene

Arriving in Bordeaux and seeing all the fountains, classic French architecture (like the gorgeous opera house), and primed and trimmed gardens, the first impression you may get is that the art scene will be equally primed and trimmed—and you'd be right. You may find various galleries showing old rugs, china, 16th-century decorative art, and landscape paintings. It's not all still-life here, though; the Bordelais are making their way into the 20th century, slowly, slowly....

▶▶**VISUAL ARTS**

By now you've gazed up at a thousand stained-glass windows on your European whirlwind tour of churches and cathedrals, and they're all looking the same. Now see how they're made at **Vitral Concept** *(24 rue St. James; Tel 05/56-51-32-80, Fax 05/56-51-19-50; Bus A, L, B, 20, 21, F, U, G to Pasteur; 9am-noon/2-7pm Mon-Fri)*. It's a workshop and gallery where you can watch artists in action creating new and repairing old stained-glass art. Chat with the restorers about the contrasting styles from then and now and how the materials have changed.

Changing exhibitions at **Galerie L'Ami des Lettre** *(5 rue Jean-Jacques Bel; Tel 05/56-79-15-34; Bus 13, 16-21 to Comédie; 10:30am-12:30pm/2:30-6:30pm Tue-Sat)* show small collections of paintings, sculptures, watercolors, and pastels from contemporary international artists. Recently they've hung artists who had works in Madrid's annual ARCO show.

Fashion is art and usually gravitates to Paris, but Frédérique Fimat has brought style to Bordeaux at her boutique **La Cour de Joséphine** *(26 rue des Remparts; Tel 05/56-44-16-77; Buses 7, 8 to Gambetta; 2-7pm Mon, 10am-7pm Tue-Sat; V, MC)*, where you'll find stunning women's clothing of the kind you see on runway models but would actually be able to wear. The *creatrice* fits you with layers, combinations of light fabrics like linen, and bright colors for spring and summer. (Considering they start at 2000F an outfit, however, you may just want to look.) The window displays change frequently to show off fashions you'd expect to see only in the City of Light.

boy meets girl

Pick-up lines can be translated into 20 languages, but they're all the same—You've got beautiful eyes, Do you come here often? My favorite here was *"Est-ce-que vous habitez chez vos parents?"* (Do you live with your parents?). The French, like many of us, are ready to take on the world—but for the moment, we have to move back in with our folks.

▶▶PERFORMING ARTS

In the Saint Pierre neighborhood is **Café-Théâtre ONYX** *(13 rue Fernand Philippart; Tel 05/56-44-26-12; Bus 1, 22, 23, 28, 91, 92 to Jean Jaurès; Box office and theater hours depend on showtime; 35-80F; No credit cards)*, an independent theater, now in its twentieth year, that brings creative comedies and comics (musical, dark, burlesque) to its small stage in cycles. For example, *Festifemmes,* a periodic week-long festival of comedirennes, artists, musicians, and actresses, shows off female humor and creativity.

Even if you're not interested in opera, Bordeaux's **Grand-Théâtre** *(Place de la Comédie; Tel 05/56-00-85-95, Fax 05/56-00-85-69; Reservation and info line 2-6pm Mon-Fri: Tel 05/56-00-85-65; Bus 13, 14, 16-21 to Comédie; Theater front desk 10am-6pm Mon-Sat; www.bordeaux-opera.com, www.opera-bordeaux.com; all events 35-330F, student/under 25 rates; AE, V, MC)* is truly grand, outside and in, and offers dance, music, theater, and perhaps, most interesting (and economical), cinema. Ask for the program in the theater or at the tourist office to see what *"ciné-scènes"* films are being shown in the Grand-Théâtre (30F!). They also show *"ciné-musique,"* Films accompanied by piano or orchestra, in a smaller associated theater. Showings are seasonal and few—hope you catch one!

Centre Jean Vigo *(6 rue Franklin; Tel 05/56-44-35-17; Bus 7, 8 to Gambetta; First session 2:15pm daily; centre@jeanvigo.com, www.cinesites. tm.fr; 37F admission, 30F Mon and Wed, 25F students; No credit cards)* shows only original-version films in theme- or director-based cycles, including big box-office hits, classics, and international cinema from *Blair Witch* to Hitchcock to Tatsumi Kumashiro. Every so often the cinema hosts lectures before the film.

Just want to veg out on a movie that has no cultural significance whatsoever? Go to the 15-screen **UGC Ciné-cité** *(13-15 rue Georges Bonnac; Tel 08/36-68-68-58, or 05/56-48-43-43; Bus 7, 8 to Gambetta; First session 11am; 48F adult, 25F students)* right in the center of the old town. Sometimes they show both French and original versions, but Julia Roberts will always play the same part.

gay scene

Bordeaux's gay and lesbian center, **Maison de l'Homosocialité** *(30/32 rue Paul Bert; Tel 05/56-01-12-03; e-mail: m.homo@netcourrier.com)* provides services, information, and support as well as hosting evening discussions, debates, and social gatherings starting at 8:30pm. From 6 to 11pm on Tuesdays, Thursdays, and Fridays a little bar, **le bar associatif,** opens up to all. A good guide, for both the town and southwestern France, is a monthly mini-magazine called *Factory,* which lists bars, restaurants, associations, events, and prints classifieds and short articles. A website to check the detailed program for the area is *www.franc.qrd.org.* There's no defined gay neighborhood, but most gay bars, restaurants, and clubs are all centrally located on the pedestrian streets around place Saint Pierre and west near the Cathédrale St. André.

fIVE-O

Like everywhere in France, there are a couple of different uniforms hitting the beat here, which tip you off as to whether they're going to give you a parking or running-with-a-scissors ticket, or if they're here for serious business. In general, cops don't make a huge stage appearance in Bordeaux. The worst they seem to do is try to confiscate skateboards.

Rainbows end at **Bistrot MAP** (*62 rue de la Devise; Tel 05/56-48-19-92; Bus 13, 16-21 to Comédie; 7pm-2am Tue-Sun, opens 7:30pm in winter; V, MC*), the bar/restaurant in the Saint Pierre area. People come for traditional southwestern French dishes like *Magret de canard entier* (duck, 78F) or creative salmon lasagna (42F) up until midnight, and to sit near those who just come for a drink. ABBA may complement either the cuisine or the conversation. Summer evenings are lively at the terrace tables and there's a wealth of flyers and mags for browsing the local gay scene.

Seven Café (*73 rue des Trois Conils; Tel 05/56-48-13-79; Buses 7, 8, 13, 14, 15, 20, 21 to Gambetta; 6pm-2am daily; No credit cards*) is a friendly little bar with mostly male customers, some women, and fading orange-and-mirror decor. Techno and funk energize you and will perhaps drag you downstairs for the Saturday and Sunday after-hours that start at 5am and break through the dawn. Drinks run 10 to 40F.

Women head to **La Reine Carotte** (*32 rue du Chai-des-Farines; Tel 05/56-01-26-68; 7pm-2am Tue-Thur, 9pm-2am Fri-Sat; Bus 1, 22, 23, 28, 91, 92 to Douane; No credit cards*) to look at the changing art exhibitions hanging in the bar...or maybe really to look at the other women. Not an aggressive atmosphere, though; a place where both men and women can drink and nibble on tapas.

CULTUrE ZOO

First, a couple of budget hints:

If you have a student ID with you (i.e., not back at the hostel), you can get in free to Musée d'Art Contemporain, Centre Jean Moulin, Musée d'Aquitaine, Musée de Arts-Décoratifs, Musée des Beaux-Arts, Musée Goupil, and Muséum d'Histoire Naturelle. The first Sunday of every month is also free at these same museums. If museums aren't your thing, there are plenty of monuments and gardens to see: esplanade de Quinconces, a tree-lined spread with an impressive fountain on the quai Louis XVIII; Notre Dame, the Baroque church tucked away near the place de la Comédie; place de la Bourse, the ex-royal palace on the river; and la Grosse Cloche, the clock tower down by the place de la Victoire.

Cathédrale Saint André (*Place Pey-Berland; Tel 05/56-52-68-10; Bus 12, 19-21,93 to Pey-Berland; 10am-6:30pm Mon, 8-11:30am/2-6:30pm Tue-Sat, till 6pm Nov-Mar, 8am-12:30pm Sun; guided visits*

festivals

Les Epicuriales, l'Art de la Fête *(info at tourist office; takes place near the Grand Théâtre; Bus 13, 16-21 to cours de XXX Juillet)*, organized by commercial Bordeaux, is now in its sixth year. "The Art of the Festival" brings eating, drinking, and music to the allées de Tourny for 17 days during the second half of June and beginning of July. Entrance is free, but you pay for food, drinks, and atmosphere at tents where Bordeaux bars, cafes, and restaurants serve up their international specialties. Summer evenings filled with gorging and drinking to music: What more could you ask for?

Of course there's a wine festival, **Bordeaux Fête Le Vin** *(Tel 05/56-006-629; bordeaux-fete-le-vin@bordeaux-tourisme.com, www.bordeaux-tourisme.com)*, a fine opportunity for discovering wine or the bottom of your glass, held from June 30 to July 2 in even-numbered years .

2:30pm Thur Jul-mid-Sept; free): The apex of Gothic architecture in the city, this ostentatious cathedral was consecrated by Pope Urban II in the 11th century but was not completed until the 16th century. Its stone facade, which features sculptures of angels and apostles in reliefs devoted to the life of Christ, remains its most distinguishing feature. Inside, its greatest treasure is a series of 13th-century sculptures on the Porte Royale or "royal door," although the 14th-century sculptures on the north door are also impressive. Its soaring 14th-century chancel contrasts dramatically with the more severe architectural style of the nave, which dates from the 13th century. The highlight of a visit, though, is not the cathedral itself, but its adjoining bell tower, Tour Pey-Berland, jutting 50 meters up into the Bordeaux cityscape, evoking *campanile* an Italian. The tower's builders feared it might collapse into the cathedral, so they constructed it 15 meters away for safety's sake. If you climb its steep 229 steps, you'll be rewarded with a panoramic vista of France's southwestern coast.

Musée d'art Contemporain *(7 rue Ferrère; Tel 05/56-00-81-50; Bus 1 to intersection rue Ferrère with quai Louis XVIII, or Bus 7, 8 to Jardin Publique; 11am-6pm Tue-Sun, till 8pm Wed, closed holidays; capc@marie bordeaux.fr; 20-30F adults, students free, noon-2pm free to all 1st Sun every month):* This museum is housed in an old harbor warehouse redesigned in a Roman style, which itself is a spacy concept. Inside hangs an ever-changing exhibit of contemporary international installations, sculptures, paintings, etc. You can pick up a publication called *Dans les Musées de Bordeaux,* which gives current exhibit information, at the tourist office.

Vinorama (*12 cours du Médoc; Tel 05/56-39-53-02; Bus 7, 8, 9 to Medoc or Bus 1 two stops after Les Chartrons if coming from center; 10:30am-12:30pm/2:30-6:30pm Tue-Sat, 2-6:30pm Sun Jun-Sept; 2-6:30pm Tue-Fri, 10:30am-12:30pm/2:30-6:30pm Sat Oct-May; 35F adults, 18F under 18*): Who's got time to go all the way out to the vineyards? Stay right in Bordeaux and sample the Romans' recipe, another from the 1800s, or one from today at this museum that gives you more of a taste through the history of wines. The brochure makes it look kinda cheesy and touristy—but hey, that's what we are, and we did come here to drink some wine.

Grand Théâtre (*Place de la Comédie*): The Neoclassic design of this massive structure may make you think you're in Rome. It's one of the "must-sees" according to many, and you'll probably see it a lot 'cause it's a conspicuous landmark. If you want to experience more than the foyer, there's a tour guided by folks from the **tourist office** for 30F [see *need to know*, below]. There are also occasional *ciné-scènes*, presentations of cult or art films within a formal, somewhat academic setting.

modification

You can walk into **Maori's Concept** (*48 rue du Pas St. Georges; Tel 05/56-44-96-96; Bus to Bus 15 to Comédie, Bus 1, 22, 23, 28 to Douane gets you in walking distance; 2-8pm Mon, noon-8pm Tue-Sat; AE, V, MC*) an average Joe, and strut out tattooed, pierced, decked and groovin' like the rest of the clubbing world. The concept is fourfold: "urban zone" for clothes (*Diesel jeans 400F*), "point bar" to sip a cafe or tea (*8-12F*), "Maori's music" to find the hottest sounds (*vinyl starts at 60F*), and piercing/tattoos to feel the pain (*piercing 100-400F, tatts 400F+*). Plop down on the velvet theater seats, groove on the poppy-colored decor, and watch the transformations begin. The staff has already reached coolness but aren't so far out there they won't talk to you, and they're in on events.

Down the road, **Le Petit Salon** (*38 rue du Pas St. Georges; Tel 05/56-44-54-02; 9:20am-9pm Tue-Fri, 9am-6pm Sat; Cuts 80-120F, color 40-130F; No credit cards*) will help you put any finishing touches on your look. Listen to music at *un volume élévé* and you won't mind waiting to get in the stylist's chair for fun modern cuts, colors, and up-dos. Photos and art hung on the exposed brick walls and tons of event-flyers keep you entertained, too.

city sports

Bikes, boards, and blades zoom by you on every corner as people easily and amazingly traverse the turns and pedestrian streets of the old center of Bordeaux. Sports are on wheels in Bordeaux, and you need to get yourself some for the day. Start out on the *quais* along the river to stretch out and warm up. **Bord'Eaux-Velos Loisirs** [see *need to know*, below] is right there to rent the single and tandem bikes, blades, and scooters that you obviously couldn't fit in your bag. As for skaters, they congregate in the **Place Pey Berland,** where "no skating permitted" signs have been posted and removed a couple of times. Skate or die.

great outdoors

Bordeaux and the surrounding areas are also well-charted for cycling. All you have to do is ask for the extensive trail maps at **Bord'Eaux-Velos Loisirs** or the **Maison de la Gironde** [see *need to know*, below] to plan a journey. You can cross the river and head into the wine country on your own, stopping wherever you want. The rental shops can also hook you up with a guided bike tour of the vineyards and wine tasting. Call to work out the details. There are weekend trips (or longer on demand) to the wine district **Entre-Deux-Mers**. For three days and two nights, breakfasts and midday meals included, it comes out to around 1000F with extras, like museums and coffee, coming out of your pocket. You bike 30 to 40km a day and sleep in little inns along the way, going from one château vineyard to the next. It's not super hardcore and they'll carry your things from stop to stop, which definitely helps if you end up buying cases of wine!

For outdoor clubs and activities, a great source is **CIJA-Centre Information Jeunesse Aquitaine** (*5 rue Duffour Dubergier and 125 cours Alsace et Lorraine; Tel 05/56-56-00-56, Fax 05/56-56-00-53; Bus 20, 21 to Pey Berland, same bus and stop for both locations; 9:30am-6pm Mon-Thur, 9:30am-5pm Fri*). It's an organization to help directionless youth like yourself with careers and all that, but it's also a great place to find brochures, flyers, and posted outdoor activities like canoeing, whitewater rafting, rock-climbing clubs, etc. You can also pick up a copy of CIJA's edition of the newspaper *Sud-Ouest*.

stuff

The central shopping district runs straight down rue Sainte Catherine and between the Place Gambetta and Cathedral Saint André, where you have time to window-shop because cars aren't allowed to zoom down most of these streets. Of course, this doesn't mean you won't have to do some tricky maneuvering through the crowds that threaten to sweep you away. If you need to go to a mall, the place des Grands Hommes, off the place Gambetta, houses a multilevel center, Gallerie des Grands Hommes, with grocery store on the bottom floor. The surrounding streets comprise a shopping area that's a bit more chic and *chèr*.

▶▶BOUND

Time to break out that high school French to read a novel? Try **La Bouquinerie Plus** (*44 place Gambetta; Tel 05/56-01-09-10; Bus 7, 8 to Gambetta; 10:30am-1pm/2-7:30pm Mon-Sat; AE, V, MC*). It's not your typical musty, dusty used bookshop with a cat sitting in the window, but big and bright. Not up to par on the French? There's a little foreign-language section to pick up a paperback, and loads of French cartoon books, *Asterix*, *Tin Tin*, and *Gaston*.

New lit for bookworms and reading machines lines the shelves of **La Machine a Lire** (*8 place du Parlement; Tel 05/56-48-03-87; Bus 1, 22, 23, 28,91, 92 to Jean Juarès or Douane, Bus 13, 16-21 to Comédie; 10am-8pm Tue-Sat, 2-7pm Mon; machine@machinalire.com, www.*

machinealire.com; AE, V, MC), set on a well-preserved 18th-century street in the center of town near place de la Bourse. It's nice to be in a big bookstore that's not a warehouse or a chain. This place has that personal touch, along with author signings and lectures.

▶▶TUNES

Strickly Hip-Hop *(18 place F. Lafargue; Tel 05/56-52-01-52; Bus A, B, G, L, N, P, 12, 34 to Ste. Catherine, or Bus 5, 6 to Ravez; 11am-1:30pm/ 2-7:30pm Mon-Sat; No credit cards),* in the Saint-Éloi district, near the Church of Saint Paul, is not exactly what the name implies—jungle, break beat, and R&B can be spun here too. Upstairs there's mostly guys' wear. The vinyl and the selection of spray paints for extra-curricular activities are in the little basement.

The place for good house, techno, jungle, trance, hard techno, and other imported electronic music is **Maori's Concept** [see *modification,* above], where four shipment arrivals a week assure that you're ahead of the game. Equipment is also for sale in case you're planning on making a surprise appearance. If you're just with the DJ, they have a selection of CDs.

▶▶DUDS

The bull-horn-and-hide bench, the bits of Mexican art, and the starred cowboy boots somehow go with the Euro-trash urban wear at **Mexicana** *(135/137 rue Ste. Catherine; Tel 05/56-48-15-63; Bus A, B, G, L, N, P, 12, 34 to Ste. Catherine, or Bus 5, 6 to Ravez; 9:30am-7:30pm Mon-Sat; AE, V, MC).* Guys and girls, outfit yourselves head to toe and stomp into a club with No Name trainers or big industrial buckled boots. Don't know where to head? Shuffle through the flyers on the table while you wait for your size.

"La fripe c'est Cheap et Chic." "Fripe" is a word to turn used into stylin'. At **Docks...Cavier** *(183 rue Ste. Catherine; Tel 05/56-91-69-56; Bus A, B, G, L, N, P, 12, 34 to Ste. Catherine or Bus 5, 6 to Ravez; 10am-7pm Mon-Sat; V, MC)* you won't have to search through racks to find the good stuff—they've done that for you. Find retro from back in the day: jeans, skirts, button-downs, all around 100 to 300F; and the blue- and rose-colored shades make everything look a bit more chic.

Flyers of gay happenings scatter the doorway of **Eric S.** *(73 rue de Remparts; Tel 05/56-01-08-00; Bus 7, 8 to Gambetta; 2-7:30pm Mon, 11am-7:30pm Tue-Sat; eric.s-bordeaux@worldonline.fr; AE, V, MC),* a clothing store for men and more men. Show off your broad shoulders and nice butt in the tribal-patterned nylon shirts (200F) and Paco designer jeans (800F), or carry it all away in the crazy hard-shell plastic backpacks (1350F).

▶▶TRINKETS

At **CineToys** *(21 rue de Cheverus; Tel 05/56-52-11-54; Bus F, G, 12, 20, 21 to Pey Berland; V, MC over 100F),* on the street running parallel to rue des Remparts, talk to the guy behind the laptop about all the cinema-related gadgets from Matrix, Austin Powers, Star Wars, etc. I almost couldn't leave without the Chewbacca backpack (279F), but really didn't know how to justify the purchase. Get your Dr. Evil figurine for *one million dollars!!* Just kidding, it's 179F.

On the opposite end of the spectrum, **Le Petit Bois** (*8 rue des Remparts; Tel 05/56-52-86-91; Bus 7, 8 to Gambetta; 10am-7pm Mon-Sat; V, MC*) is where you can be a kid again without Hot Wheels or Barbies. Everything is made out of wood, perhaps to inspire creativity. Flip ladybug yo-yos in a cat's cradle, or roll the dice to help you decide what tonight's activity will be....

EATS

At the mention of Bordeaux, wine is immediately on the mind, but Bordeaux has culinary treasures as well [see *only here*, below]. In the quartier Saint Pierre, regional French restaurants and international flavors spice up the pedestrian streets, and the rue Saint Remi, which goes from Saint

only here-wine

The **tourist office** [see *need to know*, below] organizes wine tours, which are the easiest way to see some of the famed wine châteaux, especially if you're short on time. Call or go directly to the tourist office when you get to Bordeaux to reserve your spot, because the trips fill up quickly. The half day (160F adults, 140F student) is the most popular. Leaving at 1:30pm and getting back around 7:30pm, you visit two vineyards, taste a few wines, and drive around in the coach half-listening to a witty French woman give you the low-down. The day trip, from 9:30am, includes a museum and a "tasting lunch" at 290F adults, 255F students. Either trip's a great ride to meet other kids on their whirlwind tours of Europe. Only thing is you don't get to get off the bus very often as you pass through vineyards and drive by the châteaux. There's always a couple of wine geeks, though, to keep you entertained while they ask questions to let everyone see just how much they know.

If you happen to be one of those wine geeks, you may want to consider renting a car or bike [see *great outdoors*, above] and taking off on your own to the wine regions of Médoc or Entre-Deux-Mers. Visit the **Maison du Vin** (*1 cours XXX Juillet; Tel 05/56-002-266, Fax 05/56-002-277; 9:30am-5:30pm Mon-Fri, 9:30-3pm Sat; Bus 13, 16-21 to cours de XXX Juillet; civb@vins-bordeaux.fr, www.vins-bordeaux.com*), right across the street from the general tourist office. They are the experts on wine and have all the literature to help you brush up on terminology and learn how to match wine with foods. To become a real expert, you can go to their wine school. Check their web page, *http://ecole.vins-bordeaux.com*.

TO MARKET

Le Marché des Capucins *(Place des Capucins; Bus 7, 8, 22, 23 to Capucins; 4am-1pm Mon-Sat)* is the biggest food market in town, located just east of place de la Victoire. Vendor stalls, bars, and restaurants offer you everything, including nourishment before hitting the sack after a night out. A more intimate market, set on the Garonne, **Le Marché des Chartrons** *(Place des Cartrons; Bus 1, 24 to Chartrons; 7am-1pm Tue-Sat)* is where the neighbors come to sell their goods. Taking a picnic from the market to the riverside is a delicious idea.

Catherine east to place de la Bourse, is known for dining out, and not strictly expensive 10-course extravaganzas either. You can see the fast-life-skinny-wallet lifestyle of the student reflected in the food found down towards the bottom of rue Sainte Catherine near the place Victoire: lots of fries, kebabs, and panini stands, none better than another. If you really need a fast-food burger hit, go to the **Quick** *(270 rue Ste. Catherine; Tel 05/56-31-97-48; 11am-1am daily; Combo meals start at 35F; V, MC)*, and you'll feel less guilty than passing under the golden arches. Once you reach the quite large Victoire square itself, there's a surplus of cafe/bars where you can actually sit, and all are prime for people watching, sitting, and relaxing. Eating is very social, especially in the spring and summer when you can hardly negotiate a path through the tables and chairs on the pedestrian streets.

▶▶CHEAP

Not an ordinary sandwich shop, the **Chicken Station** *(1 rue de Can-dale; Tel 05/56-94-30-00; Bus 7, 8, 20, 21 to Victoire; 11am-2:15pm, 7pm-2am Mon-Sat; No credit cards)* near the place des Victoires on a street running parallel to rue Sainte Catherine, turns up the reggae and dub beats and attracts natty dreads. Although the sandwich and the plate are both chicken, they're combined with omelettes, cheese, bacon, etc. and topped with house sauces for 15 to 22F. Wash it down with a fresh fruit milkshake—try the special banana and avocado (sounds weird, but it's delicious). It you're gonna have *another* sandwich, it might as well be eaten sitting down and chilled out.

Something a little different, filling, and reasonable is **Cassolette Café** *(20 place de la Victoire; Tel 05/56-92-94-96; Bus 7, 8, 20, 21 to Victoire; opens noon-last orders 11:30pm daily; V, MC)*. It's a popular place for locals, students, and English-speakers who like to taste a little bit of everything. It's fun to sit down in a group and check off what you want on the menu. The chipper waiter will bring food out in round clay dishes. Mini-portions of salads, omelettes, eggplant *au gratin,* curried pork, and cheeses, among other dishes, are 13F, and "maxis" are 39F. Two or three minis or a mini and a maxi are enough to satisfy.

▶▶DO-ABLE

For traditional Brazilian food any night, and Brazilian dancing on Friday and Saturdays, head for **Beija Flor** *(13 rue Villedieu; Tel 05/56-94-17-56; Bus 7, 8, 20, 21 to Victoire; 8-11pm daily; www.gei-sa.fr/BeijaFlor; Average entrée 60-70F; AE, V, MC).* To get there, start in the place de Victoire and go down cours Aristide Briand; rue Villedieu forks off of it. The *feijoada,* a dish of black beans, spicy sausage, and meats over rice, is especially satisfying. Add a hot sauce and orange slices for tropical taste to match the decor.

Italian food will generally satisfy even the pickiest of groups. At **La Mama** *(21 rue des Remparts; Tel 05/56-44-67-87; Bus 7, 8, 13, 26 to Gambetta; lunch and dinner till 11pm Tue-Sat; Menu 100F; V, MC),* you're received by the family and have all the classic Italian pasta and pizza fare, topped off by tiramisu, to drool over.

▶▶SPLURGE

The only problem with dining at **La Petite Savoie** *(27 rue des Argentiers; Tel 05/56-51-21-80; Bus 1,22,23,28 to Douane ; dinner 7pm-last order 11:30pm daily; Fixed menu around 120F; AE, V, MC)* is that your clothes and hair smell like fondue cheese when you leave, but if you're willing to *suffer,* it's recommended. Drinking and adding wine to the pot will diminish the lingering smell of the three-cheese fondue for 58F.

crashing

With quite a few options in town you can pretty much just wander the streets of the old town till you find a good option. It's not really worth it to spend the night near the station—it's out of the way, not to mention a little sketchy, and schlepping back will be a hassle when you want to be in on what's going on in the center. If your bag is really that heavy, check it at the station. Most Bordeaux hostels/hotels have no curfew and either you have a key or the door has a code which buzzes you in. The price for an average room with WC and shower ranges from 100 to 300F, and it doesn't drop for a single. When you make reservations for a room without a shower *(une douche),* make sure that at least there's a shower in the hall to use!

▶▶CHEAP

Probably the cheapest bed you'll find in town, other than the youth hostel, is **Studio** *(26 rue Huguerie; Tel 05/56-48-00-14; Bus 13, 16-21, M to Tourny; 98-130F single, 250F five people; AE, V, MC),* right near the public gardens. Its simple but clean rooms come with shower, toilet, sink, phone, and TV. You use a door code to enter and have no curfew. There's a slew of international vagabonds, and the BusAbout tour comes every few days to drop off more kids, so it's best to call ahead, even though they have 102 beds.

The **HI Youth Hostel** *(22 cours Barbey; Tel 05/56-91-59-51; Bus 7, 8 to first or second stop after train station; 72F per person; No credit cards)* is a jaunt on foot from the station down cours de la Marne with a left down cours Barbey. There's a three-night limit, and the second and third nights drop in price by 10F.

▶▶DO-ABLE

Studiotel Blayais *(17 rue Mautrec; Tel 05/56-48-17-87, Fax 05/56-52-47-57; Bus 13, 16-21 to Comédie; 220F singles and doubles; All rooms have toilet and shower; AE, MC, V),* tucked away on a short street at the top of rue Ste. Catherine and near the tourist office, is only a two-star, but the owner treats you like it was a five-star. All is in order and clean, and the proprietor can help you orient yourself with all the brochures, schedules, and maps. It's like a mini-tourist office. The details make the stay.

The two-star **Hôtel Albion** *(5 cours de la Somme; Tel 05/56-94-00-19, Fax 05/56-91-44-94; Bus 7, 8, 20, 21 to Victoire; www.hotel-albion.com; 260F single or double, breakfast 38F; AE, V, MC)* is on the south end of rue Sainte Catherine, right in the heart of the place de la Victoire nightlife. You literally walk out the door onto the plaza, which makes for convenient crashing at the end of the night. All the rooms have full bathrooms and a TV with Canal Plus (the cable station). The complimentary breakfast is a little buffet, which is more than the normal croissant and coffee.

▶▶SPLURGE

Bayonne Etche Ona *(15 cours de l'Intendance; Tel 05/56-48-00-88; Bus 13, 21 to Comédie; 400-800F room; V, MC)* adds extra cush with climate control, spacious private bathrooms, and satellite TV if you're planning on relaxing in the room. It's a proper hotel with reception desk and breakfast for 60F, but being so central (right near the tourist office), there's no lack of cafes to find a morning spot.

need to know

Currency Exchange Most **banks** will change your money, but they are closed on Saturdays and Sundays in the city center. Suburban banks are closed on Mondays and Sundays. So buy your francs before the weekend starts, or use the ATMs.

Tourist Information The main Bordeaux **tourist office** is on **12 cours du XXX Juillet** *(Tel 05/56-00-66-00; Bus 13,16-21 to cours de XXX Juillet; 9am-7pm Mon-Sat/7:30pm July and Aug, 9:30am-6:30pm Sun; www.bordeaux-tourisme.com).* You can load up your pack with brochures and maps. They also organize walking or horse-drawn tours in Bordeaux and wine tours outside the city. There's another branch at the **Gare Saint Jean** train station, in the arrivals foyer *(Tel 05/56-91-64-70; 9am-noon/1-6pm Mon-Fri, 10am-noon/1-3pm Sa-Sun).* For regional info, guidebooks, and maps on camping, biking, wining, and dining, go to the **Maison de la Gironde** *(21 cours* *de l'Intendance; Tel 05/56-52-61-40; Bus 15, 20, 21 to Comédie; www.tourisme-gironde.cg33.fr).*

Public Transportation Although buses run in the center, most sites are pretty walkable and almost as easy to get to on foot. The tourist office and info desks at the train station have bus maps. A single ride costs 7.50F; a book of ten is 53F (33F students) from the driver or a tobacconist. The single-ride ticket can be used on different buses for an hour after you first validate it. You can also buy a one-day pass for 23F or a three-day pass for 53F. Evening buses only run till around midnight. The main starting point is **place Pey Berland** by the cathedral.

Health and Emergency Emergency: *081;* Ambulance (SAMU): *15;* Fire: *18* (firefighters here are trained paramedics, too); Cops: *17;* Euro emergency: *112.* **Hôpital Pellegrin,** the main hospital, is located west of the center *(place Amélie St. André; Tel 05/56-79-56-79; Bus 11 to Pellegrin).*

Pharmacies A **green or blue neon cross** indicates pharmacies, which are located throughout town.

Telephone City code: *05/56* if you call within France, *556* if you're calling from another country; National operator: *12;* International operators: *00-33-12* plus the country code; *0/800* numbers are free, *0/836* charge you a "premium" rate.

To use most public phones in France, you need to buy a *télécarte* (phone card) at newsstands and tobacconists. The lowest denomination is 50F. Cafes and bars often have coin phones.

Airport From **Mérignac Airport** *(Tel 05/56-34-50-50)* about 11 kilometers west of Bordeaux, there's a **"Jet Bus"** shuttle that is a 30- to 45-minute ride to the following stops: place Gambetta, Grand Théâtre at Barrière Judaïque, 29 rue Esprit de Lois, quai Richelieu at "Douane" bus stop, and Gare Saint Jean, the train station. It runs every 30 minutes weekdays, every 45 minutes weekends, from 5:30am-9:30pm (10pm on weekends). A single ride costs 37F, return 60F, with a special rate if you're under 26. A taxi to the center runs you around 100F during the day.

Trains Gare Saint Jean *(Info and booking: 0/836-35-35-35; Timetable: 08/36-67-68-69; station services: Tel 05/56-33-11-83)* is a half-hour hop from the center on buses 7 and 8.

Bus lines out of the City: Gare Routière *(Rue Fondaudège; Tel 05/56-43-08-43),* near the Place Tourny just southwest of the esplanade de Quinconces, is for long distances. To jet about the Gironde region surrounding Bordeaux, like to the coast or to Langon, Libourn, Savignac, etc., there's the **Réseau Trans-Gironde** *(Tel 05/56-99-57-83).* You can get a map from the Maison de la Gironde [see *tourist info,* above].

Wheels Rental Rent bikes, blades, and "city-bug" scooters at **Bord'Eaux-Velos Loisirs** *(Quai Louis XVIII; Tel/Fax 05/564-47-31, mobile: 06/81-83-23-03; Bus 22, 23, 94, 29, 31, 91, 92 to Quinconces; 9:30am-9pm daily, closing may vary if it's a slow day; No age restrictions; 20F per hour,*

50F 1/2 day, 90F full day, 120F for 24 hours; 1000F deposit or leave your passport/ID; No credit cards). You can drill the owner in English about all the trails in the surrounding areas and perhaps go on one of his trips—or make your own over a weekend [see *city sports,* above].

Laundry *Laveries* are plentiful and are usually self-op with washers, dryers, and detergent. A load of 6-7kilos starts at 15F, drying at 2F per minute, and soap 2-5F. Here's a couple (but ask around—there could be one closer to where you're staying): **Laverie Lincoln Automatique** *(123 cours d'Alsace et Lorraine; No phone; 8am-8pm daily; Bus A, B, G, L, N, P, 12, 34 to Ste. Catherine; No credit cards).* **Repassage Laverie Montabadon** *(8 rue Lafaurie de Monbadon; Tel 05/56-52-84-16; 7am-9pm Daily; Bus 13, 16-21, M to Tourny; No credit cards).*

Postal Mail stuff from the main **La Poste** *(15 rue Judaïque; Tel 05/57-78-80-00; Bus 7, 8 to Gambetta),* almost on the Place Gambetta.

La Rochelle

For those who embrace the winds off the sea more readily than they spend hours slathered in Banana Boat oil reading a romance novel, the port city of La Rochelle offers all the mystique of *la mer* without the trappings of a typical seaside resort. Although some tourist brochures try to hype its location on the Atlantic as a beach bum's dream, La Rochelle's true charm lies more in the pictures it brings to mind of rugged fishermen and windy days along the New England coast.

Even into early summer, the salty winds tunneling through the old port chase residents through the narrow whitewashed streets as they side-step around annoyingly prevalent piles of dog poo. The overriding image, *sans* dog excrement, recalls a skewed remake of the Who's *Quadrophenia*, not so much in kids' dress or musical tastes, but more in their attitude of defiance towards the older generation. In La Rochelle, that defiance finds its voice in cheesy cover bands, brightly colored scooters, and thrift stores. Although their threads aren't especially mod, local kids have a sense of style that's lacking in Loire Valley towns to the east. Perhaps information travels more readily to a seaport, perhaps not.... At any rate, the look is a lot more calculated here. La Rochelle is a university city, so you'll find plenty of young folk here. Along with fashion-conscious guys and gals, there's plenty else to enjoy, especially after twilight, including loads of fun bars and basement music venues, a flirty pickup scene, and a summer film festival that delivers the content of Cannes without the snooty 'tude. At night the quays along the water come alive as the outdoor cafes and restaurants start hopping. By day, take advantage of the city's seaside locale and explore the **Canal de Rompsay** by canoe [see *city sports,* below], or check out the waterlogged **Fort Boyard** by boat [see *culture zoo*, below].

The tourist office publishes the most comprehensive guide to La Rochelle [see *need to know*, below], which is available there and at almost any restaurant or hotel in the city.

neighborhoods

The layout of La Rochelle is easy to figure out. The center of town and all its events are concentrated around the Vieux Port (Old Port), and you're never more than a 20-minute walk from the next spot you want to go. The town seeps out from the center in all directions, but thins into mainly industrial and residential areas with little of interest to visit or do. The exception is the few nightclubs that are a hefty walk out of center city, but these can be easily reached by cab or car.

Another effect of the diminutive size of La Rochelle is a bus system that doesn't truly operate in the center city. One central commuter line

five things to talk to a local about

1. Ninja scooters: They are everywhere in La Rochelle—pumped up, aggressive, and brightly colored beasts that tear around the port and occasionally take out a tourist or two. (Just kidding.)

2. The gentrification of the bars around the **Vieux Port.** During the day, these outdoor brasseries are crowded with all types of La Rochelle youth and adults, but at night the older folks are sucked into bars with awful cover bands or bad DJs.

3. The tourists during the film festival. Sure, every town resents that major event, which brings a million pic-snapping outsiders into city limits, but when the festival plays second fiddle to the one in a certain other French city on the Mediterranean, feelings can get pretty nasty.

4. Film, in general. At the same time that they rue their silver medal in the French film festival race, these people are French and do love their indie films. Mention Gerard Depardieu for instant laughter and the ensuing lengthy conversation on the merits and demerits of his career.

5. The Atlantic. Especially if you hail from the American East Coast or any place touching a great body of water, this can be an easy conversation starter. People here are proud of their seashore, from the old forts and fishing port to the beaches and fresh seafood.

leaves from the **place de Verdun,** a 10-minute walk from the port. But for the most part, unless the ol' feet are really hurting, it's a better idea simply to have a good pair of walking shoes or a bike to check out what La Rochelle has to offer.

hanging out

A 10-minute walk from the port, the **place de Verdun** is a wide-open space that's constantly packed with people during the day. It's a major stop for most bus lines in the city (the main reason for all the activity), but it's also a good place to watch the citizens of La Rochelle go about their daily business. The crowd is mostly students who are talking, sitting around, or riding bikes, usually shouting loudly enough about nighttime plans for you to catch a few hints for yourself.

Another, more consistently lively, trail of activity winds around the Old Port on the **quai duperre, cours des Dames,** and **quai Valin.** Every square inch of real estate is filled with some kind of bar or restaurant here, predominantly of the outdoor seating variety. Most places are easy-going about letting you lounge at their tables for hours as long as you order something to make it worth their while—a cup of coffee will do. From this vantage point of plastic chair paradise with tall drink in hand, it's easy to meet either the person at the next table or someone in the street. The action-packed quais along the port make mixing and mingling a breeze, but can also lead to close encounters between motor scooters and pedestrians, which happens a little too often for comfort.

bar scene

Apart from a few cheesy bars around the Vieux Port that attract a mostly older crowd, the bar scene in La Rochelle is all fun. For some reason most of the bartenders and owners are psyched beyond belief to have their own

boy meets girl

With a plethora of bars squeezed into such a small town, you'd think that the dating scene would be based on cruising bars and attempting to pick up members of the opposite sex over a pint. This is, however, not quite the case. People here are flirty and coy rather than blatantly looking for a homerun, and a quick and intriguing glance will get a guy much farther than slapping some money on the bar to buy a drink for "the little lady over in the corner." That said, the clubs of La Rochelle can be a bit different once the alcohol starts to seep in and the music takes over—every dance floor will have one or two of the obligatory, slobbering Casanovas who try to grind with every person in sight.

bars and to serve *you!* Expect star service wherever you choose to go, i.e., pate, various bar snacks, and good drinks aplenty.

Le Pub *(23 rue Leonce Vieljeux; Tel 05/46-41-38-03; 5pm-2am daily)* is truly one of the great French/Irish bars. While it may lack the determined decorative scheme of some of the bigger bars of similar theme, it holds its own in service, music, and quality. Here you can sit down at one of the cozy tables and dive into the complimentary bread and pate, while the owners feast on treats of their own behind the bar. With live Celtic and rock music beginning at midnight and continuing until 2 or 3am, the mood is as loud, friendly, and raunchy as a drunk uncle's picnic. Le Pub doesn't often get overly congested with visitors. It has a faithful following who know and love each other, and welcome visitors with open arms.

Jekyll & Hyde Cafe *(2 rue des Templiers; Tel 05/46-41-03-74; 4pm-2am daily)* is a new addition to La Rochelle, which is evident in everything from the over-eager owner's flashy business cards to his bumpin' Bose sound system. The decor inside attempts to copy its NYC namesake, but ends up looking instead like a high school science project overrun with taxidermy and Art Nouveau decoration. All the same, the beer selection is tops. Perhaps that's why it's so popular among young locals, who make up about three quarters of its clientele.

Located on one of the most busy nighttime streets in La Rochelle, **Bar Le Saint Nicolas** *(12 rue St. Nicolas; Tel 05/46-41-16-07; Eve-2am daily)* is a spacious establishment that probably attracts one of the hippest crowds in town. While the decor will remind you of an American road trip—the walls are decked with old license plates and vintage signs—the patrons are very certainly Franks, kitted out in all things European. The cool kids seem to favor the downstairs section, a dimly lit cavern of Lichtenstein prints and comfy couches. Upstairs, the bartenders, who double as DJs, change the CDs about once a minute but do a decent job of pleasing their audience's musical tastes.

LIVE MUSIC SCENE

Most of the major live music events, ranging from rock to salsa, in La Rochelle take place at the **esplanade Saint Jean d'Acre** *(6 rue de La Desiree; Tel 05/46-68-25-22; AE, MC, V, EC)*. This also is the site for **Festival FrancoFolie,** a yearly musical extravaganza in the middle of July (see *festivals,* below).

La Rochelle is not without its basement music scene, however, which in fact seems to creep out of the basement and into hot, stuffy venues. One such gem is **La Casamance** *(Rue du Cordouan; No phone; Most shows begin 10:30pm; 20-50F; No credit cards)* which advertises "break-core mixes" and often delivers something else entirely. Though it's difficult to see past the throbbing mass of kids sweating and screaming at the stage, the live acts are usually local Goth-looking dudes who play a skewed mix of Nine Inch Nails and Krautrock. A small bar is sandwiched between the two back walls although it might take a cattle prod laced with heavy tranquilizers to part the crowds and get to a bartender. Your best bet is simply to give in to the crowd, get hot n' sweaty, and let out some stress along with the tunes.

club scene

L'Oxford (*Complexe de la Pergola-Plage de La Rochelle, near place de la Préfecture; Tel 05/46-41-51-81; 11pm-4am daily; 60F includes one drink, 5F mandatory coat check; No credit cards*), tucked away in the large park space at the Prefecture, brings the ocean air inside to one of the most popular clubs in La Rochelle. The place remains empty until around 1am, at which point the two dance floors start to fill up with movers and shakers. The tunes are a bit outdated, but fun nonetheless. We can't deny that in a foreign country it's awfully tempting to dance to Britney Spears and Will Smith. Even more amusing is trying to learn a few French rap faves, which everyone in the club seems to know and doesn't hesitate to clap or sing along to. No one appears to mind the slightly cheesy "Miami Vice" decor of airbrushed palm trees and sandscapes or the fact that nearly every table in the club is "reserved" for phantom club goers who never actually show up. Thankfully, these little white placards only carry weight until 2am or so, when the intense bouncers in denim shirts and ties back off and let the weary dancers sit where they please.

gay scene

Although when you arrive the owner will scowl at you like Lurch and Uncle Fester's love child, once he finds out you're aware that **L'Insolite** (*12 rue Bletterie; Tel 05/46-41-90-51; 5pm-2am*) is a gay bar, the smiles and bar propaganda aren't far behind. For straight and queer crowds alike, it's a good place to listen to quality dance music where people will actually, you know, *dance*.

culture zoo

One of the best ways to explore the historical attractions of this city on the Atlantic is, unsurprisingly, by boat. For 65 to 110F, depending on the length of the ride and the sites included, you can catch most of the waterside must-sees of La Rochelle [see *great outdoors,* below]. At the tourist office [see *need to know,* below], you can address your queries to any of the four outfitters that give tours, or talk to someone who works at the tourist office, which is fairly objective about the relative merits of the offerings of each. In midsummer, there are about a half-dozen tours of the city's four ports every day. In winter, they're offered about three times a day, Saturday and Sunday only. Prices range from 60-90F per person, and last between 70 and 95 minutes each, depending on the tour and the company. Rides are very touristy, generally led by a guy speaking into a microphone in French.

Fort Boyard: Situated between the islands of **Ré** and **Oléron,** the fort was originally conceived in 1805 as a 74-cannon fortress to protect not only the two islands, but the city of La Rochelle itself. The construction was continuously delayed, however, by the difficulty of building an entire fort on a man-made sandbank. Nearly 50 years later the stunted fort still stood at only 2 meters above the water. Construction was finally completed in 1857, but by that time the defensive uses were obsolete and the fort became a military prison. You can see the fort from one of the boat tours we mentioned above, but, unfortunately, it's impossible to tour the fort itself—unless you've got some serious La Rochelle political connections.

Tour de la Lanterne, (*Tel 05/46-41-56-04; 10am-7pm daily April-Sept; 10am-12:30pm, 2-5:30pm daily Oct-Mar; Admission 25F, 15F ages*

festivals

For one week in mid-July, beginning on the second or third Sunday of the month, La Rochelle is rocked by some of the most diverse French and world musical acts around. With themed nights like *Reggae 100% Jamaican* and *Fiesta Latino-Cubaine,* the **Francofolies** has an answer for nearly every musical taste. From Monday to Saturday, starting around 10:30pm daily, three or four bands take the stage and keep things lively until the wee hours. Tickets are available at the tourist office [see *need to know,* below] from 50-175F.

The major festival in town, however, is the highly reputed **Festival International du Film de La Rochelle** (*for info year round, write to rue Saint Sabin, 75011 Paris; Tel 01/06-16-66; Fax 01/48-06-15-40; Advance reservations required*). For about two weeks at the end of June and early July, crowds from Paris and other major European cities flood into town to attend screenings, show off their tacky evening wear, and try out their new yachts on the Atlantic. All that said, if you're interested in the flavor of Cannes with slightly less snobbiness—a festival where you might actually get into a few screenings—this is the time to do it. Tickets cost from 50-200F, depending on the film.

17 and under), stands 58 meters above the harbor of Vieux Port, opposite **Tour Saint Nicolas.** Built between 1445 and 1476, it was the first lighthouse ever constructed in France. In the 18th and 19th centuries, it was turned into a jail, and during the various wars of religion in the region, the lighthouse was used as an execution tower, notably when 13 priests were tied up and tossed overboard. Come here not for exhibits but to climb the tower and feast your eyes on an Atlantic panorama that includes the offshore island of **Ile d'Oléron.**

If you're not put off by wax museums and automatons, **Musée des Automates** *(Rue de la Desiree-La Ville en Bois; Tel 05/46-41-68-08; 2pm-6pm Nov-Jan, 10am-noon/2pm-6pm Feb-May and Sep-Oct, 9:30am-7pm June-Aug; 40F adults, 25F children under 10)* can be a fascinating stop. Over 300 moving dolls and figures jerk, whirr, and hum through specially created settings—almost like figures in a penny arcade.

sports

The shop with the funny name, **Boobaloo** *(Plage de la Concurrence; Tel 05/46-41-02-24; prices vary)* is at a great central spot on the plage de la Concurrence and offers the gamut of rental possibilities from bikes to tandems to scooters. For the best cycling around, you might consider taking the 30-minute boat ride to the Ile de Ré, leaving from the Vieux Port. Local cyclists are familiar with the bike paths (no cars allowed) that crisscross and circumnavigate the placid isle. A complete circumnavigation of the island might take a seasoned cyclist a full day; about a half-dozen lesser treks are clearly outlined in a brochure handed out for free at the tourist office [see *need to know,* below]. If it's water sports you seek, a short bus ride to **Canal Canoe** *(Pont de Rompsay ave. Louise-Pinchon; Bus 4 to Rompsay SNCF; Tel 06/86-82-42-34; Adult prices 35F per hour; 75F half day; 95F full day)* guarantees a day of fun through the beautiful, tree-lined Canal de Rompsay. Test your endurance in the bow or the stern, or simply sit back and let a loved one do all the hard work while you take in the sights and sounds of the city.

great outdoors

Clustered just to the north of the mouth of the Gironde lie cluster sandy islands: **Ile d'Oléron, Ile de Ré,** and the even smaller **Ile d'Aix.** Favored by French families who flock to their beaches, the islands are dotted with pines, stone buildings, seasonal restaurants serving fresh local oysters, limestone outcroppings, and the ruins of very old windmills. A bridge between the mainland and **Ile d'Oléron** makes access to the second-largest French offshore island (Corsica is bigger) relatively easy. The bridge is at Marennes, some 35 miles south from La Rochelle. The Romans called Oléron Ularius, and for centuries it occupied a strategic position at the head of the Gironde estuary, between the two major trading ports, La Rochelle and Bordeaux. Eleanor of Aquitaine lived in the island's château in 1199, just five years before she died. Notwithstanding her banishment, she imposed legal restraints on the island and helped create a maritime code that was used centuries later as the basis for France's law of the sea. For more insights into her life, you can visit the **Musée de l'Ile d'Oléron Aliénor-d'Aquitaine,** *(37 rue Pierre Loti, St. Pierre d'Oléron; Open mid-June to mid-September only, 10am-noon, 2:30-6:30pm daily; Admission 25F; no phone).* Many visitors prefer to simply tour the island and gaze at sparkling water, miles of oyster-laden salt flats, and old churches. Many people go swimming off the island's sandy beaches. For more information about Ile d'Oléron, contact the Office de Tourisme, place Gambetta, St. Pierre d'Oléron (Tel 05/46-47-11-39); it's closed in October and every afternoon in winter.

You can take a tour from the Vieux Port of La Rochelle to **Ile de Ré.** Ile de Ré, 10 kilometers across the sea from La Rochelle, has 70 kilometers of fine white sandy beaches. The island is dominated by nature preserves riddled with bike and hiking paths. Between Easter and November, there are between five and seven departures a day. The rest of the year, there are between two and three departures every Saturday and Sunday, and about one a day on Monday to Friday. Tours allow brief promenades on some of the islands, and cost, round-trip, between 90 and 160F per person, depending on the itinerary.

Ile d'Aix, at only 600 meters wide and 3 kilometers long, has a year-round population of about 200 hearty souls, though the population swells in summer when visitors flock here to enjoy some of the sandiest beaches off the coast of La Rochelle. For the best of these, head for the southern part of the island near a series of landmark lighthouses. There are many little idyllic coves where you'll sometimes find French beach-goers baring all to the sea. The little island is split by a number of hiking trails as well.

If you can tear yourself away from the beaches you can visit either of the island's two museums, **Musée Africain** and **Musée Napoléonien** *(June-Sept 9:30am-6pm; April, Oct 9:30am-noon, 2-6pm daily; November-March 9am-noon, 2-5pm daily; Separate admission 16F adults, 12F ages 18-25, 17 and under free; Combined admission to both museums 24F, 18F ages 18-25; Tel 05/46-84-66-40 for info. about either museum),* standing in the center of the tiny town of Point Accuell. Both evoke memories of Napoléon, who spent his last three days in France here following his defeat at the battle of Waterloo. In the Napoléon museum is a collection of portraits and Waterloo memorabilia, including a copy of the defeated dictator's surrender to superior British forces. The other museum is devoted to relics of Napoléon's campaign in Egypt, including the (preserved) dromedary he rode through the desert.

Ferries, the best way of getting to the island in summer, leave from La Rochelle three or four times daily, and are operated by **Inter Iles** *(14 cours des Dames; Tel 05/46-50-51-86).* The boat ride, which lasts a little more than an hour and takes you past Fort Bayard. costs 90F round trip. The island is also connected to the mainland at La Pallice, a suburb of Rochelle. This toll bridge spans three kilometers and costs 110F round trip per vehicle.

To explore the island in summer, you can rent bikes (40F per half day, 50F per full day) from any number of fast food eateries at Port Accueill, where the ferry lands.

stuff

While La Rochelle does have plenty of shopping in the arch-covered streets of the old town (rue du Palais is the main drag) most stores cater to the more mature, womanly Paris look than the hipster-about-town. At least one visit-worthy establishment exists on the trendy **rue Saint Nicolas.**

▶▶USED AND BRUISED

A surprisingly good find in an otherwise fashion-retro city, **Welta** (*5 rue St. Nicolas; Tel 05/46-41-43-69*) is run by a hipper-than-thou staff who not only know the history of the clothes they sell, but also sport them with pride. The majority of the stock is vintage Lacoste, Polo, and Adidas (expect plenty of cool, old-school tracksuits), as well as funky side-button sweaters indigenous to the fishermen of the region. The store also stocks a small selection of belts, handbags, and other accessories.

eats

Eating in La Rochelle is limited for the most part to a predictable variety of seaside fare, at least as long as you stick to the portside *quays*. The outlying streets contain many pleasant surprises which, with a little diligence in the search, easily beat out the mainstays by the port for both quality and value.

▶▶CHEAP

Crepes, anyone? With a view of the Tour de la Lanterne and the entire old port, **Crêperie la Bigoudene** (*63 rue St. Jean du Perot; Tel 05/46-50-01-34; Mon-Sat, 8am-8pm; Sun 10am-8pm; 20-40F; No credit cards*)

fashion

There's a hint of Brighton circa 1965 floating around in La Rochelle, but no real identifiable scene arises because of it. Kids are for the most part comfortably hip in dark-colored turtlenecks, Levis, and trainers of some kind. The clothes tend to take a place on the back burner to the type of scooter or motorbike in the garage. Colorful electronic locomotion is *huge* here, not only as a means to get around but also as a status symbol—the more fluorescent, the better.

serves up crepes to take for a walk through town or to sit with in the interior terrace. This particular creperie specializes in the savory kind; the fillings, which range from spinach with goat cheese to meat ensembles, definitely pack a punch.

Brasserie La Grand'Rîve (*24 quai Duperré; Tel 05/46-41-44-53; Prix Fixe 57-135F; Main courses 70-95F; noon-3pm, 7-11pm daily; MC, V*), is one of the most appealing brasseries in La Rochelle. Set in a wood-paneled enclave of old-fashioned but functional charm, directly opposite the twin towers (*les deux tours*) for which the city is famous, this place is probably La Rochelle's best food value. The specialty is Atlantic seafood of all kinds, including oysters, shellfish, fish stews, and fish soups. Also served are such staples as filet of duckling in orange sauce and *steak au poivre*, all in a decor inspired by an English pub, complete with forest-green leather-covered banquettes. Local charm is provided by the young people of La Rochelle, who come here to eat well even when they're short of francs.

▶▶DO-ABLE

Bar/Bistro André (*5 rue Saint Jean/place de la Chaîne; Tel 05/46-41-28-24; Main courses 72-128F; Prix fixe 122F; noon-2:30pm, 7-10:30pm daily; AE, MC, V*), offers one of the best values at the port for those who want a big seafood dinner. Regrettably, this is an expensive item anywhere in France, so it's a bit of a splurge, but worth it. One plate of food at the lower end of the price scale is a big meal unto itself. This place, which has been feeding hungry sailors since 1947, offers a trio of dining rooms—one outfitted like an old-fashioned Lyonnais bistro, the other two like a captain's cabin aboard a seafaring yacht. Menu items are firmly based on the seafaring traditions of La Rochelle, and include savory versions of fish soup, all kinds of shellfish, an unusual version of home-smoked codfish (*cabillaud fumé*) served with a garlic-flavored cream sauce; a local version of *mouclade* (curried mussels); and a local saltwater fish not common in other parts of France, filet of *maigre*, served with a chive-flavored cream sauce.

For the price (and even perhaps price notwithstanding) **Le Soleil Brille Pour Tout le Monde** (*13 rue des Cloutiers; Tel 05/46-41-11-42; Tue-Sat; No credit*) is one of the most amazing restaurants in La Rochelle. The upbeat and perennially cheerful Senegalese hostess/owner/cook rules the restaurant like a mother hen protecting her chicks. That is to say if every person at every table isn't stuffed and smiling stupidly, she makes sure the situation is remedied ASAP. Whether it be through the perfect bottle of wine, extra appetizer, or homemade dessert, Le Soleil Brille is nothing short of a divine experience. Menu standouts include lamb chops, vegetarian quiche, and an indescribably tasty "apple crumble."

▶▶SPLURGE

"If you've got it, flaunt it," goes the old saying, and in the case of the most elegant restaurant in La Rochelle, the chef definitely has it. The self-named **Richard Coutanceau** (*Plage de la Concurrence; Tel 05/46-41-*

48-19; noon-2pm and 7:30-9:30pm Mon-Sat; 125F-200F main courses, 230F-430F prix fixe menu; All credit cards) brings together the fruits of the adjacent sea in a beautiful setting. The seating is within the confines of a romantic park; half the space is devoted to a tearoom, the remainder to the dining area. The best dishes come straight from the sea: We suggest any of the oysters, shellfish, or roasted bass.

crashing

It's difficult to be far from the action wherever you choose to stay in La Rochelle, which makes booking a hotel far from the headache it can be in larger, more spread-out cities. Despite their great locations and even better prices, however, most hotels are small and quite basic. It's smartest to assume that not every room will have a private shower or WC. If it's a hotel with fewer than 20 rooms, it's likely that you won't get your own private bathroom. A sink and towels are always standard, however, so if you're passing through town for a night, these smaller hotels can be a great way to save money.

▶▶CHEAP

Near the old port with a spectacular view of the two towers, **L'Ocean** (36 cours des Dames; Tel 05/46-41-31-97; 190-250F single) is a steal for the price and location alone. This tiny hotel has only 15 rooms, 8 with a view of the port, and all with cable TVs. While the accommodations are not exactly glamorous, the beds are comfortable—if you're looking for a place to sleep in after a long night of clubbing at the nearby Prefecture or cours des Dames, this is the ideal place to do it.

▶▶DO-ABLE

To stay on another street full of bars and nightlife opportunities, reserve a room at **De Bordeaux** (43 rue Saint Nicolas; Tel 05/46-41-31-22; 175-300F single), where you can roll out of bed and virtually into the venue of your choice. Like most other small, non-chain hotels in La Rochelle, De Bordeaux is nothing too fancy—but what it lacks in over-the-top bravado it makes up for in quaintness and charm. Rooms are small, cozy, and all wired with cable television. Rooms with private baths cost more.

▶▶SPLURGE

Hôtel de la Paix (14 rue Gargoulleau; Tel 05/46-41-33-44; 200-380F single; No credit cards), while not directly on the port, is located on a prime street near the place de Verdun. This charmingly decorated two-star hotel offers comfortable rooms with cable TVs and private toilets and showers. If you're flying more than solo, however, it might be wise to request a room with un grand lit (double bed) to avoid the "pushed together twin beds" scenario. A small bar/brasserie, usually open from 6am to early evening, is located on the ground floor of the hotel.

need to know

Currency Exchange Money can be changed at any bank, ATM, change office, and, in some cases, at a hotel. Automatic fast-cash bill changers are located at **Crédit Lyonnais** *(19 rue du Palais)* and **Crédit Maritime** *(9 quai Maubec).*

Tourist Information The tourist office is semi-hidden on the east end of the port at **place de la Petite Sirene-Le Gabut** *(Tel 05/46-41-14-68; 8am-7pm daily; tourisme.la.rochelle@wanadoo.fr; http:/www.Ville-laRochelle.fr).* Signs from quai Valin lead directly to the office. The tourist office will make hotel reservations for you, for a charge of 10F.

Public Transportation As mentioned earlier, La Rochelle is not a town that relies heavily on public transportation. The bus system is great to reach the train station or points north of town, but is not necessary (or really available) within the center city. Single ride (7F) and multiple-use bus passes can be purchased on the bus or by calling Tel 05/46-51-53-42.

Health and Emergency Ambulance: *15;* Police: *17;* Fire: *18;* Urgent care: *Tel 05/46-67-33-33;* **Centre Hospitalier** *(Blvd. Joffe; Tel 05/46-45-50-50; 24 hours daily).*

Pharmacies Pharmacies are located throughout town; look for the **flashing green cross. Pharmacie de Gabut** *(10 quai Georgette. Tel 05/46-41-07-97)* lies very close to the city's tourist office.

Telephone City code: *05;* Information: *12;* International operator (USA): *00/33-12-11.* Phone cards are available at most tobacco shops, post offices, and magazine shops in 50F and 100F denominations.

Airports Aeroport La Rochelle-Ile de Ré *(Tel 05/46-42-30-26 for info and reservations).*

Trains The town is served by the main station **Gare SNCF** *(Tel 08/36-35-35-35 for reservations),* located just south of the city center and easily reached by all bus lines. Six to eight trains arrive daily from both Bordeaux to the south and Nantes to the north (trip time, 2 hours), as do a handful of TGV trains from Paris (trip time, 3 hours).

Bus Lines Out of the City You can catch buses going out of the city at the train station or the **place de Verdun** *(Tel 05/46-34-02-22 for information).*

Boats La Rochelle is positively stocked with boat rentals, boat tours, and boat excursions. The Office de Tourisme [see *tourist information,* above] has a good selection of brochures on the mind-boggling selection of boating activities, which usually involve a visit to **Ile d'Aix, Ile d'Oléron, Fort Boyard,** or all three.

Bike/Moped Rental La Rochelle is the perfect town to explore by bike, with or without a motor attached. A number of places offer bike and moped rentals, including **Autoplus "Les Velos Jaunes"** *(Place de Verdun; Tel 05/46-34-02-22),* **Cyclo-Parc** *(Plage de la Concurrence; Tel 05/46-41-02-24),* and **Motive** *(Parking lot across from the Musée Maritime, Les Minimes; Tel 05/46-34-99-16).* Electric vehicles can be rented at **Electrique Autoplus** *(Espace Autoplus, place de Verdun; Tel 05/46-34-02-22).*

Laundry Self-service laundry is located at **Lavarie de la Genette** *(20 rue de la Pepiniere; Tel 05/46-67-56-25; 8am-9pm; 15-30F per load)*.

Postal La Rochelle has seven post offices scattered throughout town. The largest and most central is **La Poste** *(6 rue de l'Hôtel de Ville; Tel 05/46-30-41-30; 8am-5pm Mon-Fri, 8am-noon Sat)*.

THE LOIRE VALLEY

THE LOIRE VALLEY

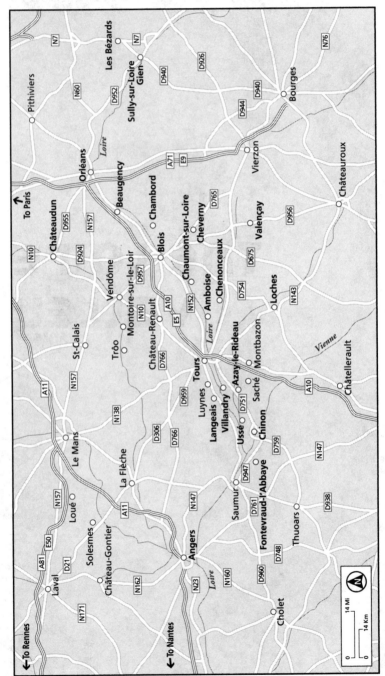

grab a pal, rent some wheels, and get ready to chill in river country. It's mostly flat and sometimes gently rolling land, full of large, open fields, and perfect for bike excursions, especially if you avoid the major highways. Professional and amateur bicyclists from all over come here to try the valley's many trails and off-road areas, so why not you?

Often passed over as the "sleepy" midsection of France, the Loire Valley is actually one of the best places to make a very personal connection with France. Its big tourist draw is châteaux, châteaux, and more châteaux: It's no surprise that a bunch of dukes and kings used to live here, and from the looks of it, a lot of them were busy trying to keep up with the Joneses. So if you really dig old stone castles in the country, this is the place to come. There's also the wild Loire River, which runs through the center of the valley. It's too swift to swim in, but it does make a nice spot for a picnic; pick up a bottle of the Valley's famous white wine before you go.

Although the Valley seems quiet and uneventful on the surface, it does have lots of activities. From town festivals and karaoke nights, it's the perfect spot to gain an insider look at France.

For more urban diversions, head to **Angers** or **Tours.** Like other cities in the region, you'll find lots of curvy, cobblestone streets within the Old Town leading to little back alleys and hidden streets. If you have the

Travel Times

* TGV (Fast Train—more expensive)

	Angers	Paris	Tours
Tours	1:00	1:00*	-
Angers	-	1:00	1:30

LIVING LARGE IN THE CHÂTEAUX

The Loire Valley is kind of like a "Once Upon a Time" ride at Disney World, but it's for real. Bike along the banks of the Loire River—one of the most thrilling rides in Europe—and you can check out incredible châteaux that have survived the French Revolution and two world wars (not to mention massive armies of tourists). The town of Tours is châteaux central—all of the best ones are within a 60-mile radius—so you can bike, drive, or take a bus from here. Most castles have free guided tours (included in the price of admission) in French with printed translations in English.

Dozens of bus companies offer tours, but the **Office de Tourisme** in the city of Tours has a much better way to go: a fleet of eight-passenger minibuses (board in front of the office, 9-9:30am and 1-1:30pm daily) that offer half- and full-day trips (two to four châteaux) for 100-185F. Entrance fees to the châteaux are not included in the price, but you get a reduced rate. The big tour buses charge 100-300F depending on the scope of the tour; call **Service Touristique de la Touraine** *(Tel 02/47-05-46-09).*

The easiest château to reach from Tours is **Azay-le-Rideau** *(Tel 02/47-45-42-04; Open daily 9am-7pm July-Aug, 9:30am-6pm Apr-June and Sept-Oct, 9:30am-12:30pm and 2-5:30pm Nov-Mar; 35F, 23F ages 12-25),* 13 miles southwest of town. Three trains run daily from Tours (30 minutes, 28F one way) to this fairy-tale Renaissance château where you can see the shimmering reflection of the dormer-

patience to spend a few days canvassing a Loire Valley town, chances are you'll leave feeling like you really know the place—unlike that daunting "where do I even begin" feeling that can take hold in a larger city.

Cities in the Valley have an inviting, smooth-around-the-edges feel to them. Many of them suffered heavy damages during World War II. This led to major reconstruction, usually in the outlying sections, which often resulted in a noticeable spiral effect. Suburbs are filled with crude, postwar buildings that serve not so much as grim reminders of the past, but as a foil to the gorgeous buildings and general *joie de vivre* you'll find in the Old Town.

Valley locals are friendly and easygoing. If you consider yourself a city kid and loathe a laid-back atmosphere, you might initially experience some culture shock when you enter the region. Folks not only smile at you when you pass them in the street, but also (gasp) may offer unsolicited help or advice if you look really lost. In a country that's famous for its more, shall we say, prideful citizens, this is nothing to scoff at.

studded roof in the moat. The château is about a 15-minute walk from the train station. Also within easy reach of Tours is the **Château of Chenonceau** (*Tel 02/47-23-90-07; Open daily 9am-7pm Mar-Sept, 9am-4:30pm Oct-Apr; 45F, 35F ages 7-15*), 16 miles east of town. This towering masterpiece has an enticing soap-opera history: Henri II gave it to his mistress, Diane de Poitiers, but his real wife, Catherine de Médici, kicked her out when Henri died (it was the favorite party site of the French aristocrats during the Renaissance). This is the Loire's most exquisite château, spanning the Cher river and flanked by gardens and woodlands. Three trains run daily from Tours (45 minutes, 36F one way); the château is about a 15-minute walk from the train station. Other must-sees include the **Château of Blois** (*37 miles northeast of Tours; Tel 02/54-90-33-33; Open daily 9am-5:50pm Oct-Mar, 10am-6:30pm Mar-June, 10am-7pm July-Aug; 35F, 20F students*), where Leonardo da Vinci was a regular on the guest list, and **Château of Chambord** (*11 miles east of Blois, bus #2 from Blois; Tel 02/54-50-40-29; Open daily 9am-6:45pm July-Aug, 9:30am-6:15pm Sept, 9:30am-5:15pm Oct-Mar; 9:30am-6:15pm Apr-June; 42F, 26F ages 12-25*), a 440-room, 13,000-acre extravagance that bankrupted its original owner, François I. There's a double-helix staircase rumored to have been designed by Leonardo da Vinci.

GETTING AROUND THE REGION

With its close proximity to Paris and the sheer number of rail lines crisscrossing the landscape, it's easy to get around the Loire Valley with the aid of a Eurorail pass. Intercity bus lines also connect some of the closer towns, like Tours and Angers. Once in the Valley, you'll find that the maximum train time between towns is usually only one or two hours max.

▶▶ROUTES

If you begin in Paris, you can connect to Angers in about one hour. From Angers, you can continue on to Tours, Le Mans, and Poitiers before looping back to the capital. Stopping in Poitiers requires several transfers when coming from Le Mans, however, so the best route to follow for this town starts in Angers or Paris and winds through Tours.

TOURS

Perched between the **Loire** and **Chere** rivers, Tours has a strong rivalry with its Loire Valley neighbor, Angers. Both are relatively small riverside cities; both rely heavily on their quaint old quarters for tourism; and both offer up their share of stained glass and ancient stone. But it's Tours that snatches up the bulk of the tourists in the region.

If Angers is the indie rock music collector, then Tours is definitely the Top 40-loving older brother. As a result, the sites here can feel a bit touristy and the locals tend to take themselves a little too seriously. But if you're looking for a more active nightlife than Angers can offer, and want to experience a Loire Valley city, it can be a great place to spend some time. It's also a good jumping-off point for visiting the nearby châteaux.

Tours locals can fancy themselves Parisians if the mood strikes. From their wooing tactics to their bar etiquette, the younger generation is like a punky kid (at least in theory). They've got a chip on their shoulder about being from a picturesque small city on the Loire, and now, with the increasing number of tourists and ensuing possibilities for diversion, they've got an attitude as well. This can be a good thing—once you win the trust of a Tours resident you'll feel that the opportunities are limitless—it's just the initial ice-breaking that can trump the less determined.

The task may seem daunting, but don't give up too soon. Not everyone has this aura of "excellence," and there are certainly plenty of people—both kids and adults—who are more than willing to help out a polite and curious traveler. A good place to start is the tourist office, which employs

five things to talk to a local about

1. *The Place Plumereau:* This square in old Tours crawls, boils, brims, and overflows with tourists during the lazy nights of summer, much to the chagrin of many locals. Do these staggering drunks bring commerce and cash to the town, or do they simply ruin an otherwise good night out when they dump a pint down your shirt? Utter small *tsks* of regret when required and bemoan the tourist situation in your own hometown. Empathy is really the best reaction and, truthfully, the only one sought.

2. *Angers, Orleans, etc:* While the popular vote places Tours above the other nearby "little Loires," locals still have a petit chip on their shoulders. Bashing other towns might make a quick friend, and so might a word of flattery about the joys of life in Tours.

3. *The neo-geo Office de Tourisme:* In an old city lined with conservatively acceptable old buildings, many feel a real distaste for the modern structure that houses the tourist office. On the other hand, you'll also find plenty of staunch supporters who dig the neon lights and large mass of glass and steel. Pick a side, but don't expect to start a riot; this is a minor issue that's more a conversation starter than thought-provoking or engaging.

4. *Social problems of any kind:* As is evident in gathering places like **La Barque** [see *hanging out,* above], the youth of Tours are genuinely concerned with the plight of their fellow men and women. Especially in student hangouts, don't be surprised to hear issues like homelessness or government ineptitude cropping up in conversation just as much as weekend plans or new music releases.

5. *Swing music:* Americans, you thought you escaped it when you left home. You foolishly imagined that lame revival swing nights were stuck squirming in the cultural gates of big cities under the Stars and Stripes. You were wrong. Swing nights are cropping up everywhere in Tours bars and clubs. The kids are psyched, and the zoot suit riot is closing in menacingly.

an overwhelming number of these friendly youth. You can also pick up information on the city here. A good basic guide is available (in French and English) that outlines everything from museums to restaurants to bars. Many restaurants, galleries, and hotels also have copies of the free guide to Tours published by the ***Groupe Ecole Superieure de Commerce et de Management,*** which is the best and most extensive guide to the city.

TOURS

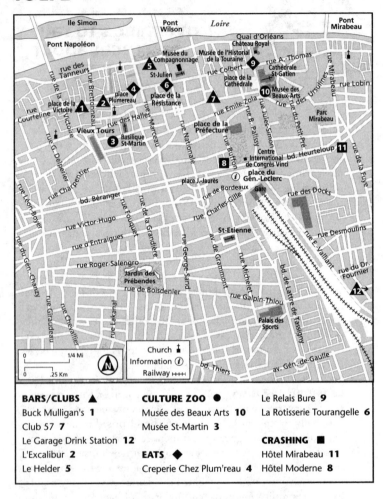

BARS/CLUBS ▲

Buck Mulligan's **1**

Club 57 **7**

Le Garage Drink Station **12**

L'Excalibur **2**

Le Helder **5**

CULTURE ZOO ●

Musée des Beaux Arts **10**

Musée St-Martin **3**

EATS ◆

Creperie Chez Plum'reau **4**

Le Relais Bure **9**

La Rotisserie Tourangelle **6**

CRASHING ■

Hôtel Mirabeau **11**

Hôtel Moderne **8**

neighborhoods

Tours proper is a sprawling maze of residential streets between the two rivers, with the true center of town cozying up against the **Loire** and extending south to the **Blvd. Thiers.** In this section you'll find *Vieux Tours,* or old Tours—a mismatched assortment of cobbled streets and amazingly beautiful old building (especially around the **Place Plumereau**). The town center is divided on a larger scale into roughly four quadrants, split by the **avenue de Grammont/rue Nationale** running north/south and the **boulevard Béranger/boulevard Heurteloup** running east/west. The old town is in the northwest quadrant, the **Hôtel de Ville** (town hall) and several museums are in the northeast quadrant, the train station is in the southeast, and a largely uneventful residential area is in the southwest. For visitors the liveliest areas are concentrated in the two northern quadrants, though several worthwhile events take place elsewhere.

The best neighborhoods for hanging out lie between the Boulevard Béranger/ Heurteloup and the river at the **place Anatole France,** and the Place Plumereau, as well as the the **place Jean-Jaures,** just south of the Boulevard Béranger. The other important square, **place du Grand Marché,** is just west of Place Plumereau. Shops, cinemas, and restaurants line the busy and congested **rue Nationale,** which can be a good starting point for exploring Tours since it cuts through the heart of the city. From here you can branch out either to the old town to the west or the cultural center to the right, both equally appealing choices.

Public transport is usually not necessary in the northern quadrants, but to reach other parts of Tours the bus is the best choice. You can pick up most bus lines near the train station, and buses run regularly throughout the day until around 11pm. A tourist train also leaves every hour (10-noon and 2-6pm, Easter-September) from the **Office de Tourisme** [see *tourist information,* below].

The open-sided bus passes through the oldest section of town as the driver gives a running commentary in French (leaflets are available in English). The fare is 30F per person.

hanging out

No, it's not just an artsy fartsy spot—the gardens at the **Musée des Beaux Arts** [see *culture zoo,* below] are free, fun, and filled with gaggles of interesting folks. The open lawn space can feel more like a greenhouse on a hot summer day, but the winding, tree-lined paths that branch out from this square of *vert* offer plenty of benches where you can have a seat or even stretch out for a little nap.

Always socially conscious, the French do it up again at **La Barque** *(118 rue Colbert; Tel 02/47-61-71-29; Bus 8 to St-Ursule; 8:30am-6pm Mon, Wed-Fri; 9am-6pm Sat-Sun; www.respublica.fr/labarque),* a combo coffee shop/shelter a couple blocks from the river that offers a place where kids, adults, dogs, etc. can hang out without the temptation of alcohol or the ubiquitous French pastime...smoking. If you want to escape those pesky fumes, this may be the only place in the entire city to do so and still communicate with other human beings. The joint is run on a purely nonprofit basis, and the workers are passionate about their cause.

bar and live music scene

If you want to do your drinking outdoors without the trappings of a bar, join the hordes of folks hanging out at place Plumereau. Travelers and locals alike gather here to drink cheap booze and trade tall tales. Pick up your supplies at **La Vinothèque** *(16 rue Michelet; Tel 02/47-64-75-27),* a 10-minute walk south of the château, in a side street that connects with the very large, very commercial rue de Bordeaux. They sell every kind of wine and whiskey you could ever need to get a buzz in as classy or as cheap a method as possible. People move the party to the bars around 6pm.

Le Helder *(7 rue Nationale; Tel 02/47-05-75-90; 9am-2am daily; All credit cards)*, located just east of the bumpin' Place Plumereau, is a nice outdoor brasserie close to the Loire, though the 35ish crowd is slightly older than in most of the bars along this plaza. It makes for a more mature, quiet night out. Good place to read a book without looking too much like a tourist—for the girls, a trait guaranteed to solicit unwanted conversation from drunk, middle-aged men.

Le Garage Drink Station *(53 bis rue du Docteur Fournier; Tel 02/47-32-90-10; Bus 6 to Dr. Fournier; 5pm-2am daily; No cover)*, a hangout for young locals, is a short bus ride or a safe 30-minute walk southeast of the city center. It has live music and a well-stocked bar. The feel is comfortably outback America, especially when live jazz acts swing on Friday nights. Most shows start around 9pm, and with names like "Alcootest Blues Band" and "Sweet Mama," how can you go wrong?

If you just can't stay away from the overwhelming supply of Irish bars cluttering the streets of France, why not pick a good one? **Buck Mulligan's** *(37-39 rue du Grand Marché; Tel 02/47-39-61-69; Bus 10, 4 to Vieux Tours; 5pm-2am daily)* has the name and the face to go with it—expect giddy Irish tunes and ample Irish brew—and a ton of Brits and Americans at the bar.

Also check out the live bands that play at extreme-sport wonderland **Riderland** [see *city sports* below].

wired

If you're willing to brave a crowd and can concentrate through loud, adolescent chatter, **L'Annexe Informatique** *(29 rue Colbert; Tel 02/47-75-10-02; Closing times vary; Opens at 12:30pm Mon-Fri, 2pm Sat, 3pm Sun; annexe.informatique@ wanadoo.fr; 20F/half hour, 30F/hour)* is the prime spot in Tours for Internet access, word processing, video games, and even just hanging out. The place can get a bit crowded during the late afternoon and early evening when every brace-toothed preteen crawls home from school and crowds around the large screens for cyber carnage. As a result, the surest way to guarantee a computer is to show up after 7pm, when the kids realize they haven't eaten all day and the crowd begins to thin. You'll also have a little free time in the afternoon to explore the flea market and other nearby diversions on rue Colbert, which is just a 5-minute walk south of the river, directly off the main thoroughfare, rue Nationale.

boy meets girl

In Tours, twentysomething and teen males seem to have forgotten about the dating game, leaving the graceful act of seduction up to older (and usually much less socially mature) men. Perhaps that's why you see so many attractive young women on the arms of substantially older men at the brasseries and out on the streets. Tours males will hit on chicks regardless of their age. No one is overly intense in his pursuit however. If you're not interested, simply ignore it or look bored and problems will die quickly and without pain. Boys, on the other hand, probably won't encounter any overzealous Mrs. Robinsons during a night out, and can instead concentrate on wooing *amours* from their own generation.

club scene

Just across the street from the Grand Théâtre in the center of the old town, **Club 57** *(57 rue de la Scellerie; Tel 02/47-05-46-90; Bus 8 to Ste-Ursule; 11pm-4am, Tue-Sat; 60-80F cover charge, includes one drink; Ladies free on Tuesdays)* has a cheesy, bad disco feel, but spins cool classics you'd expect from a high school theme dance. Practice your Travolta moves at home in the mirror, throw on some rhinestone-encrusted bell bottoms...and you'll probably be the only one in sight who looks the part. The essential thing to remember about Club 57 is that, while the promo and the music grasp for a theme, the people inside most definitely do not. While sneakers and jeans are looked down upon, there's no real costume party going on here.

Another old town bar, **L'Excalibur** *(Place Plumereau; Tel 02/47-64-76-78; Bus 4, 10 to Vieux Tours; 11pm-4am Tue-Sat; 60F cover charge includes one drink),* is right next to the landmark Central Square, place du Grand Marché. It is always packed with Tours natives and visitors from afar. This is a good place to go if you want to jam with Americans or Australians—they seem to make up the majority of foreigners here and also the majority of the dance population. Tunes range from disco faves to Top 40 hits and remixes, as well as the much-loved French rap, which gets all the locals off their high barstools and onto their feet.

arts scene

▶▶VISUAL ARTS

Like most of its Loire Valley siblings, Tours offers an art scene that leans heavily on the past for support. Ideas look to the future, however, at the **Centre de Creation Contemporaine** *(53-55 rue Marcel Tribut; Tel 02/47-66-50-00; Bus 6 to Champ-Girault; 3-7pm Tue-Sun; Closed annu-*

ally 25 Dec-1 Jan; ccc.art@wanadoo.fr; Cover 15-50F). The center, which is near the railway station (a 10-minute walk southeast of the town center), opened in 1985 with the dual mission of bringing new art into the public eye through exhibits and making that art accessible and understandable. Three to five exhibitions go up every year, keeping the schedule slower than at a regular gallery, but saving it from the dinosaur effect that takes hold of art that's unchanged in a museum setting.

Keeping things on a much smaller scale, **Galerie Sylvaine Gainier** *(99 rue Colbert; Tel 02/47-64-90-42; Bus 8 to Ste-Ursule; 2:30-7pm Tue-Sat)* shows contemporary symbolist paintings from both local and international artists. Ms. Gainier herself contributes a bit of work to the gallery, and as a result jumps at the chance to explain every piece she shows, some of it partially inspired by Gauguin. There are also a lot of other art galleries on this same narrow street, which separates the neighborhood around the cathedral from the neighborhood known as Vielle-Ville.

Musée des Beaux Arts *(18 place Francois Sicard, adjacent to the cathedral; Tel 02/47-05-68-73; Bus 8 to Ste-Ursule; 9am-12:45pm/2-6pm Wed-Mon; 30F adults, 15F students and children)* has a small but discriminating collection ranging from the Gothic era, to through the old Masters to the 18th and 19th centuries. Don't miss the religious triptychs and icons from the Middle Ages. The 15th-century *Vierge de Douleur* is a must-see for even the most ardent non-believer. Its humble and fragile beauty has universal appeal. For those into recognizable names, the museum also houses one of Rodin's studies for his famous *Monument to Balzac* as well as paintings by Boucher and Rembrandt.

CULTURE ZOO

The capital of the Touraine is used more as a center for excursions to the châteaux than as a sightseeing attraction of its own. But there are some nuggets here for those willing to hang around long enough to discover them.

Installed within the confines of the Saint-Jean chapel, **Musée St. Martin** *(3 rue Rapin; Tel 02/47-64-48-87; Bus 4,10 to Vieux Tours;*

RULES OF THE GAME

In most quarters of town, best behavior is expected at all times. Any shenanigans—from public drunkenness to simple public loudness—warrant severe looks and mumbles of disapproval. In and around the nighttime Place Plumereau, however, manners are lost and social mores forgotten as everyone slams back the booze and stumbles over the cobblestones. The mood is basically that of a large outdoor party, though attempting the same gregarious behavior during the day is probably not the best idea.

festivals

Starting the third week of every May, happy feet take over Tours during the **Festival de Danse Contemporaine,** a modern-dance festival that takes place in various parks and performance spaces throughout town. While the emphasis is on contemporary dance, the influences span centuries. One night a duo serves up a baroque performance, while the next pays a heavy tribute to John Cage and Merce Cunningham. Tickets are 80F for adults and 40F for those under 18; information is available by calling *Tel 02/47-36-46-00* or through e-mail at *info@ccnt-larrieu.com*.

9:30am-12:30pm/2-5:30pm Tue-Sat) is more of a shrine to the life of St. Martin than an actual museum. It also happens to be one of the most peaceful sites in Tours, especially if you have any fondness for ancient sculpture and art. On sunny days the stained glass of the chapel provides an eerily beautiful light that falls over the displays, adding an ethereal charm.

Sports

For all the skate rats still holding onto those glistening images of Christian Slater in *Gleaming the Cube* and pulling at the hems of their shredded Vision streetwear, **Riderland** *(23 rue Cugnot; Tel 02/47-73-91-85; Hours vary daily and by season, call for info;10F/hour, 30F/4 hours, 50F/day)* can feel like a slice of the divine. It can also feel like what it is, a crowded hangout for every kind of alternative sports fiend in a five-mile radius. The courses and setups are decent, however, and even if you don't like to ollie you can relax with a drink or sandwich. At night Riderland turns into a big ol' party, with concerts featuring local bands and the occasional contest à la ESPN's *X-Games*.

Stuff

No one ever accused Tours of being a great shopping mecca—many locals take the train to Paris when the shopping bug bites them. But it's fun to spend an hour or two browsing the streets of the old quarter around Cathedrale St. Gatien. You can also hit the area around place Plumereau, where dozens of shops lie along the narrow side-streets.

▶▶**DUDS**

Le Dressing *(120 rue Colbert; Tel 02/47-20-52-53; Bus 8 to Ste-Ursule; 2-7pm Mondays, 10:30am-1pm/2-7pm Tue-Sat)* specializes in ready-to-wear originals and accessories with a funky feel. The clothes have a cool, earthy feel, but it's the jewelry that's truly interesting. Colorful and daring

fashion

The Tours look is largely forgettable and based on function over form and decadence. The most "outrageous" dressers tend to keep their wild duds hidden until they go clubbing, and even those brave enough to try a new style on the daytime sidewalks usually only dare a cropped shirt or oddly patterned capri pant. Folksy headscarves in decidedly unfolksy patterns are hot for girls, as are sporty label shirts of any kind for boys. Much of the same Eastern influence that crept into late '90s fashion is just getting a kick-start here: think bindis, appliques and beading on jeans, and flowing peasant blouses.

jewels and minerals sparkle in brass and more delicate settings. Direct your questions to Laurence, the friendly and helpful owner.

▶▶CLUB GEAR AND BEYOND

Just when you thought Hello Kitty had finished taking over the world, there arises **Tek-Off** *(4 rue des 3 Paves Ronds; Tel 02/47-05-30-40; Bus 10, 4 to Vieux Tours).* Carrying everything from techno/house records to Sanrio pacifiers, the place is a gadget fiasco for the serious ravehead. They've also got some of the standard fare: lava lamps, naughty T-shirts, etc.—all at decent prices, which are reduced even more when you bring in a flyer (easy to find at almost any music store).

▶▶TUNES

Planet Phone *(105 rue des Halles; Tel 02/47-66-33-66; Bus 4, 10 to Vieux Tours; 10am-7pm Mon-Sat)* sounds like it shouldn't, but it does in fact have a pretty decent selection of music in addition to a wide selection of portable phones and pagers. For the kitschy, bad compilation freak, there are multiple 10F and 20F tape bins holding titles like *The Rock Album,* where on one tape you can get all the Foreigner, Blue Oyster Cult, and Toto you can stand.

▶▶BAZAAR

Wake up early on any Saturday and head down to the **rue Colbert** *(Bus 8 to Ste-Ursule)* for one of the best flea markets/junk sales around. It's 5-minute walk south from the river, directly off rue Nationale, the principal artery of the old town. The entire length of the street is filled on both sides with tables, clothing racks, and boxes of old vinyl, where, with a little patience you may uncover treasures untold. For the book freak, there are stacks of ancient hardcovers with old-school illustrations; for the movie buff, there are French film posters for everything from *New Jack City* to *Casablanca.*

Eats

▶▶CHEAP

Chez Plum'reau *(6 rue du Grand Marché; Tel 02/47-66-34-99; Bus 4, 10 to Vieux Tours; Mon-Sat 8am-10pm, Sun 10am-8pm; 20-50F; All credit cards)* is a crêperie in an ideal location to get some grub after drinking on the Place Plumereau. Situated inside one of the gorgeous mansions around the square, the atmosphere is dark and cozy, with cross-timbered walls and heavy, wooden tables. Service can be slow due to the single overworked waitress, but the food is worth hanging around for and—for some of you it's going to be nice to relax after all those shots of JD.

Established in the late 1990s, **La Souris Gourmande** *(100 rue Colbert; Tel 02/47-47-04-80; Bus 4; Noon-2pm Tues-Sat, 7-10:30pm Mon-Sat; Main courses 40-82F; MC, V)*, is devoted to whatever dish its chefs can concoct from France's legendary diversity of cheese. Menu items include both vegetarian and meat dishes, such as roasted chicken, veal, or beef, but the real allure lies in its rich assortment of crêpes, *tartes fines,* and cheese casseroles. Especially tempting are a half-dozen fondues, each made from the cheese of a different region of France. (They include Alsace, Normandy, the Dauphine, the Auvergne, the Savoie, and, in the case of Touraine, a fondue made exclusively from goat's cheese.) The dining room decor is hyper-cheerful—cows, happy cheese-eating mice, and cheese crates—but it holds no more than 30 diners at a time, so you may have a chance to hook up with some friendly locals or fellow travelers at a communal table.

▶▶DO-ABLE

For a taste of the Loire Valley, walk 10 minutès east of the old town to **Le Relais Bure** *(1 place de la Resistance; Tel 02/47-05-67-74; Bus 1 to Anatole France; Noon-3pm/7pm-midnight daily; 75-130F; All credit cards),* a popular brasserie specializing in regional cuisine. Many locals use Le Relais as a hangout and the ample outdoor seating and lively bar are big draws. The ambience indoors is light and refreshing, but it's often more fun to take an outside seat to enjoy the activity on the square. The menu goes heavy on the sauerkraut but if you're not a big fan, there's plenty of seafood dishes.

Le Lapin qui Fume *(90 rue Colbert; Tel 02/47-66-95-49; Bus 4; Noon-2pm and 8-10pm Tues-Sat; Fixed-price menus 76-150F; AE, MC, V)* is a down-to-earth bistro with banquettes, etched-glass mirrors, and a cramped, often rowdy approach to socializing and dining. Come here for a hearty, no-nonsense approach to food that derives from the kind of fare produced by thousands of French grandmothers throughout the region.

▶▶SPLURGE

Relaxed and elegant dining is a sure thing at the classy **La Rotisserie Tourangelle** *(23 rue du Commerce; Tel 02/47-05-71-21; 12:15-1:45pm/7:15-9:30pm Tue-Sat, noon-1:45 Sun; 100F-200F main courses, 90-215F prix fixe menu; All credits cards),* where the short hours are an obvious indication of the laid-back attitude. The staff is only there for two meals a day and, more often than not, has only a handful of tables to serve. This naturally leads to one of the most pleasant dining experiences you'll find in Tours (but make sure you have a reservation first!). The menu sticks to classics of the region—foie gras, sausages, sauerkraut, and duck, just to name a few.

crashing

If you're thinking about crowding more people into your room, you may have to rely on the mood of the front desk clerk. Most hotels don't have an official policy, but they'll definitely say no if they think you are serious party animals. On the other hand, if you look like you'd never trash a hotel room, they may try to accommodate you. It's a thing that has to be negotiated at the doorstep.

With a highly desirable location just a short walk from the train station and in close proximity to Place Jean-Jaures, **Hôtel Moderne** *(1 et 3 rue Victor Laloux; Tel 02/47-05-32-81; All bus lines to Jean-Jaures; 160-250F single, 258-340F double with private bath, 215F double without; Breakfast 37F)* is probably the best value in Tours. If you're willing to go without a shower and share a floor bathroom, you can get a cut-rate room on the top floor which—while in no way the height of luxe—is comfortable enough and actually kind of charming in a romantic, 18th-century kind of way. For slightly more cash, you can forgo the artist's garret feel and take one of the well-lighted and cheerful rooms on the lower floors, all equipped with showers and WCs. Beware of the curfew, however, when the front door locks at midnight, you'll need the code from the front desk to get back to your room.

Built into a quiet, downtown mansion, **Hôtel Mirabeau** *(89 bis Blvd. Heurteloup; Tel 02/47-05-24-60; All lines to Jean-Jaures; 220-310F single, 250-310F double; Breakfast 35F)* caters to business travelers in its brochure but is a cozy getaway for anyone. Each room, equipped with a television, telephone, bathtub/shower, and WC, is charmingly decorated with unique accessories. For those who can't go a second without checking their e-mail, a handful of rooms also come wired with an internet connection. Ask at the front desk for prices and details.

If these are booked, try the **Auberge de Jeunesse** *(Ave. d'Arsonval; Tel 02/47-25-14-45; Fax 02/47-48-26-59; Bus 36, 11; Single 109F, Double, Triple, Quad 89F/person; V, MC, AE, DIN)* in the south of the city; **Hôtel Regina** *(2 rue Pimbert; Tel 02/47-05-25-36; Fax 02/47-66-08-72; Single 125-175 F, Double 140-195F, Triple 220F, Quad 240F; V, MC, DIN)* in the city center; or **Hôtel Colbert** *(78 rue Colbert; Tel 02/47-66-61-56; Fax 02/47-66-01-55; Single 165-290F, Double 185-330F; V, AE)* near the Catherdral St. Gastien.

need to know

Currency Exchange ATMs and all **banks** offer the best exchange rates. The most convenient place to change bills is the automated change machines scattered throughout town.

Tourist Information The **Office de Tourisme** *(78 rue Bernard-Palissy; Tel 02/47-70-37-37; Mon-Sat 8:30am-7pm, Sun 10am-5pm [closed 12:30-2:30pm] Apr15-Oct15; Mon-Sat 9am-6pm, Sun 1:30-6pm, Oct15-Apr15; info@ligeris.com; www.ligeris.com)* is in a groovy, teched-out building near the train station, easily recognizable with its huge "Office de Tourisme" sign in neon letters. The tourist office will make hotel reservations for you if you show up in person, but they won't arrange anything in advance over the phone.

Public Transportation Tours is served by an extensive bus system that branches out to all major points of the city through suburban lines. In the center city, however, most buses run up the **rue Nationale,** so you may have a mini-trek to the far eastern and western parts of central Tours from the closest bus stop. All bus lines can be picked up at **place Jean-Jaures,** a short walk from the train station. The municipal bus service for the entire Tours region is **Autocars Fil Bleu** *(Tel 02/47-66-70-70),* which offers day passes for 27F. Most fares within Tours cost 6.90F per person, and are bought on board the bus.

Health and Emergency Ambulance: *15;* police; *17;* fire: *18;* hospital: *Tel 02/47-47-47-47;* emergency medical service: *Tel 02/47-38-33-33.* The two hospitals near Tours are **CHU Bretonneau** *(Blvd. Tonelé; Tel 02/47-47-47-47),* on the eastern perimeter of town, and **Hôpital Trousseau** *(Rte. De Loches, Tel 02/47-47-47-47),* 3 miles south of the town center.

Pharmacies Pharmacies are located throughout town; look for the **flashing green cross.**

Telephone City code: *02;* information: *12;* international operator (USA): *Tel 00/33-12-11.* Phone cards are available at most tobacco shops, post offices, and magazine shops in 50F and 100F denominations.

Airports **Aeroport de Tours** *(4 rue de l'Aerogare; Tel 02/47-49-37-00)* is 5 miles north of town. There is no public transportation or shuttle service to the town center. Taxis charge about 180F to go the distance; call **Taxi-Radio** *(Tel 02/47-20-30-40).*

Trains Tours is a 55-minute TGV ride from Paris's **Gare Montparnasse.** Nearly 10 trains per day take this route, costing 289-406F one way. Trains arrive at Tours' **Gare Routiere** *(Place du General Leclerc; Tel 02/47-05-30-49).* The train station is directly south of the old town, right below Jardin de la Préfecture, the large park that opens onto Tours' major thorooughfare, blvd. Heurteloup. It takes about 20 minutes to walk to the center of town; head west from the station to place Jean-Jaurès, then head north on rue Nationale.

Bike/Moped Rental For biking around—and out of—town, rent your wheels at **Amstercycles** *(5 rue du Rampart; Tel 02/47-61-22-23).* The tourist office will give you free maps of the area. **Velomania** *(109 rue Colbert; Tel 02/47-05-10-11).*

Laundry Wash 'n' dry your dirty duds at **Lavomatique de Tours** *(23 place Michelet; Tel. 02/47-64-91-84), right by the train station.*

Postal The main post office is located at **1 Blvd. Beranger** *(Tel 02/47-60-34-20; All bus lines to Place Jean-Jaures; 8am-5pm Mon-Fri, 8am-noon Sat).*

Internet See *wired,* above.

angers

When traveling in western Europe, it can often feel like your choices are limited to the extremes of small-town charm or big-city bustle: long walks through the woods or tall drinks under flashing lights; mind-numbing boredom or body-assaulting excess. But finding the medium—the balance most experienced travelers lust after—is easy to do in Angers. You can come away from Angers feeling like the star jock in a rural, sporty high school—a conqueror of sorts.

Angers is a place easily traversed by foot, as is evident with one glance at the cutesy, hand-drawn map you pick up at the tourist office. The majority of sites and events are located in the center city, directly southeast of the Maine River extending down to the Boulevard Foch. As you explore Angers' mostly narrow, winding central streets, it's easy to walk in circles and find yourself back at the same CD store or *boulangerie.* But fear not! After a good day or two of exploring, Angers is yours.

If châteaux (or tapestries) are your thing, then you won't want to miss the **Château d' Angers,** where a massive 335-foot-long tapestry depicts scenes from the Book of St. John in gory detail [see *culture zoo,* below]. Culture vultures will also find plenty to occupy their time at Angers' six museums, featuring everything from natural history to gothic art [see *culture zoo,* below]. The people of Angers are overwhelmingly friendly, sometimes to the point of seeming fake (or even a bit scary). They're used to having visitors solely of the business variety, since tourists often bypass Angers for the larger Tours or Orleans. But this accessibility and genuine nature of the people is what makes Angers one of the true gems of the

angers

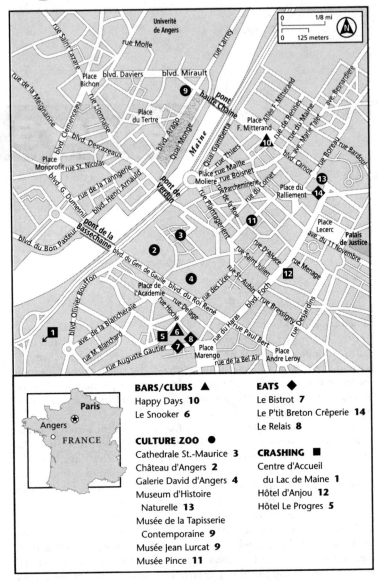

BARS/CLUBS ▲
Happy Days **10**
Le Snooker **6**

CULTURE ZOO ●
Cathedrale St.-Maurice **3**
Château d'Angers **2**
Galerie David d'Angers **4**
Museum d'Histoire
  Naturelle **13**
Musée de la Tapisserie
  Contemporaine **9**
Musée Jean Lurcat **9**
Musée Pince **11**

EATS ◆
Le Bistrot **7**
Le P'tit Breton Crêperie **14**
Le Relais **8**

CRASHING ■
Centre d'Accueil
  du Lac de Maine **1**
Hôtel d'Anjou **12**
Hôtel Le Progres **5**

Loire Valley. Unlike some of the bigger cities nearby, it feels like a real French *ville,* while still offering most of the perks of big-city life.

Although the town does feature all of the plusses that would keep the Sims happy in a virtual metropolis, don't expect discos on every corner and high fashion parading down the streets, (unless of course Alexander McQueen moves his fall collection to the Place du Ralliement). The dress code is low-key and fairly predictable and there isn't a huge bar and club scene here. On the other hand, there is a university, so you'll probably run into a fair number of students.

Angers is far from a town of rebels. The scruffy and rude street crowd that infests other French cities is refreshingly absent here, and in its place you're more likely to find young people who are, for lack of a better phrase, "just doing their thing." They're a socially conscious bunch, and they are way into their culture, both national and local. Small playhouses abound, as do stores catering to dancers, musicians, and thespians. All of the shops exhibit a team-pride kind of attitude. If you walk into a boutique that outfits dancers and want to find the best theater to see a performance or the music store with the most comprehensive Rachmaninoff collection, you'll get the info you seek.

As is often the case in a small town, asking storeowners or friendly locals is the best way to glean information and also the most gratifying, since you'll usually make a new pal in the process. The tourist office is a close runner-up, docked points only because of its decisive lack of street creds. For info on the town's history and high culture, however, it can't be beat in terms of the sheer volume of Angers propaganda it carries. Here you can also pick up *L'Ouvre-Boites,* the local youth publication (in french, *bien sur*). Though heavy on the editorials and political trash polemics, it sometimes has good listings for festivals and theater. A better choice is a quick romp through Angers's music stores and university bulletin boards, which always have flyers for live music events, clubs, and other youth-oriented activities.

neighborhoods

The layout of Angers is incredibly easy to follow and remember. The **Maine River,** dissects the town: To the north is **place Bichon, place Du Tertre,** and **place Monprofit;** to the south is the heart of town, which extends south to **boulevard Foch.** You'll find most of Angers' star attractions south of the river, including the **Chateau d'Angers** [see *culture zoo,* below] and the bars off the **place Du Ralliement.** North of the river it's mostly residential, except for the **University of Angers** and the college bars that go with it. During summer, the university basically closes down except for a few classes, but there are still enough students to let you know that this is definitely a college town.

Most of the best neighborhoods in which to spend time fall south of the river along the **rue St. Aubin,** the **rue Plantagenet,** and the **place du Ralliement.** This is the charming, postcard Angers, which retains its old-world feel. Just north of the river it's a different story: Ugly, postwar buildings surround the university, where the lawns fill up between classes, and make a great spot for people-watching.

The local public transportation system relies on bus power, which can almost entirely avoided during pleasant weather if you have good walking shoes. Angers is small enough to cover by foot; by taking the bus you miss out on exploring the small streets that give the city its character.

hanging out

Like to feel the love in the air? Take a trip to the fountain across the street from the **Hôtel d'Anjou** [see *crashing*, below], where you're sure to catch scores of couples groping, kissing, and generally enjoying each other's company. Puppy love aside, this is also a popular spot for independents on bikes or on foot—the well-worn benches are ergonomic bliss, and the BMX bandits skidding by on the asphalt provide nearly constant entertainment as they vie with the falling skateboarders for the crowd's attention. Here also is one of the best spots in the city to take in Angers as a whole, with the old town whispering sweet nothings from one side and the dingy building complexes screeching on the other.

There's always action at **Les Halles,** the main town market and also the site of the perplexingly popular CD store **CDBD** [see *tunes*, below]. Here, too, the commotion circles around a fountain—this time ringed by stairs upon which you'll find every sort of Angerian lolling about. It's mostly a younger crowd, geared out in headphones and semi-tech apparel, but the occasional mom, businessperson, or college student pops up to vary the scene.

For a respite from humans, crawl past the side entrance gates at the **Musée d'Histoire Naturelle** [see *culture zoo* below] and relax for a few minutes, an hour, whatever, beneath the huge trees. The space has the feeling of a deserted secret garden, which can be better than therapy after too much time on your feet. The air is still and quiet here, save the hum of insects, which on sunny days move unseen through the amorphous green light falling through the trees.

bar scene

For a British feel with a billiard fix, head to **Le Snooker** *(Rue de la Gare directly north of Place de la Gare; All bus lines to Gare; Eve-2am daily),* where the look is more Prince Charles than Austin Powers. The bar goes all out to present a *gestalt* devoted to that revered green-table game, complete with those annoying prints of dogs smoking and playing cards and eight pool tables in the back. The bar is always packed with students, off-duty garage mechanics, a soldier or two from the nearby military base, a few hookers, and the local butcher; you'll also catch a smattering of visitors who can appreciate a true local pub. The tables in the back are almost always occupied, but the vibe is easygoing and the players a bit closer in spirit to pool guppies than any kind of shark. Random nights will host a DJ, usually spinning some form of heavy house or techno (and also usually bros with all of the people at the bar...bad news when everyone gets drunk and decides to take their turn at the decks). Drink prices are average, but for a Brit-themed bar the beer and lager flow is at a minimum; both boys and girls favor mixed drinks and cigarettes. The place starts to clear out around 1am, so it's best to show up early to catch the action in full swing.

In a slightly more student-oriented section of town, **Happy Days** *(46 blvd. Ayrault; Bus 10 to Francois-Mitterand; Tel 02/41-88-16-02; Eve-*

boy meets girl

The mood here is definitely the antithesis of big city hookups and one night stands. Most young people, in fact, seem to be a part of either a blissfully oblivious couple or a solid group of friends who aren't out to get laid or be played. As a rule, don't expect to find a soulmate, without some serious ice breaking.

2am) offers a typical French brasserie menu, along with some of the cheapest drinks in town. For less than 50F, you can sit down to a night of drinking accompanied by one of the loudest jukeboxes and liveliest crowds in Angers. And just after exam time, watch out. This place is overrun with students celebrating their newfound freedom in *the* most raucous fashion.

LIVE MUSIC SCENE

While its facade suggests a world of waltzes and sonatas, the **Grand Theatre d'Angers** *(3 rue Louis de Romain; Bus 15 to Ralliement; Tel 02/41-24-16-40; Show times vary; Prices vary according to show, 40-130F)* does in fact feature some new and interesting spins on classical music. The *Mardis Musicaux,* or musical Tuesdays, bring some of the top acts in France—from the youthful members of Le Concert Impromptu to the world beats of the Ensemble Musique Oblique. No matter which act you catch, nearly any night spent at the Grand Theatre will be a memorable one.

CLUB SCENE

While the club scene in Angers is admittedly *very* limited and uninteresting, a ten-minute cab ride outside the city can lead to a much more interesting night of dancing. **Jungle Jane** *(Rte. de Cantenay Epinard; No phone; Eve-4am Tue-Sat; 60F includes one drink)* is so popular with the youth of Angers that any cabbie can take you straight to the front door without questions. The reason for this is up for discussion: It could be the overall kitschy jungle theme and the stuffed animal heads on the walls, or simply that the youth of Angers will fall in love with any place that has a dance floor. The music is varied to cater to the diverse crowd, though the French disco formula is definitely present. Rap, ragga, reggae, jungle (obviously), and contemporary pop hits mix in the heavy air while kids ignore their drinks and rush to the floor.

ARTS SCENE

The visual arts in Angers's center consists mostly of antique dealerships along the rue Toussaint and other, smaller streets. Most gallery space is consumed by dusty books, bronze Victorian busts, and rickety chairs—

leaving little room for paintings, drawings, or photographs. The art that does make it on the walls is usually limited to trite lithographs of seaside France.

The best place to check out this strange marriage of art and antiques, is on rue Toussaint, a small street locals refer to as *la rue Antiquaires* because of the dense concentration of antique stores. Check out **L'Atelier** (*9 rue Toussaint; Bus 16 to St Aubin; Tel 02/41-88-74-10; 11am-12:30pm/2:30pm-7pm Wed-Sat*), across the street from Château d'Angers. The gallery represents a small and varied group of six artists (all male save one) who work in mixed media, from drawing to sculpture.

The performing arts of Angers tend to fare better, which is evident in the number of theaters. For a small, intimate setting where the audience is always part of the show, check out **La Comedie** (*1 rue Cordelle; Tel 02/41-87-24-24; Bus 9 to St. Aubin; 11pm Fri & Sat; 80F adults, 60F students*). Created in 1990 and made up mostly of local performers, the troupe is talented onstage and friendly off—a stop at the theater during the week shows a hardworking team rehearsing yet always willing to take a second to talk to the public. Shows tend toward the comic so if you're looking for a place to try out a new box of tissues, this isn't it.

CULTURE ZOO

Angers serves up a staggering selection of cultural offerings, especially for such a moderately sized town, but unfortunately many need some picking through. Lucky for you, we've done it for you. A comprehensive guide to Angers's major attractions is available at the tourist office [see *need to know,* below], where you can also buy a museum *passeport.* For 25F, this pass will get you into five of the major museums. **Musée Jean Lurcat** (*4 blvd Arago; Tel 02/41-24-18-45; Tue-Sun 10am-noon and 2pm-6pm; 15F students, 25F adults*): If you only have time to visit one museum while you're in Angers, make it this one. Set within what once functioned as a hospital, it contains the town's most famous weaving, a huge tapestry ("The Song of the World") designed by Jean Lurçat, and executed in ten sewn-together panels between 1957 and 1966. It depicts an abstract conglomeration of beneficent suns, popping champagne bottles, and life cycles of birth, death, and renewal. You could skip the rest of the exhibits without feeling cheated, but if you're into strange artifacts, you might want to check out the smaller collections—everything from a magnificent pewter vessel (1720) that once contained an antidote for snake bites to a Romanesque cloister with a enchanting garden and a collection of centuries-old stonework. **Musée Pince** (*32 rue Lenepveu; Tel 02/41-88-94-27; Tue-Sun 10am-noon and 2pm-6pm; 15F students, 25F adults*): The major attraction within this small 16th-century tower is a stunning collection of Japanese masks, engravings, and ceramics on the second floor. There's also a collection of Gallo-Roman artifacts, and a small exhibit of Egyptian and Etruscan vases. **Galerie David d'Angers** (*33 bis, rue Toussaint; Tel 02/41-87-21-03; Tue-Sun 10am-noon and 2pm-6pm; 15F students, 25F adults*): Go here on a sunny day to see the way light floods the interior of

fEStIVALS, COOL ANNUAL EVENTS

Festival des Quais, a yearly arts festival, takes place over two days in mid-May and has more to do with drinking and toasting in honor of the artists than the art itself. Entry is free for all events, ranging from orchestral ensembles and jazz groups to water sports and video screenings.

Another, perhaps better, music festival to check out, during the final two weeks in May, is the **Festival Gipsy Swing,** which celebrates international music with local bombast. Performances take place at outdoor spots throughout the city, and can be seen with a variety of tickets, including one- to three-day passes *(Prices vary by event; Call 02/41-96-12-81 for information).*

this old church through the greenhouse-style roof built around 1900 (the church had fallen into ruins a hundred years earlier). Stay to check out the huge collection of plaster casts David of Angers donated to his hometown; it includes busts of celebrated Frenchmen from Balzac to Victor Hugo. **Musée de la Tapisserie Contemporaine** *(same info as Musée Jean Lurcat):* If you still haven't met your museum quotient, stop by this one to get a perspective on the weaving and tapestry industry that has been headquartered in Angers since the Middle Ages. Skip the collection of antique looms if you've had enough ancient history for the day, and check out the contemporary weavings.

Musée d'Histoire Naturelle *(43 rue Jules Guiton; Tel 02/41-86-05-84; Tue-Sun 2pm-5pm; 15F student, 25F adults):* Skip this one unless you have a major museum jones or have always secretly had a crush on Jane Hathaway, the bird-watching secretary on *The Beverly Hillbillies.* In addition to the special emphasis on ornithology, there are exhibits on geology, botany, and zoology. (Don't worry, you won't be tested afterward.)

Château d'Angers *(Tel 02/41-87-43-47; Bus 6 to Château; 9am-7pm June-Sept 15, 9:30am-12:30pm/2-6pm Sept 16-May; 35F adults, 23F seniors and students, 6F children 7-17, free for children 6 and under):* OK, yes, some people would rather dig their spleen out with a spoon than visit a fortress famous for a really big tapestry, but trust us—*this* one is a must-see. The *Apocalypse Tapestries* is a series of 77 individual pieces depicting the book of St. John in occasionally very gory detail. In a museum or textbook, this 335-foot-long piece might look like a hallway rug, but within the confines of the fortress (an impressive sight in itself), it takes on a life of its own. After checking out the artwork, you can tour the prison cells, ramparts, chapel, and other sections of the château alone or with a guide.

The tapestries at **Cathédrale St-Maurice** *(Place Freppel; Tel 02/41-87-58-45; Bus 9 to St. Aubin; 9am-7pm daily; Free admission);* were once on display here; now only a few remain to remind the visitor of what once must have been awesome sight. This cathedral, dating mostly from the 12th and 13th centuries, is a mix of Gothic and Norman features and is most easily understood with the help of the handy English-language pamphlets at the church, which detail the construction of each part of the massive structure.

modification

Although you'd never guess by looking at the friendly folk of Angers, there is at least one spot for body alteration, be it through ink or piercing. The imaginatively named **Tattoo Studio** *(68 rue Jules Guitton; Tel 02/41-87-55-28)* has a surprisingly good selection of body jewelry and a viciously loyal clientele. Patrons come back again and again, not necessarily for more modification, but usually just to hang out on the street and compare flesh wounds.

sports

A dizzying array of water-based sports can be found at Angers's youth hostel on the lake, **Centre d'Accueil du Lac de Maine** [see *crashing*, below]. A five-minute bus ride from the center of town opens up a world of opportunities for sailing, wind-surfing, canoeing, and swimming, as well as tennis, running, cycle, judo, and gymnastics.

stuff

Angers's coolest shopping streets are the rue Saint Aubin and the pedestrian zones off rue Plantagenet. The focus of most boutiques is refreshingly earthy in comparison to the chain stores that take up space in many other cities. True, the town has the tiresome Galleries Lafayettes, same as anywhere else, but this is slightly offset by the number of quaint shops that rival it.

fashion

Overall Angers fashion statement? Confused. Honey, those 6-inch jean rolls and Polo Sport sweatshirts are so over! And brother, please squeeze out of those butt-caressing trews before you hurt yourself. It isn't so much the singular items that clash however, it's the look as a whole. Girls seem to be a bit more in tune than the dudes, though some parade around in way-too-tight black pants that leave little to the imagination. Luckily, most everyone here is as skinny as a blade of grass, so they can get away with it.

▶▶DUDS

Like a Chinatown boutique with a European edge, the **Troc & Co Boutique** *(9 rue Plantagenet; Tel 02/41-86-71-39; Bus 15 to Ralliement)* has tons of colorful and fun women's clothing starting around 350F. They also have a strangely out-of-place second-hand rack that sometimes hides a few gems between the tightly packed secretary blouses and knee-length skirts.

▶▶HOLISTIC AND GROOVY

One of the few places carrying anything of a semi-holistic nature is the **Candle Shop** *(74 bis rue Plantagenet; Tel 02/41-18-15-09; Bus 15 to Ralliement; 2pm-7pm Mon, 10am-7pm Tue-Sat)*, where you can pick up scented gifts, from trendy tribal-wrapped candles to the chunky block soaps famous in France. The orange walls seem like a strange way to make merchandise appear attractive, but if you can look past the interior decoration and focus on the shelves, this is a good place to pick up a gift for anyone from a high school sister to a yoga instructor aunt.

▶▶TUNES

CDBD *(69 rue St Laud; Bus 15 to Ralliement; Tel 02/41-25-20-00; 2-7pm Mon, 10:30am-7pm Tue-Sat)* attracts a big crowd not only for its musical selection, but also for its proximity to the popular french-fry shop next door. Like most other small-town record shops in France, CDBD has a paltry offering of CDs, a better selection of music mags, and a sampling of records (mostly house/trance/techno). The owners also trade and buy CDs and DVDs if you're interested in getting some musical weight off your hands while traveling.

EATS

Like life itself in Angers, the food scene has a good balance among types of restaurants and price levels. On nearly any street, you can find something as quick as a crêpe or as involved as a six-course seafood feast.

▶▶CHEAP

Le P'tit Breton Creperie *(8 rue Pocquet de Livonniere/directly off Place Imbach; No phone; Bus 5 to Lise; Noon-2:30pm and 7-10pm Tue-Sat; Crêpes 10-25F, specialty items 30-39F; MC, V, EC)* may sound like it belongs in another part of France, but who cares when the food is so tasty. The menu is divided between traditional crêpes like banana with chocolate or savory mushroom and the specialty *galettes* of the house. Gallettes are also crêpes, but they're heartier than dessert crêpes and usually are filled with ham, cheese, or vegetables as a main course. It's difficult to choose among these, but a good starter would be the incredible *Carnac:* diced apples with vanilla ice cream and hot chocolate sauce that melts in your mouth and makes you wonder why the plate emptied so quickly.

▶▶DO-ABLE

For a quick meal at a reasonable price, check out **Le Bistrot** *(8 Place de la Gare; Tel 02/41-88-37-32; All bus lines to Gare; 11:45am-11pm daily, Open til midnight Fri and Sat; Prix fixe 65F, other items 40-100F; All credit*

TO MARKET

Les Halles, the main market center in town, is at 7 rue d'Anjou *(Bus to Place Ralliement)*. If you've never seen a skinned rabbit or a featherless chicken with three decorative plumes sticking out of its ass, this is the place. Certainly not vegetarian-friendly, but a great stop for fresh meat. Les Halles is also the location of the local Air France office, as well as several jewelry and music stores.

---

cards). Part of a business-class hotel across from the train station, Le Bistrot is the less flashy sibling of the hotel's upscale restaurant next door. Touted as the quick, yet satisfying, pit stop for visiting businesspeople, Le Bistrot gets flack from locals for its second-class status. What the hotel staff won't tell you and what most people don't know, however, is that the restaurants share one chef, ensuring that the plates coming your way under both roofs will taste basically the same, albeit with very different prices and a slight change in presentation. Most menu dishes are reliable, if in no way gourmet, and the wait staff is helpful in selecting whatever suits your mood.

For a great meal you can actually afford, go for the fixed-price meal at **Le Péché Gourmand** *(48 rue Parcheminerie; Tel 02/41-81-04-76; bus 9; Noon-3pm and 7-11pm Tues-Sat; Fixed-price lunch 78F, fixed-price dinner 98F; MC, V).* Located about 300 yards from the parking lot for the town's outdoor produce market (les Halles) and the Place du Ralliement, this restaurant serves cost-conscious but well-flavored meals. Most dishes are based on time-tested regional recipes, such as a filet of beef Rossini or roasted pigeon, both stuffed with foie gras. Or try some Basque food: small calamari fried with olive oil, garlic, and peppers, or the "cheeks" of a local freshwater fish (sander) served with shrimp. After the chef does his magic, fish cheeks taste a hell of a lot better than you might think.

▶▶SPLURGE

For a genuine taste of the Loire Valley, visit the famous chefs Gerard Pelletier and Christophe Noel at **Le Relais** *(9 rue de la Gare; Tel 02/41-88-42-51; All bus lines to Gare; Menu items 80-200F),* one of a French chain that has a down-home, one-of-a-kind feel. The clientele is mostly older, but they seem to enjoy the bright, cheerfully decorated atmosphere. Pelletier and Noel, formerly of London, are famous in Angers for their refusal to work with anything frozen, which becomes evident with the first bite of any plate they serve up.

crashing

▶▶CHEAP

Located a convenient five-minute bus ride out of center city, the **Centre d'Accueil du Lac de Maine** *(49 ave du Lac de Maine; Tel 02/41-22-32-10; Bus 6, 16 to Lac de Maine; angers.lac@wanadoo.fr; 200F double with private bath, 85F per person quad with shared bath; Breakfast included; All credit cards)* is a beautiful 150-bed getaway hostel located on 220 hectares (544 acres) of water. As a result, the water activities are plentiful [see *sports*, above], and the adjacent sports fields and track are great for those who hesitate to get their feet wet. Rooms are comfortable, standard, and safe, if not overly exciting. Campsites are also available.

If you prefer to stay in town, try the **Royal Hôtel** *(rue d'Iéna; Tel 02/41-88-30-25; Fax 02/41-81-05-75; 148F single, 200F single with private bath, 160F double, 260F double withprivate bath, 330F triple with private bath, 340F quad with private bath; Breakfast 30F; V, MC, AE)*, just a 5-minute walk from the train station in the city center, or **Hôtel des Lices** *(25 rue des Lices; Tel 02/41-87-44-10; 170F with private bath, 120F without; Breakfast 28F; V, MC, AE)*, also in the city center but just a little farther from the train station.

▶▶DO-ABLE

Hotel Le Progres *(26 rue Denis Papin; Tel 02/41-88-10-14; all bus lines to Gare; 210-280F single, 280-330F double, all with private bath; Breakfast 39F; All credit cards)* is a convenient spot to crash, close to both the train station and center city. The friendly owners and hotel staff do all in their power to ensure a pleasant stay, and are extremely knowledgeable about the ins and outs of the town.

▶▶SPLURGE

Hôtel d'Anjou *(1 Blvd. Foch; U.S. Tel 800/528-1234, Local Tel 02/41-88-24-82; Bus 10 to Foch/Lorraine; 505-905F singles or doubles, depending on amenities; Breakfast 65F; All credit cards)* is a posh little four-story number on one of the main drags in town. If it's tasteful decoration you seek in a hotel room, you can definitely find it here. Most rooms are completely remodeled with an old-town touch, garnished with fancy reproductions and an occasional antique. The wall pieces may remind you of a small love nest in a Helena Bonham Carter tear-jerker, but the furniture is comfortable, the ceilings are high, and the beds are the next best thing to home.

need to know

Currency Exchange The best exchange rates can be had at any number of Angers's **ATMs** or **banks.** There are several in front of the railway station in the Place de la Visitation. Some larger hotels also change traveler's checks, but they use the rates published in the newspaper, which are always worse than if you trekked to the ATM.

Tourist Information Located near the Château on the **place du President-Kennedy** *(Tel 02/41-23-51-11; Mon 11am-6pm, Tue-Sat*

9am-6pm, Sun 10am-1pm Oct 1-May 2; Mon-Sat 9am-7pm, Sun 10am-1pm and 2pm-6pm May 3-Sep 30), the tourist office is full of over-eager workers who jump at the chance to unload leaflets, brochures, and verbal information on any interested visitor. They'll even make hotel reservations for you if you show up in person. Here also you can pick up the 25F ticket to the major museums of Angers—a good choice for a day of culture if you can spare the time.

Public Transportation The **bus system** is reliable, if hard to comprehend on the teeny bus map. During the week buses run per the French timetables, until about 11pm, but beware that times and lines change drastically on the weekend when service is cut down to five lines that cater mostly to the suburbs rather than the center of town. Cabs are sparse, but can be called through **Allo Taxi** *(Tel 02/41-87-65-00).*

Health and Emergency Emergency *15,* police: *17;* fire: *18.* The local hospital is the **Centre Hospitalier Universitaire** *(4 rue Larrey; Tel 02/41-35-36-37),* 2 miles north of the Château, beyond the Musée Lurçat.

Pharmacies Pharmacies are located throughout town; look for the **flashing green cross.**

Telephone City code: *02;* information: *12;* international operator (USA): *Tel 00/33-12-11.* Phone cards are available at most tobacco shops, post offices, and magazine shops in 50F and 100F denominations.

Airports Aeroport Angers-Marce *(Tel 02/41-33-50-20)* is 12 miles east of the center of town and serves a few destinations throughout Europe as far east as Amsterdam and Dusseldorf. To get into Angers, you have to take a taxi; there is no bus service.

Trains The Gare SNCF *(Place de la Gare; Tel 08/36-35-35-35)* is a 10-minute walk south of the center of town.

Laundry One laundromat in the center of town is located at **15 rue Plantagenet,** open 8am-9pm daily. This one is unsupervised except for three hours in the morning after opening, but you can throw your own load in a washer for 22-42F, depending on the size.

brittany

brittany

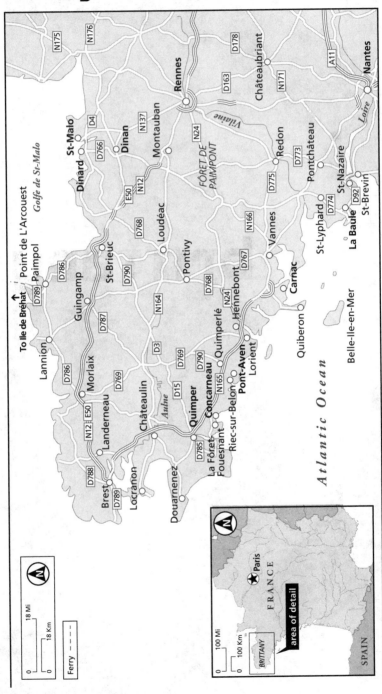

from fairy tale forests dripping with green to a lighthouse-dotted coast, Brittany is a region packed with surprises. Yet it often gets left off the average traveler's itinerary. Compared to the lights of Paris or the beaches of Cannes, Brittany offers rain, the rather bleak inland capital city of **Rennes,** and more rain. Next to the typically hyped regions of France, it's like an undiscovered middle child, patiently waiting for its turn in the spotlight.

If you're serious about seeing all of France, however, this region offers lots of opportunities that you won't find elsewhere. For one thing, there's Brittany's fierce history as a Celtic stronghold that remained independent of France until the 16th century, so you can trip out on their weird old megaliths and castles. Even now you'll find that Breton culture has been preserved, especially in western Brittany. It's just like those color photographs from your outdated French textbook: People are still wearing the white bonnets and traditional dress that your French prof raved about, at least during the festivals.

But unlike other parts of the world where the new and old worlds meet and clash, the younger generation in Brittany embraces and appreciates the culture from which it springs. College-aged kids speak the local dialect with as much ease as their grandparents, and seem eager to keep alive a tradition that separates them from the rest of the country.

This idea of separation is evident over and over here, not so much as a rebellion—although, as recently as the 1970s, Bretons did stage uprisings and agitate for independence from France—but rather in the locals' deep attachment to their region. It's easy to see why they love it: Nowhere else outside of Ireland can one get quite as lost in a sea of green than in Brittany. Bretons are also proud of their local products: oysters; rich, salty butter; chunky blue and yellow pottery; specially seasoned duck; renowned theater troupes and underground cinema; and the Pont Aven school of painting, started by Paul Gaugin.

While each smaller region of Brittany has its own definitive characteristics and quirks, the overall vibe is relaxed, refined, and comfortable. Locals are at ease with their culture and their surroundings; the aggravations of, say, the typical New Yorker are pleasantly absent throughout the region. What replaces the clenched-toothed, tight-jawed attitude is a love of the simple pleasures that are impossible to miss—bike trails, outdoor cafes, and cozy bars packed with friends. You'll be able to enjoy this laid-back vibe in **Quimper,** within shouting distance of the sea. Three-story discos and flashy chain department stores are largely absent in this region, which has impressively held on to traditions while adapting its own night diversions and shopping ops. For an edgier nightlife, head to Rennes, which despite its dreary appearance has a hoppin' youth scene.

getting around the region

Catching all of Brittany's highlights is luckily not a difficult task. Getting around the region is really a matter of picking up a few train schedules and being willing now and then to hop on a rented bike to cruise the countryside.

Major cities in Brittany are all connected by the very reliable and easy-to-follow Eurorail, and the smaller towns are easily accessible either by smaller train lines from Rennes or by car. You can pick up comprehensive time schedules at the local train stations; they aren't always available

pont-aven, pure & simple

Paul Gauguin—who never was big on city life—moved out to the Pont-Aven, an idyllic little village of white-painted houses set along the banks of the gently flowing Aven River, in 1886. Where Gauguin went, others were sure to follow, and soon Emile Bernard, Paul Sérusier, and Maurice Denis made the pilgrimage to the little town 20 miles southeast of Quimper. They established the "School of Pont-Aven," exemplified in one of Gauguin's most memorable works, "The Yellow Christ." They broke away from mainstream Impressionism, emphasizing purer colors, shunning perspective, and simplifying human figures. You can see their work—mostly dramatic seascapes and landscapes of Brittany—at the **Musée de L'Ecole de Pont-Aven** (*Place de Hotel-de-Ville; Tel 02/98-06-14-43; Open daily 10am-7pm July-Aug, 10am-2:30pm and 2-6pm the rest of the year; 25F adults, 5F ages 13-20, under 12 free*), near the tourist office. Or do the art-crawl around town to the places they lived and hung out; the tourist office (*Place de Hôtel-de-Ville, off Place Gauguin; Tel 02/98-56-96-72*), sells a walking-tour guide for 2F. You won't be alone—artists still flock here to live, work, or wait for the muse. Buses to Pont-Aven leave Quimper six times a day all summer (four the rest of the year); it's a 1-hour trip on **Transports Caoudal** (*Tel 02/98-06-04-70; 35F one way*).

Travel Times

*TGV (Fast Train—more expensive)	Quimper	Paris	Rennes
Rennes	2:10* 2:30	3:00	-
Quimper	-	5:00* 5:40	2:10* 2:30

online or in larger guidebooks. From Rennes it's easy to get to La Rochelle and other Atlantic coastal towns, once again by using the Eurorail. The Rennes–La Rochelle line also passes through Nantes.

▶▶ROUTES:

If you're pressed for time, start at the *Gare Montparnasse* in Paris and take the fast and efficient TGV westward to Quimper or Brest. Both are hefty journeys of about six hours. If you aren't up for doing solid train time, plan to stop in Rennes before heading further west; it's on the same train line and cuts the travel time in half. But if you could use a little downtime on the French rails, make the trek to Quimper first, then come back to Rennes.

If you're coming from the south, take any Eurorail line to Nantes for the transfer to Rennes.

quimper

As the modern TGV cuts through the lush, green countryside, slicing a path not only from Paris to the coast but also seemingly through times and attitudes, it becomes evident why Quimper is the perfect corner of Breton to visit. For ages visitors have complained about the frequent rain and the sometimes downright nasty weather, but under the heavy belly of western Brittany's often gray skies lies the most brilliant emerald lawn in all of France. Every leaf and peeling scrap of tree bark seems to suggest something primal and mythical, almost like a Norse fairy tale or an old Irish legend.

Quimper's ties to Ireland are not only geographical, but mental and social as well. Locals are fiercely proud of their Breton heritage, which is still reflected today in the bilingual street signs (French and Celtic-influenced Breton) and the Irish bars—the most popular nightspots in town.

Although it offers a hit-or-miss club circuit and (did we mention this before?) plenty of rain, Quimper does have an open and friendly youth scene. The ruddy local kids are smiling, large-toothed individuals who will readily help out an obviously floundering American with anything from street directions to a plan for the night. They're acutely interested in all things U.S., from fashion to slang, and they'll jump at the chance to impress you with their knowledge of words and phrases like "ass" and "get the hell out of here." They are also eager to toss out some catchphrases of their own; take advantage of the language barter! A surefire way to get chummy with the locals is to display genuine enthusiasm for their unique culture. After a few pints of Guinness in the dimly lit corners of any random Quimper nightspot, it's easy to feel like a local.

Besides hitting the bars, you can tuck into some oysters, take a hike up nearby **Mont Frugy** [see *hanging out,* below], or plan to slip away for a day at the beach nearby; the closest one is **Benodet** [see *within 30 minutes,* below]. Or, if it's August, you may want to hang around for the music fest, which features reggae, rap, and more reggae [see *festivals/cool annual events,* below]. Shopping is nothing to write home about, but if you're looking for funky Breton jewelry, or that chunky blue and yellow pottery, you'll find it here.

Unfortunately, if you don't know French, Quimper can be hard to explore through printed info alone. The town lacks a solid events paper, even in the native language, and the information from the tourist office ain't exactly the most swingin' selection. Posters and fliers for live music and club events pop up everywhere, however, and most pub-goers are eager to volunteer information on upcoming events. As a rule, if you can summon enough courage to venture an inquiry, you'll get a friendly and helpful response.

neighborhoods

Quimper is a fairly easy city to navigate on foot, with most of the main events happening in **Le Vieux Quartier**, the old-town district where most of Quimper's cool historic buildings are located. Easily found from

five things to talk to a local about

1. **Drugs:** Yes, they take them, and you can be sure they like to talk about it. Nothing hardcore goes down here, just a strong affinity for hashish and the occasional classic spliff, but all that reggae music and those chunky sweaters don't exist for nothing.
2. **The annual music festival** (see *festivals,* below).
3. **The weather:** No, not because they're particularly interested in hearing you whine about how wrinkled your shorts are getting while they rot in your suitcase or backpack, but because they take great pleasure in mocking you for your lack of stout-heartedness when confronted with Nature's follies. Oh, the shame...
4. **America:** As with most Europeans, the residents of Quimper are way into the U.S. of A.—especially when you mention any big city they may have seen in an '80s movie.
5. **The local culture:** The last thing the people of Quimper are is ashamed of their strange and wacky heritage; they embrace the culture of Brittany in every way—from language to dress to handicrafts.

quimper

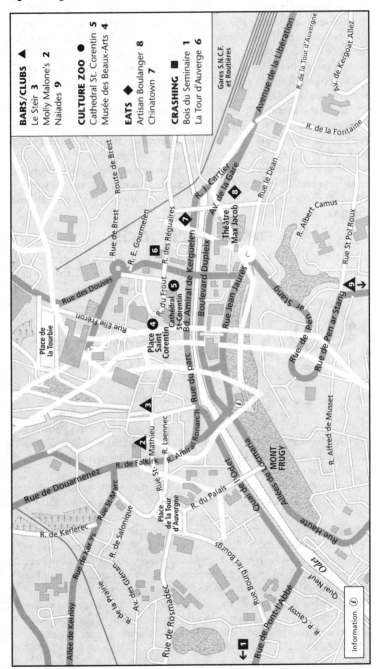

BARS/CLUBS ▲
Le Steir **3**
Molly Malone's **2**
Naiades **9**

CULTURE ZOO ●
Cathedral St. Corentin **5**
Musée des Beaux-Arts **4**

EATS ◆
Artisan Boulanger **8**
Chinatown **7**

CRASHING ■
Bois du Seminaire **1**
La Tour d'Auverge **6**

Information ℹ

any part of town, this cluster of small, twisty streets sits in the shadow of the famous **St. Corentin Cathedral** [see *culture zoo,* below] towering over the heart of Quimper. The city sits along the **Odet River,** which cuts through the center of the town north of the train station.

South of the river is an outdoorsman's paradise, dominated by large stretches of unspoiled grasslands and plentiful spots for camping. Where the green expanse ends, the second "center" of Quimper begins. It starts with **Creac'h Gwenn,** a strip of parks, tennis courts, and lawns that leads to Quimper's commercial center, the university, and the bars, clubs, and nightspots that go hand-in-hand with college students. To the west of the river is **Penhars,** a quiet, leafy, residential neighborhood that has little of interest other than the city's youth hostel at **Bois du Seminaire** [see *crashing,* below].

Since the most interesting parts of Quimper are within walking distance of the city center, exploring by foot is usually the best way to go. It's also the only way to take advantage of the many beautiful outdoor surprises that crop up in the city limits, from **Mont Frugy** [see *hanging out,* below] to the carousels in the center of town. The bus is a quick and easy way to get to those out-of-the-way spots, but it's best not to rely on public transport late at night or on Sundays. Most bus lines stop running annoyingly early (around 7pm) in Quimper, both weekdays and on the weekend, which leads to potential trouble if you don't have a car or a friend who does. Taxis are virtually nonexistent, and when they do appear the fare seems to vary depending on your cabbie.

hanging out

Any hanging out you do in Quimper should definitely be done with an umbrella. Perhaps the folks here are resigned to the weather or perhaps they just don't like outdoor dining. Whatever the reason, the brasseries and outdoor cafes that flourish in the rest of the country are in limited supply here. The best places to meet people, as a result, tend to be in the safe and dry confines of bars and pubs in the center of town. On a precipitation-free day, however, expect mass turnouts at any number of stoops, steps, and park benches throughout the town.

fIVE-O

The fuzz here keep a low profile. This isn't to say that Quimper runs amok with deviants and criminals, but what goes and what doesn't is strictly understood and followed. As a result, the police make token appearances to write parking tickets or catch a bite to eat, but otherwise keep out of the public eye.

wired

In the past few years, Internet cafes and computer stores with online access have flourished like weeds under the Quimper rain. The best rates are at **Cyber Copy** *(3 blvd. Amiral Kerguelen; Tel 02/98-64-25-15; Bus 1-8 to SNCF; 9am-7pm Mon-Sat; CYBER-COPY@wanadoo.fr; 15F/half hour, 20F/hour),* but that cozy cafe feeling is best found at **E.Com Cafe** *(7 rue du Roi Gradlon; Tel 02/-77-85-63-22; Bus 1-8 to Resistance; 8am-10pm daily in June, 8am-8pm daily other months; 50F/hour),* where the kids are cool, the music is cool, and the chairs are cool but incredibly uncomfortable. Cyber Copy is just 200 yards east of the town center, adjacent to the river; E.Com Café is on the street leading directly to the cathedral. Also check out the new kid in town, immediately opposite the produce market in the center of town: **C.com Café** *(Quai du Steir; Tel 02/98-95-81-62; 8am-10pm daily in June, 8am-8pm daily other months; 50F/hour).*

The liveliest of these common areas is the **place Saint Corentin,** bounded by the **Musée des Beaux-Arts** [see *culture zoo,* below] and the cathedral [again, see *culture zoo*]. Here also is one of the city's two carousels—deliciously (or appallingly) sacrilegious next to a famous house of God. When the sun is shining, expect the benches to be packed with people catching rays. (Note: Be sure to check out the marked difference between the locals in thick, chunky sweaters and the tourists lolling about in shorts shouting over their drippy ice cream cones.)

A trip south down the rue du Roi Gradlon takes you to a slightly less busy crowd magnet, the **Jardin de l'Eveche.** Unmarked and easily missed as just a wall with some benches in front of it, this little garden actually attracts some of the town's most interesting bums and slackers. Here tall cans of Heineken and Tuborg mix with the flowers, and tortured Quimperians scribble fervently in their little geek pads. Also common is the ubiquitous nomadic French couple, ready with German Shepherd and crusty dreads to tell you not only their life story, but also exactly why they need your last 10 francs more than you do. For those too soft to turn them down, perhaps this isn't the best spot to spend an afternoon. But if you're prepared with an "I'm busy and can't talk right now" book or dark sunglasses, it can be a damn good place to people watch.

Slightly less amenable to human spotting and more appropriate for tree hugging, the easily attainable summit of **Mont Frugy,** extending along the south bank of the Odet River, provides a peaceful and downright beautiful break from the town below. If you've ever wanted to brag about being a mountain climber, this is definitely the *mont* to attack—gradually sloping toward the low Breton sky and well trodden by eager hikers.

bar scene

As already suggested, the few scattered bars in Quimper don't hide their allegiance with the great green island to the north (perhaps because Brits came here in droves). On any given night about 10 percent of the bar population is English-speaking—mostly Brits and Americans—and in July and August that percentage goes up to about 15-20 percent. This leads to star treatment for the English speaker (especially if that English is accented with a hint of the ol' Irish brogue), and a continuous nightly diet of Guinness and umm...more Guinness.

Authenticity is key at **Molly Malone's** *(Place St.-Mathieu; Tel 02/98-53-40-42; Bus 4, 6, 7, 8 to St. Mathieu; V, MC, EC)*, where the bartenders pour the drinks slowly and to the top. Built into the belly of an old-town church (a 10-minute walk from the cathedral), this bar remains the favorite nightspot of Quimper youth. The decor is hilariously inappropriate—beer flags and Irish paraphernalia struggle against the exposed stone walls. The theme seems at once Charles Dickens and *Dr. Quinn, Medicine Woman*, complete with dangling pots and pans and a back wall covered with dusty old books. The crowd is as eclectically mixed as the decorations: from pouty girls in floppy turtlenecks to aging surfer hippies who will regale anyone willing to listen with stories of big waves and *hyper-cool* parties.

Day or night, the music is always playing at **Le Steir** *(7A place Terre au Duc; No phone; Bus 1, 2, 3, 4, 5, 6, 7, 8 to rue du Parc/Resistance; 9:30am-2am daily; V, MC EC)*, a German-looking pub with French-looking patrons who may glare at you if you go for the Touchmaster game. The nighttime crowd is much friendlier, with a mellow vibe of beer sipping and quiet chatter. It's really easy to find; less than a 2-minute walk from the cathedral.

LIVE MUSIC SCENE

Catching tunes in the flesh in Quimper tends to consist, more often than not, of "techno vibes" and "DJ stylin's" that harken back to the region's love of reggae and all things house. The best performers flock to **Le Calao** *(Rte. des Châteaux; No phone; Taxi by way of Pont L'Abbe to rte. des Châteaux; 10pm-3am daily; 40F cover before midnight, 80F midnight-close; V, MC, EC, AE)*, a three-story venue that, like a few other Quimper nightspots, boasts a park and swimming pool [see

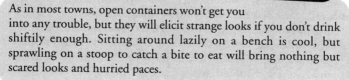

rules of the game

As in most towns, open containers won't get you into any trouble, but they will elicit strange looks if you don't drink shiftily enough. Sitting around lazily on a bench is cool, but sprawling on a stoop to catch a bite to eat will bring nothing but scared looks and hurried paces.

club scene, below]. The first floor is dedicated solely to techno and usually brings in the best live acts—DJs from Germany, France, and occasionally the States. On the upper levels you'll find a more clubby, dance-based vibe where the kids desperately attempt to get down while shaking their fists and heads to *la musique*. Don't waste your time looking for a bus—there are none. You have to take a taxi or get a ride in somebody's car. It's 9 miles west of Quimper, beside the highway leading to the sea.

club scene

The club circuit in Quimper is even more hit-or-miss than the bar scene, with only one legitimate *boite* in the city and a few more scattered around a short drive away. The pride (or the shame, according to some) of Quimper's post-bar life is **Naiades** *(Blvd. Creach Gwen; Tel 02/98-53-32-30; Bus 1 to Creach Gwen; 10pm-4am daily; 60F cover, includes one drink; V, MC, EC, AE)*, which is more of an amusement park fiasco than a nightclub. One wise Quimper resident noted that "you really only need to visit Naiades one time," and it's true. This is guaranteed to be one of the strangest nights you're likely to experience here. Not only is the club a standard shake-yer-booty kind of joint, it also houses a swimming pool with windows to the dance floor and an indoor park. Don't expect to see too many bathing beauties in the middle of the night; the pool is tiny and no one ever swims unless they're totally drunk. Once in a blue moon, a pie-eyed lass might flip off her bra and take a wee plunge, but don't get your hopes up, it's rare. The action is definitely concentrated on the moderately sized dance floor where an older crowd of folks dance to the beats in their heads and seem to ignore the beat pumping on the stereo. This is just as well, since the majority of DJ selections are outdated, "raise the hair on the back of the neck" numbers from the late '80s and early '90s. The crowd seems to dig it, though, which keeps Naiades rolling until the early morning.

festivals, cool annual events

Quimper's special ties to reggae and world music are made even more evident every summer at the **Parc des Expositions** *(First three weeks of August; Bus 3, 4, 5 to Croix des Gardens)*. Modeled after the larger international music festival in Rennes, Quimper's smaller and more subdued version is nonetheless a heavily attended and quality event which, surprise, surprise, features mostly rap, raggae, and templin acts from around the world. Locals will argue fiercely that their festival is far better than that of Rennes, and it's hard to have a conversation with anyone about music without the topic cropping up, solicited or not.

boy meets girl

The laid-back attitudes of Quimper's younger residents extends to their very friendly, unaggressive style of courting. A trip to a bar seldom ends in a torrid love affair in some artist's dusty garret...unless, that is, you want it to. Unlike the smooth talkers of Paris, the kids in Quimper are content to talk and let things happen. Those who find success are, as can be expected, those who know how to play it cool.

arts scene

Confined to a few small spaces along the rue Ste.-Catherine, the visual arts scene in Quimper suffers under the heavy hand of its ever-present rival, traditional blue and yellow pottery. Quimper is known for this chunky trademark, which chokes out the already small gallery spaces. One gallery that makes an effort at mixing several styles is the **Galerie Ste. Catherine** (*13 rue Ste. Catherine-pres Prefecture; Tel 02/98-90-18-22; Bus 1, 2, 3, 4, 5, 6, 7, 8 to Resistance; Tue-Sat, 10:30am-12:30pm, 2:30pm-7pm; EC, MC, V*). Here, between low ceilings and creaky floors, you find contemporary paintings, lithographs, and sketches by local artists in addition to bowls and plates. While the quality of the work is sometimes questionable, the attempt to bring some semblance of modern art into Quimper is definitely commendable.

The best way to take in the modern art of the town is to check out the **Centre d'Art Contemporain de Quimper** (*10 parc du 137eme R.I.; Tel 02/98-55-55-77; Bus 6, 8 to Pl. de la Tour D'Auvergne; Tue-Sat, 10am-12:30pm, 1:30pm-6pm; Sundays 2pm-5pm; www.le-quartier.net; 20F adults, 10F students, Sundays free*), adjacent to Molly Malone's Pub, a quarter-mile west of the town center. Here international (but usually regional) artists exhibit cutting-edge work, from the obsessively complex sculpture of Niek van de Steeg to the interior scenarios created by Tatiana Trouve. The curatorial staff keeps the center lively by changing shows frequently and continuously bringing in new talent, which is an impressive feat in an art world where galleries often compromise challenging new art for safe, public-friendly exhibitions.

gay scene

Unsurprisingly in a town with only a handful of good straight bars, the number of decent gay or lesbian places to hang out is miniscule. One, to be exact. Don't be scared off by the ever-present huge dog in the doorway of **L'Oreille Cassee** (*Ave. de la Gare/rue Artistide Briand; No phone; Bus 4, 6 to SNCF; 9am-2am daily; V, MC, EC*); the largely male crowd inside the thick, smokey haze is friendly and laid back. Most of the guys are regulars

12 hours in quimper

1. Climb **Mont Frugy** [see *neighborhoods, above*] with a walkman and your favorite mix tape, but don't peek until you get to the top and can look out over the spectacular town and countryside. If you're lucky and the timing is right, the perfect song and amazing view could bring tears to your eyes. Or simply a smile of physically-induced satisfaction.

2. Rest your legs and let technology do the work...Ride the top row of the carousel at **Place St. Corentin** and watch the people below sleep, eat, and talk on the benches.

3. Look at the huge allegorical paintings in the **Musée des Beaux Arts** [see *culture zoo, above*] and try to figure out the meanings, or make up a story of your own about the significance of the ever-present virginal figure descending through the clouds above the chaos of some random battlefield.

4. Walk into the cathedral [see *culture zoo, above*] after 6pm, when most of the visitors are gone, and check out the stained glass or sit down for a moment to collect your thoughts.

5. Go to a restaurant specializing in regional cuisine from the tourist guide, pretend you know what every descriptive number means on the oyster menu ("Aha, zee number three is my favorite!"), and spend a few *francs* on a plate of your own. The best place to sample the oysters is **Grand Café de Bretagne** *(18 rue du Parc; Tel 02/98-95-00-13; Noon-3pm and 7-11:30pm daily; Fixed-price menus 67-175F; MC, V)*, directly opposite the tourist office. You can slurp the succulent crustaceans for 48F per half-dozen in a belle-époque setting of polished brass, wood paneling, and etched mirrors. Ooh la la!

6. Head to **Molly Malone's** [see *bar scene, above*] to end the night in Irish-tinged splendor surrounded by the crazy patrons and ample stock of booze.

who seem to know each other. But unlike the folks at Le Steir, they welcome outsiders (with a slightly cold shoulder toward the ladies) with open arms.

CULTUre ZOO

Like many other towns, Quimper certainly has its share of cultural offerings. Two of the most interesting ones are opposite each other on the Place St. Corentin.

Musée des Beaux Arts *(40 place St-Corentin; Tel 02/98-95-45-20; Bus 3, 5, 7, 8 to St. Corentin; 10am-noon/2pm-6pm Wed-Mon; www. mairie-quimper.fr/musee; musee@mairie-quimper.fr; 25F, 15F for students)* houses an impressive collection of art with a special focus on the Pont Aven school started in the late 19th century by Paul Gauguin. Be sure to check out the exhibit devoted solely to this school, as well as the art nouveau/art deco section on the upper level. If it's contemporary art you seek, however, don't expect to find much of merit at Quimper's museum. Although it does a good job of compiling art from earlier periods, the small contemporary section on the second floor is haphazard and skippable.

The 13th-century **Cathedral St. Corentin** *(Place St. Corentin; Tel 02/98-95-06-19; Bus 3, 5, 7, 8 to St. Corentin; 9am-6:30pm daily; Free)* stands about 50 steps from the entrance to the museum and is easily identified by its two massive 250-foot towers. Even if churches aren't typically your bag, the incredible stained glass panels are a must-see—a far cry from some of the more run-of-the-mill mosaic patterns in other French cathedrals.

modification

The typical citizen of Quimper isn't exactly livin' it like he loves it with huge pierced ears, cheek spikes, or half sleeves, but if you feel the need to bleed, check out **Body Blue** *(Ave. de la Gare; Tel 06/68-72-15-89; Bus to SNCF; Mon-Sat, 2:30pm-10pm)*, a combo tattoo/piercing parlor that's only scary and dirty from the outside. The interior features the standard tattoo and piercing fare: dolphins, tribal art, and, of course, scary clowns with guns. It's about a 10-minute walk east of the center of town, but the place has had multiple addresses over the past few years—and could easily shift sites at any time without notice—so you might want to call before you show up.

sports

Aside from the aforementioned swimming pool that has made its way into the club life of Quimper, two traditional splash spectaculars exist within the city limits. The first, the **Piscine Aquarive** *(Blvd. de Creac'h Gwenn, Bus 1 to Aquarive; Tel 02/98-52-00-15; 10am-8pm daily; 40F)*, is located in the far south of town, near the university. It has several pools (including a shallow one for swimming laps and a deep one for diving), plus saunas, changing rooms, lockers, and a health-conscious snack bar. **Piscine Municipale** *(Bus 1, 8 to Piscine Municipale; Wed-Sat 3-6pm)* is more centrally located, but you can ony swim there two afternoons a week, and if hordes of screaming schoolchildren show up to splash—as they often do—the pool is closed to the public. You're much better off at Piscine Aquarive, unless you happen to be staying at the adjacent youth hostel, **Bois du Seminarie** [see *crashing*, below].

great outdoors

A really cool spot for hiking and biking is **Locronan,** a small coastal village about 20km (12.4 miles) northwest of Quimper. High on a hill, surrounded by lush farmland, Locronan is a throwback to the Middle Ages which looks like a stage set for *Sleeping Beauty.* The center of town is Grande Place, with remarkably well-preserved houses and flower gardens everywhere. And getting there is just as good as being there; hike, bike, or take a bus on a scenic inland route that cuts through the pastoral Breton countryside. About 6-8 buses per day make the 20-minute drive from Quimper to Locronan (23F one way). If you get bored hanging out in town, go to the **tourist office** *(Place de la Mairie; Tel 02/98-91-70-14)* and ask for a brochure about **Circuit pedestre,** the walking path that circles the town. You'll pass by all the major monuments, which are identified in the brochure. Still not walked out? Hit the **Montagne de Locronan** trail, beginning 2km (1.24 miles) east of town, to catch one of the most amazing panoramas in Brittany—both the farmland and the turbulent sea beyond. It's well worth the hike.

STUff

Maybe it's the natural beauty of the surrounding landscape that leads Quimperians to shun material comfort for the great outdoors, or perhaps the hipness of Paris doesn't reach this far. Whatever the reason, the shopping in Quimper is lackluster at best. Most stores tend to cluster on or near the Place Corentin and the cathedral, but the number of standouts for hip, new merchandise is decidedly few. Crystals, scary miniature dragons, pottery, and traditional threads are abundant along the **rue du Parc,** while other boutiques are randomly scattered around the cathedral and pedestrian zones.

▶▶**DUDS**
Some of the hippest women's clothing in Quimper hangs on the racks at **Chattawalk** *(53 rue Kereon, No phone; Bus 3, 5, 7, 8 to St. Corentin; 2-7pm Mon, 9:30am-12:30pm/2-7pm Tue-Sat; V, AE, MC, EC),* where

fashion

Overwhelmingly Maine hippie...not that they can help it, with the bloody miserable weather and the constant rain. Chunky alpaca sweaters, hemp bags, Aigle jackets for girls, track jackets (usually Lacoste or Adidas) for boys. For some reason your high school German teacher's velour tracksuits are still in style here; twentysomething, semi-hip-looking boys don't hesitate to rock the Herr's classic look. Tight, ultra-French trousers are only present to a small degree; it's usually far too cold to wear such flimsy material. Umbrellas and rain jackets are surprisingly obsolete in such a rainy climate—most people seem to have given in to the weather and instead walk around with wet heads and looks of smug complacency.

cute pomo gear and reasonable prices blissfully meet....Think pucker-front shirts, straight skirts, mild tech stock, etc.

▶▶TYPICAL BRETON FARE

If you must give in to the urge to pick up some of the traditional wares of Quimper or Brittany in general, a good has-all stop is **L'Iris d'Argent** (*16 rue du Parc; No phone; Bus 1, 2, 3, 4, 5, 6, 7, 8 to rue du Parc; 9am-noon/2-6:15pm Tue-Sat; DC, AE, V, MC, EC*). In the cluttered confines of this homey space, groovy Breton jewelry meets pottery meets postcards. The most impressive wares, naturally, are the jewels. Celtic-influenced silver bracelets and necklaces twist and curl in the window displays alongside deep amber amulets and earrings. Be sure to check out the postcard selection for some of the most amusing images of Brittany ever compiled in one store.

Eats

Brittany is known worldwide for the amazing oysters that leave the region by the truckload, so naturally most restaurants of any price level will have at least several oyster-based dishes on the menu. Just a short drive from the rocky Atlantic coast, Quimper is an ideal spot to sample this regional specialty. What also makes Quimper special is the number of quality restaurants and bake shops that crop up unexpectedly among the crowded and often mediocre restaurants "specializing" in shellfish.

▶▶CHEAP

While Quimper is stocked with the usual selection of *boulangeries* and *patisseries,* one stands out above the rest for quality eats. The **Artisan Boulanger** (*Ave. de la Gare/rue Artistide Briand; Bus 1-8 to SNCF; 6am-5pm Mon-Sat; 4-20F for bread or pastries; No credit cards*), has shelves overflowing with perfectly crusty baguettes and buttery chocolate croissants for under 5F. Eating one of the latter is almost a sickeningly sweet meal in itself. The bakery is a 5-minute walk east of the cathedral, along the road that leads to the train station. For some of Quimper's tastiest crêpes—probably the the least expensive meal in town—walk across the river (with the cathedral at your back) onto rue Ste.-Catherine, where you'll find a string of crêperies. You can get all kinds, from the hearty meal-in-itself variety to rich dessert crêpes, for as little as 8F (the bigger main-dish sort can cost up to 42F). Fattening? Forget about it—most Bretons eat at least two or three a day, and they look fabulous.

▶▶DO-ABLE

Chinatown (*15 blvd. de Amiral Kerguelen; Tel 02/98-95-58-68; Bus 3, 4, 5, 6, 7, 8 to Kerguelen; Noon-2pm/7-11pm daily; Closed Mon afternoon; 45-50F entrees, 110F prix fixe meal; All credit cards*) is a kitschy pan-Asian surprise, replete with dope interior design and traditional music. It's a toss-up whether the cheesy, brightly lit decor (reminiscent of a '50s sci-fi version of the future) and overly serious waitstaff are a bigger draw than the actual food. This is a happy alternative to oyster overkill. The mostly Vietnamese and Chinese dishes are generous, relatively affordable, and easy to decipher on the English/French menu. House specialties are the duck or chicken dishes; ask the waiter for specific suggestions.

▶▶**SPLURGE**

One of the best splurges in town is also a great value for what you get. **L'Assiette** *(5 bis rue Jean-Jaurès; Bus 7; Tel 02/98-53-03-65; Noon-2pm Mon-Sat; 7:30-10pm Wed-Sat; Fixed-price lunch 68F, fixed-price dinner 82F, dinner main course 100-125F; MC, V)* is a simple, down-to-earth place that has surprisingly excellent food. It is run by a local family—the Danielles—who are always friendly to all of the locals and visitors who fill their 55 seats every night. You'll get delicious Breton-style home cookery along with the Danielle family charm. "We're not too fancy," one of the family members says, "but we'll prepare you our best steaks, veal, and chicken, and we won't skimp on the portions." Go here when you're really hungry, and make sure you order the home-made soup—it's awesome.

crashing

For a town of moderate size, Quimper manages to hold onto a tradition of lodging that shuns many of the impersonal chain hotels cluttering other French cities. Even those chains that do enter Quimper somehow retain a taste of the heritage that makes the town special, whether it be through decoration or a knowledgeable hotel staff. A good guide to Quimper's hotels and hotel-restaurants can be picked up at the tourist office [see *need to know*, below]. It lists basic information about the city's lodging possibilities and provides a clear map for those interested in seeking out the best location. For the most part, any of the hotels along the avenue de la Gare, which turns into the avenue de la Liberation as it continues to the east, are affordable, comfortable, and close to the town center.

▶▶**CHEAP**

The cheapest accommodations in town are at the youth hostel at the **Bois du Seminaire,** *(6 ave. des Oiseaux; Tel 02/98-64-97-97; Bus 1, 8 to Piscine Municicpale; 70-185F per person; V, MC, AE, EC).* Unlike many other *auberges de jeunesses* in France, Quimper's youth hostel is actually located in mild proximity to the center of town. It's about a mile west of the town center; you can take the 1 or 8 bus, but it's not necessary—most locals walk it in 20 minutes. The location is cool—adjacent to the munic-ipal campground, which contains a swimming pool and a garden—but don't expect anything remotely fancy. This is about as simple a youth hostel as you'll find anywhere in France. There's a Spartan-looking com-munal kitchen, some coin-operated washing machines, and a major emphasis on the dorm-style living (rooms are for two, four, and eight). Don't forget the midnight curfew.

▶▶**DO-ABLE**

The fairly impersonal but clean and comfortable rooms at the **Relais Mercure** *(21 bis ave. de la Gare; Tel 02/98-90-31-71; Bus 1-8 to SNCF; 315-495F per person (all with private bath); V, MC, AE, EC)* are—except for the top floor—newly renovated, with comfortable beds and surprisingly spacious bathrooms. The Mercure's just a hop, skip, and a jump away from the train station—a big plus if you're only going to be in town for a day or two. Even for longer stays it's only a 10-minute walk from the major attractions in the *centre ville*.

▶▶**SPLURGE**

Next to a part of the old city ramparts, **Hôtel Gradlon** *(30 rue Brest; Bus 1 or 8; Tel 02/98-95-04-39; Fax 02/98-95-61-25; Closed Dec 20-Jan 22; 410-575F single or double; Breakfast 59F; DC, V)* is the best—and most welcoming—of the moderately priced hotels in Quimper. It's old-fashioned but not run-down at all; the 24 bedrooms (private showers) are extremely clean, and the traditional Breton furnishings make them feel really comfy-cozy. Most of the rooms are priced at the lower end of the scale (see above) except for one that has a brass bed and a Jacuzzi. The location is really great—a 3-minute walk northeast of the cathedral in the heart of the old town—and there are tons of cool cafes and brasseries nearby.

within 30 minutes

Quimper's proximity to the rugged western coast makes it a perfect jumping-off point for a day at the beach. The town is about 10 miles north of the nearest coastline where the beaches are known for pale-colored, very fine sands that attract huge crowds in summer (even when the weather is bad) and are almost deserted in winter. The closest beach-town to Quimper is **Benodet;** more remote outposts include **Île Tudy** and **Ste.-Marine,** which are separated from each other by about 5 miles of sandy beach. Almost all locals drive to the beach, but for 20-30F each way, you can take a bus from Quimper's **Gare Routière** *(immediately adjacent to the train station; Tel 02/98-90-88-89)* every 90 minutes during midsummer. Buses are marked with the final destination—usually Benodet/Beg Meil or Île Tudy/Ste.-Marine—so it's easy to see where they're headed. The beach scene here is nothing like Riviera beaches with cabanas and golden-skinned beach-boys serving up cocktails and rented towels. There's none of that—and no lifeguards either—so just pick a beach that appeals to you and hit the waves.

If you'd rather sail the sea than sleep on the beach next to it, try a boat trip from Benodet to the **Glénan Archipelago,** a rocky cluster of sand-ringed islands 9 miles off the coast. Most of the islands are undeveloped and uninhabited. You'll see lots of anchored yachts bobbing on the sea and excellent sandy beaches, but no facilities for year-round living. The only place where there is really any sign of "civilization" is the largest island, Saint-Nicolas, where there are a few summer homes scattered here and there, two cafes, and a couple of SCUBA-diving and sailing schools. The only time you can go there is between late June and mid-September, but it's really a welcome escape if you're maxed out on crowds, scenes, and sightseeing. Two outfitters sail from the Vieux-Port of Benodet every 90 minutes (110F round-trip): **Les Vedettes de l'Odet** *(Tel 02/98-57-00-58)* and **Vedettes Bigoudènes** *(Tel 02/98-66-23-46).*

need to know

Currency Exchange The best exchange rates can be had at Quimper's **ATMs** or **banks.** Some larger hotels also change traveler's checks, but they use the rates published in the newspaper, which are always worse than the ATMs.

Tourist Information The tourist office is located in a small building on the **Place de la Resistance** *(7 rue de la Deesse Place de la Resistance; Tel 02/98-53-04-05; Bus to Resistance; Mon-Sat, 9am-noon and 1:30pm-6pm Oct-Mar; 9am-12:30pm and 1:30pm-6:30pm Apr-Jun and Sep; 9am-7pm Jul & Aug; Open Sundays 10am-1pm May 1-Jun 15; 10am-1pm and 3pm-6pm Jun 15-Sep 15).* The office has a moderate selection of materials and usually only one English-speaking assistant, but all of the basic information on Quimper can be found here. They'll also make hotel reservations for you if you show up in person.

Public Transportation All bus lines are easy to access from the center of town, along the boulevard Amiral de Kerguelen. You can pick up a bus map at the *Office de Tourisme,* or call *02/-98-95-26-27* for other locations; the 7-10F bus fare cards can be purchased from the driver. Remember that buses in Quimper run on slightly different schedules than in other French towns, often stopping around 9pm during the week and earlier on the weekends.

Health and Emergency Emergency: *15;* police: *17;* fire: *18.* The hospital, **Hôpital Laennec** *(Ave. Yves Thepot; Bus 1 or 2 to Hôpital Laennec)* is a mile south of Quimper, beside the highway leading to Benodet.

Pharmacies Pharmacies are located everywhere throughout town; look for the **flashing green crosses.** The only 24-hour pharmacy is the **Pharmacie de Paris** *(32 place Terre au Duc; Tel 02/98-55-58-97; Bus 1-8 to rue du Parc; No credit cards)* and the 24-hour hours are loosely followed here. If it's closed, go to the police station for pharmaceutical assistance.

Telephone City code: *02;* information: *12;* international operator (USA): *Tel 00/33-12-11.* Phone cards are available at most tobacco shops, post offices, and magazine shops in 50F and 100F denominations.

Airports Aeroport Quimper *(Tel 02-98-94-30-30)* is 5 miles west of the center of town on the way to Brest and is easily reached by taking the shuttle bus from the train station, but there's no real schedule, so you can't count on it. The local bus company, **Transport Lecoeur** *(Tel 02/98-54-40-15),* directs its regular buses to detour into the airport to pick up passengers when a plane lands, but this service is irregular. The best way to get to and from the airport is to take a taxi. You won't have any trouble spotting them; they line up whenever a plane lands to pick up passengers. Planes arrive daily from most major cities in France.

Trains The **Gare Routiere** *(Tel 02/98-90-88-89)* in Quimper is located just south of the town center, on the Odet River. Trains arrive several times daily from Rennes *(3 hours; 150F one way)* and Paris *(6 hours; 375F one way TGV).*

Bus Lines Out of the City There is no real bus station. What buses there are pull into the area of the **Gare Routière** *(Tel 02/98-90-88-89 for bus info)* and let off passengers immediately adjacent to the train depot. There are almost no buses servicing Quimper from outside its *departement* (Le Finistère). Bus service is mainly limited to the nearby villages and some of the beach towns in summer.

Boats Don't bother asking the tourist office about boat rentals; they'll just tell you to go to Benodet, where you can arrange rentals from private boat owners during the summer. Hundreds of yachts—many belonging to wealthy Parisians—are moored in marinas in or near Benodet, the beach resort closest to Quimper. You can rent one of them—or other sailboats and motorcraft of all shapes and sizes— through **Calypso** *(Port de Plaisance, Benodet; Tel 02/98-57-15-82)* or **First Bretagne Charter** *(2 ave. de l'Odet, Benodet; Tel 02/98-57-08-44)*.

Bike/Moped Rental Quimper has no locations to rent motorized scooters. You can rent a bike for the day or weekend at **Cycles Lennez** *(13 rue Aristide Briand; Tel 02/98-53-84-41; Bus 1-8 to SNCF; 100-500F)* and **Torch'VTT** *(58 rue de la Providence; Tel 02/98-53-84-41; Bus 3, 5 to Rigoule; 60-400F)*.

Laundry Centrally located and cheap laundry service can be found at the **Lavarie** *(4 place de la Gare; Bus 1-8 to SNCF)*. Prices run from 20 to 40F, depending on size of the load; you can also drop off your dirty duds for a slightly elevated price.

Postal The main post office is **La Poste-Recette Principale** *(37 Amiral de Kerguelen; Tel 02/98-64-28-50; 8am-7:30pm Mon-Fri, 8am-noon Sat)*.

Internet See *wired*, above.

rennes

In Rennes, the grayish brown sky melts into tired looking buildings—a muted palette of postwar facades and countless clouds of cigarette smoke fused together around the rushing canals and scurrying locals. At first glance, Rennes seems like an unfriendly and even hostile city. When the temperature drops, the chill that rises from the water seems to be reflected in the hardened faces of the locals. You find yourself asking where the cheer is and not coming up with any answers. But if you stick it out past the first instinct to flee, you'll realize that Rennes has more to offer than perhaps any other city in western France, despite its tough appearance. If you don't get it at first, that's because locals like to play it low key: They don't exactly take the colonial Williamsburg approach of sidewalk banners and prolific "We love our town" signs. The city pride lives in the hearts of the people instead.

Even so, it's not an easy city to love. With the exception of the massive **Jardin des Plantes le Thabor** [see *culture zoo*, below], you'll find precious little green space, and even the water flowing through the canals and rivers, though featured on the tourist map in a cheerful cerulean blue, is a muddy shade of fish-scale brown.

This lackluster urban landscape can make it easy to get bummed out in the early hours of a visit to Rennes, but don't lose the faith right away. Like London, Dublin, Berlin, or any city that has suffered the abuse of war or climate, Rennes has more to offer than its ugly mask suggests, and its gritty surface holds together a city full of change and excitement. Why do major acts like Oasis and big-name DJs from around the world choose to play Rennes when they tour France? Because the kids in this city are cool as shit, know their music, their fashion, and their culture...and they aren't afraid to show it. It might also have something to do with the sheer numbers a band can pull in from the 40,000-plus students at **L'Universite de Rennes.** This large institution is made up of several smaller colleges devoted to science, engineering, liberal arts, mathematics, and other studies.

The average Rennes local has the same diverse tastes as any other eclectic, urban European, but with an underground twist. Nothing is more revered here than the slightly subversive; it doesn't matter what the cause. If it slams back at the majority, someone in Rennes will embrace it. Perhaps that's why rebellious minds from all over France come here, and why there's a hotbed of activity for a young traveler. While the adult tourists flock to the major cultural spots, the real action is on the streets, which are crawling with quirky kids. Extreme styles rage here, there are lots of bars, and there's always something going down (from fistfights to bonfires) on the happening **rue St.-Michel.**

The best way to find out about what's doing is to talk to people. Tons of publications come out detailing what's going on in the city, but none do a very good job of describing anything other than what movies are playing in the big cinemas or what the major political crisis of the week is. A decent pick from the melting pot of print is *La Griffe,* a free weekly cultural journal that you can pick up at the tourist office or various spots around town. It's in French, but its daily listings of concerts, gallery events, clubs, and miscellaneous *spectacles* are easy to follow.

neighborhoods

Rennes, when seen as a grid of streets on a map, looks about as easy to comprehend as the troubleshooting guide to a PC. Rivers break apart into little vein-like canals, which in turn shoot off in completely different directions. Segmented into neighborhoods, however, it really isn't that difficult. The **Vilaine River** runs east to west and cuts the town in half, providing the starting point for the center city, extending north and south.

The portion of the center city directly south of the river contains several different types of cityscape mashed tightly together, and at times unpleasantly. The **avenue Jean Janvier** is a major route towards the *quais* and the nightlife north of the river (running over the Viliane as a bridge), and leads directly to the train station at its southern tip. It's best to avoid the area west of the station past the main post office, however. This rather shady commercial/industrial wasteland, while safe during the day, can get a bit sketchy after hours.

North of the river are some of the main gathering places for both the young and old of Rennes, like the **place de la Mairie,** [see *hanging out,* below]. The major shopping streets are **rue de Coetquen** and **rue St.-Melaine** where you can find clothing boutiques, shoe stores, and book shops aplenty. Slightly farther north are some of the main drags for bar activity, including **rue St.-Melo** and the much loved and probably much more hated **rue St.-Michel** [see *only here,* below], running north-south for one block between **place St.-Michel** and **place Ste.-Anne.** Rue St. Michel and its extension, rue St.-Malo are known as *les rues de la soif* (streets of thirst) because of the dozen or so bars on either side of them. Bar crawlers love the rowdiness but neighbors hate the noise. *C'est la vie.* The bus system in Rennes covers alot of ground and is very reliable.

hanging OUT

The ominous postwar facades lining the streets of Rennes don't exactly invite you into their arms in the same way that the cozy nooks of a more intimate French city might. The banks of the Vilaine, rather than hosting scores of lounging students and tourists, often remain empty—save the odd youngster sneaking a cigarette drag while his parents shop on the streets above. The best places to hang out, as a result, tend to be the more intimate and friendly such as bars or in courtyards directly adjacent to large public structures.

One such place is the **place de la Mairie,** the large gravel courtyard between the Hôtel de Ville and **L'Opera de Rennes** [see *culture zoo,* below]. Most of the youth of Rennes meet up at the Place before heading north for barhopping or an evening meal, so linger and mingle here to pick up suggestions for a night out. The Place also offers a respite from the heavy shopping that takes place on the bordering streets—a perfect spot to drop the shopping bags and relax.

The buildings of the university are spread out enough to discourage the sort of mixing and mingling that you see at other schools of higher learning; students instead tend to congregate at their favorite bar or brasserie. If so inclined, however, the outdoor-lovin' student can take a quick jaunt across the boulevard de la Duchesse Anne to the landscaped grounds of the **Jardin des Plantes le Thabor** [see *culture zoo,* below]. Most of the students disappear in summer, so student life is not nearly as vital in July and August as it is the rest of the year. The bar scene really comes to life from autumn to late spring.

wired

A small and usually smoke-filled spot to, as the French say, *envoyer un e-mail* is at **Cybernet on Line** *(22 rue St.-Georges; Tel 02/99-36-37-41; 25F per 1/2 hour).* It has all the trappings of a cybercafe—the smoke, the loud kids playing destructive computer games, and the music—minus any semblance of food or drink. It's more of a shop than a cafe. They also do photocopying, tee shirt imprinting, and word processing for variable fees.

fIVE-O

The law enforcers of Rennes have to be more on their toes than the police in other towns in the region. It's not that crime runs rampant, mind you, but simply that the relatively larger population naturally leads to more disorderly conduct. Police are visible, if not overly talkative or friendly, and do a good job of covering ground. As a result, streets are well patrolled and safe; however, as in any urban area, you'll need some common sense when traversing the more desolate areas immediately south of the river.

bar scene

Rennes offers ample opportunity to get your drink on, with a bar for nearly every taste. These alcohol-servin' venues are lined up shoulder to shoulder along the rue St.-Michel, which fills up with people, mostly under 35, every night of the week. Many good—and less advertised—bars are tucked away a bit farther north of the St.-Michel commotion on the streets that branch off the place Hoche and rue St.-Malo. Here you can find a more mellow vibe, where students gravitate to their favorite dive night after night.

A good starting point to a night of debauchery—named after the more peaceful city gardens—**Jardin des Plantes** *(32 rue St.-Melaine; Tel 02/99-38-74-46; noon-2am daily; No credit cards)*, is a dark and homey setting where you can warm up for the night ahead. Built into a wood-timbered, Germanic *maison,* the bar stands out on the primarily boutique-y street with its commanding architecture and the raucous music escaping with every swing of the heavy door. The large wrap-around bar and spacious back room make this spot ideal for the live rock, pop, and world music acts that drop in every few weeks. Schedules for these and other citywide music events can be picked up near the entrance—for the concert-crazed traveler, this is one of the best spots in town to scope out upcoming tunefests.

If you're looking for music that's just as loud but slightly less mainstream, head to **Trinquette** *(26 rue St.-Malo; 5pm-2am daily; No credit cards)*, where a small but smug crowd of thuggy, old school punks exchange arch glances and knock back beers. Bleached hair, ratty sweatshirts, and body jewelry abound in this one-room dive covered in weird pseudo-graffiti. No one seems to pay any mind to the strange paintings, however, because the focus is on catching up with friends and harassing the bartender for song requests on the CD player—most of which are Clash bootlegs interspersed with the occasional newer hardcore favorite. No live music here, though.

Take a few steps farther down rue St.-Malo to enter a completely different world where liberty spikes and gauged ears are replaced by platform

rennes

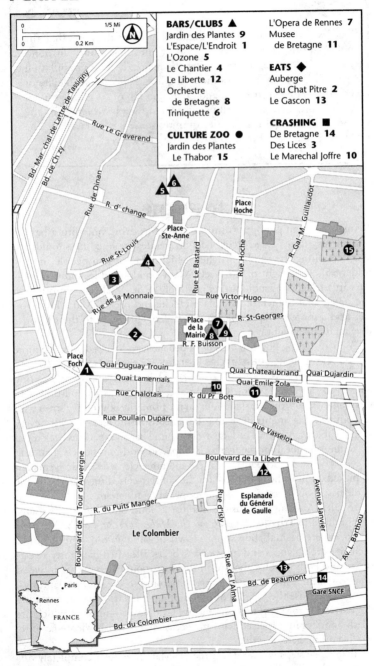

BARS/CLUBS ▲
Jardin des Plantes **9**
L'Espace/L'Endroit **1**
L'Ozone **5**
Le Chantier **4**
Le Liberte **12**
Orchestre
  de Bretagne **8**
Triniquette **6**

CULTURE ZOO ●
Jardin des Plantes
Le Thabor **15**

L'Opera de Rennes **7**
Musee
  de Bretagne **11**

EATS ◆
Auberge
  du Chat Pitre **2**
Le Gascon **13**

CRASHING ■
De Bretagne **14**
Des Lices **3**
Le Marechal Joffre **10**

sandals and midriff tops. **L'Ozone** (*9 rue St.-Malo; 5pm-2am daily; No credit cards*) jumps on the Latin music bandwagon, but doesn't quite take the clientele along for the ride. From Ricky Martin hits to more obscure salsa and merengue jams, the theme is consistently south of the border, but don't go in expecting professional booty-shakers. The brightly colored bar seems to entice patrons to remain seated rather than move to the music. L'Ozone is, however, a chatty and accessible place to hang out if you'd rather meet people than bust out your merengue.

LIVE MUSIC SCENE

Rennes attracts a number of world-recognized music acts throughout the year, whether it be to the **Transmusicales festival** [see *festivals & events,* below] or to the rock concerts held both at bars and bigger venues throughout town.

Unlike many of the stuffier orchestral ensembles of traditional European fame, the **Orchestre de Bretagne** (*42A rue St.-Melaine; Tel 02/99-275-282; Showtimes vary; www.orchestre-de-bretagne.com; 150F for youth pass to five shows, 450-1200F for 5+ show passes; All credit cards*) consists of a group of mostly young musicians who don't hesitate to stray from the beaten path. Beethoven and Bach are easily paired with lesser knowns like Louise Farrenc and Jean Cras. Unsurprisingly in a town as heritage-proud as Rennes, French composers are well represented.

Le Liberte (*Esplanade Gal de Gaulle; Tel 02/99-85-84-83; Showtimes vary; Tickets 50F and up*) books acts from Oasis to DJ Clue in a modest space near the Gare SNCF, on the southern edge of town (easily walkable from the town center). A surprising find in a seemingly out-of-the way French town, this venue brings concert-goers from all of Brittany and France to the streets of Rennes. Crowds on the night of a show can reach the high hundreds, which afterwards spill into a city which has come to accept the raucous attitudes of youth.

FESTIVALS, COOL ANNUAL EVENTS

During the first week of December, Rennes shuts down to celebrate the **Transmusicales** festival. This joyous musical event is seen as a "good dose of sun before the winter"—a chance for locals and throngs of visitors alike to drink in the fun before buttoning up their coats and working through the harsh winter. Global bands and performers from Bjork and Nirvana to Massive Attack and Marquis de Sade have shown up to celebrate with the town. After more than 20 years of the festival, it arguably remains the most anticipated event in Rennes.

club scene

Most nightclubs in Rennes are located around the hub of activity that is rue St.-Michel.

For furious, beat-driven clubbing, check out **Le Chantier** *(18 carrefour Jouaust—near Place des Lices; Tel 02/99-31-58-18; 7pm-9pm and 10pm-1am daily; 60-80F; www.rennet.org/culture/chantier)* where the DJs throw up an open mix of house, techno, straight electronica, jungle, and trance. The crowd is an eclectic mix of youngsters and slightly older, Eurotrash clubgoers who show up to support their favorite DJ—never anyone too famous, but beloved all the same. Keep in mind that these intense record spinnin' dudes (the ladies seem, sadly, to be ignored at the decks) go on after the 10pm reopening, so unless you're just taking it easy it's best to wait a bit before plunking down your cash.

To keep the party moving deep into the night, head for the "deep house" at **L'Espace/L'Endroit** *(45 blvd. de la Tour d'Auvergne; Tel 02/99-30-21-95; 11pm-5am daily; 60-90F)*. For twenty years this swanky space has been keeping its patrons happy with varied nights of diverse musical categories. For the most part, expect house mixes and typical Euro DJ cuts; although some evenings feature concert performances from rock, jazz, and rap artists. The cooly styled and dimly lit atmosphere makes it easy to feel comfortable either sitting and schmoozing or twisting and shouting—just remember that everyone here knows the words to every song (if there are any, that is), so it's probably best to catch the chorus before letting loose with the vocal stylings.

arts scene

Some of the more cutting-edge arts expositions are set up by the University of Rennes and feature not only student art, but genuinely intriguing conceptual contemporary art by outsider artists. One venue where you can catch such action is the **Galerie Art & Essai** *(19 ave. de Flandres-Dunkerque; Bus 8 or 16; Tel 02/99-14-11-42; 1pm-6pm Tue-Fri and 2pm-5pm Sat)*, where young, cutting edge artists display their work alongside emerging scientists and engineers of the university. The space is a successful merger of science and art for the Renaissance man or woman. Most exhibitions lean toward the social and political, which can be a bit heavy-handed, but are balanced nicely with highly conceptual or sometimes just plain amusing installation pieces. The Galerie is in the University sector *(La Ville Jean),* a 15-minute bus ride northwest from the center of town.

gay scene

Cafe Concert *(Rue St.-Michel; 5pm-2am; No credit cards)* is not explicitly gay, but the attractive queer waiters and barstaff don't hurt the subliminal vibe. A minimally snobby doorman scopes your entrance to the bar, but doesn't really give the halt sign to anyone except drunken fools who try to stagger in from the street. The crowd inside is mostly in their

only here

Yes, yes, we've mentioned it a million times already—but the **rue St.-Michel** truly *is* unique. In very few other cities is a street simultaneously so loved and so hated, and in no other place are the crusty hippie/punk hybrids so prevalent. All of the attitude of Rennes is compacted into a time bomb here. Sneers, jeers, and wine bottles fly even on a slow night, and if you're lucky you can catch one of the mini-fueds which have a tendency to erupt into shouting matches between rival groups before the police come to break it up. Rest assured that some kind of sidewalk shenanigans start up—whether out of sheer boredom or bitter spite, who knows—as soon as the sun goes down.

20s and early 30s, male, and extremely Euro. Fitted black trousers, collared shirts, and nice shoes are expected, although dressing under par won't get you turned away—it'll simply ensure that you remain outside the action. The crowd thickens around midnight, when clubby house music pumps over the system and people start to leave their booths for a little alcohol-induced dancing between tables. Tables are often rented out on the weekends for private parties, in which groups of smiling, well-dressed gay men and their stylish female friends sip tall ones behind the cushy booths. Also worth checking out: the most visible gay disco around, **Le Batchi** *(34 rue Vasselot; Tel 02/99-79-62-27; 10pm-3am Wed-Sun; 20-40F cover),* and a busy mingle-and-meet market, **La Bernique Hurlante** *(40 rue de St.-Malo, Tel 02/99-36-21-12; 7:30pm-1am; No cover).*

There isn't a noticeable lesbian bar scene in Rennes, but **Femmes Entre-Elles** *(La Maison des Jeunes, La Paillette; Tel 02/99-59-50-32),* a municipally funded group, throws drink-and-dance parties for women. For more information on Renne's gay scene, write to **Collective Lesbienne & Gay Pride** *(B.P. 3743, 35037 Rennes CEDEX).* Don't bother looking them up in a phone book—they don't take calls.

CULTURE ZOO

Not surprisingly in a city the size of Rennes, many opportunities exist to indulge one's cultural fetishes. From botanical gardens to world class museums, the selection can seem staggering, but a few standouts do exist within the city confines.

L'Opera de Rennes *(Place de la Mairie; Tel 02/99-28-55-87; Evening showtimes daily, exact times vary; Tickets 40F and up; V, MC, AE, DIN):* If you love opera, or if you happened to pack an extra Yves Saint Laurent

fashion

Rennes fashion may come as a shock to you after spending time in the smaller cities of Brittany and the nearby Loire Valley. In such a large city, the extreme styles which are absent in rural France crop up more forcefully than a Tyson blow to the head. Hardcore punks, skaters, mods, and even the occasional thug make their presence felt in the damp streets surrounding the Vilaine, while even the more conservative locals display a basic sense of style. An interesting sub-group crawling the pavement are the everpresent packs of bratty, Pokemon-age boys who rock sporty Adidas tracksuits or sweatshirts and toss insulting comments to passersby.

gown and want to show it off in the front row (or you simply want to spend a night out in something a bit flashier than the outfit that hasn't left your body in six days), why not try a night at the opera? This particular opera house has a tragic history filled with flames and reconstructions. Only 20 years after it was built in 1836, fire broke out, and a new building rose from the ashes. The renovations done in 1999—including a completely revamped technical system and improved seating—have made the opera house one of the most envied in all of France.

Jardin des Plantes du Thabor *(5 blvd. de la Duchesse Anne; 7:15am-9pm daily; Free admission):* Sauntering through these sprawling provincial gardens is a beautiful and free way to spend an hour or two outdoors. It has three distinct sections—a French classical garden, an English garden with fountains and exotic trees, and a standard botanical garden. On a sunny day these green spaces overflow with visitors both human and animal, losing themselves on the winding paths and under enormous trees. The jardin is also a perfect spot for the hopeless romantic: The Thabor's rose garden, dotted with classical statues, is enticing both visually and sensually.

Musée de Bretagne *(20 quai Emile Zola; Tel 02/99-28-55-84);* History buffs and philistines alike will find something of interest in this museum devoted to the culture and history of Brittany. If only to gain a further clue to Rennes' unique heritage—from the traditional bonnets and dress to the colloquial language—this cultural site is a must-see. Rotating exhibitions give an account of daily life in Brittany through the ages, including an interesting look at an artist's studio. To indulge your inner nerd, don't miss the collection of Gallic coins spanning several centuries, which might make you wish for the abolition of paper money altogether.

Sport

Test your mental prowess along with those hefty biceps with **Vertical Quest Loisirs** *(32 rue de la Marbaudais; Tel 02/99-38-79-78)*. They lead rock-climbing expeditions in and around Rennes, but they're tough to catch—their office is open about three nights a week for about an hour. The usual routine: You call, you leave a message, and they call you back.

Stuff

Most stores in Rennes have a tired feeling; the same boutiques that can be found in any number of French cities—the Pimkies, the Mod (fill in the blank here), and the Galeries Lafayettes. The city's posh shopping street is the rue le Batard, a pedestrian street adjacent to Town Hall (La Mairie). The street for hip-central stores is rue St.-Melaine, which stretches from La Vieille Ville to the Jardin des Plantes du Thabor.

▶▶DUDS

Sure, they can be found in every city, but the **Boutique Lacoste** *(4 rue Nationale; Tel 02/99-78-29-00; 10am-noon and 1pm-7pm daily)* in Rennes seems to be one of the better choices for clothes. Lacoste happens to be one of the few of the French chains to offer clothes of actual quality—at a price, of course.

▶▶TUNES

CD Bulle *(25 rue St. Melaine; Tel 02/99-27-76-70; 4-7pm Mon, 2-7pm Tue & Wed, 1-7pm Thur & Fri, 2-7pm Sat)* has a very hip feel, from the staff to the kids perusing the aisles of music. It leans toward electronic and trance, as evidenced in the dragging cuffs of the raver cargo pants drooping off the majority of the customers. It's on the street that stretches from La Vieille Ville westward toward the harbor.

▶▶CRAFTY

For locally crafted Breton pottery, sculptures, weavings, and artwork, take your francs to **Couleurs de Celtie** *(35 rue Vasselot; Tel 02/99-78-24-60; Mon-Sat 10am-6pm)* in the center of town, near the Champ de Mars, or **Ti Breiz** *(2 place Hoche; Tel 02/99-79-17-83; Mon-Sat 10am-6pm)* near town hall and the Parlement de Bretagne.

Eats

Finding places to eat in Rennes is never a headache as long as you're open to new possibilities. From themed joints to straight-up French fare, tasty and reasonably priced meals can be had throughout the city.

▶▶CHEAP

If you've always wanted to play the badass but aren't quite ready to post bail, a meal at **La Banque** *(5-7 aliée Rallier du Baty; Tel 02/99-78-13-13; Noon-2pm and 7pm-midnight Mon-Sat, closed Sat afternoon; 55-120F)* might suffice. In an old prison, this small restaurant relies on its location for publicity, and its solid chefs for quality. La Banque is actually named in honor of the owner's banking ancestors rather than any fugitive relatives or iron bar settings, though the menu contains surprises. There are choices for almost any taste—from pizzas and sandwiches, to seafood and meats. If you like a little music with your meal, go on a Saturday night to catch local DJs doing their thing on the tables.

▶▶**DO-ABLE**

When you need a little gastronomic reminder that you're vacationing in France, nothing brings the point home better than a good meal from the southwest. At the recently renovated **Le Gascon** (15 blvd. Beaumont; Tel 02/99-30-85-80; Closed Sun; 60-180F), choose from a variety of traditional plates, including foie gras and *cassoulet* (a stew, usually of beans and meat). The small dining room provides a cozy eating experience and soft lighting for any gathering.

Can't make it to the Renaissance Faire this year? Head back to the Middle Ages at **Auberge du Chat Pitre** (18 rue du Chapitre; Tel 02/99-30-36-36; Closed Sundays; 120-160F), where you can munch on "medieval cuisine" in a cool themed atmosphere. The chefs here stick to kettle creations: stews, broths, and other steaming soups. You'll also find a variety of regional foods on the menu to carve up with your stocky utensils, from oysters to foie gras.

crashing

Rennes sprawls enough to warrant some serious consideration when choosing a hotel. A handful of good hotels sit directly across the Place de la Gare from the train station, but it can be a bit of a pain to make the 20-minute walk home after a late night at most major nighttime spots. It's definitely do-able, but not terribly well advised after several drinks. If you must hoof it back to the hotel, however, stick to the main routes along the river or avenue Jean-Janvier...or just bring a friend. However, there are many more first-rate hotels closer to the river and the center of town, which are definitely a better choice if you plan to spend more than a night in town. Most of them serve complimentary breakfast, which consists of a pot of coffee, tea, or chocolate accompanied by a baguette, butter, and jam. In rare instances, you might get a slice of cheese and ham as well.

▶▶**CHEAP**

Situated in an ideal location to catch any buses along the Place de la Republique, and in close proximity to the shopping and random fun around Place de la Mairie, **Le Marechal Joffre** (6 rue du Marechal Joffre; Tel 02/99-79-37-74; 130F single without bath, 175F single with bath, 175F double without bath, 220F double with bath; Breakfast 30F; V, MC) is a small, simple, but affordable base from which to explore Rennes. All rooms are humbly furnished, have cable access, and surprisingly comfortable beds. The hotel doesn't have its own restaurant, but the hungry traveler can grab breakfast.

▶▶**DO-ABLE**

For a charming room just seconds from the train station, book a space at **De Bretagne** (7 bis place de la Gare; Tel 02/99-31-48-48; 240-300F, all with private bath; Breakfast 36F; AE, V, MC, EC), where a helpful staff makes sure your stay in Rennes is a pleasant one. All rooms are newly refurbished and equipped with cable TVs and breakfast is available daily in the cheerful and bustling dining area on the main floor.

One of the best finds in Rennes for location and price alone is **Des Lices** *(7 place des Lices; Tel 02/99-79-14-81; 270-315F single, 290-340F double; Breakfast 34F; V, MC)* the perfect spot to lay your bags if you seek the nighttime chaos of place des Lices and rue St.-Michel. The hotel pleases the younger generation yet again in its choice of cable service, opting not only for the standard channels but also for *Canal Plus* and satellite TV—ensuring that any visitors too hungover from the previous nights barcrawl can enjoy a quiet morning/afternoon with the remote control. You'll also feel in good company with the other cost-conscious semi-poor young travelers shacking up here. True, you might want to attack them for running through the halls and shouting in their native languages while you're trying to catch some sleep, but hey, it's the atmosphere, right?

Need To Know

Currency Exchange You can change traveler's checks or cash at most hotels here, but check out **ATMs** or **banks** for the best rate. You can find a good concentration of these cash machines around the town square and the *Hotel de Ville.* There is also an ATM at the train station, which unfortunately seems to be out of service more often than other machines in town.

Tourist Information The **tourist office** is located in a newly renovated spot in the Vieille, very close to the cathedral. *(11 rue St.-Yves; Tel 02/99-67-11-11; 9am-7pm Mon-Sat, 11am-6pm Sun and holidays; infos@tourisme.rennes.com).* The brown, unobtrusive building is easy to miss in the melee of construction outside, but once you're inside it's easy to navigate. The staff is mostly under 30 and very knowlegeable about both Rennes and the surrounding region.

Public Transportation All municipal buses of Rennes are operated by a government agency called **STAR** *(Place de la Mairie; Tel 02/99-79-37-37).* There is bus service throughout the entire city 6am-10pm daily, but they cover only the major neighborhoods 10pm-12:30am. Tickets can be purchased on board for 6.50F per ride, or 51F for a *carnet* of 10 tickets, available at the STAR office. Cabs are more frequent than in many other cities, most leaving from the train station. However, you can call for a car *(Tel 02/99-30-87-80)* anytime of the day or night.

Health and Emergency Police: *17;* fire: *18;* ambulance: *15.* The main hospital of Rennes is **Hôpital Pontchalliou** *(Rue Louis Guilloux; Tel 02/99-28-43-44 or 02-99-28-43-45 for info or emergencies).* It's in the University sector *(La Ville Jean),* about a 12-minute bus ride (lines 8 or 16) northwest of the center of town.

Pharmacies Pharmacies are located throughout the city; look for the **flashing green cross.**

Telephone City code: *02;* information: *12;* international operator (USA): *Tel 00/33-12-11.* Phone cards are available at most tobacco shops, post offices, and magazine shops in 50F and 100F denominations.

Airports Ten minutes south of the center city, **L'Aeroport de Rennes St. Jacques** *(11 ave. Joseph Le Brix, 35136 St. Jacques de la Lande; Tel 02/99-29-60-00; aeroport@rennes.cci.fr)* services all of France and much of western Europe. The airport can be reached easily either by taxi or **bus** *(lines 57 or 58 from Place de la Republique).*

Trains The train station in Rennes, **La Gare SNCF** *(Place de la Gare; Tel 08/36-35-35-35 for info)* is located at the intersection of **avenue Jean Janvier** and **place de la Gare.** Warning: It's easy to confuse the train and bus stations because there names are so similar and they are both located on the Place de la Gare, on the southern edge of town (a 20-minute walk from the center). Remember that the train station is **La Gare SNCF** and the bus station is **La Gare Routière.**

Bus Lines Out of the City Most travelers coming into Rennes from outside the *département* arrive by train, as Rennes is the rail center-piece for all of Brittany. Buses departing from the **Gare Routière,** immediately adjacent to the **Gare SNCF,** tend to go only to nearby towns and villages not serviced by the train. Most buses that run inside of the town of Rennes depart from the **STAR** depot in front of the Hôtel de Ville.

Bike/Moped Rental Rent bicycles of all kinds, including mountain bikes and scooters, from **Guédard Cycles** *(13 blvd. Beaumont; Tel 02/99-30-43-78).*

Laundry Take your dirty clothes to the local coin-operated laundromat: **Lavomatique** *(Place de Bretagne; No phone; Open daily 7am-11pm).*

Postal The main post office is located on the **Place de la Republique,** between the quai Emile Zola and rue Pre Botte.

Internet See *wired,* above.

normandy

normandy

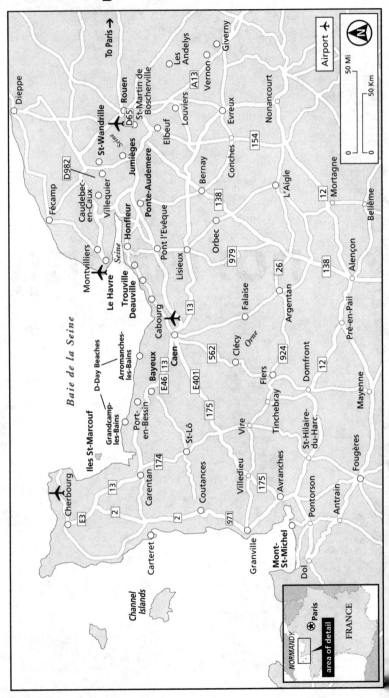

history hasn't been kind to rocky, rough-hewn Normandy—from the Vikings who first invaded the area 10 centuries ago, to the Allied forces that landed on the soft dune beaches on June 6, 1944 in that D-Day invasion we've all heard so much about. Bombing runs before and during that offensive flattened huge parts of **Le Havre, Caen,** and **Rouen,** and the battle that would finally liberate France from Germany cost 100,000 lives.

Since then, the cities in this northern region bordering the English Channel have been painstakingly rebuilt, and a few important landmarks miraculously survived the destruction. These include the fortress-like château and abbeys of William the Conqueror in Caen and the Cathédrale de Notre Dame in Rouen. Parts of Rouen were spared a good deal of destruction, and it still has some of its original old narrow streets and half-timbered buildings, so old and crooked they look like they could have inspired Cubism. You can also visit the ancient seaside abbey at **Mont Saint Michel** and Monet's old house in **Giverny,** both untouched by the war.

Keeping with the stereotype for northern France, kids in Normandy are generally less talkative upon first introduction, but warm up quickly after some conversation. Generally youth subculture in Normandy's larger regional capitals is decently developed. The most lively town for nightlife is Rouen, which is also the most appealing architecturally. Le Havre has a small number of interesting bars and concert venues, while Caen is more interesting for its tourist sites. But don't expect to do a lot of serious clubbing. When the weather is right, Le Havre's beach shines brightly, awash in a unique white light. When the sun fades behind gray clouds, Le Havre, like the region as a whole, can become depressive in a uniquely northern European way.

If you read French, ***www.lanormandie.net*** is a good resource for Normandy, with interesting articles on local attactions and hotels. For the linguistically impaired, the Official Normandy Tourist Board, the **Comité Régional de Tourisme de Normandie** *(14 rue Charles Corbeau, F27000 Evreux; Tel 02/32-33-79-00, Fax 02/32-31-19-04; normandy@imanginet.fr, www.normandy-tourism.org),* can also provide a wealth of information via e-mail or post.

getting around the region

Regionally a system of rail and bus lines connects all the major towns of both *Haute* (High) and *Basse* (Lower) *Normandie.* The trains tend to be faster, but occasionally require annoying transfers. Even more frustrating is the bus system, which runs locally but not inter-departmentally. For example, you can take a bus from Le Havre to Rouen, but not from

TRAVEL TIMES

* TGV (Fast Train—more expensive)

	Rouen	Giverny	LeHavre	Caen	Cherbourg	Mont St-Michel	Paris
Rouen	-	:40*	1:10	2:00	3:30	2:30*	1:18
Giverny	:40*	-	1:50*	2:10*	3:30*	3:00*	:50*
Le Havre	1:10	1:50*	-	1:10*	2:40*	2:30*	2:00
Caen	2:00	2:10*	1:10*	-	1:30	1:15*	1:50
Cherbourg	3:30	3:30*	2:40*	1:30	-	1:40*	3:30
Mont St. Michel	2:30*	3:00*	2:30*	1:15*	1:40*	-	3:15*

Rouen to Caen, because Caen is in Calvados and Rouen is in Seine-Maritime. Still, the bus is the fastest means of transportation between Le Havre and Caen. The best way to get around Normandy is by bike or by car. It's easiest to use ***www.bison-fute.equipement.gouv.fr*** to plan out your road trip or hitch-hiking. Within the towns of Normandy, walking is the fastest form of transportation, from the train station to the center of town. In Le Havre, which is more spread out than most cities, Bus 1 will take you to the Hôtel de Ville and then the beach front.

▶▶ROUTES

Caen is a nice, quiet starting point for a visit to Normandy. From here, because the train takes almost twice as long, it's easiest to take the bus to Le Havre, perhaps the toughest town in Normandy with its bombed-out appearance and higher crime rate. A rather spectacular bridge spans the mouth of the Seine along the autoroute between the two towns. From Le Havre, Rouen—the nicest, most happening city in Normandy—is a short car or train trip.

If you're in a pinch for time, Rouen is perhaps the most pleasant of Normandy's landlocked towns, while Le Havre, which was thoroughly destroyed in the war, enjoys a rare quality of light that you will not find in landlocked Caen or smoggy Rouen.

It's easiest to ferry to Portsmouth from Le Havre. From Caen you need to take a bus to Quistreham to catch the ferry, which is a logistical nightmare.

rouen

An important industrial town, port, and home to several universities, Rouen is situated along the Seine in a small valley. Half of the town was reduced to rubble during WWII, but fortunately the **Cathédrale de Notre Dame,** whose fleeting beauty was captured by Monet at all hours of the day, and the small but intricately laid out *vieille ville* of the beautiful *Rive Droite* were spared. Walk around the narrow streets, many for pedestrians only, window-shop at the expensive antique shops around the Cathédrale, and gaze at the impressive old half-timber, white stucco, brown-tile-roofed houses, asymmetrically held together by heavy dark crossbeams.

While Rouen's *vieille ville* is indisputably beautiful, if you hop on a tram/metro and then take a bus to the end of the line in the upper reaches of the **Rive Gauche,** you will be greeted by startlingly ugly industry, dark fumes, and ominous-smelling pits of black sludge. Only then will it make sense that Rouen is on the short list of the most polluted cities in France. Pollution has taken its toll on the Cathédrale; up close it looks like it does in Monet's paintings from a distance.

In a town where history hangs around like smoke after a fire, the kids in Rouen are extremely varied. You see natty white dreads, prim *indé* kids, athletically built sports players, and scraggly scrappy-looking intellectuals sitting together at the same table.

neighborhoods

Unless you really dig ugly industrial buildings, you'll be spending your time in Rouen in the *vieille ville*. To reach the old city from the train station,

rouen

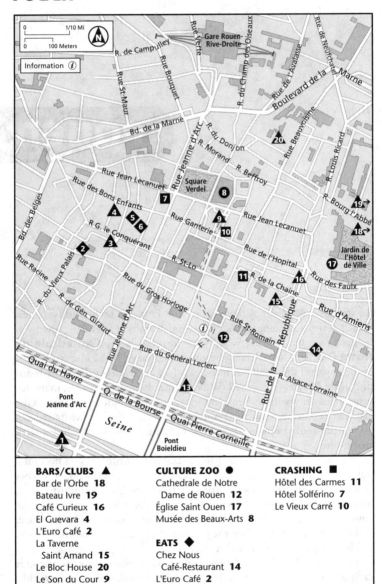

BARS/CLUBS ▲
Bar de l'Orbe **18**
Bateau Ivre **19**
Café Curieux **16**
El Guevara **4**
L'Euro Café **2**
La Taverne
  Saint Amand **15**
Le Bloc House **20**
Le Son du Cour **9**
Murphy's Irish Pub **3**
Opium **1**
XXL **13**

CULTURE ZOO ●
Cathedrale de Notre
  Dame de Rouen **12**
Église Saint Ouen **17**
Musée des Beaux-Arts **8**

EATS ◆
Chez Nous
  Café-Restaurant **14**
L'Euro Café **2**
Le Monastir **5**
Mimi la Souris **6**

CRASHING ■
Hôtel des Carmes **11**
Hôtel Solférino **7**
Le Vieux Carré **10**

head south along the main north-south route **rue Jeanne d'Arc,** which eventually becomes the Pont Jeanne d'Arc and leads into the *Rive Gauche.* Running through the center of the *vieille ville* perpendicular to rue Jeanne d'Arc is the **rue du Gros Horloge** (Street of the Great Clock), a wide pedestrian street that connects the **Cathédrale de Notre Dame,** [see *culture zoo,* below] at its eastern end, to the **place du Vieux Marché** at its western end. And once you're here, you might as well do what every tourist does at least once: From the Cathédrale de Notre Dame, walk down the rue du Gros Horlorge and check out the ornate gilt medieval timepiece that is mounted on an archway that bridges the street. Continue another 200 yards and you'll see the bizarrely ocean-wave-like **Église de Jeanne d'Arc** on the place du Vieux-Marché. Here Jeanne d'Arc was burned alive, kissing the cross she clutched. Another main roadway is the east-west-running **rue Jean Lecanuet**: The central **Square Verdel** sits on the corner where Lecanuet meet **rue Jeanne d'Arc**, and the lush **Jardin de l'Hôtel de Ville** is at its eastern end.

When getting around the city, you can take your pick from Rouen's underground metro line and extensive bus network [see *need to know,* below]. The metro runs from the train station to the suburbs, with a central stop at the Théâtre des Arts, which is also opposite the main bus information office.

hanging out

The cool kids come to sun themselves over beer, coffee, and cigarettes at **place 19 du Avril 1944,** a marble square bordered on two sides by pedestrian walkways, with rue Ganterie on the north side and rue des Fosses Louis VII on the south, while their dogs take dips in the cool water of the fountain.

Square Verdel, a couple blocks north of the place 19 du Avril and across from the **Musée des Beaux-Arts** [see *culture zoo,* below], has a beautiful natural-rock and falling-water fountain and green overarching trees. It's a great place to bring a sandwich and sun yourself. Little kids play on the rocks, and elderly guys sit on the benches and stare at the youth they left behind.

Even better for lounging are the bushy paths, running brook, and benches and tables of the **Jardins de l'Hôtel de Ville** at the eastern end of the rue Jean Lecannet. In this secluded place you're bound to find some kids enjoying the day or hanging out and drinking at night, though watch out for drunk, raving maniacs—the freaks do come out at night. Even if you think you've seen enough cathedrals to howl at the moon and make your own shrine to the devil, you'll enjoy gazing at the **Église Saint Ouen** [see *culture zoo,* below], at the north end of the park—you can't miss it. If after some quality lounging you feel the need to replenish your blood-alcohol level, continue through the park. The rue Abbey de l'Épée emerges out of the park and leads to the rue de l'Orbe. On the opposite corner, you'll find charming *quartier* (neighborhood) **Bar de L'Orbe** [see *bar scene,* below].

bar, club, and live music scene

Rouen has a pretty vibrant bar scene. There's something here for just about everyone, from those who like quiet as they consume their beverages, to sports fans who want to curse at the television, to those who can't stop their legs from shaking to the booming beat of house or the staccato of drum 'n' bass.

If an alcohol-induced escape from the crowds of tourists is what you crave, the all-wood interior of **La Taverne Saint-Amand** *(11 rue St. Amand; Tel 02/35-88-51-34; 11-2am Mon-Sat)* is quiet and calm and has a nice selection of German, Belgian, and French beers. Sit on the chairs that spill out onto the street, be served by the red-nosed barman who is said to sneak sips of the hard stuff when his wife isn't looking, and enjoy the *Rouennaise nuit* in the old town, a few steps from Abbtiale St. Quen.

Though the interior of **Le Son du Cor** *(Corner of passage de la Grande Mesure at 221 rue Eau de Robec; Tel 02/35-71-46-62; 10am-2pm)* lacks the all-wood splendor of Saint Amand, its strength is the quiet terrace perfect for drinking and the sand court for playing *boule*. The crowd at the bar, located around the corner from the Cathédrale, varies from the teenagers who bartend to thirtysomethings and aged geezers, and you can nurse your drink as long as you like.

The bartender at the neighborhood **Bar de l'Orbe** *(136 rue de l'Orbe, just behind the Hôtel de Ville in the old town; Tel 02/35-89-61-10; 11am-2am Tue-Fri; opens at 6pm Sat, 8pm Mon; 9-10pm happy-hour)* specializes in different types of shooters and makes a wicked rum and lime punch. Hang out for a couple of hours, chat with the barman in your cute-sounding but poorly accented French, and you might be one of the lucky ones to stay past closing time and take a couple of free toasts to the good life.

Clustered around the Vieux Marché are a number of joints ranging from bland to appealing. Though a bit pricey, **Murphy's Irish Pub** *(12 place Vieux Marché; Tel 02/35-71-17-33; 11am-midnight)* is the place to watch France's national soccer team win another championship. The television on the main floor is a bit small, but that doesn't stop the heavy wood pub-style high tables and chairs from filling up with twentysomethings oohing and ahhing over their team. Upstairs, there's a bit more space, with tables, chairs, and booths. More chairs and tables spill out onto the sidewalk.

Pumping commercial house music, fistfights, and loud, greasy-haired, Eurotrash of all nationalities and sexual preferences keep the neighbors up around the appropriately named **L'Euro Café** *(41 place du Vieux Marché; Tel 02/35-07-55-66; 11am-2am Sun-Thur, til 4am Fri, & Sat; www.leuro.tm.fr)* smack in the center of the old town, beside the square where Joan of Arc was burned at the stake. Decorated with bright bold colors and broken tile mosaics, the establishment has three floors. The first floor is a bar, where kids drink funny-colored drinks and occasionally spill them all over their tight white pants. The second is a restaurant serving tapas that yearn for more careful preparation. The third is a *"club cubain,"* where the fit *filles* and *garçons* try to dance on the minuscule dance floor to daily DJs. One interesting twist to the joint: Everything that goes on in the bar and club is taped and simultaneously rebroadcast for the patrons.

If you have trouble swallowing your beer to the throbbing beat of house and the ubiquitous giggles of drunk girls, and prefer something slightly cooler and more oriented toward underground music, go to the nook-like **Café Curieux** (*3 rue des Fosses Louis VIII; Tel 02/35-89-58-76; 9pm-2am Wed and Sat, 9pm-4am Thur, Fri; 10F cover; 10F beer*). This dark, strangely decorated place—on a quiet, narrow street that leads to la rue des Carmes—is the home of drum 'n' bass, big beat, and breakbeat culture in Rouen. Dig the vibe, take slow sips of brew, and listen to what's new.

Salsa, dancehall and Cuban music groove in the cigar-smoked air of **El Guevara** (*31 rue des Bons Enfants; Tel 02/35-15-97-67; Noon-2am, 5-10pm happy hour; 18F margaritas*), a red-lit, Ché-themed bar a few blocks from the place an Vieux Marché. Every night Gérard comes out from behind the bar to give free salsa lessons from 8 to 9:30pm. But revealing your American nationality when asking Gerard about the history of Fidel and Ché might make you feel like doing a cha-cha towards the door.

Live music rocks **Bateau Ivre** (*17 rue des Sapins; Tel 02/35-70-09-05; Hours vary; Shows normally start at 10pm, ticket prices vary*). Dance-hall, blues, and rock attract diverse but always young and hip crowds. Because the venue is an actual boat, the sound of the stereo system is deep. A lesser version of the Batofar in Paris, the sound waves here are not refracted by the hard cement of the city but reverberate on the hull of the ship. If you catch wind of a show from the venue's flyers around town, definitely try and catch it there.

gay scene

Le Bloc House (*138 rue Beauvoisine, near the Hôtel de Ville; Tel 02/35-07-71-97; 4pm-2am, happy hour 8-10pm*) is the longtime standard in Rouen's gay scene. Pinball machines, foos ball, and various other electronic games fight a rotating lineup of house DJs, and mostly older dudes shimmy and shake on the dance floor. If your thing is grooving on older guys, this might be the place for you.

With the rainbow flag flying from the bar to the steady swirl of house music, **XXL** (*25-27 rue de la Savonnerie; Tel 02/35-07-00-15; 4pm-2am Tue-Sat, 5pm-2am Sun*) is gay and proud, and a veritable fixture on the gay scene in Rouen. It stands in the center of town, between the cathedral and the quays of the Seine. Don't go if you don't feel like flirting, because the beat will want to make you shake your hips, and you'll have likely the best sense of rhythm in the place. Though the place is basically a guy's hangout, women will not be turned away, they just may be left out of the action.

A 15-minute walk from the center of town, **Opium** (*2 rue Malherbe [Rive Gauche]; Tel 02/35-03-29-36; 11pm-4am; No cover before midnight,*

50F after; MC, V) is perhaps Rouen's most dramatic gay club/bar with a suitably smoothly dressed clientele of well-put-together men and women. It features an obscured entrance, a DJ booth on the second floor, lush frescoes on the walls, and drag shows on Sunday nights.

CULTURE ZOO

The two principal cultural attractions of Rouen are the Cathédrale de Notre Dame and the Musée des Beaux-Arts. While the obvious wear and tear on the Cathédrale is a bit sad, you should go check it out before time inflicts any further damage on its delicate structure. The Musée des Beaux-Arts is a large and relatively important museum, with over 65 rooms of works.

Cathédrale de Notre Dame de Rouen *(Place de la Cathédrale; 8am-7pm Mon-Sat, 7:30am-6pm, closed during mass and holidays):* This massive structure, built over the course of the 14th century, was made famous in the 19th century by Monet's series of Impressionist renderings in various lights. The central portal, whose centerpiece depicts the Tree of Jesus, is embellished with statues severely damaged during WWII and has been faded by the output of the heavy industry that fills Rouen's suburbs. Its twin towers are sculpted with beautifully lacy flourish. While the interior is nothing to write home about, it does contain a couple of interesting pieces, most notably the Bookseller's Stairway on the north transept, which invokes images of medieval priests clothed in rich brocade solemnly climbing its hallowed stairs. Catch a mass on Monday, Wednesday, or Thursday at 6:30pm or Sunday at 11am and be awed by the awesome wealth and power of the Church.

Église Saint Ouen *(Place du Général-de-Gaulle; 10am-12:30pm/ 2-4:30pm Wed, Sat, Sun Jan 16-Mar 14, Nov 14-Dec 1; 10am-12:30pm/ 2-6pm Wed-Mon Mar 15-Oct 31):* The sole remains of a Benedictine abbey, this is one of the most beautiful gothic structures you'll see in France. Built between the 14th and 15th centuries, the furnishings of the church have been completely removed, leaving an empty interior atmosphere that is stark and almost spooky.

Musée des Beaux-Arts *(Place Verdel; Tel 02/35-71-28-40; 10am-6pm Wed-Mon; 20F adults, 13F students, free 18 and under):* This institution contains an impressive range of works from the Middle Ages to the 20th century. Delacroix, David, and Ingres make strong appearances in the museum's hallowed *salons*. Other works by artists such as Caravaggio, Rubens, Fragonard, and Corot only make the trip more worthwhile. Several of Monet's versions of the Cathédrale also appear among other Impressionist works.

STUFF

Globo Loco *(59 rue Jeanne d'Arc; Tel 02/35-15-00-58; 10am-12:30pm/2-7pm, closed Mon morning; MC, V)* is a skate shop of questionable utility to actual skaters. The stock is pricey, but should you desperately need a new deck or another set of wheels this is the place to come. It also carries a considerable stock of footwear and clothing, which some of Rouen's hip set have donned to keep up with the streetwear craze that is slowly sweeping across France. There is a second location at 98 rue Ganterie with a similar stock and the same hours.

EaTS

Eating in Rouen offers various options, from killer kebabs to innovative combinations of cheese and meat. If you don't see anything here you like, go to the Office de Tourisme [see *need to know,* below], which has a very good list of restaurants.

A prince among thieves, **Le Monastir** *(38 rue des Bonnes Enfants; Tel 02/35-71-71-92; 11am-2am Mon-Thur, till 4am Sat, Sun; No credit cards)* is a venerable institution among the kebab places in Rouen and often runs out of kebab meat. Order a steak sandwich and watch the surly guy behind the glass counter plop the garlic and spiced ground beef on the grill. Listen to it sizzle, and know your stomach will be very happy very soon. They also have tasty baklava. You'll find it a few blocks north of the place du Vieux Marché.

Specializing in the very French combination of meat and cheese, **Mimi la Souris** *(95 rue Ecuyère; Tel 02/35-70-80-60; noon-2pm/7-10:30pm, till 11 weekends; closed Sat lunch and Sun; lunch menus 69-89F; MC, V)* is at its best when it practices this tradition. Though suffering from surly, inattentive service, the food they put before you is quite tasty. Go for the lunch menu to keep things from getting too pricey. Located just a couple blocks northeast of the place du Veille Marché.

Next to the bombed and bullet-torn remains of the Palais de l'Archevêche, **Chez Nous** *(234 rue Martainville; Tel 02/35-89-50-02; 11am-2pm/7-midnight Tue-Sun; MC, V)* serves finely prepared, delicately flavored French standards. Order off the chalk board and ignore the sometimes flighty service. If the weather is pleasant, you'll want to eat outside and ponder the bullet-scarred walls of the Église Saint Maclou, but the sunny-colored interior is just as inviting when the weather is gray.

To MARKET

For groceries, there is the omnipresent **Monoprix** *(73 rue du Gros Horloge; Tel 02/35-70-24-44; 8:30am-9pm Mon-Sat),* the French K-mart-style superstore.

crashing

The cheap, two-star **Hôtel Solférino** *(51 rue Jean Lecanuet; Tel 02/35-71-10-07; 130-210F with sink or shower and toilet, 250F double; MC, V)* is centrally located just a seven-minute walk from the station and five from the place de Vieux Marché. Rooms are slightly worn or just antiquey, depending on whether your cup is half empty or half full, and have cute homey touches. Beds are about as soft as they get for the two-star class. There is no elevator, but each room does come with a private bath.

Some of the nicest rooms in Rouen are the highly individualized rooms at the **Hôtel des Carmes** *(33 place des Carmes; Tel 02/35-71-92-31, Fax 02/35-71-76-96; 230F single),* located a few blocks north of the Cathedral. Patchwork quilting on the bedspreads, flowers in the lobby, and even the occasional burning incense give this hotel a sense of domestic meditative calm. All rooms have showers, televisions, and telephones.

Another charming choice is the **Hôtel Le Vieux Carré** *(34 rue Ganterie; Tel 02/35-71-67-70; Fax 02/35-71-19-17; vieux-carre@ mcom.fr; 330F single, 360F with a view of garden; MC, V, AE).* With its flowered and ivy-encrusted courtyard, garden, smart *salon de thé,* and elegant dining, it is slightly more romantic than the Hôtel des Carmes, and the front desk makes you feel welcome. All rooms come with private baths. Centrally located just a few blocks north of the rue du Gros Horloge.

need to know

Currency Exchange The best places to change money are the **American Express Offices** *(25 place de la Cathédrale; Tel 02/35-89-48-60; similar hours to Office de Tourisme or the main American Express Office).* But for convenience sake, you can just go to one of the many ATMs along rue Jeanne d'Arc, in the heart of the old town: **Crédit Agricole, Crédit Lyonnais,** and **Société Générale.**

Tourist Information: The **Office de Tourisme** *(25 place de la Cathédrale; Tel 02/32-08-32-40; 9am-7pm Mon-Sat, 9:30am-12:30pm/ 2:30-6pm Sun, holidays)* provides all kinds of information, from metro and bus maps to hotel listings—they'll even make hotel reservations for you (in person only). To find out about shows and youth-oriented stuff (in French only), **Centre Information Jeunesse** *(84 rue Beauvoisine; Tel 02/35-98-38-75; 10:30am-6:30pm)* has got it all.

Public Transportation If the **TCAR/Métrobus** *(15 rue de la Petite Chartreuse; Tel 02/35-52-52-52; Route and schedule info available at the tourist office)* moves *"au rythme de la ville,"* then Rouen is a glacier. You'll find the main station on the south side of town, a block from the Seine. The tram system works well, but be prepared to wait a long

wired

The cheapest place to use the Internet is, as ever, the *Cyberposte* at the central post office [see *need to know,* below]; however, after hours you can check your e-mail at the cyber-cafe **Cybernetics** *(59 place du Vieux Marché; Tel 02/35-07-02-77; www.cybernetics.fr).* Closely linked to its website, it has a number of good search engines, including ***www.fr.yahoo.com*** and Les Pages Jaunes, the yellow pages, ***http://wfa.pagesjaunes.fr/pj.cgi,*** which is in English as well as French. Easy to find, just 2 blocks from the Musée Jean d'Arc.

The tourist office's multilingual site is located at ***www.mairie rouen.fr.*** A number of Rouen's merchants have banded together to create the slick-looking ***www.les-vitrines-de-rouen.com,*** but unless you speak French, it's of limited interest.

time for buses. The only time you'll really need to catch the bus is to go the hospital in an emergency, and then you're probably better off calling a taxi. **Radio Taxi** *(66 rue Jean Lecanuet; Tel 02/35-88-50-50)* is available 24 hours a day. Taxi stands can be found at the *gare* and along rue Sapins by the banks of the Seine.

American Express The main **American Express Office** *(1-3 place Jacques-Le Fleur; Tel 02/-32-08-19-20; 8:45am-noon/1:30-6pm Mon-Fri)* holds mail, supplies new cards if yours gets lost or stolen, and changes money.

Health and Emergency Police: *17;* Ambulance: *15;* Fire department: *18.* Rouen's central hospital is **C.H.U.** *(1 rue de Germont; Tel 02/32-88-89-90; Bus 4 to C.H.U. stop; www.chu-rouen.fr/homeng.html).*

Pharmacy There is a pharmacist at the C.H.U., and another in the center of town: **Pharmacie André Arnaud** *(91 rue Général Leclerc; Tel 02/35-98-12-91 9:00am-7:00pm Mon-Sat).*

Trains The **Gare SNCF** *(Place Bernard Tissot; Tel 08/36-35-35-35)* is located at the north end of rue Jeanne d'Arc, on the Rive Droite, a 10-minute walk from the *Vieille Ville.* Trains leave Paris Saint Lazare almost every hour for the 70-minute trip at a cost of 115F. For schedules, call *Tel 08/36-35-35-35.*

Bike/Moped Rental There's a bike rental outfit in the heart of the old town, near the place du Vieux-Marché: **Rouen Cycles** *(45 rue Saint Eloi; Tel 02/35-71-34-30).*

Buses From the **Gare Routière** *(25 rue des Charrettes; Tel 02/35-52-92-00)* and **Compagnie Normande d'Autobus (CNA)** buses leave for a variety of locations in Normandy, like Le Havre and Dieppe, but take a good deal longer than the train. Use them for trips along route des Abbayes. Several buses a day leave for Caudebec-en-Caux.

Laundry Looking for a laundromat? Go to **Lavomatique** *(56 rue Cauchoise; Tel 02/35-70-57-58)*. If you're looking for it on a map, rue Cauchoise opens directly onto the place du Vieux-Marché.

Postal The **Poste Principale** *(45 rue Jeanne d'Arc; Tel 02/35-15-66-73; 7am-8pm Mon-Fri, 8am-noon Sat; Has photocopiers, telephones, and a* Cyberposte iMac, as well as the usual postal services.

Internet See *wired,* above.

giverny

Fifty miles northeast of Paris, on the border between Île-de-France and Normandy, the charmingly modest 19th-century home of Claude Monet has been carefully restored by the foundation that bears his name. Monet first came to Giverny in 1883 and lived here the rest of his life, often visited by his friends. Though you may have been turned off by the Monet posters adorning every other college dorm room in America, visiting Giverny will help you understand his work and his goal of capturing the quality of light using innovative brushwork and composition. The only thing to see in Giverny is Monet's home and gardens, so you probably won't want to stay any longer than a day. Getting there is a bit of a chore, so be prepared to leave early and get back late [see *need to know*, below]. You can also book tours from Paris through **American Express** *(Tel 01/42-27-58-80)* or **Cityrama** *(Tel 01/44-55-61-00),* in which case you get to ride in a big bus and feel like a big lazy tourist.

Though the place can be overrun with middle-aged tourists on weekends, the Claude Monet Foundation *(Rue Claude-Monet Parc Gasny; Tel 02/32-51-28-21; 10am-6pm Tue-Sun Apr-Oct; Closed Nov-Mar; 35F, students 20F, gardens only 25F, students 19F)* is well worth a short trip, if just for the gardens. The gorgeously overgrown, brightly blossoming gardens with rhododendrons, *nymphéas,* wisteria, and weeping willows surround the water-lillied pond, the reflections of which the artist continued to paint even as his eyesight faded. Sit on a bench and admire the flowers (which bloom from April to October), or cross the Japanese bridge and watch the reflections of butterflies and dragonflies skitter across the dappled surface of the pond, and you will feel like you are dreaming.

need to know

Cars Getting to Giverny from Paris is difficult unless you are blessed with a **car,** in which case you can just take **Autoroute de l'Ouest** (Port Saint Cloud) toward Rouen, getting off at the Bonniere exit and following the signs to Vernon, the closest town to Giverny. Cross the bridge over the Seine and then follow the signs to Giverny. Unless you're traveling during the weekend, the trip should take about an hour.

Trains Trains leave Paris's **Gare Saint Lazare** every couple of hours for the 50-minute trip to Vernon. From the train station, take a **taxi,** ride the **shuttle bus** *(12F),* or rent a **bicycle** *(55F a day with deposit)* and bike to Monet's home.

Eats You'll probably want to bring picnic supplies from Paris for your day trip. If you do need to gorge yourself on food while in Giverny, you'll find grocers and other small food stores along the **rue d'Al-buféra** in Giverny. If you feel like a sit-down meal, try the **Auberge du Vieux Moulin** *(21 rue de la Falaise; Tel 02/32-51-46-15; Noon-3pm 7:30pm-10pm Tue-Sat; Prix fixe menus 98f-158f; MC, V),* which is a five-minute walk from Monet's home and has reasonably good country-style French cooking.

Le havre

Though Le Havre was reconstructed after being nearly obliterated in WWII [see *conspiracy theory,* below], and retains its original street plan, it is strikingly horizontal and sprawling compared to most other French cities. Auguste Perret, the architect who began the massive reconstruction, and the Socialist and Communist municipal governments that completed it, seem to have taken a few hints on urban development from beyond the Iron Curtain. Certainly, the vaguely Stalinist architecture of Hôtel de Ville and its large imposing square make the individual feel small in much the same way Lubyanka, the former headquarters of the KGB in Moscow, does, and the 350-foot tower and geometrically arrayed heavy cement and stained-glass of **Église Saint Joseph** make it look much more like a temple to modern man's might than a church.

Though the architecture of this coastal city is somewhat curious and definitely different from other French cities, what really sets Le Havre apart, even from other parts of *Normandie,* is the quality of its light. On bright sunny days the light reflected by the sea bathes the town in a brilliant white sheen. Unfortunately, Le Havre, with its proximity to England, shares a fair bit of those gray English skies for much of the year. So it seems fitting that the people who you'll meet in Le Havre seem to have equal doses of lightness and darkness in them, to which their sometimes humorously snide remarks hint.

Though you'll likely only be in Le Havre long enough to transfer from the train to the ferry (or vice versa), it is nice to know that nightlife options do exist, should you end up here overnight. The presence of the small, regional Université du Havre lends the city a vaguely collegiate nightlife, in which a sojourn to the town bars—with some proper guidance from the locals to the post-bar-closing after-hours party—could turn into an evening of orgiastic consumption. Kids from the university put out a flyer-pamphlet of the shows and gigs going on in and around town and throughout most of *Haute* and *Basse Normandie*. It's called **Bazart** *(107 rue Général Sarrail; Tel 02/35-43-62-79)*, and you can pick it up around town in the cooler youth-oriented bars and establishments. Remember, though, that the under-25 population drops off sharply in June, when school lets out, and doesn't pick up again until late August.

neighborhoods

You'll want to avoid the trashy area around the train station and concentrate most of your lounging around the **beachfront** and the neighborhoods between **avenue Paris,** which runs roughly north-south, and **avenue Foch,** the elegant main drag that is wider than Paris's Champs Elysées, and runs east-west. From the train station, head east on **boulevard Strasbourg,** which leads directly to the main square, the **place de l'Hôtel de Ville.** Past that point, it becomes avenue Foch and runs out to the sea. If you don't want to make the 15-minute walk into town from the station, hop on **Bus 1,** which runs up avenue Strasbourg/avenue Foch all the way out to the beachfront. The **University** is north of the train station. The **ferry stations** are on the **Bassin de la Manche,** south and southwest of the **Espace Oscar Niemeyer** [see *culture zoo,* below].

hanging out

When the sun shines, the town shimmers in brilliant white light, and there's no better place to be than on the **beachfront,** with its very 1950s Art Deco-ish apartment buildings. Le Havre was granted the official title of Seaside Resort by the French government in 1999—apparently, a rather distinguished moniker. Given this new status, an effort was made to make the beach/sea areas as accommodating as possible. A large-scale sanitation plan was enacted to make the water clean and clear. There are changing rooms, hot showers, information desks, equipment rental stations, and anything else a beach-goer would need to have an entertaining day. And, though they may not quite fit in with the city's sanitation plan, there are also several striking pieces of excellent graffitti and spray-can art. Or perhaps, if you have sins to repent from a reckless journey, you could kill some time enjoying the kaleidoscopic interior of **Église Saint Joseph** [see *culture zoo,* below].

The mile-and-a-half rock beach has a **half pipe** *(Opposite tourist office, behind swimming pool; Open dusk to dawn; Free)* for skate-boarders and in-line-skaters alike, though expect there to be a lot more adolescent, snot-nosed in-liners than real skaters. They also promenade up and down the cement boardwalk doing curlicues, obviously picked up from watching professional ice skating. At night, the town's skaters, never short on machismo or bravado, hang out at the **L'Abri-Cotier** [see *bar scene,* below], where they stick out like sore thumbs. Besides having girls wrapped around their arms like tight sweaters, they sport baggy pants and

le havre

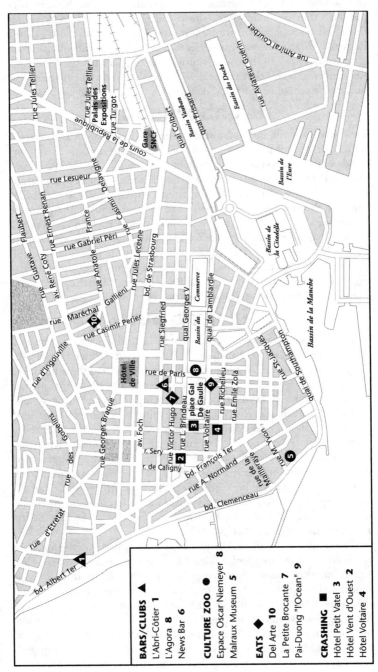

cocked baseball caps. Like everywhere else, skaters are the "bad boys" of Le Havre.

bar scene

Though Le Havre may seem slim on cool bars, the nifty bars that it does have make up for the absence of competitors.

One part *tiki* bar, one part beach-house bungalow, **L'Abri-Cotier** *(24 blvd. Albert 1er Front de Mer or 35 rue Guillemard; Tel 02/35-42-51-20; 2:30pm-2am daily, 11am for lunch in the summer)* is frequented by Le Havre's hip set, including, but not limited to, snide indie rockers and raucous skaters. However, what makes this beachside bar worthwhile are the kind, hip guys who run it and the hip-hop, soul, house, and groove that kids spin on the weekends. During the summer, even though most of the clientele is still dormant from debauched drinking the night before, they open at 11am and serve tasty salads. Take your plate outside on the front terrace and soak up Le Havre's brilliant light.

News Bar *(100 rue de Paris; No phone; 8am-10pm Tue-Thur, till 2am Fri, Sat; Closed Mon)* fills nightly with domesticated bikers and rowdy baby boomers downing the cheap brew and shaking a leg to sixties rock. A single woman might be cautious about coming here alone, but needn't worry any more here than elsewhere in France. The presence of baby boomers and their young kids tends to dampen the rough behavior of some of the tougher, rowdier customers at the bar.

In the **Espace Oscar Niemeyer** [see *culture zoo*, below], the lounge-like **L'Agora** *(Tel 02/32-74-09-70; Show times vary; Cover varies; MC, V)* has a well-stocked, hip bar and hosts cool live music of every conceivable genre, from hip-hop and ragga to *indé* (indie), metal, and blues, with artists from as far away as America, Jamaica, and Cuba. Inquire at the venue for a show schedule or check the leaflet *Bazart*, available around town.

arts scene

It is easy to find the contemporary art scene in Le Havre: Just look for the big white cone. That cone, the **Espace Oscar Niemeyer** [see *culture zoo*, below] houses both the **Cinéma l'Eden** *(Tel 02/35-21-28-70; closed July, Aug; 40F)*, which plays both classic foreign films and recent releases with French subtitles (in V.O.), and the **Maison de la Culture du Havre** *(Tel 02/35-19-10-10; Box office open 1:30-7pm Tue-Sat; Tickets from 50F)*, the center of the performing arts in Le Havre, which has theatrical productions from September through June.

culture zoo

Culture in Le Havre is a paradox to some visitors who sneer at the city's 1950s architecture, but there are two stops essential to anyone who wants a glimpse of what Le Havre has to offer: the **Espace Oscar Niemeyer** and the **Musée Malraux**.

conspiracy theory

The complete and utter destruction of Le Havre in 1944 has left ample room for conspiracy theories as to the reasoning behind the destruction. The Germans had essentially vacated the town, but British bombers continued to blast away, reducing the town to rubble and leaving hundreds of thousands homeless. There are still streaks of resentment expressed *en famille* about the excessive destruction of England's primary commercial rival for shipping in the channel. Despite the ongoing local conjecture, however, two things should be remembered: The British were not operating as loose cannons but were under the command of U.S. general Dwight Eisenhower at the time, and since then nearly all of the "secrets" of WWII (even those that embarrass the Allies) have been revealed under the Freedom of Information Act and nothing has proven the Havre conspiracy theory. Still, old wounds heal very slowly. Sensitivity to such cultural issues as the legacy of WWII—and the United States' current economic hegemony and cultural imperialism—goes a long way in winning the respect of the French.

Espace Oscar Niemeyer *(Ave. Paris, two blocks from the place de l'Hôtel de Ville):* Affectionately known as *Le Volcan* (The Volcano), this swooping, almost cooling tower–like, conical-shaped arts center houses **L'Agora** bar-lounge-concert space [see *bar scene,* above], the **Cinéma l'Eden,** and the **Maison de la Culture du Havre** [see *arts scene,* above, for both]. It was designed by the Brazilian architect Oscar Niemeyer, who is famous for designing another enormously impractical project, Brazil's ill-conceived capital, Brasilia. Locals are affectionate toward the tripped-out asymmetrical building, even though it hasn't exactly aged perfectly—the white plaster exterior is stained and cracking in spots.

Musée André-Malraux *(2 blvd. Clémenceau; Tel 02/35-19-62-62; 11am-6pm Mon-Fri, till 7pm Sat, Sun; Closed Tue, holidays):* Ringed with running water, this sharp steel, aluminum, and glass museum makes excellent use of Le Havre's inspired light. The building reinterprets the interaction between Le Havre's land, light, and water in a truly interesting fashion. Paintings by Boudin, Dufy, and other pre-Impressionists and Impressionists are laid out in a meaningful way and lit as naturally as possible.

CITY SPORT

If you've got cash and time to spend in Le Havre, check in with the Secretariat of the **Club Nautisme et Plaisance Le Havre** *(27 rue de la Mailleraye; Tel 02/35-21-27-27-85; 8am-noon/2-5:30pm Mon Tue Thur Sat, till 7 Wed, till 4 Fri Apr-Nov; cnph@wanadoo.fr)*, located at the large marina. The club specializes in fast boats for competition and offers day-long as well as more involved classes. It also runs the **École Française de Voile** from the beginning of July to the first week of August, offering six-week classes in small vessel and catamaran sailing (750-930F). You can get half-day (120F) and full-day (230F) lessons that focus less on competition racing and more on the general mechanics of sailing at **Génération Voile** *(Ste. Nautique Havraise (SRH)/ Société des Régates, quai Eric Tabarly; Tel 02/35-42-41-21)*. You can also sign on as an unpaid "apprentice" aboard a yacht that stays out on the seas for weeks at a time. Sailing in Le Havre, like everywhere, is the sport of the upper middle class. A good command of French is absolutely required, because the helpful Secretariat is unused to dealing with foreigners and instruction is only in French.

Crazed kids who don't mind the goose-bumping and testicle-shrinking northern Atlantic waters of *La Manche* windsurf in front of the beach. The high winds and low waves make it a perfect spot to practice and get your bearings on the board. Check the weather by calling *02/32-74-03-60*, or dial the electronic weather report line of Météo France at *08/36-68-08-08*. Complete equipment is available to rent or to buy at **Sport Maximum** *(122 blvd. Clemenceau; Tel 02/35-21-09-05, Fax 02/35-42-38-57; 9:30am-noon/1:30-7:15pm)*.

EATS

A couple of blocks south of the Place Gal de Gaulle, **Dai-Duong "L'Ocean"** *(67 rue Richelieu; Tel 02/35-22-52-82; noon-2pm/7-9pm; three-course menu with drink around 100F)* is a quiet, lace-curtained, homey establishment. But don't be put off by the simple look of the place—they serve seriously sumptuous Vietnamese-French fusion cuisine. Order the thankfully strong, colorful beach umbrella *cocktail de la maison* and treat yourself to the tasty shrimp chips that taste like they just jumped out of the deep-fat-fryer, as you peruse the lengthy menu.

On the opposite side of the place Gal de Gaulle, the classy **La Petite Brocante** *(75 rue Louis Brindeau; Tel 02/35-21-42-20; 11am-3pm/6:30pm-midnight Mon-Sat; Entrees 65-125F)* serves classic French dishes without being too rich or over-the-top, in an interior with the leisurely and colorful feel of a Toulouse-Lautrec print. Come look pensive and sample some of the Lyonnaise cheese imported from the south. One of the most cost-effective restaurants in Le Havre, **Les Nuages dans la Tasse** *(93 ave. Foch; Tel 02/35-21-64-94; noon-2pm Mon-Sat, 7-10pm Thurs-Sat; main courses 48-68F, beer 13-16F/glass; MC, V)*, is set in a battered-but-cozy, endlessly busy dining room outfitted with posters of vintage American cars and paintings by local artists. It's cheap and cheerful, with a wide choice of main-course salads, baked tarts—including vegetarian—that can be a meal in themselves, and a series of platters that feature tripe, *andouillette* (chitterling sausages), couscous, *pave* of rump-steak, and breast of duckling. Located in the heart of the commercial zone, it's especially popular at lunchtime. The only drawback is that it's open only three evenings a week, but then you can always try the micro-brew along with your pepper steak at *Le Brasseur des Halles (8-10 rue Bernardin de St. Pierre, close to place Oscar Niemeyer; Tel 02/35-21-41-19; 11am-2pm and 6-11pm Mon-Sat; Main courses 35-74F; MC, V).* This place brews five different beers; you can see the large copper fermentation tanks from any seat on the ground floor. Most of the street level is devoted to a 40-foot-long wooden bar where tons of young people meet after work to drink, gossip, and chow down on French comfort food: pepper steak with fries, sole *meunière, blanquette de veau,* calves' liver, and an assortment of fresh fish.

If your palette craves something more Mediterranean, try the pizza and *crostini* of **Del Arte** *(Centre Commercial René Coty R3, 22 rue Casimir Perrier; Tel 02/32-74-95-12; 11am-4pm and 6-11pm daily).* The dark, varnished-wood interior, glossy pictographic menu, and tall white hats the chefs wear as they flip pizza in the exposed open-air kitchen resemble those of a high-end American chain restaurant, but the food here is actually quite sophisticated and good, and even if the pizza tends to sag in the middle. On bright days there's a nice terrace on which to enjoy the sunshine. Though you may scrupulously avoid malls at home, the adjacent Commercial Centre René Coty makes for an interesting after-dinner stroll, if just for comparison to your local version.

crashing

While in Le Havre, you'll want to stay in the neighborhood between avenue Paris and avenue Foch because of its proximity to the avenues themselves, as well as the beachfront. The more expensive hotels in Le Havre tend to be more distinctive, and the one-and two-star hotels are textbook examples of bland.

The **Hôtel Voltaire** *(14 rue Voltaire; Tel 02/35-19-35-35, Fax 02/35-19-35-30; 150-210F single, 180-240F double)* is a classic one-star hotel located on the second floor of a low-slung and elevatorless building. It's clean, cheap, convenient, and characterless, but you do get TV in your room. Mattresses and towels are thin but not too thin, and the television only has 10 or so channels.

The two-star **Hôtel Le Petit Vatel** *(86 rue Louis Brindeau; Tel 02/35-41-72-07, Fax 02/35-21-37-86; 230-250F single, 250-280F double)* is a Volvo of a hotel—"boxy but good"—yet still pretty close to bland. Bright reds spice up the lobby and intense orange decorates a few of the rooms making it ever so slightly more colorful than the Voltaire. Predictably, the mattresses are more comfy, furniture is newer, and cable television is longer in the channel department. You get a private bath with every room too.

The three-star **Hôtel Vent d'Ouest** *(6 rue de Caligny; Tel 02/35-42-50-69, Fax 02/35-42-58-00; 460-560F single, 480-580F double, breakfast 45F, Parking 40F)* is distinguished by its overdone interior decoration, with antiqued furniture and hyper-pretty printed drapes and bed linens. Each floor of the three-story hotel is decorated in a different theme: mountain, country, and naval. All rooms have super-cushy beds and their own toilets and baths, and the location, close to the beach, makes it hard to beat.

need to know

Currency Exchange You can change money most easily at the central **post office,** and there is a 24-hour ATM run by **Société Générale** *(Tel 02/35-41-41-41)* on the place Léon Meyer in the center of town.

Tourist Information The **Office de Tourisme** *(186 blvd. Clémenceau; Tel 02/32-74-04-04, Fax 02/35-42-38-39; 9am-7pm Mon-Sat, 2:30-6pm Sun summer, 9am-6:30pm Mon-Sat, 10am-1pm Sun winter; www.normandy-tourism.org),* located along the waterfront, makes hotel reservations for weary visitors, and dispenses dry information about the town, only matched by the dryness of its website. For those who like to have their hand held, the office also provides various guided theme tours around town.

American Express One of two offices in Normandy (the other is in Rouen), Le Havre's **American Express office** *(57 quai George V; Tel 02/35-19-05-93; 8:45am-noon/1:30-6pm, closed Sat, Sun)* provides travel assistance and card member services and is helpful, even if having an American Express card in France generally is not.

Health and Emergency Police: *17;* medical emergency: *15* or *Tel 02/32-73-32-74;* Hôpital du Havre *(55 rue Gustave Flaubert; Tel 02/32-72-38-50)* Medical facilities are also available close to the marina. If you are injured at the beach, call or head across the street to the corner of rue Mailleraye and rue Augustin Normand, where there is a small **medical complex** including a **sports therapist** *(Tel 02/35-42-00-42),* a **general practitioner** *(Tel 02/35-55-54-35),* and a **pharmacist.**

Public Transportation While Le Havre is a sprawling city in French terms, by American standards it is still rather small. The only time you'll need to take a **bus** is for traveling between the *gare* and the beachfront, in which case you hop on **Line 1.** Buses, operated by **Bus Océane** *(115 rue Jules Lecesne; Tel 02/35-19-75-75)* tend to run on the slow side, so it's almost always just as fast to walk. Tickets are 8F and can be purchased from the bus driver. **Radio Taxi** *(Gare SNCF; Tel 02/35-25-81-81)* can be called 24 hours a day.

Trains The **Gare Centrale** *(Cours de la République; Tel 08/36-35-35-35)* is located at the end of boulevard Strasbourg and its intersection with cours de la République.

Bus Lines out of the City The **Gare Routière** *(Blvd. de Strasbourg)* is located directly across the street from the Gare Centrale. **Autocar Gris** *(Tel 02/35-27-04-25)* runs daily to Étretat-Fecamp. **Bus Verts du Calvados** runs daily trips to Honfleur-Deauville, Trouville-Cabourg-Caen, and Pont-L'Eveque-Lisieux, and has an express to Caen. **CNA** *(Tel 02/35-52-92-29)* runs trips to Rouen along the Seine River valley.

Boat Irish Ferries *(Gare Maritime; Tel 02/32-23-44-44; Eurail pass accepted, otherwise 400-650F)* runs trips to Rosslare and Cork, Ireland. **P&O European** *(Quai de Bostom, off Ave. Lucien-Corbeaux; Tel 08/03-01-30-13, 190F)* runs trips to Portsmouth. The Irish Ferries depart from a dock at the very southern end of avenue Paris. The P&O Portsmouth Ferries depart from a neighboring dock, further down the Bassin de La Manche. There is a shuttle that runs once a day from the train station to the ferries at 2pm and costs 8F.

Postal Poste Centrale *(62 rue Jules Siegfried; Tel 02/32-92-59-00; 8am-7pm Mon-Fri, 10am-noon/2-5pm Sat).*

caen

A sometimes sleepy town on the banks of the Orne River, Caen was almost flattened by bombing during WWII. The main tourist draws, the **Château** and two Romanesque and Gothic **abbeys** founded by William the Conqueror and his keep-it-in-the-family cousin and wife, Mathilda, were thankfully spared and are the best reason to visit this little town [see *culture zoo,* below, for both]. The architecture of this capital of *Basse Normandie* is not nearly as distinctive as that of Le Havre or Rouen, and is ultimately as bland as its nightlife. The city primarily distinguishes itself as an administrative and commercial center for the region. Kids abound, but they lack cool clubs and bars in which to get down. While here, you'll want to take the time to be a "good tourist" and check out the sites, and then lay low at night. You can pretty much walk to all the sites, except the WWII museum, which you can reach by bus.

neighborhoods and hanging out

Caen's modern **city center** is just south of the sprawling grounds of the **Château de Caen** [see *culture zoo,* below]. In the center, you'll find several pedestrian shopping streets and larger boulevards, including the main **avenue du 6 Juin,** which runs southeast from the city center, across the **Orne River,** and out to the train station. The few remnants of Caen's old city can be found east of the Château grounds around **rue du Vaugueux.**

You'll find kids sunning themselves on the hilly field surrounding the ramparts of William the Conqueror's **Château,** where you can chill and enjoy the view from the rampart walls and watchtowers. The green grounds of the Château make a great place to kick back after a jaunt to one or both of the **abbeys,**—it lies equidistant between the two—or to the **Musée des Beaux-Arts** [see *culture zoo*, below, for all three], which is located within the walls on the south side of the grounds.

Located on a bright, open square in front of the city's theater, **Café du Théâtre** *(3 rue des Jacobins; Tel 02/31-86-18-43; 7am-8pm daily; 15F beer; No credit cards)* is a pleasant place to people-watch, have a cheap beer, and enjoy the day. The interior is nothing to write home about, decorated with standard dark varnished wood, but a table on the square is *the* place to relax during the summer months.

From the cafe, explore **rue Saint Pierre, rue de Bras,** and **rue Strasbourg** for a plethora of other cafes and brasseries.

bar and club scene

As we said, the nightlife here is rather pale. But if a long day of sightseeing leaves you thirsty for some action, there are a few options, most of which are huddled at the north end of rue du Vaugueux, above the Château grounds.

Sitting on the west side of the château, the **Café des Beaux-Arts** *(88 rue de Geôle; Tel 02/31-86-43-21),* like Caen itself, is so laid-back it's horizontal. Laze about with the locals young and old as they play pinball, chat, and let the reggae, jazz, and salsa coming from the stereo set the pace. This is definitely the most appealing nightlife option.

If you really must get your groove on, there are two options, neither of which will give you much trouble at the door. The better of the two, **Le Chic** *(Rue de Prairies St. Gilles; Tel 02/31-94-48-72; 10pm-2am Thu-Sat; Cover varies),* is up north of the Château. It attracts a young, relatively hip crowd with blaring disco. South of the Château, **Joy's/Le Paradis** *(10 rue de Strasbourg; Tel 02/31-85-40-40; 10pm-2am Thu-Sat; Cover varies)* gets down with its techno self every weekend.

Le Cabaret Joyeux *(Place du 36e Régiment d'Infanterie; Tel 02/31-34-99-00; 11pm-5am daily; Cover varies)* is the most popular gay bar here in Caen. As the name suggests, it's got an exuberant vibe.

culture zoo

There are four big complexes of the cultural attractions in Caen: the Château grounds, which contains the Musée des Beaux-Arts; the Abbaye des Hommes, which contains the Église Saint Étienne; the Abbaye aux Dames; and the Mémorial. While the Château has vast walls, imposing gates, and green grounds on which to hang out, nothing except the exterior remains of William the Conquerer's original castle. The interior of the Château was completely destroyed during WWII and today the castle walls merely contain a modern Musée des Beaux-Arts.

Le Mémorial de Caen *(Esplanade Dwight-Eisenhower; Tel 02/31-06-06-44; Bus 17 to Memorial; 9am-7pm, till 9pm mid-July-mid-Aug; 72F adults, 63F students):* This is the only museum dedicated to peace in a region that saw the ravages of WWII like few other places in Europe. The bilingual French-English exhibits neatly outline the economic, social, and political movements that brought Europe to the brink of self-destruction.

caen

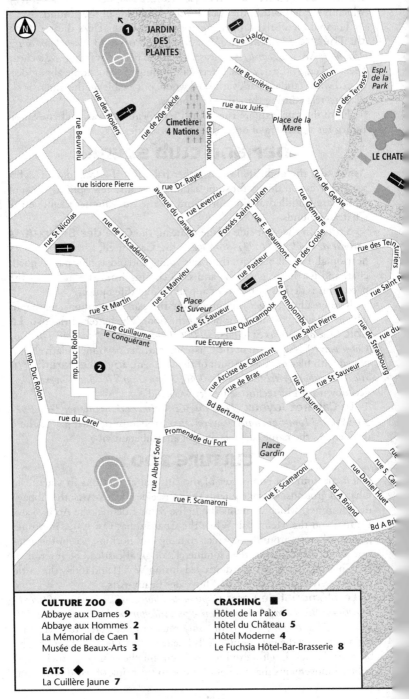

CULTURE ZOO ●
Abbaye aux Dames **9**
Abbaye aux Hommes **2**
La Mémorial de Caen **1**
Musée de Beaux-Arts **3**

EATS ◆
La Cuillère Jaune **7**

CRASHING ■
Hôtel de la Paix **6**
Hôtel du Château **5**
Hôtel Moderne **4**
Le Fuchsia Hôtel-Bar-Brasserie **8**

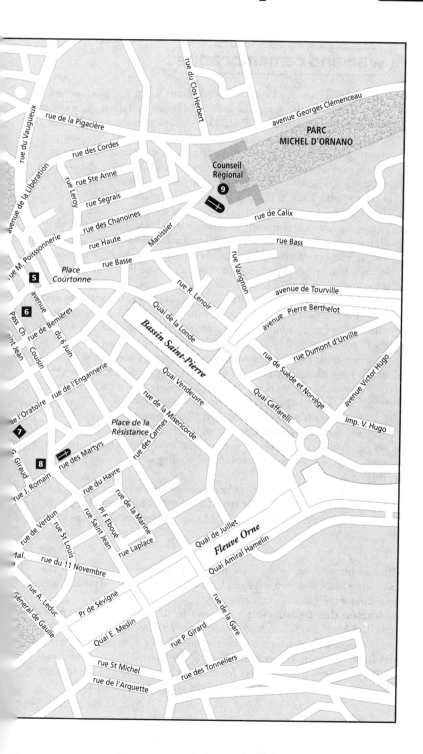

war and remembrance

On June 6, 1944, the United States Military, with the assistance of Canadian and British forces, launched the largest and most audacious military attack in history. Over 128,000 troops converged, by air and by sea, upon a 50-mile stretch of desolate (save for the Nazi troops awaiting their arrival) beach along the Normandy coast. American troops were deployed first at points Utah and Omaha (the American military's renowned codenames given to these previously unheard-of seaside spots); later in the day British and Canadian forces secured beaches Juno, Gold, and Sword. Throughout the course of "the longest day," Allied forces relentlessly bombed, battled, and bayonetted their Nazi foes in order to gain a substantial foothold from which to advance deeper into France. History is of course proof that the mission was a success, and rather expediently at that—Paris was liberated less than a week after the battle's conclusion. Yet with casualties totalling close to 200,000 by the three-month campaign's close (nearly 2,500 troops were downed on the first day alone), there is no underestimating the impact this event had on Allied forces and the generation from which they came.

The people of France have far from forgotten the intrepid actions of the men who participated in the harrowing battles on the beaches of Normandy, and as proof there are monuments, memorials, and museums throughout the area paying homage to them.

The **Caen Memorial Museum** [see *culture zoo*, below] is an absolute must-see as much for its comprehensive explanation of the social and political forces that created the Great War, as for its singular dedication to peace and mutual understanding as a means to avoiding further conflict.

About 35km northwest of Caen, is one of the most well-known of all D-day memorials, the **Normandy American Cemetery,** *(Tel 02/31-51-62-00; 9am-6pm daily May-Sept, 9am-6pm daily Oct-Mar).*

After an intense visit to the museum, check out one of the films in the exhibition space and then relax and let it all sink in for several hours while you wander the gardens of the museum.

Musée des Beaux-Arts *(Château; Tel 02/31-30-47-70; 9:30am-6pm Wed-Mon; 25-20F adult, 10F student, free 18 or younger and Wed):* This nicely designed modern space houses a collection of 17th-century French and Italian works as well as some paintings by Rubens, Boucher, and van der Weyden. Some strangely cool Modern pieces also crop up here, making it well worth a visit after a stroll around the ramparts of the Château.

Whether you're ardently opposed to war in all its forms, or still think it's the best way to make a boy a man, if you're not moved by a visit to this spot you're most likely a robot. Located on a cliff overlooking Omaha beach (the initial landing point of American forces on D-day) in Colleveille-sur Mer, over 9,000 white crosses and Stars-of-David cover the cemetery's 170 acres. Something of a WWII equivalent of the Vietnam memorial, thousand of veterans and families of the fallen come to the cemetery each year to pay homage to the boys who never made it home.

Further west of Omaha, in Pointe du Hoc, is **Musée des Rangers** *(14450 Grandcamp-Maisy; Tel 33/2-31-92-33-51),* a commemoration of Col. James Rudder and his elite Ranger task force (with a name like that, you just know they were cool). The museum chronicles the creation of the team and their subsequent capture of Point du Hoc. The area of Point du Hoc itself, with its scarred and ragged cliffs, is actually something of a living memorial to the conflict and is alone worth the trip.

Unfortunately, the best way to see these memorials is via car. From Paris, take A-13 west to Caen, continuing west on E-46 to Bayeux. From Bayeaux, take D6 north until you hit the coast. Take D514 west along the coast past Port-en-Bessin, the spots start to appear soon after. Your one and only bus option is **Bus Verts** *(Tel 02/31-92-02-92),* which runs to all the important spots along the coast. Call for schedule details.

The Battle of Normandy is an unforgettable event in French history, and probably one of the few times that Americans were unconditionally admired (maybe with the exception of that whole French New Wave thing), so listen: Take a break from your boozin' and your clubbin' and find out just how brave your grandpa and his war buddies really were.

Abbaye aux Hommes *(Esplanade Jean-Marie-Louvel; Tel 02/ 31-30-42-81; 8:15am-7:30pm daily; Free):* Attached to the Église Saint Étienne this abbey was founded by William the Conqueror in the 11th century. The church's twin 276-foot Romanesque towers and 15th-century Gothic, spired elaborations offer a dramatic vision of the faith of old Europe. God-fearing William began the abbey to secure his chances of reaching heaven's gates. Be sure to check out the hand-carved wooden portal doors and the wrought iron staircase for their exceptional craftsmanship.

Abbaye aux Dames *(Place de la Reine-Mathilde; Tel 02/31-06-98-98; 2-5:30pm daily; Free):* Unlike the ornate Abbaye aux Hommes, the Dames impresses with its elegant simplicity and clean Romanesque lines. Unfortunately its spires were destroyed during the 100 Years War, but Queen Mathilda, William the Conqueror's wife (and kissing cousin), rests undisturbed in the beautifully vaulted 12th-century choir. Thankfully, she was spared the cruel fate of William, whose body was first desecrated by the Huguenots in a 1562 uprising and then destroyed during the revolution. The abbey is about a two-minute walk east of the Château.

EATS

A colorful Martha Stewart-meets-Provence color scheme is perhaps the first thing you will notice about **La Cuillere Jaune** *(17 rue de l'Oratoire; Tel 02/31-50-19-94; 11:45am-2pm/7pm-midnight, closed Sat, Sun lunch; MC, V),* a cheaply priced, home-style restaurant with a nice private terrace. Light, delicious, seasonal dishes, friendly, attentive service, and a garden-like terrace (even if the patio chairs are plastic) make for delightful summer dining. During the summer, try the fresh smoked fish and grapefruit salad.

crashing

Staying in Caen is reasonably cheap, but on the whole the hotels are rather a dull affair. Cheap hotels swarm around the train station, but the 20-minute walk from the center is annoying and a bit creepy late at night.

Across the street from the mossy Église Saint Jean, the budget one-star **Hôtel Le Fuchsia** *(98 place St.-Jean; Tel 02/31-86-14-50, Fax 02/31-86-15-55; 100-190F single, 150-230F double; MC, V)* is attached to a brasserie of the same name and is decorated in pastels, as its name might imply. Planters with bright-colored petunias hanging off the first- and second-floor windows welcome visitors. Rooms are clean and comfortable, albeit with thin mattresses and small televisions. You can get rooms with private bath or shower (all have private toilet), and there is no elevator.

Another reliable bet is **Hôtel de France** *(10 rue de la Gare, 14000 Caen; Tel 02/31-52-16-99; Fax 02/31-83-23-16; 200-300F double).* Located across the street from the train station, this simple yet quaint six-story brick house comes equipped with TVs and comfortable beds to rest your weary bones. Although the furnishings are relatively basic, some rooms have been known to sport some pretty funky colors that you won't see in your everyday French hotel (did someone say fuchsia?). There's a restaurant, but it only accommodates group tours staying at the hotel.

Located along one of Caen's main drags, the two-star **Hôtel du Château** *(5 ave. du 6 Juin; Tel 02/31-86-15-37, Fax 02/31-86-58-08; 150-240F single, 220-280F double, breakfast 35F; MC, V)* has pink neon lights and a somewhat flashy entry way, but nothing could be more different than the actual rooms, which taken together could be a case study of the Euro-bland hotel aesthetic: generic Formica finishes and absolutely forgettable furniture. But where it counts, the Château has got it: cushy mattresses, large televisions, and clean showers and toilets.

You had better make reservations if you want to stay in the centrally located, reasonable, three-star **Hôtel Moderne** *(116 blvd. Maréchal Leclerc; Tel 02/31-86-04-23, Fax 02/31-85-37-93; 340-560F single, 410-610F double, 51F breakfast; MC, V, AE).* All rooms have comfortable beds, toilets, showers, and minibars, and are furnished with modern but less-than-attractive furniture. Breakfast is served on the fifth floor, with a panoramic view of Caen and a choice of newspapers.

need to know

Currency Exchange Banks will make all currency transactions. They are open Monday-Saturday, on Sundays, the **Caen Memorial,** if you're in the neighborhood, can make exchanges. ATMs are no help at all unless you have a bank card.

Tourist Information The **Office de Tourisme** *(Hôtel d'Escoville; 12 place Saint Pierre; Tel 02/31-27-14-14, Fax 02/31-27-14-18; All bus lines to Château 9:30am-7pm Mon-Sat, 9:30am-1pm/2-5pm Sun holidays; 10am-1pm/2-6pm Mon-Sat, 10am-1pm Sun winter; tourismeinfo@ville caen.fr, www.ville-caen.fr; MC, V, AE)* offers Internet access as well as a wealth of information on Caen and the Calvados region as a whole. It also books hotel rooms and changes money at reasonable rates.

Public Transportation CTAC *(15 rue de Geôle; Tel 02/31-15-55-55),* the city bus transportation, is reasonably efficient, but unnecessary for traveling around the city center. The only times you'll need it is to head to the **Mémorial,** the **Auberge de Jeunesse,** or the hospital. Tickets are 6.20F, 16.5F for an all-day pass and 53F for a *carnet* of 10 tickets. For **taxis** call *02/31-94-15-15* or *02/31-52-17-89.*

Health and Emergency SAMU Ambulance Service: *15;* Gendarmerie and police: *17;* firefighters: *18.* Your medical service options are the **Centre Hospitalier Regional Universitaire (CHRU)** *(Ave. de la Côte de Nacre; Tel 02/31-06-31-06; Bus 6,8 13 to stop **CHU**; Open for emergencies 24 hours daily, and non-medical emergencies 10am-8pm daily)* or the **Hôtel de Police** *(Rue Docteur Thibout de la Fresnaye; Tel 02/31-29-22-22; Open for emergencies 24 hours daily, and non-emergencies 8:25am-noon/2-6pm daily).*

Pharmacy Located right off the avenue 6 du Juin, which runs from the train station to the château, **Pharmacie Madelaine** *(3 place de la Résistance; Tel 02/31-86-24-39)* is able to fulfill just about all of your over-the-counter medicinal needs.

Trains The **Gare SNCF** *(Place de la Gare; Tel 02/36-35-35-35; Buses 1, 3, 5, 6, 7, 9, 10, 12, 15, 16, 23 to SNCF)* is located just south of town (about a half-hour walk) and sends trains hourly to Paris Saint Lazare. The trip takes an hour and 45 minutes and costs approximately 174F.

Buses The **Bus Verts du Calvados Depot** *(Tel 02/31-44-77-53; Information Tel 0/801-214-214),* located next to the train station, has express regional service to Le Havre for 122F.

Ferries Brittany Ferries *(Outristreham Gare Maritime; Tel 02/31-36-36-00; 320F mid-July-Aug, 280F Apr-June Sept, Oct, 180F Nov-Mar)* has three departures daily to Portsmouth from Outristreham's *gare maritime*. There is a 20F shuttle bus from Caen's *gare* to the ferry. The trip from Caen to Outristreham takes 25 minutes and the ferry takes six hours.

Postal The **Post Office** *(Rue Georges Lebret; Tel 02/31-39-35-75; 8am-7pm Mon-Fri, 10-noon/2pm-5pm Sun)* has all the usual postal operations.

cherbourg

Although a pleasing greyscale for the hungover, bloodshot eyes arriving by ferry from parties in Portsmouth, England, the town of Cherbourg is hardly a site to star on the map. This port city is, simply, just what the term implies—boats come in, boats drop off cargo, boats leave. The hustle 'n' bustle surrounding other famous ports simply isn't here; if you do find yourself stopping in Cherbourg from points north, it's best to treat the city as a stepping stone to the rest of Normandy and France and ignore the temptation to scour the side streets for hidden activity. Not that there are many appealing streets to explore, mind you—the central waterway, **Bassin du Commerce,** effectively separates the hardly lively western side of town from the ghostly shadows of the eastern half. In the west you'll spot the occasional Cherbourg resident, but mostly boatmen whistling through dirty teeth while they search for a bite to eat.

While nightlife may not be Cherbourg's waving banner of hope, if you do find yourself stuck in town there are a few options for distraction. Cherbourg was born as a major port after getting some pretty crazy artificial breakwaters; if you're into high seas adventure without the peg leg and eye patch, it is rather awe inspiring to watch the crashing waves from the **Fort du Roule**, situated off avenue Étienne LeCarpentier, southeast of the train station (on the lifeless side of the river). It sits high atop the town so you can get a view of the port. It is also the site of the **Musée de la Libération** *(10am-6pm daily Apr-Sept, 10am-6pm Tue-Sun, 9:30am-noon/2-5:30pm Mon Oct-March; Films 20F)*, a little museum packed with photographs and posters detailing the Nazi occupation, liberation, and reconstruction of Normandy, which is a worthwhile stop if you have time between ferry and train. There's also the beach itself, which while quite passable is hardly the seaside getaway the town's online propaganda makes it out to be. A "seaside family resort town"? *Non non, mon cheri....*

bar scene

The two most popular bars in town draw a young, fun, international crowd (a lot of Brits in town for a night or so) and have brasserie sections where you can fortify yourself with seafood after tanking up on wine and booze. Both places are in the center of Cherbourg: **Le Fifty's Diner** *(5-*

7 place Général-de-Gaulle; Tel 02/33-43-58-20) serves both American and traditional French food; **Bar-Brasserie Le Commerce** *(42 rue François la Vieille; Tel 02/33-53-18-20)* serves French-style brasserie food and seafood.

eats

Eating well in Cherbourg is thankfully a breezier task than one might suspect. Seafood spots abound (no surprise there), along with some more land-based restaurants and the twice-weekly **fresh food market** *(Tue and Thur until 5pm; Place de Gaulle and place Centrale).*

For a complete—albeit fairly cheesy—feel o' the sea, check out **La Moulerie** *(73 rue au Blé; Tel 02/33-01-11-90; Closed Sun, Mon lunch; Entrées 45-120F).* Here you'll find mostly mussels, with sides of a more British persuasion (read: lots of potatoes). Each dish is available with a variety of homemade sauces, though our suggestion is to stay away from the weirder sounding options—there's a reason they sound strange to the ear. The mustard wine sauce is, however, surprisingly yummy—you'll want to mop it up with some greasy chips after you're through.

A quick fix in center city can be had at **Tea Time** *(39 rue Maréchal Foch; Tel 02/03-94-46-47; Entrées 30-70F),* which serves up the typical brasserie fare—from sandwiches or panini to salads or heftier main dishes.

crashing

Most hotels in Cherbourg are quite similar, making almost any selection on the western side of town a safe bet. Don't expect Internet access or a Jacuzzi spa; Cherbourg's accommodations don't cater to the business or jet set. What you will find are modest prices, comfortable rooms, and a good-enough place to rest your bones before moving on out of town.

One of the most popular hotels is the **Hôtel Moderna** *(28 rue de la Marine; Tel 02/33-43-05-30; 140-200F double),* situated in a desirable central location and usually filled with the most tourists. Farther down the street you'll find the **Hôtel Renaissance** *(4 rue de l'Église; Tel 02/33-43-19-16; 140-190F double),* another heavily selected spot. Both of these hotels offer cut-rate rooms without showers (great if you're only spending the night and want to save some cash) or larger rooms with shower facilities.

For a room near the tourist office and right next to the port, stop by **La Régence** *(42 quai de Caligny; Tel 02/33-43-05-16; 160-250F double)* a more gussied-up version of its neighbors, if only for the extended TV package and more attractive bedspreads.

And, if you really feel the need to visit and vacate Cherbourg as quickly as possible, plunk down the change for a room at **Hôtel de la Gare** *(10 place Jean-Jaurès; Tel 02/33-43-06-81; 140-200F double),* a homely little number right next to the station.

need to know

Currency Exchange Exchange traveler's checks and cash at banks or ATMs for the best rates, or at most hotels for a slightly higher fee. The biggest concentration of banks is on quai Alexandre III, around the tourist office. Some of the most visible ATMs in the center of town and around the train station include **Crédit Agricole** *(87 rue du Val-de-Saire; 10 rue de l'Ancien Quai)* and **Crédit Maritime Mutuel** *(55 rue Maréchal Foch).*

Tourist Information The **tourist office** *(2 quai Alexandre III; Tel 02/33-93-52-02; June-Aug, Mon-Sat 9am-6:30pm; Sept-May Mon 1:30-6pm, Tue-Fri 9am-noon and 1:30-6pm, Sat 9am-noon)* is near the center of town. They will make hotel reservations for you at no charge.

Public Transportation Cherbourg's bus system centers around the train station at the **Autogare** *(Tel 02/33-44-32-22, weekdays 8:45am-noon/2-6:30pm, for information)* and runs intermittently throughout the small town. Fare is 5.80F, and tickets can be bought on board. There is also a bus whose sole purpose is to run between the ferry terminal and the tourist office. It makes the trip 3-10 times a day, depending on the season, and tickets, which you buy on board, are 5F.

Health and Emergency Police: *17;* fire: *18;* ambulance: *15.*

Pharmacies Pharmacies are located throughout town; look for the flashing green cross.

Trains and Buses Cherbourg's **Gare SNCF** *(Ave. Francois-Miller/place Jean-Jaurès; Tel 02/33-57-50-50)* connects the small town to several destinations including Paris and Caen. The regional bus line, **STN** *(Tel 02/33-85-50-00),* runs to campsites and spots of interest near Cherbourg, and leaves from the Autogare [see above].

Boats Boats are a big deal in this port town, connecting Cherbourg with both England and Ireland. The quickest ride is via **Superstar Express** service to Portsmouth, which takes about 2 hours and 45 minutes on **P&O** *(Tel 02/03-85-65-70; 5-6 runs per day).* Slower rides are available to England on **Brittany Ferries** *(Tel 02/33-88-44-88; 1-2 runs per day)* or to Ireland on **Rosslare** *(Tel 02/33-44-28-96; 1-2 runs per day).* The ferry terminal is 3km northeast of the train station; unless you're in the mood for a long walk through a dull town, it's best to take the bus between them [see above].

Laundry Just off Place Centrale in center city, there is a **laundrette** at 62 rue au Ble *(7am-10pm daily).*

MONT ST-MICHEL

With all the *rues* and *places* "Saint Michel" in Rennes, one wonders where all this buzz originates. The answer, of course, is the famous and historic Mont Saint Michel, a stunning little summit on a rocky islet connected to the Golfe de Saint Malo by causeway. If you make the journey out here, be prepared for plenty of schlocky souvenir stands, and a serious walk up **Grand Rue** through hordes of tourists to reach the famous **abbey** *(Tel 02/33-89-80-00; 9am-5:30pm daily May-Sept [mass daily at 12:15pm];*

9:30am-4:30pm Oct-Apr [mass daily at 12:15pm]; Admission free)—albeit a walk made beautiful by the 15th- and 16th-century houses lining the street (still, for the most part, inhabited by wealthy locals). If you can get into the right mindset, it's sort of like a melodramatic Hollywood epic—minus shrieking Mel Gibson and warpaint. Visitors from the entire world over make the trek to visit the abbey, some out of religious curiosity, but most simply to view the stunning mix of architectural styles—from the Gothic choir to the pink granite refectory from the early 1200s—that make up the structure that saved France from invaders during the Medieval era.

Many think of revolutionary and independent France simply in terms of the 19th-century revolution, but it was here at Mont Saint Michel that the concept of a free-standing France was truly birthed—centuries before that event, during the darkest years of France's occupation by the English.

Once you're finished with the free stuff—walking and exploring of the *abbey* itself—you can opt to visit any of the three smaller attractions surrounding the *abbey*. There's the **Archéoscope** *(Tel 02/33-48-09-37),* a small theater presenting shows on the history of the abbey, the **Musée Maritime et Archéologique** *(Tel 02/33-60-14-09),* a historical and geographical showcase that illustrates the region surrounding Mont Saint Michel, and the **Musée Grevin** *(Tel 02/33-60-07-01),* a small museum trawling the history of the *abbey.* Conveniently, all are open the same hours *(9:30am-5:30pm daily)* and charge the same admission price *(45F for adults; 30F for those under 16).* You can get a combined pass *(75F for adults, 45F for those under 16),* which is a good value if you're *really* into discovering every aspect of Mont Saint Michel, but honestly the attractions can feel a bit touristy. If you're running short on dough (or even if you're not...) it might be best simply to appreciate the natural beauty of the surrounding area—including the famous and sometimes ferocious tides and quicksands—and the amazing *abbey* itself, rather than splurging on the tourist attractions.

Staying near the Mont is gonna cost you—it's best to make this a daytrip. But if you miss the last train out of town, there are options. If you've got the gear, you can sleep for cheap at **Camping du Mont Saint Michel** *(2km out of Mont Saint Michel on D976 toward Pontorson; Tel 02/33-60-09-33; Open mid Feb-mid Nov; 22F per person, 20F per tent and car; 220F per bungalow).* Besides grassy fields for pitching tents, they also offer little two-person wooden bungalows, complete with bathroom facilities, which are a nice compromise between roughing it and true comfort. And speaking of comfort, you'll find plenty of it at the cushy, expensive hotels in town. The most reasonable of the lot is **Les Terraces Poulard** *(Grand Rue; Tel 02/33-60-14-09, Fax 02/33-60-37-31; mere.poulard.mtstmichel@wanadoo.fr, www.mere-poulard.fr; 300-900F per room; All credit cards),* housed in two village houses—one medieval, one from the 1800s—that are joined at the hip. They price their rooms based on the quality of the view, so if you don't mind opening your shades to street-level traffic, you can have a comfy bed, private bath, and your very own TV without completely breaking the bank. The English-speaking staff is very sweet, and there's a moderately priced restaurant that serves decent regional (read: seafood) specialties accompanied by a gorgeous view of the bay. It's the first hotel on your left as you walk up the hill.

If your tum is grumbling, you can have a sit-down at one of the over-priced touristy restaurants, or grab picnic supplies at the **supermarché** *(2km out of Mont St.-Michel on D976 toward Pontorson; 8am-8pm, closed Sun, mid Feb-Oct)*, conveniently located next to the Camping du Mont Saint Michel. If you do feel the need to be waited on, try the **restaurant in the Hôtel du Mouton-Blanc** *(Grand Rue; Tel 02/33-60-05-62; Lunch and dinner daily; Fixed-price menus 70-255F; All credit cards).* Soak in the Norman aesthetic in the *über*-rustic dining room, with its rough wooden walls and stone accents, or choose a seat on the terrace and gaze out to sea. The food is all lovely, from the roast pork in cider sauce to the mussels in cream sauce.

need to know

Tourist Info The **Office de Tourisme** *(In the Corps de Garde des Bour-geois, at the left of the town gates; Tel 02/33-60-14-30; 9am-noon/2-5:45pm Mon-Sat, till 7pm with no lunch break in July and August)* will give you all the brochures and info you desire.

Bus Mont Saint Michel can be most easily reached by bus, from Rennes. One provider is **Les Couriers Bretons** *(Tel 02/99-56-79-09 for reser-vations and info, which sends buses from Rennes to Mont-Saint Michel 2-5 times a day, depending on the season).*

planning your trip

In the pages that follow, we've compiled everything you need to know to handle the practical details of planning your trip—what documents you'll need, how to use French currency, how to find the best airfare, when to go, and more—as well as basic info on the regions of France and it's art and architecture.

The regions in brief

No other country concentrates such a stunning diversity of sights and scenes into so compact an area as France does. It encompasses each of the characteristics that make up Europe: the north's flat, fertile lands; the central Loire Valley's rolling green hills; the east's snowcapped alpine ranges and hordes of young skiers; the southwest's towering Pyrénées; the west's sprawling vineyards (most willing to spot you a free taste of their goods); the Massif Central's plateaus and rock outcroppings; and the southeast's lushly semitropical Mediterranean coast, perfect for kicking back with an umbrella-topped cocktail.

All these regions are within easy traveling range of Paris (conveniently located in the center of the country) and each other. The train trip from the capital is just 4 hours to Alsace, 5 to the Alps, 7 to the Pyrénées, and 8 to the Côte d'Azur. France's National Railroads (SNCF) operate one of the finest lines in the world, with impressively fast service to and from Paris (though trains tend to crawl on routes unconnected with the capital).

If you decide to rent a car—though the train covers tucked away spots quite nicely—you'll find some 44,000 miles of roadway at your disposal, most in good condition for fast long-distance driving. (But try not to stick to the Route Nationale network all the time. Nearly all of France's scenic splendors lie along secondary roads, and what you'll lose in mileage you'll more than make up for in enjoyment.) France is a great place to discover by bicycle, and those secondary roads are well-suited for long, meandering rides.

A "grand tour" of France is nearly impossible for the average visitor, who doesn't have a lifetime to explore the country. If you want to get to know a province in depth, it's good to devote a week to a specific region if you can; you may have a more rewarding trip if you concentrate on getting to know two or three areas in greater depth and at a leisurely pace rather than racing around, trying to cram in too much. You're going to be faced with hard choices about where to go in your limited time, so with this in mind, we've summarized the highlights of each region for you.

ÎLE DE FRANCE (INCLUDING PARIS) The Île de France is an island only in the sense that its boundaries (following about a 50-mile radius from the center of Paris) are delineated by rivers with odd-sounding names like Essonne, Epte, Aisne, Eure, and Ourcq, plus a handful of canals. It was in this temperate basin that France was born. This region's spectacular attractions include **Paris, Versailles, Fontainebleau,** and **Notre-Dame de Chartres,** yet it also incorporates endless dreary suburbs and even Disneyland Paris. Despite creeping industrialization, pockets of verdant charm remain, including the **forests** of **Rambouillet** and **Fontainebleau.**

THE NORTH France's northern region is often ignored by North Americans unless they happen to be there catching a ferry. In summer, French families arrive by the thousands to visit Channel beach resorts like **Le Touquet-Paris-Plage.** This district is heavily industrialized and (like neighboring Champagne) has always been horribly war-torn. The region's best-known port, **Calais,** was a bitterly contested English stronghold on the French mainland for hundreds of years. Ironically, Calais functions today as the port of disembarkation for the ferries, hydrofoils, and Chunnel arrivals from Britain. **Notre-Dame Cathedral** in **Amiens,** the medieval capital of Picardy, is a treasure, with a 140-foot-high nave—the highest in France.

CHAMPAGNE Every French monarch since 496A.D. was crowned at **Reims,** and much of French history revolved around this holy site and the fertile hills ringing it. Joan of Arc was burned at the stake thanks partly to her efforts to lead her dauphin through enemy lines to Reims. Directly in the path of any invader wishing to occupy Paris, both Reims and the fertile Champagne district have been awash in more blood throughout the centuries, including the terrible World War I battles of Somme and Marne. There are industrial sites concentrated among patches of verdant forest, and the steep sides of valleys are sheathed in vineyards.

The 78-mile road from Reims to Vertus, one of the three **Routes du Champagne,** takes in a trio of wine-growing regions that produce 80% of the bubbly used for celebrations around the world.

ALSACE-LORRAINE Between Germany and the forests of the Vosges is the most Teutonic of France's provinces: **Alsace,** with cosmopolitan **Strasbourg** as its capital. Celebrated for its cuisine, particularly its foie gras and *choucroute* (sauerkraut), this area is home to villages whose half-timbered designs will make you think of the Black Forest. **Lorraine,** birthplace of Joan of Arc and site of the industrial center of **Mulhouse,** witnessed countless bloody battles during the world wars. Its capital, **Nancy,** is the proud guardian of a grand 18th-century plaza: Place Stanislaus. The much-eroded peaks of the **Vosges** forest, the closest thing to a wilderness left in France, offer rewarding hiking.

BURGUNDY Few trips will prove as rewarding as several leisurely days spent exploring Burgundy, with its splendid old cities like **Dijon.** Besides being famous for its cuisine (*boeuf and escargots à la bourguignonne,* for example), the district contains, along its Côte d'Or, hamlets whose names are synonymous with great wines.

THE MASSIF CENTRAL/AUVERGNE The rugged heartland of south-central France, this underpopulated district contains ancient cities, unspoiled scenery, and an abundance of black lava, from which many area buildings were created. Hiking opportunities, along with other outdoor pleasures, abound.

According to Parisians, the Massif Central is provincial with a vengeance—and the locals work hard to keep it that way. From historic Clermont-Ferrand, the well-preserved medieval capital of the province of the Auvergne, you can head out into the surrounding **Parc Naturel Régional des Volcans d'Auvergne.**

THE RHÔNE VALLEY & THE FRENCH ALPS A fertile area of alpine foothills and sloping valleys in eastern and southeastern France, the upper Rhône Valley ranges from the cosmopolitan French suburbs of the Swiss city of Geneva to the northern borders of Provence. The district is thoroughly French, unflinchingly bourgeois, and dedicated to preserving the gastronomic and cultural traditions that have produced some of the most celebrated chefs in French history.

Only 2 hours by train from Paris, the region's cultural centerpiece, **Lyon,** is France's "second city." You can explore the Rhône Valley en route from northern climes to Provence and the south. The Rhône Valley is also the "doorway" to the French Alps. This area's resorts rival those of neighboring Switzerland and contain some incredible scenery: snowcapped peaks, glaciers, and alpine lakes. **Chamonix** is a world-famous ski resort facing Mont Blanc, Western Europe's highest mountain. Annecy is a charming little canal-filled town that sits on the edge of an alpine lake.

During summer in the Alps you can enjoy such spa resorts as **Evian** and the calm and restful 19th-century resorts ringing Lake Geneva.

PROVENCE One of France's most fabled regions flanks the Alps and the Italian border along its eastern end and incorporates a host of sites the rich and famous have long frequented. Premier destinations are **Aix-en-Provence,** associated with Cézanne; Arles, "the soul of Provence," captured so brilliantly by Van Gogh; **Avignon,** the 14th-century capital of Christendom during the papal schism; and **Marseille,** a port city established by the ancient Phoenicians (in some ways more North African than French). The **Camargue,** on the western edge of Provence, is the name given to the steaming marshy delta formed by two arms of the Rhône River. Rich in bird life, it's famous for its flat expanses of tough grasses and for fortified medieval sites. The strip of glittering coastal towns along Provence's southern edge is known as the Côte d'Azur (see below).

CÔTE D'AZUR & THE FRENCH RIVIERA The fabled gold-plated Côte d'Azur (Blue Coast) has become hideously overbuilt and spoiled by tourism. Even so, the names of its resorts still evoke glamour and excitement. July and August are the most crowded, but spring and fall can be a delight. **Nice** (pronounced niece) is the biggest city along this coast, and the most convenient base for exploring the area. The independent principality of **Monaco,** the most fabled piece of real estate along the Côte d'Azur, occupies less than a square mile. Along the coast are some sandy beaches, but many are rocky or pebbly. Topless bathing is common, especially in **St. Tropez,** and some of the restaurants here are fabled citadels of conspicuous consumption. This is not just a place for sun and fun, however. Dozens of artists and their patrons have littered the landscape with world-class galleries and art museums.

Teeny tiny **Monaco** (1.21 square miles in all) is technically an independent nation, but you'd hardly know it. Document requirements for travel to Monaco are exactly the same as those for travel to France, and there are virtually no border patrols or passport formalities at the Monégasque frontier. *Tip:* Unless you're traveling with tails and major moolah, don't even try to get into the casinos in Monte Carlo.

If you'd like information specifically about the principality of Monaco, contact the **Monaco Government Tourist and Convention Bureau,** 565 Fifth Ave., 23rd Floor, New York, NY 10017; Tel 212/286-3330, Fax 212/286-9890. Most of its facilities (along with its consulate) are in New York at the above address.

In London, the office is at 3/18 Chelsea Garden Market, The Chambers, Chelsea Harbour, London SW10 OXF; Tel 029/7352-9962, Fax 020/7352-2103.

LANGUEDOC-ROUSSILLON & THE PYRÉNÉES Languedoc may not be as chic as Provence, but it's also less frenetic and more affordable. Roussillon is the rock-strewn arid French answer to ancient Catalonia, just across the Spanish border. **Toulouse,** the bustling pink capital of Languedoc is a great place start your visit here. Heading toward the border with Spain, you might stop at the small town of **Foix,** then into **The Parc National des Pyrénées,** the national park crisscrossed with gorgeous hiking trails. In the isolated villages and towns of the Pyrénées, the old folkloric traditions, strongly permeated with Spanish influences, continue to thrive.

THE BASQUE COAST Extending west to the Atlantic coast, the rugged Pyrénées have formed a natural boundary between France and Spain since prehistoric times. The Basques, one of Europe's most unusual cultures, flourished within the sheltered valleys of the mountain range. The Basque influence is felt to this day throughout the adjacent areas of the country, and of course, in northern Spain as well. Clustered together at the coast, you'll want to stop in **Bayonne, Anglet,** and **St.-Jean-Pied-de-Port,** as well as resorts like **Biarritz,** which in the 19th century attracted the French aristocracy.

BORDEAUX WINE COUNTRY & THE MID-ATLANTIC COAST
Flat, fertile, and frequently ignored by North Americans, this region incorporates towns pivotal in French history, such as **La Rochelle,** and wine- and liquor-producing villages whose names are celebrated around the world. **Bordeaux,** the district's largest city, has an economy firmly based on wine merchandising and boasts truly grand 18th-century architecture. Traveling inland toward the Massif Central, you'll want to venture into the Dordogne & Périogord region the site of some of Europe's oldest prehistoric settlements. For biking or just indulging in a totally decadent gourmet meal, the region is among the top vacation spots in France. In the Périogord, traces of Cro-Magnon settlements are evidenced by the cave paintings at Les Eyzies. The Dordogne is the second-largest *département* (French equivalent of an American state). Some of France's most unusual châteaux were built in the valley of the Dordogne during the early Middle Ages, and many of the towns that grew here are spectacularly beautiful. The region is, unfortunately, no longer undiscovered, as retirees from abroad have moved into the elegant stone manor houses dotting the banks of the many rivers.

THE LOIRE VALLEY This area includes two ancient provinces, **Touraine** (centered on **Tours**) and **Anjou** (centered on **Angers**). It was beloved by royalty and nobility until Henry IV moved his court to Paris. Head here to see the most magnificent castles in France. Irrigated by the Loire River and its many tributaries, this valley produces many superb and reasonably priced wines.

BRITTANY Jutting out into the Atlantic, the westernmost (and one of the poorest) region of France is known for its rocky coastlines, Celtic roots, frequent rains, and ancient dialect, which is akin to the Gaelic tongues of Wales and Ireland. Many French vacationers love the seacoast (rivaled only by the Côte d'Azur) for its sandy beaches, high cliffs, and relatively modest prices (by French standards, anyway).

NORMANDY This region will forever be linked to the 1944 D-Day invasion. Some readers consider their visit to the D-Day beaches the most emotionally worthwhile part of their trip to France. Normandy boasts 372 miles of coastline and a long-standing maritime tradition. It's a popular weekend getaway from Paris, starting with **Giverny.** Many glamorous hotels and restaurants thrive here, especially around the casino town of Deauville. This area has hundreds of half-timbered houses reminiscent of medieval England, and mighty ports like **Cherbourg** and **Le Havre,** where the Seine flows into the English Channel. Normandy's great attractions include **Rouen's** cathedral, the abbey of Jumièges, and medieval Bayeux.

VISITOR INFORMATION

Your best source of information before you go is the **French Government Tourist Office (www.fgtousa.org),** which can be also reached at the following addresses:

In the United States, at 444 Madison Ave., 16th floor, New York, NY 10022 *(Tel 212/838-7800);* 676 N. Michigan Ave., Suite 3360, Chicago, IL 60611-2819 *(Tel 312/751-7800);* or 9454 Wilshire Blvd., Suite 715, Beverly Hills, CA 90212-2967 *(Tel 310/271-6665).* To request information, you can also try France on Call *(Tel 410/286-8310).*

In **Canada,** contact the Maison de la France/French Government Tourist Office, 1981 av. McGill College, Suite 490, Montreal, H3A 2W9 *(Tel 514/288-4264).*

In the **United Kingdom,** contact the Maison de la France/French Government Tourist Office, 178 Piccadilly, London, W1V 0AL *(Tel 020/7399-3540; Fax 020/7493-6594).*

In **Ireland,** call the Maison de la France/French Government Tourist Office, 10 Suffolk St., Dublin 2, Ireland *(Tel 01/679-0813).*

In **Australia,** contact the French Tourist Bureau, 6 Perth Ave., Xarralumia, NSW 2000, Australia *(Tel 02/6216-0100; Fax 02/9221-8682).*

In **New Zealand,** there's no representative, so you can contact the Australia phone or fax listed above.

You'll also want to check out the Online Directory in the next chapter.

ENTRY REQUIREMENTS & CUSTOMS

PASSPORTS & VISAS

All foreign (non-French) nationals need a valid passport to enter France.

The French government no longer requires visas for U.S. citizens, providing they're staying in France for less than 90 days. For longer stays, U.S. visitors must apply for a long-term visa, residence card, or temporary-stay visa. Each requires proof of income or a viable means of support in France and a legitimate purpose for remaining in the country. Applications are available from the **Consulate Section of the French Embassy,** 4101 Reservoir Rd. NW, Washington, DC 20007 Tel 202/944-6000; or from the **Visa Section of the French Consulate,** 10 E. 74th St., New York, NY 10021, Tel 212/606-3689. Visas are required for students planning to study in France even if the stay is for less than 90 days.

At the moment, citizens of Britain, Canada, New Zealand, Switzerland, Japan, and European Union countries do not need visas.

Australians do need visas to enter France. They're available from the **French Consulate,** Consulate General, 31 Market St., 26th Floor, Sydney, NSW 2000; Tel 02/9261-5931.

South Africans also need visas to enter France. They're available from the **French Consulate,** 2 Dean St., Cape Town 8001, Tel 0421/23-15-75, Fax 021/24-84-70.

WHAT YOU CAN BRING INTO FRANCE Customs restrictions for visitors entering France differ for citizens of the European Union and for citizens of non-EU countries. Non-EU nationals can bring in duty-free 200 cigarettes, 100 cigarillos, 50 cigars, or 250 grams of smoking tobacco. This amount is doubled if you live outside Europe. You can also bring in 2 liters of wine and 1 liter of alcohol over 22 proof and 2 liters of wine 22 proof or under. In addition, you can bring in 50 grams of perfume, a quarter liter of eau de toilette, 500 grams of coffee, and 200 grams of tea. Visitors ages 15 and over can bring in other goods totaling 300 F ($48); for those 14 and under the limit is 600 F ($96). (Customs officials tend to be lenient about general merchandise, realizing that the limits are unrealistically low.)

Citizens of European Union countries can bring in any amount of goods as long as these goods are intended for their personal use and not for resale.

WHAT YOU CAN BRING HOME Returning U.S. citizens who have been away for 48 hours or more are allowed to bring back, once every 30 days, $400 worth of merchandise duty-free. You'll be charged a flat rate of 10% duty on the next $1,000 worth of purchases. Be sure to have your receipts handy. On gifts, the duty-free limit is $100. You cannot bring fresh foodstuffs into the United States; canned foods, however, are allowed. For more information, contact the **U.S. Customs Service** Tel 202/927-6724; www.customs.ustreas.gov., and request the free pamphlet *Know Before You Go.* It's also available on the Web at www.customs.ustreas.gov.

Citizens of the U.K. who are returning from a European Community (EC) country will go through a separate Customs Exit (called the "Blue Exit") especially for EC travelers. In essence, there is no limit on what you can bring back from an EC country, as long as the items are for personal use (this includes gifts), and you have already paid the necessary duty and tax. However, customs law sets out guidance levels. If you bring in more than these levels, you may be asked to prove that the goods are for your own use. Guidance levels on goods bought in the EC for your own use are 800 cigarettes, 200 cigars, 1kg smoking tobacco, 10 liters of spirits,

90 liters of wine (of this not more than 60 liters can be sparkling wine), and 110 liters of beer. For more information, contact **HM Customs & Excise,** Passenger Enquiry Point, 2nd Floor Wayfarer House, Great South West Road, Feltham, Middlesex, TW14 8NP, Tel 020/8910-3744 (Tel 44/181-910-3744 from outside the U.K.); or consult their Web site at www.hmce.gov.uk.

For a clear summary of Canadian rules, visit the comprehensive Web site of the Canada Customs and Revenue Agency at **www.ccra-adrc.gc.ca.** You can also write for the booklet *I Declare,* issued by **Revenue Canada,** 2265 St. Laurent Blvd., Ottawa K1G 4KE, Tel 613/993-0534. Canada allows its citizens a $750 exemption, and you're allowed to bring back duty-free 200 cigarettes, 2.2 pounds of tobacco, 1.5 liters of liquor, and 50 cigars. In addition, you're allowed to mail gifts to Canada from abroad at the rate of Can$60 a day, provided they're unsolicited and don't contain alcohol or tobacco (write on the package "Unsolicited gift, under $60 value").

Citizens of Australia should request the helpful Australian Customs brochure *Know Before You Go,* available by calling Tel 1-300/363-263 from within Australia, or Tel 61-2/6275-6666 from abroad. For additional information, go online to www.dfat.gov.au and click on Hints for Australian Travellers. The duty-free allowance in Australia is A$400 or, for those under 18, A$200. In addition, Australian citizens can bring back 250 cigarettes or 250 grams of loose tobacco, and 1.125 liters of alcohol.

For New Zealand customs information, contact the **New Zealand Customs Service,** 50 Anzac Ave., P.O. Box 29, Auckland, Tel 09/359-6655, www.customs.govt.nz. The duty-free allowance for New Zealand is NZ$700. Citizens over 17 can bring in 200 cigarettes, or 50 cigars, or 250 grams of tobacco (or a mixture of all three if their combined weight doesn't exceed 250 grams); plus 4.5 liters of wine and beer, or 1.125 liters of liquor.

money honey

France is one of the world's most expensive destinations. But, to compensate, it often offers top-value food and lodging. Part of the problem is the value-added tax (VAT in English, or TVA in French), which tacks between 6% and 33% on top of everything.

It's expensive to rent and drive a car in France (gasoline is costly, too), and flying within France costs more than flying within the United States. Train travel is relatively inexpensive, however, especially if you purchase a railpass.

Remember that prices in Paris and on the Riviera will be higher than those in the provinces. Three of the most touristed areas—Brittany, Normandy, and the Loire Valley—have reasonably priced hotels and scads of restaurants offering superb food at moderate prices.

THE FRENCH FRANC

The basic unit of French currency is the franc (F), which consists of 100 centimes. Coins are issued in units of 5, 10, 20, and 50 centimes, plus 1,

2, 5, and 10 francs. Notes are denominated in 20, 50, 100, 200, 500, and 1,000 francs.

All banks are equipped for foreign exchange, and you'll find exchange offices at the airports and airline terminals. Banks are open Monday through Friday from 9am to noon and 2 to 4pm. Major bank branches also open their exchange departments on Saturday from 9am to noon.

When converting your home currency into francs, be aware that rates may vary. Your hotel will offer the worst rate. In general, banks offer the best, but even they charge a commission, depending on the transaction. Whenever you can, stick to the big banks of France, like Crédit Lyonnais, which usually offer the best rates and charge the least commission. Always make sure you have enough francs for *le week-end.*

If you need a check denominated in French francs before your trip (for example, to pay a deposit on a hotel room), contact **Ruesch International,** Tel 800/424-2923. Ruesch performs a wide variety of conversion-related services, usually for $5 to $15 per transaction. You can also inquire at a local bank.

WHAT'S UP WITH THE EURO?

The euro, the new single European currency, became the official currency of France and 10 other countries on January 1, 1999, but not in the form of cash. (There are still no euro banknotes or coins in circulation—payment in euros can only be made by check, credit card, or some other bank-related system.)

The French franc will remain the only currency in France for cash transactions until December 21, 2001, when more and more businesses will start posting their prices in euros alongside those in French francs, which will continue to exist for a while longer. Over a maximum 6-month transition period, French franc banknotes and coins will be withdrawn from circulation.

The symbol of the euro is a stylized **E,** which actually looks like an uppercase C with a horizontal double bar through the middle; its official abbreviation is EUR.

Although at this time, very few, if any, French hotel and restaurant bills are actually paid in euros, there will be an increasing emphasis on the new pan-European currency.

ATMS

ATMs are linked to a national network that most likely includes your bank at home. **Cirrus/MasterCard** (Tel 800/424-7787; www.mastercard.com/atm/) and **PLUS/Visa** (Tel 800/843-7587; www.visa.com/atms) are the two most popular networks; check the back of your ATM card to see which network your bank belongs to. Use the 800 numbers to locate ATMs in your destination. Cirrus is linked to Credit Lyonnais, Banque Nationale de Paris, Ceile de France, and Societé Generale. PLUS is linked to Societé Generale, Banque National de Paris, Carte Bleue Group, and Credit Lyonnais. You can also ask your bank for a list of overseas ATMs. Be sure to check the daily withdrawal limit. Also, make sure you have a

PIN number that you can use in Europe. Depending on the number of digits in your PIN, you may not be able to use your ATM abroad.

TRAVELER'S CHECKS

Traveler's checks are something of an anachronism from the days before the ATM made cash accessible at any time. These days, traveler's checks seem less necessary because most cities have 24-hour ATMs that allow travelers to withdraw small amounts of cash as needed right from their own bank accounts, although you might be subject to a small fee for doing so. But some travelers still prefer the security offered by traveler's checks, since you can get a refund if they're lost or stolen, if you've kept a record of their serial numbers.

You can get traveler's checks at almost any bank. **American Express** offers checks in denominations of $10, $20, $50, $100, $500, and $1,000. You'll pay a service charge ranging from 1% to 4%. You can also get American Express traveler's checks over the phone by calling Tel 800/221-7282 or 800/721-9768; you can also purchase checks online at www.americanexpress.com. AmEx gold or platinum cardholders can avoid paying the fee by ordering over the telephone; platinum cardholders can also purchase checks fee-free in person at AmEx Travel Service locations (check the Web site for the office nearest you). American Automobile Association members can obtain checks fee-free at most AAA offices.

Visa offers traveler's checks at Citibank branches and other financial institutions nationwide; call Tel 800/227-6811 to locate the purchase location near you. MasterCard also offers traveler's checks through Thomas Cook Currency Services; call Tel 800/223-9920 for a location near you.

If you carry traveler's checks, be sure to keep a record of their serial numbers (separately from the checks, of course), so you're ensured a refund in case they're lost or stolen.

CREDIT CARDS

Credit cards are invaluable when traveling. They are a safe way to carry money and provide a convenient record of all your expenses. You can also withdraw cash advances from your credit cards at any bank (though you'll start paying hefty interest on the advance the moment you receive the cash, and you won't receive frequent-flyer miles on an airline credit card). At most banks, you don't even need to go to a teller; you can get a cash advance at the ATM if you know your PIN number. (If you've forgotten your PIN number or didn't even know you had one, call the phone number on the back of your credit card and ask the bank to send it to you. It usually takes 5 to 7 business days, though some banks will provide the number over the phone if you tell them your mother's maiden name or pass some other security clearance.)

Almost every credit card company has an emergency 800-number that you can call if your wallet or purse is stolen. They may be able to wire you a cash advance off your credit card immediately, and in many places, they can deliver an emergency credit card in a day or two. Citicorp Visa's U.S.

emergency number is Tel 800/336-8472. American Express cardholders and traveler's check holders should call Tel 800/221-7282 for all money emergencies. MasterCard holders should call Tel 800/307-7309.

when to go

July and August are the worst months. Parisians desert their city, leaving it to the crowds of tourists and the businesses that cater to them.

The best time to come to Paris is off-season, either in the uncommonly long spring (April through June) or the equally extensive autumn (September through November), when the tourist trade has trickled to a manageable flow and everything is easier to come by—from Métro seats to good-tempered waiters. The weather, however, is temperate throughout the year.

Hotels used to charge off-season rates during the cold, rainy period from November through February, when tourism slowed; now, however, they're often packed with business clients, trade fairs, and winter tour groups in those months, and there's less incentive for hoteliers to offer big reductions. Airfares, however, are still cheaper in these months, and more promotions are available. They rise in the spring and fall, peaking in the heavily trafficked summer months when tickets will cost the most.

Don't come to Paris in the first two weeks of October without a confirmed hotel reservation. The weather's fine, but the city is jammed for the annual motor show, when the French indulge their passion for cars.

WEATHER

France's weather varies considerably from region to region and sometimes from town to town as little as 12 miles apart. Despite its north latitude, Paris never gets very cold—snow is a rarity. The hands-down winner for wetness is Brittany, where Brest (known for the mold that adds flavor to its bleu cheeses—probably caused by the constant rainfall) receives a staggering amount of rain between October and December. The rain usually falls in a kind of steady, foggy drizzle and rarely lasts more than a day. May is the driest month.

The Mediterranean coast in the south has the driest climate. When it does rain, it's usually heaviest in spring and autumn. (Cannes sometimes receives more rainfall than Paris.) Summers are comfortably dry—beneficial to humans but deadly to much of the vegetation, which (unless it's irrigated) often dries and burns up in the parched months.

Provence dreads *le mistral* (an unrelenting, hot, dry, dusty wind), which most often blows in winter for a few days but can last for up to 2 weeks.

For up-to-the-minute weather forecasts, you can get updates from the Weather Channel by calling Tel 900/WEATHER in the United States (95¢ per minute). The 24-hour service reports on conditions in Paris and several other large cities throughout France.

france calendar of events

In France, holidays are known as *jours fériés*. Shops and many businesses (banks and some museums and restaurants) close on holidays, but hotels and emergency services remain open. For more options, see the **festivals and events** sidebars thorughout the book.

The main holidays—a mix of both secular and religious ones—include New Year's Day (January 1), Easter Sunday and Monday (April 15 to 16 in 2001; March 31 to April 2 in 2002), Labor Day (May 1), V-E Day in Europe (May 8), Whit Monday (May 19), Ascension Thursday (40 days after Easter: May 25 in 2001; May 10 in 2002), Bastille Day (July 14), Assumption of the Blessed Virgin (August 15), All Saints' Day (November 1), Armistice Day (November 11), and Christmas (December 25).

JANUARY

Monte Carlo Motor Rally. The world's most venerable car race. For more information, call Tel 92/16-61-66. Usually mid-January.

International Ready-to-Wear Fashion Shows (Le Salon International de Prêt-à-porter), Parc des Expositions, Porte de Versailles, Paris 15e (Tel 01/44-94-70-00). Here you'll see what the public will be wearing in 6 months. Mid-January to mid-February.

FEBRUARY

Carnival of Nice. Float processions, parades, confetti battles, boat races, street music and food, masked balls, and fireworks are all part of this ancient celebration. The climax follows the 113-year-old tradition of burning King Carnival in effigy, an event preceded by Les Batailles des Fleurs (Battles of the Flowers), during which members of opposing teams pelt one another with flowers. Make your hotel reservation well in advance. For information or reservations, contact the Nice Convention and Visitors Bureau, 1 esplanade Kennedy (BP 4079), 06302 Nice CEDEX 4 (Tel 04/92-14-48-00; Fax 04/92-14-48-03). Mid-February to early March.

MARCH

Foire du Trune, on the Neuilly Lawn of the Bois de Vincennes, Paris. This mammoth amusement park operates daily from 2pm to midnight. Call Tel 01/46-27-52-29. End of March to late May.

APRIL

The 24-hour Le Mans Motorcycle Race. For information, contact Automobile Club de l'ouest (Tel 02/43-40-24-24).

International Marathon of Paris. Runners from around the world compete. Call Tel 01/41-33-15-68. First weekend in April.

Son-et-Lumière (Sound-and-Light) Shows, Loire Valley. April to September.

MAY

Anniversary of the End of World War II, Paris and Reims. Though the capitulation of the Nazis was signed on May 7, 1945, the celebration lasts several days in Paris, and with even more festivity in Reims. May 5 to 8.

Cannes Film Festival. Movie madness transforms this city into a media circus, with daily melodramas acted out in cafes, on sidewalks, and in hotel lobbies. Great for people-watching. Reserve early and make a deposit. Getting a table on the Carlton terrace is even more difficult than procuring a room. Admission to some of the prestigious films is by invitation only.

There are box-office tickets for the less important films, which play 24 hours. For information, contact the Festival International du Film (FIF), at 99 blvd. Des Malesherbes, 75008 Paris (Tel 01/45-61-66-00; Fax 01/45-61-87-60). Two weeks before the festival, the event's administration moves en masse to the Palais des Festivals, esplanade Georges-Pompidou, 06400 Cannes (Tel 04/93-39-01-01). May 10 to 21.

French Open Tennis Championship, Stade Roland-Garros, 16e (Métro: Porte d'Auteuil). The Open features 10 days of Grand Slam men's and women's tennis. European and South American players traditionally dominate on the hot, red, slow, dusty courts. To get tickets call Tel 01/97-43-48-60. Late May to early June.

JUNE

Monaco Grand Prix. Hundreds of cars race through the narrow streets and winding corniche roads in a surreal blend of high-tech machinery and medieval architecture. For more information, call Tel 01/42-96-12-23. June 1 to 4.

Le Prix du Jockey Club (June 1 at 2pm) and the **Prix Diane-Hermès** (June 8 at 2pm), Hippodrome de Chantilly. Thoroughbreds from as far away as Kentucky and Brunei, as well as mounts owned by European aristocrats, compete in a very genteel race that's broadcast around France and talked about in horsey circles around the world. On race days, as many as 30 trains depart from Paris's Gare du Nord for Chantilly, where they are met with free shuttle buses to the track. Alternatively, buses depart on race days from Place de la République and Porte de St-Cloud, on a schedule that coincides with the beginning and end of the races. Call Tel 01/49-10-20-30 for information on this and on all other equine events in this calendar.

Cinéscénie de Puy du Fou, son-et-lumière at the Château du Puy du Fou, Les Epesses (Poitou-Charentes). With a cast of 650 actors, dozens of horses, laser shows, and a soundtrack by famous actors, it celebrates the achievements of the Middle Ages. For information, call Tel 02/51-64-11-11. Early June to early September.

Les Nocturnes du Mont-St.-Michel. This is a sound-and-light tour through the maze of stairways and corridors of one of Europe's most impressive medieval monuments. Performances are Monday to Saturday evenings from June to mid-September. In the off-season, performances are on Saturday and Sunday only. For more information, call Tel 02/33-89-80-00.

Festival de St.-Denis. This series presents 4 days of music in the burial place of the French kings, a grim early Gothic monument in Paris's industrialized northern suburb of St.-Denis. Call Tel 01/48-13-06-07 for information; Métro: St-Denis-Basilique. June 13 to 16.

Paris Air Show. This is where the military-industrial complex of France shows off enough high-tech hardware to make anyone think twice about invading La Patrie. Fans, competitors, and industrial spies mob the exhibition halls of Le Bourget Airport for a taste of what Gallic technocrats have wrought. For information, call Tel 01/53-23-33-33. Mid-June in alternate years only. The 2001 dates are June 15 to June 19.

The 24-Hour Le Mans Car Race. For information, contact Automobile Club de l'ouest (Tel 02/43-40-24-24). June 17 to 18.

Festival Chopin, Paris. Everything you've ever wanted to hear from the Polish exile who lived most of his life in Paris. Piano recitals are held in the Orangerie du Parc de Bagatelle. For information, call Tel 01/45-00-22-19. June 17 to July 14.

Gay Pride Parade, Paris. A week of expositions and parties climaxes in a massive parade patterned after those in New York and San Francisco. It begins at place de l'Odéon and proceeds to place de la Bastille, then is followed by the Grand Bal de Gay Pride at the Palais de Bercy, a major convention hall/sports arena. For information, contact Centre Gai et Lesbien, 3 rue Keller, 75011 Paris (Tel 01/43-57-21-47). June 24, 2001.

La Villette Jazz Festival. Some 50 concerts are held in churches, auditoriums, and concert halls in all neighborhoods of the Paris suburb of La Villette. Past festivals have included Herbie Hancock, Shirley Horn, Michel Portal, and other artists from around Europe and the world. For information, call Tel 08/03-30-63-06. Late June to early July.

JULY

Colmar International Music Festival, Colmar. Different classical musical concerts are held in various public buildings of one of the most folkloric towns in Alsace. For more information, call Tel 03/89-20-68-92. July 1 to July 15.

Le Grand Tour de France. Europe's most prominent, most highly contested, and most overabundantly televised bicycle race pits crews of wind-tunnel-tested athletes along an itinerary that detours deep into the Massif Central and ranges across the Alps. The race is decided at a finish line drawn across the Champs-Elysées. For information, call Tel 01/41-33-15-00. July 3 to 21.

Festival d'Avignon. One of France's most prestigious theater events, this world-class festival has a reputation for exposing new talent to critical acclaim. The focus is usually on avant-garde works in theater, dance, and music by groups from around the world. Make hotel reservations early. For information, call Tel 04/32-74-32-74 or Fax 04/90-82-95-03. July 5 to July 30.

Festival d'Aix-en-Provence. A musical event par excellence, featuring everything from Gregorian chant to melodies composed on computer synthesizers. The audience sits on the sloping lawns of the 14th-century papal palace for operas and concerts. Local recitals are performed in the medieval cloister of the Cathédrale St-Sauveur. Make advance hotel reservations and bring written confirmation with you. Expect heat, crowds, and traffic. For information, contact the Festival International d'Art Lyrique et Academie Europeénne de Musique, Palais de l'Ancien Archevêche, 13100 Aix-en-Provence (Tel 04/42-17-34-34; Fax 04/42-66-13-74). July 7 to 28.

Les Chorégies d'Orange, Orange. One of southern France's most important lyric festivals presents oratorios and choral works by master performers whose voices are amplified by the ancient acoustics of France's best-preserved Roman amphitheater. For information, call Tel 04/90-34-24-24. July 12 to August 1.

Bastille Day. Celebrating the birth of modern-day France, the nation's festivities reach their peak in Paris with street fairs, pageants, fireworks, and feasts. In Paris, the day begins with a parade down the Champs-Elysées and ends with fireworks at Montmartre. No matter where you are, by the end of the day you'll hear Edith Piaf warbling "La Foule" (The Crowd), the song that celebrated her passion for the stranger she met and later lost in a crowd on Bastille Day. July 14.

Paris Quartier d'Eté. These 4 weeks of music evoke the style of the pop orchestral music of an English village green. The setting is either the Arènes de Lutèce or the Cour d'Honneur at the Sorbonne, both in the Latin Quarter. The dozen or so concerts are usually grander than the outdoorsy setting would imply and include performances by the Orchestre de Paris, the Orchestre National de France, and the Baroque Orchestra of the European Union. Spin-offs of this include plays and jazz concerts. For information, call Tel 01/44-94-98-00 or Fax 01/44-94-98-01. July 15 to August 15.

Nice Jazz Festival. This is the biggest, flashiest, and most prestigious jazz festival in Europe, with world-class entertainers. Concerts begin in early afternoon and go on until late at night (sometimes all night in the clubs) on the Arènes de Cimiez, a hill above the city. Reserve hotel rooms way in advance. For information, contact the Grand Parade du Jazz, Cultural Affairs Department of the city of Nice (Tel 04/93-92-82-82; Fax 04/93-92-82-85). July 22 to 29.

St-Guilhem Music Season, St-Guilhem le Désert (Languedoc). This festival of baroque organ and choral music is held in a medieval monastery. For information, call Tel 04/67-63-14-99. July 25 to August 19.

AUGUST

Festival Interceltique de Lorient, Brittany. Traditional Celtic verse and lore are celebrated in the Celtic heart of France. The 150 concerts include 3,500 classical and folkloric musicians, dancers, singers, and painters from all over. Traditional Breton pardons (religious processions) take place in this once-independent maritime duchy. For information, call Tel 02/97-21-24-29. First week of August.

Festival International de Folklore et Fête de la Vigne (Les Folkloriades), Dijon, Beaune, and about 20 villages of the Côte d'Or. At the International Festival of Folklore and Wine in Dijon, dance troupes from around the world perform, parade, and participate in folkloric events in celebration of the famous wines of Burgundy. For information, contact the Festival de Musique et Danse Populares, 27 blvd. de la Tremouille, 21025 Dijon (Tel 03/80-30-37-95; Fax 03/80-30-23-44). Late August and early September.

SEPTEMBER

Festival Musique en l'Île. A series of concerts, mostly dignified masses composed between the 17th and late 19th centuries, are given within medieval churches in the 4th, 5th, and 6th arrondissements. Sites include

St-Louis-en-l'Île, St-Severin, and St-Germain-des-Prés. Call Tel 01/43-55-47-09 for more information. September 5 to October 17.

Festival d'Automne, Paris. One of France's most famous festivals in France is also one of its most eclectic, concentrating mainly on modern music, ballet, theater, and modern art. Tickets cost 100 F to 300 F ($18 to $54), depending on the venue. For details, call or write to the Festival d'Automne, 156 rue de Rivoli, 75001 Paris (Tel 01/53-45-17-01; Fax 01/53-45-17-01). During the festival itself, call Tel 01/53-45-17-17 to reserve tickets for any of the events. Mid-September to mid-December.

International Ready-to-Wear Fashion Shows (Le Salon International de Prêt-à-porter), Parc des Expositions, Porte de Versailles, Paris. Late September.

OCTOBER

Perpignan Jazz Festival. Musicians from everywhere jam in what many visitors consider Languedoc's most appealing season. For information, call Tel 04/68-66-30-30. Throughout October and November.

Festival d'Automne, Paris. Ballet performances, both classical and modern, are presented, along with theatrical performances, contemporary music performances, and exhibitions of modern art. The venues occur all over town. Throughout October.

Paris Auto Show, Parc des Expositions, near the Porte de Versailles in western Paris. This is the showcase for European car design, complete with glistening metal, glitzy attendees, lots of hype, and the latest models from world automakers. Check Pariscope for details or contact the French Government Tourist Office (see "Visitor Information" earlier in this chapter), or call Tel 01/56-88-22-40. Fifteen days in early October.

Prix de l'Arc de Triomphe. France's answer to England's Ascot is the country's most prestigious horse race, culminating the equine season in Europe. Hippodrome de Longchamp, 16e (Tel 01/49-10-20-30). Early October.

NOVEMBER

Festival d'Automne, Paris. Throughout November.

Armistice Day, nationwide. In Paris, the signing of the controversial document that ended World War I is celebrated with a military parade from the Arc de Triomphe to the Hôtel des Invalides. November 11.

Les Trois Glorieuses, Clos-de-Vougeot, Beaune, and Meursault. The country's most important wine festival is celebrated in three Burgundian towns. Though you may not gain access to many of the gatherings, there are enough wine tastings and other amusements to keep you occupied. Festivities include wine auctions from some of the district's most historic cellars. Reserve early or visit as part of day trips from any of several nearby villages. Confirm information by contacting the Office de Tourisme de Beaune, rue de l'Hôtel-Dieu, 21200 Beaune (Tel 03/80-26-21-30). Third week in November.

City of Paris's Festival of Sacred Art. This dignified series of concerts is held in five of the oldest and most recognizable Paris churches. For information, call Tel 01/44-70-64-10. Mid-November to mid-December.

DECEMBER

Festival d'Automne, Paris. Through late December.

The Boat Fair (Le Salon International de la Navigation de Plaisance). Europe's most visible exposition of what's afloat and of interest to whole-salers, retailers, individual boat owners (or wanna-bes), and anyone involved in the business of waterborne holiday-making. Parc des Exposi-tions, Porte de Versailles, Paris, 15e (Tel 01/41-90-47-10; Fax 01/41-90-47-00; Métro: Porte de Versailles). The fair lasts for 8 days in early December.

Fête des Lumières, Lyon. In honor of the Virgin, lights are placed in thousands of windows throughout the city. December 8 until sometime after Christmas.

Foire de Noël, Mougins. Hundreds of merchants, selling all manner of Christmas ornaments and gifts, descend on Mougins, a small but choice village in Provence, to herald the Christmas spirit. December 11 and 12.

Christmas Fairs, Alsace (especially Strasbourg). More than 60 Alsa-tian villages celebrate a traditional Christmas. The events in Strasbourg have continued for some 430 years. Other towns with noteworthy cele-brations are Mu[um]nster, Selestat, Riquewihr, Kaysersberg, Saverne, Wissembourg, and Than. Late November to December 24.

Fête de St-Sylvestre (New Year's Eve), nationwide. In Paris, it's most boisterously celebrated in the Quartier Latin around the Sorbonne. At midnight, the city explodes. Strangers kiss strangers and boulevard St.-Michel and the Champs-Elysées become virtual pedestrian malls. December 31.

health & insurance

STAYING HEALTHY

In most cases, your existing health plan will provide all the coverage you need. Be sure to carry your identification card. You should check to see whether you are fully covered when away from home; HMO's are particularly unlikely to provide such coverage. If your, or your par-ents', plan won't cover you, look into the Council on International Education Exchange (CIEE) described in Tips for Travelers with Spe-cial Needs, under Students, below. They can provide health insurance for students and non-students under 26. Under Travel Insurance below, we also list some resources that combine medical coverage with their other options.

If you suffer from a chronic illness, consult your doctor before your departure. For conditions like epilepsy, diabetes, or heart problems, wear a Medic Alert Identification Tag (Tel 800/825-3785; www.medicalert.org), which will immediately alert doctors to your condition and give them access to your records through Medic Alert's 24-hour hot line. Member-ship is $35, plus a $15 annual fee.

Pack prescription medications in your carry-on luggage. Carry written prescriptions in generic, not brand-name form, and dispense all prescription medications from their original labeled vials. Also bring along copies of your prescriptions in case you lose your pills or run out.

Contact the **International Association for Medical Assistance to Travelers** (IAMAT; Tel 716/754-4883 or 416/652-0137; www.sent-edex.net/~iamat). This organization offers tips on travel and health concerns in the countries you'll be visiting, and lists many local English-speaking doctors.

TRAVEL INSURANCE

Comprehensive insurance programs, covering basically everything from trip cancellation and lost luggage to medical coverage abroad and accidental death, are offered by the following companies: **Access America** (Tel 800/284-8300; www.accessamerica.com); **Travel Guard International** (Tel 800/826-1300; www.travel-guard.com); and **Travelex Insurance Services** (Tel 888/457-4602; www.travelex-insurance.com).

Trip-cancellation insurance is a good idea if you have paid a large portion of your vacation expenses up front (say, by booking a charter flight, or purchasing a package deal). Trip-cancellation insurance costs approximately 6% to 8% of the total value of your vacation.

The other two types of insurance, however, don't make sense for most travelers. Rule number one: Check your existing policies before you buy any additional coverage.

As we note above, your existing health insurance should cover you if you get sick while on vacation—but you should always check before you go to see whether you are fully covered when away from home.

For lost or stolen luggage, your (or, often, your parents') homeowner's or renter's insurance should provide coverage. The airlines are responsible for losses up to $2,500 on domestic flights if they lose your luggage (finally upped in early 2000 from the old 1984 limit of $1,250); if you plan to carry anything more valuable than that, keep it in your carry-on bag.

If you do require additional insurance, try one of the companies listed above. But don't pay for more than you need. If you need only trip-cancellation insurance, don't purchase coverage for lost or stolen property.

special needs

FOR STUDENTS The best resource for students is the **Council on International Educational Exchange,** or CIEE, 6 Hamilton Place, Boston, MA 02108. They can set you up with an ID card (see below), and their travel branch, **Council Travel Service** (Tel 800/226-8624; www.counciltravel.com), is the biggest student travel agency operation in the world. It can get you discounts on plane tickets, railpasses, and the like. Ask them for a list of CTS offices in major cities so you can keep the discounts flowing (and aid lines open) as you travel.

From CIEE you can obtain the student traveler's best friend, the $20 International Student Identity Card (ISIC). It's the only officially acceptable form of student identification, good for cut rates on railpasses, plane tickets, and other discounts. It also provides you with basic health and life insurance and a 24-hour help line. If you're no longer a student but are still under 26, you can get a GO 25 card from the same people, also for $20, which will get you the insurance and some of the discounts (but not student admission prices in museums).

In Canada, **Travel CUTS,** 200 Ronson St., Suite 320, Toronto, ONT M9W 5Z9 (Tel 800/667-2887 or 416/614-2887, or 020/7528-6113 in London; www.travelcuts.com), offers similar services. **Usit Campus,** 52 Grosvenor Gardens, London SW1W 0AG (Tel 020/7730-3402; www.usitcampus.co.uk), opposite Victoria Station, is Britain's leading specialist in student and youth travel.

FOR TRAVELERS WITH DISABILITIES Facilities for travelers with disabilities are certainly above average in Europe, and nearly all modern hotels in France now provide rooms designed for persons with disabilities. However, older hotels (unless they've been renovated) may not provide such important features as elevators, special toilet facilities, or ramps for wheelchair access.

The new high-speed TGV trains are wheelchair accessible; older trains have special compartments for wheelchair boarding. On the Paris Métro, those with disabilities are able to sit in wider seats provided for their comfort. Guide dogs ride free. But some stations don't have escalators or elevators, so these present problems.

There are agencies in the United States and France that can provide advance-planning information. Knowing in advance which hotels, restaurants, and attractions are wheelchair accessible can save you a lot of frustration—firsthand accounts by other travelers with disabilities are the best.

The **Association des Paralysés de France,** 17 blvd. Auguste-Blanqui, 75013 Paris (Tel 01/40-78-69-00), is a privately funded organization that provides documentation, moral support, and travel ideas for individuals who use wheelchairs. In addition to the central Paris office, it maintains an office in each of the 90 départements of France and can help find accessible hotels, transportation, sightseeing, house rentals, and (in some cases) companionship for paralyzed or partially paralyzed travelers. It's not, however, a travel agency.

Travelers with disabilities may also want to consider joining a tour that caters specifically to them. One of the best operators is **Flying Wheels Travel,** 143 West Bridge (P.O. Box 382), Owatonna, MN 55060 (Tel 800/535-6790). They offer various escorted tours and cruises, with an emphasis on sports, as well as private tours in minivans with lifts.

Other helpful organizations are the **American Foundation for the Blind,** 11 Penn Plaza, Suite 300, New York, NY 10001 (Tel 800/232-5463 or 212/502-7600); **The Lighthouse, Inc.,** 111 E. 59th St., New York, NY 10022 (Tel 800/829-0500 or 212/821-9200; www.lighthouse.org); and the **New York Society for the Deaf,** 817 Broadway, 7th floor, New York, NY 10003 (Tel 212/777-3900 TTY/voice; www.nysd.org).

In the United Kingdom, **RADAR** (Royal Association for Disability and Rehabilitation), Unit 12, City Forum, 250 City Rd., London ECIV

8AF (Tel 020/7250-3222; Fax 020/200-0212), publishes holiday "fact packs" (three in all), which sell for £2 each or a set of all three for £5. The first one provides general information, including planning and booking a holiday, insurance, finances, and useful organization and holiday providers. The second outlines transport and equipment, transportation available when going abroad, and equipment for rent. The third deals with specialized accommodations.

Another good resource is the **Holiday Care Service,** 2nd floor, Imperial Buildings, Victoria Road, Horley, Surrey RH6 7PZ, UK (Tel 01293/774-535; Fax 01293/784-647), a national charity that advises on accessible accommodations for elderly and persons with disabilities. Once a member, you can receive a newsletter and access to a free reservations network for hotels throughout Britain and, to a lesser degree, Europe and the rest of the world.

FOR GAY & LESBIAN TRAVELERS Paris vies with London and Amsterdam as Europe's gay and lesbian capital. France is one of the world's most tolerant countries, and Paris, of course, is the center of French gay life, though gay and lesbian establishments exist throughout the country as well, especially on the Riviera.

Before going to France, both lesbians and gay men will want to check out our "Gay Scene" write-ups for each location throughout this book. Frommer's *Gay & Lesbian Europe* is another good source.

"Gay Paree," with one of the world's largest homosexual populations, has dozens of gay clubs, restaurants, organizations, and services. Other than the publications listed below, one of the best sources of information on gay and lesbian activities is **Centre Gai and Lesbien,** 3 rue Keller, 75011 (Tel 01/43-57-21-47; Métro: Bastille). Well equipped to dispense information, and to coordinate the activities and meetings of gay people from virtually everywhere, it's open daily from 2 to 6pm. Sundays, they adopt a format known as Le Café Positif, and feature music, cabaret, and information about AIDS and the care for and prevention of sexually transmitted diseases.

SOS Écoute Gay (Tel 01/44-93-01-02) is a gay hot line, theoretically designed as a way to creatively counsel persons with gay-related problems—the phone is answered by volunteers, some of whom are not as skilled and helpful as others. A phone counselor responds to calls Monday and Wednesday 8am to 10pm; Tuesday, Thursday, Friday 6 to 8pm.

Another helpful source is **La Maison des Femmes,** 163 rue de Charenton, 12e (Tel 01/43-43-41-13; Métro: Reuilly-Diderot), offering information about Paris for lesbians and bisexual women and sometimes sponsoring informal dinners and get-togethers. Call any Wednesday from 4 to 7pm for further information.

Gai Pied's publication *Guide Gai* (revised annually) is the best source of information on gay and lesbian clubs, hotels, organizations, and services—even restaurants. Lesbian or bisexual women might also like to pick up a copy of Lesbia, if only to check out the ads. These publications and others are available at Paris's largest and best-stocked gay bookstore, **Les Mots à la Bouche,** 6 rue Ste.-Croix-de-la-Bretonnerie, 4e (Tel 01/42-78-88-30). Hours are Monday through Saturday from 11am to 11pm, Sunday from 2 to 8pm. Both French- and English-language publications are available.

If you want help planning your trip, **The International Gay & Lesbian Travel Association** (IGLTA; Tel 800/448-8550 or 954/776-2626; www.iglta.org), can link you up with the appropriate gay-friendly service organization or tour specialist. With around 1,200 members, it offers quarterly newsletters, marketing mailings, and a membership directory that's updated quarterly. Members are kept informed of gay and gay-friendly hoteliers, tour operators, and airline and cruise-line representatives.

Out and About (Tel 800/929-2268 or 212/645-6922; www.outand about.com) has been hailed for its "straight"(ha, ha) reporting about gay travel. It offers a monthly newsletter packed with good information on the global gay and lesbian scene. There are also two good, biannual English-language gay guidebooks, both focused on gay men but including information for lesbians as well. You can get the Spartacus International Gay Guide or Odysseus from most gay and lesbian book stores, or order them from Giovanni's Room (Tel 215/923-2960) or from A Different Light Bookstore (Tel 800/343-4002 or 212/989-4850; www.adlbooks.com). Both lesbians and gays might want to pick up a copy of Gay Travel A to Z ($16). The Ferrari Guides (www.q-net.com) is yet another very good series of gay and lesbian guidebooks.

General gay and lesbian travel agencies include **Family Abroad** (Tel 800/999-5500 or 212/459-1800; gay and lesbian); and **Above and Beyond Tours** (Tel 800/397-2681; mainly gay men).

flying from north america

Flying time to Paris is about 7 hours from New York or Washington, D.C., 8 hours from Atlanta or Miami, 9 hours from Chicago, and 11 hours from Los Angeles.

The two Parisian airports—Orly and Charles de Gaulle—are almost even bets in terms of convenience to the city's center, though taxi rides from Orly might take a bit less time than those from de Gaulle. Orly, the older of the two, is 8 miles south of the center, whereas Charles de Gaulle is 14 miles northeast. In April 1996 the last of Air France's flights to Orly from North America was rerouted to Charles de Gaulle (Terminal 2C). U.S. carriers tend to land at both airports in equal measure.

Most airlines divide their year into roughly seasonal slots, with the lowest fares between November 1 and March 13. Shoulder season (October and mid-March to mid-June) is only slightly more expensive. We think it's the ideal time to visit France.

THE MAJOR AIRLINES

American Airlines (Tel 800/433-7300; www.aa.com) offers daily flights to Paris from Dallas/Fort Worth, Chicago, Miami, Boston, and New York.

British Airways (Tel 800/AIRWAYS) offers flights from 18 U.S. cities to Heathrow and Gatwick airports in England. From there, you can book any number of British Airways flights to Paris.

Continental Airlines (Tel 800/231-0856; www.flycontinental.com) provides nonstop flights to Paris from Newark and Houston. Flights from Newark depart daily, while flights from Houston depart four to seven times a week, depending on the season.

Delta Airlines (Tel 800/241-4141; www.delta-air.com) is one of the best choices for those flying to Paris from the southeastern United States or the Midwest. There's a nonstop from Atlanta to Paris every evening. Delta also operates daily nonstop flights from both Cincinnati and New York. Note that Delta is the only airline offering nonstop service from New York to Nice.

US Airways (Tel 800/428-4322; www.usairways.com) offers daily nonstop service from Philadelphia to Paris.

The French national carrier, **Air France** (Tel 800/237-2747; www.air france.com), offers daily or several-times-a-week flights between Paris and such North American cities as Atlanta, Boston, Chicago, Cincinnati, Houston, Los Angeles, Mexico City, Miami, Montreal, New York, Newark, San Francisco, Toronto, and Washington D.C.

Canadians usually choose **Air Canada** (Tel 800/776-3000 in North America; www.aircanada.ca), which offers daily nonstop flights to Paris from Toronto and Montréal. Two of Air Canada's flights from Toronto are shared with Air France and feature Air France aircraft.

Icelandair (Tel 800/223-5500; www.icelandair. com) offers direct flights from North America to Europe via its hub in Reykjavik, Iceland. They offer service from Boston, New York, Baltimore/Washington, Minneapolis/St. Paul, Orlando, and Halifax (Canada) to Paris. We think they're one of the coolest ways to get to Europe, not only because of the great service, but because of their Take-A-Break program: you can take up to a 3-day layover in Iceland on any of their flights (in either direction) for no extra charge.

FLYING FOR LESS: TIPS FOR GETTING THE BEST AIRFARES

1. Watch for sales. You'll almost never see them during the peak summer vacation months of July and August, or during the Thanksgiving or Christmas seasons; but at other times, you can get great deals. In the last couple of years, there have been amazing deals on winter flights to Paris. If you already hold a ticket when a sale breaks, it may even pay to exchange your ticket, which usually incurs a charge of between $50 and $150, depending on the airline and the ticket.

2. If your schedule is flexible, ask if you can secure a cheaper fare by staying an extra day or by flying midweek. (Many airlines won't volunteer this information.)

3. Consolidators, also known as bucket shops, are a good place to find low fares. Consolidators buy seats in bulk from the airlines and then sell them back to the public at prices below even the airlines' discounted rates. Their small boxed ads usually run in the Sunday travel

section of your newspaper, at the bottom of the page. **Council Travel** (Tel 800/226-8624; www.counciltravel.com) and **STA Travel** (Tel 800/781-4040; www.sta.travel.com) cater especially to young travelers, but their bargain basement prices are available to people of all ages. **Travel Bargains** (Tel 800/AIR-FARE; www.1800airfare.com) was formerly owned by TWA but now offers the deepest discounts on many other airlines, with a 4-day advance purchase. Other reliable consolidators include **1-800-FLY-CHEAP** (www.1800flycheap.com); **TFI Tours International** (Tel 800/745-8000 or 212/736-1140), which serves as a clearinghouse for unused seats; or "rebators" such as **Travel Avenue** (Tel 800/333-3335 or 312/876-1116).

4. Book a seat on a charter flight. Most charter operators advertise and sell their seats through travel agents, thus making these local professionals your best source of information for available flights. Before deciding to take a charter flight, however, check the restrictions on the ticket: You may be asked to purchase a tour package, to pay in advance, to be amenable if the day of departure is changed, to pay a service charge, to fly on an airline you're not familiar with (this usually is not the case), and to pay harsh penalties if you cancel—but be understanding if the charter doesn't fill up and is canceled up to 10 days before departure. Summer charters fill up more quickly than others and are almost sure to fly, but if you decide on a charter flight, seriously consider cancellation and baggage insurance (see Health & Insurance, above).

5. Search for deals on the Web. It's possible to get some great deals on airfare, hotels, and car rentals via the Internet. See the online directory in the next chapter for more information about travel Web sites that can save you money.

GETTING THERE FROM EUROPE
BY PLANE

From London, **Air France** (Tel 0845/084-5111) and **British Airways** (Tel 0345/222111 in the U.K. only) fly frequently to Paris with a trip time of only 1 hour. These airlines alone operate up to 17 flights daily from Heathrow, one of the busiest air routes in Europe. Many commercial travelers also use regular flights originating from the London City Airport in the Docklands.

Direct flights to Paris also exist from other major cities in the U.K., such as Manchester, Edinburgh, and Southampton. Contact Air France, British Airways, or **British Midland** (Tel 0870/607-555) for details.

There are no hard-and-fast rules for British travelers interested in getting the best deals for European flights, but do bear the following points in mind. Daily papers often carry advertisements for companies offering cheap flights. Highly recommended companies include **Trailfinders** (Tel 020/7937-5400), which sells discounted fares, and **Avro Tours** (Tel 0181/715-0000), which operates charters. In London, there are many ticket consolidators (who buy inventories of tickets from airlines and then resell them) in the neighborhoods of Earl's Court and Victoria Station that offer cheap fares. CEEFAX, a British television information service (received by many private homes and hotels), presents details of package holidays and flights to Europe and beyond.

You can reach Paris from any major European capital. Your best bet would be to fly on the national carrier, Air France, which has more connections into Paris from European capitals than any other airline. From Dublin, try **Aer Lingus** (Tel 800/223-6537; www.aerlingus.com), with the most frequent flights into Paris from Ireland. From Amsterdam, the convenient airline for Paris is **KLM** (Tel 800/374-7747; www.klm.nl).

BY TRAIN

Paris is one of Europe's busiest rail junctions, with trains arriving at and departing from its many stations every few minutes. If you're already in Europe, you may want to go to Paris by train. Even if you don't, the cost is relatively low—especially in comparison to renting a car.

Railpasses as well as individual rail tickets within Europe are available at most travel agencies or at any office of **Rail Europe** (Tel 800/4-EURAIL in the U.S.) or Eurostar (Tel 800/EUROSTAR in the U.S.). Their Internet address is www.raileurope.com.

BY BUS

Bus travel to Paris is available from London as well as many other cities throughout the Continent. In the early 1990s, the French government established strong incentives for long-haul buses not to drive into the center of Paris. The arrival and departure point for Europe's largest bus operators, **Eurolines France,** is a 35-minute Métro ride from central Paris, at the terminus of Métro line 3 (Métro: Gallieni), in the eastern suburb of Bagnolet. Despite this inconvenience, many people prefer bus travel. Eurolines France is located at 28 ave. du Général-de-Gaulle, 93541 Bagnolet (Tel 08/36-69-52-52).

Long-haul buses are equipped with toilets, but they also stop at mealtimes for rest and refreshment. The price of a round-trip ticket between Paris and London (a 7-hour trip) is 490 F ($78.40) for passengers 26 or over, and 430 F ($68.80) for passengers under 26.

Because Eurolines does not have a U.S.-based sales agent, most people wait until they reach Europe to buy their tickets. Any European travel agent can arrange these purchases. If you're traveling to Paris from London, you can contact **Eurolines (U.K.) Ltd.,** 52 Grosvenor Gardens, Victoria, London SW1; or call Tel 0990/143219 for information or for credit-card sales.

BY CAR

The major highways into Paris are the A1 from the north (Great Britain and Benelux); the A13 from Rouen, Normandy, and other points of northwest France; the A10 from Bordeaux, the Pyrénées, France's southwest, and Spain; the A6 from Lyon, the French Alps, the Riviera, and Italy; and the A4 from Metz, Nancy, and Strasbourg in eastern France.

BY FERRY FROM ENGLAND

Ferryboats and hydrofoils operate day and night, in all seasons, with the exception of last-minute cancellations during particularly fierce storms.

Many Channel crossings are carefully timed to coincide with the arrival/departure of major trains (especially those between London and Paris). Trains let you off a short walk from the piers. Most ferries carry cars, trucks, and massive amounts of freight, but some hydrofoils take passengers only. The major routes include at least 12 trips a day between Dover or Folkestone and Calais or Boulogne. Hovercraft and hydrofoils make the trip from Dover to Calais, the shortest distance across the Channel, in just 40 minutes during good weather, whereas the slower-moving ferries might take several hours, depending on weather conditions and tides. If you're bringing a car, it's important to make reservations, as space below decks is usually crowded. Timetables can vary depending on weather conditions and many other factors.

The leading operator of ferryboats across the channel is **P&O Stena Lines** (BritRail Tel 800/247-7268 for reservations within North America, or 0870/600-0611 in England). It operates car and passenger ferries between Portsmouth, England, and Cherbourg, France (three departures a day; 4 1/4 hours each way during daylight hours, 7 hours each way at night); between Portsmouth and Le Havre, France (three a day; 5 1/2 hours each way). Most popular of all are the routes it operates between Dover and Calais, France (25 sailings a day; 75 minutes each way), costing $41 (U.S.) one-way.

The shortest and by far the most popular route across the Channel is between Calais and Dover. Hoverspeed operates at least 12 hovercraft crossings daily; the trip takes 35 minutes. It also runs a SeaCat (a catamaran propelled by jet engines) that takes slightly longer to make the crossing between Boulogne and Folkestone; the SeaCats depart about four times a day on the 55-minute voyage. For reservations and information, call **Hoverspeed** (Tel 800/677-8585 for reservations in North America or 08705/240-241 in England). Typical one-way fares are 25 F ($4) per person.

If you plan to transport a rental car between England and France, check in advance with the rental company about license and insurance requirements and additional drop-off charges. And be aware that many car-rental companies, for insurance reasons, forbid transport of one of their vehicles over the water between England and France. Transport of a car each way begins at 75 F ($12). A better idea is to ask about a car exchange program (Hertz's is called "Le Swap"), in which you drop off a right-hand drive car and pick up a left-hand drive vehicle at Calais.

UNDER THE CHANNEL

Queen Elizabeth and the late French president François Mitterrand officially opened the Channel Tunnel in 1994, and the **Eurostar Express** now has daily passenger service from London to both Paris and Brussels. The $15 billion tunnel, one of the great engineering feats of our time, is the first link between Britain and the continent since the Ice Age. The 31-mile journey takes 35 minutes, although the actual time spent in the Chunnel is only 19 minutes.

Eurostar tickets, for train service between London and Paris or Brussels, are available through **Rail Europe** (Tel 800/4-EURAIL for information). A one-way first class nonrefundable ticket costs $199, or else $239 if refundable. In second class a nonrefundable one-way ticket goes for $119, or else $159 if refundable.

In London, make reservations for Eurostar at Tel 0990/300003 (accessible in the United Kingdom only); in Paris at Tel 01/44-51-06-02; and in the United States at Tel 800/EUROSTAR. Chunnel train traffic is roughly competitive with air travel, if you calculate door-to-door travel time. Trains leave from London's Waterloo Station and arrive in Paris at Gare du Nord.

LE SHUTTLE

The Chunnel accommodates not only trains, but also passenger cars, charter buses, taxis, and motorcycles. Le Shuttle, a half-mile-long train carrying motor vehicles under the English Channel (Tel 0990/353535 in the U.K.), connects Calais, France, with Folkestone, England, and vice versa. It operates 24 hours a day, 365 days a year, running every 15 minutes during peak travel times and at least once an hour at night.

With Le Shuttle, gone are weather-related delays, seasickness, and a need for reservations. Before boarding Le Shuttle, you stop at a toll booth to pay, and then pass through Immigration for both countries at one time. During the ride, you travel in bright, air-conditioned carriages, remaining inside your car or stepping outside to stretch your legs. An hour later, when you reach France, you simply drive off.

getting around france by train

With some 50 cities in France linked by the world's fastest trains, you can get from Paris to just about anywhere else in the country in just a few hours. With 24,000 miles of track and about 3,000 stations, SNCF (French National Railroads) is fabled throughout the world for its on-time performance. You can travel first or second class by day and in couchette or sleeper by night. Many trains carry dining facilities.

If you plan much travel on European railroads, get the latest copy of the **Thomas Cook European Timetable of Railroads.** This comprehensive 500-plus-page book documents all Europe's mainline passenger rail services with detail and accuracy. It's available in North America from the **Forsyth Travel Library,** 226 Westchester Ave., White Plains, NY 10604 (Tel 800/367-7984), at a cost of $27.95, plus $4.95 postage (priority airmail in the U.S. and $6.95 U.S. for shipments to Canada).

IN THE UNITED STATES

•For more information and to purchase railpasses (see below) before you leave, contact **Rail Europe** at 500 Mamaroneck Ave., Suite 314, Harrison, NY 10528 (Tel 800/677-8585; Fax 914/682-3712).

IN CANADA

•**Rail Europe** offices are at 2087 Dundas St. E., Suite 105, Mississauga, ON L4X 1M2 (Tel 800/361-7245 or 905/602-4195; Fax 905/602-4198).

IN LONDON

•SNCF maintains offices at **French Railways,** 179 Piccadilly, London W1V 0BA (Tel 0345/48-49-50; Fax 020/7491-9956).

IN PARIS

•For train information or to make reservations call **SNCF** at Tel 08/36-35-35-35. You are charged at the rate of 3 F (50¢) per minute to use this service. You can also go to any local travel agency, of course, and book tickets. A simpler way to book tickets is to take advantage of the Billet-terie or ticket machines in every train station. If you know your PIN, you can use credit cards such as American Express, MasterCard, and Visa to purchase your ticket.

FRENCH RAIL PASSES Working cooperatively with SNCF, Air Inter Europe, and Avis, Rail Europe offers three flexible cost-saving railpasses that can reduce travel costs considerably.

The **France Railpass** provides unlimited rail transport throughout France for any 3 days within 1 month, costing $205 in first class and $175 in second. You can purchase up to 6 more days for an extra $30 per person per day. Costs are even more reasonable for two adults traveling together: $328 for first class and $280 in second. Children 4 to 11 travel for half price.

The **France Rail 'n Drive Pass,** available only in North America, combines good value on both rail travel and Avis car rentals and is best used by arriving at a major rail depot, then striking out to explore the countryside by car. It includes the France Railpass (see above), and use of a rental car. A 3-day rail pass (first class) and 2 days' use of the cheapest rental car (with unlimited mileage) is $204 per person (assuming two people traveling together). It's $187 per person for the second-class rail pass and the same car; you can upgrade to a larger car for a supplemental fee. Solo travelers pay from $289 for first class and $255 for second.

EURAILPASSES For years, many in-the-know travelers have been taking advantage of one of Europe's greatest travel bargains: the **Eurailpass,** which permits unlimited first-class rail travel in any country in Western Europe except the British Isles (good in Ireland). Passes are for periods as short as 15 days or as long as 3 months and are strictly non-transferable.

The pass is sold only in North America. A Eurailpass is $554 for 15 days, $718 for 21 days, $890 for 1 month, $1,260 for 2 months, and $1,558 for 3 months. Children 3 and under travel free providing they don't occupy a seat (otherwise they're charged half fare); children 4 to 11 are charged half fare. If you're under 26, you can purchase a Eurail Youth-pass, entitling you to unlimited second-class travel for $388 for 15 days, $499 for 21 days, $623 for 1 month, $882 for 2 months, and $1,089 for 3 months. Regardless of the pass you buy, you'll have to pay an extra supplement if you want to take a high-speed TGV train anywhere in France.

Remember that a train pass or ticket by itself does not guarantee you a seat; it merely gets you transportation from one place to another. On crowded trains and during busy times of year, you'll have to make a seat reservation (and pay for the privilege—usually an additional $8 per person) if you want to be sure of sitting somewhere other than on top of your luggage. Many of the trains have couchettes (sleeping cars), which also cost extra. Obviously, the 2- or 3-month traveler gets the greatest economic advantages; the Eurailpass is ideal for such extensive trips. With the pass you can visit all of France's major sights, from Normandy to the Alps, then end your vacation in Norway, for example. Eurailpass holders are entitled to considerable reductions on certain buses and ferries as well.

Travel agents everywhere, and railway agents in such major cities as New York, Montreal, and Los Angeles, sell Eurailpasses. You can also purchase them at the North American offices of CIT Travel Service, the French National Railroads, the German Federal Railroads, and the Swiss Federal Railways.

The **Eurail Flexipass** allows you to visit Europe with more flexibility. It's valid in first class and offers the same privileges as the Eurailpass. However, it provides a number of individual travel days that you can use over a much longer period of consecutive days. That makes it possible to stay in one city for a while without losing days of rail travel. There are two passes: 10 days of travel in 2 months for $654, and 15 days of travel in 2 months for $862.

With many of the same qualifications and restrictions as the previously described Flexipass is a **Eurail Youth Flexipass.** Sold only to travelers under 26, it allows 10 days of travel within 2 months for $458, and 15 days of travel within 2 months for $599.

getting around france by car

Frankly, Europe's rail networks are so well developed and so inexpensive, we recommend that you rent a car only for the same reasons you would enjoy—even more—getting around by bike: For exploring areas little serviced by rail lines, such as Brittany, rural Burgundy, and the Dordogne. Or take trains between cities and rent a car only on the days when you want to explore independently.

Driving time in Europe is largely a matter of conjecture, urgency, and how much sightseeing you do along the way. Driving time from Paris to Geneva is 5½ hours minimum. It's 2½ hours from Paris to Rouen, 3½ hours to Nantes, and 4 hours to Lyon. The driving time from Marseille to Paris is a matter of national pride, and tall tales abound about rapidly the French can do it. With the accelerator pressed to the floor, you might conceivably make it in 7 hours, but we always make a 2-day journey of it.

RENTALS Renting a car in France is easy. You'll need to present a passport, a valid driver's license, and a valid credit card. You'll also have to meet the minimum age requirement of the company. (For their least expensive cars, this is 21 at Hertz, 23 at Avis, and 25 at Budget. More expensive cars at any of the above-mentioned companies might require that you be at least 25.) It usually isn't obligatory, at least within France, but certain companies, especially the smaller ones, have at times asked for the presentation of an International Driver's License, even though this is becoming increasingly superfluous in Western Europe.

Note: The best deal is usually a weekly rental with unlimited mileage. All car-rental bills in France are subject to a whopping 19.6% government tax, among the highest in Europe. And though the rental company won't usually mind if you drive your car across the French border—into, say, Germany, Switzerland, Italy, or Spain—it's often expressly forbidden to transport your car on any ferryboat, including the dozens that ply the waters of the Channel to England.

Unless it's already factored into the rental agreement, an optional collision-damage waiver (CDW) carries an extra charge of 110 F to 125 F ($17.60 to $20) per day for the least expensive cars. Buying this will usually eliminate all but $250 of your responsibility in the event of accidental damage to the car. Because most newcomers aren't familiar with local driving customs and conditions, we highly recommend that you buy the CDW, though you should check with your credit-card company first to see if they'll cover this automatically when you rent with their card (they may cover damage to the car but not liability, so make sure you understand this clearly). At some of the companies the CDW won't protect you against the theft of a car, so if this is the case, ask about buying extra theft protection. This cost is 45 F ($7.20) extra per day.

Automatic transmission is considered a luxury in Europe, so if you want it you'll have to pay dearly.

Budget (Tel 800/472-3325 in the U.S. and Canada; www.bud getrentacar.com) maintains about 30 locations in Paris, with its largest branch at 81 ave. Kléber, 16e (Tel 01/47-55-61-00; Métro: Trocadéro). For rentals of more than 7 days, you can pick up a car (at least in most cases) in one French city and drop it off in another, but there are extra charges. Drop-offs in cities within an easy drive of the French border (including Geneva and Frankfurt) incur no extra charge; however, you can arrange drop-offs in other non-French cities for a reasonable surcharge.

Hertz (Tel 800/654-3001 in the U.S. and Canada; www.hertz.com) maintains about 15 locations in Paris, including offices at the city's airports. The main office is at 27 rue St-Ferdinand, 17e (Tel 01/45-74-97-39; Métro: Argentine). Be sure to ask about any promotional discounts.

Avis (Tel 800/331-2112 in the U.S. and Canada; www.avis.com) has offices at both Paris airports, as well as an inner-city headquarters at 5 rue Bixio, 7e (Tel 01/44-18-10-50; Métro: École-Militaire), near the Eiffel Tower.

National (Tel 800/227-3876 in the U.S. and Canada; www.national alcar.com) is represented in Paris by Europcar, whose largest office is at 165 bis rue De Vaugirard (Tel 01/44-38-61-61; Métro: St.-Sulpre). It has offices at both Paris airports and at about a dozen other locations. Any of its offices can rent you a car on the spot, but to qualify for the lowest rates it's best to reserve in advance from North America.

Two U.S.-based agencies that don't have Paris offices but act as booking agents for Paris-based agencies are **Kemwel Holiday Auto** (Tel 800/678-

0678; www.kemwel.com) and **Auto Europe** (Tel 800/223-5555; www.autoeurope.com). These companies can make bookings in the U.S. only, so call before your trip.

GASOLINE Known in France as *essence,* gas is extraordinarily expensive for those accustomed to North American prices. All but the least expensive cars usually require an octane rating that the French classify as essence super, the most expensive variety. Depending on your car, you'll need either leaded (*avec plomb*) or unleaded (*sans plomb*). Filling a medium-size car will cost between $45 and $65.

Beware of the mixture of gasoline and oil sold in certain rural communities called *mélange* or *gasoil;* this mixture is for very old two-cycle engines.

Note: Sometimes you can drive for miles in rural France without encountering a gas station, so don't let your tank get dangerously low.

DRIVING RULES Everyone in the car, in both the front and the back seats, must wear seat belts. Drivers are supposed to yield to the car on their right, except where signs indicate otherwise, as at traffic circles.

If you violate the speed limits, expect a big fine. Those limits are about 130 kilometers per hour (80 m.p.h.) on expressways, about 100 kilometers per hour (60 m.p.h.) on major national highways, and 90 kilometers per hour (56 m.p.h.) on small country roads. In towns, don't exceed 60 kilometers per hour (37 m.p.h.).

MAPS For France as a whole, most motorists opt for the Michelin map 989. For regions, **Michelin** publishes a series of yellow maps that are quite good. Big travel-book stores in North America carry these maps, and they're commonly available in France (at lower prices). One useful feature of the Michelin map (in this age of congested traffic) is its designations of alternative *routes de dégagement,* which let you skirt big cities and avoid traffic-clogged highways.

BREAKDOWNS/ASSISTANCE A breakdown is called *une panne* in France, and it's just as frustrating here as anywhere else. Call the police at Tel 17 anywhere in France and they'll put you in touch with the nearest garage. Most local garages have towing services. If your breakdown occurs on an expressway, find the nearest roadside emergency phone box, pick up the phone, and put a call through. You'll immediately be connected to the nearest breakdown service facility.

BY PLANE
Regrettably, there are very few competitors in the rarefied world of domestic air travel within France. **Air France,** which recently acquired Air Inter Europe, is the 800-pound gorilla in this field, serving about eight cities in France and eight others in Europe. Airfares tend to be much higher than they would be for comparable distances in the U.S., and discounts are few and far between. Sample round-trip fares between

Paris and Nice sell for 2,300 F ($368); Paris to Bordeaux is 2,240 F ($358.40); Paris to Toulouse is 2,260 F ($361.60). Air travel time from Paris to most anywhere in France is about an hour.

Tips on Shopping

France is the market of continental Europe—a jumble of products, colors, crafts, and cutting-edge style. Though its retail reputation has grown through fashion and style, the truth is that this is a country where shopping at the local produce market is a quasi-religious experience, where the dime stores are as much fun as (if not more) the major department stores, and where many of the best things in life can be found in a *parapharmacie*—a newfangled concept that marries tons of drugstore/health-care/beauty products with a discount system.

Factory outlets are opening up *droit* and *gauche*, whereas the old factories continue to sell wares straight from their hometown and the new factories have opened boutiquelike shops to hawk overruns to the public.

Add to all this a tradition of the finest antiques in the world (plus heaps of fun junk and what locals call *brocante*) and you have the makings of a spree even a nonshopper will love.

Here are some tips about items you may find irresistible for yourself or gift-giving for the folks back home:

FOOD & WINE Spectacular breads, cheeses, mustards, chocolates, wines, and fresh produce abound. *Tip:* You can buy chocolates in grocery stores, but these are commercial chocolates. If you want to know what everyone's raving about, save up a few francs and head to the chocolatiers in Lyon or Paris, preferably in the cooler months, and begin your own taste test. In Paris, the big outlets are La Maison du Chocolat and Christian Constant.

FASHION You can find knockoffs of the latest trends all over France, at more-than-affordable prices, in the two major dime-store chains. Every major city has a Monoprix (owned by Galeries Lafayette) or Prisunic (owned by Au Printemps); some have both.

BEAUTY PRODUCTS & PERFUMES Regular designer makeup at retail may be the same price in France as in the States—or possibly more expensive in France. But at a "duty-free" (nonairport variety) store or a discounter where you can qualify for *détaxe,* you'll see anywhere from 20% to 45% melt off your bill. Paris offers the most duty-free stores and bigger discounts on name-brand goods, but any city with a tourist business (Nice, Cannes, Monaco, Biarritz) will have at least one discounter.

Note that French perfume lasts longer than the U.S. counterpart of the same scent (it's made with potato alcohol, not grain alcohol). French perfume makers, especially the top-of-the-line designer names (like Chanel and Dior), are cracking down on the recent move toward discounting. But, basically, if you don't qualify for détaxe, you should be able to get a flat 20% discount in duty-free stores in Paris and in major cities in the provinces. The airport offers a 13% discount. Warning: Don't buy American brands of fragrance in Europe, even at a duty-free shop—they're more expensive than at home.

CRAFTS The main faïence cities are in the north, stretching from Rouen in the northeast to Quimper on the Atlantic coast. You'll find tiles in the south (check out Salernes), and Moustier Ste.-Marie in Provence is known for a specific type of faïence with animals. Soap making is an art in the south of France, with soap makers dotting Marseille and Provence. L'Occitane, a Provençal brand, is now sold in its own boutiques in assorted Provence towns and in Paris.

SHIPPING IT HOME
Shipping costs will possibly double your cost on goods; you'll also pay U.S. duties on the items if they're valued at more than $50. The good news is that détaxe is automatically applied to any item shipped to an American destination—no need to worry about the 1,200 F minimum. However, some stores have a $100 minimum for shipping. You can also walk into any PT&T (post office) and mail home a Jiffy bag or small box of goodies. French do-it-yourself boxes can't be reopened once closed.

HOW TO GET YOUR VAT REFUND
French sales tax, or VAT (value-added tax), is now a hefty 19.6%, but you can get most of that back if you spend 1,200 F ($190) or more at any participating retailer. Most stores participate, though discount perfume shops usually peg the minimum at 1,200 F net, which actually works out to an equivalent pretax amount of 1,600 F to 1,700 F ($254 to $270). They then deduct the 20% discount so you're back where you started, at 1,200 F. Since this sounds more complicated than it is, ask!

The name of the refund is *détaxe,* meaning exactly what it says. You never really get the full 19.6% back, but you can come close.

After you spend the required minimum amount, ask for your détaxe papers; fill out the forms before you arrive at the airport and allow at least half an hour for standing in line. All refunds are processed at the final point of departure from the EU, so if you're going to another EU country, you don't apply for the refund in France.

Mark the paperwork to request that your refund be applied to your credit card so you aren't stuck with a check in francs that you can't cash. Even if you made the purchase in cash, you can still get the refund put on a credit card. This ensures the best rate of exchange. While you can get cash in some airports, if you don't take the cash in French francs you'll lose money on the transaction.

If you're considering a major purchase, especially one that falls between 1,200 F to 2,000 F ($192 to $320), ask the store policy before you get too involved—or be willing to waive your right to the refund.

france online

This is not a comprehensive list, but a discriminating selection to get you started. Recognition is given to sites based on their content value and ease of use. Inclusion here is not paid for—unlike some Web-site rankings, which are based on payment. Finally, remember this is a press-time snapshot of leading websites; some undoubtedly will have evolved, changed, or moved by the time you read this.

TRAVEL-PLANNING WEB SITES

By Lynne Bairstow

WHY BOOK ONLINE?

Online agencies have come a long way over the past few years, now providing tips for finding the best fare, and giving you suggested dates or times to travel that yield the lowest price if your plans are at all flexible. Other sites even allow you to establish the price you're willing to pay, and they check the airlines' willingness to accept it. However, in some cases, these sites may not always yield the best price. Unlike a travel agent, for example, they may not have access to charter flights offered by wholesalers.

All major airlines also have their own websites and often offer incentives (bonus frequent-flyer miles or Net-only discounts, for example) when you buy online or buy an e-ticket.

The best of the travel planning sites are now highly personalized; they store your seating preferences, meal preferences, tentative itineraries, and credit-card information, allowing you to quickly plan trips or check agendas.

In many cases, booking your trip online can be better than working with a travel agent. It gives you the widest variety of choices, control, and the 24-hour convenience of planning your trip when you choose. All you need is some time—and often a lot of patience.

WHO SHOULD BOOK ONLINE?

Online booking is best for travelers who want to know as much as possible about their travel options, for those who have flexibility in their travel dates, and for bargain hunters.

One of the biggest successes in online travel for both passengers and airlines is the offer of last-minute specials, such as American Airlines' weekend deals or other Internet-only fares that must be purchased online. Another advantage is that you can cash in on incentives for booking online, such as rebates or bonus frequent-flyer miles.

Business and other frequent travelers also have found numerous benefits in online booking, as the advances in mobile technology provide them with the ability to check flight status, change plans, or get specific directions from hand-held computing devices, mobile phones, and pagers. Some sites will even e-mail or page a passenger if their flight is delayed.

Online booking is increasingly able to accommodate complex itineraries, even for international travel. The pace of evolution on the Net is rapid, so you'll probably find additional features and advancements by the time you visit these sites. The future holds ever-increasing personalization and customization for online travelers.

ONLINE BARGAINS

There's nothing airlines hate more than flying with lots of empty seats. The Net has enabled airlines to offer last-minute bargains to entice travelers to fill those seats. Most of these are announced on Tuesday or Wednesday and are valid for travel the following weekend, but some can be booked weeks or months in advance. You can sign up for weekly e-mail alerts at the airlines' own sites (see the box below listing the airlines' Web addresses) or check sites that compile lists of these bargains, such as Smarter Living or WebFlyer (see below). To make it easier, visit a site that will round up all the deals and send them in one convenient weekly e-mail.

Important Note: See "Flying to France from North America" in chapter 2 for the Web addresses of airlines serving France. These sites offer schedules and flight booking, and most have pages where you can sign up for e-mail alerts for weekend deals and other late-breaking bargains.

1travel.com. *www.1travel.com*
Here you'll find deals on domestic and international flights and hotels. 1travel.com's Saving Alert compiles last-minute air deals so you don't have to scroll through multiple e-mail alerts. A feature called "Drive a little using low-fare airlines" helps map out strategies for using alternate airports

to find lower fares. And Farebeater searches a database that includes published fares, consolidator bargains, and special deals exclusive to 1travel.com. *Note:* The travel agencies listed by 1travel.com have paid for placement.

Bid for Travel. *www.bidfortravel.com*
Bid for Travel is another of the travel auction sites, similar to Priceline (see below), which are growing in popularity. In addition to airfares, Internet users can place a bid for vacation packages and hotels.

Cheap Tickets. *www.cheaptickets.com*
Cheap Tickets has exclusive deals that aren't available through more mainstream channels. One caveat about the Cheap Tickets site is that it will offer fare quotes for a route, and later show this fare is not valid for your dates of travel—most other websites, such as Expedia, consider your dates of travel before showing what fares are available. Despite its problems, Cheap Tickets can be worth the effort because its fares can be lower than those offered by its competitors.

LastMinuteTravel.com. *www.lastminutetravel.com*
Supliers with excess inventory come to this online agency to distribute unsold airline seats, hotel rooms, cruises, and vacation packages. It's got great deals, but an excess of advertisements and slow-loading graphics.

Moment's Notice. *www.moments-notice.com*
As the name suggests, Moment's Notice specializes in last-minute vacation deals. You can browse for free, but if you want to purchase a trip you have to join Moment's Notice, which costs $25.

SkyAuction.com. *www.skyauction.com*
An auction site with categories for airfare, travel deals, hotels, and much more.

Smarter Living. *www.smarterliving.com*
Best known for its e-mail dispatch of weekend deals on 20 airlines, Smarter Living also keeps you posted about last-minute bargains.

Travelzoo.com. *www.travelzoo.com*
At this Internet portal, more than 150 travel companies post special deals. It features a Top 20 list of the best deals on the site, selected by its editorial staff each Wednesday night. This list is also available via an e-mailing list, free to those who sign up.

WebFlyer. *www.webflyer.com*
WebFlyer is a comprehensive online resource for frequent flyers and also has an excellent listing of last-minute air deals. Click on "Deal Watch" for

a round-up of weekend deals on flights, hotels, and rental cars from domestic and international suppliers.

ONLINE TRAVELER'S TOOLBOX

Exchange Rates. *www.x-rates.com*
See what your dollar, or pound is worth in French francs.

Foreign Languages for Travelers. *www.travlang.com*
Learn basic terms in more than 70 languages and click on any underlined phrase to hear what it sounds like. (*Note:* Free audio software and speakers are required.) They also offer hotel and airline finders with excellent prices and a simple system to get the listings you are looking for.

InnSite. *www.innsite.com*
Listings for inns and B&Bs around the globe (even a "floating hotel"—a six-cabin barge—moored on Paris's Quai Henri IV.) Find an inn at your destination, have a look at images of the rooms, check prices and availability, and then send e-mail to the innkeeper if you have further questions. This is an extensive directory of bed and breakfast inns, but only includes listings if the proprietor submitted one. (*Note:* It's free to get an inn listed.) The descriptions are written by the innkeepers, and many link to the inns' own websites.

ismap.com. *www.ismap.com*
Locate almost any address in France with this neat interactive map that identifies nearby points of interest with icons that link to sites with more information.

U.S. Customs Service Traveler Information. *www.customs.ustreas.gov/travel/index.htm.*
HM Customs & Excise Passenger Enquiries. *www.open.gov.uk.*
Canada Customs and Revenue Agency. *www.ccra-adrc.gc.ca.*
Australian Customs. *www.dfat.gov.au*
New Zealand Customs Service. *www.customs.govt.nz*
Planning a shopping spree and wondering what you're allowed to bring home? Check the latest regulations at these thorough sites.

Visa ATM Locator. *www.visa.com/pd/atm*
MasterCard ATM Locator. *www.mastercard.com/atm*
Find ATMs in hundreds of cities around the world. Both include maps for some locations and both list airport ATM locations, some with maps.

The Weather Channel. *www.weather.com*
Weather forecasts for cities around the world.

Top Web Sites for France

By Cheryl Pientka

Most of the following sites give users the option of using English or French. Though many of them will first come up in French, follow the icons for English versions. If it's not evident at first, scroll down to find an American or British flag.

GENERAL SITES FOR FRANCE

Enjoy France. *www.enjoyfrance.com*
Search for a restaurant, hotel, guest house, or ski resort around the country. Most listings include basic contact information and photos.

FranceWay. *www.franceway.com*
Full of suggestions for your trip to France. Especially heavy on information about Paris, this guide covers dining, lodging, and transportation. A section called "Prepare Your Trip" offers short articles on duty-free shopping, visa requirements, information for people with disabilities, and a list of French consulates in the U.S.

Maison de la France. *www.franceguide.com*
The official site of the French Government Tourist office is a practical guide to France with advice on using transportation and finding the accommodation that's right for you. The calendar of events links to other sites, and the Regions section includes brief cultural articles on each part of the country.

Travel France. *www.bonjour.com*
Pick one of the country's regions and peruse a directory of links to attractions, tour operators, and city tourism offices. Check out the hints for getting around Paris, learn about events taking place around the country, learn basic French phrases (you'll need to download free RealPlayer).

PARIS GUIDES

Aeroports de Paris. *www.paris-airports.com*
For the Charles de Gaulle and Orly airports, find, listings of hotels, restaurants, and car rental agencies. The parking map and accessibility information may be helpful for disabled travelers.

Bonjour Paris. *www.bparis.com; AOL Keyword: Bonjour; CompuServe: Go: Paris*
One of the most comprehensive and fun websites about life in Paris today, written from an American expatriate point of view. Hotel recommendations and travel tips for Paris abound. Message boards debate cultural differences between the French and Americans, and offer readers' restaurant, food, and wine picks. The Travel Tips section is especially helpful for new travelers to France.

Paris Pages. *www.paris.org*
There's so much information on this site that it sometimes takes a while to download. Lodging reviews are organized by area of the city and the monuments that stand nearby. The city guide includes an event calendar, shop listings, map of attractions with details about each, and photo tours.

Paris Tourist Office. *www.paris-touristoffice.com*
Get a calendar of events, and contact information and the closest Métro stops for museums, lodging, restaurants, and nightlife. Tour parks and gardens and discover Paris's trendy arrondissements.

Paris Zagat. *www.zagat.com*
You must register (it was free as of this writing) to access this site. Choose Paris from the pull-down menu and see what other travelers have to say about the local cuisine and service.

RATP (Subway and Buses). *www.ratp.fr/index.eng.html*
Paris Métro and bus maps as well as street maps to the city will help get you around. Download a free version of Adobe Acrobat to view some of the street maps. RATP links to Subway Navigator, which shows you how to use the Métro from one point to another.

Smartweb: Paris. *www.smartweb.fr/paris*
This city guide shows the big attractions, such as the Louvre and Eiffel Tower, and includes history, photos, admission fees, and hours. Navigate the shopping and gallery listings organized by district and preview the airports' terminals. Click on maps to get the weather and subway information.

PROVENCE & THE FRENCH RIVIERA

Avignon and Provence. *www.avignon-et-provence.com*
Restaurant reviews (many restaurants provide their menus), museum listings, ideas for outdoor activities, and lots of history about the popes of Avignon, in addition to practical information for emergencies and classified ads.

Beyond the French Riviera. *www.beyond.fr*
A thorough alphabetical list of villages with maps, directions, and hotel and restaurant information, as well as photos, history, and excursions.

Cannes Online. *www.cannes-on-line.com*
The city's promotional site includes uncritical hotel listings, a city map, and an events calendar.

Nice. *www.nice-coteazur.org*
The in-depth outline of guided tours around the city makes this site worthwhile. You can also search for a hotel by criteria you select.

Provence Touristic Guide. *www.provence.guideweb.com*
Dig into the Leisure and Culture section for pictures, exhibit descriptions, and contact information for museums. A directory of hotels and guest houses includes photos and some online reservations. Visitors can refer to travel guides for wine and antiques.

Provence Web. *www.provenceweb.fr*
Addresses for hotels, restaurants, and activities for 600 towns in Provence and Camargue, Luberon, and Verdon.

Riviera Côte d'Azur. *www.crt-riviera.fr*
Excursions and outdoor activities around the Côte d'Azur are arranged by season. Take a photo tour to see where you might go hiking or four-wheeling. Find out where you can get a Carte Musée Côte d'Azur, the pass good at 62 museums on the Riviera.

St. Tropez Tourism Office. *www.nova.fr/saint-tropez*
Some of the links on this site (most notably restaurants and beaches) had expired at press time. Others are in French or poor English. The site has expanded to include the villages of the surrounding peninsula and has photos and links to the e-mail of hotels and restaurants. Many of the hotels listed are chains, however, and feature other locations in addition to those in St-Tropez.

BORDEAUX & THE ATLANTIC COAST
Bordeaux Office of Tourism. *www.bordeaux-tourisme.com*
Most of the cultural information and travel tips here are fairly general. However, a nice photo gallery in the "City" section shows pictures of Bordeaux's architecture. Information is provided on 82 hotels and 12 restaurants.

Pays Basque.com. *www.paysbasque.com*
Click on the tiny British flag in the top right hand corner of this site to discover the mountains, beaches, towns, restaurants and hotels in the southwest corner of France.

Real South West of France: 123 Voyage. *www.123voyage.com/realsw*
Read lengthy descriptions about villages and attractions throughout the southwest of France. Though the lodging listings are ad-based, they include photos and offer a good idea of what to expect in this beautiful region.

Touradour.com. *www.touradour.com*
Listings for 64 hotels on the Basque coast, and more than 1,100 inland, as well as history of the region, extensive sports and activities, and links to maps and local transportation information. You'll also find lists of addresses for scooter and bike rentals. Restaurants appear in the individual town sections.

Tour of Bordeaux. *www.bordeaux.com*
Wine lovers, get ready. Read up on which wines from the region fit your taste. Also consult the dining and lodging reviews and download free QuickTime VR software to take a virtual tour of town.

BURGUNDY & THE RHONE VALLEY
Burgundy: Land of Great Art and Good Living. *www.burgundy tourism.com*
A regional map directs wine enthusiasts to the area's vineyards, and photos and brief background on nearby castles show off the local architecture. Information on restaurant and lodging and sports and leisure activities is also provided.

Lyon Convention and Visitors Bureau. *www.lyon-france.com*
An attractive site with an excellent "City Guide" section includes directions on arriving by car and plane, public transportation, maps, foreign exchange offices, and travel tips.

BRITTANY
Brittany Holiday Guide. *www.brittany-guide.com*
Thorough descriptions with photos of places of interest, hotels and guest houses, transportation information (including roadwork), history, and an events calendar for the region.

Region Bretagne. *www.region-bretagne.fr*
Get the basics from the "Tourism" section, then see the "Leisure" section, which includes outdoor activities such as hiking and horseback riding. Otherwise, this site offers little substance in its dining and lodging sections.

NORMANDY
French Tourism Board for Normandy. *www.normandy-tourism.org*
Hotel descriptions and information on museums and attractions organized by town. Check out the D-Day section that highlights Battle of Normandy places of interest. An interactive parks and gardens list takes you to photos and information about the many gardens in the region. Check out the "Sports & Leisure" section with its details about the region's many golf courses.

Giverny and Vernon. *www.giverny.org*
Visitors to the old stomping grounds of Claude Monet will find loads of useful travel and transportation information at this basic site. Find details on the area's castles, museums, and places of archaeological interest. Don't miss the tips on avoiding the crowds (avoid Sundays and bank holidays).

LOIRE VALLEY
Châteaux and Country. *www.chateauxandcountry.com*
Scroll down to the bottom of the home page and click on the American flag in the right-hand corner for the English version. A comprehensive

site with photos, driving directions, castle hours, and admission prices, and, where applicable, castle lodging prices. Discover the France of the kings by following the "historical journeys" mapped here. You can search for châteaux in five regions of France.

Loire Net. *www.loire.net*
With photos, descriptions, and reviews, this guide to the Loire Valley shows off the historic châteaux, museums, and other attractions.

West Loire. *www.cr-pays-de-la-loire.fr/eng.htm*
Pictures of château-accommodations give a nice preview of your trip. Read the brief descriptions of golf courses, local cuisine, spas, and museums.

GETTING AROUND
Rail Europe. *www.raileurope.com*
Rail Europe lets you buy Eurail, Europass, and Brit Rail railroad passes online, as well as Eurostar tickets to and from London via the Channel Tunnel, rail and drive packages, and point-to-point travel in 35 European countries. Even if you don't want a railpass, the site offers invaluable first- and second-class fare and schedule information to the most popular European rail routes.

SNCF (Railroad). *www.sncf.fr*
Schedule and fare information for main French and European railroad lines. You can reserve or purchase tickets online and pick up the ticket at a station or ticket vending machine (your credit card is required for this) or have it sent to you.

Subway Navigator. *http://metro.ratp.fr:10001/bin/cities/english*
An amazing site with detailed subway route maps for Paris, Lyon, Marseille, and some other French cities.

E-MAIL ON THE ROAD

You don't have to be out of touch just because you don't carry a laptop while you travel. Web browser–based free e-mail programs make it much easier to stay in e-touch.

Just open a **freemail** account at a browser-based provider, such as **MSN Hotmail** (*hotmail.com*) or **Yahoo! Mail** (*mail.yahoo.com*). Both are equally reliable, but Hotmail tends to handle attachments better (both sending and receiving). AOL users should check out *AOL Netmail* (*aol.com*), and **USA.NET** (*www.usa.net*) comes highly recommended for functionality and security. You can find hints, tips, and a mile-long list of *freemail* providers at *www.emailaddresses.com*.

In France, web connection is easily available not only at Internet cafes, but also at copy shops, and cash- and credit-card Internet-access machines (often available in hotel lobbies or business centers). The **Net Café Guide** (*www.netcafeguide.com/mapindex.htm*) will help you locate Internet cafes at hundreds of locations around the globe.

hostels appendix

The source for all hostel listings and hostel-resource information below was the website for the Fédération Unie des Auberges de Jeunesse (FUAJ), a member of the International Youth Hostel Federation: **www.fuaj.org.** The FUAJ is the French link in a chain of 6,000 youth hostels located in 66 countries; there are over 186 hostels in France alone. Membership in the FUAJ enables travelers to stay and take part in hostel activities in France and abroad, as well as allows you to use its International Booking Network (IBN) to make reservations. Contact one of the main regional offices (listed below) directly for more information on membership and IBN reservations.

Website information is subject to error of course, and is constantly being updated. Please check the site, **www.fuaj.org,** or get in touch with the individual hostel or one of the regional offices, before planning your trip.

Rates range from 31-72F per person, but are based on a category designation and may vary by season. Refer to the website **www.fuaj.org,** or check with a regional office or the hostel itself for current rates.

REGIONAL FUAJ OFFICES
FUAJ National Center in Paris
FUAJ Centre National F.F./IBN
27 rue Pajol
75018 Paris
Tel: 01/44-89-87-27
Fax: 01/44-89-87-10/49
E-mail: centre-national@fuaj.org
Métro: La Chapelle, Marx Dormoy,
    Gare du Nord (RER B)
Hours: 9:30am-6pm Mon-Fri, 10am-
    5pm Sat

FUAJ Branches in Paris
Antenne Beaubourg
9 rue de Brantôme
75003 Paris
Tel: 01/48-04-70-40 (voyages)
Tel: 01/48-04-70-30 (transports)
Fax: 01/42-77-03-29
Métro: Châtelet les Halles, Hôtel de
    Ville, Rambuteau
Hours: 11am-12:30pm/1:30-6:45pm
    Mon; 10am-6:45pm Tues-Fri; 10am-
    5:30pm Sat
Antenne République
4, blvd. Jules Ferry
75011 Paris
Tel: 01/43-57-43-28
Fax: 01/3-57-53-90
Métro: République, Parmentier,
    Oberkampf

FUAJ Regional Branches
FUAJ Champagne F.F.
Centre International de Séjour
Parc Léo Lagrange-Allée Polonceau
51100 Reims
Tel: 03/26-40-52-60
Fax: 03/26-47-35-70

FUAJ Île et Vilaine F.F./IBN
Auberge de Jeunesse
10-12 Canal St.-Martin
35700 Rennes
Tel: 02/99-33-22-33
Fax: 02/99-59-06-21

FUAJ Isère F.F./IBN
Auberge de Jeunesse
10 ave. du Grésivaudan
38130 Echirolles

Tel: 04/76-09-33-52
Fax: 04/76-09-38-99

FUAJ Lorraine F.F.
7 rue des Trinitaires
57000 Metz
Tel: 03/87-75-23-98
Fax: 03/87-76-17-59

FUAJ Montpellier F.F./IBN
Auberge de Jeunesse-Rue des Écoles
    Laïques
Impasse Petite Corraterie
Rue des Écoles Laïques
34000 Montpellier
Tel: 04/67-60-32-22
Fax: 04/67-60-32-30

FUAJ Nord F.F./IBN
10 rue de Malpart
59000 Lille
Tel: 03/20-57-13-57
Fax: 03/20-57-13-69

FUAJ Poitou F.F./IBN
1 allée Roger Tagault
86006 Poitiers
Tel: 05/49-30-09-70
Fax: 05/49-30-09-79

INDIVIDUAL HOSTELS
Aix-en-Provence
Auberge de Jeunesse
Ave. Marcel Pagnol 3
13090 Aix-en-Provence
Tel: 04/42-20-15-99
Fax: 04/42-59-36-12
E-mail: n/a
Open: Feb 1-Dec 20
Desk hours: n/a

Aix-les-Bains
Auberge de Jeunesse
Promenade du Sierroz
73100 Aix-les-Bains
Tel: 04/79-88-32-88
Fax: 04/79-61-14-05
E-mail: aix-les-bains-@fuaj.org
Open: Dec 23-Jan 7, Feb 5-Nov 5 for
    individuals; all year for groups
Desk hours: 7-10am/6-10pm

Albi
MJC
Rue de la République 13
81000 Albi
Tel: 05/63-54-53-65
Fax: 05/63-54-61-55
E-mail: n/a
Open: All year
Desk hours: 7-9pm; 8-9pm Sat, Sun,
and holidays

Anglet
A.J. "Gazté Etxea"
Rte. des Vignes 19
64600 Anglet
Tel: 05/59-58-70-00
Fax: 05/59-58-70-07
E-mail: biarritz@fuaj.org
Open: Jan 20-Dec 20
Desk hours: 8:30am-10pm

Angoulême
Auberge de Jeunesse
Parc de Bourgines
16000 Angoulême
Tel: 05/45-92-45-80
Fax: 05/45-95-90-71
E-mail: angouleme@fuaj.org
Open: Jan 4-Dec 18
Desk hours: n/a

Annecy
Auberge de Jeunesse
Rte. du Semnoz 4
74000 Annecy
Tel: 04/50-45-33-19
Fax: 04/50-52-77-52
E-mail: n/a
Open: All year except Dec 15-25
Desk hours: 7am-11pm
May 1-Sept 30; 7am-1pm/4pm-10pm
Oct 1-Mar 31

Anzin
A.J. "Du Parc Mathieu"
Rue des Martyrs 43
59410 Anzin
Tel: 03/27-28-21-00
Fax: 03/27-28-21-01
E-mail: n/a
Open: All year
Desk hours: 8-10am/5-10pm

Arles
Auberge de Jeunesse
Ave. Foch 20
13200 Arles
Tel: 04/90-96-18-25
Fax: 04/90-96-31-26
E-mail: n/a
Open: Feb 5-Dec 20
Desk hours: 7-10am/5pm-midnight
summer; 7-10am/5-11pm winter

Arras
Auberge de Jeunesse
Grand Place 59
62000 Arras
Tel: 03/21-22-70-02
Fax: 03/21-07-46-15
E-mail: arras.aj@free.fr
Open: Feb 1-Nov 30
Desk hours: 7:30am-noon/5-11pm

Autrans
A.J. "Les Hirondelles"
Les Gaillards
38880 Autrans
Tel: 04/76-94-77-15
Fax: 04/76-94-77-89
E-mail: autrans@fuaj.org
Open: All year
Desk hours: 8am-12:30pm/5-8pm

Avrillé les Ponceaux
Auberge de Jeunesse
"Pause-Gâtines" rue des Tilleuils
37340 Avrillé
Tel: 02/47-24-96-00 or 02/47-25-14-45
Fax: 02/47-48-26-59
E-mail: n/a
Open: July 1-Aug 31 for individuals; all
year for groups
Desk hours: 5-10pm

Banize
Centre d'Hébergement Lou Pélélé
Centre d'Hébergement et d'Animation
Puy Joint
23120 Banize
Tel: 05/55-66-00-63
Fax: 05/55-66-02-07
E-mail: n/a
Open: All year
Desk hours: n/a

Bayeux
"Family Home"
Rue Général de Dais 39
14400 Bayeux
Tel: 02/31-92-15-22
Fax: 02/31-92-55-72
E-mail: n/a
Open: All year
Desk hours: n/a

Beaugency
Auberge de Jeunesse
Rte. de Châteaudun 152
45190 Beaugency
Tel: 02/38-44-61-31
Fax: 02/38-44-14-73
E-mail: beaugency@fuaj.org
Open: Mar 1-Dec 31
Desk hours: n/a

Beaulieu Sur Dordogne
Auberge de Jeunesse
La Riviera Limousine Place du Monturu
19120 Beaulieu Sur Dordogne
Tel: 05/55-91-13-82
Fax: 05/55-91-26-06
E-mail: beaulieu@fuaj.org
Open: Apr 1-Nov 5 for individuals; all
   year for groups booking in advance
Desk hours: 6-9pm (Oct 1-Nov 5:
   please call before your arrival)

Belfort
"Résidence Madrid" FJT Belfort
Rue de Madrid 6
90000 Belfort
Tel: 03/84-21-39-16
Fax: 03/84-28-58-95
E-mail: n/a
Open: All year
Desk hours: 8:30-12:30pm/2-7:30pm,
   closed Sun mornings

Belle-Île-en-Mer
Auberge de Jeunesse
Haute Boulogne Belle-Ile
56360 Le Palais
Tel: 02/97-31-81-33
Fax: 02/97-31-58-38
E-mail: belle-ile@fuaj.org
Open: Jan 3-Dec 24
Desk hours: 8-10am/6-8pm

Besançon
Foyer Mixte De Jeunes Travailleurs
FJT "Les Oiseaux"
Rue des Cras 48
25000 Besançon
Tel: 03/81-40-32-00
Fax: 03/81-40-32-01
E-mail: n/a
Open: All year
Desk hours: 9am-7pm, till 6pm Sun

Bétête
Centre animation hébergement et tourisme
Abbaye de Prébenoit
23270 Bétête
Tel: 05/55-80-78-91
Fax: 05/55-80-86-80
E-mail: n/a
Open: Apr 1-Nov 1
Desk hours: n/a

Biarritz
A.J. "Aintziko Gazte Etxea"
Rue Chiquito de Cambo 8
64200 Biarritz
Tel: 05/59-41-76-00 or 05/59-58-70-00
Fax: 05/59-41-76-07 or 05/59-58-70-07
E-mail: biarritz@fuaj.org
Open: Jan 20-Dec 20
Desk hours: 8:30am-10pm

Blois "Les Grouëts"
Auberge de Jeunesse
Rue de l'Hôtel 18
Pasquier Les Grouëts
41000 Blois
Tel: 02/54-78-27-21
Fax: 02/54-78-27-21
E-mail: blois@fuaj.org
Open: Mar 1-Nov 15
Desk hours: 6:45-10am/6-10:30pm

Blois Montivault
A.J. "Levée de la Loire"
Cedex 181
Monlivault
41350 Vineuil
Tel: 02/54-78-27-21
Fax: 02/54-78-27-21
E-mail: n/a
Open: July 1-Aug 31
Desk hours: n/a

Boulogne sur Mer
Auberge de Jeunesse
Place Rouget de Lisle
62200 Boulogne sur Mer
Tel: 03/21-99-15-30 or 03/21-99-15-35
Fax: 03/21-99-15-39
E-mail: boulogne-sur-mer@fuaj.org
Open: Feb 1-Dec 23
Desk hours: 9am-noon Sept-Mar; 8am-
    1pm Apr-Aug

Bourges
A.J. "Jacques Coeur"
Rue Henri Sellier 22
18000 Bourges
Tel: 02/48-24-58-09
Fax: 02/48-65-51-46
E-mail: bourges@fuaj.org
Open: Jan 17-Dec 17
Desk hours: n/a

Brive la Gaillarde
Auberge de Jeunesse
Ave. du Maréchal Bugeaud Parc Mon-
    jauze 56
19100 Brive
Tel: 05/55-24-34-00
Fax: 05/55-84-82-80
E-mail: aj.brive@wanadoo.fr
Open: Jan 16-Dec 14
Desk hours: 8am-noon/2-10pm; 8am-
    noon/6-10pm Sat and Sun

Cadouin
Auberge de Jeunesse
Place de l'Abbaye
24480 Cadouin
Tel: 05/53-73-28-78
Fax: 05/53-73-28-79
E-mail: n/a
Open: Feb 1-Dec 15
Desk hours: n/a

Caen
FJT "Robert Rême"
Rue Eustache Restout 68
14000 Caen
Tel: 02/31-52-19-96
Fax: 02/31-84-29-49
E-mail: n/a
Open: June 1-Sept 30
Desk hours: 7am-10pm

Cahors
FJT
Rue Frédéric Suisse 20
46000 Cahors
Tel: 05/65-35-64-71 or 05/65-53-97-02
Fax: 05/65-35-95-92
E-mail: n/a
Open: All year
Desk hours: 9am-noon/2-7pm

Cancale
Auberge de Jeunesse
Port Picain
35260 Cancale
Tel: 02/99-89-62-62
Fax: 02/99-89-78-79
E-mail: cancale@fuaj.org
Open: All year except Jan 3-31
Desk hours: 8am-1pm/5-10pm May-
    Sept; 9am-1pm/6-8pm Oct-Apr

Cap-Ferret
Auberge de Jeunesse
Ave. de Bordeaux 87
33970 Cap-Ferret
Tel: 05/56-60-64-62
Fax: n/a
E-mail: n/a
Open: July 1-Aug 31
Desk hours: 7:30am-1pm/6-9pm

Cap-Fréhel
Auberge de Jeunesse
La ville Hardieux
22240 Fréhel
Tel: 02/96-41-48-98
Fax: 02/96-41-48-98
E-mail: n/a
Open: Apr 1-Sept 15
Desk hours: 8:30am-12:30pm/6-10pm

Carcassonne
Auberge de Jeunesse
Rue du Vicomte Trencavel "La Cité
    Médiévale"
11000 Carcassonne
Tel: 04/68-25-23-16
Fax: 04/68-71-14-84
E-mail: carcassonne@fuaj.org
Open: Feb 1-Dec 15
Desk hours: 7am-11pm (minimum ser-
    vice 11pm-7am)

Cassis
A.J. La Fontasse
13260 Cassis
Tel: 04/42-01-02-72
Fax: n/a
E-mail: n/a
Open: Mar 2-Jan 9
Desk hours: 7:30-10am/
  5-11pm

Cepoy / Montargis
Auberge de Jeunesse
Quai du Port 25
45120 Cepoy
Tel: 02/38-93-25-45
Fax: 02/38-93-19-25
E-mail: n/a
Open: Feb 1-Dec 19
Desk hours: 8am-noon/6-10pm

Cernay
Auberge Internationale de la Jeunesse
Ave. Faubourg de Colmar 16
68700 Cernay
Tel: 03/89-75-44-59
Fax: 03/89-75-87-48
E-mail: n/a
Open: All year except Dec 25-31
Desk hours: 5-10pm winter till 11pm
  summer

Chalons en Champagne
A.J. "L'Embellie"
Square Antral
Rue Kellermann 6
51000 Chalons en Champagne
Tel: 03/26-68-13-54
Fax: n/a
E-mail: n/a
Open: All year
Desk hours: 24 hours

Chamonix Mont-Blanc
Auberge de Jeunesse
Montée Jacques Balmat Les Pèlerins
  d'en Haut 127
74400 Chamonix Mont-Blanc
Tel: 04/50-53-14-52
Fax: 04/50-55-92-34
E-mail: Chamonix@fuaj.org
Open: Dec 10-May 10, May 18-Oct 1
  for individuals; all year for groups
Desk hours: 8am-noon; 5-10pm

Chamrousse
A.J. Le Saint Christophe
38410 Chamrousse
Tel: 04/76-89-91-31
Fax: 04/76-89-96-66
E-mail: chamrousse@fuaj.org
Open: Dec 1-May 1, June 1-Sept 15
Desk hours: 8am-12:30pm/
  5-7:30pm

Chaumont
FJT
Rue de Carcassonne 1
52000 Chaumont
Tel: 03/25-03-22-77
Fax: n/a
E-mail: n/a
Open: All year
Desk hours: 3-9pm

Chauny
Auberge de Jeunesse
Blvd. de Bad Kostritz
02300 Chauny
Tel: 02/23-52-09-96
Fax: 02/23-39-90-92
E-mail: n/a
Open: All year
Desk hours: 7-10am/
  5-10pm

Cherbourg
Auberge de Jeunesse
Rue de l'Abbaye 55
50100 Cherbourg
Tel: 02/33-78-15-15
Fax: 02/33-78-15-16
E-mail: n/a
Open: Jan 4-Dec 23
Desk hours: 9am-noon/
  6-11pm

Cholet "Les Pâquerettes"
FJT "Les Pâquerettes"
Rue de la Casse 5 - B.P. 316
49303 Cholet Cedex
Tel: 02/41-71-36-36
Fax: 02/41-62-62-22
E-mail: n/a
Open: June 15-Sept 15
Desk hours: 9am-8pm Mon-Fri; 10am-
  5pm Sat

Choucan en Brocéliande
Auberge de Jeunesse
Choucan Paimpont
35380 Plelan le Grand
Tel: 02/97-22-76-75
Fax: n/a
E-mail: n/a
Open: May 1-Sept 30
Desk hours: n/a

Clermont-Ferrand
A.J. "Cheval Blanc"
Ave. de l' U.R.S.S. 55
63000 Clermont-Ferrand
Tel: 04/73-92-26-39
Fax: 04/73-92-99-96
E-mail: n/a
Open: Mar 1-Oct 31
Desk hours: 7-10am/5-11pm

Colmar
A.J. "Mittelharth"
Rue Pasteur 2
68000 Colmar
Tel: 03/89-80-57-39
Fax: 03/89-80-76-16
E-mail: n/a
Open: All year except Dec 16-31
Desk hours: 5-11pm winter, till mid-
    night summer

Creil
Centre des Cadres Sportifs
Rue du Général Leclerc 1
60100 Creil
Tel: 03/44-64-62-20
Fax: 03/44-64-62-29
E-mail: n/a
Open: All year
Desk hours: 6-9pm

Dieppe
Auberge de Jeunesse
Rue Louis Fromager Quartier Janval de
    Dieppe 48
76550 Saint Aubin sur Sciè
Tel: 02/35-84-85-73
Fax: 02/35-84-89-62
E-mail: n/a
Open: Mar 15-Oct 15
Desk hours: 8-10am/5-10pm

Dinan
A.J. "Le Moulin de Méen" Vallée de la
Fontaine des Eaux
22100 Dinan
Tel: 02/96-39-10-83
Fax: 02/96-39-10-62
E-mail: dinan@fuaj.org
Open: All year
Desk hours: 8am-noon/4-11pm

Dole
A.J. "Le Saint Jean"
Place Jean XXIII B.P. 164
39101 Dole
Tel: 03/84-82-36-74
Fax: 03/84-79-17-69
E-mail: n/a
Open: All year
Desk hours: 11:30am-2:30pm Mon-Fri;
    6pm-8am Sat-Sun

Dunkerque
Auberge de Jeunesse
Place Paul Asseman
59140 Dunkerque
Tel: 03/28-63-36-34
Fax: 03/28-63-24-54
E-mail: n/a
Open: Jan 2-Dec 20
Desk hours: 6-11pm

Eu / Le Tréport
Centre des Fontaines
Rue des Fontaines B.P. 123
76260 Eu Cedex
Tel: 02/35-86-05-03
Fax: 02/35-86-45-12
E-mail: n/a
Open: Jan 5-Dec 19
Desk hours: 6-9pm

Evian les Bains
C.I.S.
Ave. de Neuvecelle B.P. 31
74500 Evian les Bains Cedex
Tel: 04/50-75-35-87
Fax: 04/50-75-45-67
E-mail: jptreil@cur-archamps.fr
Open: All year
Desk hours: 8am-10pm

Fontaine de Vaucluse
Auberge de Jeunesse
Chemin de la Vignasse
84800 Fontaine de Vaucluse
Tel: 04/90-20-31-65
Fax: 04/90-20-26-20
E-mail: n/a
Open: Feb 15-Nov 15
Desk hours: 8-10am/5-10pm

Fontenay-le-Comte
Foyer Sud Vendéen "Les 3 Portes"
Rue des Gravants 16 B.P. 347
85206 Fontenay le Comte Cedex
Tel: 02/51-69-13-44
Fax: 02/51-69-04-23
E-mail: n/a
Open: June 15-Sept 15
Desk hours: 9am-8pm

Fréjus
Auberge de Jeunesse
Chemin du Counillier
83600 Fréjus
Tel: 04/94-53-18-75
Fax: 04/94-53-25-86
E-mail: n/a
Open: Feb 1-Dec 20; Groups: call in
    advance
Desk hours: closes at 9:30pm

Gannat
Auberge de Jeunesse
Maison des Cultures et Traditions Route
    de Saint Priest
03800 Gannat
Tel: 04/70-90-12-67
Fax: 04/70-90-66-36
E-mail: n/a
Open: Apr 1-Oct 10
Desk hours: 9am-7pm

Granville
Centre Régional de Nautisme
Blvd. des Amiraux
50400 Granville
Tel: 02/33-91-22-62
Fax: 02/33-50-51-99
E-mail: n/a
Open: Jan 3-Dec 21
Desk hours: 3-11pm

Gray
FJT
Rue André Maginot 2
70100 Gray
Tel: 03/84-64-99-20
Fax: 03/84-64-99-29
E-mail: le-foyer@wanadoo.fr
Open: All year
Desk hours: 8am-noon/2-7pm

Grenoble Echirolles
Auberge de Jeunesse
Ave. du Grésivaudan 10
38130 Echirolles
Tel: 04/76-09-33-52
Fax: 04/76-09-38-99
E-mail: grenoble-echirolles@fuaj.org
Open: All year
Desk hours: 7:30am-11pm Mon-Sat;
    7:30-10am/5-11pm Sun

Guillestre
"Les Quatre Vents"
"La Rochette" B.P. 22
05600 Guillestre Cedex
Tel: 04/92-45-04-32
Fax: 04/92-45-04-32
E-mail: n/a
Open: Dec 1-Sept 30
Desk hours: n/a

Ile de Groix
Auberge de Jeunesse
Fort du Méné
56590 Île de Groix
Tel: 02/97-86-81-38 or 02/97-86-85-53
Fax: 02/97-86-52-43
E-mail: n/a
Open: Apr 1-Oct 15
Desk hours: 9-11:30am/6-8pm

Imphy
Résidence "Georges Bouqueau"
Rue Jean Sounié 8
58160 Imphy
Tel: 03/86-90-95-20
Fax: 03/86-38-31-87
E-mail: n/a
Open: All year
Desk hours: n/a

Inzinzac Lochrist
Auberge de Jeunesse
Ferme du Gorée
56650 Inzinsac Lochrist
Tel: 02/97-36-08-08 or 02/97-36-00-83
Fax: 02/97-36-90-63
E-mail: n/a
Open: Mar 1-Oct 15; All year if booked
in advance
Desk hours: 6-9pm, till 10pm July and
Aug

La Clusaz
Auberge de Jeunesse
Rte. du Col de Croix Fry "Les Etages"
B.P. 47
74220 La Clusaz Cedex
Tel: 04/50-02-41-73
Fax: 04/50-02-65-85
E-mail: la-clusaz@fuaj.org
Open: Dec 17-Sept 26 for individuals;
All year for groups booking in advance
Desk hours: 8am-9pm

La Foux d'Allos
A.J. Neige et Soleil
"Les Chauvets"
04260 La Foux d'Allos
Tel: 04/92-83-81-08
Fax: 04/92-83-83-70
E-mail: n/a
Open: Dec 1-Apr 25, June 10-Sept 15
Desk hours: 8-10am/5-8pm

La Palud sur Verdon
A.J. "L'Immense Botte de Paille"
Départementale 23
04120 La Palud sur Verdon
Tel: 04/92-77-38-72
Fax: 04/92-77-38-72
E-mail: n/a
Open: Mar 1-Oct 31
Desk hours: 7-10am/5-9pm

La Rochelle
Auberge de Jeunesse
Ave. des Minimes B.P. 305
17013 La Rochelle Cedex
Tel: 05/46-44-43-11
Fax: 05/46-45-41-48
E-mail: n/a
Open: Jan 1-Dec 18

Desk hours: 8am-12:30pm/1:30-
7:30pm/8:30-10:30pm; 8am-
11:30pm summer

La Toussuire
Auberge de Jeunesse
La Toussuire
73300 Fontcouverte
Tel: 04/79-56-72-04
Fax: 04/79-83-00-93
E-mail: n/a
Open: Nov 30-Apr 30, July 1-Sept 14
Desk hours: 6-11pm

Lannion
A.J. "Beg Leguer"
Plage de Goalagorn
22300 Lannion
Tel: 02/96-47-24-86
Fax: 02/96-37-02-06
E-mail: n/a
Open: Apr 15-Sept 15 for individuals;
All year for groups booking in advance
Desk hours: 10am-noon/6-8pm
A.J. "Les Korrigans"
Rive Gauche
Rue du 73ème territorial 6
22300 Lannion
Tel: 02/96-37-91-28
Fax: 02/96-37-02
E-mail: lannion@fuaj.org
Open: All year
Desk hours: 9am-9pm; 7am-11pm
summer

Lautenbach
A.J. "Dynamo"
La Schellimatt
68610 Lautenbach
Tel: 03/89-74-26-81
Fax: n/a
E-mail: n/a
Open: Weekends & school period
Desk hours: 24 hours

Le Mans
FJT "Le Flore"
Rue Maupertuis 23
72000 Le Mans
Tel: 02/43-81-27-55
Fax: 02/43-81-06-10
E-mail: florefjt@cybercable.tm.fr

Open: All year
Desk hours: 10am-7pm

Le Mazet Saint Voy
La Ferme du Besset "La Bataille"
43520 Le Mazet Saint Voy
Tel: 04/71-65-00-35
Fax: 04/71-65-05-44
E-mail: n/a
Open: All year
Desk hours: 9am-noon/2-5pm

Le Mont Dore
A.J. "Le Grand Volcan"
63240 Le Mont Dore
Tel: 04/73-65-03-53
Fax: 04/73-65-26-39
E-mail: le-mont-dore@fuaj.org
Open: All year
Desk hours: 8am-9pm

Le Puy en Velay
Centre Pierre Cardinal
Rue Jules Valles 9
43000 Le Puy en Velay
Tel: 04/71-05-52-40
Fax: 04/71-05-61-24
E-mail: n/a
Open: All year; Closed weekends and
   holidays Oct 1-Mar 31
Desk hours: 7:30am-noon/2-10pm

Le Trayas /Théoule sur Mer
Auberge de Jeunesse
Ave. de la Véronèse Le Trayas 9
06590 Théoule sur Mer
Tel: 04/93-75-40-23
Fax: 04/93-75-43-45
E-mail: n/a
Open: Feb 15-Jan 2
Desk hours: 8-10am/5:30-10pm May-
   Aug; 5:30-9pm Sept-Apr

Les Aldudes
Association Ecole des Buissons
Urtxintxenea Route d'Urepel
64430 Les Aldudes
Tel: 05/59-37-56-58
Fax: 05/59-37-56-58
E-mail: urtxintx@aol.com
Open: Feb 15-Dec 15
Desk hours: From 9am

Les Deux Alpes
A.J. "Les Brûleurs de Loups"
38860 Les Deux Alpes
Tel: 04/76-79-22-80
Fax: 04/76-79-26-15
E-mail: les-deux-alpes@fuaj.org
Open: Dec 5-May 2, June 20-Sept 5 for
   individuals; All year for groups by
   reservation
Desk hours: 8:30am-11pm

Les Gets
A.J. Les Farfadets "Le Poncet"
74160 Les Gets
Tel: 04/50-79-14-86
Fax: n/a
E-mail: n/a
Open: All year
Desk hours: n/a

Les Rousses
Auberge de Jeunesse
Le Bief de la Chaille 2400
39220 Les Rousses
Tel: 03/84-60-02-80
Fax: 03/84-60-09-67
E-mail: n/a
Open: Dec 20-Apr 24, May 11-Sept 25
   for individuals; All year for groups
Desk hours: 5-10pm May-Sept

Lille
Auberge de Jeunesse
Rue Malpart 12
59000 Lille
Tel: 03/20-57-08-94
Fax: 03/20-63-98-93
E-mail: lille@fuaj.org
Open: Feb 1-Dec 20
Desk hours: 7am-noon/2pm-1am, till
   2am summer

Lorient
Auberge de Jeunesse
Rue Victor Schoelcher 41
56100 Lorient
Tel: 02/97-37-11-65
Fax: 02/97-87-95-49
E-mail: n/a
Open: Jan 8-Dec 22
Desk hours: 8-10:30am/
   5:30-10pm

Lourdios-Ichère
Estivade d'Aspe Pyrénées
"Maison Pelou"
64570 Lourdios-Ichère
Tel: 05/59-34-46-39
Fax: 05/59-34-48-04
E-mail: n/a
Open: All year
Desk hours: 9am-6pm

Lyon
Auberge de Jeunesse du Vieux Lyon
Montée du Chemin Neuf 41-45
69005 Lyon
Tel: 04/78-15-05-50
Fax: 04/78-15-05-51
E-mail: lyon@fuaj.org
Open: All year
Desk hours: 7am-noon/2pm-1am

Lyon (South)
Auberge de Jeunesse
Rue Roger Salengro 51
69200 Vénissieux
Tel: 04/78-76-39-23
Fax: 04/78-77-51-11
E-mail: lyonsud@fuaj.org
Open: Jan 17-Dec 23
Desk hours: 7am-noon/2:30pm-
    12:30am Apr 1-Sept 30; 7am-
    noon/3:30-11pm Oct 1-Mar 31

Manosque
Auberge de Jeunesse
Parc de la Rochette
04100 Manosque
Tel: 04/92-87-57-44
Fax: 04/92-72-43-91
E-mail: n/a
Open: All year
Desk hours: 8am-noon/5-10pm

Marseille
A.J. "Château de Bois Luzy"
Allée des Primevères
13012 Marseille
Tel: 04/91-49-06-18
Fax: 04/91-49-06-18
E-mail: n/a
Open: All year
Desk hours: 7:30am-noon/
    5-10:30pm

A.J. "Bonneveine"
Impasse Bonfils Ave. Joseph Vidal
13008 Marseille
Tel: 04/91-73-21-81
Fax: 04/91-73-97-23
E-mail: marseille-bonneveine@fuaj.org
Open: Feb 1-Dec 21
Desk hours: 7am-11pm

Menton
Auberge de Jeunesse
Plateau Saint Michel
06500 Menton
Tel: 04/93-35-93-14
Fax: 04/93-35-93-07
E-mail: n/a
Open: Feb 1-Nov 15
Desk hours: 7am-noon/5-10pm

Metz
"Carrefour"
Rue Marchant 6
57000 Metz
Tel: 03/87-75-07-26
Fax: 03/87-36-71-44
E-mail: ascarrefour@wanadoo.fr
Open: All year
Desk hours: 24 hours
Auberge de Jeunesse
Allée de Metz Plage 1
57000 Metz
Tel: 03/87-30-44-02
Fax: 03/87-33-19-80
E-mail: aubjeumetz@aol.com
Open: All year
Desk hours: 7-10am/5-10pm

Millau
FJT "Sud Aveyron Accueil"
Rue Lucien Costes 26
12100 Millau
Tel: 05/65-61-27-74
Fax: 05/65-61-90-58
E-mail: n/a
Open: All year
Desk hours: 9am-noon/2-6pm

Montpellier
Auberge de Jeunesse
Rue des Ecoles Laïques Impasse Petite
    Corraterie
34000 Montpellier

Tel: 04/67-60-32-22
Fax: 04/67-60-32-30
E-mail: n/a
Open: Jan 10-Dec 17
Desk hours: 8am-midnight

Montreuil Sur Mer
A.J. "La Hullotte"
Citadelle Rue Carnot
62170 Montreuil Sur Mer
Tel: 03/21-06-10-83
Fax: 03/21-06-10-83
E-mail: n/a
Open: Mar 1-Oct 30
Desk hours: 10am-6pm

Morzine-Avoriaz
A.J. "Holiday Campus"
La Coutettaz
74110 Morzine
Tel: 04/50-79-14-86
Fax: same as phone
E-mail: n/a
Open: Dec 24-Apr 22, June 14-Sept 12
Desk hours: 5-9pm

Mulhouse
Auberge de Jeunesse
Rue de l'Ilberg 37
68200 Mulhouse
Tel: 03/89-42-63-28
Fax: 03/89-59-74-95
E-mail: n/a
Open: Jan 11-Dec 18
Desk hours: 8am-noon/5-11pm, till
    midnight summer

Nancy
Château de Réémicourt
Rue de Vandoeuvre 149
54600
Tel: 03/83-27-73-67
Fax: 03/83-41-41-35
E-mail: n/a
Open: Jan 2-Dec 23
Desk hours: 7:30am-10:30pm

Nantes
Auberge de Jeunesse
Place de la Manu 2
44000 Nantes
Tel: 02/40-29-29-20

Fax: 02/51-12-48-42
E-mail: nanteslamanu@fuaj.org
Open: All year
Desk hours: 9am-1pm/3-11pm
Résidence "Port Beaulieu"
Blvd. Vincent Gâche 9
44200 Nantes
Tel: 02/40-12-24-00
Fax: 02/51-82-00-05
E-mail: n/a
Open: July 1-Aug 31
Desk hours: 8am-midnight
FJT
Place Sainte Elisabeth 1
44042 Nantes Cedex 01
Tel: 02/40-20-63-63
Fax: 02/40-20-63-79
E-mail: n/a
Open: All year
Desk hours: 8am-10pm

Nice
Auberge de Jeunesse
Rte. Forestière du Mont-Alban
06300 Nice
Tel: 04/93-89-23-64
Fax: 04/92-04-03-10
E-mail: n/a
Open: All year
Desk hours: 7am-noon/5pm-midnight

Nîmes
Auberge de Jeunesse
La Cigale
Chemin de L'auberge de Jeunesse 257
30900 Nîmes
Tel: 04/66-68-03-20
Fax: 04/66-68-03-21
E-mail: nimes@fuaj.org
Open: Apr 28-Dec 31
Desk hours: 7:30am-11:30pm winter;
    24 hours summer

Nouvelle-Calédonie/Nouméa
Nouméa City Hostel
B.P. 767 51 bis, rue Olry
98845 Nouméa Cedex
Tel: 06/87-27-58-79
Fax: 06/87-25-48-17
E-mail: n/a
Open: All year
Desk hours: 7:30-10am/5-7:30pm

Oinville Sur Montcient
A.J. "Relais Randonnée"
Impass, 10 bis, rue de Gournay
78250 Meulan
Tel: 01/34-75-33-91
Fax: 01/34-75-33-91
E-mail: n/a
Open: All year
Desk hours: 9am-1pm/5-10pm

Paimpol
A.J. Château de Kerraoul
22500 Paimpol
Tel: 02/96-20-83-60
Fax: 02/96-20-96-46
E-mail: paimpol@fuaj.org
Open: All year
Desk hours: 8am-10pm

Paris
Auberge "Jules Ferry"
Blvd. Jules Ferry 8
75011 Paris
Tel: 01/43-57-55-60
Fax: 01/43-14-82-09
E-mail: paris.jules-ferry@fuaj.org
Open: All year
Desk hours: 24 hours

Auberge de Jeunesse
Rue des Sept Arpents 24
93310 Le Pré Saint Gervais
Tel: 01/48-43-24-11
Fax: 01/48-43-26-82
E-mail: paris.cite-des-sciences
   @fuaj.org
Open: All year
Desk hours: 24 hours

Auberge "Léo Lagrange"
Rue Martre 107
92110 Clichy
Tel: 01/41-27-26-90
Fax: 01/42-70-52-63
E-mail: paris.clichy@fuaj.org
Open: All year
Desk hours: 24 hours

Auberge "Le d'Artagnan"
Rue Vitruve 80
75020 Paris
Tel: 01/40-32-34-56

Fax: 01/40-32-34-55
E-mail: paris.le-dartagnan@fuaj.org
Open: All year
Desk hours: 24 hours

Parthenay
Auberge de Jeunesse Periscope
Rue Blaise Pascal 16
79200 Parthenay
Tel: 05/49-95-46-89 or 05/49-95-26-32
Fax: 05/49-94-64-85
E-mail: periscope@district-partenay.fr
Open: All year
Desk hours: 7:30am-7pm

Pau / Gelos
FJT "Logis des Jeunes"
Base de Plein Air
64110 Gelos
Tel: 05/59-06-53-02
Fax: 05/59-11-05-20
E-mail:
   logis.des.jeunes.pau@wanadoo.fr
Open: All year
Desk hours: 4-11pm

Périgueux
Foyer de Jeunes Travailleurs
Rue des Thermes Prolongés
24000 Périgueux
Tel: 05/53-06-81-40
Fax: 05/53-06-81-49
E-mail: FGTDordogne@wanadoo.fr
Open: All year
Desk hours: from 4pm

Perpignan
Auberge de Jeunesse
Parc de la Pépinière Ave. de la Grande
   Bretagne
66000 Perpignan
Tel: 04/68-34-63-32
Fax: 04/68-51-16-02
E-mail: n/a
Open: Jan 20-Dec 20
Desk hours: 24 hours

Phalsbourg
Centre Européen de Rencontre
Rue du Général Rottembourg 6
57370 Phalsbourg
Tel: 03/87-24-37-37

Fax: 03/87-24-13-56
E-mail: n/a
Open: All year
Desk hours: 8am-10pm

Plouguernevel
Village Vacances de Kermarc'h
22110 Plouguernevel
Tel: 02/96-29-10-95
Fax: n/a
E-mail: n/a
Open: All year
Desk hours: 9am-noon/
   4-5pm

Poggio Mezzana
A.J. "La Villanella"
20230 Poggio Mezzana
Tel: 04/95-38-50-10
Fax: 04/95-38-50-11
E-mail: n/a
Open: Apr 1-Oct 30
Desk hours: 8am-12:30pm/
   4-8pm

Poitiers
Auberge de Jeunesse
Allée Roger Tagault 1
86000 Poitiers
Tel: 05/49-30-09-70
Fax: 05/49-30-09-79
E-mail: poitiers@fuaj.org
Open: Jan 3-Dec 24
Desk hours: 7am-noon/4-11pm Mon-
   Fri; 7am-1pm/5-11pm Sat-Sun

Pontarlier
Auberge de Jeunesse
Rue Jouffroy 2
25300 Pontarlier
Tel: 03/81-39-06-57
Fax: 03/81-39-06-57
E-mail: n/a
Open: Dec 20-Nov 11
Desk hours: 5:30-10pm

Pontivy
Auberge de Jeunesse
Île des Récollets
56300 Pontivy
Tel: 02/97-25-58-27
Fax: 02/97-25-76-48

E-mail: n/a
Open: All year (to get Desk except
   summer)
Desk hours: 6-9:30pm

Pontorson
Centre Duguesclin
Rue Patton 21
50170 Pontorson
Tel: 02/33-60-18-65
Fax: 02/33-60-18-65
E-mail: aj@ville-pontorson.fr
Open: All year
Desk hours: 8-11am/5-10pm

Puichéric
Auberge de Jeunesse
Rue Marcellin Albert 2
11700 Puichéric
Tel: 04/68-43-73-81
Fax: 04/68-43-71-84
E-mail: n/a
Open: All year
Desk hours: 7am-11pm

Quiberon
"Les Filets Bleus"
Rue du Roch Prio 45
56170 Quiberon
Tel: 02/97-50-15-54
Fax: n/a
E-mail: n/a
Open: May 1-Sept 30
Desk hours: 8:30am-9:30pm

Quimper
Auberge de Jeunesse
Ave. des Oiseaux 6
29000 Quimper
Tel: 02/98-64-97-97
Fax: 02/98-55-38-37
E-mail: n/a
Open: Jan 5-Dec 23
Desk hours: 8-11am/5-9:30pm

Redon
FJT "Mapar"
Rue Chantebel 2 B.P. 101
35603 Redon Cedex
Tel: 02/99-72-14-39
Fax: 02/99-72-16-53
E-mail: MAPAR@wanadoo.fr

Open: June 1-Aug 31
Desk hours: 9am-10pm Mon-Thur, till
7pm Fri; 9am-noon/3-7pm Sat; 3-
7pm Sun

Reims
Centre International de Séjour
Parc L.o Lagrange Allée Polonceau
51100 Reims
Tel: 03/26-40-52-60
Fax: 03/26-47-35-70
E-mail: n/a
Open: Jan 2-Dec 24
Desk hours: 7am-10:30pm

Rennes
Auberge de Jeunesse
Canal Saint Martin 10-12
35700 Rennes
Tel: 02/99-33-22-33
Fax: 02/99-59-06-21
E-mail: n/a
Open: Jan 3-Dec 24
Desk hours: 7am-11:30pm

Roanne
A.J. "Centre Jeunesse P.Bérégovoy"
Rue Fontenille 4
42300 Roanne
Tel: 04/77-72-52-11
Fax: 04/77-70-66-28
E-mail: n/a
Open: All year
Desk hours: 8am-noon/2-10pm

Rochefort Sur Mer
"Logis Etape"
Rue de la République 20
17300 Rochefort Sur Mer
Tel: 05/46-82-10-40 or 05/46-99-74-62
Fax: 05/46-99-21-25 or 05/46-99-74-62
E-mail: jeunesserochefort@neotech.fr
Open: July-Aug
Desk hours: 8-10am/from 5:30pm

Rodez
A.J. "Les Quatre Saisons"
Blvd. des Capucines 26 - Onet-le-
Château
12034 Rodez cedex 09
Tel: 05/65-77-51-05 or 05/65-77-51-01
Fax: 05/65-67-37-97

E-mail:
ASSOC.FJT.Gd.Rodez@wanadoo.fr
Open: All year
Desk hours: 8:30am-12:30pm/5-
6:30pm/8-9:30pm

Rodome
A.J. Ferme Equestre H'Val
11140 Rodome
Tel: 04/68-20-32-22
Fax: 04/68-20-76-10
E-mail: h_val@club-internet.fr
Open: Feb 15-Nov 15
Desk hours: 8am-10pm

Saint Brévin les Pins
A.J. "La Pinède"
Allée de la Jeunesse 1
44250 Saint Brévin les Pins
Tel: 02/40-27-25-27
Fax: 02/40-64-48-77
E-mail: n/a
Open: Feb 8-Oct 9, Nov 1-Jan 2
Desk hours: 9am-12:30pm/6-9pm

Saint Brieuc
A.J. Manoir de la Ville Guyomard
"Les Villages"
22000 Saint Brieuc
Tel: 02/96-78-70-70
Fax: 02/96-78-27-47
E-mail: saint-brieuc@fuaj.org
Open: All year
Desk hours: 8am-noon/5-9pm

Saint Gaudens
FJT "Le Vénasque"
Rue de la Résidence 3
31804 Saint Gaudens Cedex
Tel: 05/61-94-72-73
Fax: 05/61-94-72-74
E-mail: n/a
Open: Jan 2-Dec 30
Desk hours: 8am-12:30pm/2-11 Mon-
Fri; 5-11pm Sat; 6-11pm Sun and hol-
idays

Saint Guen
Auberge de Jeunesse
Rue du Sénéchal 10
22530 Saint Guen
Tel: 02/96-28-54-34

Fax: 02/96-26-01-56
E-mail: n/a
Open: Apr 1-Nov 1
Desk hours: 5-9pm

Saint Junien

A.J. de Saint Amand
Rue de Saint Amand 13
87200 Saint Junien
Tel: 05/55-02-22-79
Fax: 05/55-02-22-79
E-mail: n/a
Open: All year
Desk hours: 8am-10pm

Saint Malo

C.R.I. "Patrick Varangot"
Ave. du R.P. Umbricht 37 B.P. 108
35407 Saint Malo Cedex
Tel: 02/99-40-29-80
Fax: 02/99-40-29-02
E-mail: n/a
Open: All year
Desk hours: 24 hours

Saint Martin des Olmes

Auberge de Jeunesse
Le Bourg Saint Martin des Olmes
63600 Ambert
Tel: 04/73-82-01-38 or 04/73-82-69-88
Fax: 04/73-82-01-38
E-mail: n/a
Open: Feb 15-Nov 15 for individuals;
  All year for groups
Desk hours: 8-10:30am/5-10pm

Saint Mihiel

Auberge de Jeunesse
Rue Sur Meuse 12
55300 Saint Mihiel
Tel: 03/29-89-15-06 or 03/29-89-09-78
Fax: n/a
E-mail: n/a
Open: Apr 3-Nov 30 for individuals; all
  year for groups by reservation
Desk hours: 6pm

Saintes

Auberge de Jeunesse
Place Geoffroy Martel 2
17100 Saintes
Tel: 05/46-92-14-92

Fax: 05/46-92-97-82
E-mail: saintes@fuaj.org
Open: All year
Desk hours: 7am-noon/2:30-10:30
  winter, till 11pm summer

Salies De Bearn

Auberge de Jeunesse
Rte. du Padu
64270 Salies De Bearn
Tel: 05/59-65-06-96
Fax: 05/59-65-06-96
E-mail: n/a
Open: All year
Desk hours: 7-9pm

Saverne

Château des Rohans
67700 Saverne
Tel: 03/88-91-14-84
Fax: 03/88-71-15-97
E-mail: saverne@fuaj.org
Open: Jan 15-Dec 15
Desk hours: n/a

Savines le Lac

A.J. "Les Chaumettes"
05160 Savines le Lac
Tel: 04/92-44-20-16
Fax: 04/92-44-24-54
E-mail: n/a
Open: Apr 1-Nov 30
Desk hours: 8:30am-8:30pm

Seez-les-Arcs

A.J. "La Verdache"
73700 Seez
Tel: 04/79-41-01-93
Fax: 04/79-41-03-36
E-mail: seez-les-arcs@fuaj.org
Open: Dec 19-Sept 30 for individuals;
  All year for groups
Desk hours: 9am-noon/2-5pm

Serre-Chevalier

Auberge de Jeunesse
Le Bez B.P. 2
05240 Serre-Chevalier 1400
Tel: 04/92-24-74-54
Fax: 04/92-24-83-39
E-mail: serre-chevalier@fuaj.org
Open: All year

Desk hours: 8:30am-8:30pm winter and
summer; 9am-noon/2-8pm other seasons

Séte
A.J. "Villa Salis"
Rue du Général Revest
34200 Séte
Tel: 04/67-53-46-68
Fax: 04/67-51-34-01
E-mail: n/a
Open: Jan 15-Dec 15
Desk hours: 8am-2pm/6-11pm;
7:30am-11pm June 16-Sept 15

Strasbourg
A.J. "Parc du Rhin"
Rue des Cavaliers B.P. 58
67017 Strasbourg Cedex
Tel: 03/88-45-54-20
Fax: 03/88-45-54-21
E-mail: strasbourg.parc-du-
rhin@fuaj.org
Open: All year except Dec 21-31
Desk hours: 24 hours

A.J. "René Cassin"
Rue de l'Auberge de Jeunesse 9
67200 Strasbourg
Tel: 03/88-30-26-46
Fax: 03/88-30-35-16
E-mail: n/a
Open: Feb 1-Dec 31
Desk hours: 7am-12:30pm/1:15-
7:30pm/8:15-11:30pm

Camping de la Montagne Verte
Rue Robert Forrer 2
67200 Strasbourg
Tel: 03/88-30-25-46
Fax: 03/88-27-10-15
E-mail: n/a
Open: May 1-Oct 31 and
Dec 1-Dec 31
Desk hours: 7am-12:30pm/1:30-
7:30pm/8:30-10:30pm

Tarascon
Auberge de Jeunesse
Blvd. Gambetta 31
13150 Tarascon

Tel: 04/90-91-04-08
Fax: 04/90-91-54-17
E-mail: tarascon@fuaj.org
Open: Mar 1-Dec 15
Desk hours: n/a

Tarbes
Foyer de Jeunes Travailleurs
Rue Alsace Lorraine 88
65000 Tarbes
Tel: 05/62-38-91-20
Fax: 05/62-37-69-81
E-mail: FJT.TARBES@wanadoo.fr
Open: All year
Desk hours: 8am-11pm

Thionville
A.J. Centre Européen de Séjour
Place de la Gare 3
57100 Thionville
Tel: 03/82-56-32-14
Fax: 03/82-56-16-06
E-mail: n/a
Open: All year
Desk hours: 9-10am/5-9pm

Thouars
FJT "Hector Etoubleau"
Blvd. du 8 Mai 5 B.P. 77
79102 Thouars Cedex
Tel: 05/49-66-22-40
Fax: 05/49-66-10-74
E-mail: n/a
Open: All year
Desk hours: n/a

Tignes
A.J. "Les Clarines"
Les Boisses
73320 Tignes
Tel: 04/79-41-01-93 or 04/79-06-35-07
Fax: 04/79-41-03-36
E-mail: tignes@fuaj.org
Open: June 28-May 2 for individuals;
All year for groups
Desk hours: 9am-noon/2-5pm

Tours
Auberge de Jeunesse
Ave. d'Arsonval Parc Grandmont
37200 Tours

Tel: 02/47-25-14-45
Fax: 02/47-48-26-59
E-mail: n/a
Open: All year
Desk hours: 8-11am/4-10pm

Trébeurden

A.J. "Le To'no"
22560 Trébeurden
Tel: 02/96-23-52-22
Fax: 02/96-15-44-34
E-mail: n/a
Open: Jan 1-Nov 20
Desk hours: 8:30-10am/6-8pm

Troyes /Rosiéres

Auberge de Jeunesse
Chemin Sainte Scholastique
10430 Rosiéres
Tel: 03/25-82-00-65
Fax: 03/25-72-93-78
E-mail: troyes-rosieres@fuaj.org
Open: All year
Desk hours: 8am-10pm

Val-Cenis Lanslebourg

Auberge de Jeunesse
Hameau des Champs
73480 Lanslebourg Mont Cenis
Tel: 04/79-05-90-96
Fax: 04/79-05-82-52
E-mail: n/a
Open: Dec 1-Apr 30, June 15-Sept 20
  for individuals; May 15-June 15 for
  groups by advance booking
Desk hours: 8am-noon/4:30-10:30pm

Ventron

A.J. Les Roches
Chemin de Fondronfaing 8
88310 Ventron
Tel: 03/29-24-19-56
Fax: n/a
E-mail: n/a
Open: All year
Desk hours: 5-8pm

Verdun

A.J. du Centre Mondial de la Paix
Place Monseigneur Ginisty
55100 Verdun

Tel: 03/29-86-28-28
Fax: 03/29-86-28-82
E-mail: n/a
Open: Aug 1-Dec 31
Desk hours: 8am-noon/5-11pm

Vernon

Centre d'Hébergement "Ile de France"
Ave. l'Île de France 28
27200 Vernon
Tel: 02/32-51-66-48
Fax: 02/32-21-23-41
E-mail: n/a
Open: Apr 1-Sept 30
Desk hours: 7-10am/6-10pm

Verzy

Auberge de Jeunesse
Rue du Bassin 16
51380 Verzy
Tel: 03/26-97-90-10
Fax: n/a
E-mail: n/a
Open: Mar 1-Nov 30
Desk hours: 7:30-10am/5-10pm

Vesoul

A.J. de Vaivre
Ave. des Rives du lac
70000 Vaivre-Montoille
Tel: 03/84-76-48-55 or 03/84-76-22-86
Fax: 03/84-75-74-93
E-mail: n/a
Open: All year
Desk hours: 8-10am/5-8pm

Vezelay

Auberge de Jeunesse
Rte. de l'Etang
89450 Vezelay
Tel: 03/86-33-24-18
Fax: 03/86-33-24-18
E-mail: n/a
Open: Feb 1-Dec 31 (reservations
  required)
Desk hours: 5:30-7pm

Vienne

M.J.C.
Quai Riondet 11
38200 Vienne

Tel: 04/74-53-21-97
Fax: 04/74-31-98-93
E-mail: n/a
Open: All year except Sundays Sept 16-
May 15
Desk hours: 5-8pm Sept 16-May 15; 6-
9pm May 16-Sept 15

Vierzon
Auberge de Jeunesse
Rue François Mitterrand 1
18100 Vierzon
Tel: 02/48-75-30-62
Fax: 02/48-71-19-03
E-mail: vierzon@fuaj.org
Open: Feb 1-Dec 24
Desk hours: 5-10pm

Villefranche de Rouergue
FJT du Rouergue
12200 Villefranche de Rouergue
Tel: 05/65-45-09-68
Fax: 05/65-45-62-26

E-mail: n/a
Open: All year
Desk hours: 9am-10pm

Woerth
Auberge de Jeunesse
Rue du Moulin 10
67360 Woerth
Tel: 03/88-54-03-30
Fax: 03/88-09-58-32
E-mail: woerth@fuaj.org
Open: Mar 1-Dec 1
Desk hours: 8-10am/5-11pm

Yvetot
Auberge de Jeunesse
Rue de la Brigeuterie 4
76190 Yvetot
Tel: 02/35-95-37-01
Fax: n/a
E-mail: n/a
Open: Apr 1-Jan 31
Desk hours: from 7:30am/12

glossary of useful french terms

A well-known character is the American or lapsed Canadian who returns from a trip to France and denounces the ever-so-rude French. But it is often amazing how a word or two of halting French will change their dispositions. At the very least, try to learn a few numbers, basic greetings, and—above all—the life raft, *Parlez-vous anglais?* (Do you speak English?). As it turns out, many people do speak a passable English and will use it liberally, if you demonstrate the basic courtesy of greeting them in their language. Go out, try our glossary, and don't be bashful. *Bonne chance!*

▶▶BASICS

English	French	Pronunciation
Yes/No	**Oui/Non**	wee/nohn
OK	**D'accord**	dah-*core*
Please	**S'il vous plaît**	seel voo *play*
Thank you	**Merci**	mair-*see*
You're welcome	**De rien**	duh ree-*ehn*
Hello (during daylight hours)	**Bonjour**	bohn-*jhoor*
Good evening	**Bonsoir**	bohn-*swahr*
Good-bye	**Au revoir**	o ruh-*vwahr*
What's your name?	**Comment vous appellez-vous?**	ko-mahn-voo-za-pell-ay-*voo?*
My name is	**Je m'appelle**	jhuh ma-*pell*
Happy to meet you	**Enchanté(e)**	ohn-shahn-*tay*
How are you?	**Comment allez-vous?**	kuh-mahn-tahl-ay-*voo?*

Fine, thank you, and you?	**Trés bien, merci, et vous?**	tray bee-ehn, mare-ci, ay *voo?*
So-so	**Comme ci, comme ça**	kum-*see*, kum-*sah*
I'm sorry/excuse me	**Pardon**	pahr-*dohn*
I'm so very sorry	**Désolé(e)**	day-zoh-*lay*
That's all right	**Il n'y a pas de quoi**	eel nee ah pah duh *kwah*

GETTING AROUND/STREET SMARTS

English	French	Pronunciation
Do you speak English?	**Parlez-vous anglais?**	par-lay-voo-ahn-*glay?*
I don't speak French	**Je ne parle pas français**	jhuh ne parl pah frahn-*say*
I don't understand	**Je ne comprends pas**	jhuh ne kohm-*prahn* pas
Could you speak more loudly/more slowly?	**Pouvez-vous parler plus fort/ plus lentement?**	Poo-*vay*voo par-lay ploo for/ploo lan-te-*ment?*
Could you repeat that?	**Répetez, s'il vous plaît**	ray-pay-*tay,* seel voo play
What is it?	**Qu'est-ce que c'est?**	kess-kuh-*say?*
What time is it?	**Qu'elle heure est-il?**	kel uhr eh-*teel?*
What?	**Quoi?**	kwah?
How? or What did you say?	**Comment?**	ko-*mahn?*
When?	**Quand?**	kahn?
Where is?	**Où est?**	ooh-eh?
Who?	**Qui?**	kee?
Why?	**Pourquoi?**	poor-*kwah?*
here/there	**ici/là**	ee-*see*/ lah
left/right	**à gauche/à droite**	a goash/a drwaht
straight ahead	**tout droit**	too-drwah
I'm American/	**Je suis américain(e)/**	jhe sweez a-may-ree-*kehn/*
Canadian/	**canadien(e)/**	can-ah-dee-*en/*
British	**anglais(e)**	ahn-*glay (glaise)*
Fill the tank (of a car), please	**Le plein, s'il vous plaît**	luh plan, seel-voo-*play*
I'm going to	**Je vais à**	jhe vay ah
I want to get off at	**Je voudrais descendre à**	jhe voo-*dray* day-son drah-ah
airport	**l'aéroport**	lair-o-*por*
bank	**la banque**	lah bahnk
bridge	**pont**	pohn
bus station	**la gare routière**	lah gar roo-tee-*air*
bus stop	**l'arrêt de bus**	lah-*ray* duh boohss
by means of a bicycle	**en vélo/par bicyclette**	uh vay-low, par bee-see-*clet*
by means of a car	**en voiture**	ahn vwa-*toor*
cashier	**la caisse**	lah *kess*
cathedral	**cathédral**	ka-tay-*dral*
church	**église**	ay-*gleez*
dead end	**une impasse**	ewn am-*pass*

driver's license	permis de conduire	per-*mee* duh con-*dweer*
elevator	l'ascenseur	lah sahn *seuhr*
entrance (to a building or a city)	une porte	ewn port
exit (from a building or a freeway)	une sortie	ewn sor-*tee*
gasoline	du pétrol/de l'essence	duh pay-*trol*/de lay-*sahns*
ground floor	rez-de-chausée	ray-de-show-*say*
highway to	la route pour	la root por
hospital	l'hôpital	low-pee-*tahl*
insurance	les assurances	lez ah-sur-*ahns*
luggage storage	consigne	kohn-*seen*-yuh
museum	le musée	luh mew-*zay*
no entry	sens interdit	sehns ahn-ter-*dee*
no smoking	défense de fumer	day-*fahns* de fu-may
on foot	à pied	ah pee-*ay*
one-day pass	ticket journalier	tee-kay jhoor-nall-ee-*ay*
one-way ticket	aller simple	ah-*lay* sam-pluh
police	la police	lah po-*lees*
rented car	voiture de location	vwa-*toor* de low-ka-see on
round-trip ticket	aller-retour	ah-*lay* re-*toor*
second floor	premier étage	prem-ee-*ehr* ay-*taj*
slow down	ralentir	rah-lahn-*teer*
store	le magazin	luh ma-ga-*zehn*
street	rue	roo
suburb	banlieu, environs	bahn-*liew,* en-veer-*ohn*
subway	le métro	le may-tro
telephone	le téléphone	luh tay-lay-*phone*
ticket	un billet	uh *bee*-yay
ticket office	vente de billets	vahnt duh bee-*yay*
toilets	les toilettes/les WC	lay twa-*lets*/les vay-*say*
tower	tour	toor

NECESSITIES

English	**French**	**Pronunciation**
I'd like	Je voudrais	jhe voo-*dray*
a room	une chambre	ewn *shahm*-bruh
the key	la clé (la clef)	la clay
How much does it cost?	C'est combien?/ Ça coûte combien?	say comb-bee-*ehn?*/sah coot comb-bee-*ehn?*
That's expensive	C'est cher/chère	say share
Do you take credit cards?	Est-ce que vous acceptez les cartes de credit?	es-kuh voo zaksep-*tay* lay kart duh creh-*dee?*
I'd like to buy	Je voudrais acheter	jhe voo-dray ahsh-*tay*
aspirin	des aspirines/ des aspros	deyz ahs-peer-*een*/ deyz ahs-*proh*

cigarettes	**des cigarettes**	day see-ga-*ret*
condoms	**des préservatifs**	day pray-ser-va-*teef*
dictionary	**un dictionnaire**	uh deek-see-oh-*nare*
dress	**une robe**	ewn robe
envelopes	**des envelopes**	days ahn-veh-*lope*
gift	**un cadeau**	uh kah-*doe*
handbag	**un sac**	uh sahk
hat	**un chapeau**	uh shah-*poh*
magazine	**une revue**	ewn reh-*vu*
map of the city	**un plan de ville**	unh plahn de *veel*
matches	**des allumettes**	dayz a-loo-*met*
necktie	**une cravate**	uh cra-*vaht*
newspaper	**un journal**	uh zhoor-*nahl*
phonecard	**une carte téléphonique**	uh cart tay-lay-fone-*eek*
postcard	**une carte postale**	ewn carte pos-*tahl*
road map	**une carte routière**	ewn cart roo-tee-*air*
shirt	**une chemise**	ewn che-*meez*
shoes	**des chaussures**	day show-*suhr*
skirt	**une jupe**	ewn jhoop
soap	**du savon**	dew sah-*vohn*
socks	**des chaussettes**	day show-*set*
stamp	**un timbre**	uh *tam*-bruh
trousers	**un pantalon**	uh pan-tah-*lohn*
writing paper	**du papier à lettres**	dew pap-pee-*ay* a *let*-ruh

IN YOUR HOTEL

English	French	Pronunciation
Are taxes included?	**Est-ce que les taxes sont comprises?**	ess-keh lay taks son com-*preez?*
balcony	**un balcon**	uh bahl-cohn
bathtub	**une baignoire**	ewn bayn-*nwar*
for two occupants	**pour deux personnes**	poor duh pair-*sunn*
hot and cold water	**l'eau chaude et froide**	low showed ay fwad
Is breakfast included?	**Petit déjeuner inclus?**	peh-*tee* day-jheun-*ay* ehn-*klu?*
room	**une chambre**	ewn *shawm*-bruh
shower	**une douche**	ewn dooch
sink	**un lavabo**	uh la-va-*bow*
suite	**une suite**	ewn sweet
We're staying for ... days	**On reste pour ... jours**	ohn rest poor ... jhoor
with air-conditioning	**avec climatization**	ah-*vek* clee-mah-tee-zah-ion
without	**sans**	sahn
youth hostel	**une auberge de jeunesse**	oon oh-bayrge-duh-jhe-*ness*

IN THE RESTAURANT

English	French	Pronunciation
I would like	Je voudrais	jhe voo-*dray*
to eat	manger	mahn-*jhay*
to order	commander	ko-mahn-*day*
Please give me	Donnez-moi,	doe-nay-*mwah*,
	s'il vous plaît	seel voo play
an ashtray	un cendrier	uh sahn-dree-*ay*
a bottle of	une bouteille de	ewn boo-*tay* duh
a cup of	une tasse de	ewn tass duh
a glass of	un verre de	uh vair duh
a plate of breakfast	une assiette de le	ewn ass-ee-*et* duh luh
	petit-déjeuner	puh-*tee* day-zhuh-*nay*
cocktail	un apéritif	uh ah-pay-ree-*teef*
check/bill	l'addition/la note	la-dee-see-*ohn*/la noat
dinner	le dîner	luh dee-*nay*
knife	un couteau	uh koo-*toe*
napkin	une serviette	ewn sair-vee-*et*
platter of the day	un plat du jour	uh plah dew jhoor
spoon	une cuillère	ewn kwee-*air*
Cheers!	A votre santé!	ah vo-truh sahn-*tay*!
Can I buy you a drink?	Puis-je vous	*pwee*-jhe voo *zahsh*-tay
	acheter un verre?	uh *vaihr*?
fixed-price menu	un menu	uh may-*new*
fork	une fourchette	ewn four-*shet*
Is the tip/service included?	Est-ce que le service	ess-ke luh ser-*vees* eh
	est compris?	com-*pree*?
Waiter!/Waitress!	Monsieur!/Mademoiselle!	mun-*syuh*/mad-mwa-*zel*
wine list	une carte des vins	ewn cart day van
appetizer	une entrée	ewn en-*tray*
main course	un plat principal	uh plah pran-see-*pahl*
tip included	service compris	sehr-*vees* cohm-*pree*
wide-ranging sampling	menu dégustation	may-*new*
of the chef's best efforts		day-gus-ta-see-*on*
drinks not included	boissons non comprises	bwa-*sons* no com-*pree*

NUMBERS & ORDINALS

English	French	Pronunciation
zero	zéro	*zare*-oh
one	un	oon
two	deux	duh
three	trois	twah
four	quatre	*kaht*-ruh
five	cinq	sank
six	six	seess
seven	sept	set

eight	huit	wheat
nine	neuf	noof
ten	dix	deess
eleven	onze	ohnz
twelve	douze	dooz
thirteen	treize	trehz
fourteen	quatorze	kah-*torz*
fifteen	quinze	kanz
sixteen	seize	sez
seventeen	dix-sept	deez-*set*
eighteen	dix-huit	deez-*wheat*
nineteen	dix-neuf	deez-*noof*
twenty	vingt	vehn
twenty-one	vingt-et-un	vehnt-ay-*oon*
twenty-two	vingt-deux	vehnt-*duh*
thirty	trente	trahnt
forty	quarante	ka-*rahnt*
fifty	cinquante	sang-*kahnt*
sixty	soixante	swa-*sahnt*
sixty-one	soixante-et-un	swa-*sahnt*-et-*uh*
seventy	soixante-dix	swa-sahnt-*deess*
seventy-one	soixante-et-onze	swa-sahnt-et-*ohnze*
eighty	quatre-vingts	kaht-ruh-*vehn*
eighty-one	quatre-vingt-un	kaht-ruh-vehn-*oon*
ninety	quatre-vingt-dix	kaht-ruh-venh-*deess*
ninety-one	quatre-vingt-onze	kaht-ruh-venh-*ohnze*
one hundred	cent	sahn
one thousand	mille	meel
one hundred thousand	cent mille	sahn meel
first	premier	preh-mee-ay
second	deuxième	*duhz*-zee-em
third	troisième	*twa*-zee-em
fourth	quatrième	*kaht*-ree-em
fifth	cinquième	*sank*-ee-em
sixth	sixième	*sees*-ee-em
seventh	septième	*set*-ee-em
eighth	huitième	*wheat*-ee-em
ninth	neuvième	*neuv*-ee-em
tenth	dixième	*dees*-ee-em

THE CALENDAR

English	French	Pronunciation
Sunday	dimanche	dee-*mahnsh*
Monday	lundi	luhn-*dee*
Tuesday	mardi	mahr-*dee*
Wednesday	mercredi	mair-kruh-*dee*
Thursday	jeudi	jheu-*dee*

Friday	**vendredi**	vawn-druh-*dee*
Saturday	**samedi**	sahm-*dee*
yesterday	**hier**	ee-*air*
today	**aujourd'hui**	o-jhord-dwee
this morning/ this afternoon	**ce matin/cet après-midi**	suh ma-*tan*/set ah-preh mee-*dee*
tonight	**ce soir**	suh *swahr*
tomorrow	**demain**	de-*man*

FOOD

Note: To order any of these items from a waiter, simply preface the French-language name with the phrase, "Je voudrais" (jhe voo-*dray*), which means, "I would like ..." *Bon appétit!*

English	**French**	**Pronunciation**
Lamb	**De l'agneau**	Duh l'ahn-*nyo*
Chicken wings	**Des ailes de poulet**	Dayz ehl duh poo-lay
Sirloin	**De l'aloyau**	Duh l'ahl-why-*yo*
Steak	**Du bifteck**	Dew beef-*tek*
Stewed meat with white sauce, enriched with cream and eggs	**De la blanquette**	Duh lah blon-*kette*
Marinated beef braised with red wine and served with vegetables	**Du boeuf à la mode**	Dew bewf ah lah *mhowd*
Brains	**De la cervelle**	Duh lah ser-*vel*
Double tenderloin, a long muscle from which filet steaks are cut	**Du Chateaubriand**	Dew sha-tow- bree-*ahn*
Chicken, stewed with mushrooms and wine	**Du coq au vin**	Dew cock o vhaihn
Frogs' legs	**Des cuisses de grenouilles**	*Day cweess duh gre noo yuh*
Haunch or leg of an animal, especially that of a lamb or sheep	**Du gigot**	*Dew jhi-*goh
Ham	**Du jambon**	*Dew jham-*bohn
Rabbit	**Du lapin**	*Dew lah-*pan
Beef stew	**Du pot au feu**	*Dew poht o fhe*
Chicken	**Du poulet**	*Dew poo-*lay
Rolls of pounded and baked chicken, veal, or fish, often pike, usually served warm	**Des quenelles**	*Day ke-*nelle
Sweetbreads	**Des ris de veau**	*Day ree duh voh*
Kidneys	**Des rognons**	*Day row-*nyon
Filet steak, embedded with fresh green or	**Un steak au poivre**	*Uh stake o pwah-*vruh

black peppercorns,
flambéed and served
with a cognac sauce

Veal	**Du veau**	*Dew voh*
Eel	**De l'anguille**	Duh l'ahn-*ghwee*-uh
Mediterranean fish soup or stew made with tomatoes, garlic, saffron, and olive oil	**De la bouillabaisse**	Duh lah booh-ya-*besse*
Pike	**Du brochet**	Dew broh-*chay*
Shrimp	**Des crevettes**	Day kreh-*vette*
Herring	**Du hareng**	*Dew ahr*-rahn
Lobster	**Du homard**	*Dew oh*-mahr
Oysters	**Des huîtres**	Dayz *hoo*-ee-truhs
Wolf fish, a Mediterranean sea bass	**Du loup de mer**	*Dew loo-duh-* mehr
Mussels	**Des moules**	*Day moohl*
Mussels in herb-flavored white wine with shallots	**Des moules marinières** *mar-ee-nee*-air	*Day moohl*
Fish (freshwater) and fish (saltwater)	**Du poisson de rivière,** *or* **poisson d'eau douce/ du poisson de mer**	*Dew pwah-sson duh* ree-vee-aire, *dew pwah-sson d'o* dooss/ *dew pwah-sson duh* mehr
Smoked salmon	**Du saumon fumé**	*Dew sow-mohn fu*-may
Tuna	**Du thon**	*Dew tohn*
Trout	**De la truite**	*Duh lah tru*-eet
Butter	**Du beurre**	Dew bhuhr
Sauerkraut	**De la choucroute**	Duh lah chew-*kroot*
Snails	**Des escargots**	Dayz ess-car-*goh*
Liver	**Du foie**	Dew fwoh
Goose liver	**Du foie gras**	Dew fwoh grah
Bread	**Du pain**	Dew pan
Potted and minced pork and pork by-products, prepared as a roughly chopped pâté	**Des rillettes**	*Day ree*-yett
Rice	**Du riz**	*Dew* ree
Pineapple	**De l'ananas**	Duh l'ah-na-*nas*
Eggplant	**De l'aubergine**	Duh l'oh-ber-*jheen*
Cabbage	**Du choux**	Dew *shoe*
Lemon/lime	**Du citron/du citron vert**	Dew cee-*tron*/dew cee-*tron* vaire
Spinach	**Des épinards**	Dayz ay-pin-*ar*
Strawberries	**Des fraises**	Day frez
Green beans	**Des haricots verts**	*Day ahr-ee-coh* vaire
Orange	**Une orange**	*Ewn or-an*-jhe

Grapefruit	**Un pamplemousse**	*Uh pahm-pluh*-moose
Green peas	**Des petits pois**	*Day puh-tee* pwah
French fried potatoes	**Des pommes frites**	*Day puhm* freet
Potatoes	**Des pommes de terre**	*Day puhm duh* tehr
Grapes	**Du raisin**	*Dew ray*-zhan
Beer	**De la bière**	Duh lah bee-*aire*
Drinks not included	**Boissons non compris**	*Bwa-son nohn com*-pree
Coffee	**Un café**	Uh-ka-*fay*
Coffee (with milk)	**Un café au lait**	Uh ka-fay o *lay*
Coffee (with cream)	**Un café crg´me**	Uh ka-fay krem
Coffee (decaf)	**Un café decaffeiné (un déca; slang)**	Un ka-fay day-kah-fay-e-*nay* (uh day-kah)
Coffee (black)	**Un café noir**	Uh ka-fay-nwahr
Coffee (espresso)	**Un espresso (un express)**	Un ka-fay ek-*sprehss*-o (uh ek-*sprehss*)
Orange juice	**Du jus d'orange**	*Dew joo d'or-an*-jhe
Water	**De l'eau**	Duh lo
Milk	**Du lait**	*Dew* lay
Tea	**Du thé**	*Dew tay*
Herbal tea	**Une tisane**	*Ewn tee*-zahn
White wine	**Du vin blanc**	*Dew vhin blahn*
Red wine	**Du vin rouge**	*Dew vhin rooj*
Thick custard dessert with a caramelized topping	**De la crème brûlée**	Duh lah krem bruh-*lay*
Cheese	**Du fromage**	*Dew fro* mahjz
Cake	**Du gâteau**	*Dew gha*-tow
Vanilla ice cream	**De la glace à la vanille**	*Duh lah glass a lah vah*-ne-*yuh*
Tart	**Une tarte**	*Ewn tart*
Caramelized upside-down apple pie	**Une tarte tatin**	*Ewn tart tah*-tihn
Sour heavy cream	**De la crème fraîche**	Duh lah krem *fresh*
Mustard	**De la moutarde**	*Duh lah moo*-tard-*uh*
Pepper	**Du poivre**	*Dew pwah*-vruh
Salt	**Du sel**	*Dew* sel
Sugar	**Du sucre**	*Dew suh*-kruh
In the style of Burgundy, usually with red wine, mushrooms, bacon, and onions	**A la Bourguignon**	Ah lah Boor-geehn-nyon
Method of cooking whereby anything (including fish, meat, fruits, or vegetables) is simmered in a reduction of its own fat or juices	**Un confit**	Uh khon-feeh

Cooked over a wood fire	**Cuit au feu de bois**	Kwee o fhe duh *bwoi*
A method of food	**à la Lyonnais**	*Ah lah lee-ohn*-nehz
	preparation native to	
	Lyon and its region,	
	that usually includes	
	wine sauce accented	
	with shredded and	
	sautéed onions	
Cooked in parchment paper	**En papillotte**	*Ehn pah-pee*-yott
Minced and potted meat,	**Une terrine**	
seasoned and molded into		
a crock		*Ewn tair*-ee
Puff pastry shell	**Vol-au-vent**	*Vhol-o*-vhen

about the authors

Known variously to women across the world as the boy that put the "oohh" in oh-la-la, **Anthony Joseph Laudato** recently graduated from Columbia University with nothing to show for it except a degree in comparative literature, the God-given talents of asset management/acquisition, and a kick-ass collection of commemorative coins. For a post-bac breath of fresh air, he is studying up on cabala and comma placement, becoming a connoisseur of manicures, and cultivating the fine arts of management consulting. Traveling France—and indeed the third world over—in search of the ultimate in silken skin softeners, whipped cream, and other delights, it was only under duress that Kristen Couse, Balliett and Fitzgerald's maitre d'editorial convinced him to share some of his accumulated secrets to good travel and easy living. But now you have her to thank for his insight. Thank you, Kristen!

Veronica Kirk-Clausen is a writer from San Francisco. She was hoping to become a professional chef, but decided to pursue travel writing instead...and it was a good decision, since she's not much of a cook! But she can make a mean baguette-and-cheese sandwich (best if eaten in the Parc de la Tete d'Or in Lyon while watching a game of pétanque!)

Shannon Connelly is a New York based writer whose freelance works appear in several publications, including current shelf hit *Sexy New York City* and the ill-fated 1995 journal, *Mod Tendencies*. Research for this guide comprised Miss Connelly's second trip to France—one she remembers best for *Le Gibus*, dodgy hotel bed springs, questionable photos, and surprised restaurant waiters. Following the obvious travel-writing bliss, Shannon enjoys made-for-TV movies, seedy bars, and cleaning.

Amanda Buttinger lives on the coast of summer outdoor cafes in the capital of Spain with a Basque star of the stage. She doesn't get hungry for lunch until at least two, and has made savoring café con leche after the meal and digesting every other moment in life a profession. Along with having a new sobrin@, there are plenty of Spanish tapas and wine on the menu in her future. She continues to be seduced by travel writing. Every time she says it's the last... till they ask her again. In the mean time, she's workin' like she doesn't need the money, lovin' like she's never been hurt, and dancin' like she's under the spotlight.

Every year, millions of people fly directly over Iceland on their way to Europe. Many of them are asleep. The smart ones are flying Icelandair.

That's because Icelandair has flights to more than 20 European cities including Amsterdam, Frankfurt, Glasgow, London and Paris, with easy connections through Reykjavik. And travelers on their way to Europe via Icelandair can stop over "Take a Break" in Iceland for up to three nights at no additional air fare.

Many species of birds also stop over in Iceland on their way to European breeding grounds.

Typically, the birds are not sleeping.

NOTES

NOTES